WITHDRAWN

WITHDRAWN

CONTROL
OF
HUMAN BEHAVIOR

Roger Ulrich
Western Michigan University

Thomas Stachnik
John Mabry
Illinois Wesleyan University

Scott, Foresman and Company

PREFACE

The purpose of this book is to make available a volume of readings which encompasses a broad range of contributions to the control of human behavior. The time has arrived when all those who seek to modify human behavior can benefit by a knowledge of the principles of behavior derived .from its experimental analysis. Although our contributors are behavioral scientists, we hope our audience will include everyone interested in human behavior and its control.

The level at which the instructor might wish to introduce this book could vary considerably. Our intention was to produce a self-contained collection of readings which would require little or no previous training in psychology. A careful reading of the section titled "Principles and Methods in the Experimental Analysis of Behavior" should provide the beginning student with sufficient background to profit from the remainder of the readings. More advanced students would find much to interest them in sections dealing with the applications, fallacies, and implications of behavior control.

It is our opinion that the book has sufficient flexibility to be useful throughout a wide spectrum of training requirements. In fact, it was the editors' own need for this kind of volume in courses ranging from introductory psychology through abnormal, experimental, and senior readings courses which prompted the publication of this collection.

We are grateful to a number of persons for their assistance and encouragement, but in particular we would like to acknowledge the help given by Dr. G. S. Reynolds of the University of California, San Diego, and Mrs. Kay Mueller, both of whom made many valuable comments regarding content and format.

We also wish to express our indebtedness to our students, whose reactions to some of these articles over a number of years have provided us with valuable feedback. The final selection of articles reflects the judgment, not only of the editors, but of their students as well.

Roger Ulrich
Thomas Stachnik
John Mabry

Library of Congress Card No. 66-14832
Copyright © 1966 by Scott, Foresman and Company, Glenview, Illinois 60025
All rights reserved. Printed in the United States of America
Regional offices of Scott, Foresman and Company are located in
Atlanta, Dallas, Glenview, Palo Alto, and Oakland, N.J.

CONTENTS

CONTROL
OF
HUMAN BEHAVIOR

INTRODUCTION

The history of man's attempts to control the behavior of his fellows is a long one. Ancient and modern masters have pondered techniques for obtaining more work from their slaves, while the slaves, in turn, have plotted to reduce their masters' demands. Mothers and teachers have struggled to train children. The bizarre activities of the so-called lunatic or insane have further stimulated man's efforts to discover better methods for the control of human beings. The behavior of the criminal, the enemy, and even the friend have all, at times, called for control. Thus the contents of this book, which represent some of the latest efforts at and techniques for the control of human behavior, should not come as a surprise to anyone.

What, precisely, is behavioral control? It is simply the manipulation of the environmental conditions to which an organism is exposed so as to bring about a definite behavioral result: to produce new behavior, to maintain or change the organism's tendency to engage in current behavior, or to eliminate past behavior.

The development of more successful methods of behavioral control has, until recently, proceeded by a sort of natural selection. Whether a new method was discovered by chance, insight, or actual design, it tended to remain in use if successful and to be discarded if it was not.

This century, however, has seen the beginnings of a conceptual and methodological system for developing and testing new methods of control. At the foundation of this system is the observation that behavior is consistently preceded by *causes*. Recognition of these causal relationships is not new. Descartes, for example, noted the similarity between the reflexive behavior of the mechanical figures installed in seventeenth century parks and the reflex reaction of animals and men.

The *science* of behavioral control, however, was born in the laboratory with the discovery of the *conditioned reflex*. Pavlov demonstrated that, through experimental manipulation, regular, predictable relationships could be established between changes in the behavior of the living organism and the environments to which it was exposed. Careful changes in the environment and subsequent changes in behavior were produced time and again. Each bit of knowledge broadened the base on which a more complete understanding of behavioral principles rested. As more and more relationships were discovered, it became increasingly possible to control behavior by reproducing the conditions which had been experimentally proved to precede behavioral change.

Thus, over the years, behavioral scientists have worked on the premise that human behavior, like other natural phenomena, is subject to natural laws. Through a careful experimental analysis, laws of behavior have been derived which have increased man's understanding far in excess of what was once thought possible. Careful laboratory studies, first with animals and later with men, slowly built up a store of knowledge which eventually allowed for the extension of both method and principle to settings beyond the confines of the laboratory. The educational institution, the outpatient clinic, the mental institution, advertising, business, industry, and the military have all felt the influence of the science of control. The applications of the principles of behavioral control are reaching out toward every corner of our culture.

In spite of and, in fact, because of the success of this new approach, there has been considerable resistance to its application and development. People simply do not want to admit the possibility of being completely controlled by outside sources—a possibility which has arisen as a result of the achievements of this new science.

A growing interest in and concern over this possibility of control is evident in many aspects of our culture. The topic is discussed in the pages of our newspapers and magazines. Books such as *The Brain Watchers* and *The Hidden Persuaders*[1] are read by large segments of our population. Other books such as *1984, Brave New World*, and *The Manchurian Candidate*[2] deal with the potential horrors of controlled human behavior. Arguments and debates are heard concerning the practical and moral implications of such a power. In what areas should such techniques be applied? Who shall use them? To control whom and to what ends? The possibility of a really effective science of human behavior has caused man to re-examine some of his most basic ideas concerning his own nature and his future.

Yet, in spite of this concern, debate, and re-examination, the fact that many benefits have already resulted from these techniques of control is perhaps the strongest argument for their continuation and advancement. The control of man's actions does not necessarily involve the type of outcome pictured by novelists. A more carefully planned society can just as easily be a more pleasant and rewarding society. Although, because of the effectiveness of these techniques of control, projected dangers can be real and must be considered, the benefits to date have been great and the potential benefits are greater still.

The truth of the matter is often less frightening than the fictions we devise while still in ignorance. If the facts of behavioral control are hidden or made to seem intolerable, no one will benefit. On the other hand, the more complete our understanding of the nature and techniques of human control, the greater our chance to use them for our own betterment.

Although there is much which remains to be explained, the methods of science have provided an ever increasing understanding of human behavior. The use of this information is being extended daily. Furthermore, the results of these extensions are there for all to see. It is for this purpose that the following pages are presented. Here is evidence. Certainly the possibility of planning human behavior carries with it many pitfalls and responsibilities. But the facts are with us, and, if accepted and properly used, they can indeed provide the seeds for a better society.

---

1 Martin L. Gross' *The Brain Watchers* (Random, 1962) is an attack on psychological testing, while Vance Packard's *The Hidden Persuaders* (McKay, 1957) purports to be an exposé of modern advertising techniques.

2 George Orwell's *1984* (Harcourt, 1949) and Aldous Huxley's *Brave New World* (Doubleday, 1932) are projections of future "controlled" societies. Richard Condon's *The Manchurian Candidate* (McGraw, 1959) is a fantasy involving Chinese Communist "brain-washing" techniques.

THE SCIENTIFIC ANALYSIS OF BEHAVIOR

1

1

ASSUMPTIONS UNDERLYING
THE CONTROL OF HUMAN BEHAVIOR

Throughout this collection, there are many examples of the control of human behavior, and behind them all lies a set of assumptions. The purpose of the following papers is to help clarify these assumptions.

The most basic assumption underlying the control of human behavior states that man, like other elements of the universe, is subject to lawful causality. Grünbaum, in his "Causality and the Science of Human Behavior," offers a series of arguments in defense of this position. But perhaps more striking than his fine analysis of the arguments involved is the light which Grünbaum sheds on the nature of causality itself and its progeny, determinism. Readers who share this assumption of causality and also those to whom it seems improbable, impossible, or even frightening should find his treatment thought-provoking and, hopefully, enlightening.

Once the assumption of causality is made, and as long as the causes are available for manipulation, the assumption that extensive control of human behavior is possible naturally follows. Skinner, in "Freedom and the Control of Men," not only states that behavioral control is possible, but goes on to assert that it is inevitable, desirable, and, in fact, prevalent today. In keeping with his optimistic approach to the existence of control, Skinner calls into question the traditional notion of "freedom." Rather than seeing freedom and control locked in deadly conflict, Skinner, in a sense, sees a new, more positive kind of freedom emerging as the *product* of control—the freedom of man to, as he says, achieve "control of the world of which he is a part . . . [and to] learn at last to control himself."

Causality and the science of human behavior

ADOLF GRÜNBAUM

It is not uncommon to find that even those who have complete confidence in the continued success of the scientific method when applied to inanimate nature are highly skeptical of its applicability to the study of human behavior. Some go so far as to assert quite categorically that the methods of the natural sciences are in principle incompetent to yield predictions of man's individual or social behavior. Thus, for example, Dilthey and his followers in the *Geisteswissenschaften* movement[1] insist on the methodological autonomy of psychology and the social sciences, claiming that intelligent goal-seeking, which is so characteristic of man, calls for a method differing *toto genere* from that of the physical sciences.

Several important arguments have been offered against the hypothesis that cause-effect relationships exist in human behavior. These arguments are intended to deny the possibility of making the predictions which only the existence of such relationships would render feasible. In this article I shall attempt to show that the arguments in question are invalid and that there are good reasons for accepting the causal hypothesis against which they are directed. Many of the ideas to be discussed here have been previously outlined or developed by other authors in diverse contexts; wherever possible, references are given to these writings.

Before analyzing critically some of the reasons which have been given for supposing that human behavior is inherently unpredictable, I wish to point out several important consequences of this widely held belief, and also of its denial. It is essential to state explicitly what these consequences are, since few of the proponents of this doctrine realize all of its implications.

If human behavior, both individual and social, does not exhibit cause-effect sequences, then the scientific method is essentially irrelevant to the elucidation of the nature of man, and both scientific psychology and the social sciences are permanently barred from achieving the status of sciences. This conclusion follows, since it is the essence of a scientific explanation in any field outside of pure mathematics to "explain" a past phenomenon or predict a future event by showing that these are instances of a certain law (or laws) and that their occurrence is attributable to the fact that the conditions for the applicability of the relevant law(s) were satisfied. Therefore, scientific or rational learning from past experience consists in ascertaining causal regularities from which to anticipate the future. Accordingly, to deny the existence of uniformities in human behavior, both individual and social, is to assert that significant lessons cannot be drawn from the past and that man's future is capricious and elusive. Nevertheless, some historians and social scientists tell us that the absence of causal law is the distinguishing feature of their subject as contrasted with the natural sciences. In the same breath, they maintain that the only way in which individuals and nations will become manageable is by a drastic intensification in the cultivation of the social studies. It is plain that this position is untenable. For nothing can be learned from history regarding the wise conduct of international relations, if no such wisdom is to be found in history. The distinction between wisdom and foolishness in practical affairs first becomes meaningful through the existence of cause-effect relationships in human behavior and by reference to the predictions which the existence of these relationships makes possible. Rules for managing individuals and nations can be based only on causal laws which tell us that *if* such and such is done, it is likely that the outcome will be thus and so, either in all cases or in an explicitly stated percentage of cases. It is useless to bemoan the great gap between our mastery of physical nature and our scientific understanding of man, if one denies

From *American Scientist*, 1952, **40**, 665-676.

1 In the latter part of the nineteenth century, W. Dilthey spearheaded an influential movement whose representatives claimed that the theoretical task of the natural sciences is fundamentally different from that of the social sciences and humanities. The aim of the natural sciences was said to be generalization, whereas the social sciences were held to seek the articulation of individuality.

the existence of the conditions which alone would make a scientific analysis of man possible. Only if human behavior does display some kind of causal law is it significant to emphasize the need for closing the dangerous gap between man's control over physical nature and his scientific knowledge of himself lest he destroy himself.

By contrast, the assumption that causal laws are discoverable in human behavior presents enormous possibilities. For in this case we can ask the social scientist to ascertain what means will bring about given ends. Thus it is possible to get a factually true rather than an emotional answer to some of the burning questions of our time. For example, we could hope for an authentic answer to the question, What system of organizing economic relationships will in fact lead to the maximum satisfaction of certain types of human needs? Whatever the answers to such questions, they would merit the assent of all rational men who share the same goals. To be sure, the history of physical science does record the defiance and acrimony evinced by men whose theories failed to be confirmed by the evidence. Nevertheless, we have learned to reject physical theories which fail to pass the test of observable fact, no matter how ingenious the theory or how dear it may be to our hearts when first propounded. For this reason the history of physical science is in a sense the history of discarded theories. What an advance toward sanity it would be, if it were equally generally accepted that theories of human nature, like physical theories, need careful, disciplined checking through observation. In our time, the ordinary person is very much aware of the need for scrupulous care in ascertaining the facts of nature but will hold forth dogmatically and evangelically about the alleged facts of "human nature." Despite the serious divisions among mankind today, most scientific knowledge concerning inanimate nature commands assent among thinking men everywhere. It would seem, therefore, that scientific knowledge of man, specifying the requirements for attaining given ends, would also merit such universal assent. In so far as this assent would actually be forthcoming, it would constitute a partial step toward human brotherhood.

So much for the implications of rival answers

to the issue under discussion. Let us now deal directly with the merits of the answers themselves.

ARGUMENTS AGAINST CAUSALITY IN HUMAN BEHAVIOR, AND THEIR REFUTATION

There are four arguments which I wish to consider against the hypothesis that causality is present in human behavior. These are:

1. Human behavior is not amenable to causal description and therefore not predictable, since each individual is unique and not exactly like anyone else.

2. Even if there is a causal order in the phenomena of human behavior, it is so complex as to elude discovery permanently.

3. In the physical sciences, a present fact is always determined by past facts, but in human behavior present behavior is oriented toward future goals and thus "determined" by these future goals.

4. If human behavior were part of the causal order of events and thereby in principle predictable, it would be futile to attempt to make a choice between good and evil, meaningless to hold men responsible for their deeds, unjust to inflict punishment, and naive to take seriously such remorse or guilt as is professed for past misdeeds. In short, the argument is that to assume the principle of causality in human behavior is incompatible with the known fact that people respond meaningfully to moral imperatives.

In the following pages I shall try to show that all four of these arguments are the result of superficial or specious analysis. The fourth has been by far the most influential and was invoked in the pages of this journal a few years ago (Petrunkevitch, 1945).

ARGUMENT FROM THE UNIQUENESS OF HUMAN INDIVIDUALS

This objection to the possibility of constructing a scientific psychology rests on several misunderstandings of the meaning of causality in science. To remove these misunderstandings it must be pointed out that *all* particulars in the world are unique, whether they are physical objects like trees, physical events like light flashes, or human beings. The mere assertion that a thing is a particular, means that it is in one way or another unique, different from all other objects of its own kind or of other kinds. Every insignificant tick of my watch is a unique event, for no two ticks can be simultaneous with a given third event. With respect to uniqueness, each tick is on a par with Lincoln's delivery of the Gettysburg address! It is clear, however, that the uniqueness of physical events does not prevent them from being connected by causal laws, for present causal laws relate only *some* of the features of a given set of events with *some* of the features of another set of events. For example, frictional processes are accompanied by the development of heat in so far as they are frictional, whatever else they may be. A projectile fired under suitable conditions will describe a parabolic orbit regardless of the color of the projectile, its place of manufacture, and so on. Since the cause-effect relation is a relation between *kinds* of events, it is never necessary that all the features of a given cause be duplicated in order to produce the same kind of effect. It follows that when scientific psychologists assume the existence of causal laws for human behavior, this standpoint is not incompatible with the existence of great individual differences among men, nor does it infringe on the uniqueness and dignity of each particular person.

Every individual is unique by virtue of being a distinctive assemblage of characteristics not precisely duplicated in any other individual. Nevertheless, it is quite conceivable that the following psychological law *might* hold: If a male child having specifiable characteristics is subjected to maternal hostility and has a strong paternal attachment at a certain stage of his development, he will develop paranoia during adult life. If this law holds, then children who are subjected to the stipulated conditions would in fact become paranoiacs, however much they may have differed in other respects in childhood and whatever their other differences may be once they are already insane.

A variant of the argument against scientific psychology is that no psychologist can ever feel exactly like each of the diverse people whose feelings and behavior he is trying to understand. This form of the argument contains an additional misconception of the kind of understanding or explanation that is sought by science—the impression that in order to explain aspects of human experience or behavior scientifically, the psychologist must himself directly have the experience in question in all its complexity. One who objects to scientific psychology on these grounds virtually equates scientific understanding with genuinely empathic understanding. To understand a phenomenon scientifically, however, is, in the first place, to know the conditions necessary for its occurrence. A physician interested in understanding cancer (including the psychic consequences of that disease) is not interested in becoming a cancer victim himself but only in knowing the conditions associated with the occurrence and non-occurrence of cancer. Strictly empathic understanding may have great heuristic value and sometimes aesthetic value as well. However, from the standpoint of achieving scientific understanding and making the predictions which such mastery makes possible, the empathic method in psychology and in history (Dilthey) is quite insufficient.

THE ARGUMENT FROM THE COMPLEXITY OF HUMAN BEHAVIOR

This argument, it will be recalled, is to the effect that human behavior involves so complex a proliferation of factors that it is futile to attempt to unravel them. A glance at the history of science will deprive this point of view of such plausibility as it may possess. Consider what a person advancing such an argument about psychology today would have said about the physics of motion before the time of Galileo. Probably he would have said that it is hopeless to attempt to reduce the vast diversity of terrestrial and celestial motions to a few simple laws of motion. Before the rise of scientific chemistry, this kind of person would have dismissed the possibility of reducing the seemingly unsurveyable variety of substances in nature to some 96 elements. This argument rests its case on what is not known, and therefore, like all such arguments, it has no case.

THE ARGUMENT FROM THE "DETERMINATION" OF THE PRESENT BY THE FUTURE IN GOAL SEEKING HUMAN BEHAVIOR

If a person is now taking action toward the realization of a future goal, it is argued that the immediate action is the effect of a future cause — a kind of causation not encountered among physical phenomena. The answer to this contention is that, not the future goal-event, but rather the present expectation of its realization causally controls forward-looking behavior. Indeed, the goal sought may never be attained. Moreover, both the motives for achieving the given goal and the contemplation of action in its behalf function as antecedent conditions in the same way as the causal factors in physical phenomena. Thus in motivational situations causal determination is quite unaffected by the ideational reference of motives to the future (Hempel and Oppenheim, 1948; Jeans, 1945).

THE ARGUMENT FROM MORAL CHOICE

The name "determinism" is applied to the thesis that all phenomena, including those of human behavior, fall into causal patterns. This formulation of determinism is logically objectionable in some respects, but it will suffice for this discussion. It is clear that determinism is one of the key (regulative) principles of all scientific research. The denial of determinism is called "indeterminism," and the indeterminist argument from moral choice to be considered here has been summarized by a critic somewhat as follows (Schlick, 1939): If determinism is true, then my will also is always determined by my character and my motives. Hence I do not make free choices and should not be held responsible for my acts, since I can do nothing about my decisions and cannot help doing what I do. If the determinist is right, I have not chosen either my motives or my character; my motives come to me from both external and internal causes and my character is the necessary product of the influences which have been effective during my lifetime. Thus determinism and moral responsibility are incompatible. Moral responsibility presupposes freedom, that is, exemption from causality.

The question before us is whether the argument of the indeterminist is valid. Before arguing that the answer to this question is emphatically in the negative, I wish to distinguish between two types of determinism and attempt to show that they must each be objectionable to the indeterminist, once he has set forth his argument from moral choice.

The first type of determinism is the 100 per cent type, which maintains that under specifiable conditions a specifiable outcome will occur in all cases. For example, whenever a metal is heated (under ordinary conditions) it will expand. The second type of determinism is the statistical type, which maintains (roughly) that under specifiable conditions a certain result will occur but only in an explicitly stated percentage of cases. An instance of this is the statement that of all the people born in slums, 80 per cent will commit a crime at some time during their lifetime. The claim which I wish to make first is that if the moral argument of the indeterminist were valid against the 100 per cent type of determinism, it would also have relevance against the statistical type of determinism. This point is particularly important, since many indeterminists attempt to acknowledge the incontestable existence of an impressive measure of regularity in human behavior by emphasizing that they object on moral grounds only to the 100 per cent type of determinism and not to the statistical type.

To establish my case, let us suppose that, contrary to fact, we knew that all hunters are subject to the following 100 per cent deterministic law: All hunters commit homicide at some time after returning from jungle life. The indeterminist would say that if these hunters were really subject to such a causal law, they could not help becoming murderers and therefore we should have no right to punish them for their crimes. What would the position taken by the indeterminist have to be if we had a statistical type of law stating with near certainty that, of all the people born in slums, in the long run 80 per cent will commit a crime at some time during their lifetime? To be sure, this statistical law would not entitle us to say that any particular individual(s) born in the slums will become criminal; hence, it does not preclude the possibility that some particular person (or persons) be among the 20 per cent whose conduct is legal and that, to this extent, the person in question be regarded as having acted "freely" in the indeterminist sense. In so far as responsibility is an individual matter, it might even seem that our statistical law would permit the indeterminist to employ his own criteria for assigning individual responsibility to as many as 20 per cent of those persons originating in the slums. But if the 80 per cent who actually did commit a crime at some time during a long interval of time were simultaneously brought to trial before a judge holding the indeterminist point of view, the statistical law in question would deny him the logical right of making individual assignments of responsibility; this law would not enable the judge to designate among the culprits any one or any group of whom it could meaningfully be said that they "could" have avoided the crime by being among the 20 per cent who did, in fact, avoid it. For if a procedure for carrying out such a designation were possible—which it is not—the statistical law would remind us that not only all the remaining defendants arraigned before the judge but also some of those actually belonging to the 20 per cent *could then not have helped* violating the statutes. This means that if over a long period of time we select all those having originated in a slum and not guilty of any crime, the remainder having a similar origin will *always* as a matter of fact commit a crime and will constitute 80 per cent of those born in slums. Thus by the indeterminist's own criteria for assigning responsibility, the judge would not be able to carry out such an assignment individually as he must, because sufficient causality is assured by the statistical law to preclude his doing so consistently with indeterminist premises. If the indeterminist denies the justice of punishment, as he does in the case of 100 per cent determinism, he cannot assent to the punishment of individuals belonging to groups concerning which statistical laws make only a statistical prediction of conduct. Accordingly, the indeterminist must have moral objections to 100 per cent determinism and statistical determinism alike. This means that he must be a foe of the belief that any kind of scientific study of man is possible!

To establish the invalidity of the moral argument offered by the indeterminist, I shall now try to show that there is no incompatibility be-

tween the deterministic assumptions of scientific psychology on the one hand and the meaningful assignment of responsibility, the infliction of punishment, and the existence of feelings of remorse or guilt on the other.

CAUSALITY AND MORAL RESPONSIBILITY

The first point to be made clear is that determinism should never be identified with the prescientific and primitive doctrine of fatalism. The fatalist says that regardless of what we do, the outcome will be the same. By contrast, the determinist says that *if* we do such and such, *then* the effect will be thus and so. The fatalist thinks that if you go into combat, and if "some bullet has your name on it," you will be killed no matter what you do. Thus he would say that when a natural disaster occurs, it does not matter whether you are at the scene of the disaster or not; if you are not there but are "destined to die" that day, you will be destroyed some other way. The determinist maintains that a person will die on a certain day only if the conditions which lead to death materialize for that person on that day, as indeed they do at some time for each of us. Unlike fatalism, determinism allows causal efficacy to human actions.

The second point to keep in mind is that physical laws do not in any sense force bodies to behave in a certain way, but merely describe how, as a matter of fact, they do behave. Similarly, psychological laws do not force us to do or desire anything against our will. These laws merely state what, as a matter of fact, we do or desire under certain conditions. Thus if there were a psychological law enabling us to predict that under certain conditions a man will desire to commit a certain act, this law would not be making him act in a manner contrary to his own desires, for the desire would be his. It follows that neither the causes of our desires nor psychological laws, which state under what conditions our desires arise, compel us in any way to act in a manner contrary to our own will.

An illustration will show that district attorneys are determinists, since they assume in their work a definite causal connection between motives and acts. In a recent French film we find a district attorney married to a rather unsophisticated lady whom he had been suspecting of violating her marital vows. While speaking to her, he found a seemingly innocent way of mentioning the name of his rival. She promptly gulped, and then tried to maintain with studied innocence that she had had no motive at all for gulping. He insisted that she had had a very definite motive, and as it turned out he was right.

It should not be thought that the indeterminist is now prepared to surrender, for he has yet to use his strongest weapon. Says he: "We are all familiar with the fact that when we look back upon past conduct, we frequently feel very strongly that we could have done otherwise. If the determinist is right in saying that our behavior was unavoidably determined by earlier causes, this retrospective feeling of freedom either should not exist or else it is fraudulent. In either case, the burden of proof rests upon him." The determinist gladly accepts this challenge, and his reply is as follows: Let us carefully examine the content of the feeling that on a certain occasion we could have acted other than the way we did, in fact, act. What do we find? Does the feeling we have inform us that we could have acted otherwise *under exactly the same external and internal motivational conditions?* No, says the determinist, this feeling simply discloses that we were able to act in accord with our strongest desire at that time, and that we could indeed have acted otherwise if a different motive had prevailed at the time.

Thus the determinist answer is that the content of this "consciousness of freedom" consists in our awareness that we were able to act in response to our strongest motive at the time[2] and that we were not "under compulsion" in that sense. But the determinist reminds us that our feeling of "freedom" does not disclose that, given the motives which acted on us at the time and given their relative strength and distribution, we could have acted differently from the way in which we did, in fact, act. Neither do we feel that we could have responded to the weaker of two contending motives, or acted without a cause or motive, or chosen the motives which acted upon us. Since the retrospective feeling of freedom that we have does not report any of these results, its deliverances contain no facts incompatible with the claim of the determinist.

The analysis we have offered is applicable at once to the case of remorse, regret, or guilt. We sometimes experience remorse over past conduct when we reconsider that conduct in the light of *different* motives. Once we bring a different set of motives to bear on a given situation, we may feel that a different decision is called for. If our motives do not change, we do not regret a past deed no matter how reprehensible it would otherwise appear. Regret is an expression of our emotion toward the disvalue and injustice which issued from our past conduct, as seen in the light of the new motives. The regret we experience can then act as a deterrent against the repetition of past behavior which issued in disvalue. If the determinist expresses regret concerning past misconduct, he is applying motives of self-improvement to himself but not indulging in retroactive self-castigation or blame. Retroactive blame is futile, since the past will never return again. Thus, by responsibility the determinist does not mean retroactive blameworthiness, but rather liability to reformative or educative punishment. Punishment is educative in the sense that when properly administered it institutes counter-causes to the repetition of injurious conduct. The determinist rejects as barbarous the primitive vengeful idea of retaliatory punishment. He fails to see how the damage done by the wrongdoer is remedied by the mere infliction of pain or sorrow on the culprit, unless such infliction of pain promises to act as a *causal* deterrent against the repetition of evil conduct. We recall that the indeterminist accused the determinist of cruelly punishing people who, if determinism is true, cannot help acting as they do. The determinist now turns the tables on his antagonist and accuses him of being gratuitously vengeful, on the grounds that the indeterminist is committed by his own theory to a retaliatory theory of punishment. The indeterminist cannot consistently expect to achieve anything better than retaliation by inflicting punishment; for were he to admit that punishment will causally influence all or some of the criminals, then he would be abandoning the

2 The claim that we act in response to our strongest conscious or unconscious motive is not a covert tautology (see Schlick, 1939, Ch. II).

basis of his entire argument against the determinist. We see that determinism does not entail the doctrine *tout comprendre, c'est tout pardonner.*

What does the determinist believe about the application of punishment? From his point of view, punishment should be administered to the person upon whom the decisive motive acted, for that person is the essential junction of causes, and it is he who is likely to cause.harm again if unpunished. Thus the doctrine of the determinist does not commit him to punishing the parents or social environment of the culprit for the culprit's deeds, even though they are the basic cause of his misconduct. Such a procedure would be of no avail if the aim is to rehabilitate the wrongdoer. There are . . . cases, however, in which the determinist does not apply punishment. When a person is acting under compulsion, he is being prevented from implementing his own desires. In that event, his internal state is irrelevant to what he does. Since his internal state needs no reforming, punishment would be completely misplaced in such a case. . . .

It is apparent that the entire problem of responsibility can be solved within the domain of deterministic assumptions. Thus the issue is not *whether* conduct is determined but rather *by what factors* it is determined, when responsibility is to be assigned (Frank, 1932). Far from facing insuperable difficulties with the problem of responsibility, the determinist and the scientific psychologist now challenge the indeterminist to provide a logical foundation for the penal system.

OTHER ARGUMENTS OF THE INDETERMINIST

It is sometimes said that, when applied to man, the deterministic doctrine becomes untenable by virtue of becoming self-contradictory. This contention is often stated as follows: "The determinist, by his own doctrine, must admit that his very acceptance of determinism was causally conditioned or determined. Since he could not help accepting it, he cannot argue that he has chosen a true doctrine." To justify this claim, it is first pointed out rightly that determinism implies a causal determination

of its own acceptance by its defenders. Then it is further maintained, however, that since the determinist could not, by his own theory, help accepting determinism, he can have no confidence in its truth. Thus it is asserted that the determinist's acceptance of his own doctrine was forced upon him. I submit that this inference involves a radical fallacy. The proponent of this argument is gratuitously invoking the view that if our beliefs have causes, these causes *force* the beliefs in question upon us, against our better judgment, as it were. Nothing could be further from the truth. My belief that I am now looking at symbols on paper derives from the fact that their presence is causally inducing certain images on the retinas of my eyes, and that these images, in turn, cause me to infer that corresponding symbols are actually present before me. The reason why I do not suppose that I am now addressing a group of students in a classroom is that the images which the students would produce are not now in my visual field. The causal generation of a belief in no way detracts from its reliability. In fact, if a given belief were not produced in us by definite causes, we should have no reason to accept that belief as a correct description of the world, rather than some other belief arbitrarily selected. Far from making knowledge either adventitious or impossible, the deterministic theory about the origin of our beliefs alone provides the basis for thinking that our judgments of the world are or may be true. Knowing and judging are indeed causal processes in which the facts we judge are determining elements along with the cerebral mechanism employed in their interpretation. It follows that although the determinist's assent to his own doctrine is caused or determined, the truth of determinism is not jeopardized by this fact; if anything, it is made credible.

We have yet to consider the bearing of developments in atomic physics on this problem, since a number of writers have argued that these developments provide evidence for the indeterminist position.

It is known that for measurements in the domain of subatomic dimensions, the Heisenberg Uncertainty Relation comes into play. This relation states that for a given uncertainty or vagueness in the value of an observable quantity like position, there is a definite limit, imposed by the laws of nature, on the accuracy with which the simultaneous value of another empirical quantity like velocity can be known, and that this limit is independent of the particular apparatus or method used in the determination. Since the apparatus used in measurement disturbs the system under observation, it would seem that the possibilities for refining measurements are not unlimited and that the dream of classical physics can therefore never come true. No refinement of experimental technique could ascertain the present values of the observables of a physical system accurately enough to enable us to make a *precise* prediction of the future values. Consequently, the new quantum mechanics is content to specify the frequencies or probabilities with which different values will be found in a given set of measurements. These probability predictions are thus based on a statistico-determinism for the micro-processes of subatomic physics rather than upon the 100 per cent type of determinism which prevails in the physics of the macrocosm.

What are the implications of this situation for the controversy between the philosophical indeterminist and the scientific psychologist? In his *Atomic Theory and the Description of Nature*, Bohr (1934) gives several reasons for supposing that the most precise experimentally ascertainable knowledge of the momentary state of the constituent particles of the nervous system and of the external stimuli affecting it permits only a statistical prediction and not a completely detailed prediction of the fate of these stimuli in the nervous system. Nevertheless, there are important reasons why the philosophical indeterminist can derive no comfort from this situation. It has already been shown that if the moral argument for indeterminism is to be valid, statistico-determinism is objectionable along with 100 per cent determinism. For genuine free will would prevail only if the quantum theory were to conclude that all human acts (macrophenomena) can occur with the same frequency. But the theory does not make this assertion at all. The microscopic probabilities yielded by the theory are such that the acts which a macroscopic psychology would predict are overwhelmingly likely to occur. From the standpoint of the macrophenomena of human conduct a 100 per cent type of determinism holds, to all intents and purposes.

As Cassirer (1937) has stated, the extent of the determination of human behavior is so great that the free will of the philosophical indeterminist can find no refuge in it. Schrödinger (1945) has aptly summarized these conclusions in the following words:

"According to the evidence . . . the space-time events in the body of a living being which correspond to the activity of its mind, to its self-conscious or any other actions, are (considering also their complex structure and the accepted statistical explanation of physico-chemistry) if not strictly deterministic at any rate statistico-deterministic. To the physicist I wish to emphasize that in my opinion, and contrary to the opinion upheld in some quarters, *quantum indeterminacy* plays no biologically relevant role in them, except perhaps . . . in such events as meiosis, natural and X-ray-induced mutation and so on . . . let me regard this as a fact, as I believe every unbiased biologist would, if there were not the well-known, unpleasant feeling about 'declaring oneself to be a pure mechanism.'"

CONCLUSION

In this paper an attempt has been made to show that the arguments advanced against the possibility of a scientific study of man are without foundation. Of course, the truth of either strict determinism or statistico-determinism has not been established conclusively; for this cannot be done by logical analysis alone, but requires actual success in the scientific search for uniformities. Since the important arguments against determinism which we have considered are without foundation, the psychologist need not be deterred in his quest and can confidently use the causal hypothesis as a regulative principle, undaunted by the *caveat* of the philosophical indeterminist.

For a later viewpoint on this subject by Adolf Grünbaum, please see "Science and Man" by Adolf Grünbaum from *Perspectives in Biology and Medicine*, Vol. 5, No. 4 (Summer 1962). Copyright 1962 by the University of Chicago Press.

Freedom and the control of men

B. F. SKINNER

The second half of the twentieth century may be remembered for its solution of a curious problem. Although Western democracy created the conditions responsible for the rise of modern science, it is now evident that it may never fully profit from that achievement. The so-called "democratic philosophy" of human behavior to which it also gave rise is increasingly in conflict with the application of the methods of science to human affairs. Unless this conflict is somehow resolved, the ultimate goals of democracy may be long deferred.

I

Just as biographers and critics look for external influences to account for the traits and achievements of the men they study, so science ultimately explains behavior in terms of "causes" or conditions which lie beyond the individual himself. As more and more causal relations are demonstrated, a practical corollary becomes difficult to resist: it should be possible to *produce* behavior according to plan simply by arranging the proper conditions. Now, among the specifications which might reasonably be submitted to a behavioral technology are these: Let men be happy, informed, skillful, well behaved, and productive.

This immediate practical implication of a science of behavior has a familiar ring, for it recalls the doctrine of human perfectibility of eighteenth- and nineteenth-century humanism. A science of man shares the optimism of that philosophy and supplies striking support for the working faith that men can build a better world and, through it, better men. The support comes just in time, for there has been little optimism of late among those who speak from the traditional point of view. Democracy has become "realistic," and it is only with some embarrassment that one admits today to perfectionistic or utopian thinking.

The earlier temper is worth considering, however. History records many foolish and unworkable schemes for human betterment, but almost all the great changes in our culture which we now regard as worthwhile can be traced to perfectionistic philosophies. Governmental, religious, educational, economic, and social reforms follow a common pattern. Someone believes that a change in a cultural practice — for example, in the rules of evidence in a court of law, in the characterization of man's relation to God, in the way children are taught to read and write, in permitted rates of interest, or in minimal housing standards — will improve the condition of men: by promoting justice, permitting men to seek salvation more effectively, increasing the literacy of a people, checking an inflationary trend, or improving public health and family relations, respectively. The underlying hypothesis is always the same: that a different physical or cultural environment will make a different and better man.

The scientific study of behavior not only justifies the general pattern of such proposals; it promises new and better hypotheses. The earliest cultural practices must have originated in sheer accidents. Those which strengthened the group survived with the group in a sort of natural selection. As soon as men began to propose and carry out changes in practice for the sake of possible consequences, the evolutionary process must have accelerated. The simple practice of making changes must have had survival value. A further acceleration is now to be expected. As laws of behavior are more precisely stated, the changes in the environment required to bring about a given effect may be more clearly specified. Conditions which have been neglected because their effects were slight or unlooked for may be shown to be relevant. New conditions may actually be created, as in the discovery and synthesis of drugs which affect behavior.

This is no time, then, to abandon notions of progress, improvement or, indeed, human perfectibility. The simple fact is that man is able, and now as never before, to lift himself by his own bootstraps. In achieving control of the world of which he is a part, he may learn at last to control himself.

From *American Scholar*, Winter 1955-1956, **25**, special issue, 47-65.

II

Timeworn objections to the planned improvement of cultural practices are already losing much of their force. Marcus Aurelius was probably right in advising his readers to be content with a haphazard amelioration of mankind. "Never hope to realize Plato's republic," he sighed, ". . . for who can change the opinions of men? And without a change of sentiments what can you make but reluctant slaves and hypocrites?" He was thinking, no doubt, of contemporary patterns of control based upon punishment or the threat of punishment which, as he correctly observed, breed only reluctant slaves of those who submit and hypocrites of those who discover modes of evasion. But we need not share his pessimism, for the opinions of men can be changed. The techniques of indoctrination which were being devised by the early Christian Church at the very time Marcus Aurelius was writing are relevant, as are some of the techniques of psychotherapy and of advertising and public relations. Other methods suggested by recent scientific analyses leave little doubt of the matter.

The study of human behavior also answers the cynical complaint that there is a plain "cussedness" in man which will always thwart efforts to improve him. We are often told that men do not want to be changed, even for the better. Try to help them, and they will outwit you and remain happily wretched. Dostoevsky claimed to see some plan in it. "Out of sheer ingratitude," he complained, or possibly boasted,

"man will play you a dirty trick, just to prove that men are still men and not the keys of a piano. . . . And even if you could prove that a man is only a piano key, he would still do something out of sheer perversity—he would create destruction and chaos—just to gain his point. . . . And if all this could in turn be analyzed and prevented by predicting that it would occur, then man would deliberately go mad to prove his point."

This is a conceivable neurotic reaction to inept control. A few men may have shown it, and many have enjoyed Dostoevsky's statement because they tend to show it. But that such perversity is a fundamental reaction of the human organism to controlling conditions is sheer nonsense.

So is the objection that we have no way of knowing what changes to make even though we have the necessary techniques. That is one of the great hoaxes of the century—a sort of booby trap left behind in the retreat before the advancing front of science. Scientists themselves have unsuspectingly agreed that there are two kinds of useful propositions about nature—facts and value judgments—and that science must confine itself to "what is," leaving "what ought to be" to others. But with what special sort of wisdom is the non-scientist endowed? Science is only effective knowing, no matter who engages in it. Verbal behavior proves upon analysis to be composed of many different types of utterances, from poetry and exhortation to logic and factual description, but these are not all equally useful in talking about cultural practices. We may classify useful propositions according to the degrees of confidence with which they may be asserted. Sentences about nature range from highly probable "facts" to sheer guesses. In general, future events are less likely to be correctly described than past. When a scientist talks about a projected experiment, for example, he must often resort to statements having only a moderate likelihood of being correct; he calls them hypotheses.

Designing a new cultural pattern is in many ways like designing an experiment. In drawing up a new constitution, outlining a new educational program, modifying a religious doctrine, or setting up a new fiscal policy, many statements must be quite tentative. We cannot be sure that the practices we specify will have the consequences we predict, or that the consequences will reward our efforts. This is in the nature of such proposals. They are not value judgments—they are guesses. To confuse and delay the improvement of cultural practices by quibbling about the word *improve* is itself not a useful practice. Let us agree, to start with, that health is better than illness, wisdom better than ignorance, love better than hate, and productive energy better than neurotic sloth.

Another familiar objection is the "political problem." Though we know what changes to make and how to make them, we still need to control certain relevant conditions, but these have long since fallen into the hands of selfish men who are not going to relinquish them for such purposes. Possibly we shall be permitted to develop areas which at the moment seem unimportant, but at the first signs of success the strong men will move in. This, it is said, has happened to Christianity, democracy, and communism. There will always be men who are fundamentally selfish and evil, and in the long run innocent goodness cannot have its way. The only evidence here is historical, and it may be misleading. Because of the way in which physical science developed, history could until very recently have "proved" that the unleashing of the energy of the atom was quite unlikely, if not impossible. Similarly, because of the order in which processes in human behavior have become available for purposes of control, history may seem to prove that power will probably be appropriated for selfish purposes. The first techniques to be discovered fell almost always to strong, selfish men. History led Lord Acton to believe that power corrupts, but he had probably never encountered absolute power, certainly not in all its forms, and had no way of predicting its effect.

An optimistic historian could defend a different conclusion. The principle that if there are not enough men of good will in the world the first step is to create more seems to be gaining recognition. The Marshall Plan (as originally conceived), Point Four, the offer of atomic materials to power-starved countries—these may or may not be wholly new in the history of international relations, but they suggest an increasing awareness of the power of governmental good will. They are proposals to make certain changes in the environments of men for the sake of consequences which should be rewarding for all concerned. They do not exemplify a distinterested generosity, but an interest which is the interest of everyone. We have not yet seen Plato's philosopher-king, and may not want to, but the gap between real and utopian government is closing.

III

But we are not yet in the clear, for a new and unexpected obstacle has arisen. With a world of their own making almost within reach, men of good will have been seized with distaste for their achievement. They have uneasily rejected opportunities to apply the techniques and findings of science in the service of men, and as the import of effective cultural design has come to be understood, many of them have voiced an outright refusal to have any part in it. Science has been challenged before when it has encroached upon institutions already engaged in the control of human behavior; but what are we to make of benevolent men, with no special interests of their own to defend, who nevertheless turn against the very means of reaching long-dreamed-of goals?

What is being rejected, of course, is the scientific conception of man and his place in nature. So long as the findings and methods of science are applied to human affairs only in a sort of remedial patchwork, we may continue to hold any view of human nature we like. But as the use of science increases, we are forced to accept the theoretical structure with which science represents its facts. The difficulty is that this structure is clearly at odds with the traditional democratic conception of man. Every discovery of an event which has a part in shaping a man's behavior seems to leave so much the less to be credited to the man himself; and as such explanations become more and more comprehensive, the contribution which may be claimed by the individual himself appears to approach zero. Man's vaunted creative powers, his original accomplishments in art, science, and morals, his capacity to choose and our right to hold him responsible for the consequences of his choice—none of these is conspicuous in this new self-portrait. Man, we once believed, was free to express himself in art, music, and literature, to inquire into nature, to seek salvation in his own way. He could initiate action and make spontaneous and capricious changes of course. Under the most extreme duress some sort of choice remained to him. He could resist any effort to control him, though it might cost him his life. But science insists that action is initiated by forces impinging upon the individual, and that caprice is only another name for behavior for which we have not yet found a cause.

In attempting to reconcile these views it is important to note that the traditional democratic conception was not designed as a description in the scientific sense but as a philosophy to be used in setting up and maintaining a governmental process. It arose under historical circumstances and served political purposes apart from which it cannot be properly understood. In rallying men against tyranny it was necessary that the individual be strengthened, that he be taught that he had rights and could govern himself. To give the common man a new conception of his worth, his dignity, and his power to save himself, both here and hereafter, was often the only resource of the revolutionist. When democratic principles were put into practice, the same doctrines were used as a working formula. This is exemplified by the notion of personal responsibility in Anglo-American law. All governments make certain forms of punishment contingent upon certain kinds of acts. In democratic countries these contingencies are expressed by the notion of responsible choice. But the notion may have no meaning under governmental practices formulated in other ways and would certainly have no place in systems which did not use punishment.

The democratic philosophy of human nature is determined by certain political exigencies and techniques, not by the goals of democracy. But exigencies and techniques change; and a conception which is not supported for its accuracy as a likeness – is not, indeed, rooted in fact at all – may be expected to change too. No matter how effective we judge current democratic practices to be, how highly we value them or how long we expect them to survive, they are almost certainly not the *final* form of government. The philosophy of human nature which has been useful in implementing them is also almost certainly not the last word. The ultimate achievement of democracy may be long deferred unless we emphasize the real aims rather than the verbal devices of democratic thinking. A philosophy which has been appropriate to one set of political exigencies will defeat its purpose if, under other circumstances, it prevents us from applying to human affairs the science of man which probably nothing but democracy itself could have produced.

IV

Perhaps the most crucial part of our democratic philosophy to be reconsidered is our attitude toward freedom – or its reciprocal, the control of human behavior. We do not oppose all forms of control because it is "human nature" to do so. The reaction is not characteristic of all men under all conditions of life. It is an attitude which has been carefully engineered, in large part by what we call the "literature" of democracy. With respect to some methods of control (for example, the threat of force), very little engineering is needed, for the techniques or their immediate consequences are objectionable. Society has suppressed these methods by branding them "wrong," "illegal," or "sinful." But to encourage these attitudes toward objectionable forms of control, it has been necessary to disguise the real nature of certain indispensable techniques, the commonest examples of which are education, moral discourse, and persuasion. The actual procedures appear harmless enough. They consist of supplying information, presenting opportunities for action, pointing out logical relationships, appealing to reason or "enlightened understanding," and so on. Through a masterful piece of misrepresentation, the illusion is fostered that these procedures do not involve the control of behavior; at most, they are simply ways of "getting someone to change his mind." But analysis not only reveals the presence of well-defined behavioral processes, it demonstrates a kind of control no less inexorable, though in some ways more acceptable, than the bully's threat of force.

Let us suppose that someone in whom we are interested is acting unwisely – he is careless in the way he deals with his friends, he drives too fast, or he holds his golf club the wrong way. We could probably help him by issuing a series of commands: don't nag, don't drive over sixty, don't hold your club that way. Much less objectionable would be "an appeal to reason." We could show him how people are affected by his treatment of them, how accident rates rise sharply at higher speeds, how a particular grip on the club alters the way the ball is struck and corrects a slice. In doing so we resort to verbal mediating devices which emphasize and support certain "contingencies of reinforcement" – that is, certain relations between behavior and its consequences – which strengthen the behavior we wish to set up. The same consequences would possibly set up the behavior without our help, and they eventually take control no matter which form of help we give. The appeal to reason has certain advantages over the authoritative command. A threat of punishment, no matter how subtle, generates emotional reactions and tendencies to escape or revolt. Perhaps the controllee merely "feels resentment" at being made to act in a given way, but even that is to be avoided. When we "appeal to reason," he "feels freer to do as he pleases." The fact is that we have exerted *less* control than in using a threat; since other conditions may contribute to the result, the effect may be delayed or, possibly in a given instance, lacking. But if we have worked a change in his behavior at all, it is because we have altered relevant environmental conditions, and the processes we have set in motion are just as real and just as inexorable, if not as comprehensive, as in the most authoritative coercion.

"Arranging an opportunity for action" is another example of disguised control. The power of the negative form has already been exposed in the analysis of censorship. Restriction of opportunity is recognized as far from harmless. As Ralph Barton Perry said in an article which appeared in the Spring, 1953, *Pacific Spectator*, "Whoever determines what alternatives shall be made known to man controls what that man shall choose *from*. He is deprived of freedom in proportion as he is denied access to *any* ideas, or is confined to any range of ideas short of the totality of relevant possibilities." But there is a positive side as well. When we present a relevant state of affairs, we increase the likelihood that a given form of behavior will be emitted. To the extent that the probability of action has changed, we have made a definite contribution. The teacher of history controls a student's behavior (or, if the reader prefers, "deprives him of freedom") just as much in *presenting* historical facts as in suppressing them. Other conditions will no doubt affect the student, but the contribution made to his behavior by the presentation of material is fixed and, within its range, irresistible.

The methods of education, moral discourse, and persuasion are acceptable not because they recognize the freedom of the individual or his right to dissent, but because they make only *partial* contributions to the control of his behavior. The freedom they recognize is freedom from a more coercive form of control. The dissent which they tolerate is the possible effect of other determiners of action. Since these sanctioned methods are frequently ineffective, we have been able to convince ourselves that they do not represent control at all. When they show too much strength to permit disguise, we give them other names and suppress them as energetically as we suppress the use of force. Education grown too powerful is rejected as propaganda or "brain-washing," while really effective persuasion is decried as "undue influence," "demagoguery," "seduction," and so on.

If we are not to rely solely upon accident for the innovations which give rise to cultural evolution, we must accept the fact that some kind of control of human behavior is inevitable. We cannot use good sense in human affairs unless someone engages in the design and construction of environmental conditions which affect the behavior of men. Environmental changes have always been the condition for the improvement of cultural patterns, and we can hardly use the more effective methods of science without making changes on a grander scale. We are all controlled by the world in which we live, and part of that world has been and will be constructed by men. The question is this: Are we to be controlled by accident, by tyrants, or by ourselves in effective cultural design?

The danger of the misuse of power is possibly greater than ever. It is not allayed by disguising the facts. We cannot make wise decisions if we continue to pretend that human behavior is not controlled, or if we refuse to engage in control when valuable results might be forthcoming. Such measures weaken only ourselves, leaving the strength of science to others. The first step in a defense against tyranny is the fullest possible exposure of controlling techniques. A second step has already been taken successfully in restricting the use of physical force. Slowly, and as yet imperfectly, we have worked out an ethical and governmental design in which the strong man is not allowed to use the power deriving from his strength to control his fellow men. He is restrained by a superior force created for that purpose—the ethical pressure of the group, or more explicit religious and governmental measures. We tend to distrust superior forces, as we currently hesitate to relinquish sovereignty in order to set up an international police force. But it is only through such counter-control that we have achieved what we call peace—a condition in which men are not permitted to control each other through force. In other words, control itself must be controlled.

Science has turned up dangerous processes and materials before. To use the facts and techniques of a science of man to the fullest extent without making some monstrous mistake will be difficult and obviously perilous. It is no time for self-deception, emotional indulgence, or the assumption of attitudes which are no longer useful. Man is facing a difficult test. He must keep his head now, or he must start again—a long way back.

V

Those who reject the scientific conception of man must, to be logical, oppose the methods of science as well. The position is often supported by predicting a series of dire consequences which are to follow if science is not checked. A recent book by Joseph Wood Krutch, *The Measure of Man,* is in this vein. Mr. Krutch sees in the growing science of man the threat of an unexampled tyranny over men's minds. If science is permitted to have its way, he insists, "we may never be able really to think again." A controlled culture will, for example, lack some virtue inherent in disorder. We have emerged from chaos through a series of happy accidents, but in an engineered culture it will be "impossible for the unplanned to erupt again." But there is no virtue in the accidental character of an accident, and the diversity which arises from disorder can not only be duplicated by design but vastly extended. The experimental method is superior to simple observation just because it multiplies "accidents" in a systematic coverage of the possibilities. Technology offers many familiar examples. We no longer wait for immunity to disease to develop from a series of accidental exposures, nor do we wait for natural mutations in sheep and cotton to produce better fibers; but we continue to make use of such

accidents when they occur, and we certainly do not prevent them. Many of the things we value have emerged from the clash of ignorant armies on darkling plains, but it is not therefore wise to encourage ignorance and darkness.

It is not always disorder itself which we are told we shall miss but certain admirable qualities in men which flourish only in the presence of disorder. A man rises above an unpropitious childhood to a position of eminence, and since we cannot give a plausible account of the action of so complex an environment, we attribute the achievement to some admirable faculty in the man himself. But such "faculties" are suspiciously like the explanatory fictions against which the history of science warns us. We admire Lincoln for rising above a deficient school system, but it was not necessarily something *in him* which permitted him to become an educated man in spite of it. His educational environment was certainly unplanned, but it could nevertheless have made a full contribution to his mature behavior. He was a rare man, but the circumstances of his childhood were rare too. We do not give Franklin Delano Roosevelt the same credit for becoming an educated man with the help of Groton and Harvard, although the same behavioral processes may have been involved. The founding of Groton and Harvard somewhat reduced the possibility that fortuitous combinations of circumstances would erupt to produce other Lincolns. Yet the founders can hardly be condemned for attacking an admirable human quality.

Another predicted consequence of a science of man is an excessive uniformity. We are told that effective control—whether governmental, religious, educational, economic, or social—will produce a race of men who differ from each other only through relatively refractory genetic differences. That would probably be bad design, but we must admit that we are not now pursuing another course from choice. In a modern school, for example, there is usually a syllabus which specifies what every student is to learn by the end of each year. This would be flagrant regimentation if anyone expected every student to comply. But some will be poor in particular subjects, others will not study, others will not remember what they have been taught, and diversity is assured.

Suppose, however, that we someday possess such effective educational techniques that every student will in fact be put in possession of all the behavior specified in a syllabus. At the end of the year, all students will correctly answer all questions on the final examination and "must all have prizes." Should we reject such a system on the grounds that in making all students excellent it has made them all alike? Advocates of the theory of a special faculty might contend that an important advantage of the present system is that the good student learns *in spite of* a system which is so defective that it is currently producing bad students as well. But if really effective techniques are available, we cannot avoid the problem of design simply by preferring the status quo. At what point should education be deliberately inefficient?

Such predictions of the havoc to be wreaked by the application of science to human affairs are usually made with surprising confidence. They not only show a faith in the orderliness of human behavior; they presuppose an established body of knowledge with the help of which it can be positively asserted that the changes which scientists propose to make will have quite specific results—albeit not the results they foresee. But the predictions made by the critics of science must be held to be equally fallible and subject also to empirical test. We may be sure that many steps in the scientific design of cultural patterns will produce unforeseen consequences. But there is only one way to find out. And the test must be made, for if we cannot advance in the design of cultural patterns with absolute certainty, neither can we rest completely confident of the superiority of the status quo.

VI

Apart from their possibly objectionable consequences, scientific methods seem to make no provision for certain admirable qualities and faculties which seem to have flourished in less explicitly planned cultures; hence they are called "degrading" or "lacking in dignity." (Mr. Krutch has called the author's *Walden Two* an "ignoble Utopia.") The conditioned reflex is the current whipping boy. Because conditioned reflexes may be demonstrated in animals, they are spoken of as though they were

exclusively subhuman. It is implied, as we have seen, that no behavioral processes are involved in education and moral discourse or, at least, that the processes are exclusively human. But men do show conditioned reflexes (for example, when they are frightened by all instances of the control of human behavior because some instances engender fear), and animals do show processes similar to the human behavior involved in instruction and moral discourse. When Mr. Krutch asserts that " 'Conditioning' is achieved by methods which by-pass or, as it were, short-circuit those very reasoning faculties which education proposes to cultivate and exercise," he is making a technical statement which needs a definition of terms and a great deal of supporting evidence.

If such methods are called "ignoble" simply because they leave no room for certain admirable attributes, then perhaps the practice of admiration needs to be examined. We might say that the child whose education has been skillfully planned has been deprived of the right to intellectual heroism. Nothing has been left to be admired in the way he acquires an education. Similarly, we can conceive of moral training which is so adequate to the demands of the culture that men will be good practically automatically, but to that extent they will be deprived of the right to moral heroism, since we seldom admire automatic goodness. Yet if we consider the end of morals rather than certain virtuous means, is not "automatic goodness" a desirable state of affairs? Is it not, for example, the avowed goal of religious education? T. H. Huxley answered the question unambiguously: "If some great power would agree to make me always think what is true and do what is right, on condition of being a sort of clock and wound up every morning before I got out of bed, I should close instantly with the offer." Yet Mr. Krutch quotes this as the scarcely credible point of view of a "proto-modern" and seems himself to share T. S. Eliot's contempt for ". . . systems so perfect / That no one will need to be good."

"Having to be good" is an excellent example of an expendable honorific. It is inseparable from a particular form of ethical and moral control. We distinguish between the things we *have* to do to avoid punishment and those we *want* to do for rewarding consequences. In a culture which did not resort to punishment we should never "have" to do anything except with respect to the punishing contingencies which arise directly in the physical environment. And we are moving toward such a culture, because the neurotic, not to say psychotic, by-products of control through punishment have long since led compassionate men to seek alternative techniques. Recent research has explained some of the objectionable results of punishment and has revealed resources of at least equal power in "positive reinforcement." It is reasonable to look forward to a time when man will seldom "have" to do anything, although he may show interest, energy, imagination, and productivity far beyond the level seen under the present system (except for rare eruptions of the unplanned).

What we have to do we do with *effort*. We call it "work." There is no other way to distinguish between exhausting labor and the possibly equally energetic but rewarding activity of play. It is presumably good cultural design to replace the former with the latter. But an adjustment in attitudes is needed. We are much more practiced in admiring the heroic labor of a Hercules than the activity of one who works without having to. In a truly effective educational system the student might not "have to work" at all, but that possibility is likely to be received by the contemporary teacher with an emotion little short of rage.

We cannot reconcile traditional and scientific views by agreeing upon *what* is to be admired or condemned. The question is whether anything is to be so treated. Praise and blame are cultural practices which have been adjuncts of the prevailing system of control in Western democracy. All peoples do not engage in them for the same purposes or to the same extent, nor, of course, are the same behaviors always classified in the same way as subject to praise or blame. In admiring intellectual and moral heroism and unrewarding labor, and in rejecting a world in which these would be uncommon, we are simply demonstrating our own cultural conditioning. By promoting certain tendencies to admire and censure, the group of which we are a part has arranged for the social reinforcement and punishment needed to assure a high level of intellectual and moral industry. Under other and possibly better controlling systems, the behavior which we now admire would occur, but not under those conditions which make it admirable, and we should have no reason to admire it because the culture would have arranged for its maintenance in other ways.

To those who are stimulated by the glamorous heroism of the battlefield, a peaceful world may not be a better world. Others may reject a world without sorrow, longing, or a sense of guilt because the relevance of deeply moving works of art would be lost. To many who have devoted their lives to the struggle to be wise and good, a world without confusion and evil might be an empty thing. A nostalgic concern for the decline of moral heroism has been a dominating theme in the work of Aldous Huxley. In *Brave New World* he could see in the application of science to human affairs only a travesty on the notion of the Good (just as George Orwell, in *1984,* could foresee nothing but horror). In a recent issue of *Esquire,* Huxley has expressed the point this way: "We have had religious revolutions, we have had political, industrial, economic and nationalistic revolutions. All of them, as our descendants will discover, were but ripples in an ocean of conservatism — trivial by comparison with the psychological revolution toward which we are so rapidly moving. *That* will really be a revolution. When it is over, the human race will give no further trouble." (Footnote for the reader of the future: This was not meant as a happy ending. Up to *1956* men had been admired, if at all, either for causing trouble or alleviating it. Therefore —)

It will be a long time before the world can dispense with heroes and hence with the cultural practice of admiring heroism, but we move in that direction whenever we act to prevent war, famine, pestilence, and disaster. It will be a long time before man will never need to submit to punishing environments or engage in exhausting labor, but we move in that direction whenever we make food, shelter, clothing, and labor-saving devices more readily available. We may mourn the passing of heroes but not the conditions which make for heroism. We can spare the self-made saint or sage as we spare the laundress on the river's bank struggling against fearful odds to achieve cleanliness.

VII

The two great dangers in modern democratic thinking are illustrated in a paper by former Secretary of State Dean Acheson. "For a long time now," writes Mr. Acheson,

"we have gone along with some well-tested principles of conduct: That it was better to tell the truth than falsehoods; . . . that duties were older than and as fundamental as rights; that, as Justice Holmes put it, the mode by which the inevitable came to pass was effort; that to perpetrate a harm was wrong no matter how many joined in it . . . and so on. . . . Our institutions are founded on the assumption that most people follow these principles most of the time because they want to, and the institutions work pretty well when this assumption is true. More recently, however, bright people have been fooling with the machinery in the human head and they have discovered quite a lot. . . . Hitler introduced new refinements [as the result of which] a whole people have been utterly confused and corrupted. Unhappily neither the possession of this knowledge nor the desire to use it was confined to Hitler. . . . Others dip from this same devil's cauldron."

The first dangerous notion in this passage is that most people follow democratic principles of conduct "because they want to." This does not account for democracy or any other form of government if we have not explained why people *want* to behave in given ways. Although it is tempting to assume that it is human nature to believe in democratic principles, we must not overlook the "cultural engineering" which produced and continues to maintain democratic practices. If we neglect the conditions which produce democratic *behavior*, it is useless to try to maintain a democratic *form* of government. And we cannot expect to export a democratic form of government successfully if we do not also provide for the cultural practices which will sustain it. Our forebears did not discover the essential nature of man; they evolved a pattern of behavior which worked remarkably well under the circumstances. The "set of principles" expressed in that pattern is not the only true set or necessarily the best. Mr. Acheson has presumably listed the most unassailable items; some of them are probably beyond question, but others —concerning duty and effort—may need revision as the world changes.

The second—and greater—threat to the democracy which Mr. Acheson is defending is his assumption that knowledge is necessarily on the side of evil. All the admirable things he mentions are attributed to the innate goodness of man, all the detestable to "fooling with the machinery in the human head." This is reminiscent of the position, taken by other institutions engaged in the control of men, that certain forms of knowledge are in themselves evil. But how out of place in a democratic philosophy! Have we come this far only to conclude that well-intentioned people cannot study the behavior of men without becoming tyrants or that informed men cannot show good will? Let us for once have strength and good will on the same side.

VIII

Far from being a threat to the tradition of Western democracy, the growth of a science of man is a consistent and probably inevitable part of it. In turning to the external conditions which shape and maintain the behavior of men, while questioning the reality of inner qualities and faculties to which human achievements were once attributed, we turn from the ill-defined and remote to the observable and manipulable. Though it is a painful step, it has far-reaching consequences, for it not only sets higher standards of human welfare but shows us how to meet them. A change in a theory of human nature cannot change the facts. The achievements of man in science, art, literature, music, and morals will survive any interpretation we place upon them. The uniqueness of the individual is unchallenged in the scientific view. Man, in short, will remain man. (There will be much to admire for those who are so inclined. Possibly the noblest achievement to which man can aspire, even according to present standards, is to accept himself for what he is, as that is revealed to him by the methods which he devised and tested on a part of the world in which he had only a small personal stake.)

If Western democracy does not lose sight of the aims of humanitarian action, it will welcome the almost fabulous support of its own science of man and will strengthen itself and play an important role in building a better world for everyone. But if it cannot put its "democratic philosophy" into proper historical perspective —if, under the control of attitudes and emotions which it generated for other purposes, it now rejects the help of science—then it must be prepared for defeat. For if we continue to insist that science has nothing to offer but a new and more horrible form of tyranny, we may produce just such a result by allowing the strength of science to fall into the hands of despots. And if, with luck, it were to fall instead to men of good will in other political communities, it would be perhaps a more ignominious defeat; for we should then, through a miscarriage of democratic principles, be forced to leave to others the next step in man's long struggle to control nature and himself.

2

PRINCIPLES AND METHODS IN THE EXPERIMENTAL ANALYSIS OF BEHAVIOR

The increased plausibility of the term "control" as applied to human behavior reflects an increasingly effective technology of behavioral control. Originally generated in the animal laboratory, this technology has only recently been applied systematically to human behavior. The justification for applying to humans the same techniques which have been shown to maximize or minimize the chances that an animal will behave in a certain way under given conditions is simply that the techniques have, in fact, proved effective with humans as well.

An understanding of the technology of behavioral control should be based on a knowledge of the science from which it came. The purpose of this section is to examine the basic principles and techniques of the science of behavior as it stands today.

The articles presented in this section share a common terminology, restricted for the most part to observable behavior, on the one hand, and to the relevant features of its controlling environment on the other. The general principles of the science of behavior relate the behavior to the environment and are most simply described as statements or rules for altering behavior in a highly reproducible fashion.

The general principles for the prediction and control of animal and human behavior have been abstracted from laboratory experiments. A principle is accepted as sound only when it has been demonstrated to apply to each individual organism, under the conditions of the experiment. This emphasis on replication from individual to individual, in contrast to concern with the average of a group, has somewhat erroneously been termed "single organism" research. The experimental results and principles have not, as the misnomer suggests, been generalized from the behavior of a single animal. Rather the validity and power of a principle rests on the demonstration that it influences the behavior of each organism in the same way.

Establishing the criterion for replication at the level of the individual organism dictates another feature of the present methodology. One of its hallmarks is the establishment of a stable pattern of performance, called a behavioral baseline, as the dependent variable. Changes in the independent variables — the environment — are then studied as they affect the stable baseline of behavior. More conventional experimental designs, convinced of the inevitability of individual differences, have used many experimental subjects for relatively short periods of time. The methodology described in this section studies the most powerful experimental variables available for modifying behavior by providing for each organism an experimental history of long duration. This minimizes the effect of the organism's previous experience on its performance in the experiment. Under such well-controlled conditions, changes in the dependent variable, the behavior, can be attributed with great certainty to the relevant independent variables.

The articles in this section, taken together, exemplify these characteristics, but each displays unique features which recommend its inclusion. The lead article, by Michael and Meyerson, gives a readable and concise summary of the important principles which comprise a major portion of the working knowledge of the behavioral technician. These principles are stated in precise, concrete terms and share the reliability attainable in the laboratory.

As has been suggested, the principles which define the major working relations within an empirical science cannot be separated from the procedures which generate the knowledge. In his article, Verhave emphasizes the specific methods and procedures used in the experimental analysis of behavior. Many of the principles discussed in the preceding article receive concrete illustration in examples from the laboratory.

For those who picture scientific methodology as a set of cut-and-dried procedures to be applied in a mechanical fashion, Sidman's "Normal Sources of Pathological Behavior" should help dispel such illusions. The author conducts an exciting tour of the scientist's adventures with his subject matter. The major aim is the continual refinement of techniques and procedures to a point where the behavioral data virtually speak for themselves. The clinical implication of this excellent episode comes from the demonstration that a type of "neurotic" behavior, persistent and out of phase with the current environment, is produced by slightly different combinations of the same variables which produce normal, adaptive behavior. Although the notion that disordered behavior shares a continuum with more orderly forms is not new, the production and manipulation of such behavior is usually outside the clinical experience. As in experimental medicine, such healthy and vigorous explorations may well be the source of future clinical knowledge.

In the experimental analysis of behavior, considerable reliance has been placed on information provided by infra-human subjects. While the evolutionary continuity of species lends some credence to the relevance of these principles to human behavior, direct evidence requires the actual application of the procedures to human behavior. In Holland's "Human Vigilance," we are reminded that important variables from the animal laboratory can be profitably extended to human beings in specific as well as in more general cases. In his experiment, Holland succeeds in making explicit processes which previously were described as implicit, inaccessible properties of the experimental subject. Manipulation of the schedule of signal presentations, in an observing task, for example, effectively altered the "expectancy" of the subject, as revealed by the sensitive changes in the rate at which the subject gave himself opportunities to observe the signals. The subject's "expectancy" was analyzed in terms of the observing response and the variables that controlled it. Terms such as "expectancy" come only to have descriptive value in view of the increased explicitness of the behavior and its controlling variables.

In each of the papers included in this section, an active interaction between the scientist and his subject matter is evident. The major concepts, principles, and procedures are all intimately concerned with altering behavior in a direct and explicit fashion. While subsequent sections will briefly recount portions of this material which are particularly relevant to the research or application discussed there, the papers contained in the present section are recommended highly as a convenient source for an understanding of the technological base from which such research and application have issued.

A behavioral approach to human control

JACK MICHAEL AND LEE MEYERSON

A behavioral approach to human control does not consist of a bag of tricks to be applied mechanically for the purpose of coercing unwilling people. It is part of a highly technical system, based on laboratory investigations of the phenomena of conditioning, for describing behavior and specifying the conditions under which it is acquired, maintained, and eliminated.

Much more knowledge of conditioning and its broad field of applicability to human behavior is available today than can be appreciated by those who have only vague recollections of the glandular and motor responses of the dogs studied by Pavlov.

It is the major purpose of this paper to describe, in a didactic way, a portion of the new knowledge that has been obtained. Starting from definitions of specialized concepts and terminology, mastery of which will permit further reading of the technical literature, an overview is given of a descriptive and explanatory system of behavior that has relevance for [many applied areas]. . . .

It is necessary to understand at the outset that the familiar characterization of behavior as a function of the interaction of hereditary and environmental variables is accepted, not with the lip service that is sometimes given before fleeing to hypothetical constructs of inner behavior determiners that are neither heredity nor environment, but with utmost seriousness.

The consequences of this orientation should be made explicit: Inherited genetic and constitutional determiners are not under the control of, or subject to, direct experimentation by behavioral scientists. This means that the only channel open . . . for influencing human behavior is through changes in the environment. Additionally, certain environmental manipulations, such as separating a person from his frontal lobes or administering drugs that have psychopharmacological effects, are not available to psychologists and educators. The phenomenon with which [we] deal, then, is behavior, and the independent variable which controls behavior must be the environment. A behavioral system attempts to specify, without reference to unobservable, hypothetical inner-determining agents, the conditions and the process by which the environment controls human behavior.

A BEHAVIORAL SYSTEM[1]

Respondent Conditioning

Certain physical events in the environment are related to certain human muscular and glandular activities in a relatively invariable way. A light shined in the eye elicits a constriction of the pupil. An acid solution placed on the tongue elicits secretion by the salivary gland. Such physical events are called stimuli and the muscular and glandular activities are called responses. Some of these stimulus-response relationships or reflexes are present at birth, and in humans most of them are involved in maintaining the internal economy of the body or protecting it against harmful external conditions.

From *Harvard Educational Review*, 1962, **32**, 382–402. Originally titled "A Behavioral Approach to Counseling and Guidance."

1 The principles of the system presented here are based on data reported by a great many people. Most studies within the last 5 years were reported in the *Journal of the Experimental Analysis of Behavior*.

The statements about avoidance are based in large part on work done by Murray Sidman and his associates. Statements about punishment are based primarily on the work of N H. Azrin and his associates. A more complete treatment of the material basic to this systematic presentation is available in J. G. Holland and B. F. Skinner, *The Analysis of Behavior* (New York: McGraw-Hill, 1961) and in B. F. Skinner's earlier work, *Science and Human Behavior* (New York: Macmillan, 1953). Similar material has been presented in several shorter papers, like the present one. . . . Two of these are especially valuable in their thoroughness and in their detailed discussion of practical applications of research findings. They are C. B. Ferster's "Reinforcement and punishment in the control of human behavior by social agencies," *Psychiatric Research Reports*, 1958, **10**, 101–118; and M. Sidman's "Operant techniques," in Arthur J. Bachrach (Ed.), *Experimental Foundations of Clinical Psychology* (New York: Basic Books, 1962).

A stimulus which is not a part of a reflex relationship becomes a *conditioned stimulus* for the response by repeated, temporal pairing with an *unconditioned stimulus* which already elicits the response. This new relationship is called a *conditioned reflex;* and the pairing procedure is called *respondent conditioning.*

In general, conditioning does not produce permanent effects. If the conditioned stimulus is presented frequently in the absence of the unconditioned stimulus, a procedure called *extinction,* it loses its eliciting properties.

The procedures for producing conditioning and extinction were first explored systematically by I. P. Pavlov, and respondent conditioning is an area of continued interest and active investigation.

However, if conditioning phenomena were limited in applicability to the transfer of eliciting effects from reflex stimuli to other stimuli, the field would be of little importance in understanding human behavior. Most of the behavior that is of interest to society does not fit the paradigm of the reflex. There is in general no identifiable eliciting stimulus for the broad class of "voluntary" activity called by B. F. Skinner *operant* behavior. The basic operation of respondent conditioning, however, the systematic temporal pairing of stimulus conditions, is of some significance since a portion of almost any kind of stimulus effect can be transferred to a new stimulus by the procedure of pairing the two stimuli.

Operant Conditioning

Whereas for reflexes and conditioned reflexes the event of critical explanatory importance is the eliciting stimulus preceding the response, for a large class of non-reflex behavior the critical events are the environmental consequences of the behavior. Such behavior can be said to "operate" on the environment, in contrast to behavior which is "respondent" to prior eliciting stimuli.

It is convenient to group the kinds of stimulus events which are consequences of acts into three major classes in terms of their effects on operant behavior.

Positive reinforcers. These stimulus events are defined by the observation that the behavior

which preceded them has a higher probability of occurrence under similar conditions in the future. Such events are often called rewards and described as pleasant. Some of these positive reinforcers are of biological significance to the organism such as food, water, sexual contact, and some are of acquired significance such as praise, affection, grades, money.

Negative reinforcers or aversive stimuli. These events are defined by the observation that behavior which preceded their removal is more likely to occur under similar conditions in the future. The common aversive stimuli are those we call painful or unpleasant such as extreme heat or cold, blows on the surface of the body, distortions of certain inner organs as in a stomach ache, very loud sounds or very bright lights. Another class of aversive stimuli are those whose properties are acquired during our lifetimes such as social disapproval, criticism, nagging, threat.

The operation of presenting a positive reinforcer contingent upon a response is called *positive reinforcement.* The operation of removing an aversive stimulus contingent upon a response is called *negative reinforcement.*[2] Both operations are called *operant conditioning* and both increase the future frequency of the response which preceded them.

No consequence and neutral stimuli. Responses continue to occur if they receive either positive or negative reinforcement. They cease if followed by no consequence or by neutral stimuli. The procedure of allowing behavior to occur without reinforcement is called *operant extinction,* and can be contrasted with *respondent extinction* which is the procedure of allowing a conditioned stimulus to occur without pairing it with an unconditioned stimulus.

It should be noted that none of the above statements constitutes postulates, axioms, assumptions or issues of theoretical controversy. The definitions are simply descriptions of observed relationships. Some events serve as reinforcers and some do not. The determination of what constitutes a reinforcer for a

---

2 Negative reinforcement should not be confused with punishment which is the presentation of an aversive stimulus contingent on a response.

particular organism is an empirical problem, although of course, it is often very helpful to have studied biologically similar organisms or those inhabiting similar environments. In the case of humans, the reinforcers of biological significance are apparently very similar to those of other mammals and are fairly well known. On the other hand, the specification of the events of acquired reinforcing value for an individual human requires either a contemporary investigation or considerable knowledge of his environmental history.

Conditioned reinforcers. Only a small proportion of the important consequences of human behavior are the unconditioned reinforcers attributable to biological characteristics. Other consequences, *conditioned reinforcers,* acquire their reinforcing properties as a function of experience. It appears that an event becomes a conditioned reinforcer in some degree simply by being paired with another reinforcer. However, most of the conditioned reinforcers that are important in human affairs are, in addition, stimuli in the presence of which further behavior is reinforced. In common sense terms, most conditioned reinforcers are means to an end which may be an unconditioned reinforcer or another conditioned reinforcer. For example, a match for a smoker will serve as a reinforcer for the behavior which procured it because it makes possible the further behavior of striking it and lighting the cigarette.

Some conditioned reinforcers are specific to particular unconditioned reinforcers as when signs regarding the serving of food, pictures of food, and menus, function as conditioned reinforcers for humans who are momentarily reinforceable with food. Some conditioned reinforcers, however, because they have been paired with many different unconditioned and conditioned reinforcers and because they have been means to many different ends almost become ends in themselves. Reinforcers that have this property, such as money, social approval, successful manipulation of the physical environment, affection, and others are called *generalized conditioned reinforcers.*

Common sense, automaticity, and superstitious behavior. It may seem that to emphasize the pleasant and unpleasant consequences of acts through "rewards and punishments" is nothing new. The effects described above have long been known and used in an intuitive way, but they also have long been misunderstood. The strengthening effect of a reward is commonly understood in terms of a rational process. It seems only natural that a person will repeat that which he can see will benefit him, and perform again those acts which he believes will terminate unpleasant conditions. However, the effect does not depend on a rational process at all. The foreseeing of consequences or the ability to state the relation between the consequence and the behavior which produced it is unnecessary. Any behavior which is followed by reinforcement—in all of the many species studied, and above all in man—is more likely to occur again in the same or a similar situation. This could be called the *automaticity* of the effect of reinforcement. To increase the occurrence of a particular class of behavior, it is necessary only to ensure that reinforcement occurs relatively soon after the behavior.

The automaticity effect is most dramatically demonstrated in what is called "superstitious behavior." When reinforcement follows behavior, even though the behavior did not produce or in any sense cause the reinforcement, it is called *accidental reinforcement.* Behavior which is developed as a function of accidental reinforcement was whimsically referred to as superstitious behavior in a study with pigeons (Skinner, 1948a) and the term has become a quasi-technical term in the behavioral field. Humans, probably because of their more complex environment, provide many more examples of superstitious behavior than lower animals. The verbalizations and unique motor activities of gamblers and the unnecessary postures and movements seen in sports activities are examples of the effects of accidental contingencies of reinforcement.

Shaping

Inasmuch as an operant response must first occur before it can be followed by reinforcement, one might suppose that operant conditioning cannot be used to produce new behavior. However, the detailed topography of a response—the particular muscle actions, including force and speed of various muscle components—varies from one occurrence to another. To produce new behavior then, or behavior that has not appeared in the response repertoire before, it is sufficient to selectively reinforce one of the variations in topography which resulted from the previous reinforcement, while allowing the other variations to extinguish. This has the effect of producing a further class of variations from which one may again differentially reinforce some and allow others to extinguish, and so on.

For example, in teaching a child to talk, his efforts to pronounce a particular word will at first be reinforced rather uncritically. Eventually, some of the variations will resemble accepted pronunciation more than others and receive selective reinforcement while other variations are allowed to extinguish. These events have the effect of producing a class of responses which come ever closer to the correct pronunciation than the last reinforced response, and the selective reinforcement can be applied again. This procedure for producing new behavior is called *shaping*. It is essentially the differential reinforcement of successive approximations to some complex form of behavior. It is the technique which animal trainers use to produce unusual and entertaining behaviors in their subjects, and it is the technique whereby humans acquire the complex response topographies of speech, athletic abilities and other motor skills.

Stimulus Control of Operant Behavior

Although the emphasis in describing operant behavior has been on the reinforcement occurring subsequent to the response, stimulus control is implied in the phrase concluding the principle of operant conditioning—if an operant response is followed by reinforcement it is more likely to occur *under similar conditions* in the future. The simplest principle of stimulus control is that the future probability of response is highest when the stimulus conditions resemble most closely those existing at the moment of previous reinforcement. The expression "resemble most closely" must be analyzed in some detail, but first a description is needed of a typical experimental situation

in which the effects of stimuli on operant behavior are studied. A lower animal rather than a human is described as the subject in this example because stimulus control in humans is confounded by their extensive training regarding the relevance of certain classes of stimuli (see "discrimination training" below). A food-deprived monkey is placed in a small chamber containing a movable foot pedal, and reinforced with food for pressing the pedal. Suppose that the chamber is illuminated by a relatively bright overhead light, a moderately loud tone of 1000 cycles per second plays constantly, and a small translucent disc above the pedal, at eye level, is illuminated from behind with a bright green light. Although none of these stimulus conditions can be said to elicit the response, they all come to exert some control over its probability, for if any of them is changed, the tendency to respond will be temporarily lowered. Of course, if we continue to reinforce in the presence of the changed stimuli, responding will recover and the class of stimulus conditions controlling the response will be broadened. If, instead of changing only one of the stimulus conditions, we change all of them, the tendency to respond will be very low. In brief, any change from the stimulus conditions that existed at the moment of reinforcement will reduce the tendency to respond, and the greater the change, the greater the reduction.

There is, however, a vagueness in this formulation. How can the extent to which a changed stimulus condition resembles the original one be evaluated? For example, can we predict for a specific monkey whether changing the tone will reduce his tendency to respond more than turning off the overhead light? We cannot. It is an empirical question. To some extent the similarity of different stimulus conditions will depend on the biological characteristics of the species. But in part, as in the case of reinforcers, the importance to the individual organism of the various aspects of the stimulus condition will depend on the previous history of that particular organism.

In the situation described above a change in color on the translucent disc would not be expected to change the tendency to respond very much because the disc color is only a small part of the total stimulus situation. By skilled use of the procedures of reinforcement and extinction, however, we can bring about the more precise type of stimulus control that is called *discrimination*. If we change the color from green to red, and in the presence of the red disc we do not reinforce the pedal response, it will become less frequent, i.e., extinguish. If we then restore the color and in its presence pedal pressing is again reinforced and so on, alternating the two conditions, the control of the disc color over the pedal response will become quite strong. This procedure is called *discrimination training*. If in the presence of a stimulus a response is reinforced, and in the absence of this stimulus it is extinguished, the stimulus will control the probability of the response in high degree. Such a stimulus is called a *discriminative stimulus*.

Almost all important human behavior is under the control of discriminative stimuli. Although part of the educational process involves extensive shaping, particularly for motor skills, the educator's major efforts are directed toward the development of *discriminative repertoires*, or in common terminology, knowledge. Many details regarding the building of discriminative repertoires have been discovered in the experimental laboratory, and these findings are now beginning to see systematic exploitation in the field of programmed instruction.

The development of effective discriminative repertoires for interpersonal behavior is also a topic of great importance for those dealing with the practical control of behavior, and although the principles of discrimination are the same when the stimuli to be discriminated are the behaviors of other people, the details of application remain to be worked out.

A beginning has been made in applying basic principles of discrimination to verbal behavior, language, and communication. This is presently seen to be a field composed of one discriminative repertoire under the control of the many features of the physical and social environment, with additional repertoires controlled by features of the first (Skinner, 1957b).

Schedules of Intermittent Reinforcement

Thus far discussion has centered on the role of reinforcement in simply making a response

more likely to occur in the future, in shaping up novel topographies or forms of response, and in bringing a response under the control of a particular stimulus condition. But reinforcement does not lose its relevance once an adequate topography has been developed and the behavior is under proper stimulus control. It has additional effects that may be treated according to the schedule by which reinforcement is given.

An important characteristic of much behavior is that it is repeated, either because the appropriate stimulus conditions persist or because they recur. Having learned to ask a parent for a cookie a child can immediately ask for another, and another. This behavior must eventually cease because of temporary changes in the parent's disposition to provide the reinforcer, because the reinforcer loses its effectiveness by satiation, or for other reasons, but there will be other occasions for similar behavior to occur. If every occurrence of such a repeatable response is followed by reinforcement the behavior will continue until other variables exert control. On the other hand, if reinforcement is discontinued altogether the behavior will cease.

Between the extremes of *continuous reinforcement* where every relevant response is reinforced and *extinction* where there is no reinforcement there are many situations where responses are only occasionally reinforced. Such *intermittent reinforcement* might be expected to produce an effect intermediate between continuous reinforcement and extinction, but that is not the case. The situation is much more complex. A schedule of intermittent reinforcement is actually a way of arranging reinforcement contingencies regarding the passage of time, the number of responses, or both. The complexity arises from the varied and intricate ways in which these temporal and number contingencies can be combined and interrelated in natural and laboratory environments, and from the extreme sensitivity of the behavior of organisms to such conditions.

Ratio reinforcement. There is a large class of schedules involving solely a number contingency, and this is usually specified in terms of the ratio of responses to reinforcements. Industrial piecework pay is an example of ratio reinforcement, as is the pay-off schedule provided by the "one-armed bandit" of the gambling house. The principal characteristic of such schedules is that the more rapidly one works the more frequently one is reinforced. Behavior conforms to this kind of requirement by occurring at a high rate. Another feature of this kind of schedule is that very large amounts of work per reinforcement can be tolerated, but to avoid premature extinction the organism must approach such conditions gradually by first being exposed to less stringent requirements. A third feature is that simple ratio reinforcement does not have self-corrective properties. Any temporary reduction in the tendency to respond simply delays the ultimate reinforcement. Vicious circles can easily develop where the less one responds the less one gets, and therefore the less one responds in the future.

Interval reinforcement. Another class of schedules involves only temporal contingencies. The most commonly studied arrangements are those where the probability of a response being reinforced increases as a simple function of the passage of time, and under these conditions the frequency of responding generally reflects the changing probability of reinforcement. An example from daily life is the behavior of telephoning someone who is not at home. One cannot hasten his return home by rapid re-dialing, as in ratio reinforcement, but the probability of making the connection and completing the call increases as time passes. If the interval varies randomly, response frequency is relatively constant over time. If the interval is constant, responding increases in frequency as the time for reinforcement approaches. In such schedules the rate of responding is directly related to the frequency of reinforcement. Only moderate response rates are generated by interval reinforcement but when the reinforcement is discontinued altogether, responding decreases in frequency very slowly compared with behavior which has been continuously reinforced. Resistance to extinction is high. In contrast to the ratio schedules described earlier, interval schedules in general

are self-corrective. Any temporary reduction in response frequency is counteracted by receiving the next reinforcement after fewer unreinforced responses, and this restores the tendency to respond.

Much more complex arrangements of temporal and number contingencies occur in the human physical and social environment, and also in the behavior laboratory. Fortunately the field is somewhat systematized and it is becoming increasingly possible to predict the effects of new arrangements on the basis of what is known about their components.

Intermittent reinforcement and motivation. In addition to its general theoretical relevance in illuminating the effects of reinforcement contingencies, intermittent reinforcement is of considerable practical significance because of its relationship to the traditional field of motivation. The well-motivated person is one who works at some activity with persistence, even though his reinforcement is long delayed. He is also a person who can put out a very large amount of work with only an occasional reward. It is not evident, however, that these properties are *in* the person or that the behavior cannot be produced by manipulating the environment. Variable interval schedules generate great persistence in the face of non-reinforcement, and ratio schedules produce large amounts of work for the minimum number of reinforcements. Not only good motivation but the pathologically "driven" behavior that is said to characterize the gambler can be generated in the laboratory by programing the same kind of variable ratio schedule that acts on the gambler. Similarly when a child cries and begs his parents with great persistence and intensity to take him with them rather than leave him with a baby sitter, we are likely to say something like "he *wants* very much to go with them." The work on intermittent reinforcement tells us very clearly that just such a performance could be generated by acquiescing to the child's requests after only mildly intense and slightly persistent entreaties at first and then slowly raising the requirement. Whether any particular sample of behavior arose in this way is an empirical question.

Deprivation and Satiation

Not all motivational problems fit the paradigm described above. Deprivation and satiation have two major effects on behavior which cannot at present be reduced to the effects of any of the biological or environmental variables discussed previously.

Food, water, sexual activity, activity in general, and some other similar unconditioned reinforcers will serve as reinforcers only if the organism has been deprived of them. Satiation weakens and deprivation strengthens the effectiveness of these reinforcers. This is one major effect of this variable. In addition, deprivation with respect to a reinforcer results in an increased likelihood of occurrence of all the behavior that has in the past been reinforced with it.

Stated in terms of food, for example, the first effect is that as deprivation time increases, food becomes a more powerful reinforcer. As eating continues, food loses its reinforcing capacity. The second effect is seen in that food-seeking behavior becomes more frequent as time since last eating increases, and less frequent as eating proceeds. This second effect cannot at present be reduced to the first, since the increase in food-seeking behavior can be observed even before reinforcement has been received.

The study of deprivation-satiation variables appears to come closest to the traditional field of motivation, but there are many cases where these variables are *not* relevant but it is common to infer them. For example, one man may show strong persistent behavior directed toward socio-sexual relations with women, and another may show very little such behavior. The customary explanations is in terms of sex drive, with the implication that equivalent periods of deprivation affect the two men differently or that one is more deprived than the other. It is more likely in our culture that differences of this magnitude are due largely to different histories of intermittent reinforcement although again this interpretation would require independent evidence in any particular case. Laboratory studies with lower animals indicate quite clearly that variables such as frequency of reinforcement and kind of schedule can cause variations in frequency and persistence of behavior that are greater than the variations generated by deprivation.

It would also be a mistake to infer a history of specific deprivation from the knowledge that a particular event will function as a reinforcer. In the case of ordinary conditioned reinforcers this mistake would not usually be made —the fact that the sight of a telephone is reinforcing certainly doesn't suggest telephone deprivation, since a telephone is so obviously a means to an end. The generalized conditioned reinforcers, however, of affection, attention, money, because they are means to many different ends, erroneously might be assumed to be subject to the deprivation effect in themselves.

In summary then, deprivation and satiation are critical determiners of the momentary effectiveness of a number of reinforcers, and of the momentary strength of large classes of responses. But to pattern all "motivational" problems on this model would be to neglect other equally if not more important determiners.

Emotion

It is customary to consider emotion as respondent behavior, but operant aspects of emotion can also be specified. Like deprivation, emotional variables affect a large class of operant responses. For example, a person who is ordinarily described as fearful not only shows the respondent effects such as a more rapid heart rate, moist palms and dry throat, but also he shows an increased tendency to engage in all those operant behaviors which have in the past been reinforced by escape from current or similarly difficult situations. Further, those aspects of his repertoire which ordinarily receive positive reinforcement in this situation are weakened. His tendencies to run away, to hide, to seek help from other individuals, are all increased, whereas his tendencies to eat, play, and engage in normal social behaviors are decreased. These phenomena presently are not well understood.

The operations which produce behavioral changes in respondent and operant repertoires under emotion have not yielded to efforts to develop a simple classification scheme. Furthermore, the class of responses which are altered by any particular operation contain such a large component of acquired behaviors that the similarities between different individuals are of little systematic value. However, although an empirical description and ordering of the responses which change with emotion presently are limited, the principles whereby already developed repertoires can be transferred from one stimulus condition to another are somewhat better understood. The operation of temporal pairing is relevant. Any stimulus which is systematically present during an emotional condition will produce some of the respondents and some of the change in the operant repertoire that characterize the emotional condition when it is presented alone. Practical use of principles in this field has been under investigation in the U.S.S.R. ever since the earliest work of Pavlov. More recently, however, a group of British investigators have made very successful deliberate applications of emotional conditioning principles to the treatment of abnormal behavior (Eysenck, 1960).

Aversive Control

Escape and avoidance. An environmental arrangement in which an organism's response can terminate an already present aversive stimulus is called an *escape* procedure. It is negative reinforcement, and operant conditioning of the response is the result. When behavior can prevent or delay the onset of the aversive stimulus the procedure is called *avoidance,* and this arrangement also will result in the development and maintenance of operant behavior. Avoidance cannot be considered as a simple case of negative reinforcement, however, since there is often no obvious stimulus termination immediately following the response. Turning off an alarm clock that has already begun to ring is an example of escape behavior, but pushing in the stop before it begins to ring is avoidance.

Examples of this kind of control are easily found in parent-child interactions. Children's cleanliness activities are often maintained as escape behavior where the aversive stimulus is the nagging verbal behavior of a parent. Sometimes these activities constitute avoidance

behavior. Here the aversive stimulus is criticism, scolding, or being made to wash over again. Later, when children go to school their studying behavior is often maintained as avoidance behavior, where the aversive stimulus is again criticism, failing grades, or removal of privileges. The distinction between behavior for positive reinforcement and the avoidance paradigm is illustrated in the following not uncommon interchange between parent and child. The child is told to do something and asks "What will I get if I do?" whereupon the parent replies "You'll get something if you don't!"

Laboratory findings with avoidance behavior have indicated several characteristics of this kind of control which are closely related to behavior disorders of many kinds. In the first place, successful avoidance behavior will by its very nature prevent the discovery that the aversive stimulus has been discontinued, and when this is coupled with the extraordinary persistence of such behavior it suffices to explain many human activities that serve no current function.

Another finding relevant to behavior problems is the fact that occasional presentations of the aversive stimulus without respect to the organism's behavior will maintain the avoidance repertoire almost indefinitely. In this way, even though the bad thing that one is avoiding is no longer related to one's behavior, so long as it occurs once-in-a-while the avoidance repertoire may persist.

A final point concerns the conditions under which the escape or avoidance repertoire will occur. In escape behavior the presentation of the aversive stimulus produces immediate strength in the escape repertoire and the escape repertoire is not readily seen in the absence of the aversive stimulus. In avoidance, the presentation of stimuli which have in the past accompanied that or other aversive stimuli strengthen the avoidance repertoire, but an even stronger effect is seen when the aversive stimulus itself is presented momentarily. To maintain behavior in this manner it is necessary to maintain the threat of aversive stimulation.

Punishment. Technically, punishment refers to the operation of presenting an aversive stimulus contingent upon a response, or removing a positive reinforcer contingent upon a response.[3] It is widely used in our culture to reduce the frequency of behavior, and according to "common sense" psychology is often described as opposite in effect from reward. As rewards strengthen behavior, so punishments are believed to weaken it. Considerable experimental evidence is now available regarding the effects of this operation, which turn out to be quite complex.

One kind of complexity arises because whereas the strengthening effects of reinforcement can be studied in isolation, the weakening effects of punishment can only be studied by superimposing them on preceding or ongoing strengthening effects. This is not only a methodological problem. In practical affairs the question of the efficacy of punishment seldom arises except with respect to behavior that has at least moderate probability of occurrence.

It is difficult to generalize about this competition between reinforcement and punishment since the parameters of the positive reinforcement and the aversive stimulus used are critical, as is the availability of alternative responses which are reinforced and/or punished to varying degrees. However, it is probably safe to say that when no other response but the punished one can obtain positive reinforcement, and with positive reinforcers like food, it takes very severe punishment to effectively reduce the frequency of the behavior.

Added to this complication is the fact that an aversive stimulus may have some effects because it is aversive, but it also has other stimulus effects. By the principle of stimulus control mentioned earlier an aversive stimulus can reduce the frequency of responding if the stimulus constitutes a change from the conditions which existed during previous reinforcement, regardless of its aversive characteristics. And since reinforcement often occurs in the same situation as punishment, an aversive stimulus, as a result of some systematic relation to the reinforcement, can acquire even more complex stimulus properties, such as those of a discriminative stimulus, or even a conditioned positive reinforcer.

Finally, there is a complication in interpreting the effects of punishment in human interactions that is brought about by the fact that a person who punishes may for a time be less disposed to provide any ordinary positive reinforcement. If this is the case, punishment systematically precedes a period of extinction. This arrangement results in a reduction in some behavior — but not due to the aversive effects of the punishment. On the other hand, punishers sometimes show a greater disposition to provide positive reinforcement shortly after they have administered punishment. This results in a temporary increase in some kinds of behavior, and, under proper conditions, even a future increase in the punished behavior.

Any stimulus which is paired temporally with an aversive stimulus acquires some of its properties. Such stimuli are called *conditioned aversive stimuli* or conditioned negative reinforcers. Aversive stimuli and conditioned aversive stimuli, in addition to producing the effects described above are also classed as emotional variables, because of their respondent effects and their effects on large classes of operant responses. This emotional effect enters into and further complicates various kinds of aversive control. It also appears to be responsible for various deleterious changes in certain internal organs. Because of this, and for many other reasons, aversive control is in most cases socially undesirable although it is apparently not completely avoidable.

This concludes the presentation of the basic empirical principles of this behavior system. Of course, many details have been omitted, but the major relations have been covered. Further development of this system is proceeding along two lines: workers in experimental laboratories are constantly discovering new details, improving imprecise relations, and sometimes revealing new major principles; others working in applied settings are developing a behavioral technology based on these basic principles.

---

3 Common sense usage often has punishment synonymous with what is referred to here as an aversive stimulus or, even more broadly, as aversive control.

Recent developments in the experimental analysis of behavior

THOM VERHAVE

In his "An Introduction to the Study of Experimental Medicine," Claude Bernard (1865) wrote: "I am convinced, in experimental sciences that are evolving, and especially in those as complex as biology, discovery of a new tool for observation or experiment is much more useful than any number of systematic or philosophic dissertations. Indeed, a new method or a new means of investigation increases our power and makes discoveries and researches possible which would not have been possible without its help" (p. 171).

Bernard's point certainly is well demonstrated by B. F. Skinner's discovery of frequency of responding as a dependent variable in the investigation of the factors controlling voluntary behavior (1956, 1957a). In 1930, Skinner described an experimental method that, with various modifications by many subsequent workers, has become "a fixture in modern experimental research on behavior" (Keller and Schoenfeld, 1950, p. 42). The paper described a way of measuring the rate of eating by a white rat. The method involved: 1) an experimental cage containing a device for giving a small pellet of food to a hungry rat each time the animal pushed open the swinging door of a foodbin at one end of his chamber; and 2) a mechanism for automatically recording the rate of panel pushing or eating. Today, as in Skinner's original studies, the rate of responding usually is recorded as a cumulative curve on a modified kymograph. A pen moves across a paper tape driven by a slowly revolving cylinder. The pen, driven by a ratchet device, moves in the vertical direction a short uniform distance with each response. The resulting sloping line therefore is proportional to the rate of responding.

Figure 1 is an illustration of the construction of a cumulative record of behavior. The step-wise nature of the record is obvious in this figure because of the excessively large time and response units selected for illustrative purposes. In contemporary work involving many different species, appropriate paper speeds

and unit steps are chosen in such a way that the rates to be studied give convenient slopes. It may be noted that at no point does the experimenter intervene for purposes of interpretation of the records generated by a cumulative recorder. The cumulative recording data presented in this paper are photographic reproductions of records made by the animals themselves (Ferster and Skinner, 1957; Skinner, 1938).

In laboratory experiments selection of a response is based on the following considerations: 1) The response should be objectively measurable. 2) The behavior should be able to be executed easily by the subject. 3) The experimental subject should be able to respond repeatedly without fatigue (Skinner, 1957a).

In experiments with pigeons, the birds are trained to strike at (peck) a small translucent plastic key mounted at the height of the beak

From *Proceedings of the Eleventh Research Conference,* sponsored by the American Meat Institute Foundation, at the University of Chicago, March 26-27, 1959.

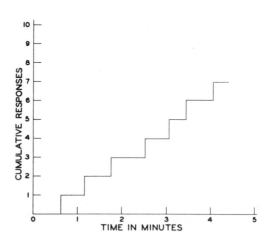

Figure 1. *Illustration of the construction of a cumulative record.*

in one of the walls of a small cage as shown in Figure 2. In some experiments a bird may make as many as 70,000 pecks during a 4-1/2 hour experimental period (Ferster and Skinner, 1957). With pigeons, rates of key-pecking may vary between zero and 15 pecks per second.

Figure 3 is an illustration of a cumulative record as "drawn by" an animal. The curve shows the cumulative record of a rat on a variable-interval schedule of reinforcement (Ferster and Skinner, 1957). In this particular experiment the animal pressed a small lever mounted in one of the walls of a small cage. Pressing of the lever was rewarded by a small food pellet at various different intervals since the previous reward. During the periods between rewards the animal was free to press the lever, however, without being reinforced. In this illustrative experiment the intervals between payoffs ranged from 5 to 120 sec. The mean interval between rewards was 1 minute. The scale of the record is indicated by the insert in the figure, which shows a small set of co-ordinates containing some representative slopes.

This experiment, as all contemporary work, was programmed automatically by means of electrical relay circuits. Data were recorded automatically by means of running-time meters, impulse counters and a cumulative recorder.

The consequences of Skinner's initial modest and seemingly trivial experiment have been staggering. Ever since 1930, and at a positively accelerated rate the end of which is not yet in sight, hundreds of rats and pigeons, as well as mice, turtles, chimpanzees, fish, cats, dogs, college students, mentally defective persons, psychotic patients and naval trainees, have been pushing doors, pressing levers, nosing plastic disks, and pulling all sorts of switches, unwittingly producing cumulative records.

In all these experiments the behavior of the subjects is controlled by the consequences. In the experiment with the rat that was previously used as an illustration, the consequence of pressing the lever was the occasional pellet of food received by doing so. Such consequences of behavior, ranging from water, candy and chicken feed to "a pat on the back by the boss," are some of the most powerful factors that alter the rate or frequency of voluntary behavior. With this type of behavior the organism usually acts upon his environment, thus producing changes in it. Skinner proposed the term "operant behavior" because the organism operates on his environment (Skinner, 1938, 1953). Every step towards a door reduces the distance between the walker and the door, to use a down-to-earth illustration. These changes in the environment, produced by the organism itself, subsequently change the organism, affecting its future behavior. Because of these feed-back effects

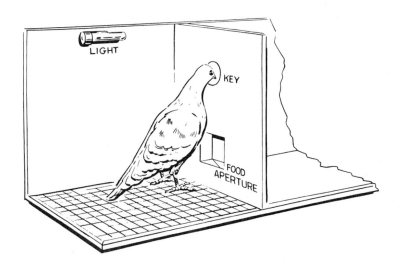

Figure 2. *Illustration of an experimental cage used for operant-conditioning research with pigeons.*

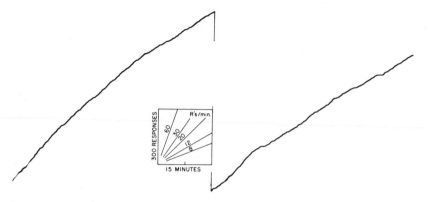

Figure 3. Performance of a rat under variable-interval reinforcement.

Figure 4. Characteristic performance by a rat under fixed-interval reinforcement.

of what in daily life are usually called rewards and punishments, the present area of research might be thought of as a kind of experimental cybernetics.

The data in Figure 3 illustrate the fact that responding can be maintained by reinforcing the behavior only intermittently. Many fascinating phenomena have been discovered by the use of "intermittent reinforcement" procedures. A large volume of research dealing with the effects of various "schedules of reinforcement" has recently been published (Ferster and Skinner, 1957).

Figure 4 shows a typical performance of a rat on a frequently used schedule of reinforcement. In this experiment the animal was reinforced by the presentation of a measured amount (1/2 cc) of sweetened condensed milk by means of a dipper. The schedule of reinforcement was a 12-minute fixed-interval (FI) schedule (Ferster and Skinner, 1957); lever pressing was reinforced at intervals of 12 minutes. When a reinforcement was received, pressing the lever became ineffective until a 12-minute recycling timer ran out, closing the electrical circuit between the lever and the dipper. The dipper was accessible for

a 10-second period, long enough to give the animal a chance to clean out the cup of milk. The reinforcement period was followed by a 5-minute time-out period during which all the lights in the cage were turned off. At the end of this 5-minute break, a light came on above the lever and the 12-minute timer was started again. Figure 4 shows a sample portion of the cumulative record obtained during a session after a considerable amount of training. The animal had been previously exposed for more than 100 hours to the schedule.

In this experiment the cumulative recorder pen was automatically reset to the bottom of the recorder at the end of each 5-minute time-out period after each reinforcement. Reinforcements are indicated by small oblique marks on the record, like the one near the arrow. In the short sample of the performance shown in Figure 4 the onset of the light above the lever started at "a." The first reinforcement was not given until 12 minutes later (at the arrow). It can be seen that the animal started responding at a very low rate that, as time passed, accelerated into a fairly stable terminal rate at "b" maintained until reinforcement occurred. During the 5-minute time-out periods the animal did not respond at all. This is indicated by the flat horizontal stretch of record that appears after each reinforcement. During the subsequent 12-minute fixed-interval periods, responding did not start until a few minutes after onset of the light above the lever (at "d"), which coincided with the return of the pen to the baseline (at "e"). Abortive starts are made occasionally (at "f"). A smooth gradual acceleration with an occasional pause may be seen at "g." The overall characteristic pattern of performance shows fairly gradual, positively accelerated scallops in each fixed interval period (Ferster and Skinner, 1957; Skinner, 1938). A characteristic performance when the intervals between reinforcement are not fixed is shown in Figure 3.

As P. Dews (1958a) has recently pointed out, the performance of an organism on a fixed-interval schedule, whether rat (Skinner, 1938), pigeon (Ferster and Skinner, 1957), or human

being (Holland, 1958[1]), is not what one would expect. In discussing the effects of certain pharmacological agents on the pecking rate of pigeons before a scientifically oriented lay audience, he explicitly emphasized that cumulative curves "should be taken at their face value." One should "not sit in judgment of the intelligence" of the animal in these experiments. The trained experimenter has learned to view his cumulative records with the same detached objectivity with which a physical chemist looks at an infrared absorption spectrum. "One would not try to put oneself in the place of a molecule being irradiated to decide which wave lengths one would expect to be absorbed."

It is also very easy to talk about the timing behavior of an animal under these conditions of reinforcement. It might be pointed out, however, that it makes no more sense to state

1 See pages 53-64 of this volume.

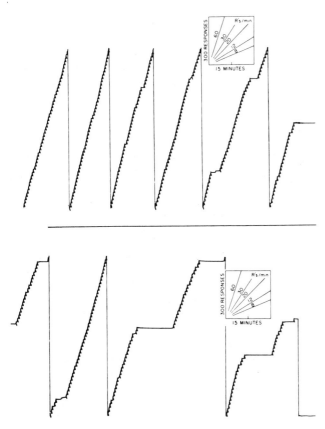

Figure 5. *Typical performance by a monkey under fixed-ratio reinforcement. Reinforcements occurred at the vertical marks on the record.*

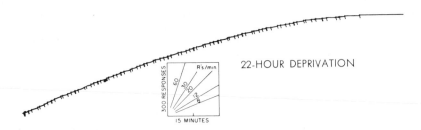

Figure 6. *Performance of a rat under variable-interval reinforcement and low deprivation. Reinforcements occurred at the vertical marks on the record.*

that an animal is timing (or has a sense of time) than it would be to say the same thing about a condenser in a resistor-condenser circuit. The only important questions concern the relevant experimental variables that control the performance.

The effects of piecework schedules, among others, have also been extensively investigated (Ferster and Skinner, 1957). Figure 5 shows the cumulative response record of a monkey pressing a lever for water as a reinforcement. The monkey is on piecework in the sense that only each 28th response is reinforced. Such a reward schedule is called a fixed-ratio (FR) schedule of reinforcement.

If one compares the curves of Figures 3 and 5 some interesting differences are apparent. Whereas the rat of Figure 3 works steadily at a fairly constant rate, the monkey works in spurts. Small but definite pauses are observable after each reinforcement for the animal on the ratio schedule. These pauses become more frequent and their duration increases as the number of rewards received increases. Satiation records of animals working on a variable-interval schedule of reinforcement look quite different. Figure 6 shows the cumulative record of a rat on a one-minute variable-interval schedule pressing a lever for water as a reward. In this case the curve is negatively accelerated and levels off smoothly.

The difference in performance in the various experiments described so far is due to the particular schedules of reinforcement employed. They are not specific for a certain species or type of reward used. Similar results have been obtained with many different species and other reinforcements. . . .

The phenomena of operant conditioning

are not restricted to animals. As a matter of fact most of our daily activities involve operant behavior. Anyone in the possession of a watch with a large sweep second hand can demonstrate to himself some of the basic principles.

A lecturer standing in front of a fairly small audience makes an especially good subject. Many speakers let their eyes wander from person to person. Before "conditioning," the experimenter should determine the number of times the speaker looks at him during a given period, e.g., 10 minutes. This allows one to calculate the pre-experimental control rate of the response involved. Subsequently one can start reinforcing this behavior. From now on, every time the speaker looks at him the experimenter should smile or nod, meanwhile keeping a record of the frequency of the speaker's behavior during successive 5-minute intervals. It is not uncommon to triple or even quadruple the frequency of the "looking-at-the-experimenter" behavior within a 20-minute period.

Laboratory studies of operant conditioning have not been limited to behavior controlled by rewarding or pleasant consequences. One of the more frequent methods of controlling behavior, both in animals and in man, employs so-called aversive consequences, or punitive measures (Skinner, 1953). In daily ·life such "negative reinforcers" may range from physical abuse to fines and ridicule. A negative reinforcer can be defined as a behavioral consequence that induces organisms to act in order to escape from it or to prevent it from happening entirely (avoidance).

The use of electric shock in animal behavior research has been common practice for decades. However, laboratory techniques for

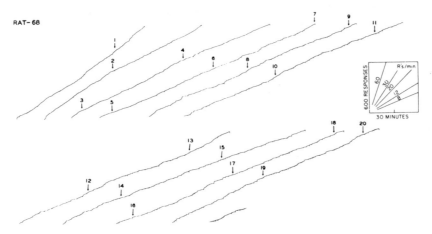

RAT-68

Figure 7. *Performance of a rat that avoids shock by pressing a lever under the Sidman procedure. The numbers indicate successive hours. The occurrence of a shock is indicated by a vertical mark on the record.*

generating stable rates of responding controlled by aversive consequences were not available until 1953. In that year M. Sidman disclosed a technique that opened up the entire field of avoidance behavior (1953a). An extensive experimental analysis of escape and avoidance behavior as well as of the effects of punishment is currently being pursued in several laboratories.

In Sidman's initial series of avoidance experiments, rats were given an electric shock through a grid floor at regular intervals unless a lever was depressed by the animal. Each lever depression reset the timer that controlled the shock and thus delayed its occurrence. If, for example, each response reset a 30-second timer, a minimum interval of 30 seconds was insured between avoidance behavior and shock. By continuously pressing the lever within 30-second intervals the rat would not get shocked at all. The time interval with which each response postpones the shock (the response-shock, or RS, interval) does not have to be equal to the time interval between shocks (the shock-shock, or SS, interval) when no responding occurs at all. As in Skinner's original experiment, Sidman's technique permits using the rate of responding as a continuous and direct indicator of the effects of experimental manipulations.

A sample of the lever-pressing behavior of a rat during a 21-hour long session is shown in Figure 7. Neither food nor water was avail-

able to the animal during the experimental session. The interval between shocks and the time interval with which each press postponed the shock were 30 seconds. Since the slopes of the curves are the only relevant feature of a cumulative record, white space has been cut out of the original record and the separate segments have been brought closer together to facilitate reproduction. Shocks are indicated by the oblique marks on the record. An interesting and characteristic aspect of the performance is the warm-up effect at the beginning of the session. When the animal was first put into the experimental cage the rate of responding was low and the animal received a large number of shocks. This phenomenon occurs regularly at the beginning of a new session. The reasons for it are not yet very well understood. The cumulative record shows that the number of shocks per hour increases as the session continues. The first six to eight hours, however, show a stable response as well as shock rate.

Much higher rates than the one shown by the rat of Figure 7 can be generated by certain modifications of Sidman's original procedure. Instead of requiring the animal to make only one press to reset the shock timer, one can train the animal to press several times to postpone the shock. Figure 8 shows the various rates of responding of a rat when eight presses are required to reset the shock-timer (Verhave, 1959b). The four panels from top to bottom

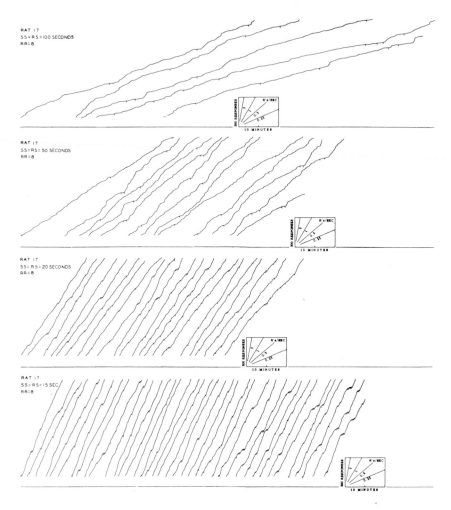

Figure 8. *Performance of a rat that avoids shock by pressing a lever under a modified Sidman procedure. The performance during 4 different sessions is shown. Shocks occurred at the vertical marks on the record.*

show the rate of responding during four six-hour sessions when each lever press postponed the shock for 100, 50, 20 and 15 seconds, respectively. These data show that, as in Sidman's original procedure, the rate of responding is a function of the time period by which each response postpones the shock (Sidman, 1953b; Verhave, 1959b).

The avoidance procedures can be used very effectively to restrict an animal's repertoire and limit it almost exclusively to the emission of a single kind of behavior selected arbitrarily by the experimenter.

Williams and Teitelbaum (1956) recently employed such a technique to force satiated rats to drink exorbitantly large quantities of water. Similar procedures could be used to make animals overeat. The degree of control exerted by the avoidance schedules discussed here and operant-conditioning techniques in general is remarkable and frightening in its implications for human behavior. The basic contingencies involved, the postponement or reduction of an aversive consequence, are common in the daily control of human behavior (Skinner, 1953). . . .

The experimental investigation of the control over operant behavior by aversive contingencies has not been limited to animals. Hefferline in recent ingenious experiments generated pure Sidman-type avoidance behavior in humans (Hefferline, *et al.*, 1959). Fortunately for both experimenter and subjects, the aversive reinforcers employed were innocuous.

The subjects were relaxed in a semi-reclining chair. Recording electrodes were taped to the right hand to pick up thumb twitches. Other, dummy, electrodes were attached to various other parts of the body. The subjects were led to believe that the experimenter was interested in changes in body tension when noise was occasionally superimposed on music. During the experiment, music and noise were fed through earphones. The music consisted of semiclassical selections and the noise was a loud hum generated by a signal tracer. Music only was played during the first 10 minutes of a session during which the experimenter determined the frequency of the response before avoidance conditioning. Thereafter the noise was introduced and from then on each muscle twitch turned the noise off for 15 seconds. As in Sidman's experiments with animals, responses during the 15-minute noise-free periods reset the 15-second timer, postponing the noise for another 15-second period. Subjects conditioned rapidly, first escaping from the noise and subsequently avoiding it. Interestingly enough, when the subjects were questioned after the experiments, they showed no evidence of suspecting that they had in any way control over the noise. According to Hefferline the subjects "expressed annoyance at the noise, not only because it was unpleasant in itself, but also because it interrupted the music at times when they were particularly absorbed in it." They reported that "the situation became more tolerable after the experimenter cut down the length of the noise periods." The subjects were completely unaware of their behavior!

All of the above described experiments have illustrated two kinds of consequences by means of which behavior can be established and maintained. A person who drops a coin into a Coca-Cola machine demonstrates behavior determined by a positive reinforcer. The rat that terminates electric shock by pressing a lever demonstrates behavior controlled by a negative reinforcer. Another example of the latter is provided by Chicagoans

who flock to the beaches of Lake Michigan in order to escape the heat of a summer day.

On the basis of the many illustrations given so far, the reader will have little trouble in understanding the definitions of these two kinds of reinforcements. 1) The term "positive reinforcer" is a label for those behavioral consequences that increase or maintain the frequency of behavior when presented, that is, when they are made contingent upon a certain bit of behavior. 2) A "negative reinforcer" is a behavioral consequence that *also increases* or maintains behavior but when *its removal* is made contingent upon a particular response (Keller and Schoenfeld, 1950; Skinner, 1953). Both reinforce, i.e., they increase or maintain behavior. Because of this empirical fact the meanings of these technical terms no longer agree with the popular concepts of reward and punishment. According to these conceptions, rewards "stamp in" behavior while punishment "stamps out" behavior. The effect of punishment in the layman's sense, however, is far from simple. In agreement with our more technical definition of a negative reinforcer, it has been shown experimentally that punishment is only effective because it strengthens (conditions) competing avoidance behavior (Skinner, 1953). The general topic of punishment is a large one and the problems are complex. Because of limitations of space, these issues cannot be further discussed here.

A little reflection concerning the technical definition of a positive reinforcer gives rise to the following question: 1) What happens when we make the *removal* of a positive reinforcer (such as money) contingent upon behavior (as in the case of a fine)? This particular case has been extensively investigated recently with chimpanzees and pigeons by C. B. Ferster. He demonstrated that the removal of a positive reinforcer has effects similar to those that can be obtained by the presentation of a negative reinforcer (Ferster, 1957, 1958a).

In one of Ferster's experiments (1957), chimpanzees were trained to press a telephone key that occasionally, on a variable-interval schedule, produced food. The key would only pay off, however, when an overhead light was turned on. Since responding in the absence of the light was never reinforced, the chimps

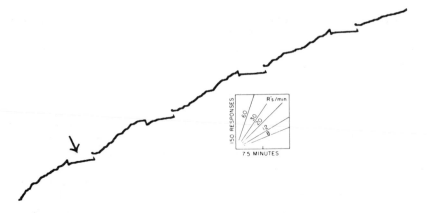

Figure 9. *Suppression of lever-pressing behavior of a rat during a warning stimulus.*

soon stopped pressing in its absence. The chimps were trained in such a manner that by turning the light on or off, the experimenter could start or stop the responding of the animal. After this preliminary training, a red light, called the pre-time-out, or pre-aversive, stimulus, was installed next to the key. This light would come on every 15 minutes for 2-1/2 to 3 minutes. If, during the last 20 seconds of the pre-time-out period, the animal pressed the key, a one-hour time-out from the variable-interval schedule followed as indicated by the absence of the overhead light. However, if the animal did not respond during the final 20 seconds of the pre-time-out warning period, no time-out would occur. The next chance for getting a long one-hour "layoff" would come again 15 minutes later when the red light came on again.

The resulting performance looked very much like the one illustrated in Figure 9. This cumulative record, however, shows the behavior of a rat on a 1-minute variable-interval schedule pressing a lever with water used as reinforcement. Every 10 minutes a tone came on for 5 minutes as indicated by the dip in the record (see arrow). An electric shock was administered to the animal unless the rat did not press the lever during the last 30 seconds of the 5-minute warning period. It is obvious from the record that the animal hardly responded towards the end of these warning periods as indicated by the flattening out of the cumulative record. Data similar to those of Figure 9

were obtained by Azrin (1956) using pigeons.

On the basis of his experiments Ferster (1957) concluded that "The suppression of the base-line behavior by the stimulus preceding the time out from the variable-interval schedule of reinforcement establishes the time out as an aversive event having properties similar to those of electric shock. The time out as an aversive event can be extrapolated to most aversive control in human behavior, where noxious stimuli such as corporal punishment or electric shock are rarely used."

I may mention at this point that if the reinforcement contingencies in the last two experiments were changed in such a way that the animal had been required to increase his rate of responding by a certain amount, the experimental situation would have been almost analogous to the conditions that confront the driver of a car at an intersection controlled by traffic lights. The amber traffic light has the same function as Ferster's pre-time-out stimulus, being followed after a few seconds by a red light during which the driver has to stop his car. It is doubtful whether anybody would care to argue that the red light is not aversive. The amber pre-time-out and the red time-out lights are occasionally superimposed upon the intermittently positively reinforced behavior of driving a car. Similar to Ferster's chimpanzees, many drivers have a strong tendency to increase their rate of movement, by stepping on the gas pedal, if they are close to an intersec-

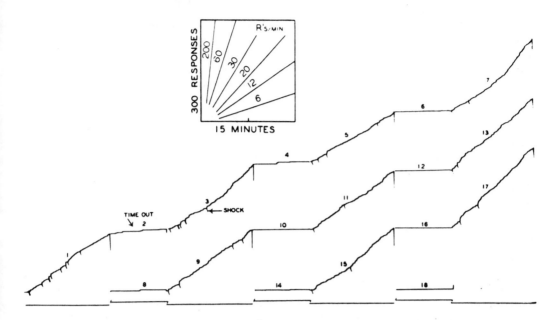

Figure 10. Performance of a rat in an avoidance procedure involving a discrimination between tone-on and tone-off periods. Tone-on periods, correlated with a time-out from the avoidance schedule, occurred during the even-numbered flat stretches in the cumulative record (baseline pen up). Shocks are indicated by the vertical marks on the record.

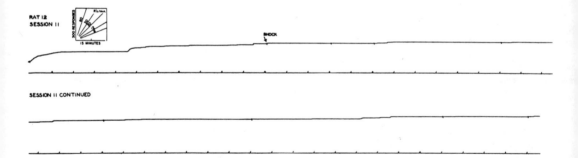

Figure 11. Performance of a rat on the avoidance lever in a procedure identical to that described for Figure 10 except that the rat can produce the time-out from the avoidance schedule himself by pressing a second lever in his cage. The time-out from the avoidance period was present whenever the baseline pen was in the down position.

tion when the yellow light appears. This often dangerous behavior could easily be eliminated by removing the amber pre-time-out stimulus. A few cities recently have switched to systems in which all approaches of an intersection are simultaneously red for a certain length of time. Whether this was done to eliminate the amber light as a pre-time-out stimulus is doubtful.

There is an interesting opposite to the control of behavior by "time out from positive reinforcement" (Ferster, 1958a). The author and Murray Sidman (at the Walter Reed Army Institute for Medical Research) are currently investigating the case where a response is conditioned and maintained by a time out from a stimulus associated with the avoidance schedules described previously. It follows from our definition of a negative reinforcer that its removal should be rewarding.

In one of the author's experiments a certain arbitrary stimulus, for example a 433 cycle/sec. tone, is made aversive to a rat by always being associated with a Sidman-type avoidance schedule. During several 6-hour experimental sessions, given every other day, the animal was first taught to discriminate between tone-on and tone-off periods, which alternated every 10 minutes. During the 10-minute tone-off period, the avoidance schedule was in effect. During the tone-on period the animal was released from the avoidance schedule: when the rat did not respond, he did not get shocked. Within a few sessions under these conditions, the animal learned not to respond during the time-out but went back to work immediately when the tone went off again. A typical performance of a rat is shown in Figure 10. In the next phase of the experiment the rat is given control over the occurrence of the time-out periods. Pressing a second lever will produce a 10-minute time out from the shock-avoidance schedule. As is shown by the record of the animal in Figure 11, this animal produces one time out after another, spending hardly any time in the stimulus associated with the avoidance schedule.

The preceding discussion has shown that stable behavioral processes in the individual organism can be demonstrated and objectively recorded by means of operant-conditioning procedures. Because of the extensive control over behavior obtained with these methods, it is not surprising that investigators with different interests have become involved in this area. . . .

In summary, the techniques for the experimental analysis of voluntary behavior described in this paper employ the frequency with which an organism performs a certain arbitrary bit of behavior as a basic datum for study. Apparatus and certain well-established experimental results were discussed. The methods described provide continuous and objective records of the rate of responding of individual subjects during extended experimental sessions. It was pointed out that accurate and extensive prediction and control of the behavior of individual organisms as diverse as rats, pigeons and chimpanzees could be achieved. . . .

Normal sources of pathological behavior

MURRAY SIDMAN

While they were once held to be incompatible, clinical and experimental medicine have lived together so long and so harmoniously that they are now recognized to be at least common-law partners. The bond that united them was the thesis, ably demonstrated and eloquently expounded by Claude Bernard, that pathological states may be manifestations of normal processes — normal, not according to any statistical criterion, but in the sense that they carry on a lawful existence independently of their pathological manifestations. The study of disease and the study of normal physiological functions have thus come together within a deterministic framework. Clinical medicine has developed a truly experimental foundation and looks to basic science for future progress.

With respect to pathologies of behavior, however, clinical practice and laboratory experimentation have yet to achieve a satisfactory working partnership. The origin of pathology in normal behavioral processes is beginning to be recognized (see, for example, Mowrer, 1950; Skinner, 1953), but in a not very large segment of current experimental or clinical practice. Experimental and clinical psychologists alike seem to equate the two terms *abnormal* and *disorderly*. Thus, when an experimenter isolates a lawful behavioral phenomenon, he is likely to consider that its very lawfulness removes it from the realm of clinical interest. Similarly, the clinician who does ven-

From *Science*, 8 July 1960, **132**, 61–68.

ture into the laboratory will, more often than not, try to demonstrate the absence of lawfulness in some behavioral phenomenon. Neither worker seems to give much thought to the possibility that maladaptive behavior can result from quantitative and qualitative combinations of processes which are themselves intrinsically orderly, strictly determined, and normal in origin.

I shall try to demonstrate a case of this sort here. The clinician may not have available, when I have finished, any new diagnostic or therapeutic tool, but if he can relate the events in my story to these introductory remarks, we may move somewhat closer to an experimental foundation for clinical psychology. The point of view must generate a practice before it can show practical results. The course that has proven so fruitful in medicine should also yield rich dividends in psychology.

ESTES-SKINNER EXPERIMENT

In a paper on "Some quantitative properties of anxiety," W. K. Estes and B. F. Skinner (1941) described the changes produced in the lever-pressing activities of a rat by the sounding of a tone and administration of an electric shock when the tone ended. Observation by Estes and Skinner of the world about them —clinical observation, so to speak—had led these investigators to suspect that the term *anxiety* was often applied to behavior occurring during sequences of events similar to the tone and shock. The authors selected the laboratory rat as the subject for their experiment; but it was assumed that under similar circumstances other animals would behave in a similar fashion, and this assumption has subsequently been confirmed to a remarkable extent.

In the experiment, a rat is placed in a small chamber. The rat is first trained to press a lever projecting from the wall; as reinforcement it gets small food pellets from a tray underneath the lever. Next, the mechanism connecting the lever to the food-delivery system is scheduled so that lever pressing produces food only once every 4 minutes. As established by earlier experiments (Skinner, 1938), on this schedule, a hungry rat will press the lever at a fairly steady rate.

The investigation proper is now begun, with experimental sessions lasting 1 hour. During each session the tone is sounded (through a phone in the chamber) once or twice, for 3 minutes at a time, and at the termination of the tone the rat receives a brief, unavoidable shock through the grill on which it stands. The food-reinforcement schedule remains in effect at all times, including the period when the tone is sounding. After a number of sessions the effect of the tone is to diminish greatly the rate at which the rat presses the lever. This phenomenon is called conditioned suppression.

We repeated the Estes-Skinner experiment in our laboratory, using a rhesus monkey as the subject and making the food pellets available at irregular intervals. Again, the result was conditioned suppression. As the record reproduced in Figure 1 shows, when the tone sounded the monkey pressed the lever at a much slower rate. After the shock was administered, the monkey pressed the lever at its usual rate.

The disruption of ongoing activity is quantitatively reproducible for the same animal, for animals of the same or different species, and for animals in tests of behavior other than lever pressing. Yet this lawful phenomenon has pathological characteristics. As the animal reduces the rate at which it presses the lever, there is a resultant loss of food; this response would seem to have no adaptive value. Instead of pressing the lever, the animal displays other forms of behavior, which may range from complete immobility to agitated, intense, and apparently aimless locomotor activity, all accompanied by signs of autonomic upset.

APPLICATIONS OF THE
ESTES-SKINNER TECHNIQUE

The small perturbation in the cumulative response curve of Figure 1 may not correspond to one's favorite definition of anxiety. As Schoenfeld (1950) has noted, ". . . anxiety in its multifarious nonoperational meanings is a perfectly bad word. . . ." But that is not the issue here. The fact remains that we have a simple technique for producing a profound change in an organism's behavior, a change that appears to be characteristic of a pathological condition. The simplicity of the manipulation should not deceive us. Whenever a simple operation is found to exert a powerful behavioral effect, we may suspect that the phenomenon can be widely generalized. In the present case, furthermore, the simple operation of exposing an organism to the stimulus-shock sequence leads to behavioral consequences of an exquisite complexity.

After it was first described, in 1941, the Estes-Skinner experiment received almost no experimental attention for a period of 10 years. It was finally resurrected by Hunt and Brady (1951), who, with their collaborators, made it the basis of a productive research program. At first Hunt and Brady were interested in conditioned suppression not so much for its own sake as for its potentialities as a tool in studying other things. Their initial investigations, for example, dealt with electroconvulsive therapy. After their subjects, white rats, had developed a full-blown conditioned suppression, ceasing to press a lever when they heard the clicking noise which preceded shock, they were given a series of electroconvulsive "treatments." On being returned to the experimental chamber they no longer reacted to the clicker. Instead of being disrupted, the animals behaved normally during the warning stimulus. Electroconvulsive shock had "cured" them of their anxiety.

A long and revealing series of experiments followed, elucidating additional aspects of electroconvulsive shock treatment. In these experiments, Brady and Hunt (1955) employed conditioned suppression in much the same way as the physiologist, for example, utilizes the techniques of chemistry to investigate metabolic processes. Little more was learned of the behavioral processes themselves. But as additional uses were developed for the Estes-Skinner technique, greater attention was given to the behavioral processes, the initially silent partner in this study of a "cure." It is instructive both for the experimentalist and the clinician to follow at least part of the course of this development.

Another problem to which the suppression technique was applied was that of the effects of certain types of damage to the central nervous system. For example, if a clicking noise of mild intensity is sounded while a thirsty rat

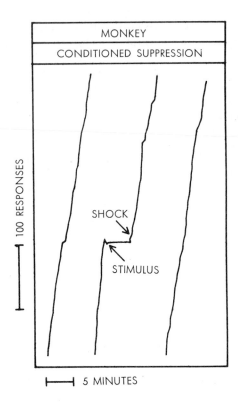

Figure 1. *An illustration of the Estes-Skinner conditioned suppression phenomenon. Responses are recorded cumulatively, with the pen automatically resetting to the base line after every 450 responses. The introduction of the clicking noise is indicated by the slight oblique downward displacement of the pen at the first arrow. The shock, which immediately follows termination of the tone, occurs at the point where the pen displacement is rectified, indicated by the second arrow.*

is pressing a lever to obtain occasional small drops of water, and an unavoidable shock is delivered to the rat when the clicker stops, the animal will eventually cease pressing the lever while the clicker is on. We then make a surgical lesion in the rat's septal forebrain region. When placed in the experimental situation again after it has recovered from the operation, the rat presses the lever for water in the same way as it did before. But when the clicker sounds, the animal does not reduce its rate of lever pressing to the degree that it did prior to the operation. The septal lesion tends to attenuate the conditioned suppression in much the same way as electroconvulsive shock does (Brady and Nauta, 1955).

Certain drugs also change the reaction of both monkeys and rats to the warning clicker. Animals given reserpine over a long period, for example, gradually resume their normal rate of lever pressing during clicker stimuli which precede electric shock (Brady, 1956; Sidman, 1956a). Like electroconvulsive therapy, reserpine apparently cures their disturbed behavior.

There is a similar effect when rats and monkeys are rewarded for lever pressing not by food but by intracranial electrical stimulation via permanently implanted electrodes. (Intracranial electrical stimulation seems to function as a reward for the animal. The basic observation is that the animal will work for electrical stimulation in certain brain areas just as it will work for food; it is not necessary to assume that the animal derives pleasure from the electrical stimulus.) But, whereas an animal working for food will cease its lever-pressing activities after a series of clicker-shock experiences, the same animal, when working for electrical stimulation of the brain, will continue to press the lever while the clicker sounds (Brady, 1958a). Though both function as rewards, brain stimulation and food cause animals to react differently in an anxiety situation.

As far as the behavioral processes were concerned, we had not, at this point, progressed much beyond the original Estes-Skinner phenomenon. But the behavioral perturbation that often accompanies the warning stimulus shows both an order and a complexity which help us to understand behavioral pathology. One more application of the technique will show how we were led to consider conditioned suppression as of interest in its own right.

A research program was under way to test the notion that behavioral phenomena and the functioning of the pituitary-adrenocortical system are correlated. On the endocrine side, John Mason and his collaborators had developed a reliable technique for measuring blood levels of 17-hydroxycorticosteroids in monkeys (Harwood and Mason, 1952) and were engaged in a series of studies to determine the anatomical and physiological properties of the system. On the psychological side, we set out to determine whether this system could be activated by behavioral methods. One of our successful ventures involved the Estes-Skinner technique. When blood samples were taken from monkeys before and after their exposure to the Estes-Skinner procedure we found that a marked elevation had occurred in the plasma level of 17-hydroxycorticosteroids (Mason, et al., 1957). But in this application we were forced to depart, to a certain extent, from the original procedure. All of the departures were dictated by practical necessity, but they had revealing systematic consequences.

A first change was required when we found we could not use the laboratory rat. Nearly all previous work on conditioned suppression had been performed with this useful animal, but unfortunately it did not have a sufficient quantity of blood for repeated steroid measure-

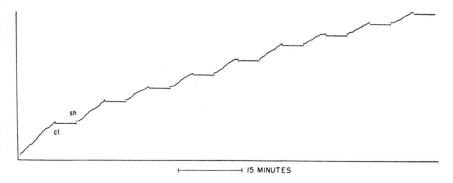

|—————————————| 15 MINUTES

Figure 2. Cumulative record of lever pressing. Five-minute periods of clicking alternated with 5-minute periods of silence. The introduction of the clicking noise is indicated by the slight oblique downward displacement of the pen and is marked Cl at the first presentation. The shock occurs at the point where the pen displacement is rectified. The first shock is marked Sh.

ments. We therefore turned to the monkey. In the initial experiments with the monkey, as in previous work, we combined stimulus and shock only once or twice during any given session. While our subjects did display elevation of steroid levels in these first tests, the elevations were not as consistent as we felt requisite for further investigation. Following a procedure developed by Azrin (1956) we therefore subjected the monkeys to a large number of stimulus-shock sequences during each experimental session and, when this procedure showed signs of success, went on to a schedule in which stimuli of 5 minutes' duration were programmed every 10 minutes. Findings under these conditions gave us clean and reproducible base lines; the animals ceased to respond during each stimulus but began to press the lever again almost immediately after each shock (see Figure 2). Correlated with this relatively stable behavior was a reliable and large elevation in steroid level.

Was this, however, a pure example of behavioral stress, or was the shock a necessary part of the picture? In order to answer this question we attempted to run test sessions in which we gave the subjects the warning stimuli as usual but no shock. Would the stimuli alone, without shock, increase the output of 17-hydroxycorticosteroids? The procedure, unfortunately, did not allow us to answer this question. When the shock was discontinued the animals pressed the lever at their usual high rate during the warning stimuli. There was no longer any conditioned suppression or any rise in steroid level.

We solved the problem by following the stimuli with shock only intermittently. The monkeys received shock after 25 percent of the warning stimuli in each session; the remaining stimuli were not followed by shock. Then, in subsequent test sessions, we again presented the warning stimuli to the subjects without shock. Consistent with the general principle that intermittent reinforcement prolongs the process of extinction was the finding that a diminished rate of lever pressing and a rise in steroid level were elicited by the warning stimuli alone.

But the story is not a continuous chronicle of success. It was necessary to keep each monkey working consistently for extended periods of time, pressing the lever steadily but ceasing to press when the clicker sounded. Stable behavior was required if further investigation was to continue. But when the modified Estes-Skinner procedure had been in effect for some time, the monkey's behavior began to deteriorate. An example may be seen in Figure 3. The contrast with the regularity shown in Figure 2 is striking. The subject now presses the lever at a very uneven rate between stimuli, with suppression sometimes continuing even after the clicker is silent. Occasionally, as at the points marked a, the animal ceases lever pressing immediately before the noise is introduced. During the stimulus period there is evidence of temporal discrimination: as indicated at b, the animal continues pressing the lever during the early minutes of the stimulus; then suppression occurs. Another strange phenomenon is indicated at c: after a period of suppression, the monkey begins to press the lever at a low, steady rate which continues until it receives the shock.

This breakdown of the behavioral base line is

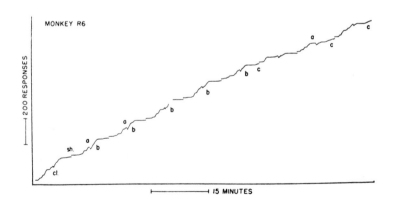

Figure 3. Cumulative record obtained under the same conditions as those of Figure 2, but at a later stage. See text for explanation of a, b, *and* c.

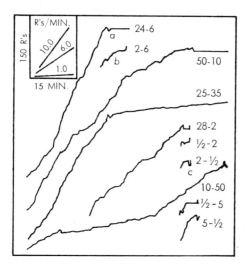

Figure 4. *Sample cumulative records made in tests with periods of clicking and of silence of various lengths. The first number of each pair designates the number of minutes of silence; the second, the number of minutes of clicking. The oblique downward displacement of each curve indicates the point at which clicking was introduced.*

the kind of phenomenon that suggests pathology. We may well conclude that the behavior is pathological but not on the grounds that it is disorderly. The anomalies which began to appear in the behavioral records appeared to be disorderly only because we were not at the time able to identify the controlling variables. Unless we could gain some understanding of the behavioral processes at work here, we could not apply the technique to the problem of behavior-endocrine interaction. Out of our investigations, then, there emerged a new appreciation of the behavioral complexities with which we had been working. Our first attempts to unravel these complexities seemed to multiply them, producing behavior which, if not pathological, was certainly bizarre, but we were eventually able to show that even the most bizarre performances were under the control of orderly and manipulable factors. In no sense did they represent deviations from lawful behavior.

Reinforcement Cost

From the several changes we had made in the basic Estes-Skinner procedure, we selected two temporal variables for further study. These were (i) the period during which the clicker sounded and (ii) the period during which the clicker was silent. Using white rats as subjects, we systematically manipulated these two periods (Stein, *et al.,* 1958). Much to our surprise, we found that such manipulation reproduced several of the phenomena shown in Figure 3. The most general finding, however, was that both temporal variables controlled the degree of conditioned suppression, but only when they were considered in relation to each other. An animal would press the lever at a very slow rate during a clicking period of a given duration only if there were relatively long intervals of silence between clicking periods. An example may be seen in the upper two curves of Figure 4. With 24-minute periods of silence, the subject makes only a few responses during a 6-minute clicking period (at *a*). Suppression is nearly complete. But when the periods of silence are reduced to 2 minutes, the animal responds considerably more often during a 6-minute clicking period (at *b*). Similarly, as may be seen further down in Figure 4, with 2-minute periods of silence and 1/2-minute clicking periods the subject again fails to respond (at *c*). Complete suppression reappears.

We now knew how to maintain a stable conditioned suppression in the subjects of our steroid studies and in other applications of the Estes-Skinner technique, but the real plum was another observation which illuminated the process through which the animals' behavior was controlled by the temporal variables. The subjects of the experiment had been deprived of water, and the reinforcement for lever pressing was a small drop of water. We noticed that the number of drops of water the animals received was relatively constant, about 90 percent of the maximum possible, regardless of the effectiveness of the clicker in diminishing the rate at which they pressed the lever. But, it will be recalled, conditioned suppression causes the animal to miss reinforcements, for it is only by pressing the lever that a drink can be obtained. In other words, the animals displayed conditioned suppression only to the extent that they could do so without missing more than 10 percent of their drinks. Thus, if the clicking period was short relative to the period of silence, the animal could cease pressing the lever during the clicking and still miss relatively few drinks in the course of an experimental session. On the other hand, if the clicking period was relatively long, complete cessation of lever pressing would cause the animal to lose most of the available drinks.

Although more work must be done before the phenomenon is entirely clear, we might say, at this point, that the animals manifest anxiety only to the extent that they can afford to do so in terms of reinforcement cost.

Aversive Interactions

A unique feature of the Estes-Skinner technique is its use of changes in the organism's ongoing behavior to measure the consequences of an independent but concurrent experimental operation. The effect of the warning stimulus may be described, in most general terms, as a disturbance in the pattern of behavior in progress at the time the stimulus appears. As we have seen, one form of disturbance is complete cessation of the behavior. It seems reasonable to suppose that the variables which control the base-line activity also have a role in determining the effect of the warning stimulus. In one of the few attempts yet made to verify this supposition, Brady found that rats reacted to a warning stimulus with conditioned suppression even when they received the water in accordance with several different types of schedules. However, when the stimulus was then presented without any shock, it was found that the type of reinforcement schedule did influence the length of time it took the animals to resume their normal rate of lever pressing (Brady, 1955). The variables controlling the normal behavior pattern, then, did affect the temporal course of the animals' "rehabilitation."

All demonstrations of conditioned suppression up to this point had one feature in common. Food or water reinforcement was always used to maintain the subjects' base-line behavior. What would be the consequence of presenting the clicker-shock sequences while the subjects were pressing a lever to avoid electric shocks?

In the experiments described below, monkeys were the subjects, and the experimental space was similar to, but larger than, that previously described for the rat. We first conditioned the monkeys to press a lever by the simple expedient of giving them a brief shock whenever 20 seconds elapsed without a lever depression. Each time they pressed the lever they postponed the shock for 20 seconds (Sidman, 1953a). After the animals had settled down to a relatively stable rate of avoidance responding we introduced the clicker and unavoidable shock sequence, using the earlier schedule of 5-minute clicking periods alternating with 5-minute periods of silence.

The immediate result was that the animals pressed the lever at approximately three times their normal rate, both when the clicker was on and when it was silent. In fact, they responded sufficiently often to avoid all avoidable shocks; the only shocks they received were the unavoidable ones (Sidman, et al., 1957). The monkeys then gradually slowed down to their normal rate of lever pressing. But they returned to their normal rates more rapidly when the clicker was silent than when it was sounding. There was, therefore, an intermediate phase in which they pressed the lever at a higher rate during the clicking periods than during the periods of silence. This reversal of the Estes-Skinner observation caught our interest.

We eliminated the avoidable shocks but continued to administer the unavoidable ones. The monkeys ceased lever pressing, as was to have been expected, during the periods of silence. But for a long time they persisted in lever pressing during the clicking periods. Figure 5 shows the striking reversal of the usual conditioned suppression; the animal practically never responds during periods of silence or during the initial minutes of the clicking periods. But as the time approaches for shock, the monkey begins to press the lever rapidly and continues until it receives the shock. Immediately after the shock, it again ceases pressing, and another cycle begins.

This phenomenon is called conditioned facilitation.

Does conditioned facilitation during the clicking period represent a breakdown of the lawfulness to which we have become accustomed in our experience with the Estes-Skinner technique? From an adaptive point of view, the facilitation of lever pressing makes no more sense than does suppression. The shock is inevitable, and the animal's high response rate during the stimulus represents only so much wasted energy. It would take very little stretching of the imagination to class this behavior as pathological. Yet, as we shall see, it results from normal processes at work in a slightly unusual setting.

When an animal that is pressing a lever for food is first exposed to the clicker-shock sequence it may initially cease pressing both when the clicker is on and when it is silent, even though it receives shock only while the clicker is on. This may be thought of as a generalized effect of unavoidable shock. A corresponding generalized effect, an over-all increase in response rate, is initially observed when the lever pressing has served to postpone

shock. In their first stages, then, the two effects are opposite in direction but similar, perhaps, in origin.

A second stage occurs when the initially generalized effect of shock is channeled into the clicking period. A monkey working for food returns to its normal rate of lever pressing during periods of silence but continues to display suppression during the clicking periods. Similarly, a monkey pressing the lever to avoid shock returns to its normal response rate during periods of silence but continues to display conditioned facilitation during the clicking periods.

If this were the whole story, both the suppression and the facilitation might well be construed as emotional reactions to the unavoidable shock, the precise form of the reaction depending upon the subject's past experience of shock. Perhaps some such formulation could encompass the observations thus far discussed. But one additional observation does not fit. Under appropriate conditions, some of which I discussed above, the conditioned suppression becomes fixed at the second stage. The conditioned facilitation, on

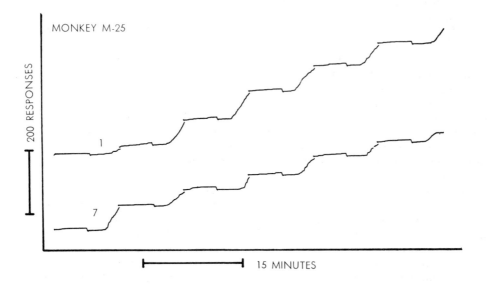

Figure 5. *Response facilitation during the period of clicking prior to shock. The introduction of clicking is marked by the downward displacements in the record. The lower curve is actually continuous with the upper one, but has been displaced for compact presentation. The first and seventh clicking periods of the session are labeled.*

the other hand, goes through a third phase. It disappears. It is really a transitory phenomenon, though its life span and magnitude are sufficiently great to merit both experimental and clinical attention. The impermanence of the facilitation places it in a different category from the suppression.

We can, however, hold on to the notion that avoidance conditioning is a prerequisite if the animal's rate of lever pressing is to increase, rather than decrease, during the clicking periods. If an organism has learned a successful shock-avoidance response, what is more appropriate, in a situation in which shocks occur, than that very response? The source of control of the facilitation may be the normal processes which govern the subject's previously acquired avoidance behavior. But we are still faced with the fact that the animal actually cannot avoid the shocks. On many occasions the monkey is almost immediately punished by the shock for its increased rate of lever pressing during the clicking period. How can we reconcile the inevitability of the shock with an explanation based upon the normal and orderly processes that underlie successful avoidance behavior?

The difficulty is more apparent than real, but I have not simply been building up a straw man. I have examined the problem in detail because its simple solution reveals a form of behavioral control which, because of its subtlety, one might easily overlook. In the actual relations between the shock and facilitated lever pressing two facts are to be noted. First, the monkey receives only one shock during each 5-minute clicking period; hence, only an extremely small proportion of its lever-pressing responses are actually punished. From the subject's point of view, lever pressing, by which it has in the past effectively avoided shocks, seems to remain largely successful. Avoidance of shock still reinforces lever pressing, even though the relation is a spurious one. The monkey's behavior during the clicking period is nonadaptive because the rules of the environment have changed and the changes have not yet elicited appropriate response modification. The occasional shocks only serve as false discriminative cues to keep the animal behaving in a fashion appropriate to the former circumstances.

The second point concerns the temporal rela-

tion between response and shock implied by the term *punishment*. The time interval that elapses between an unavoidable shock and the immediately preceding lever response is variable. In other respects the situation is exactly the same as that during the original avoidance conditioning. Originally, the monkey postponed the shock for 20 seconds each time it pressed the lever. Now, the shock sometimes occurs 2 seconds after a response, sometimes 200 seconds after, sometimes 20 seconds after, and so on. We have already demonstrated that animals will continue to avoid shock successfully when we systematically vary the amount of time they postpone shock with each lever press (Sidman and Boren, 1957). In the present case, the variation is governed not by the experimenter but by the vagaries of the subject's own lever-pressing. The contingencies are spurious, but the control they exercise is real.

In its late stages at least, facilitation during the clicking period may properly be understood as avoidance behavior which the monkey continues to manifest because of a combination of historically real and currently adventitious contingencies. It is not nearly as general a phenomenon as conditioned suppression; it requires an organism with a particular type of behavioral history, and it requires a unique set of current circumstances which serve to perpetuate the processes that stem from this history even after they are no longer relevant to the demands of the environment.

Direct manipulation of the monkey's behavioral history in a subsequent experiment effectively demonstrated its relevance. In the first phase of the experiment we conditioned the monkey to press the lever by reinforcing it with food. Once the monkey was pressing the lever at a steady rate, we introduced the clicker-shock sequences until a conditioned suppression developed during the clicking period.

The next step was to add an avoidance component to the subject's behavioral repertoire. We disconnected the food-delivery mechanism, the clicker, and the mechanism that delivered the unavoidable shock. Pressing the lever now served to postpone shocks for 20 seconds. Finally, the monkey was again given the opportunity to procure food by pressing the lever without receiving shocks at any time. The variables were the same as in the first phase of the experiment, but the monkey's experience with shock was different.

When we again introduced the clicker-shock sequences the avoidance history proved to be dominant. Whenever the clicker sounded the monkey pressed the lever at a much higher rate, even though it was working for food (Herrnstein and Sidman, 1958). By interpolating a period of avoidance conditioning between the two stages of the Estes-Skinner procedure we had changed conditioned suppression to facilitation. The conclusion seems inescapable that the facilitation represents a form of avoidance behavior, irrational perhaps, certainly not effective, but nonetheless derived from identifiable and orderly sources of control.

A final set of experiments provided us with an unexpected view of the twisted fashion in which normal behavioral processes can manifest themselves (Sidman, 1958). Our initial aim was simple enough. We had seen that the effect on a given response of a stimulus that precedes a shock will depend upon the history of that response. If we now select for simultaneous observation two different responses, one of which the monkey has used to procure food and the other of which it has used to avoid shock, will a warning stimulus generate two concurrent but opposite reactions in a single animal?

To answer this question, we made two opportunities simultaneously available to the monkey. Hanging down from the ceiling of the chamber was a chain, and pulling this chain occasionally paid off with food, while pressing a lever mounted on a wall of the chamber postponed shocks for 20 seconds. Both the food schedule and the avoidance program were in effect concurrently. The monkey adjusted appropriately to the contingencies, sometimes pulling the chain and sometimes pressing the lever.

Clicker-shock sequences were then introduced, and the avoidable shocks—shocks previously governed by lever pressing—were eliminated. The only shocks the monkey received were the unavoidable ones that followed the clicking periods. In line with previous findings, we expected the monkey, during the clicking period, simultaneously to reduce its rate of chain pulling, displaying conditioned suppression, and to increase its rate

of lever pressing, displaying conditioned facilitation.

In fact, the animal's rates of response for both chain pulling and lever pressing rose during the clicking periods. There was no evidence of suppression. Rates for both types of response were relatively low during periods of silence. This was the pattern for a response with an avoidance history, yet we had not provided the food-reinforced response with such a history. Did this mean that the lawfulness revealed in the prior experiments is missing when two response systems within a single organism are simultaneously exposed to the Estes-Skinner procedure? Such an interpretation would be consistent with the classical view of behavior pathology, and, if we had accepted it, we should have stopped work at that point. As it turned out, however, our resistance to the classical view permitted us to round out the story. The final experiments not only revealed orderly processes but, in addition, permitted us to explain some material classically considered pathological.

We found that our monkey's two concurrent responses were not entirely independent. For example, we returned the animal to the initial training procedure in which it produced food occasionally by pulling the chain and avoided shock by pressing the lever. We then disconnected the feeding mechanism. But even though no food was forthcoming, the animal continued to pull the chain at a relatively high rate. The monkey stopped pulling the chain only after we had also disconnected the shock, thereby causing it to stop pressing the lever. Only with the cessation of avoidance behavior did the monkey cease pulling the chain. It seemed clear that the food-reinforced behavior was being controlled in some way by the avoidance contingency, even though no such control was demanded by the experimental arrangements. The process through which this control developed is a most fascinating one, for it takes us, in a manner of speaking, into the "inner life" of our animal subjects.

We have already described the facilitating effect of the warning clicker as a case of adventitiously reinforced, or "superstitious," avoidance behavior. (I use the term *superstitious* in the operational sense in which Skinner uses it, to describe a situation in which a particular response is correlated only by chance with a reinforcing state of affairs (Skinner, 1948a). Even though the behavior may not actually produce the reinforcement, and though the correlation may not even be advantageous to the organism, the reinforcing effect is not thereby weakened.) The monkey's behavior during the stimulus period is reinforced by the seeming avoidance of shocks. We, as experimenters, know that the animal would not have received shocks anyway, even if it had not pressed the lever, but our monkey is a prisoner of its behavioral history.

The subject was free to make the two possible responses in any sequence. If it frequently pulled the chain and then pressed the lever, the pattern might become established as superstitious avoidance. If the monkey could speak, it might well tell us that it was avoiding the shock by first pulling the chain and then pressing the lever. The chain-pulling response, though reinforced with food, might also develop an avoidance component, which would explain the increased rate of chain pulling during a clicking period.

Being both unable and unwilling to rely upon the verbal report of our subject, we made an experimental search for adventitious reinforcement processes. We found that the monkey was actually making the two responses in sequences of the sort that would favor the development of a superstitious avoidance pattern. There was only a low probability that the animal would pull the chain twice without pressing the lever in between; the vast majority of chain pulls were followed by lever presses. There was abundant opportunity for chain pulling to be correlated accidentally with the avoidance of shock.

There remained only the task of breaking up the alternation pattern and thereby eliminating the avoidance component of the food-reinforced response. This was accomplished by utilizing a bit of behavioral technology. Up till now only an occasional chain pull had paid off on a temporal schedule. The schedule was changed so that the animal had to pull the chain a fixed number of times to procure food. Since such a schedule favors the reinforcement of rapid bursts of responses (Skinner, 1938; Ferster and Skinner, 1957), there should be a tendency for the monkey to make several chain-

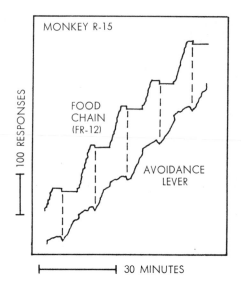

Figure 6. Concurrent cumulative records for chain pulling and lever pressing. The portions of the records displaced obliquely downward denote clicking periods that preceded shock. The broken lines connect temporally corresponding points (introduction of clicking) on each curve.

pulling responses in succession before switching to the lever.

The new schedule accomplished its purpose. The likelihood that the animal would press the lever after only a single chain pull decreased markedly. Instead, the monkey showed a marked tendency to pull the chain several times before pressing the lever. The typical pattern of bursts and pauses may be seen in the upper curve of Figure 6.

Figure 6 also indicates that we eliminated the superstitious avoidance component of the food-reinforced response. For now, when we introduce the clicker-shock sequence there is no increase in the monkey's rate of chain pulling. The clicking simultaneously suppresses the food-reinforced response and facilitates the avoidance response. Although both forms of response exist simultaneously in the same organism, each is affected by the clicking according to its own history.

It has been necessary to report the experiments in such detail in order to illustrate the complete normality of the processes underlying our initial finding of facilitation in both responses. In tracking these processes down, we have seen how they may act to produce some bizarre manifestations. Thus, behavior which has no real connection with the shock must nevertheless be diagnosed as avoidance behavior, spuriously maintained as part of an avoidance pattern. Then, this behavior, already under spurious control, perpetuates itself during the clicking period by seemingly permitting the animal to avoid shocks that would not have occurred anyway. Such behavior may be called "second-order superstition." If this is "sick" behavior, the processes that generate and maintain it are healthy enough.

Whether these particular experimental phenomena are indeed basic to the understanding, diagnosis, and treatment of clinically observed behavior pathology remains an open question. But there can be no doubt that such experimental manipulation has the necessary power and subtlety to uncover processes relevant to clinical observations. The clinical psychologist need no longer seek his experimental foundations among demonstrations of behavioral chaos. The experimentalist, too, would do well to cultivate an interest in pathology as a source of insight into normal behavioral processes.

Human vigilance

JAMES G. HOLLAND

Current interest in the classical problem of sustained efficiency in monotonous perceptual tasks has centered around situations in which human beings are required to monitor some display in search of critical, but infrequent, signals. Such tasks are numerous and of considerable practical importance. In air defense systems, operators must search radarscopes for extremely infrequent enemy targets. Increased automation requires human monitoring of equipment which seldom fails. In addition, cases involving assembly-line inspection of products represent another large group of monitoring tasks in which the critical signals may arise relatively infrequently.

Recent work on operators monitoring displays having infrequent signals indicates a drop in the percentage of signals detected as time on watch progresses. Mackworth (1948) has shown a decrement in the subject's ability to detect signals as a two-hour watch progressed. The signals were double steps of a clock hand which normally stepped 0.3 inches every second but had 24 double steps per hour. Similar decrements have been demonstrated when subjects were required to detect targets on simulated radar displays. Field studies also have shown the decrement as time on watch passes. . . . In addition, Bakan (1955), using a modified threshold measurement technique, has demonstrated a decrement in a brightness discrimination task.

Not all investigators have found a decrement. One investigator (Fraser, 1950), using the clock test, has shown an increased variance in the number of detections as the watch progresses, but no average decrement. Others (Broadbent, 1953), using latency of detection of non-transient signals as a criterion, rather than the percentage of signals detected, have found an increase in variance but no increase in the average latency of detection.

Whether a decrement is found or not, the fact is clear that many signals well above absolute threshold are not detected either early or late in the session. Furthermore, if the frequency of signals increases, there is an increase in the percentage of signals detected. For example, Deese (Deese and Ormond, 1953) found

From *Science,* 11 July 1958, **128**, 61–67.

that with a display simulating a search-radar 'scope and using 10, 20, 30, or 40 targets per hour during a three-hour watch, 46, 64, 83, and 88 percent were detected, respectively.

In order to "account for" the decrement and the relation between signal frequency and detection probability, an abundance of theoretical constructs have been offered. The results obtained are said to reflect declines in, or waxing and waning of, attention, vigilance, or fatigue. Mackworth (1948) tentatively postulated an excitatory state termed "vigilance" which is opposed by an inhibitory state that parallels the concept of external inhibition found in the literature on classical conditioning. More recently, Adams (1956) has used Hull's I_R (reactive inhibition) in a similar manner. The performance decrement is supposed to be a partial extinction phenomenon reflecting the build-up of the inhibitory state. When a verbal message to the effect that the subject should "do even better for the rest of the test" was delivered, the percentage of signals detected returned to the initial level. This is explained as disinhibition and thus as evidence for the existence of an inhibitory state. When a 1-hour break was provided, again the performance returned to the initial level. This is said to reflect spontaneous recovery from the inhibitory state.

Several investigators have employed expectancy as an explanatory concept. Mackworth (1950), Broadbent (1953), and Deese (1955) have used it to "explain" (i) the greater over-all percentage of detections when the number of signals per session increases, and (ii) the increased probability of detection for the longer intersignal times that is observed when a signal-by-signal analysis is made. [The latter finding has not always been confirmed (Bartlett, *et al.*, 1955; Deese and Ormond, 1953).] In addition, Broadbent has used the idea of stimulus selectivity (that is, attention or set) to explain not only the findings concerning monitoring behavior but classical conditioning as well.

In addition to these theories relative to psychic and conceptual states, a physiological theory has been advanced. Deese (1955) suggested that the waking center of the hypothalamus may be involved and that the activity of the center depends on an influx of sensory stimulation. According to this theory, as it applies to problems of detecting infrequent signals, a varied sensory input is necessary to maintain the excitatory state in this center and thus to maintain a high level of detection.

NEED FOR AN ATHEORETIC APPROACH

The various theories have all been developed to account for a rather meager set of data. The parameters influencing the monitoring of low-signal-frequency displays are as yet poorly explored, with the result that inconsistencies are found among the findings. In view of this state of affairs it might be well to forego the luxury of developing explanatory concepts until the empirical relations are better established.

Indeed, the necessity for theories has been sensibly challenged by Skinner (1950) with regard to theories of learning. Theories, in Skinner's sense, are explanations of data that make use of events at another level of observation and are not to be equated with empirically defined concepts which refer to the behavioral level of observation. The latter permit generalization of empirical principles. His arguments seem at least as relevant to theories of "vigilance."

Such entities as vigilance, attention, inhibition, expectancy, and waking-center activity all fall into the category of theories, as defined above. They, like concepts in learning theories, are "at some other level of observation, described in different terms, and measured, if at all, in different dimensions." (Skinner, 1950, p. 193). These concepts give the appearance of explaining the data because of the syntax of the statements. The subject is said to make a detection because he is, at that moment, vigilant or attentive or expecting a signal. But the concepts are no less mysterious than the phenomena they purport to explain. There remains the task of discovering the events which influence vigilance, attention, or expectancy. Once having done this, we may be little better off than if we had simply searched for the conditions controlling the probability of detection, since this is assumed to be directly related to the intervening explanatory concept.

The argument that theories generate research does not seem to apply to theories in this area. With one exception (Deese and Ormond, 1953), the theories seem to have been offered as explanations of data already collected. But even should they generate research in the future, it is by no means obvious that this research would be of greater significance than research directed toward an empirical and behavioral systematization of the field.

However, the use of theories is by no means surprising in view of the types of measure used. In practice, only the percentage of signals detected, latency of detection, or change in threshold intensity is measured. The investigator is then faced with the problem of saying . what it is that changes during the monitoring task. It is unsatisfactory to say that the percentage of signals detected *is* the vigilance rather than a *result* of vigilance, attention, or expectancy, just as the learning theorist is unsatisfied in saying that decrease in errors *is* learning. Instead of proceeding to search for a satisfactory datum on the behavioral level of observation, the investigator postulates events for other levels of observation. Signal detection is said to *reflect* states of vigilance, attention, or expectancy. The result of this is that the search for an appropriate behavioral datum is impeded, and in its place assumed causes are used which are mental, physiological, or conceptual events not describable in behavioral terms.

One approach to discovering a satisfactory datum is to consider the behavior which may be involved in monitoring and then to determine the variables which control that behavior. Success in detecting signals may depend on the emission of responses which will make the de-

tection possible. These could be responses of orienting toward the correct portion of the display and fixating or scanning the display. Such responses can be termed observing responses in that they bring about the observation of signals.[1] Furthermore, these observing responses might follow the same principles as instrumental responses and thus be subject to control by the same type of environmental variables. It is suggested that the observing responses which make detections possible follow the principles of operant behavior. The reinforcement for these observing responses could be the detection of the signals. That is to say, the detection itself could exert control over the rate or probability of emission of observing responses in exactly the same manner as food reinforcement controls the rate of operant responses in animals.

SIGNAL DETECTION AS REINFORCEMENT

In order to evaluate this formulation of "vigilance" it was first necessary to determine whether signal detection really could serve to reinforce an observing response. To do this, subjects (Navy enlisted men), working in the dark, were required to report deflections of a pointer on a dial; but the pointer could be seen only when the subject pressed a key which provided a brief flash of light that illuminated

1 For a use of a similar type of response applied to discrimination learning problems, see Reid (1953) and Wykoff (1952).

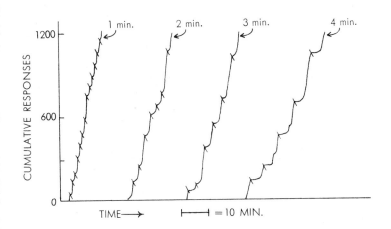

Figure 1. Cumulative response records for 1-, 2-, 3-, and 4-minute fixed-interval schedules of pointer deflections. Detections are indicated by lines cutting across the records.

the face of the dial. When the key was pressed, the light flashed for a period of only 0.07 second, even if the subject held the key down. Thus he had to release and redepress the key to obtain another look at the dial. When the subject observed a pointer deflection he reported it by pressing another key, which reset the pointer. The pointer remained deflected until this key was pressed. The deflections of the pointer were programmed so as to make possible various schedules of detections (or reinforcements). Each subject was advised that his only aim should be to make as many detections as he could and to reset the pointer as rapidly as possible. At the end of each session he was informed of the number of detections made and the average time per detection. He was not informed that the experimenter was in any way concerned with the frequency with which he flashed the light. Cumulative response records were made of his responses on the light-flashing key. This type of recording, commonly used in operant conditioning, consists of a pen which moves in small discrete steps across the recorder paper as responses are made, while the paper moves slowly in a direction perpendicular to the direction of pen movement. The result is a tracing in which the slope of the line reflects the rate of responding.

In order to determine whether signal detection can serve as reinforcement for observing behavior, various schedules of signal presentation were used, analogous to the scheduling of more conventional reinforcers, such as food and water, employed in operant conditioning with animals. Throughout all of the various schedules to be discussed below the subjects were *never* told anything about the nature of the schedule.

Fixed interval

The first schedules used were of the fixed-interval type. Five subjects began with a ½-minute fixed-interval schedule. That is to say, the needle was deflected ½ minute after each detection and remained deflected until it was reset by the subject. After eight 40-minute sessions, the interval was increased to 1, 2, 3, and finally 4 minutes, with eight successive sessions on each.

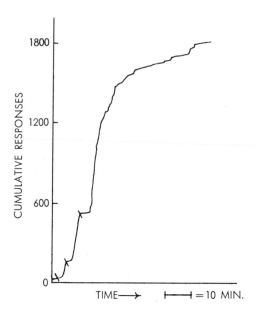

Figure 2. *Cumulative response record showing effect of withholding pointer deflections following a fixed-interval schedule. After three detections (indicated by lines cutting across the record) no further pointer deflections occurred.*

Figure 1 presents data from comparable portions of records for a typical subject on several schedules, all of different fixed intervals. Each curve is a segment of record from the last session which the subject had on the indicated fixed interval. The individual curves are displaced along the horizontal axis. The lines cutting across the records indicate signal detections. Shortly after each detection there is a period in which no observing responses are emitted, as indicated by the flat portions of the curves. Then responding (observing) resumes in an accelerated fashion and reaches a high rate before the next signal. These "scallops" are analogous to those obtained with animals working for food reinforcement on a fixed-interval schedule. In either case the data represent a temporal discrimination. Responses immediately after reinforcement are not reinforced, so a discrimination is formed for "no responding following reinforcement." Responding resumes after time passes and the conditions become appropriate for reinforcement.

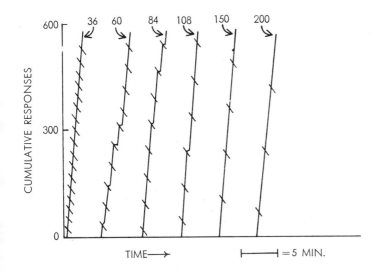

600

300

0

CUMULATIVE RESPONSES

36 60   84   108   150   200

TIME⟶   ⊢——⊣ = 5 MIN.

Figure 3. Cumulative response records for 36-, 60-, 84-, 108-, 150-, and 200-response fixed-ratio schedules of pointer deflections. Detections are indicated by lines cutting across records.

Examining the records, one could, if so inclined, speculate that they reflect "fluctuations of attention" or the course of "subjective expectancies." However, the temptation to do so should not be great since the dependency of observing rate on detection, or reinforcement, is clear. To postulate states accompanying the changes in observing rate adds nothing of use in controlling or predicting the observing rate.

Additional insight into the role of signal detection is provided when no further signals occur (that is, during extinction). Extinction data are provided in Figure 2 for the same subject for whom data were given in Figure 1. This is a complete record for a 1-hour session. Three signals were first provided on the 4-minute fixed-interval schedule which had maintained the observing behavior for six previous sessions; then no further signals were provided. Following each signal detection in the early portion of the record, the characteristic fixed-interval scallops are found. After the third and final detection there is again a scallop, with the high rate continuing for a time and then gradually declining to a very low value. This decline in rate of observing response is dependent upon the absence of signal detection. It cannot be interpreted as physiological fatigue, since on other schedules higher rates have been maintained, without decrement, for more than three hours.

Fixed ratio

To pursue further the analogy between signal detection and reinforcement as found in typical operant conditioning situations, fixed-ratio schedules were employed. These schedules make reinforcement contingent on the number of responses emitted rather than on the passage of time. To begin with, seven subjects were tested on a fixed-ratio schedule of 36 responses per detection. That is, a needle deflection occurred only after 36 observing responses were made following the immediately preceding detection. After six 40-minute sessions on this schedule the ratio was increased, in blocks of six sessions, to 60, 84, 108, 150, and finally 200 responses per detection. Presented in Figure 3 is a family of curves for the various ratios for a typical subject. These curves are equivalent segments of the subject's final sessions on the indicated schedules. Tests with these schedules, unlike most monitoring tasks, permit the subject to minimize the number of signals by not responding. Instead, however, he tends to maximize the number of signals by emitting responses at a high rate. Occasionally short breaks or periods of no responding occur, but only immediately following a detection. These results are also characteristic of those obtained with conventional reinforcement on fixed-ratio schedules.

An additional demonstration of the control exerted by the schedule of signal detection or reinforcement is seen in the extinction following fixed-ratio schedules. A 1½-hour extinction record is presented in Figure 4 for the same subject for whom data were given in Figure 3. Three needle deflections were provided on the 200-response ratio schedule which he had experienced for the preceding six sessions. After that, no more signals were given. The second portion of the record, following resetting of the pen at the vertical line, is continuous with the first. This record resembles extinction following fixed-ratio reinforcement with animals but is decidedly unlike typical extinction following fixed-interval reinforcement (see Figure 2). Instead of the gradual decline seen for extinction following fixed-interval schedules, the rate, when the subject responds at all, is high. Immediately after the last reinforcement the subject continues at his normal rate for more than 800 responses. He then begins showing occasional periods of no responding, but in each case responding resumes at the original high rate. As extinction progresses the periods of no responding increase, but, throughout the session, when there is a single response there is a run of responding at the high rate that prevailed during reinforcement.

Previous analysis (Skinner, 1950; Ferster and Skinner, 1957) has indicated that the form of the extinction curves for various schedules depends on the presence or absence of conditions which were present at the moments of reinforcement in the past. In the case of fixed-ratio schedules there tends to be reinforcement for groups of closely spaced responses (see Skinner, 1938). Thus, high rates are reinforced, and these high rates come to characterize ratio schedules. As a result, when a response is made during extinction, conditions are like those that prevailed at the time of reinforcement. During extinction, therefore, intermediate rates are lacking. The subject either responds rapidly or not at all.

Multiple schedule

It has also proved possible in operant conditioning to generate behavior appropriate to

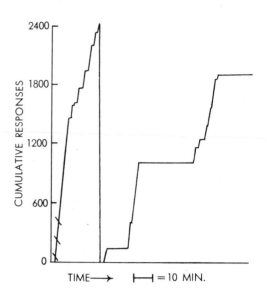

Figure 4. *Cumulative response record showing extinction following a 200-response fixed-ratio schedule of pointer deflections. After three detections (indicated by lines cutting across the record) no further pointer deflections occurred.*

more than one schedule in a single organism during the same session (Ferster and Skinner, 1957). To do so, stimuli are provided to indicate which schedule is in effect at a given moment. The stimuli used have been alternation of schedules (called mixed schedules), different colored stimulus lights, or both. I have successfully combined a 40-response fixed-ratio and a 3-minute fixed-interval schedule, using four subjects. These tests began with six 40-minute sessions in which a small red light indicated a fixed ratio of 23 responses to be in effect and a small green light indicated a ½-minute fixed interval to be in effect. The order of appearance for these two schedules was randomly determined. Then for sessions 6 through 11, the schedules were changed to a 40-response fixed ratio and a 3-minute fixed interval. These two schedules were alternated regularly. Then for the twelfth and final 40-minute session the two schedules appeared randomly, with only the stimulus light providing the basis for discrimination. A typical record for this session is presented in Figure 5. The 3-minute fixed-interval portions of the record are labeled *I,* and the 40-response fixed-ratio portions are labeled *R.* It can be seen that when the interval was in effect (green light on) the subject's observing rate provided the fixed-interval scallop. (There is a rougher grain to the scallop than to that found in Figure 1. This is probably due to the experience on fixed-ratio schedules.) When the fixed-ratio schedule was in effect (red light on), the subject's observing rate was that typical for fixed-ratio reinforcement. Thus, like other operant behavior, the observing response can be brought under stimulus control. There remains no need to appeal to another level of analysis by speaking of "attention" being dependent on "context" or "meaning." Such proposed constructs are unnecessary when the control exerted by the schedule of detection under correlated stimuli can be directly demonstrated.

Differential reinforcement of low rates

One further schedule which attests to the control of observing rate by detections is one which makes detections (reinforcements) contingent on low rates of responding. Two subjects were placed on such a schedule. The needle was deflected only after they had failed to emit an observing response for 30 seconds. A record of one subject's fourth 1-hour session

is presented in Figure 6. It can be seen that this schedule provides a very low rate of responding, like that found in other operant conditioning experiments for which similar schedules were used. The few short bursts of higher rates tend to occur after the subject responded just a little sooner than the required 30 seconds. Even this detail parallels results with animals working for food on this schedule (Sidman, 1956b).

Conclusion

The results reported thus far demonstrate that signal detections can control the rate or probability of emission of observing responses. Furthermore, this control is of the same nature as that exerted by conventional reinforcers, thereby permitting the conclusion that signal detections serve as reinforcements for observing responses.

OBSERVING RATES AND "VIGILANCE"

There remains the problem of determining whether the schedules used in classical vigilance studies will generate observing rates which parallel the probability-of-detection data found in those studies. A decrement in probability of detection during the course of a session has been shown (Deese and Ormond, 1953) for 20 signals per hour when the signals were arranged randomly through the session with

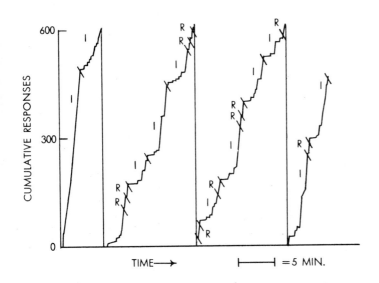

Figure 5. Cumulative response record for a multiple schedule consisting of a 3-minute fixed interval (I) and a 40-response fixed ratio (R). Lines cutting across the record indicate detections.

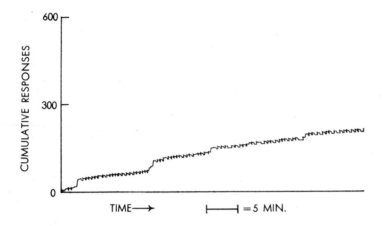

Figure 6. Cumulative response record for differential reinforcement of a low rate. Downward deflection of the pen indicates pointer deflection, and upward deflection indicates detection. Pointer deflections occurred only after no observing response was emitted for 30 seconds.

the intersignal times drawn from a rectangular distribution. Such a schedule, in operant conditioning terms, would be a variable-interval schedule having an average interval of 3 minutes. Four subjects were placed on this schedule. Figure 7 shows the records for two of these subjects during their first session. (Vigilance studies frequently have only one session.) These records were chosen by way of illustration because these two subjects were the two extremes in terms of decrement of response rate as the session progressed. All four subjects showed periods of lower observing rates in the latter portions of the session. The drop in rate as the session progresses is brought about by the fact that reinforcement frequency is insufficient to maintain the higher initial rate, which results in part from the subject's past experience. However, some decline does continue to appear within each session for as many as 18 additional 1-hour sessions. Similarly data on pigeons (Ferster and Skinner, 1957) show a within-session decline in rate on a variable-interval schedule when the average interval is long. Furthermore, the drop in observing rate parallels the frequent finding, in vigilance studies, of a decline in the percentage of signals detected.

It has also been demonstrated in vigilance studies that the percentage of signals detected increases as the signal frequency increases. To determine whether rate of observing responses also increases, two subjects were tested on various variable-interval schedules; first there were three 1-hour sessions in which the average interval was 15 seconds (240 per hour), then

the interval was increased, in blocks of three sessions, to 30 seconds (120 per hour), 1 minute (60 per hour), and finally 2 minutes (30 per hour). In each case the distribution of intervals was rectangular, varying from 5 seconds to double the average interval. In Figure 8 there is shown a family of curves for one subject for these various average intervals. These records are for the first 3000 responses of the final session on each schedule. It can clearly be seen that the rate of observing is highest for the high signal rate and decreases as the signal rate decreases. Again this finding parallels the results of classical vigilance studies in the higher percentage of detection for higher signal rates, and at the same time it parallels other operant conditioning research with variable-interval reinforcement which also shows high response rates to be associated with schedules having a low average interval.

The curvature seen in the records in Figure 8 is also of some interest. For the average interval of 2 minutes there is a decline in observing rate as the interval progresses, while for the 15- and 30-second average intervals there is an increase in observing rate. The decrease shown in the case where the smallest number of signals is used is another illustration of a decrement in "vigilance." When larger numbers of signals are used, the "vigilance" literature reports and the present study shows that the decline during the session disappears. Actually, most studies are incapable of showing a rise in probability of detection because the signal is set so that initial detection is nearly always made.

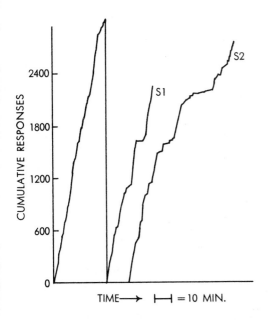

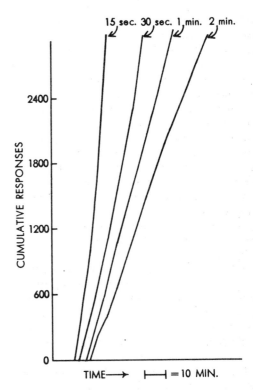

Figure 7. *Cumulative response records for the first session for two subjects (S1 and S2) on a variable-interval schedule with average interval of 3 minutes (rectangular distribution ranging from 5 seconds to 6 minutes).*

OBSERVING BEHAVIOR WITH THE MACKWORTH SCHEDULE

Additional evidence for the adequacy of the observing-behavior analysis of "vigilance" is seen when the schedule used by Mackworth (1948) is employed in the present study. The aims of this study were (i) to determine whether the schedule of signals actually used by Mackworth would confirm the data on decrement in percentage of detections found by him and at the same time provide data on decrement in observing rate, and (ii) to determine whether the data on observing rate would parallel the data on percentage of signals detected. In all of the experiments reported above, signals which remained until detected (nontransient signals) were used in order that the schedule of detections would be under the experimenter's control. The result was that signals could never be missed. But in order to determine whether

Figure 8. *Cumulative response records for variable-interval schedules with average intervals of 15 seconds, 30 seconds, 1 minute, and 2 minutes, respectively (rectangular distributions ranging from 5 seconds to double the average interval). All records are from the same subject. In each case the record was made after three previous sessions on the schedule.*

the typical vigilance measure of percentage of signals detected is paralleled by the observing rate, it was necessary to make the signal automatically disappear if it was not detected within a short time (these are called transient signals). The general procedure was identical with that previously used except for the fact that when the needle was deflected it returned to its original position after 1¼ seconds unless the subject previously detected and reset it in the usual fashion by pressing the key which indicated a detection. The schedule of pointer deflections was identical with the schedule of double jumps used by Mackworth in his clock tests, which stand as the classics in the area of vigilance. This sequence of intervals between needle deflections was ¾, ¾, 1½, 2, 2, 1, 5, 1, 1, 2, 3, and 10 minutes, in that order, and the sequence was repeated four times during the 2-hour sessions. Thus there were twelve signals each half-hour, the shortest interval between signals being ¾ minute and the longest, 10 minutes. Sixteen subjects served in two 2-hour sessions. Cumulative records were made of their observing responses. In addition, a record was kept of their successes and failures in making detections.

In Mackworth's studies, as well as in the present study, there were some important individual differences. Mackworth found that 29 percent of his subjects missed not more than one signal in the last three half-hour periods. In the present study 39 percent of the subjects missed not more than one signal in the entire two hours. The vigilance decrement is thus due to the performance of the other subjects. It turns out that the high-detection subjects show rather different observing response rates than the others. Therefore, in treating the data the subjects were divided into two groups—a high-detection group, made up of those who missed not more than one signal in a 2-hour session, and a low-detection group, made up of those who missed more than one signal per session.

The results for both the percentage of signals detected and for observing responses are summarized in Figure 9. The data for the two 2-hour sessions are combined and show the means for each half-hour period for both measures. The curve labeled *D-H* (open circles) represents the percentage-detection data for the high-vigilance group. It shows, of course, nearly perfect detection throughout, since this was the basis for assignment to this group. The curve labeled *R-H* (open triangles) shows the mean number of observing responses for this high-vigilance group. Interestingly, these subjects actually show a rise in response rate as the session progressed. Their percentage-detection data cannot reflect this rise because these subjects are already detecting nearly all the signals. It is probable that this group has an increased detection efficiency which cannot be revealed by the detection measure. Classical

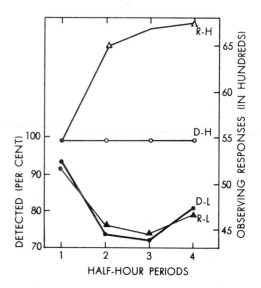

Figure 9. *Mean percentage of signals detected and mean number of observing responses per half-hour period for a two-hour session on the Mackworth schedule. Curve R-H, observing response data for the high-detection group; curve D-H, detection data for the high-vigilance group; curve R-L, observing response data for the low-detection group; curve D-L, detection data for the low-detection group.*

vigilance studies have had no measure of observing rate and therefore have been unable to show such a phenomenon.

The low-vigilance group's detection results are shown in the curve labeled *D−L* (solid circles) and their observing response results, in the curve labeled *R−L* (solid triangles). By the second half-hour there is a drop both in the percentage of signals detected and in the rate of observing responses. In the first half-hour members of this group detected 93 percent of the signals and emitted an average of approximately 5100 observing responses, while in the second half-hour they detected 74 percent of the signals and emitted an average of about 4550 observing responses. The drop from the first to the second half-hour is significant at the 1 percent level for both measures. The slight decline from the second to the third half-hour is not significant for either measure. But the rise in the fourth half-hour is significant at the 5 percent level for both measures. This end-spurt is probably due to the fact that the subjects knew that the session was 2 hours long. Mackworth found no such end-spurt, but other studies (Deese and Ormond, 1953) have shown that knowledge of the length of the session can produce such an effect.

In general, then, the vigilance decrement found by Mackworth was confirmed in this study, and a parallel decrement in observing rate was shown as well. It should be recalled that detections (that is, reinforcements) on variable-interval schedules show that the lower the rate of signals, the lower the rate of responding (see Figure 8). Thus, when signals are missed, this might have the effect of lowering the rate, since the subject is then on a different variable-interval schedule with a higher average interval.

One further factor may have an influence on the response rate in this study. When transient signals are used, the situation is analogous to work with animals in which a variable-interval schedule is used, with the added contingency that when the program is set up for reinforcement, the animals have only a brief time in which to respond before reinforcement is no longer available. Such a schedule (Ferster and Skinner, 1957) used with animals (called "variable interval with limited hold") has shown that the use of a limited hold considerably increases the rate of response over that for the same variable-interval schedule with unlimited hold. This presumably results from the differential reinforcement of high rates, since high rates of responding are more likely to be reinforced in the case of limited hold. There may well be an analogous effect in this study. Those subjects who detect almost all signals are very probably being reinforced for high response rates, with the result that their rate increases and thus maintains maximum detection proficiency.

ADDITIONAL PARALLELS BETWEEN RESPONSE RATE AND DETECTION DATA

The similarity in the shapes of the curves in Figure 9 for the observing rate data and the detection data for the low-detection group

offers support to the position that the finding of classical vigilance studies could reflect observing behavior. Additional evidence may be adduced for this in parallels between vigilance data and work on operant behavior from animal laboratories. For example, (i) Mackworth (1950) finds that giving subjects 10 milligrams of benzedrine raises the level of detection. Similarly Brady (1956) has shown that doses of benzedrine administered to rats provide high response rates when the rats are on a variable-interval schedule. (ii) In addition, Mackworth (1950) has shown that high room temperatures result in lower levels of detection; and, similarly, animals on a variable-interval schedule show lower response rates when the room temperature is high.[2] (iii) Nicely and Miller (1957) have investigated the effect of unequal spatial distribution of signals on a radar display. The strobe line rotated at 6 revolutions per minute. One quadrant had signals on an average of one every five rotations, while the remainder of the display had signals on an average of one every 30 rotations. Nicely and Miller found that the percentage of signals detected increased for the high signal-frequency area and declined for the low signal-frequency area. After 30 minutes the detection-data curve for the high signal-frequency area had approached a higher asymptote than had that for the low signal-frequency area. This situation is analogous to a multiple schedule having a 40-second average variable-interval schedule with one stimulus (one area) and a 5-minute average variable interval with another stimulus (the other area). Ferster and Skinner (1957) have shown that animals on such a multiple schedule show a lower response rate in the presence of the stimulus correlated with the long variable interval than in the presence of the stimulus correlated with the short variable interval. (iv) It has been demonstrated that rest periods restore the detection efficiency to nearly what it was at the beginning of the session (Mackworth, 1948; Adams, 1956). Similarly, Ferster and Skinner (1957) have found that response rates on variable-interval schedules are increased by interspersing rest periods.

---

2 R. J. Herrnstein, personal communication.

CONCLUSIONS AND IMPLICATIONS

This analysis has demonstrated that detections of signals can serve as reinforcements for observing responses and, further, that the detection data of vigilance studies may reflect the observing response rates generated by the particular schedules employed. Thus a means of analysis is provided which does not appeal to a nonbehavioral level.

In other vigilance studies the observing behavior has probably been fixation and scanning with the head and eyes as well as perhaps more subtle responses. It would be of interest to extend the present technique to some of these responses, although for many problems the topography of the response may be unimportant and the present methods entirely sufficient.

So far as application is concerned, the striking fact is the rather precise control exerted by the environment over the human operator's observing behavior. Thus, in a man-machine system it should be possible for the machine to maintain control over the operator's monitoring behavior. The ideal manner for exerting such control remains to be worked out. It is hoped that this will be the goal of much additional research in this area. But one obvious way is to provide a high rate of realistic artificial signals on a schedule which would provide the desired observing rate. The most promising schedule for many situations would be a variable-interval schedule of signals having a short duration, like the limited hold in animal work. Other do's and don'ts of the engineering of monitoring tasks must be worked out. To this end it is clear that the abundant amount of systematic research on operant behavior that has been done with animals should be a fruitful source of ideas for developmental research as well as for educated guesses in designing man-machine systems requiring monitoring by human beings.

3

EARLY EXAMPLES
OF THE ANALYSIS OF HUMAN BEHAVIOR

To place modern methodologies and concepts in perspective, it seems appropriate to examine some early examples of the analysis and control of human behavior. The studies included in this section are two such examples. They are among the earliest successful, systematic attempts to manipulate human behavior in experimental settings.

Watson and Rayner's study of a conditioned fear response in a young child must now be considered a classic. Predictably, coming out of the 1920's, the behavior involved is respondent. At that time, John Watson and other behaviorists had eagerly adopted the concepts and methodology developed by Pavlov and had attempted to account for human behavior in terms of chains of conditioned reflexes. This study contributed to the trend in two respects: (1) by demonstrating that the procedures which had been used successfully with animals were also relevant to human behavior, and (2) by experimentally producing a fear response by respondent conditioning techniques.

For those psychologists who felt that even the everyday activities of man—running, walking, talking, driving, etc.—cannot be adequately accommodated within Pavlov's framework, E. L. Thorndike's work at the turn of this century provided an additional model. The fact that certain, "instrumental" behaviors were repeated when followed by desirable consequences Thorndike called the "Law of Effect." In 1938, B. F. Skinner contributed to a formalization of the distinction between the methodologies of Pavlov and Thorndike by calling the former "respondent" and the latter "operant" conditioning.

It is from this lineage that Fuller's work with a "vegetative" human being can be traced. Although, needless to say, many other investigations of operant behavior followed the work of Thorndike, most of these investigations used infra-human subjects. Fuller's work is among the first which successfully and systematically manipulated the operant response of a human subject.

It is obvious that these two papers can only barely suggest the numerous studies which might have been included in this section. They are, however, presented as important representatives from the history of behavioral analysis.

Conditioned emotional reactions

JOHN B. WATSON AND ROSALIE RAYNER

In recent literature various speculations have been entered into concerning the possibility of conditioning various types of emotional response, but direct experimental evidence in support of such a view has been lacking. If the theory advanced by Watson and Morgan (1917) to the effect that in infancy the original emotional reaction patterns are few, consisting so far as observed of fear, rage and love, then there must be some simple method by means of which the range of stimuli which can call out these emotions and their compounds is greatly increased. Otherwise, complexity in adult response could not be accounted for. These authors without adequate experimental evidence advanced the view that this range was increased by means of conditioned reflex factors. It was suggested there that the early home life of the child furnishes a laboratory situation for establishing conditioned emotional responses. The present authors have recently put the whole matter to experimental test.

Experimental work has been done so far on only one child, Albert B. This infant was reared almost from birth in a hospital environment; his mother was a wet nurse in the Harriet Lane Home for Invalid Children. Albert's life was normal: he was healthy from birth and one of the best developed youngsters ever brought to the hospital, weighing twenty-one pounds at nine months of age. He was on the whole stolid and unemotional. His stability was one of the principal reasons for using him as a subject in this test. We felt that we could do him relatively little harm by carrying out such experiments as those outlined below.

At approximately nine months of age we ran him through the emotional tests that have become a part of our regular routine in determining whether fear reactions can be called out by other stimuli than sharp noises and the sudden removal of support. Tests of this type have been described by the senior author (1919) in another place. In brief, the infant was confronted suddenly and for the first time successively with a white rat, a rabbit, a dog, a monkey, with masks with and without hair, cotton wool, burning newspapers, etc. A permanent record of Albert's reactions to these objects and situations has been preserved in a motion picture study. Manipulation was the most usual reaction called out. *At no time did this infant ever show fear in any situation.* These experimental records were confirmed by the casual observations of the mother and hospital attendants. No one had ever seen him in a state of fear and rage. The infant practically never cried.

Up to approximately nine months of age we had not tested him with loud sounds. The test to determine whether a fear reaction could be called out by a loud sound was made when he was eight months, twenty-six days of age. The sound was that made by striking a hammer upon a suspended steel bar four feet in length and three-fourths of an inch in diameter. The laboratory notes are as follows:

"One of the two experimenters caused the child to turn its head and fixate her moving hand; the other, stationed back of the child, struck the steel bar a sharp blow. The child started violently, his breathing was checked and the arms were raised in a characteristic manner. On the second stimulation the same thing occurred, and in addition the lips began to pucker and tremble. On the third stimulation the child broke into a sudden crying fit. This is the first time an emotional situation in the laboratory has produced any fear or even crying in Albert."

We had expected just these results on account of our work with other infants brought up under similar conditions. It is worth while to call attention to the fact that removal of support (dropping and jerking the blanket upon which the infant was lying) was tried exhaustively upon this infant on the same occasion. It was not effective in producing the fear response. This stimulus is effective in younger children. At what age such stimuli

From *Journal of Experimental Psychology*, 1920, **3**, 1–14.

lose their potency in producing fear is not known. Nor is it known whether less placid children ever lose their fear of them. This probably depends upon the training the child gets. It is well known that children eagerly run to be tossed into the air and caught. On the other hand it is equally well known that in the adult fear responses are called out quite clearly by the sudden removal of support, if the individual is walking across a bridge, walking out upon a beam, etc. There is a wide field of study here which is aside from our present point.

The sound stimulus, thus, at nine months of age, gives us the means of testing several important factors. I. Can we condition fear of an animal, *e.g.,* a white rat, by visually presenting it and simultaneously striking a steel bar? II. If such a conditioned emotional response can be established, will there be a transfer to other animals or other objects? III. If after a reasonable period such emotional responses have not died out, what laboratory methods can be devised for their removal?

I. THE ESTABLISHMENT OF CONDITIONED EMOTIONAL RESPONSES

At first there was considerable hesitation upon our part in making the attempt to set up fear reactions experimentally. A certain responsibility attaches to such a procedure. We decided finally to make the attempt, comforting ourselves by the reflection that such attachments would arise anyway as soon as the child left the sheltered environment of the nursery for the rough and tumble of the home. We did not begin this work until Albert was eleven months, three days of age. Before attempting to set up a conditioned response we, as before, put him through all of the regular emotional tests. *Not the slightest sign of a fear response was obtained in any situation.*

The steps taken to condition emotional responses are shown in our laboratory notes.

11 Months 3 Days

1. White rat suddenly taken from the basket and presented to Albert. He began to reach for

rat with left hand. Just as his hand touched the animal the bar was struck immediately behind his head. The infant jumped violently and fell forward, burying his face in the mattress. He did not cry, however.

2. Just as the right hand touched the rat the bar was again struck. Again the infant jumped violently, fell forward and began to whimper.

In order not to disturb the child too seriously no further tests were given for one week.

11 Months 10 Days

1. Rat presented suddenly without sound. There was steady fixation but no tendency at first to reach for it. The rat was then placed nearer, whereupon tentative reaching movements began with the right hand. When the rat nosed the infant's left hand, the hand was immediately withdrawn. He started to reach for the head of the animal with the forefinger of the left hand, but withdrew it suddenly before contact. It is thus seen that the two joint stimulations given the previous week were not without effect. He was tested with his blocks immediately afterwards to see if they shared in the process of conditioning. He began immediately to pick them up, dropping them, pounding them, etc. In the remainder of the tests the blocks were given frequently to quiet him and to test his general emotional state. They were always removed from sight when the process of conditioning was under way.

2. Joint stimulation with rat and sound. Started, then fell over immediately to right side. No crying.

3. Joint stimulation. Fell to right side and rested upon hands, with head turned away from rat. No crying.

4. Joint stimulation. Same reaction.

5. Rat suddenly presented alone. Puckered face, whimpered and withdrew body sharply to the left.

6. Joint stimulation. Fell over immediately to right side and began to whimper.

7. Joint stimulation. Started violently and cried, but did not fall over.

8. Rat alone. *The instant the rat was shown the baby began to cry. Almost instantly he turned*

sharply to the left, fell over on left side, raised himself on all fours and began to crawl away so rapidly that he was caught with difficulty before reaching the edge of the table.

This was as convincing a case of a completely conditioned fear response as could have been theoretically pictured. In all, seven joint stimulations were given to bring about the complete reaction. It is not unlikely had the sound been of greater intensity or of a more complex clang character that the number of joint stimulations might have been materially reduced. Experiments designed to define the nature of the sounds that will serve best as emotional stimuli are under way.

II. WHEN A CONDITIONED EMOTIONAL RESPONSE HAS BEEN ESTABLISHED FOR ONE OBJECT, IS THERE A TRANSFER?

Five days later Albert was again brought back into the laboratory and tested as follows:

11 Months 15 Days

1. Tested first with blocks: He reached readily for them, playing with them as usual. This shows that there has been no general transfer to the room, table, blocks, etc.
2. Rat alone. Whimpered immediately, withdrew right hand and turned head and trunk away.
3. Blocks again offered. Played readily with them, smiling and gurgling.
4. Rat alone. Leaned over to the left side as far away from the rat as possible, then fell over, getting up on all fours and scurrying away as rapidly as possible.
5. Blocks again offered. Reached immediately for them, smiling and laughing as before.

The above preliminary test shows that the conditioned response to the rat had carried over completely for the five days in which no tests were given. The question as to whether or not there is a transfer was next taken up.

6. Rabbit alone. The rabbit was suddenly placed on the mattress in front of him. The reaction was pronounced. Negative responses began at once. He leaned as far away from the animal as possible, whimpered, then burst into tears. When the rabbit was placed in contact with him he buried his face in the mattress, then got up on all fours and crawled away, crying as he went. This was a most convincing test.

7. The blocks were next given him, after an interval. He played with them as before. It was observed by four people that he played far more energetically with them than ever before. The blocks were raised high over his head and slammed down with a great deal of force.

8. Dog alone. The dog did not produce as violent a reaction as the rabbit. The moment fixation occurred the child shrank back and as the animal came nearer he attempted to get on all fours but did not cry at first. As soon as the dog passed out of his range of vision he became quiet. The dog was then made to approach the infant's head (he was lying down at the moment). Albert straightened up immediately, fell over to the opposite side and turned his head away. He then began to cry.

9. The blocks were again presented. He began immediately to play with them.

10. Fur coat (seal). Withdrew immediately to the left side and began to fret. Coat put close to him on the left side, he turned immediately, began to cry and tried to crawl away on all fours.

11. Cotton wool. The wool was presented in a paper package. At the end the cotton was not covered by the paper. It was placed first on his feet. He kicked it away but did not touch it with his hands. When his hand was laid on the wool he immediately withdrew it but did not show the shock that the animals or fur coat produced in him. He then began to play with the paper, avoiding contact with the wool itself. He finally, under the impulse of the manipulative instinct, lost some of his negativism to the wool.

12. Just in play W. put his head down to see if Albert would play with his hair. Albert was completely negative. Two other observers did the same thing. He began immediately to play with their hair. W. then brought the Santa Claus mask and presented it to Albert. He was again pronouncedly negative. . . .

From the above results it would seem that emotional transfers do take place. Furthermore it would seem that the number of transfers resulting from an experimentally produced conditioned emotional reaction may be very large. In our observations we had no means of testing the complete number of transfers which may have resulted. . . .

III. "DETACHMENT" OR REMOVAL OF CONDITIONED EMOTIONAL RESPONSES

Unfortunately Albert was taken from the hospital the day the above tests were made. Hence the opportunity of building up an experimental technique by means of which we could remove the conditioned emotional responses was denied us. Our own view, expressed above, which is possibly not very well grounded, is that these responses in the home environment are likely to persist indefinitely, unless an accidental method for removing them is hit upon. The importance of establishing some method must be apparent to all. Had the opportunity been at hand we should have tried out several methods, some of which we may mention. (1) Constantly confronting the child with those stimuli which called out the responses in the hopes that habituation would come in corresponding to "fatigue" of reflex when differential reactions are to be set up. (2) By trying to "recondition" by showing objects calling out fear responses (visual) and simultaneously stimulating the erogenous zones (tactual). We should try first the lips, then the nipples and as a final resort the sex organs. (3) By trying to "recondition" by feeding the subject candy or other food just as the animal is shown. This method calls for the food control of the subject. (4) By building up "constructive" activities around the object by imitation and by putting the hand through the motions of manipulation. At this age imitation of overt motor activity is strong, as our present but unpublished experimentation has shown.

INCIDENTAL OBSERVATIONS . . .

The Freudians twenty years from now, unless their hypotheses change, when they come to analyze Albert's fear of a seal skin coat—assuming that he comes to analysis at that age—will probably tease from him the recital of a dream which upon their analysis will show that Albert at three years of age attempted to play with the pubic hair of the mother and was scolded violently for it. (We are by no means denying that this might in some other case condition it.) If the analyst has sufficiently prepared Albert to accept such a dream when found as an explanation of his avoiding tendencies, and if the analyst has the authority and personality to put it over, Albert may be fully convinced that the dream was a true revealer of the factors which brought about the fear.

It is probable that many of the phobias in psychopathology are true conditioned emotional reactions either of the direct or the transferred type. One may possibly have to believe that such persistence of early conditioned responses will be found only in persons who are constitutionally inferior. Our argument is meant to be constructive. Emotional disturbances in adults cannot be traced back to sex alone. They must be retraced along at least three collateral lines—to conditioned and transferred responses set up in infancy and early youth in all three of the fundamental human emotions.

Operant conditioning of a vegetative human organism

PAUL R. FULLER

While it is maintained (Hilgard, 1948) that a large part of human behavior is operant in nature, the majority of experiments in operant conditioning have been performed with infra-human organisms. Classical conditioning experiments, however, have been conducted with both normal and subnormal human Ss.

Razran (1933) reports experiments in classical conditioning with some feeble-minded Ss. Osipova (1926) found that subnormal children formed conditioned responses to shock faster than normal children. Segal (1929), working in Lenz's laboratory, attempted to condition a salivary response in an 18-yr.-old idiot but had little success, probably due in part to S's reluctance to have the saliometer attached. Shastin (1930) was able to establish a conditioned response in a 15-yr.-old cretin. Wolowick (1929) established a conditioned response in a sickly, retarded 6-yr.-old. On the whole, however, few experiments have been done in conditioning feeble-minded Ss.

Recently an opportunity was offered us to conduct an operant conditioning experiment on an 18-yr.-old inmate of a feeble-minded institution, whose behavior was that of a 'vegetative idiot.' The term 'vegetative' describes well his condition. He lay on his back and could not roll over; he could, however, open his mouth, blink, and move his arms, head and shoulders, to a slight extent. He never moved his trunk or legs. The attendant reported that he never made any sounds; but in the course of the experiment vocalizations were heard. He had some teeth but did not chew. He had been fed liquids and semi-solids all his life. While being fed, he sometimes choked and would cough vigorously.

According to his medical record he had a clonic seizure shortly after birth, and these seizures had continued at irregular intervals throughout his life. No other pertinent information could be obtained from the records or from the institution's physician. S had been in the institution for almost a year and had increased in weight from 30 to 50 lb. during his stay. His activity had also increased slightly.

The conditioning apparatus consisted of a syringe filled with warm sugar-milk solution — the reinforcing stimulus. The response selected to condition was a movement of S's right arm to a vertical or nearly vertical position. This arm was selected because we observed that he moved it about a third as frequently as his left arm.

S was deprived of food for 15 hr. Then, when he moved his right arm, a small amount of the sugar-milk solution was injected into his mouth. Two experiments were conducted. In the first, an assistant recorded the responses and time. In the second, a polygraph was so arranged that movements with either arm and head were recorded.

The first experiment was conducted early in June, 1948. There was one session of 20 min. each day. During the first session the rate of response was 0.67 per min. During the fourth session the rate increased to 1.67 per min. Since we lacked adequate apparatus to record the responses, the experiment was discontinued at that time to be repeated later in June.

During the interim between experiments, S was fed as usual by the attendant who stuffed food into S's mouth when he was still. S was being reinforced for not moving during the regular feeding situation while during the experiment the reinforcing stimulus followed the movement of the right arm. It could be expected, therefore, that the rate of response at the beginning of the second experiment would be less than the rate at the end of the first. This was true; the rate of response was low, less than 1 per min. During the first 10 min. of the first session of the second experiment, S was merely observed and his movements recorded. During the next 10 min., the tube with milk in it was held in position close to S's mouth. A slight increase in the rate of his right arm movements was observed but it could hardly be termed significant. The rate for the whole 20 min. was less than 1 per min.

From *American Journal of Psychology*, 1949, **62**, 587–590.

Conditioning was then begun. Every time the right arm was raised to a vertical position, the milk was injected into S's mouth. There were movements in which the arm was not raised to a vertical position, and at the other extreme, there were times when not only the arm, but the head and shoulders also were moved. These were not reinforced because the attempt was to condition a discrete movement rather than a gross, generalized one. No appreciable increase in rate was observed during the first session.

The next morning, in a 40-min. session, a total of 45 reinforcements were given S as compared with 24 the previous day. The rate of his responses rose to 1.12 per min. If we had counted the responses in which the shoulders as well as the right arm were raised, the rate would have been 1.8 per min. A brief experimental session was held that evening after only a 5-hr. food-deprivation. After 19 responses in 16 min., S fell asleep.

The fourth and final session took place the next morning. S made definite and discrete responses at the rate of 3 per min. He would lift his arm and open his mouth immediately. In the beginning of the experiment this sequence of movements had not been observed. This looked like anticipation of the reinforcing stimulus. The rate of three responses per min. allowed just enough time for the milk to be injected into S's mouth and be swallowed. The rate of responding during the fourth session was more than three times as great as during the first.

During the first sessions there was an increase in movements of the left as well as the right arm, but in the last two sessions of the second experiment these unreinforced movements dropped out almost completely, as did the gross movements in which S raised his arm, head and shoulders. The response was well differentiated during the final period.

Immediately following the 30 min. conditioning, during which S's responses averaged 3 per min., an extinction period was begun. For the first 30 min. of extinction, the rate of S's responses was maintained at almost as high a level as during conditioning. Then the rate decreased until by the seventieth minute of extinction it approached zero. After the seventy-second minute, no more responses were observed. The shape of the extinction curve is similar to what is considered a 'typical' extinction curve following continuous reinforcement during operant conditioning. During extinction, S's movements gradually became more generalized; the left arm, which had moved very little in the last two sessions, moved more frequently after the rate of movement of the right arm noticeably decreased.

An interesting feature of this study is the example it affords of phylogenetic overlap. While of normal human parentage, this organism was, behaviorally speaking, considerably lower in the scale than the majority of infra-human organisms used in conditioning experiments—dogs, rats, cats.

The attending physicians of the institute in which S was an inmate thought it was impossible for him to learn anything—according to them, he had not learned anything in the 18 years of his life—yet in four experimental sessions, by using the operant conditioning technique, an addition was made to his behavior which, at his level, could be termed appreciable. Those who participated in or observed the experiment are of the opinion that if time permitted, other responses could be conditioned and discriminations learned. For years many psychologists have experimented exclusively with infra-human Ss, and they have expressed a preference for the simple, less variable behavior of the lower organisms in the laboratory. Perhaps by beginning at the bottom of the human scale the transfer from rat to man can be effected.

APPLICATIONS OF BEHAVIOR CONTROL

u

4

BEHAVIOR MODIFICATION IN EDUCATIONAL SETTINGS

It has been suggested by critics of the American educational system, particularly following Russia's launching of Sputnik I, that a thorough re-examination of our methods and aims is in order. That such a re-examination is underway is apparent in the public interest in such new techniques as teaching machines, team teaching, the ungraded primary, and homogeneous grouping.

A number of experimental psychologists have participated in the movement to reassess current techniques. The actual and potential contribution of these men stems from their efforts to apply to educational settings the principles which, in the laboratory, have met with success in shaping and maintaining complex behavior in a wide range of species.

The most widely publicized of these contributions has been the teaching machine — the outward manifestation of the technology of programmed instruction. Holland, in his description of some of the teaching machines now in use and his review of some of the main principles of programmed instruction, is especially careful to distinguish between teaching machines as gadgetry and as a part of a true technology of education.

Fox's careful and complete analysis of the behavioral repertoire known as "study habits" should be as welcome as a fresh spring breeze, both to the teacher who tries to advise on "study habits" and to the student who must actually use them. The main contribution of this analysis is its attention to bringing the *initiation* of study behavior under stimulus control, since such initiation is obviously pre-requisite to study.

Keller presents an equally fresh approach to teaching methods and course structuring in his design for a first course in psychology. The student is allowed to progress at his own rate, yet must attack the material in the proper order. Entertaining "lectures" are used as reinforcement, and there is a notable absence of aversive control such as examinations.

Another aspect of behavior in educational settings is that known as classroom discipline: the generation and maintenance of desirable behavior and the elimination of undesirable behavior. One method of achieving discipline is through the use of the Premack principle, which states that an opportunity to perform behavior of high probability (behavior which is reinforcing to the organism) can be used to reinforce less probable behavior (behavior which is not in itself reinforcing). Homme and his associates have successfully used the Premack principle to achieve a high degree of control over such improbable behavior in preschoolers as sitting quietly in chairs and looking intently at a blackboard.

In a similar vein is the Zimmermans' report of two case studies of "emotionally disturbed" boys. By altering the consequences of tantrum behavior—by removing the social reinforcement that maintained it—the authors readily produced acceptable, productive classroom behavior. The results of this study bring into focus an extremely important question for the educator: to what extent in an educational setting do we inadvertently reinforce the very behavior we designate as undesirable?

These new and effective methods have several characteristics in common. In all cases, the behavior itself is dealt with directly, to produce definite, behavioral results. This direct approach allows the elimination of intervening variables such as "need for attention," "low motivation," "positive attitude," and other internal states that are difficult to define and manipulate. The behavior is subjected to operant analysis and is controlled by response-dependent consequences.

Some years ago, in the days of the Three R's, less efficient educational techniques might have been acceptable. But today achievement of literacy is not enough. In view of truly incredible technological advances, our schools must be able to develop complex skills in our young people, skills which were unheard of as little as twenty-five years ago. Techniques such as those presented in the following papers may be, in part, what our educational system needs in order to meet many of the challenges it faces today.

Teaching machines: An application of principles from the laboratory

JAMES G. HOLLAND

Much has been said of teaching machines recently—but the emphasis has tended to be on the gadgets rather than on the much more significant development of a new technology of education initiated by B. F. Skinner (1954b, 1958). The technology does use a device called a teaching machine, which presents a finely graded series of problems and provides immediate "reward" or reinforcement for the student's correct answers. But emphasis on machines has tended to obscure the more important facets of the new technology based on application of principles from the laboratory. The machines of today are not necessarily better than those of yesterday. Indeed, adequate machines could have been built hundreds of years ago. The movement today is not simply the mechanization of teaching, but instead the development of a new technology—a behavioral engineering of teaching procedures.

This history of unsuccessful teaching machines illustrates the relatively greater importance of the technique as opposed to the gadgets. The first teaching machine was patented 93 years ago. There have since been

From *Journal of the Experimental Analysis of Behavior,* 1960,·**3**, 275–287.

Figure 1. *Student working at a write-in machine.*

behavior. Such a technology became possible with the realization that we are actually referring to a verbal repertoire (Skinner, 1957b) controlled by the same laws as other behavior. The old, defunct explanatory concepts of knowledge, meaning, mind, or symbolic processes have never offered the possibility of manipulation or control; but behavior, verbal or otherwise, can be controlled with ease and precision.

While machines are not the essential or defining aspect of this technology, they do play an important role in providing some of this fine control the technology requires. We will now examine several machines and notice the advantages they offer.

At Harvard there is a self-instruction room with ten booths, each containing a machine such as the one shown in Figure 1. The student gets one set of material from the attendant and places it in the machine. He closes the machine and begins his studies.

This machine presents one item of material at a time. The subject reads the statement, which has one or more words missing, and he completes it by writing in the answer space. He then raises the lever and a small shutter opens, revealing the correct answer. Simultaneously, his answer is moved under glass, where it can be read and compared with the now-exposed correct answer. After comparing his answer with the correct answer, the student indicates to the machine, with an appropriate movement of the lever, whether his answer was correct or incorrect, and the next item appears in the window. He repeats all items answered wrong after he completes the set of items. He does not repeat correctly answered items.

A critical feature of the machine is that it provides immediate reinforcement for correct answers. Being correct is known to be a reinforcer for humans. In machine teaching, reinforcement is immediate. We know from laboratory work (Perin, 1943) that a delay between a response and its reinforcement of a few seconds will greatly reduce the effectiveness of the reinforcement. Adult human subjects can sustain at least small delays; nevertheless, any delay makes reinforcement less effective.

Although other techniques such as programmed workbooks (Homme and Glaser,

a series of patents and a promising burst of activity initiated by Sidney Pressey (1926) in the 1920's. None of these early efforts really caught hold. But during this period in which the idea of mechanized teaching has been latent, the science of behavior has developed principles which permit extremely precise control of behavior. This new technology is not only the so-called automation of teaching, but is an attempt to obtain the kind of behavioral control shown possible in the laboratory.

We have, of course, seen other practical applications of scientific psychology. We are all familiar with the development of a technology of testing, which permits placing an individual in situations suited to his abilities. We are also familiar with another technology called human engineering, which fits machines and jobs to the capacities of man. One places a man in a job that suits him; the other alters the job to suit the man; *neither* attempts to alter or control man's behavior.

For years in the laboratory we have controlled the behavior of experimental subjects—both animal and human—by a widening array of principles and techniques. The new technology of education is the application of behavioral laws in modifying or controlling

1959) and flashcards are sometimes used in this new behavioral technology, they offer less control. Teaching machines eliminate undesirable forms of responses which would also be successful in obtaining the right answer. For example, the teaching machine insures that the student answers before peeking at the indicated answer. There is a strong temptation to glance ahead with only a poorly formulated, unwritten answer when programmed workbooks or flashcards are used.

This write-in machine is a prototype of the most common machine. There is another machine used for teaching young children material which consistently has a single possible answer. In the machine the constructed answer is automatically compared with the true answer. The child is presented a problem, perhaps a statement such as 2 + 2 =____, and he must provide the 4. By moving a slider appropriately, he can insert the 4 into the answer space. He then turns the crank, and the next item appears immediately, so that immediate reinforcement is provided.

Both of the machines we have seen thus far require the student to compose the answer. Figure 2 shows a machine for a less mature organism who cannot yet compose an answer. This machine can be used for teaching pre-

school children (Hively, 1960). There is a large top window and three small windows. In the large window, there is some sort of problem; and in the three smaller windows, there are three alternative choices. For example, in the machine as seen in the picture, the subject chooses one of the three alternatives which has the same form as the sample, independent, in this case, of color or size. When the correct choice is made, the next frame is presented.

A teaching machine for a still lower organism is shown in Figure 3. This pigeon, with the aid of a teaching machine, has learned to hit the name plaque appropriate for a color projected above him. The principal difference between this and the other machines is that food reinforcement is used. With humans, simply being correct is sufficient reinforcement—pigeons will not work for such meager gains.

Enough of machines. They should not be allowed to obscure the truly important feature of the new technology, namely, the application of methods for behavioral control in developing programs for teaching. We need to say no more about the well-known principle of immediate reinforcement. Our second principle is also well known. Behavior is learned only when it is *emitted* and reinforced. But in the classroom, the student performs very little,

Figure 2. *Child working on the preverbal machine. In the upper rectangular window is a sample which is to be matched with a figure in one of the three lower windows. If the child presses the correct lower window, the material advances to the next frame. In this case, the match is in terms of form, with size and color irrelevant.*

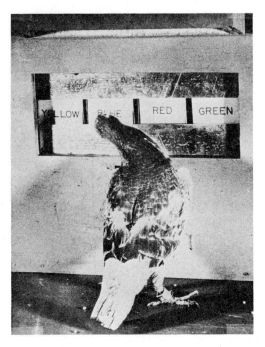

Figure 3. *A pigeon "naming colors." The pigeon pecks the color name corresponding to the color of the light projected above him.*

verbally. However, while working with a machine, the student necessarily emits appropriate behavior, and this behavior is usually reinforced because the material is so designed that the student is usually correct. Not only is reinforcement needed for learning, but a high density of correct items is necessary because material which generates errors is punishing. Laboratory experiments (Azrin, 1956) have shown that punishment lowers the rate of the punished behavior. In our experience with teaching machines, we have also observed that students stop work when the material is so difficult that they make many errors. Furthermore, they become irritated, almost aggressive, when errors are made.

The third important principle is that of gradual progression to establish complex repertoires. A visitor once asked if Skinner had realized that pigeons were so smart before he began using them as subjects. The answer given by a helpful graduate student was that they weren't so smart before Skinner began using them. And indeed they weren't. The be-

havior developed in many experiments is like that developed in the classroom. Both are complex operants. Both require a careful program of gradual progression. We cannot wait for a student to describe the content of a psychology course before reinforcing the performance; nor can we wait for a pigeon to emit such an improbable bit of behavior as turning a circle, facing a disk on the wall, pecking it if lit, and then bending down to a now-exposed food tray and eating. When developing a complex performance in a pigeon, we may first reinforce simply the behavior of approaching the food tray when it is presented with a loud click. Later, the pigeon learns to peck a key which produces the click and the food tray. Still later, he may learn to peck this key only when it is lit, the peck being followed by the loud click and approach to the food tray. In the next step, he may learn to raise his head or hop from one foot to another, or walk a figure eight, in order to produce the lighted key which he then pecks; the click follows, and he approaches the food tray. This principle of gradual progression runs through many of the teaching-machine techniques. Both human and avian scholars deserve the same careful tutorage. The teaching-machine program moves in very finely graded steps, working from simple to an ever-higher level of complexity. Such a gradual development is illustrated in Table 1 by a few items taken from a psychology program.[1]

The principle of gradual progression serves not simply to make the student correct as often as possible, but it is also the fastest way to develop a complex repertoire. In fact, a new complex operant may never appear except through separately reinforcing members of a graded series (Keller and Schoenfeld, 1950). Only this way can we quickly create a *new pattern* of behavior. The pigeon would not have learned the complex sequence necessary to receive the food if it had not learned each step in its proper order. Obviously, a child can't begin with advanced mathematics, but neither can he begin with $2 + 2 = 4$ — even this is too complex and requires a gradual progression.

---

1 This program, prepared by J. G. Holland and B. F. Skinner, is entitled *A self-tutoring introduction to a science of behavior.*

Table 1. *Items from the psychology program (11). These items illustrate the gradual development of a new concept.*

Item	Correct Answer	Percentage of Students Giving the Answer
1. Performing animals are sometimes trained with "rewards." The behavior of a hungry animal can be "rewarded" with _____.	Food	96
2. A technical term for "reward" is reinforcement. To "reward" an organism with food is to _____ it with food.	Reinforce	100
3. *Technically* speaking, a thirsty organism can be _____ with water.	Reinforced	100
50. A school teacher is likely, whenever possible, to dismiss a class when her students are rowdy because she has been _____ by elimination of the stimuli arising from a rowdy class.	Reinforced	92
51. The teacher who dismisses a class when it is rowdy causes the frequency of future rowdy behavior to (1) _____, since dismissal from class is probably a(n) (2) _____ for rowdy children.	(1) Increase (2) Reinforcement	86
54. If an airplane spotter never sees the kind of plane he is to spot, his frequency of scanning the sky (1) _____. In other words his "looking" behavior is (2) _____.	(1) Decreases (2) Extinguished (or: Not Reinforced)	94

Our fourth principle is, in a sense, another form of gradual progression—one which involves the gradual withdrawal of stimulus support. This we shall call fading. This method will be illustrated with some neuroanatomy material.[2] Figure 4A is a fully labelled cross section of the medulla oblongata. This is placed before the student while he works with a large set of items pertaining to the spatial arrangement of the various structures. For example, "posterior to the cuneate nuclei are the _____." The answer is: "the cuneate fasciculi." After many such items, he begins another set and has another picture (Figure 4B); but now the structures before him are labelled only with initials. A new set of items again asks a long series of questions pertaining to the spatial position of the various structures. For example, "between the gracile and the trigeminal nuclei are _____." The answer is the "cuneate nuclei." After many more items, he proceeds to a new set and the next picture. This time (Figure 4C), the picture is unlabelled. Again, he goes through a series of new items, not simple repetitions of the previous ones, but items pertaining to the same problem of the spatial location of the different structures. This set is followed by still another but with no

2 This material has been prepared by D. M. Brethower in collaboration with the present author, and it is being used at Harvard for research purposes.

picture at all. He is now able to discuss the spatial position of the structures without any visual representations of the structures before him. In a sense, he has his own private map of the medulla. He may further demonstrate his newly acquired ability by accurately drawing the medulla. The neuroanatomy example is an elaborate example of fading. Fading is also applied in a more simple form in constructing verbal programs without pictorial displays. A single item may in one sentence give a definition or a general law and in a second sentence in that same item, an example in which a key word is omitted. This would be followed by a new example in the next frame, but with the definition or law lacking.

This brings us to our fifth principle: control of the student's observing and echoic behavior. In the classroom the student is often treated as though he were some kind of passive receiver of information, who can sop up information spoken by the teacher, written on the blackboard, or presented by films. But all of these are effective only insofar as the student

has some behavior with respect to the material. He must listen carefully, or read carefully, thus engaging in usually covert echoic behavior. Ineffectiveness of classroom techniques is often credited to "inattention" or poor "concentration." It has been shown (Reid, 1953; Wyckoff, 1952) that if a discrimination is to be learned, adequate observing behavior must first be established. We have further found that observing behavior, or speaking loosely, "attention," is subject to the same forms of control as other behavior (Holland, 1958[3]). This control of observing behavior is of prime importance. When the student becomes very "inattentive" in the classroom, the teaching material flows on; but with a machine, he moves ahead only as he finishes an item. Lapses in active participation result in nothing more than the machine sitting idle until the student continues. There is, however, a more subtle aspect to the control of observing behavior than this obvious mechanical one. In many of the

_____

3 Pages 53–64 of this volume.

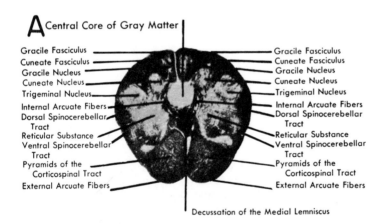

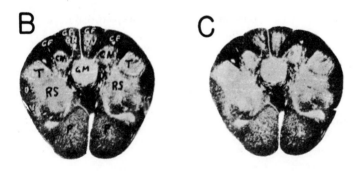

Figure 4. An illustration of the technique of fading. Section A is in front of the student while he is working on the earliest items of a neuroanatomy program; Section B is in front of the student for later items; and Section C, for still later items.

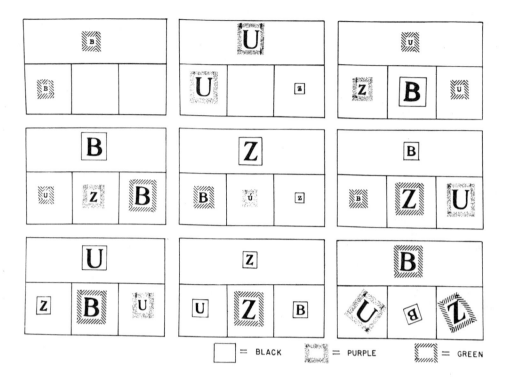

Figure 5. *Selected items from a program which teaches young children to respond in terms of the abstract property of form. The upper rectangle in each of the frames is the sample. The child must pick the alternative which corresponds to the sample in form. The color of each letter, as it appeared in the program, is indicated by the various shaded areas.*

examples we have seen, success in answering the problem depends only on the student's careful observation of the material in front of him at the moment. This may be illustrated by more material from the psychology program. A graph showing stimulus-generalization data is in front of the student while he works on the machine. In the program he may complete a statement: "As the wave length changes in either direction from the wave length present during reinforcement, the number of responses _____." The answer is "decreases." The item serves only to control the behavior of observing the data. Of course, many more such items are used to discuss the same data.

This principle of controlled observation extends to the details of writing a single item. For example, "Two events may have a common effect. An operant reinforced with two reinforcers appropriate to different deprivations will vary with _____ deprivations." The

answer is "two" or "both." Here, the programmer's choice of the omission serves to insure a careful reading of the item. *Only* those parts of an item which must be read to correctly complete a blank can safely be assumed to be learned.

Our sixth principle deals with discrimination training. In learning spoken languages, for example, it is necessary to be able to identify the speech sounds. A student may listen to a pair of words on a special phonograph which repeats the passage as many times as he desires. The visual write-in machine instructs him to listen to a specific passage. For example, the student may hear two words such as: "sit, set." He listens as many times as he needs and then writes the phonetic symbols in the write-in machine. He then operates the machine, thereby exposing the true answer and providing immediate reinforcement for his correct discrimination.

However, little academic education is *simple* discrimination. More often, it is abstraction or concept formation. An abstraction is a response to a single isolated property of a stimulus. Such a property cannot exist alone. Redness is an abstraction. Anything that is red has other properties as well—size, shape, position in space, to name a few. There are red balls, red cars, red walls. The term red applies to all of them, but not to green balls, blue cars, or yellow walls. To establish an abstraction (Hovland, 1952, 1953), we must provide many examples. Each must have the common property, but among the various examples there must be a wide range of other properties. This is best illustrated by examples from the preverbal machine shown in Figure 5.

These are from a program[4] which teaches a child to respond to the abstract property of form. In each item, the upper figure is the sample and the lower three are the alternatives. While developing a program for establishing an abstraction, we remember our earlier principles and move through a gradual progression. The first several items would be like the first one; here, there is a sample and a single match, the other two being blank. The sample and its match are exactly alike at this stage. After many such items, we would begin to have others like the next one, in which the sample and its match again correspond in size, color, and form—but an additional incorrect alternative has been added which differs from the sample in all these aspects. Later, we move on to frames

with three choices; again, the sample and its match correspond exactly. Next, the sample and the match may differ in some property such as color, in the case of the next item shown, or size in the next. It is essential that the program contain many items among which the sample and correct match differ in all properties except the one providing the basis for the abstraction. Otherwise, the abstraction will be incomplete because the extraneous property will share some of the control over the abstract response. As we move on with additional examples, the sample and the correct match differ both in color and in size, and the incorrect alternatives are beginning to share some of the extraneous properties with the sample. The student continues with many such problems in which the only common property between the sample and the correct match is the shape, regardless of size and color. Even now our abstraction may be incomplete. We have kept the figures in only one orientation. Therefore, we also have a series in which the samples are rotated as in the next item. A great deal of academic education consists of trying to teach abstractions. Concepts such as force, reinforcement, supply and demand, freedom, and many, many other possible examples are all abstractions. Furthermore, in the academic setting, the student seldom adequately forms abstractions. The trigonometry student commonly uses triangles with the right angle as one of the two lower angles. If the triangle is rotated 90°, so that the right angle is upward, the student often does not recognize it as a right triangle. Neither is an abstraction developed simply by learning a definition. The psychology student who learns the definition of reinforcement in formal terms and is acquainted with a laboratory example of food reinforcement may not realize the horrible consequences of sending his girl friend flowers to end an argument. Thus, in the psychology program, we follow the pattern in the preverbal example to develop a new concept. Wide ranges of examples are analyzed which differ in as many aspects as possible, each still having the common property which characterizes the concept.

The last principle I shall discuss is really a question of a methodology which has served so

Figure 6. *"Boy, do we have this guy conditioned. Every time I press the bar down he drops a pellet in."*

4 This program was prepared by B. F. Skinner.

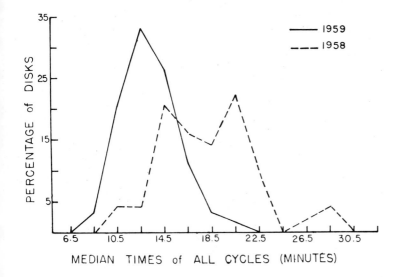

Figure 7. Frequency distributions for the median times to complete the disks or "lessons" for the revised (1959) and unrevised (1958) psychology program. Raw frequencies were converted to percentages to equate the area under the curves.

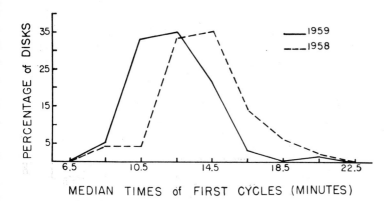

Figure 8. Frequency distributions for the median times to complete only the first cycles for the revised (1959) and unrevised (1958) psychology program. Raw frequencies were converted to percentages to equate the area under the curves.

well in the laboratory. This principle is to let the student write the program. A few years ago, the cartoon shown in Figure 6 was published in the *Columbia Jester*.

The rat leaning on the bar is saying to the other rat: "Boy, do we have this guy conditioned. Every time I press the bar down, he drops a pellet in." Although said in jest, it is true that the rat controls the experimenter's behavior. When interesting things are observed about the rat's behavior, the control circuits are rewired to investigate the interesting new facet of behavior. In a sense, the rat is wiring the control circuit. Similarly, the behavioral engineer who prepares good teaching-machine material must be under the control of the student's responses. When the student has trouble with part of a program, the programmer must correct this. The student's answers reveal ambiguities in items; they reveal gaps in the program and erroneous assumptions as to the student's background. The answers will show when the program is progressing too rapidly, when additional prompts are necessary, or when the programmer should try new techniques. When unexpected errors are made, they indicate deficiencies *not* in the student but in the program.

The most extensive experience with this principle of modifying the program to fit the student has been at Harvard with the psy-

Table 2. *A comparison of the students' errors in using the revised (1959) and unrevised (1958) program in psychology.*

. .	Percent Errors	Percent Items Improperly Scored by Students
1958	20.1	3.6
1959	11.0	1.4

chology program. In 1958, we had a program consisting of 48 disks or lessons of 29 frames each. After using the program and making a detailed, item-by-item analysis of the students' answers, we diagnosed the particular deficiencies in the program and revised it accordingly. The program was also extended to cover a larger amount of subject matter; and in 1959, it consisted of 60 disks. You have already seen a few items from the course. After using the revised material in 1959, we evaluated the extent of its improvement. Table 2 shows the percentage of errors on the first 20 disks for each of the 2 years.

The revision eliminated about half the errors. The last column of the table gives percentage of improper self-scoring by the students. Revision also cut these scoring errors approximately in half. Furthermore, the revision decreased the time required to complete the material. Although the second year's material had more disks—60 as opposed to 48—it actually required the average student about 1 hour less to complete the work than the shorter, first version had done. Frequency distributions on the median times in minutes for completion of the various disks are shown in Figure 7. These are the times required for the median student to move through each set of material answering every item once and to repeat items answered incorrectly. Notice the considerable time required for many disks in the first year's material. Primarily, this was because students repeated the larger number of items missed in the first cycle.

But the improved material provided faster performance, even when the delay due to repetition of incorrectly answered items is not considered. The frequency distributions for the first cycle only are provided in Figure 8. These data exclude the time used in repeating items. Here, too, the revision produced slightly more rapid progress.

Such careful tailoring of material to fit the student is impossible with most teaching techniques. With teaching machines, as in no other teaching technique, the programmer is able to revise his material in view of the students' particular difficulties. The student can write the program; he cannot write the textbook.

We have seen that the principles evolved from the laboratory study of behavior have provided the possibility for the behavioral engineering of teaching. This new technology is thoroughly grounded in some of the better-established facts of behavioral control. The future of education is bright if persons who prepare teaching-machine programs appreciate this, and appropriately educate themselves in a special, but truly *not* esoteric, discipline. But it is vital that we continue to apply these techniques in preparing programs. The ill-advised efforts of some of our friends, who automatize their courses without adopting the new technology, have an extremely good chance of burying the whole movement in an avalanche of teaching-machine tapes.

Effecting the use of efficient study habits

LJUNGBERG FOX

THE PROBLEM

Self-instructional materials do not escape the old problem of poor study habits; indeed, they cannot help but emphasize it. No matter how logical and clear the teaching materials, if the student does not study there is no teaching at all. Even instruction in "effective study habits" is not free of this iron law. Such excellent analyses of effective study habits as Robinson's (1946) are useful only to the extent that they can be transmitted to students. It is one thing for the student to listen and follow the exposition of effective study habits; it is another thing for him to put these habits to use outside the classroom. And no matter how successful self-instructional materials may eventually prove, schools will for some time to come depend upon traditional assignments and texts. They will depend on them long enough to justify attention to improving the manner in which students use available methods of learning.

The work on effective study habits to date represents a considerable array of reasonably sound advice to students. Robinson's Survey Q3R method, as an example, is a system of study far superior to those commonly used by students. Although further analysis could probably improve on the Survey Q3R method, it would be sufficient accomplishment to put this system into wide use. Typical methods for study habit instruction in colleges suffer several disadvantages. They usually require a trained counselor or teacher who must work with small classes to be effective. If every student who could significantly gain from it were enrolled in a remedial study section, a medium-sized college might require about 300 semester hours of trained instructor time each year. The typical college is not in a position to reach all students. Moreover, such courses seldom have the reputation for success necessary to induce students to enroll. Extraneous motivation is usually required to fill up even existing sections. In addition, the urgent needs of borderline students reduce the time devoted to better students. In short, such tuition is an extra financial burden to the college, and reaches too few students.

It attests to the importance of the problem that poor study habits are a recurrent concern of educators despite the fact that the problem has been around for a long time. A college could not discharge its responsibility to produce graduates if it adhered to the standards of education that its faculty values. With that responsibility outweighing all others, it is the student, in the final analysis, who sets the standard of education. He sets this standard by his study behavior. Students are the most important instructors in the college. No matter how brilliant the lectures or how good the facilities, most students would fail if they did not teach themselves by study outside the classroom, and it should be conceded that most of them would pass if they studied arduously and received only assignments from their professors. It would seem that a concern for the improvement of college instruction would lead us first to examine the methods of studying. That the student is seldom thought of as an instructor, in the truest sense of the word, is really the most startling indictment of our prevalent educational philosophy. When we see the student as what he is—the primary tool of educational methodology—the problem of establishing effective study habits takes priority over all others faced by a college. The issue of efficient education pivots on the study behavior of the student. Our technical concern for the improvement of education has been for matters tangential to this behavior. Study habit is not merely a small but persistent problem of education—it is a fundamental issue. What I describe and propose here is an interim approach that will make do with the materials already available while improving the student's execution of typical assignments.

The importance of study habits extends beyond the formalities of subject-matter education. The products of poor study habits are both cause and consequence of much of what

From *Journal of Mathetics*, 1962, 1, 75 – 86.

is called "personal maladjustment." The problem is a frequent occasion for visits of students to college clinic and counseling centers. That the consequences of poor study habits are fundamental expressions of repeated failure should give pause to those who would discount the problem as simply a manifestation of some more basic disorder. Four years of nagging anxiety combined with either failure or compensating behaviors of cheating, meaningless memorizing (cramming), and disguising ignorance, must have their effect. The problem may have far more relevance to what is called mental hygiene than is commonly believed.

SOME BEHAVIORS CHARACTERIZING POOR STUDY HABITS

The promotion of effective study demands both an analysis of the constituent behaviors and an analysis of the existing behaviors that compete with them. Whereas this analysis has often been provided, a description of these behaviors in the present context will further the understanding of the program described here.

The act of studying, regardless of efficiency, is not usually under adequate stimulus control, either by time or by place. The student may study physics at random occasions and at any place he may happen to be on those occasions. Thus, he is subject to all the interfering behaviors conditioned to those occasions. No one occasion becomes uniquely related to study. Even where the student has established regular places and times for study, the immediately preceding occasion is likely to produce behavior competing with that of going to the place of study. He studies physics in the library at ten o'clock if he can resist the reinforcement involved in having coffee with his friends. . A student's actual study behavior consists largely of acts indirectly relevant to, even competitive with, learning. More than anything else, to study is to read; to read is to peruse written matter as one would peruse a novel or newspaper. To study is to underline passages in a text. But why? Underlining is not the behavior one desires to learn. The underlined passages may be later recognized as important material, but usually we wish the student to reproduce this material, not point to it. To study is to copy into a notebook. But copying behavior itself hardly constitutes education, and generally wastes time.

These common conceptions of study behavior are not only unrelated to effective learning behavior, they more than likely interfere with it. Since the material to be learned is often aversive, and since others agree that copying, reading and underlining constitute study, the student may believe that he has discharged his responsibility by carrying out these behaviors. Moreover, these behaviors are usually accompanied by just enough learning to maintain them. If he fails a test he commonly complains that unrealistic demands were made of him.

Typical reading behavior is not an efficient learning method. Students will read several pages before they become aware of what they are doing. Even then, they frequently do not know what the chapter is all about. They will press on to new material before they understand necessary concepts that went before. And, of course, they underline and copy. Recitation is minimal and review is merely re-reading that which they did not master the first time.

Many study methods have been developed to cope with these difficulties. These methods, if used, can produce decided improvement. The difficulty with the methods lies hidden in the phrase, "if used." The student can be impressed with the plausibility of a method when it is described to him, as the dogpaddler can be convinced of the superiority of the Australian Crawl. These methods rely heavily on recitation, as they should. However, it is one thing to convince a student that recitation is the essential mechanism of learning, it is another to get him to outline the chapter while sitting on a closed book. Recitation is hard work, and its worthy consequences seem distantly related; the reinforcers of this hard work are considerably delayed. And even if the student has mastered an effective technique, there remains the problem of getting him to study in the first place. This, then, is the first problem facing us: how to provide the conditions that will place the *initiation* of study by students under effective stimulus control. All other developments come to nothing if the control of this first step is missing.

This is what is to be established: (a) placing the initiation of study under stimulus control, (b) making the study occasion an effective stimulus for behaviors similar to what counselors call good study habits, and (c) making it possible to accomplish this at a reasonable cost while using few professionals and reaching many students.

A pilot attempt to apply reinforcement principles to these problems has been conducted. The method was sufficiently successful to justify its serving as a point of departure, at least a beginning which can be experimentally modified. In this pilot attempt, volunteers were sought from among freshmen and sophomore college students. Students were told that the experimenter believed he had a method that would require them to study only in the day time and would lead to an improvement in grades; evenings and weekends would be free. Five students were chosen: two above and three below the college achievement average. They met with the experimenter individually every day for five to ten minutes. At the outset they were required to give a careful analysis of their schedules, including social activities. Considerable information was obtained about their usual habits of study.

On the first day of counseling, a student who had a free period at ten o'clock, immediately after his physics class, was told that he should begin building his regimen by going to the library every day at that time. The student had indicated previously that he had always intended to do this but never got around to it. He was further instructed to leave on the first floor of the library all his books except those relevant to physics. He was to go to a specified room (little used) and proceed to study physics. If he experienced discomfort or began to daydream, he should leave the library immediately and join his friends at coffee, see his girl, or do whatever he pleased. He was instructed that he must, under no condition, remain to study further. He was told that once he decided to leave, he was to read one page of the physics text carefully or solve the easiest problem assigned to him and then leave immediately, even though his interest had been renewed.

These instructions were written down for him, and it was stressed that he should follow them to the letter. He was told that failure to follow them might result in the counselor's refusal to work with him. On the next day the student was questioned about the details of what he had done, and if he had violated any part of the instructions. He was warned that further violation might lead to the termination of the counseling. After the first day no great difficulty was found in students following the instructions. Each day thereafter the student was told that he was to increase the amount of work he performed after he decided to leave the study room. He was to read one page more than the day before (more or less depending upon the nature of the material). The counselor ignored other courses, telling the student to do as he liked about them so long as he did not study them in the specified room. Gradually the student came to spend all of the hour studying physics. After the first few days there were no further increments in the amount of material required to study, and the student was told that if he finished this amount (say, three physics problems or five pages of reading) he was free to repeat exactly that amount of work if he wanted to. If he wished, he could repeat that amount again and again as long as he had made an independent decision each time. When this regimen had been established for a full week, the experimenter began scheduling an additional course. A different room was designated, and appropriate hours set aside. Always the experimenter began with the course which gave the student the most trouble, and worked toward his easiest course. Eventually, every course was so scheduled, and the student was spending the whole of one hour each day on each course. The experiment was incomplete, but a regular study schedule had been established. The student was still unable to cover all assignments in the allotted time, and he was told to take care of the extra work in any way he pleased as long as he did not use the rooms set aside for daytime study.

Pause here to analyze what was done. Each of the steps described above was suggested by a simple behavior principle. a) First of all, we were trying to make maximal use of available reinforcers. The physics student, for example, had expressed some anxiety over his inability to live up to his resolution to study each day at ten o'clock. This failure was produced by a combination of the aversive nature of the study and competition with social reinforcers. By requiring him to remain only a short time in the study room, and by giving him the option to leave at will *as a formal requirement of the procedure,* we minimized the aversive conditions of his having to forego completely the competing social engagements and of having to read difficult material for an hour. Possibly of greater importance, we may have reduced aversive features when we made the option to abandon study an approved procedure rather than a display of student irresponsibility. Next, we provided the conditions for positive reinforcement when we saw to it that the student complete an assignment before leaving, even though the assignment was small and dictated by the counselor: a counselor represents University authority in the student's thinking. b) We used the principle of successive approximations by requiring the student to master only a small part of the program of studying before he went on. It is easier to establish consistent visits to the library than it is to establish this while also trying to get him to remain an hour at hard work. c) We used our knowledge of reinforcement schedules when we broke the study assignment into small parts. The act of studying every set of four pages received reinforcement — probably in the form of satisfaction over the completion of an assignment as well as the earning of a right to leave the situation. In technical terms we put the student on a fixed-ratio schedule of reinforcement, requiring a fixed amount of work to be done for reinforcement. It is well established that such a schedule produces high rates of work and increased resistance to extinction (giving up). If the fixed-ratio schedule is "strained," requiring too much work for a given reinforcement, not only will extinction occur, but the task takes on added aversive character and boredom may be heightened. Study assignments often represent strained ratios, the student having a great deal of work to do for rather vague promises of reinforcement. We have broken up the work into small ratios and depended, in part, on escape from the aversive character of the traditional conditions of study. We have increased the ratio gradually,

just as we train laboratory subjects to work at high ratios by slow increments. d) Finally, we have produced these effects under a consistent set of stimuli, taking care that these stimuli serve only as occasions for study — study which terminates in reinforcement. This, in turn, adds to the reinforcement value of the study room itself, according to the principle of conditioned reinforcement.

DEVELOPING EFFICIENT STUDY BEHAVIOR

Since this paper is concerned with promoting study behavior using available materials, a gross analysis of study behavior is indicated. We chose to begin with the analysis of Robinson (1946), called the Survey Q3R Technique, making modifications where needed. SQ3R is an abbreviation for "survey," "question," "read," "recite" and "review." "Survey" indicates reading over the bold face and italicized headings in a chapter, and serves to give an overall picture of the material to be studied. It also serves as a one minute warm-up. "Question" means going over the material a second time and formulating questions suggested by headings. This sets the student to look for specific answers while reading. "Reading" refers to reading without underlining or note-taking. "Recitation" indicates outlining or otherwise reciting the material while the book is closed. *It is during recitation that the student is emitting the essential behavior to be learned;* reading is like watching someone else perform. "Review" can take place in the form of checking the outline against the book or re-reading the chapter, for errors of omission and commission.

Previous experience tells us that it is easy to establish surveying behavior; a bit more difficult to establish questioning; and extremely difficult to establish recitation habits. Reading is like watching someone else do it, and this is easy enough; recitation is composing, and this is work inherently more difficult and less practiced than reading.

In our exploratory attempt to establish effective study techniques in five students, we used the method of successive approximation, just as we had in establishing the behavior of spending time in the study room. Only after attendance in the study room was well established did we instruct him to begin with "survey." We explained how and why the survey was to be done and told him to spend not more than a minute surveying a section. In the next session we had him describe how he surveyed the material, and corrected him where he used the method incorrectly. When "survey" came to be routine, we instructed him to begin the questioning phase. At first, we had him ask only one question for each bold face heading, then gradually required him to ask more and more questions. An approximate time limit was set for this phase. Once "survey" and "question" were well established, we began an analysis of his reading habits (reading tests are useful here). He was instructed to stop all underlining and note taking, and we gave him a time limit to meet — so many pages in five minutes — the speed being a fraction below his average speed for the type of material. He was instructed to read only to answer those questions he had previously asked or those that occurred to him as he read. From time to time, the reading speed standard was increased until he had reached a comfortable but reasonable rate. No attempt was made to make him a speed reader. During this period we began developing "recitation." At first we told him to stop at the end of each section, to close his book and sit on it (literally),[1] and to spend three minutes — *no more* — outlining what he had read. When this had been well established we increased the recitation time by about a minute a day until he had reached an optimum. This optimum was established by the experimenter on the basis of the type of material and the number of pages. While the recitation time was being increased, we initiated review training. The student was told to open his book immediately after recitation and rapidly peruse the material for errors of commission. A short period of time was set for this review and was increased each day to a limit. Next, we had him seek errors of omission. Finally, when his original reading time had reached the desired value, and when recitation had become fairly easy, the student was instructed to re-read the whole section for review within a reasonable time limit. Throughout this procedure the student was kept on a schedule in which he made an independent decision after each section to stay and study or to leave and play.

While this description covers only the highlights of the actual work with a typical student, it should serve to exemplify the way to apply the principles of behavior to a complex situation where little control is ordinarily possible. It might be said that we were teaching the student to apply the principles. And this is fundamental: the behavior involved in applying behavior principles is also subject to those principles. We tried to make it easy for him to apply these principles to his own study behavior.

The results of our pilot study were promising. Each of the five students remained with us for the college quarter. During the second quarter they reported the continued use of the method, and all demonstrated a significant improvement in grades: the smallest average rise was one letter grade, the highest was four (one student advanced from an F average to a B average). Four of the students now accomplished all their study in the day, and had evenings and weekends free. One required two hours on Saturday morning to complete his work.

MODIFICATIONS AND EXTENSIONS

The pilot study left more to be desired. It appears that greater progress could have been made if training in the SQ3R technique had begun earlier. Variations in these details need to be tried. Improvements will be discovered only by more intensive and precise investigation of the behavior of a single student. It will be necessary to develop means for obtaining more reliable measures of the students' adherence to schedules, actual time spent in the study room, and so on. Always it must be kept in mind, however, that such an investigation as this one defeats its purpose if it becomes too involved. This is inherently a gross method of improving self-instruction.

Some concern can be directed toward special problems of different subject-matters. For example, in directing the schedules of gradu-

---

1 This is important: it discourages both looking at the book and slumping in the chair.

ate students preparing for language reading examination, we have achieved some success with little effort and time. Many of these special arrangements can be developed into more efficient procedure with little expense or trouble. A description of the highlights of some work in learning to read French will serve to illustrate what we mean by special applications.

We obtained volunteers from among graduate students who were below the required reading proficiency for French, but capable of making their way through a foreign language with greater ease than a beginner. These students simply were not practicing on a regular schedule, although their resolutions were good. The practice was tiresome and interesting events competed with it. We established a special place for this practice, provided copies of a French journal, a stop watch, graph paper, pencils, and a ruler. We diagnosed the difficulty as a matter of strained ratios of reinforcement combined with lack of good stimulus control and inadequate information about true progress (which we assumed to represent reinforcement in this case). We attempted to do away with these difficulties with the following procedures.

The students were scheduled at a time convenient to them. They were told to spend approximately ten minutes each day in the practice room, and that our methods would lead them to the required proficiency level within a short time. Each was told that he had to follow the instructions to the letter or lose the privilege of our counsel. We numbered the ordinates of the graph paper to designate the average hourly rate of reading in words per hour; the abscissa represented successive practice trials. A line was drawn parallel to the abscissa and intersecting the ordinate at the rate required by the graduate school, say 400 words an hour. They were instructed to start their stopwatches and begin a written translation of a French passage. The first passage was 25 words in length. The student translated one passage and recorded his time. A chart enabled him to calculate the hourly rate, and he was instructed to plot this rate on the graph paper provided. He had fulfilled the day's requirement when one passage had been translated, but he was told that he could translate as many more as he liked as long as he spent no more than one hour. After several days, the passages were increased to 50 words and later to 100 words.

These conditions provided all the ingredients for success in getting the student to maintain a steady practice schedule. Very quickly each came to spend the entire hour almost every day, although never required to spend more than ten minutes. The small fixed ratios and the immediate knowledge of results were sufficient to maintain this behavior and to place it under the control of a consistent set of stimulus conditions. The first exercise was a requirement; after that, the curve of progress or regression was a built-in challenge which he did not have to take. Rarely did a student leave the room until he had translated a passage with greater speed than on any previous trial. Thus, he left the room each day strongly reinforced. It was unnecessary to instruct him not to leave until he had exceeded his previous performance. No student was content to reach the standard proficiency mark, and all continued beyond this until continued improvement was difficult to realize. On days of little progress a student would leave early, thereby protecting himself from unknown sources of inefficiency.

SEMI-AUTOMATION OF COUNSELING

The time spent with the student by a professional counselor can be reduced in three ways: by substituting for some of the professional's work a set of written instructions; by using other students wherever possible; and by the use of machinery. A feasible means of exploiting these resources is yet to be worked out. It is possible that each student could be given an IBM card on which he recorded his schedule and other pertinent information. This card, when inserted into a machine, could produce a set of instructions tailor-made to his requirements. The machine would punch the card so that the next insertion would yield the second set of instructions. It may be even more efficient to train students as counselors to carry out this same routine, freeing the professional to devote his time to special cases. A workable instruction book might be developed that would adequately serve most students.

A personal course in psychology

FRED S. KELLER

I would like you to imagine that you have recently agreed to help establish a department of psychology. It is to be complete in every respect, with all the major specializations and at every level of training from the first course to the most advanced, in a university that is just being formed, and in a country where no such department now exists. Together with four young psychologists and former pupils as co-workers, you are expected to take a constructive part in procuring a complete staff, purchasing equipment, outfitting a library, designing a department building, and—especially—developing a curriculum of study. You have been assured of financial and moral support, and you have been told to be as bold and experimental as you wish in the program you adopt.

Imagine, too, that, in a few months, you will have awaiting you, at the university's opening, a group of perhaps 100 students, fairly well grounded in language, mathematics, arts, and the other sciences, who want basic psychological training. You and your colleagues, with a few assistants, working in temporary quarters and with limited facilities, are expected to introduce them to psychology and to carry them thereafter as far as they may want to go.

To start you on your way, you and your colleagues have spent a month or more in visiting colleges, universities, hospitals, and research centers, where psychology is taught in one way or another. You have talked with interested teachers and researchers about your problem; you have examined shops, laboratories, libraries, classrooms, and clinics. You have taken notes on everything and tried to extract from every experience something of value for your project. You have bought some books and ordered some equipment. And you have sat down together at the end of your travels to decide upon your next objective. What is it going to be?

Under such conditions, I suggest that your first concern would be the introductory course and those 100-odd students who will be enrolled therein. There is only *one* introductory course, and it is, or should be, a key course and a foundation for the work to come. While teaching it, you and your co-workers can prepare for the courses that immediately follow. At the same time, you can begin your search for a distinguished staff of teachers at the more advanced levels. These new teachers will, in turn, help you design and equip your workshops and laboratories, stock your library, give form and clearer purpose to your program, and, finally, help you design your building. Right now, your job is to get ready for those 100 young men and women who will be there to greet you when the school bell rings.

But what sort of first course will you teach? There's much talk today of an educational reawakening; much dissatisfaction throughout this country with our aims, our methods, and the results we now achieve. Will you try to export a course that is under fire at home? Perhaps you, yourself, have complained about the failure of your teaching—talked about the inefficiency of the lecture system, the evil of examinations, the meaninglessness of letter and number grades, the short-term retention of course content, and the rigid frame of hours, days, and weeks within which each course of study is presumed to fit. Perhaps you have even expressed a willingness to change these things, if you could only escape from the "system." Now you have your chance. What are you going to do?

The kind of course I'm going to suggest has never been taught. It won't work. It conflicts with the natural tendencies of man. It has nothing new about it. Even if it worked, it could only teach reinforcement theory. It might be all right somewhere else, but it won't go here. And I think you will find, in the last analysis, that it is against the law. So, having anticipated some of your criticisms, let me tell you more about it.

It is a course with lectures, demonstrations,

Paper read at American Psychological Association, Philadelphia, August, 1963.

discussions, laboratory hours, and "homework." The lectures and demonstrations are infrequent and primarily inspirational: Ideally, they are interesting, informative, and memorable — even entertaining. Once the course has started, they are provided at suitable places along the way, but only for those students who have reached a point that guarantees an appreciation of their content. For students who do not qualify until a later date, a recording of the lecture and, if possible, the demonstration, is available. Attendance at either lectures or demonstrations, however, is entirely optional, and no examination is based upon them.

Discussions, with one's peers or with an instructor, or both, are provided at certain times for those students who desire them and, as in the case of lectures and demonstrations, if they have earned the privilege. These discussions are also recorded and may be listened to again by any of the participants. Needless to say, the discussions are never to be used as examining devices by the teacher. They are primarily for the student, who has won the right to ask questions or to express himself with respect to the work he has been doing in the laboratory or at home.

The laboratory work itself begins on the second or third day of the course, and is its most important feature. Each student has his own private and well-equipped little room or cubicle, for a certain time each day (say an hour and a half), on five or six days of the week. There he works alone, or perhaps with a partner, under the general supervision of a laboratory assistant who has no more than nine other students in his charge at the time. The student's daily task begins when he has qualified for it — for example, when he has turned in a report of the preceding day's experiment, answered two or three questions on the last reading assignment, studied a description of his laboratory mission for the day, or done all of these things.

The experiments themselves are carefully planned to let each student discover for himself the operation of certain well-established principles of behavior; to teach him some basic skills in the use of equipment and the treatment of data; and to lead him from minimal to maximal responsibility in the writing of reports.

When a laboratory task has been completed (and *only* then), the student receives the assignment that will prepare him for the next. This is his "homework." It may include textbook study — plain or programmed; the reading of an article or technical report, carefully edited or supplemented to make it fully clear, and provided with a few key questions like those he may be asked at the beginning of his next laboratory session; and other readings may be given solely as a reward for work completed and to whet the appetite for more.

Besides preparing him for further laboratory missions, lectures, demonstrations, and conferences, this "homework" is intended to broaden the student's perspective by teaching him to generalize from the laboratory to many other situations of human life. It aims to encourage thinking in the direction of both research and practical application. And, finally, it is meant to provide the student with at least a nodding acquaintance with the great variety that goes by the name of psychology today.

The assistant's functions in such a course are very important. He is the one who prepares and checks equipment, collects reports, passes out work material and assignments, and records, in each student's individual log-book, each important step along the route — including the time of arrival and the number of set-backs, if any, before reaching port. He will also collect any student complaints, requests, comments, or suggestions (in writing), which he then passes on to the course director or other designated person.

The teachers, in a course like this, are not as conspicuous as they were under the old order. Their work-load and responsibility, however, are as great as before — especially during the first year's operation. They are the ones who design, in every minute detail and, initially, for just one student, each day's teaching program; and they are the ones who re-design this program in the light of student performance and assistants' reports. They must also stand ready to give an occasional lecture or preside at a demonstration; they must sometimes be available for conference or discussion with qualified students; and they must be prepared to read an occasional student paper. Their general loss in visibility to their students, which might be aversive to long-time performers on the classroom stage, is perhaps offset by the improved reception of their messages when given and, more generally, the increased status of their academic position.

When all the course requirements have been met, the course is at an end. At this point, the student's log-book is examined by the course director, who records the achievement, places the book in the department files, and takes a few moments, perhaps, to offer his congratulations. No final examination is given, no course grade, no reward for speed of attainment, and no punishment for delay. Examining and teaching were inseparable parts of the same educational process; and something better than a letter or a number is available, in a list of the goals that were reached and the time it took to reach them. The student is ready for Course No. 2, a new log-book, a new cubicle, a new assistant, a new body of fact and skills, and, probably, a new teacher. But this is not, at the moment, our concern.

I have sketched for you, during the past few minutes, a more or less imaginary first course in psychology, and I have suggested its more or less imaginary origin. More or less. Pilot research in this kind of teaching is already going on at several places in this country, although not exclusively aimed at first-course needs; and a full-scale test is now being planned for the first course itself, along the lines I have suggested here, at the new University of Brasilia, in Brazil, beginning in 1964. If success attends these ventures, it might well be that some such personal-course method of instruction could be applied in other sciences and at other levels of education.

Use of the Premack principle in controlling the behavior of nursery school children

L. E. HOMME, P. C. deBACA, J. V. DEVINE, R. STEINHORST AND E. J. RICKERT

Premack's principle (Premack, 1959) can be stated: if behavior B is of higher probability than behavior A, then behavior A can be made more probable by making behavior B contingent upon it.

In a preliminary exploration of nursery school procedures, three 3-yr-old subjects (Ss) were available three hours a day, five days a week, for about one month. On the first day, in the absence of any aversive control, verbal instructions usually had little effect on the Ss' behavior. When they were instructed to sit in their chairs, Ss would often continue what they were doing—running around the room, screaming, pushing chairs, or quietly working jigsaw puzzles. Taking Premack seriously, such behaviors were labeled as high probability behaviors and used in combination with the signals for them as reinforcers. These high probability behaviors were then made contingent on desired behaviors. For example, sitting quietly in a chair and looking at the blackboard would be intermittently followed by the sound of the bell, with the instruction: "Run and scream." The Ss would then leap to their feet and run around the room screaming. At another signal they would stop. At this time they would get another signal and an instruction to engage in some other behavior which, on a quasi-random schedule, might be one of high or low probability. At a later stage, Ss earned tokens for low probability behaviors which could later be used to "buy" the opportunity for high probability activities.

With this kind of procedure, control was virtually perfect after a few days. For example, when Ss were requested to "sit and look at the blackboard" (an activity which in the past had intermittently been interrupted by the signal for some higher probability behavior), they were under such good control that an observer, new on the scene, almost certainly

From *Journal of the Experimental Analysis of Behavior,* 1963, **6,** 544.

would have assumed extensive aversive control was being used.

An examination of high probability behaviors quickly showed that many, if not most of them, were behaviors which ordinarily would be suppressed through punishment. Extrapolating from this we were able to predict the reinforcing properties of some behaviors which had never been emitted. For example, throwing a plastic cup across the room and kicking a waste basket had never been observed but proved to be highly reinforcing activities after they had once been evoked by instructions. (Some unpredicted behaviors proved to be highly reinforcing, e.g., pushing the experimenter around the room in his caster-equipped chair.)

In summary, even in this preliminary, unsystematic application, the Premack hypothesis proved to be an exceptionally practical principle for controlling the behavior of nursery school *S*s.

The alteration of behavior in a special classroom situation

ELAINE H. ZIMMERMAN AND J. ZIMMERMAN

The classroom behavior of two emotionally disturbed boys was altered by arranging and manipulating its consequences.

The boys, in-patients in a residential treatment center (LaRue D. Carter Memorial Hospital), attended the first author's English class daily for 1 hr as part of an educational therapy program. There were three boys in the class, each receiving individual attention.

CASE I

Subject 1 (S-1) was 11 years old. He appeared to have no organic disorder and was of normal intelligence. In early class sessions, whenever S-1 was called upon to spell a word which had previously been studied and drilled, he would pause for several seconds, screw up his face, and mutter letters unrelated to the word. Following this, the instructor (*E*) consistently asked him to sound out the word, often giving him the first letter and other cues, encouraging him to spell the word correctly. Only after *E* had spent considerable time and attention would the boy emit a correct response. The procedure was inefficient and profitless for improving the boy's spelling behavior. In fact, it may have been maintaining the undesirable pattern, since over the first 10 or 15 class sessions, consistently more time and attention were required of *E* to obtain a correct spelling response.

While "studying" in class, S-1 would obtain sheets of paper, wrinkle them, and throw them away, laughing as he caught *E*'s eye or that of one of the other students.

The Change in Approach

After several weeks in class, S-1 was quizzed via paper-and-pencil test on a lesson based on 10 spelling words, with time allotted for study and review. He handed in a paper with a muddled combination of barely legible letters. Immediately, *E* asked him to go to the blackboard. Her instructions were simply: "We will now have a quiz. I will read a word and you will spell it correctly on the board." She read the first word, and the subject misspelled it 10 or more times on the board. During this time, *E* sat at her desk, ignoring S-1, apparently busy reading or writing. Each time S-1 misspelled the word, he glanced at *E*; but she did not respond. The boy erased the word and tried again, several times repeating "I can't spell it," or "I can't remember how," etc. Although ignored, the boy made no effort

From *Journal of the Experimental Analysis of Behavior,*
1962, **5**, 59 – 60.

to sit down or leave the room. After approximately 10 min, he spelled the word correctly; E looked up at him immediately, smiled, and said, "Good, now we can go on." She read a second word; and after a similar series of errors and verbal responses, S-1 spelled the word correctly. With each successive word (through 10 words), the number of inappropriate (unreinforced) responses decreased, as did the latency of the correct response. At the end of the quiz, E took the boy's spelling chart, wrote an "A" on it, and praised him. She then asked the subject to help her color some Easter baskets. They sat down together, and chatted and worked.

Thereafter, attention in the form of smiling, chatting, and physical proximity was given only immediately after the emission of desired classroom behavior or some approximation of it in the desired direction. Undesirable behavior was consistently ignored. As a result of a month of this treatment, the frequency of bizarre spelling responses and other undesirable responses declined to a level close to zero per class session. At the conclusion of this study, the boy was working more efficiently, and was making adequate academic progress.

CASE II

Subject S-2 was an 11-year-old boy, who, like S-1, had no apparent organic disorder and was also of normal intelligence. In initial class sessions, S-2 emitted behavior considered undesirable in the classroom context with high frequency. He displayed temper tantrums (kicking, screaming, etc.), spoke baby talk, and incessantly made irrelevant comments or posed irrelevant questions.

Several times a week, attendants dragged this boy down the hall to one of his classes as the boy screamed and buckled his knees. On several of these occasions, the boy threw himself on the floor in front of a classroom door. A crowd of staff members inevitably gathered around him. The group usually watched and commented as the boy sat or lay on the floor, kicking and screaming. Some members of the group hypothesized that such behavior seemed to appear after the boy was teased or frustrated in some way. However, the only observable

in the situation was the consistent consequence of the behavior in terms of the formation of a group of staff members around the boy.

Observing one such situation which occurred before E's class, E asked the attendant to put the boy in the classroom at his desk and to leave the room. Then E closed the door. The boy sat at his desk, kicking and screaming; E proceeded to her desk and worked there, ignoring S-2. After 2 or 3 min, the boy, crying softly, looked up at E. Then E announced that she would be ready to work with him as soon as he indicated that he was ready to work. He continued to cry and scream with diminishing loudness for the next 4 or 5 min. Finally, he lifted his head and stated that he was ready. Immediately, E looked up at him, smiled, went to his desk, and said, "Good, now let's get to work." The boy worked quietly and cooperatively with E for the remainder of the class period.

The Handling of Tantrums, Irrelevant Verbal Behavior, and Baby Talk

Each time a tantrum occurred, E consistently ignored S-2. When tantrum behavior was terminated, E conversed with the boy, placed herself in his proximity, or initiated an activity which was appealing to him. After several weeks, class tantrums disappeared entirely. Because the consequence of tantrum behavior varied in other situations, no generalization to situations outside the classroom has been observed.

Furthermore the frequency of irrelevant verbal behavior and of baby talk declined almost to the point of elimination following the procedure of withholding attention after the emission of such behavior. On the other hand, when S-2 worked quietly or emitted desirable classroom behavior, E addressed him cordially and permitted some verbal interchange for several seconds. When a lesson was being presented to the class at large and S-2 listened attentively, E reinforced him by asking him a question he could answer or by looking at him, smiling at him, etc. The reinforcement was delivered intermittently rather than continuously because: (a) reinforcing every desired response of one student was impossible since

5

PRINCIPLES AND CONTROL OF SOCIAL BEHAVIOR

Social behavior involves the interaction of two or more organisms with one another or their action together in relation to a common environment. Obviously much of human behavior is social. Although most of the experimental studies of human behavior have dealt with individual behavior, some initial attempts have been made to give behavioral, experimental definitions to various social behaviors such as cooperation, competition, leadership, and imitation. With the establishment of these behavioral definitions, further efforts have been made to manipulate social behaviors experimentally, and to describe the principles on which they operate by using the same operational and conceptual framework that has proved so effective in describing and controlling individual behavior.

The papers presented in this section are representative of such efforts to analyze and control social behavior. The first paper, by Cohen, is a fine example of the research being conducted in this direction. It demonstrates exceptionally well the relevance of the free-operant method to research on social variables. In addition, Cohen attempts to relate, in an informal way, the social behavior of subjects in an experimental setting to their behavior in nonexperimental settings such as the home.

The second paper, by Baer and Sherman, shows that imitative behavior can be established and eliminated in young children through techniques of reinforcement and extinction. More important, in their study, the reinforcement of one imitative behavior generalized to the imitation of other, different behaviors whose imitation was not directly reinforced. Thus, imitation itself seemed to become a mode of behavior which was established as a whole, no matter what specific behavior was being imitated.

The final paper, by Hingtgen, gives an example of similar research on social variables in a less controlled setting. It demonstrates the generation and maintenance of social behavior in autistic children, who had previously had very little social behavior of any kind in their repertoires.

Although the value of the contributions already made should not be minimized, it is obvious that the surface of this area has barely been scratched. The papers in this section provide a brief summary of the work done to date and a glimpse into the future of the experimental analysis of social behavior.

Justin and his peers: An experimental analysis of a child's social world

DONALD J. COHEN

The techniques of the experimental analysis of individual behavior developed in the researches of Pavlov, Watson, and Skinner have only recently been extended to human activities involving more than one person (Azrin and Lindsley 1956; Skinner, 1953). The methods of free operant conditioning allow for a sensitive control of particular variables and for analysis of changes in behavior through time. This experimental approach is thus methodologically suitable for the study of social transactions which are continuous (Argyle, 1957) and which can be shown to be related to particular classes of environmental events. While interviewing and questionnaire techniques can be used to obtain data on retrospective reports of behavior and attitudes or dispositions, the free operant method can be used in the analysis of ongoing behavior and the changes in behavior which occur when people confront each other in a social situation. Also, while field observation is usually inexact and open to observer bias, the free operant method allows for scientific control and precision in response definition and measurement.

The first free operant experimental analysis of human social behavior (Azrin and Lindsley 1956) demonstrated the possibility of generating cooperative behavior in young children through the scheduling of candy reinforcements. The cooperative behavior could be extinguished by withholding the reinforcements and regenerated through the rescheduling of the reinforcements.

In this present paper, a new instrument for the experimental analysis of social behavior is briefly described. The results of analysis of the social behavior of a particular young person are discussed. These results demonstrate that the young man behaves differently towards people with whom he has different nonexperimentally determined relations. Nonexperimental observations of the social behavior of the subjects support the clinical validity of the experimental findings.

METHOD

Subjects

The social behavior of Justin, a normal 13-year-old, is studied in relation to people with whom he has different relationships. The five people involved in this analysis of Justin's social profile are his brother (age 16), sister (age 14), close friend (age 13), mother, and a stranger (age 14).

Apparatus

The experimental environment employed throughout the experiments was two adjacent 6-ft. square rooms. Each room was equipped with a standard operant conditioning panel on one wall (Figure 1) as described by Lindsley (1956). Mounted on each panel was a metal plunger; the plunger could be pulled with little effort and in some experiments has been pulled up to several thousand times within 90 minutes with no signs of fatigue. Located on each panel was a small bin into which the reinforcements (pennies and candy) were dropped. The two adjacent rooms were separated by a clear plexiglass window through which the subjects could see each other when seated in front of the operant panels. . . .

Controlling and recording apparatus was located behind the experimental rooms in an adjoining area from which the experimental rooms were observed through concealed periscopes. A white noise generator delivered covering noise to concealed speakers in each room. The noise was maintained just loud enough to prevent any discussion between the subjects.

From *Child Development*, 1962, **33**, 697–717.

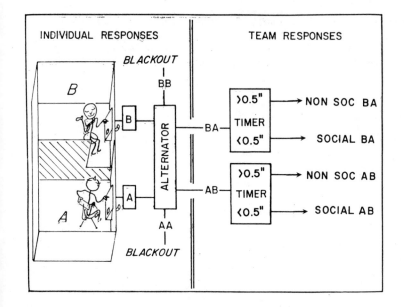

Figure 1. *Schematic drawing of apparatus and response definition for individual and team responses. Each room is equipped with a metal plunger; movement of the plunger produces an electric impulse which is electrically defined into individual and team responses as shown in the block diagram.*

Response Definition

There are two major response definition categories: team responses and individual responses (Figure 1). The latter involves only one subject, the former requires the participation of both. All response categorization was performed automatically by switching circuits. As individual *A* pulled his plunger, an impulse shortener converted the movement into an electric impulse of .06 sec. duration. Similarly, *B*'s response was converted into an electric impulse. The impulses were fed into a sequence analyzer which categorized the responses into four groups: *A* followed by *B* (*AB*); *B* followed by *A* (*BA*); *A* followed by *A* (*AA*); *B* followed by *B* (*BB*). *AB* and *BA* were team responses; *AA* and *BB* were individual responses.

In order to facilitate the study of socially defined, or team, behavior, the individual responses were mildly punished. The punishment for an *AA* consisted of *A*'s room being darkened for 2.5 sec. during which a pure tone (500 cycles) was sounded through his speaker (see Ferster and Skinner, 1957, p. 35). When either *A* or *B* was being blacked out, no responses entered the sequence analyzer.

The team responses are further defined on the basis of the temporal relationship between the two responses. An *A* response

followed within .5 sec. by a *B* response is a *Social AB*. An *A* response followed within any period of time greater than .5 sec. is a *Nonsocial AB*. Social BA and Nonsocial BA responses are defined analogously. The value of .5 sec. was chosen on the basis of exploratory investigation. The probability that a second response would follow the first within .5 sec. by chance alone (and without the production of *AA* or *BB* responses) was found to be slight. Team and individual responses of each category were simultaneously recorded on separate cumulative recorders and digital counters. The cumulative records provide a continuous measure of the ongoing social behavior throughout an experimental session.

Reinforcement Contingencies

Cooperation is operationally defined in this study as behavior in which both subjects are involved and in which both are reinforced. Competition is defined as behavior in which both subjects are involved and only one is reinforced. That is, cooperation and competition are team responses which are differentiated on the basis of the reinforcement, or "pay-off," contingency. The horizontal rows of Table 1 list the four team responses that are differentially reinforced; the columns are the type of social

Table 1. *Table of reinforcement contingencies used to differentially reinforce team responses. Double italicized entry (AB) indicates that both subjects are reinforced for a team response. Single italicized entry (A or B) indicates which single subject is reinforced for a team response. An empty square indicates that the team response is programmed for extinction. [The controlled leadership condition required that a particular subject lead; the uncontrolled condition did not.]*

Team Response Reinforcement Contingencies

	Uncontrolled leadership		Controlled leadership			
	Cooperation	Competition	A leads coop.	B leads coop.	A leads comp.	B leads comp.
Social AB	AB	B	AB		B	A
Social BA	AB	A		AB		A
Non-soc AB		A			A	
Non-soc BA		B				B

behavior that is defined by the programmed reinforcement contingency. The italicized letters in the squares specify who is reinforced for each particular team response. Double entries (*AB*) indicate that both subjects are reinforced for that team response (cooperation). Single entries (*A* or *B*) indicate that only one subject is reinforced (competition). Empty squares indicate that no reinforcement is delivered for that team response (extinction). Individual responses (*AA* and *BB*) are never positively reinforced. [Uncontrolled leadership refers to the case where reinforcement was delivered regardless of which subject (*A* or *B*) led. Controlled leadership required that the team response be made in a particular order.] . . .

The schedule of reinforcement was continuous (crf): for every reinforced team response a penny or piece of candy dropped into either one or both reinforcement bins on the operant panels (see Bijou, 1957). Punishment was also on a continuous (crf) schedule: for every punished individual response (*AA* or *BB*) the punished subject (*A* or *B*) was blacked out as described above.

Reinforcement consisted of a mixture of pennies and candy in an approximate ratio of four pennies to one candy (an assortment of gumdrops, pieces of chocolate, and other small candies).

Experimental Situation

The two subjects were brought to the labora-

tory together by the experimenter. They were given a minimal amount of information concerning what was to take place, with instructions limited to the following: "You are going to play a game. You can keep all you get." The subjects were then placed in the adjoining rooms in which the lights were dimmed. No other information was given the subjects at any time during the experimental session. All changes in behavior thus were generated by specific, controlled changes in the experimental conditions or resulted from the "dynamic" aspects of social interaction.

To clarify the experimental procedure, the first few moments of a *characteristic* experimental session will be outlined. The subjects were placed in the adjacent rooms; they sat down in front of the panels. The room lights went from dim to bright. . . . The subjects waited a minute or two and then explored the operant conditioning panels. They pulled the metal plungers. The initial reinforcement contingency was uncontrolled leadership during cooperation; that is, regardless of which subject led, so long as the other pulled his plunger within .5 sec., both were reinforced. *A* pulled his plunger; *B* pulled his within .5 sec. This constitutes a *Social AB* response. The room lights dimmed and a light went on in the reinforcement bin on each panel (conditioned reinforcer). A penny (reinforcement) fell into the reinforcement bin in each room and the lights remained dim for 5 sec. (the conditioned reinforcement cycle). The room lights brightened. *B* pulled his plunger and *A* followed

Table 2. *Justin's social profile.*

Team Justin and . . .	Uncontrolled Leadership	Controlled Leadership		Uncontrolled Competition
		Justin's lead reinforced	Other's lead reinforced	
Brother	Justin leads. Long acquisition. Individual responses.	Long acquisition. Brother persists in leading.	Shorter acquisition. Justin slow to follow.	
Friend	Justin leads; halts friend's attempts to lead.	Rapid acquisition.	Rapid acquisition. Justin slow to follow.	Alternation of leadership.
Stranger	Stranger leads strongly.			Unstable competition becomes alternation of leadership.
Sister	Sister leads strongly.	Rapid acquisition. Bursts of sister responding.		Competition.
Mother	Mother leads strongly.	Rapid acquisition. Bursts of mother responding.	Rapid acquisition.	Alternation of leadership.

Note. No entry — condition not used.

within .5 sec. This is a *Social BA.* The rooms were dimmed and a reinforcement delivered to each bin. When the lights brightened again, *B* pulled his plunger twice in a row (*BB*). A sequence of two responses by the same subject (individual responding) was mildly punished. *B*'s room darkened while a pure tone was delivered to his speaker for 2.5 sec. (black out *B*). When the lights went on again, either *A* or *B* could have led, and, so long as the other followed within .5 sec., both were reinforced by a penny dropping into both bins. . . .

Questionnaire Results: Brief Survey

Each subject was asked to answer an informal questionnaire composed of sentences to be completed and several direct questions. The quotations in this paper attributed to the subjects are drawn mainly from the answers given to this questionnaire. . . .

Summary and Discussion

The average reinforcement received by each subject for each experimental session was over $6.25. Most of the candy was eaten in the rooms. All the subjects in these experiments have asked if they could return to the laboratory. Sensitive behavioral analysis requires such highly motivated behavior.

A summary of Justin's experimentally determined social profile is presented in Table 2. A synopsis of the social behavior of the five teams in four different reinforcement contingencies (see Table 1) demonstrates the differences in Justin's social behavior in each team.

Justin led those people with whom he had previous nonexperimental experience of leadership, his brother and his friend. His sister who "mothers" him and his mother look strikingly similar during cooperation: both were strong leaders during uncontrolled leadership and both exhibited resistance to following him by bursts of inappropriate leadership responding when they were not reinforced for leading. With Justin and the friend, the stranger, and his mother, the competitive contingency was converted into complex cooperation. Justin and his sister displayed strong competition.

Justin has occupied more of his parents' attention than any of the other six children in the family, and the results of this family situation are reflected in the experimental analysis. Both his older brother and his immediately younger sister (age 12, not used in this experiment) have had psychiatric treatment for behavioral problems. The 12-year-old sister suffered from trichotillomania[1] but is now recovered; his older brother still shows signs of [earlier behavior problems]. Justin's older sister (age 14) manifests her envy and aggression by "mothering" him; his older brother manifests his by trying to underrate Justin's accomplishments and by trying to prevent further achievement. These Justin-sister and Justin-brother interactions are evidenced in the experimental analysis by the slow development of cooperation and control of leadership (Justin-brother) and the strong leadership accompanied by true competition (Justin-sister). The experimental analysis is validated by such statements as Justin's mother's in relation to her children: "They are the most competitive, aggressive group you ever met." The experimental analysis has successfully evaluated the type of expression given the "competitive, aggressive" family spirit.

Justin and his friend had a long history of extra-experimental cooperation. Their experimental behavior is fully cooperative with immediate alternation of leadership during programmed competition. Justin and the stranger had no history of extra-experimental cooperation; after initial competition during programmed competition, their experimental behavior changed into the more complex form of cooperation. Justin and his brother had a long history of competition and aggression; their experimental behavior is marked by a large number of nonteam responses, long periods of acquisition, persistence of nonreinforced leading, and the other occurrences noted above.

The results of these experiments clearly demonstrate that Justin's social behavior is differentially controlled by reinforcement. However, the dynamic properties of his social behavior are controlled by his previous extra-experimental relations with his teammates. Different patterns with different teammates prove that the method is sensitive to different social relationships. Further, the results of the experimental analysis are validated by the information gathered from the questionnaires and interviews. The experimental analysis, [however], indicates that the actual social behavior of an individual may contradict the statements made by that person concerning the social transaction (e.g., Justin and his mother).

The experimental analysis adds definiteness and precision to the non-experimental information concerning the subject's social interactions. Also, it is possible to further refine the type of behavior engaged in by the subjects as manifestations of such clinically relevant concepts as aggression, competition, unwillingness to follow, etc. For example, an analysis of unwillingness to follow has shown that it is expressed in both (a) leading when not being reinforced for leading and (b) hesitancy to respond after the leader has responded. Both (a) and (b) are manifested in the same experimental social circumstances by different individuals. . . .

CONCLUSIONS

The experimental determination of five different dynamic patterns of cooperative and competitive leadership between a young man and five other persons clearly demonstrates the sensitivity of this free operant method to important social variables. The close similarity between the experimentally measured patterns and the extra-experimental relationships as determined by questionnaires and interviews demonstrates that these experimental measures have high validity. The method permits a laboratory analysis of a child's social world.

---

1 A persistent urge to pull out one's own hair.

Reinforcement control of generalized imitation in young children

DONALD M. BAER AND JAMES A. SHERMAN

The term "imitation" has seen much use in the literature of child psychology. However, experimental work in this area has often failed to invoke its most powerful meaning. In experimental situations, behavior frequently has been called imitative because it resembled that of a model previously observed by the subject. But there rarely has been any guarantee that the *similarity* of the two behaviors was functional in producing the behavior in the observer. Instead, it has been common to require the observer to learn a reinforced response after having watched a model perform the same response and receive reinforcement for it. The observer often does profit from this observation of a correct performance. However, it is quite possible that he does so because certain stimuli of the situation have been paired with the sight of the reinforcement secured by the model. Since the sight of reinforcement should be a powerful secondary reinforcer, observational learning, not of a similar response, but of the cues which will facilitate that response may very well take place. When the observer is placed in the situation, his learning (of what typically is the only reinforced response in the situation) is speeded by his previously acquired sensitivity to the cues in the situation.

For example, a child may watch a model turn a crank on a green box and receive nothing, then turn a crank on a red box and receive reinforcement consistently and repeatedly. As a result of this observation, the observer subsequently may learn the same discrimination more quickly than a control subject. This may be due simply to the establishment of red as a discriminative cue for reinforcement. The observer is better reinforced for approaching red than green as a consequence of his observation, and thereby is more likely to turn the crank on the red box and be reinforced by it. There is no need in this example to assume that the *similarity* of his crank-turning response and the model's is involved. The similarity may lie in the eye of the experimenter rather than in the eye of the observer, and, in this situation, only a similar reponse will be reinforced. Hence the similarity is both forced and (perhaps) irrelevant.

However, there can be a more powerful use of imitation in the experimental analysis of children's learning if it can be shown that similarity per se functions as an important stimulus dimension in the child's behavior. The purpose of the present study is to add another demonstration of this role of similarity to the small body of literature already produced (e.g., Bandura and Huston, 1961) and to show the function of certain social reinforcement operations in promoting responding along the dimension of similarity in behavior. Specifically, a response is considered which is imitative of a model but never directly reinforced. Instead, other responses, also imitative of a model, are controlled by reinforcement operations. The strength of the unreinforced imitative response is then observed as a function of these reinforcement operations. An animated talking puppet, used previously in studies of social interaction with children (Baer, 1962b), serves both as a model to imitate and as a source of social reinforcement.

METHOD

Apparatus

The apparatus was an animated talking puppet dressed as a cowboy and seated in a chair inside a puppet stage. The puppet was capable of making four kinds of responses: (1) raising and lowering his head, or *nodding*; (2) opening and closing his mouth, or *mouthing*; (3) *bar-pressing* on a puppet-scaled bar-pressing apparatus located beside his chair, almost identical in appearance to a regular-sized bar-pressing apparatus located beside the child; and (4) *talking*, accomplished by playing E's voice through a loudspeaker mounted behind the puppet's chair, while the puppet's jaw was worked in coordination with the words being spoken. (For a more complete description and a photograph, cf. Baer, 1962b.)

From *Journal of Experimental Child Psychology*, 1964, 1 (1), 37–49.

First Sequence of Procedures

Introduction. The experiment was conducted in a two-room mobile trailer-laboratory (Bijou, 1958) parked in the lot of a day-care nursery. *E* observed the child and puppet through a one-way mirror from the other room. The child sat in a chair immediately in front of the puppet stage. An adult assistant, *A*, brought the child to the laboratory, introduced him to the puppet, seated him in his chair, and then sat in a screened corner of the room, out of the child's sight. The introduction for the first session was, "This is Jimmy the puppet. He wants to talk to you. And this (pointing) is your bar. See, it's just like Jimmy's bar, only bigger (pointing). Do you know how it works?" The usual answer was "No," in which case *A* demonstrated a bar-press, saying "Now you try it." (Some children pressed the bar without demonstration.) *A* then said, "You can talk to Jimmy now." On all later sessions, *A* said simply, "Hello Jimmy, here's (child's name) to talk to you again," and, to the child, "Now you can talk to Jimmy again."

After *A*'s introduction, the puppet raised his head and began speaking to the child. He followed a fairly standard line of conversation, starting with greetings, and progressing through expressions of pleasure over the chance to talk with the child to alternating questions about what the child had been doing and colorful stories about what the puppet had been doing. This type of conversation was maintained, throughout all the sessions; the social reinforcement procedures used as the independent variable in this study were interjected within the conversation according to the experimental design.

Operant level. The first session was to acquaint child and puppet and to collect an operant level of the child's bar-pressing, imitative or otherwise. Shortly after the puppet began talking to the child, he began to press his bar, alternating between a slow rate of 1 response per 15 seconds and a fast rate of about 3 responses per second. The puppet's bar-pressing was recorded on a cumulative recorder.

The operant level period was interrupted after 5–10 minutes of the puppet's bar-

pressing for a special procedure. The special procedure was designed to establish whether the child could generalize from the puppet's bar to his own. After the puppet had stopped bar-pressing, he would nod twice and say, "This is my head. Show me your head." Invariably, the child would move his head or point to it. The puppet then said, "Good," and began mouthing, saying, "This is my mouth. Show me your mouth." The child would move his mouth or point to it. Then the puppet said "Good," and bar-pressing twice, said, "This is my bar. Show me your bar." Some children imitated the response; some pointed to their bar. A few did neither; of these, some appeared puzzled, and others tentatively reached for the puppet's bar. These were the children the procedure was designed to detect. In their cases, the puppet explained that they had a bar of their own and helped them find it, which usually sufficed to produce either a bar-press or a pointing toward the bar. The puppet gave no reinforcement for the bar-pressing response, and instead resumed the conversation about his adventures or the child's. With some subjects there then followed another 5–10 minutes of bar-pressing by the puppet to determine whether this procedure in itself had promoted imitative bar-pressing by the child. No imitative bar-pressing ever did develop as a result of this procedure alone in the children subjected to it. For the rest of the subjects, this extra portion of the operant level period was dropped.

Still another 5–10 minutes of bar-pressing by the puppet was sometimes displayed. On these occasions, the puppet took up a very approving line of conversation, dispensing a great deal of "Good," "Very good," and "You're really smart" to the child. This was to determine the effect of noncontingent social reinforcement on the child's imitative bar-pressing. However, no child subjected to this procedure ever developed imitative bar-pressing as a result. The other subjects had a similar kind of noncontingent approval incorporated into the earlier portions of their operant level periods.

The typical rate of imitative bar-pressing during operant level periods was zero. In fact, of 11 children seen in this study, only one showed a slight tendency to imitate the puppet's bar-pressing, but this disappeared early in her operant level period. Two others showed a non-imitative bar-pressing rate during the initial session.

Reinforcement of some imitative responses. After collecting the child's operant level of bar-pressing, the puppet stopped bar-pressing and began to present a series of other responses one after another at first, and then at scattered points in his conversation. Each time he would first ask the child, "Can you do this?" These responses consisted of nodding, mouthing, and a variety of nonsense statements (such as "Glub-flub-bug," "One-two-three-four," or "Red robins run rapidly"). In each case, if the child imitated the responses, the puppet reinforced the child's response with approval, consisting mainly of the words "Good," "Very good," and "Fine." Almost without exception, the children did imitate virtually every response the puppet presented in this way, and after a few reinforcements, the puppet stopped asking "Can you do this?" in preface to the response.

After the child was consistently imitating each of these other responses without the prefatory "Can you do this?", the puppet resumed bar-pressing, alternating fast and slow rates. He continued to display nodding, mouthing, and verbal nonsense statements at scattered points in his conversation, and maintained a continuous schedule of reinforcement for every imitation of these by the child. The child's bar-pressing from this point on was the basic dependent variable of the study. An increase over operant level in this never-reinforced[1] bar-pressing by the child, especially insofar as it matched the puppet's bar-pressing, would be significant: It would be attributable to the direct reinforcement of the other responses (nodding, mouthing, and verbal). These responses have very slight topographical resemblance to bar-pressing; they are like it essentially in that they all are imitative of a model's behavior. Thus an increase in imitative bar-pressing by the child would indicate that similarity of responding per se was a functional dimension of the child's behavior, that is, similarity of responding could be strengthened as could responding itself.

This program of reinforcement for all imitative responding (other than bar-pressing) was usually begun during the first session. With some children, it was started early in their second session. Children were seen as many as 7 sessions in the course of the study. These sessions were separated by 3–7 days.

RESULTS

In the design of this study, both individual and group performances are relevant to the central question. If any child showed a significant increase in imitative bar-pressing over his operant level, as a result of direct reinforcement of other imitative responses, this would demonstrate the functional role of similarity in behavior for that child. Hence each child represented an experiment in himself. As a group, the sample allows some estimation of the probability of the effect occurring in children from this population.

Of 11 children studied, 4 failed to show any development of an imitative bar-pressing response during the course of reinforcement of nodding, mouthing, and verbal imitations. Two of these were the only two children showing a high level of non-imitative bar-pressing during their operant level periods. The remaining 7 children showed varying degrees of increase in bar-pressing, as illustrated in Figure 1. This figure shows 4 records, selected to indicate the range of increase in bar-pressing obtained. A fact not always apparent in these records (necessarily compressed for publication) is that virtually every bar-pressing response by the child occurs closely following a response (or response burst) by the puppet, and hence is clearly imitative.

FURTHER PROCEDURE AND RESULTS

The increased imitative bar-pressing by some of the children was brought about by reinforcement of other imitative responding by the child (nodding, mouthing, and verbal performances). Further procedures were developed to show the dependence of the

---

1 On one occasion with one child, a bar-press was accidentally reinforced. This will be noted in the results.

generalized imitative bar-pressing on this reinforcement. These procedures were of two kinds: extinction of the other imitative responding, and time-out from the other imitative responding.

Extinction of Imitation

Extinction was instituted with two children, one of whom had developed a near-perfect rate of imitative bar-pressing, the other showing a low rate. After a stable rate of imitative bar-pressing had been established by each child, the puppet stopped giving any reinforcement for imitation of his nodding, mouthing, or verbal nonsense performances (imitation of which in the immediate past he had reinforced continuously). However, he continued performing these actions at the same rate. He also continued to reinforce the child at the same rate, but at appropriate points in the child's conversation rather than for imitation. This continued for several sessions, until the child had shown a stable or marked decrease

in imitative bar-pressing. Then reinforcement was shifted back to imitations of nodding, mouthing, or verbal nonsense performances and maintained as before, until the child showed a stable or marked increase in imitative bar-pressing. As usual, bar-pressing was never reinforced.

The subjects chosen for this procedure were S1 and S4 of Figure 1; both were girls. Their records (Figure 2) include the early sessions that show operant level and the development of generalized imitation, already seen in Figure 1, as a baseline against which the effect of extinction of other imitative responding is seen. (Sessions 4 and 5 are omitted from the record of S4 because they are virtually identical in procedure and performance to Session 3 and would needlessly enlarge Figure 2 if included.) It is clear that S1 was very responsive to the extinction and reinforcement operations: Her near-perfect rate of imitative bar-pressing weakened considerably after nearly one complete session of extinction for other imitative responding, but promptly recovered its near-perfect

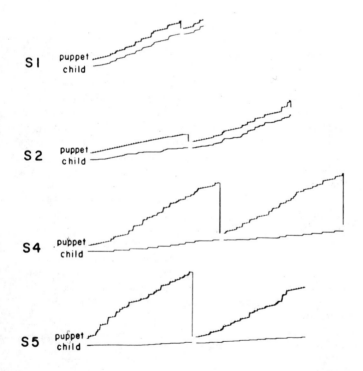

Figure 1. The development of generalized imitative bar-pressing in four representative Ss.

aspect when reinforcement was resumed.[2] The record of S4 shows the same pattern, but the differences are not so apparent. This may be due to the low rate of imitative bar-pressing induced in S4 under the previous reinforcement conditions. Sighting along the curve, however, will make clear the same pattern of rate changes apparent in the record of S1.

Time-out from Imitation

Time-out procedures were instituted with two other children, one of whom had a high rate of imitative bar-pressing, and the other only a modest rate. After a stable rate of imitative bar-pressing had been established by each child, the puppet ceased providing any nodding, mouthing, or verbal nonsense performances for the child to imitate, hence eliminating any reinforcement of imitation by eliminating the previously established cues for the occurrence of imitation. Social reinforcement was continued at the same rate, but was delivered for appropriate comments in the child's conversation rather than for imitation.

This time-out was continued until the child showed a stable or marked decrease in imitative bar-pressing. Then the puppet resumed performances of nodding, mouthing, and verbal nonsense statements, and shifted his reinforcement back to the child's imitations of these performances until the child showed a stable or marked increase in imitative bar-pressing. Then the whole cycle of time-out and reinforcement was repeated in exactly the same way. Bar-pressing, of course, was never reinforced.

The subjects chosen for this procedure were S2 of Figure 1 and S3, both girls. Their records are shown in Figure 3. (The early portion of the record of S2 has already been seen in Figure 1.) It is apparent that the time-out condition produced a quick and drastic weakening of imitative bar-pressing in

---

2 In the case of S1, it can be seen that the effects of extinction are markedly stronger with the beginning of Session 4, and that the effects of resumed reinforcement, clear in the last half of Session 5, are even more pronounced with the beginning of Session 6. This interaction between session changes and experimental conditions remains an unexplained complication of the data; however, it need not greatly alter the conclusions drawn.

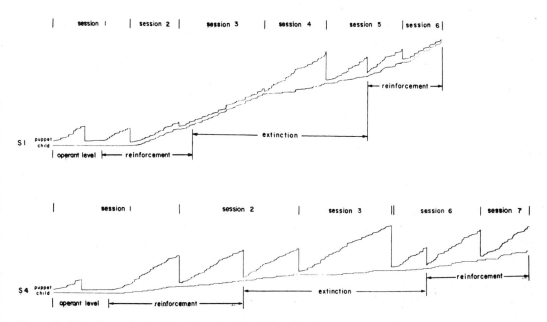

Figure 2. *The effects of extinction of previously reinforced imitation on generalized imitative bar-pressing in two Ss.*

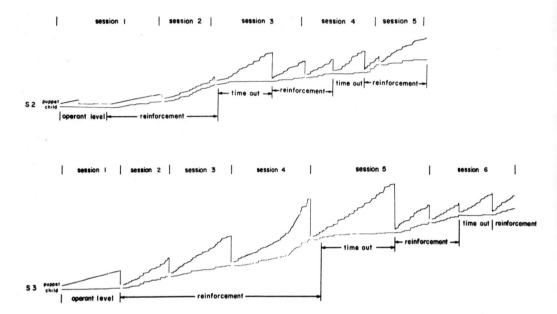

Figure 3. *The effects of time-out from reinforced imitation on generalized imitative bar-pressing in two Ss.*

these children, and that a resumption of reinforcement of other imitative responses, when these were again displayed by the puppet for the child to imitate, quickly generalized to the nonreinforced imitative bar-pressing. (By accident, S3 received one reinforcement for bar-pressing during Session 1. It is assumed that the effect of this single reinforcement was negligible.)

DISCUSSION

In this study, social reinforcement has been used to strengthen a set of behaviors directly. The responses of nodding, mouthing, and saying nonsense syllable chains have been established through instructions ("Can you do this?") and reinforcement, and maintained with reinforcement. These responses have in common the fact that they are all imitative of a model's behaviors and that the child does them only when the model does. It is in this context that the strengthening of imitative bar-pressing becomes significant. Bar-pressing was never reinforced directly; nor was the child ever instructed to bar-press imitatively. (The simple

instructions dealing with the child's bar — "Show me your bar" — never promoted imitative bar-pressing in the children observed specifically for this possibility.) Bar-pressing has little physical or topographical resemblance to nodding, mouthing, and verbal nonsense chains. What it does have in common with these responses is the fact that it too is imitative of one of the model's performances. Hence its strengthening, following the direct strengthening of nodding, mouthing, and verbal responses, may be attributed to generalization along a dimension of similarity between the child's response and the model's response. In other words, the child is responsive to the stimulus of similarity between responses per se, apparently independently of the particular physical stimuli involved in specific responses.

It can be important to demonstrate that similarity between behaviors of model and child can be a functional stimulus dimension. Such a demonstration would be essential in at least some reinforcement analyses of imitation, especially in any analysis trying to show that imitation should be a strong response in a child, even when it does not produce extrinsic reinforcement. One such analysis might proceed as follows:

In the ordinary course of his early life, a child will form many hundreds of discriminations that involve the sight or sound of a model's behavior as a cue for a response by the child which achieves the same (or a similar) reinforcing outcome. In effect, in all such situations, the child is in a position to learn what response on his part reproduces the effect produced by the model's behavior. Many times, the world will be such that only a response similar in physical make-up or topography will reproduce the same effect. For example, many times a child will need to get through a latched door. He will often observe an older or more skillful model turn the knob and pass through. The child will eventually differentiate his own behavior to the point where it succeeds in opening the door. But doors are such that very few responses will succeed, and consequently the child's behavior will be very similar to the model's. In this situation, and in many others like it, the stimulus of similarity between the child's behavior and the model's is consistently programmed and sets the occasion for reinforcement of the child. Given enough of these situations, of adequate consistency and variety, the stimulus of similarity between behaviors in general may become discriminative for reinforcement. Since a stimulus which is discriminative for reinforcement becomes (secondarily) reinforcing in its own right, then responses which produce similarity between behaviors will thereby be strengthened. Responses of the child which "produce similarity" are those responses which have a topography that the child can compare to the topography of the model's responses, e.g., he can see both his response and the model's or can hear both. Hence the child will become generally "imitative," and, if similarity has great strength as a discriminative and therefore reinforcing stimulus, imitative behavior will be correspondingly more prevalent and apparently autonomous.

Certain details of procedure in this study may be worthy of note. One involves the fact that noncontingent social reinforcement given by the puppet to the child was not sufficient to induce imitation of the puppet. Furthermore, once a generalized imitation had been set up, noncontingent reinforcement was not sufficient to maintain it. Only when other imitative responses were being reinforced would imitative bar-pressing (never directly reinforced) remain at any strength. The puppet would, as the design required, shift his reinforcement from imitative responses to other appropriate moments in the interactions, but the general amount and spacing of this reinforcement remained the same. Hence the effects on imitative bar-pressing noted here cannot be attributed to the simple presence or absence of reinforcement, but rather are related to its contingent or noncontingent use. This is at some variance with the results of other studies (cf. Bandura and Huston, 1961), in which a prior condition of noncontingent social reinforcement from a model evoked more imitation of the model from the child than otherwise. This may be due to the particular response used in this study to observe generalized imitation, which was bar-pressing. Bar-pressing may be an unusual response for a young child and may have relatively little resemblance to the strong responses already in his repertoire. For this reason, it may be a relatively inefficient response with which to demonstrate a generalized imitation of the puppet. On the other hand, it may be that while similarity between behaviors is reinforcing for children, this reinforcing value is closely dependent on similarity remaining discriminative for at least some reinforcement in the situation. Possibly, when similarity clearly is no longer discriminative for reinforcement, it loses its own reinforcing function rather quickly. It will take an extensive program of research to provide useful data on this question, but the question may well be worth it, since such arguments about imitation can figure heavily in a conceptual account of socialization or "identification."

Another point, possibly important, is that all of the subjects showing imitation were girls. Since the group sampled was composed largely of girls, this may not be unusual. However, the puppet was clearly a male cowboy, and since cross-sex interactions are prevalent where social reinforcement is involved (especially with young children), it may be that later data will demonstrate that the sex of the subject and the model is an important variable. No conclusion is possible from the present data.

Finally, the increased imitative bar-pressing demonstrated here is not simply part of a generalized increase in activity; its clearly imitative nature denies that. Furthermore, it was apparent to the observers that there was no general increase of other observable activities as imitative bar-pressing developed in the child.

Shaping cooperative responses in early childhood schizophrenics: II. Reinforcement of mutual physical contact and vocal responses

JOSEPH N. HINGTGEN AND FRANK C. TROST, JR.

Recent studies have demonstrated that operant conditioning techniques can be effectively employed in the analysis and modification of psychotic behavior (Skinner, 1954a; Lindsley, 1960, 1962b, 1963a; Ayllon and Haughton, 1962). Reinforcement methods have also been used to alter other forms of abnormal human behavior (Flanagan, Goldiamond, and Azrin, 1958; Bijou and Orlando, 1961; Barrett, 1962). Ferster and DeMyer (1961, 1962) have reported success in applying these same methods to control and maintain new response patterns in early childhood schizophrenics.[1]

In a previous study from this research center, cooperative responses were shaped in three pairs of early childhood schizophrenics using operant conditioning techniques (Hingtgen, et al., 1965). These children had been observed to show little or no social interaction with their peers. Candy reinforcement, formerly obtained in a non-social situation, was made contingent upon the emission of cooperative responses (operation of levers in proper sequence by both subjects). As the cooperative behavior increased in frequency, physical (bodily) contact and other apparent social interaction (vocal responses), although never directly reinforced by the experimenter, increased during the daily sessions. However, these forms of new behavior were not maintained outside the experimental situation.

The present study was designed to shape cooperative responses (mutual physical contact combined with vocal responses) in two pairs of early childhood schizophrenics. It was hypothesized that, if these responses were shaped through direct reinforcement, the new behavior would be maintained beyond the controlled environment for longer periods of time.

METHOD

Four early childhood schizophrenics, diagnosed as autistic (A) or autistic-symbiotic (A-S), served as subjects for this study. The diagnosis was made following DeMyer's categories of Schizophrenic Disorders of Childhood as previously described (Hingtgen, et al., 1965). All subjects had been observed to initiate little or no physical contact (bodily contact) with their peers, and were reported to make few vocal responses. The relevant subject variables are presented in Table 1.

The experimental sessions were given in a room 15 ft. long, 8 ft. wide, and 9 ft. high, illuminated by eight 40-watt fluorescent lights. A one-way window was used for continuous observation of the subjects and the filming of a number of sessions.[2] Many devices (color wheel, electric organ, movie projector, phonograph, etc.) were mounted on the walls of the room, but only a coin vendor and food vendor were operative during this experiment.

Located below each of the six columns of the food vendor was a coin slot. The columns could be operated independently by putting a coin in the proper slot. A transparent plastic

Paper read at American Psychological Association, Los Angeles, September, 1964.
1 Examples of such research appear on pages 169−202 of this volume.
2 An 8mm film (black and white, 15 minutes), which shows the two pairs of children during various stages of the shaping procedure, is available on request from the senior author.

Table 1. *Subject variables in two pairs of early childhood schizophrenics.*

Subjects	Pair I		Pair II	
	T.M.	S.M.	N.R.	B.P.
Sex	M	M	F	M
Age (years-months)	5−0	5−6	7−6	5−3
Communicative speech	none	none	none	none
Patient status*	day	in	in	in
Months of hospitalization	15	29	39	19
Months of previous experience in operant conditioning	12	12	10	12
Diagnosis	A−S	A−S	A	A

*day=day care; in=in patient

cover enclosed the columns so that the different foods (M & M's, malt balls, crackers, and dry cereal) could be seen by the children.

Cooperative and vocal responses made by the subjects were recorded on individual counters and cumulative recorders. A remote control panel, mounted below the observation window, permitted the experimenter to deliver or withhold reinforcement at the appropriate times. Anecdotal reports were recorded for each session.

Each subject was seen individually for 30-minute sessions before the cooperative and vocal shaping was initiated. During this time an FR 15 schedule of reinforcement was in effect, which required pressing the coin lever 15 times to obtain a coin. This coin could then be used in the food vendor. Following this preliminary training, the children were given two experimental sessions per day: a morning session in which *one* subject was reinforced for vocal responses, and an afternoon session in which *two* subjects were reinforced for cooperative responses.

The procedure for shaping vocal responses was as follows: The child was placed in the room alone and was rewarded initially for making any sound (hum, cough, sneeze, giggle). These sounds were continuously reinforced until a stable rate of responding was obtained. Then reinforcement was withheld until a more discrete sound was made. Finally, reinforcement was given only for such sounds as 'ah,' 'ba,' 'uh,' 'ta,' 'da,' 'loo,' and 'ma,' which were considered to be recognizable syllables. During the final stages of the shaping procedure, reinforcement was given on a VR 3

schedule of reinforcement, with an average of one coin for every three responses.

The procedure used in shaping the cooperative responses was as follows: Both subjects of a pair were placed in the room together. The shaping was divided into four steps.

Step 1 — Reinforcement was given for one subject touching the other with his hand. This response was gradually shaped using the method of successive approximation, i.e., reinforcement was initially given for physical proximity, then "accidental" bodily contact, and finally for actual hand to body contact.

Step 2 — Reinforcement was contingent upon physical contacts accompanied by vocal responses, i.e., either subject touching the other with his hand and making a vocal response.

Step 3 — Reinforcement was given only when one subject touched another with both hands and made a vocal response.

Step 4 — Reinforcement was contingent upon both subjects touching each other with both hands and both making a vocal response.

Each new step was introduced when a stable rate of responding was achieved on the previous step. During the entire shaping procedure, no verbal instructions or demonstrations were given to the subjects by the experimenter.

RESULTS AND DISCUSSION

Mean response rates for both vocal and cooperative responses are presented in Table 2. In addition, responses on the coin lever are

Table 2. *Mean response rates of two pairs of early childhood schizophrenics during shaping of vocal and cooperative behavior.*

Condition	Pair I				Pair II		
	T.M.			S.M.	N.R.		B.P.
FR 15	33.33			35.00	31.80		33.75
	Vocal	Coop.	Vocal		Vocal	Coop.	Vocal
Step 1	4.77	2.51	6.81		0.51	2.78	5.31
Step 2	9.78	3.79	6.90		0.61	2.60	5.88
Step 3	8.22	3.34	8.64		0.35	1.65	5.64
Step 4	6.33	2.47	8.16		0.44	2.02	6.45

All rates are given in responses per minute. Each mean is based on at least five days of stable responding. Cooperative responses are given for pairs rather than individual subjects. The definition of a cooperative response varied for each step of the shaping (see Method). The response rate during the FR 15 preliminary training period is the number of coin lever presses per minute. Vocal response rates represent only those responses made during the morning sessions for each of the steps in the shaping of the cooperative behavior.

given for those sessions in which the children were working alone in the room on an FR 15 schedule of reinforcement. The similar rates on the FR 15 schedule indicate that the subjects did not differ greatly when working on a simple non-social task.

The vocal response rate obtained during the morning sessions increased during the course of the experiment in all but one subject. N.R. never progressed beyond grunts, giggles, etc., which were made at very low rates. During the vocal response sessions of Step 4 all other subjects were making sounds which were recognizable as syllables.

It was possible to shape the final cooperative response in an average of 46 sessions for both pairs. For Pair II, since N.R. never adequately learned the vocal response, only B.P. was required to make the vocal response during the various stages of the shaping procedure. N.R., however, was required to make the appropriate physical contacts.

Figure 1 presents cumulative records for the early stages and the final stages of shaping. The more uniform rate of response obtained during Step 4 is an indication of the learning of the final form of the cooperative response. During the four steps, the cooperative responses were maintained at very low but stable levels.

In Pair I an average of 90 social interactions was obtained for each session. Pair II made an average of 68 per session. These interactions ranged from the one hand contact in Step 1 to the two hand mutual contact plus vocal response in Step 4. The number of interactions recorded during these sessions was significantly greater (p<.01)[3] than the total number of physical contacts and vocal responses observed in a series of toy play observations with the same pairs of children.[4] These observations were made under conditions comparable to the present experiment, but no responses were reinforced.

Throughout this experiment only one coin was given for each cooperative response. As a consequence competitive behavior, seldom observed on the ward, occurred frequently in each pair. Pushing, tugging, pinching, and hugging responses were initiated by each child to prevent his partner from getting a coin. While one child was often dominant in securing coins, the other received sufficient reinforcement to maintain the cooperative response rate. During these periods of intense interaction, eye-to-eye contact was measurably increased over that observed on the ward.

---

3 Determined by use of t-test.
4 Ellen V. Piers and J. R. Tilton, personal communication.

Affect appeared to be more appropriate in that the children laughed and smiled when cooperation was going well and expressed anger and aggression when there was a break in the cooperative behavior.

In the previous study (Hingtgen, *et al.*, 1965) in which physical contact and vocal responses were indirectly reinforced, the cooperative responses were not observed to generalize beyond the experimental situation. In this study, however, both physical contact and vocal responses were observed on the ward and in the home, although this behavior was directed towards adults rather than peers.

Two examples of this behavior are given below: (1) T.M. became fascinated with the water hose his father was using. He touched his father with both hands and said, "ba, ba." Thereafter, his father allowed him to play with the hose whenever T.M. made this response. On the ward T.M. initiated verbal responses and physical contacts to receive rides on the slide and trampoline. (2) B.P. used both physical contact and vocal responses to obtain gum, candy, and rides on the trampoline when he was on the ward.

Two weeks after this study was completed, the children were returned to the experimental rooms where they immediately began to engage in social interaction. These data suggest that reinforcement techniques could be used as a therapeutic tool for increasing social and vocal behavior of early childhood schizophrenics.

SUMMARY

Four non-verbal early childhood schizophrenics, previously observed to initiate little or no social interaction with their peers, were individually reinforced with candy for making vocal responses during daily morning sessions. In afternoon sessions the children were paired and reinforced for cooperative responses (mutual physical contact combined with vocal responses).

The procedure for shaping cooperative behavior was as follows: (1) reinforcement was given for each physical contact, i.e., the hand of either subject touching the other subject; (2) reinforcement was given only for physical contacts accompanied by a vocal response;

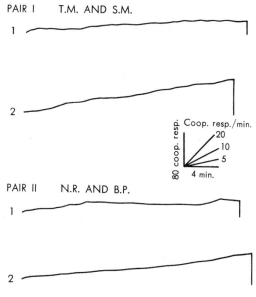

Figure 1. *Cumulative cooperative responses of two pairs of early childhood schizophrenics. Record 1 curves for each pair are typical of the early stages of shaping in Step 1 (simple hand to body contact). Record 2 curves represent the stable rate obtained during Step 4 when mutual bodily contact plus vocal responses were required for reinforcement.*

(3) reinforcement was contingent upon one subject touching the other with two hands and making a vocal response; (4) both subjects were required to touch each other with both hands and make vocal responses.

Mutual physical contact within the two pairs of schizophrenic children was shaped in an average of 46 sessions. Vocal responses were shaped in all but one subject. The number of interactions recorded during reinforcement sessions was significantly greater than the number of physical contacts and vocal responses measured in a series of toy play observations with the same children.

This study indicated that schizophrenic children, who previously initiated little or no physical interaction with their peers, are capable of such interactions under properly controlled environmental conditions. The data suggested that reinforcement techniques could be used as a therapeutic tool for increasing social and vocal behavior of early childhood schizophrenics.

6

MODIFICATION OF DISORDERED BEHAVIOR

This section contains a sampling of attempts to modify various behavioral disorders using the principles of behavioral analysis and control. The specific disorders and settings involved vary a great deal, but the techniques employed are similar. For example, the behavioral therapist believes that the disordered behavior *is* the malady to be treated. Altering the disordered behavior is not felt to be merely a futile treatment of the surface manifestation of a "deeper" problem.

This approach is quite different from the usual clinical view of disordered behavior which holds that maladaptive responses are only symptomatic of a basic, underlying problem. Direct treatment of the troublesome behavior, then, is thought to be a temporary measure at best, since the underlying cause is expected to produce another symptom which will in turn call for treatment. This replacement of an old behavioral problem by a new one is known as "symptom substitution."

Although the reappearance of a new behavioral disorder after the elimination of an old one has been observed in many cases, there may be an explanation for this phenomenon other than "symptom substitution." For example, when a disordered behavior has been successfully eliminated, other undesirable responses may easily be emitted by the organism before an adaptive behavior can be found as a substitute. While the clinician may call these new, nonadaptive behaviors "symptoms," to the behavioral therapist they are simply new behaviors of the sort constantly emitted by organisms developing appropriate adaptive behavior.

Furthermore, it is possible that much of this substitution may be attenuated by not only extinguishing the nonadaptive behavior, but by concurrently shaping and reinforcing an adaptive behavior which can replace the extinguished nonadaptive behavior. This procedure has been successful in experimental settings and appears to have considerable clinical value.

In addition to the possibility that "symptom substitution" is in part an avoidable phenomenon, other advantages recommend the direct behavioral approach. The most obvious advantage is the readiness with which observable, manipulable behaviors can be treated. Whereas the "underlying causes" of behavioral disorders are often ill-defined and considered inaccessible to treatment by any but the most highly trained professionals, the disordered behavior itself is usually relatively easy to study. In all of the cases reported in this section, the behavior has been clearly analyzed and defined, and a specific, concrete procedure for treating the disorder has been carried out. In almost all cases, the therapeutic apparatus and procedure, once they are designed and formulated by the professional, can be operated and administered by nonprofessionals after a short period of training. Often the patient can serve as his own therapist.

Another advantage of direct treatment of disordered behavior lies in the breaking of possible symptom→underlying cause→symptom circularity. For example, Wickes, in his account of a behavioral treatment of enuresis, points out that often the "anxiety" considered the underlying cause of the problem behavior disappeared when the bed-wetting stopped. In many cases, the enuresis, by aggravating interpersonal, parent-child relationships, may have been the cause of the "anxiety" rather than the symptomatic result. Thus, at least in some cases, behavioral therapy is not only a convenient, but an ultimately effective treatment of the person's "problem" as a whole.

Perhaps the most refreshing aspect of these articles is their specificity in telling the rehabilitation worker, doctor, parent, teacher, or patient — whoever is concerned with the modification of disordered behavior — precisely what they are to *do* to alter the behavior in question. The contrast between such behavioral therapy and the more esoteric procedures involved in other forms of therapy provides a new and exciting approach to old and troublesome problems.

Self-control procedures in personal behavior problems

ISRAEL GOLDIAMOND[1]

The present discussion will be concerned with the application of self-control procedures to the solution of certain limited behavioral problems.

Often one person comes for help from another because he cannot cope with problems that face him. The appropriate behaviors are not available. The means by which the behavioral deficit can be overcome are varied. Simple instructions often suffice, as when the subject cannot study because he does not have the assignment. On the other hand, the subject may not be able to study because he cannot allocate his time appropriately, because he daydreams at his desk, or because he engages in other behaviors which come under the general heading of lack of self-control. In these cases, simple instructions will not remedy the deficit since the subject himself knows what it is. He has often tried to instruct himself to behave appropriately, but with little success. Indeed, the numerous jokes surrounding New Year's resolutions indicate both the prevalence of the problem, and the ineffectiveness of its instructional solution, whether imposed by others or by one's self in self-instruction.

The specific behavioral deficit, or presenting problem, is often part of a larger context of deficits. Rather than trying to overcome the presenting deficit directly, the therapist may turn his attention to other, "deeper" behaviors or behavioral deficits. In this case, the presenting problem is considered a symptom, by exactly the same defining operations that make a skin rash a symptom. Here, the dermatologist states that to get rid of the rash he will treat in addition something else, possibly a blood imbalance, rather than only treating the rash itself (Goldiamond, Dyrud, and Miller, 1965). For example, we know of one case where a woman assumed a fetal posture for three days after an argument with her husband. She was restored to mobility by direct modification of this behavior. It can be argued that a woman who maintains control over her husband by such extreme behaviors is so lacking in more appropriate behaviors that her treatment will require considerably more than the two hours which restored her mobility. This case may be an example of treating a symptom, since behaviors other than the presenting complaint may also require modification. However, the "underlying" problem can still be considered

From *Psychological Reports*, 1965, **17**, 851–868.

1 The author is the current recipient of the Research Career Development Award, 1963–1968, at the Institute for Behavioral Research. He is also on appointment as Professor of Psychology, Arizona State University, Tempe.

as a behavioral one: in this case, the absence of those behaviors whereby wives normally control their husbands. Yet this general deficit also may be treated directly, as in our research on stuttering where we have, within the laboratory, replaced stuttering by fluent and rapid speech in 30 of 30 cases run thus far (Goldiamond, 1965b). Indeed, one of our stuttering patients, who had been suicidal, became able to read bedtime stories to her children at home, and certain other personal problems at home cleared up because her stuttering cleared up. Some of her other behaviors were accordingly symptomatic of stuttering (Goldiamond, 1965a), as we have defined "symptom."

If there is a danger in premature assignment of behavioral deficits as symptomatic, there is also a danger in premature assumption that the alteration of the presenting problem is the final solution. Further analysis in light of current knowledge will undoubtedly both modify and confirm practice in this area.

Classification of behavior as a problem for treatment or as a symptom may also be an economic or contractual matter. For example, in a marital problem, the presenting complaint may be cleared up in a short period of time, but other problems are sometimes uncovered which may require extensive treatment. At what point is the implicit contract between patient and therapist (cf. Sulzer, 1962) to treat the marital behaviors extended to behaviors in other areas? The answer to this question must depend on the extent to which the subject can afford the treatment or can afford not to get it, that is, can do without it. It would be nice to have a new car when the present one seems to require extensive repairs, but there may be other considerations such as a piano or a child's education. For going to and from work, minor adjustments may be sufficient. The economy may also be behavioral: is it worth the upset?

The present discussion will be limited to cases where the concern was with a specified behavioral problem. These cases should be interpreted in the context of the foregoing discussion: namely, that the procedures used are not intended to question other more extensive procedures, which may be necessary for other kinds of behavioral deficits.

The discussion will be concerned with self-control (Skinner, 1953) and procedures for its establishment. The procedures to be discussed center around the position that behavior is not an emergent property of an organism nor a property solely of its environment, but is described by a functional relation between the two. More technically, given a specified behavior B and a specified environmental variable x, a lawful relation can be found, such that $B=f(x)$, under certain empirical constraining conditions c. This implies that when the constraints c are set up, and x is set at a stipulated value, then B will have a stipulated value, given by the value of $B=f(x)$. When the experimenter sets x at that value, *he* will get the B stipulated. This defines the experimental control of behavior which has been demonstrated repeatedly in operant and other laboratories. When the subject himself sets x at that value, *he* will get his own B, as stipulated. This defines self-control.

If you want a specified behavior from yourself, set up the conditions which you know will control it. For example, if you cannot get up in the morning by firmly resolving to do so and telling yourself that you must, buy and set an alarm clock. Within this context, the Greek maxim, "Know thyself," translates into "Know thy behaviors, know thy environment, and know the functional relation between the two." Although the relation between an alarm clock and waking up is a simple and familiar one, other relations are neither this simple nor this familiar. There have, however, been developed in laboratories of operant behavior a body of known functional relations between behavior, and programs and other procedures which can alter even more complex behavior systematically. Self-control derived from such research can take at least two forms. One is to instruct the subject to set up the procedures which change his environment and which thereby bring his behavior under different control. I shall present some cases to this effect. Another form is to train him in the functional analysis of behavior, and have him try to determine for himself the procedures which he should apply. This approach will also appear in the following cases.

Inherent in both types of self-control is the problem posed by the tremendous gap between theory and practice. The same theory may dictate numerous alternative methods or solutions, but all may not be equally available, practical, or applicable. The operant paradigm suggests that there are at least twelve different ways to maintain or attenuate behavior (cf. Holz and Azrin, 1963). Which are appropriate to the problem?

One way of selecting effective practical measures is to have S report back to E every week with his results. This hour becomes a session for analysis of data and discussion of changes in procedure. In the laboratory, operant procedures are so arranged that relations between ongoing behavior and its conditions are continuously observed and recorded. Through successes and failures, Es may learn to analyze behavior and conditions and may develop a "feel" for their data, as do other behavioral practitioners in interaction with their subject matter, for example, skilled psychiatrists. Hopefully, such a program of systematic trial and analysis will sensitize S to his own behavior and his own conditions. By training S in control procedures to the extent that these exist and are applicable, we are providing for self-enhancement and self-actualization (Rogers, 1951). Of the individuals who can apply control procedures, S is the one most concerned with his behavior and is most in contact with it, its conditions, and its consequences. Initially E is the consultant, and eventually S becomes his own E. The procedures may be limited to Ss who are intellectually capable of such analysis or who are not otherwise incapacitated. Our Ss were mainly college students. Where systematic training in behavior analysis was used, the sessions started with individual tutorials in behavior analysis, homework assignments from standard texts (Holland and Skinner, 1961), and readings. Given this intellectual base, we could move on to discussions of the problem in question.

Our first cases were referrals from clinical psychologists who felt that we should work on some of the simpler overt problems, while they tackled their deeper meanings. One of these was a young man who was overweight, and another was a girl who had difficulty studying.

These two problems yielded, for these Ss,

to procedures involving *stimulus control*. The program with the young lady started with human engineering of her desk. Since she felt sleepy when she studied, she was told to replace a 40-watt lamp with a good one and to turn her desk away from her bed. It was also decided that her desk was to control study behavior. If she wished to write a letter, she should do so, but in the dining room; if she wished to read comic books, she should do so, but in the kitchen; if she wished to daydream, she should do so, but was to go to another room; at her desk she was to engage in her school work and her school work only.

This girl had previously had a course in behavioral analysis and said, "I know what you're up to. You want that desk to assume stimulus control over me. I'm not going to let any piece of wood run my life for me."

"On the contrary," I said, "you *want* that desk to run you. It is you who decides when to put yourself under the control of your desk. It is like having a sharpened knife in a drawer. You decide when to use it; but when you want it, it is ready."

After the first week of the regimen, she came to me and gleefully said, "I spent only ten minutes at my desk last week."

"Did you study there," I asked.

"Yes, I did," she said.

"Good," I said, "let's try to double that next week."

For the next few weeks we did not meet, but she subsequently reported that during the last month of the semester she was able to spend three hours a day at her desk for four weeks in a row, something she had been unable to do previously. When she sat at her desk she studied, and when she did other things she left her desk. The variable maintaining this increase in behavior as the semester drew to an end was apparently the forthcoming final examinations.

With regard to the young man who overate, stimulus control, chaining, and withdrawal of reinforcement were used. The stimulus for overeating is normally not food (Ferster, Nurnberger, and Levitt, 1962). In our culture, food is normally hidden; it is kept in a refrigerator or cupboard. In the cafeteria, where it is in the interests of the management to get people to eat, food is exposed.

The initial strategy for slimming the young man was to bring his eating behavior under the control of food alone, since food is normally not available as a stimulus. He was instructed to eat to his heart's content and not to repress the desire. He was, however, to treat food with the dignity it deserved. Rather than eating while he watched television or while he studied, he was to devote himself to eating when he ate. If he wished to eat a sandwich, he was to put it on a plate and sit down and devote himself exclusively to it. Thus, reinforcing consequences such as watching television or reading would be withdrawn when he engaged in the behaviors of preparing the food, eating, and cleaning up. Responding to the refrigerator in between meals resulted in withdrawal of such consequences, as did going to the refrigerator while watching television. Television, studying, and other stimuli would lose their control of initiating the chain of behaviors and conditions that terminated in eating. Within one week, the young man cut out all eating between meals. "You've taken the fun out of it," he said to me. We then worked on the contents of the meals as well, and he stopped attending sessions. I met him about three months later; he was considerably slimmer and remarked that he needed neither me nor the clinical psychologist to solve his problems. He could handle them himself.

No claim is made that all problems should be treated in this manner, or that the Ss had no other problems. The aim was to alter the specified behavior. We started out with the simplest procedures. Had these not been effective, we would have tried others. Some more complex cases will be presented next.

An interesting aspect of these and other cases as well was the fact that in a very short time the Ss ran off by themselves to apply the procedures they had learned. In some cases, I would have preferred more extensive interchange, and wondered how clinical psychologists were able to keep Ss coming week after week. Finally I attributed the tenure of the relationship to what might be called the Scheherazade effect. Scheherazade, as you will recall, became the consort of a king who killed each bedmate after one night, having generalized the infidelity of a previous wife to all women. Scheherazade told him a story on the first night, which was not completed by dawn. The king paroled her for the second night to hear the rest of the story, and having been reinforced, she repeated her behavior. The schedule maintained such behavior for 1001 nights, and the result is known as the *Arabian Nights*.

Few things are more interesting and will sustain behavior better than support for talking about one's self; one is never finished in 50 minutes. Hence, such discussions may maintain therapy sessions and allow the therapist to interact with the patient over an extended period of time. An individual tutorial may serve the same function.

MARITAL CASE 1

The husband in this case was a young man, 29, who was working on his master's degree. His wife was taking my course in behavioral analysis, and they both decided that he should come to see me about their marriage, which both wanted to maintain. The issue, as S told me, was that his wife had committed the "ultimate betrayal" two years ago with S's best friend. Even worse, it was S who had suggested that the friend keep his wife company while he was in the library at night. Since that time, whenever he saw his wife, S screamed at her for hours on end, or else was ashamed of himself for having done so and spent hours sulking and brooding. Since the events that led to the "betrayal" were an occasion for bringing home the first lesson on the consequences of behavior, we started from there.

Relation of Behavior to its Consequences

Early discussions concerned the analysis of behavior in terms of its consequences. S's behavior provided stimuli for his wife's behavior. If he wished his wife to behave differently to him, then he should provide other stimuli than the ones which produced the behaviors he did not like. There was considerable analysis of such interactions. This conceptualization of behavior was apparently new to S, who took detailed notes; and I have discovered it to be new to many other Ss as well.

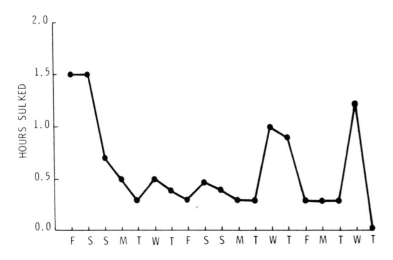

Figure 1. *Graph kept of sulking behavior.*

Stimulus Change

Altering the consequences of operant behavior will alter the behavior itself. However, this process may take a considerable amount of time. One of the most rapid ways to change behavior is by altering the conditions under which it usually occurs. This is called *stimulus change*, or the effects of novel stimuli. If the novel stimuli are then combined with new behavioral contingencies designed to produce different behavior, these contingencies are apt to generate the new behavior much more rapidly than they would in the presence of the old stimuli.

As part of the program of establishing new stimuli, S was instructed to rearrange the use of rooms and furniture in his house to make it appear considerably different. His wife went one step further and took the occasion to buy herself a new outfit.

Establishment of New Behavior

Since it was impossible for S to converse in a civilized manner with his wife, we discussed a program of going to one evening spot on Monday, another on Tuesday, and another on Wednesday.

"Oh," he said, "you want us to be together. We'll go bowling on Thursday."

"On the contrary," I said, "I am interested in your subjecting yourself to an environment where civilized chit-chat is maintained. Such is not the case at a bowling alley."

I also asked if there were any topic of conversation which once started would maintain itself. He commented on his mother-in-law's crazy ideas about farming. He was then given an index card and instructed to write "farm" on it and to attach a $20 bill to that card. The $20 was to be used to pay the waitress on Thursday, at which point he was to start the "farm" discussion which hopefully would continue into the taxi and home.

Stimulus Control

Since in the absence of yelling at his wife S sulked, and since the program was designed to reduce yelling, S's sulking was in danger of increasing. S was instructed to sulk to his heart's content, but to do so in a specified place. Whenever he felt like sulking, he was to go into the garage, sit on a special sulking stool, and sulk and mutter over the indignities of life for as long as he wished. When he was through with his sulking, he could leave the garage and join his wife. He was instructed to keep a daily record of such behavior and bring it to each session. The graph is presented in Figure 1. Sulking time had been reported as

7 hours on the preceding day, and, with occasional lapses, it was reported as dropping to less than 30 minutes before disappearing entirely. The reported reversals and drops were occasions for discussions.

Since the bedroom had been the scene of both bickering and occasional lapses, the problem was presented of changing its stimulus value when conjugality was involved. If this could be done consistently, eventually the special stimuli might come to control such behavior. The problem was to find a stimulus which could alter the room entirely and would be easy to apply and withdraw. Finally, a yellow night light was put in, was turned on when both felt amorous, and was kept turned off otherwise. This light markedly altered the perceptual configuration of the room.

Records

Daily notes of events were kept in a notebook, as was the graph. *S* took notes of the discussions with *E*. These notes were discussed at each weekly session.

One of the notions which *S* held very strongly was that his wife's behavior stemmed from some inaccessible source within her, and that many of his own behaviors likewise poured out from himself. In this context, the final sharp rise in the sulking curve was discussed. "The whole procedure won't work," he said, "my wife doesn't need me as much as I need her." The psychiatric message was that he had no control over his wife, but I chose to ignore this message in favor of a didactic one on the behavioral definition of needs. He was asked how he knew what his wife's needs were. Was he an amoeba slithering into her tissues and observing tissue needs? Was he a mind reader? After my repeated rejection of subjective definitions of needs, he redefined the problem behaviorally, namely, that his wife behaved a certain way less than he did. He said that stated this way it sounded silly, but I said, "No, it's a problem to you and not silly."

What were these behaviors? They apparently included such dependency behaviors as asking him to do things for her. "When was the last time she asked you to do something for her?" I asked. He replied that the previous day she asked him to replace a light bulb in the kitchen. Had he done so, I asked. No, he said. He then was asked to consider the extinction of pigeon behavior and took notes to the effect that, if he wished his wife to act helpless, he should reinforce dependency by doing what she asked.

A discussion on needs and personality ensued. "If by personality all that is meant is my behavior," he said, "then my personality changes from one moment to the next, because my behavior changes," he stated.

"I should hope so," I said.

"Well, what is my true personality; what is the true me?" he asked.

"Do you have a true behavior?" I asked.

He reported this as a viewpoint he had never considered; his previous training had been in terms of being consistent to his self, and of searching for "thine own self (to which he could) be true." He took extensive notes.

The next week he came in and stated: "I did something last week that I have never done before in my life. When I teach in classrooms I am able to manage my students, but when I talk to tradespeople I find I am very timid and allow myself to be cheated. Well, last week my carburetor gave out. I knew if I went to the garage they would make me buy a new one even though I have a one-year's guarantee. I sent my wife down to the garage instead. She is a real scrapper. She came back with a new carburetor. It didn't cost us a cent. Why should I have to be all things to all men? In school I control things, but with tradespeople I don't. So what?"

These weekly sessions continued during ten weeks of the summer term. After the initial training, *S* was assigned homework along with his wife who was taking the course in behavioral analysis. The weekly discussions were centered around behavioral analysis and how it might apply to his problems.

During the course of one of the sessions, *S* started to talk about his childhood and was summarily cut off.

"Shouldn't I talk about this with a psychologist?" he asked. "Isn't this one of the things that interests you? Doesn't it affect me now?"

"Look," I said, "a bridge with a load limit

of three tons opens in 1903. The next day, a farmer drives eighteen tons over it; it cracks. The bridge collapses in 1963. What caused the collapse?"

"The farmer in 1903," he said.

"Wrong," I said, "the bridge collapses in 1963 because of the cracks that day. Had they been filled in the preceding day, it would not have collapsed. Let's discuss the cracks in your marriage."

At the end of the period, there was no sulking in the garage and the partners were able to commune.

MARITAL CASE 2

This case concerned a young couple who had been married almost 10 years; their sexual relations throughout marriage had been limited to about two contacts a year. Both husband and wife ascribed the difficulty to the husband. Both Ss were professionals, intelligent, were socially well at ease, and highly regarded by their friends and the community. They were Roman Catholic, and determined to maintain the marriage, but the wife thought she might be driven into extra-marital relations. Both felt that, if only they could get started, the behavior might carry itself.

Husband and wife were seen separately every week, for one hour each. Both were instructed to discuss with me only that which they could discuss with each other, since I would make constant cross reference between the two sessions.

Various procedures were assayed by the subjects, but proved ineffective. Fondling was repulsed. *Playboy* was recommended to initiate amorous activity, but the husband fell asleep reading it. During the lesson on deprivation, the wife stated: "I am at my wit's end as to how to shape his behavior. I don't know what reinforcements I have. The characteristic of good reinforcement is that it can be applied immediately and is immediately consumed. I could withhold supper, but that is not a good reinforcer because I can't turn it off and on. I can't apply deprivation, because that's my problem. I don't know what to do."

The husband was a rising business executive who took evening courses and whose time was

so tight that he had to schedule almost every minute of his day. We discussed the possibility of his scheduling his wife in the appointment book for two evenings a week. He thought this might work, but his wife was a bit more dubious. These appointments were kept two weeks in a row, but then lost their control. We then discussed the nature of the control over behavior exerted by discriminative stimuli, of which instructions are one example (Goldiamond, 1966). There were differential consequences attached to keeping and not keeping the business appointments, but no differential consequences had been attached to meeting or not meeting appointments with his wife. Hence, the instructions lost their control (Ayllon and Azrin, 1964).

Both subjects were extremely well-groomed. Their clothing was always in best array. The wife visited the beautician once a week and the husband went to the barber every other week. In the session following the failure of control by the appointment book, the husband suggested that they might attach the opportunity to visit the beautician or barber as consequences to keeping the appointments. In the event that the appointments were not kept, the visits would not be allowed and could be resumed only when the appointments had been kept. His wife also felt that this would be extremely effective.

The next week, both showed up somewhat bedraggled. Thereafter, they were not bedraggled and the appointments were kept for the rest of that semester, at least.

As an incidental effect of the sessions, the Ss attempted to apply behavioral analysis to other problems as well. They mentioned a staff party which had been held at their home. The behavior of an inefficient secretary was being discussed.

"But you're using aversive control," one of the participants said.

"Well, she has no behaviors that I can reinforce her for," was the answer.

STUDY CASE 1: HANDWRITING

S was a seventeen-year-old high school senior of normal intelligence, who was 28th in a class of 28 and whose handwriting was illegible. He was a referral from a school psychologist.

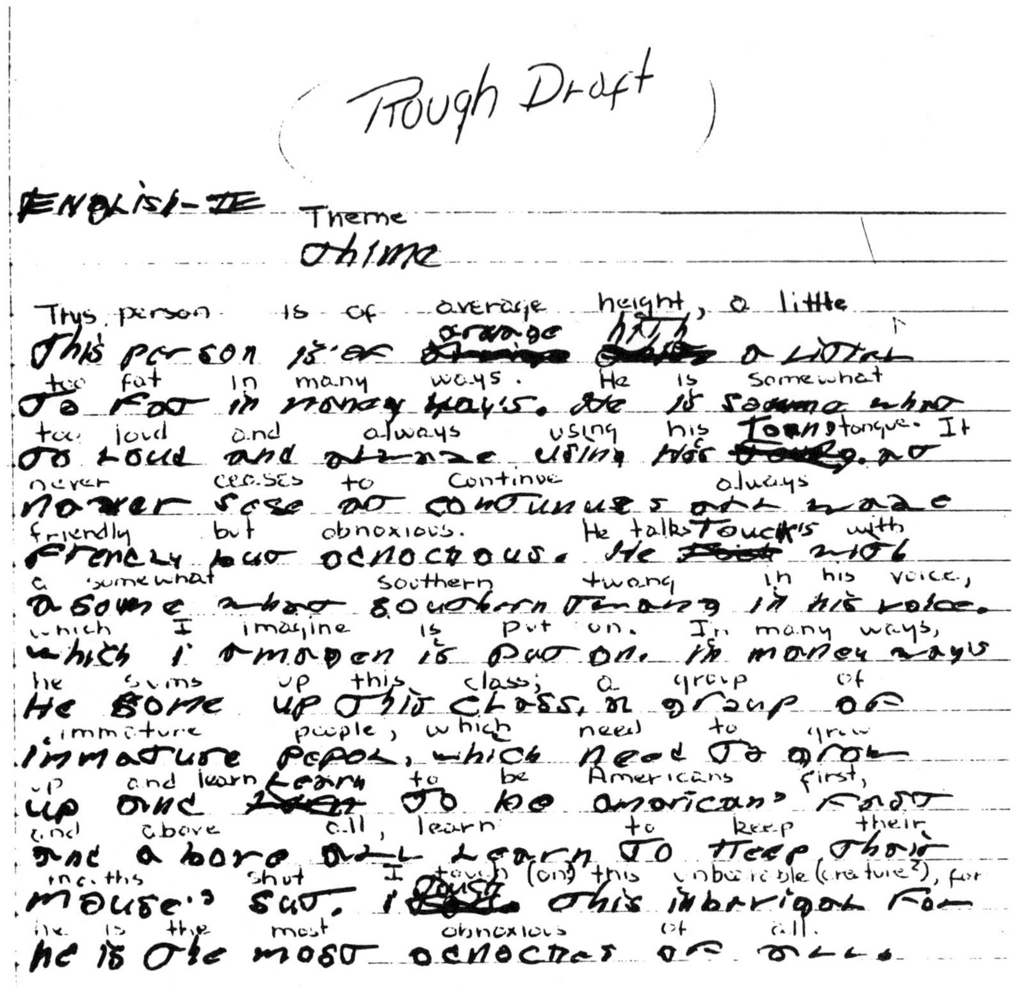

Rough Draft

ENGLISH-IE Theme
Chime

This person is of average height, a little
too fat in many ways. He is somewhat
too loud and always using his tongue. It
never ceases to continue always
friendly but obnoxious. He talks with
a somewhat Southern twang in his voice,
which I imagine is put on. In many ways,
he sums up this class; a group of
immature people, which need to grow
up and learn to be Americans first,
and above all, learn to keep their
mouse? shut. I touch (on) this unbearable (creature?), for
he is the most obnoxious of all.

Figure 2. *Sample of initial handwriting; translation appears above line.*

An example of his early handwriting is given in Figure 2. Lettered lines of translation alternate with cursive lines of handwriting. During the first session, I asked S to sit at my desk and write from dictation. He leaned forward to write, but no part of his hand or arm touched paper or desk; the entire force of his shoulder and arm was transmitted to the pencil point, making fine control impossible. Since the primary grades, no one had ever observed his writing behavior; they had, however, criticized its product. I instructed him to keep his arm on the table and to manipu-

late his pencil from the wrist and fingers. Some simple physics were explained to him. Sheets of onion skin were interlaced with carbon paper, and he was given exercises requiring modulation of force so that he would go through five sheets, four sheets, three sheets, and two sheets. He was instructed to print.

At a later session, his letter size being erratic, he was asked to letter the familiar, "Now is the time. . ." phrase. Figure 3 presents that initial attempt. The paper is lined, and the writing starts out filling up the space between the lines. The writing becomes smaller and

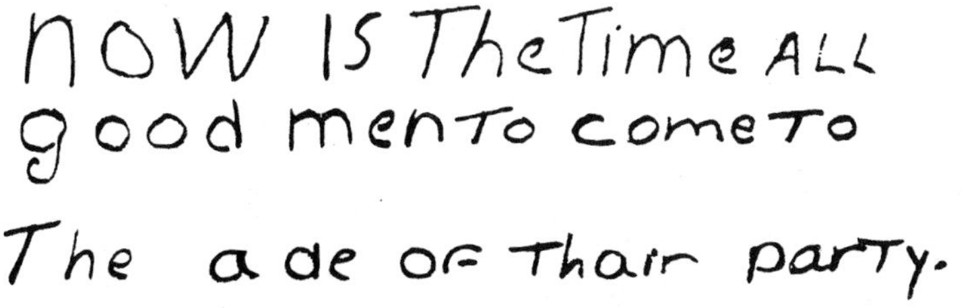

NOW IS The Time ALL
good menTo comeTo
The a de of Thair parTy.

Figure 3. *Stimulus control of ensuing letter size by writing T as capital of same size as preceding letter.*

smaller. This tendency can be traced to the letter T. In all cases, T is the same size as the preceding letters, and is also a capital. Since capital letters are followed by small letters, these T's control the size of the small letters that follow them. The first T in the second line produces a row of smaller letters following it, and the first T in the third line takes off from this size and again cuts down the size of the following letters until the final T produces a tinier Y. S was instructed to write his T's so that they were larger than the preceding letters. Figure 4 reiterates the control this letter had over the following letters. The letters which follow T are smaller than T, but since T is above the line they stay within the line. The effect has been reversed, demonstrating a causal relation. Incidentally, since T is the second most frequently used letter in English, it is a powerful source of control. In a later session, S was instructed to differentiate between capital and small T.

The passage presented is the same as that in Figure 2. The change in legibility is evident. The numerous spelling errors are of interest. As long as the writing is undecipherable, spelling errors can not be noted and corrected.

Many letters contain similar forms. For example, the letters a, b, d, o, p, and q all contain a complete circle of the same size. These circles are modified in letters such as c and e. S was instructed to bring an assortment of buttons to the session and a suitable button was found for him to use for these letters, with other buttons for other letters. He was also instructed in other principles of writing. He practiced at home and brought his material in weekly. After a period of lettering, S was instructed to link his letters in an effort to produce cursive writing.

His handwriting improved markedly during this period, and he rose from 28th in his class to 13th. The undergraduate assistant[2] who worked with him at home paid him money for lines completed and, as long as this procedure was used, S's handwriting was legible and showed evidence of training. When this pay was dropped, the handwriting deteriorated. Although legible handwriting was now contingent upon reinforcement, differential rein-

2 I wish to express my appreciation to Mr. Richard David, then an undergraduate psychology major, who brought S to and from sessions and assisted in them.

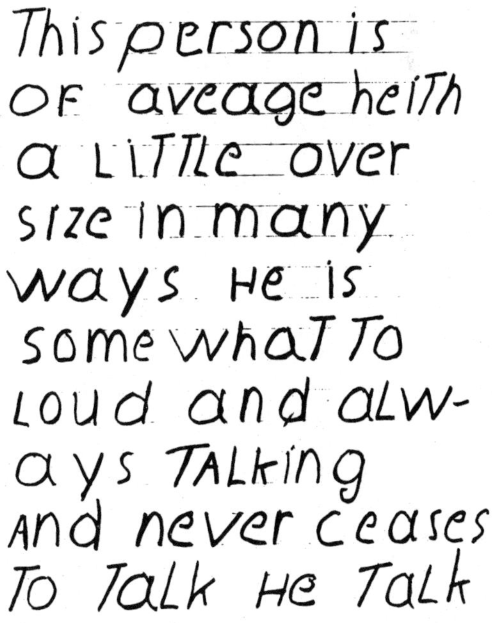

This person is OF aveage heiTh a LiTTle over size in many ways He is some whaT To Loud and always TALKing And never ceases To Talk He Talk

Figure 4. *Reversal of effect by writing T above line.*

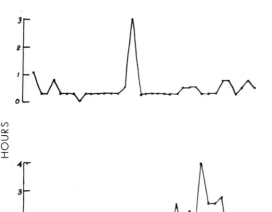

Figure 5. *Daily study charts for class with one examination (upper), and class with daily recitations (lower).*

forcement alone would not have produced the new behavior. Indeed, without making them contingent upon a program to alter behavior, differential consequences may be ineffective and may result in aversive control, as did the nagging and the poor grades he consistently obtained. Now that S has the new behavior, differential consequences can be applied to maintain it; hopefully, these will be provided by society. The requirement of extrinsic consequences was probably related to difficult conditions at home. He had no desk or work place, and he lived alone with his mother.

Several conclusions can be drawn from this case. One is that observation of the behavior itself may on occasion be far more useful than observation of its end product. Another is that behavior may be controlled by the very stimuli that the behavior itself produces, as in the size of the letters following T. A third is that merely establishing a behavior will not necessarily maintain it. The consequences which maintain it must be considered, but, as a fourth conclusion, these consequences should often be related to a program of behavioral modification. Penalizing his poor writing be-

havior, as his teachers had done, did not eliminate that behavior. It did, however, bring him in for treatment.

STUDY CASE 2: STUDY PROBLEM

This case involved a junior in college who was being expelled because of his academic record. Inasmuch as I had given him one of his D's, he came to me for advice. I told him that I would try to get him reinstated, providing he put himself under my control. He agreed and was given a conditional year. S's parents were professionals. Two siblings were at prominent Eastern universities. S was alert, and his I.Q. tests were within the range of college populations.

S had never actually studied. Accordingly, a self-control regimen for studying was introduced following some of the procedures which were discussed earlier. A daily record was kept of the total number of hours spent in study, for each course and for the total day.

At that time S studied for an average of six hours a day, but his study hours were not evenly distributed among the various classes. Figure 5 presents the study curves for two different courses. The upper curve depicts minimal studying, except for one peak. Guess when the test was given? This fixed interval curve characterizes the behavior of pigeons, as well. The lower part of the curve represents the studying pattern for a language class which involved a daily recitation. S studied at regular intervals. These curves so impressed me that I instituted daily quizzes in my classes, and was gratified to see the averages rise.

Every week, S brought his notebooks, his examinations, and his weekly records for inspection and discussion. Different procedures for keeping notes were developed for each course. In the foreign language, for example, a separate sheet was kept for masculine and feminine nouns, and for each verb class. Grammatical classes represent similar ways of treating a word. By putting words of the same grammatical class together, there may be generalization from the changes learned for one word to the changes learned for another. Flash cards may not lend themselves to such generalization.

S was taught to outline social science texts. He was asked to be a detective and resurrect the author's outline (where he had one). Red and black ink were used for headings and entries. The outlines were topical rather than sentence outlines. This required restating the sentences in his words, rather than copying them from the book.

In English, we were both at a loss. Several novels were required, and neither one of us knew what should be considered. We used the conventional procedure to find out, namely, the first exam. This told us what the instructor considered to be the terminal behaviors.

At the end of the first semester, *S*'s grades changed from the two D's and three E's of the preceding semester to two C's and two D's. Although this was an improvement, one class was dropped. I was disturbed since I felt that, with this much study and careful outlining, *S* should have obtained A's. A more detailed analysis was then undertaken.

S was taking a course in international trade, for which a knowledge of geography is requisite. He said that he knew his geography quite well and was asked to draw a map of South America. Figure 6 presents the map he drew. Brazil extends from sea to shining sea. The body of water above Venezuela is designated Lake Maracaibo, and Bolivia is north of Peru and abuts on Venezuela.

I asked *S* what grade he would assign himself for this map, and he looked at it confidently and said, "Oh, 75 per cent or a C." I said that I would give him 20 per cent. Incidentally, in work with other *S*s since then who have trouble with history, I have often found that they lack knowledge of geography, and even of map-reading. Accordingly, historical movements become disconnected facts which have to be learned for each case.

This map may be used to exemplify a behavioral definition of stupidity. Many behaviors require other behaviors as prerequisites for their acquisition and maintenance. It is possible that, in one form of stupidity, the prerequisites to the attempted behavior are absent, as well as those discriminative behaviors which differentiate the presence of adequate behaviors from their absence. Stated otherwise, the person we call stupid is lacking certain behaviors, but behaves as if he is not so

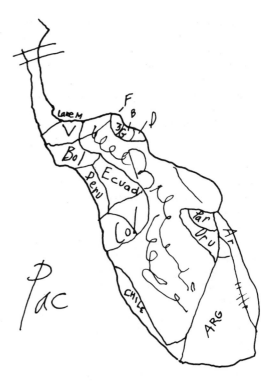

Figure 6. *Map of South America drawn from memory by college junior taking a course in international trade.*

lacking. He does not know to ask. He confidently undertakes assignments and often starts out successfully. However, where the new behaviors require older ones and these are missing, we may obtain the egregious blunders we call stupid. The blunders may be unpredictable to us simply because, in a long sequence, there are too many places in which deficits can occur for us to have come across every one.

These behavioral deficiencies were found in one area after another. Since *S* was taking courses which had as prerequisites other courses, which he had passed with D's, he was being required to acquire new behaviors when the prerequisite foundation for them was rather shaky. Accordingly, we "regressed" to the freshman texts in those courses in which he had obtained a D.

But there were deficiencies here, as well. In the economics texts, Humpty-Dumpty was quoted to the effect that words meant what *he* intended them to mean. The point here was that the economist's use of words might differ from their common usage. Humpty-Dumpty appeared in red in S's notes. S knew that Humpty-Dumpty was an egg who fell. I asked why the egg led his paragraph, and could obtain no answer. It turned out that S had not read *Alice in Wonderland*, nor any of the childhood classics, nor for that matter *Tom Swift*, nor even comic books. He simply did no home reading as a child.

I had obtained excellent control over S's behavior, but this was like successfully getting someone to work six hours a day copying Chinese letters with a brush, without his ever having learned how to hold a brush or what the significant calligraphic nuances were. I suggested a program of visiting the art galleries, listening to concerts, reading the classics, and otherwise acquiring the behaviors relevant to our cultural heritage.

There are two types of behavioral sequences. In one type of sequence, called the *chaining* sequence, a chain of behavior is maintained by the consequences attached to the last element in the chain. Thus, Lundin (1961) reports a rat who went through various behavioral gyrations, then up five stories and down an elevator. All of these behaviors were maintained by the food he received at the end. In this type of sequence, the order of training is the *reverse* of the chronological order in which the sequence of behavior is performed. The pressing of the lever for food was established first. This was made contingent upon manipulation of the elevator. Then the ride in the elevator was made contingent upon the preceding step and so on. The entire chain was maintained by the food. Thus, if the product of education is not reinforcing, the behaviors which lead to it may not be maintained. Chaining was also exemplified in the weight reduction case, when watching television no longer served as a consequence of going to open the refrigerator.

Another type of sequence, which we shall call the *systematic* sequence, is exemplified in the case of this student. A systematic sequence can be compared to a course or an educational curriculum: the acquisition of one behavior depends upon the *prior* existence of another, just as the acquisition of new knowledge depends upon a grasp of other presupposed knowledge. Thus, in order to learn algebra, we must know how to read. In order to learn to read, a certain degree of socialization must first occur. Such curricula exist not only in academic subjects, but are implicit in other types of behavior as well. It is entirely possible, for example, that certain behaviors necessary for marital success presuppose the existence of other interpersonal behaviors, whose acquisition depends upon the existence of yet other behaviors.

Stated otherwise, there are behavioral curricula involved in almost all behaviors. Where the present behavioral deficit exists because an earlier behavior was not acquired, a procedure which attempts to correct the ongoing deficit must consider some of the earlier deficits of which the present one may be an outgrowth. When this is true, in contrast to the first marital case presented, discussion of childhood may be necessary.

The cases presented here have involved different behavioral deficits. Although the content or the topography of these and other behaviors differ, the functional relations of such differing behaviors to their environment may be similar. This may be true not only where the differences are in such categories as marital or academic, both of which involve human behavior, but also where the differences categorize species. Pigeons peck, and people talk. Topographically these are different behaviors. However, if the consequences which maintain pecking are scheduled in a certain manner, and the (quite different) consequences which maintain speech are scheduled in the same manner, then the differing behaviors of pecking and speech will undergo similar changes in rate. It is upon this functional, or dynamic, similarity in the relation of behavior to its environment that the possibility of the extension of procedures from the laboratory to the clinic rests. It also suggests that problems in the clinic may be used for research in the laboratory.

The cases presented here demonstrate a simple application of certain self-control procedures derived from the laboratory. As was explicitly indicated earlier, they are not intended to supplant or question other more complex procedures (for a more extended analysis see Goldiamond, Dyrud, and Miller, 1965). However, we are currently examining some of these complex procedures, and are discovering that the explicit language of the laboratory may be very useful in analyzing and describing some of the behavioral transactions and changes that go on in other forms of psychotherapy (Goldiamond, Dyrud, and Miller, 1965).[3] Developments in other areas where explicit analysis is utilized may be considered for their relevance to psychotherapy, and psychotherapy, by a reverse lend-lease, may suggest areas of investigation under more controlled procedures (Goldiamond, 1966).

Laboratory research has necessarily been characterized by a simplicity of procedures and concepts, and their extension to the solution of complex human problems requires considerable precaution and careful examination. Nevertheless, these procedures and concepts may provide methods for the analysis and restatement of complex problems in observable and manipulable terms and may thereby assist in the explicit assessment of behavioral change and effectiveness.

The cases presented here involve behavioral problems which could be analyzed by the Ss themselves. This training of S to become his own therapist is one of the goals of most branches of psychotherapy. The method used to accomplish this will depend on the state of the art, the nature of the problem, S's past history, and social and other constraints upon S's behavior. In some cases, these factors may dictate a strategy of not instructing S, or not having him define the problem or discover its solution immediately, since such a procedure may disrupt other behaviors and the consequences currently maintaining them.[4] The course of treatment might then be considerably different from any of those discussed here. Other problems and possible procedures could be cited as well. But the cases presented here suggest that, in some areas at least, simple procedures can lead to complex changes.

3 Research being performed under contracts DA-49-193-MD-2628 and DA-49-193-MD-2448 between the Office of the Surgeon General and the Institute for Behavioral Research and the Washington School of Psychiatry, respectively. These projects involve collaboration between Jarl Dyrud, M.D., Miles Miller, M.D., and the author.

4 I am indebted to Jarl Dyrud for this observation.

Laboratory control of thumbsucking by withdrawal and re-presentation of reinforcement

DONALD M. BAER

Positive reinforcement may be withdrawn from young children by showing them movie cartoons and programming interruptions of both picture and sound track. Making such withdrawal contingent upon a response effectively reduces its frequency (Baer, 1961); and the delay of such withdrawal by responding can set up stable avoidance behavior (Baer, 1960). In the present study, this withdrawal technique is used to produce temporary control of thumbsucking in three young children who are persistent thumbsuckers. The usual account of thumbsucking attributes it to inner tensions and conflicts (Spock, 1946, p. 211), to its self-reinforcement consequences (Fenichel, 1945, p. 63), or to a history of deprivation of sucking experience during infancy (Roberts, 1944). Palermo (1956) has summarized what experimental evidence exists, and argued that thumbsucking may be interpreted as a learned response which reduces anxiety. In this context, it would seem valuable to show to what extent thumbsucking may be modified by current environmental control, using explicit stimulus consequences of the response.

From *Journal of the Experimental Analysis of Behavior,* 1962, **5**, 525–528.

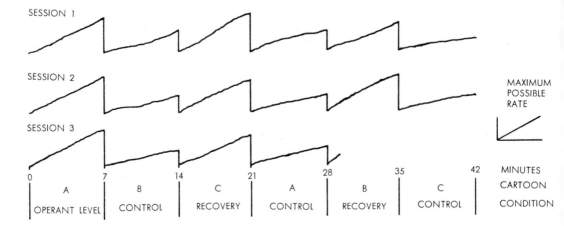

Figure 1. *Cumulative thumbsucking curves of a single subject under alternating conditions of Control and Recovery.*

PROCEDURE

The first *S* was a 5-year-old boy from a local nursery school, who had seen the same three cartoons each session, for eight sessions separated from one another by 2 or 3 days. He showed great enjoyment, laughing and mumbling throughout, and also sucked his thumb virtually 100% of each 21-min session. During these eight preliminary sessions, the subject had seen the cartoons without interruption or any other experimental treatment. (A bar was located close to his right hand for collecting an extensive operant level; however, the operant level of bar pressing was zero throughout all of these sessions.) Thus, *S* was well adapted, but experimentally naive.

The general procedure was identical to that described in an earlier paper (Baer, 1960). The *S* was conducted to the experimental room by a young female adult, *A*, who seated him before a movie screen built into one wall of the room. She then sat behind a partition in a corner of the room. Cartoons were projected on the screen from the experimenter's control and observation room on the other side of the wall. During each of the eight preliminary sessions, three 7-min cartoons were shown without break or interruption. During each of the three experimental sessions reported here, *S* was shown the same three cartoons twice, without any break between cartoons, in the sequence A, B, C, A, B, C. Thumbsucking was recorded on a Gerbrands cumulative recorder which stepped one response for every three cumulative seconds of thumbsucking. Observing through a one-way mirror, the experimenter held down a key on an otherwise automatic programmer whenever *S*'s thumb was in his mouth. The programmer pulsed the recorder for every 3 sec the key was depressed. Under punishment conditions, the programmer turned off the projector lamp and opened the loudspeaker's voice coil as long as the key was depressed so that sight and sound of the cartoons were withdrawn.

During the experimental sessions, *S* was shown cartoon A without punishment; was punished for all thumbsucking during B (a Control period); allowed C as a Recovery period; punished again for all thumbsucking during the second (Control) showing of A; allowed the second showing of B as a Recovery period; and punished again for all thumbsucking during the second (Control) showing of C.

RESULTS AND DISCUSSION

Cumulative thumbsucking for the three experimental sessions is shown in Figure 1 (a photographic reproduction of a tracing of the original record). The paper speed in the

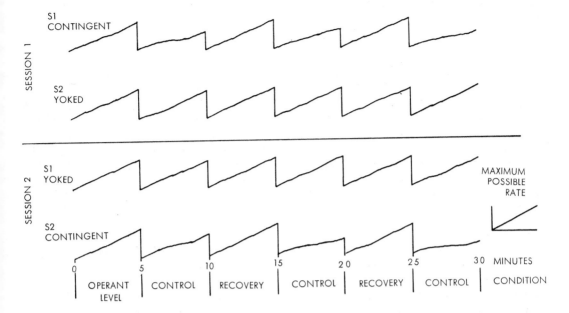

Figure 2. *Cumulative thumbsucking curves of two subjects, one experiencing contingent withdrawal/re-presentation and the other yoked, under alternating conditions of Control and Recovery.*

recorder was 22 in. per hr; thus, maximum slope was not steep. (Note the "maximum possible rate" in the figure.) During the first showing of A in each session (operant level), the rate of thumbsucking was very nearly maximal. For the first session, recovery during C was equal to the level established during A, but recovery during the second showing of B was less. However, during the second and third sessions, recovery was typically strong and prompt. The pattern was similar for responses under the Control conditions. During the first session, succeeding Control periods were progressively more effective in decreasing rate; during the second and third sessions, the rate was quite uniformly and effectively lowered during all Control conditions.

The S left after seeing only four cartoons during the third session, saying he had "seen enough." This may be attributed to the periods of punishment undergone. On the other hand, it should be recalled that S had seen each cartoon a total of 13 times, at 2- or 3-day intervals: satiation is not unreasonable, punishment or not.

The prompt and strong recovery of thumbsucking during the Recovery periods of the second and third sessions, coupled with the immediate weakening of the response during Control periods, may suggest a rapid process of discrimination of the schedule components, rather than a generalized suppression of thumbsucking through punishment. At any rate, the response remained weak only during punishment, a typical enough result. Further experimental manipulation was frustrated by the "graduation" of S from nursery school 1 week later.

The procedure used to establish this temporary control of the thumbsucking response was a complex one. It involved withdrawal of reinforcement; re-presentation of reinforcement; and the contingency of withdrawal for thumbsucking and re-presentation for removal of the thumb from the mouth. In an attempt to show the role of the contingent use of these operations, compared with their random or non-contingent use, two other 5-year-old boys were studied in a yoked situation.

In this situation, the two Ss sat side by side and watched the same cartoons projected on the screen before them. A small room-divider was placed between them so that they could not observe each other as they watched the cartoons. Two observers watched the Ss, each recording the thumbsucking of one S on separate cumulative recorders.[1] (The recorders were housed in boxes in a distant room, so that their clicking was inaudible to the Ss or Es.) The Ss were shown cartoons for a total of 30 min per session. No experimental procedures were used in the first three sessions, because the operant level of thumbsucking in this new situation was found to change steadily from uncharacteristically low values toward higher rates. By the end of the third session, both Ss showed stable rates of thumbsucking near 100%. Two experimental sessions, labelled Session 1 and Session 2 in Figure 2, followed on successive days. In Session 1, S1 experienced alternating 5-min periods of continuous cartoons and contingent withdrawal/re-presentation of the cartoons. And S2, sitting beside him and watching the same screen, hence had a yoked withdrawal/re-presentation of the cartoons during the same alternate intervals. However, in his case, these operations had only a random contingency with his thumbsucking behavior. The next day, during Session 2, the roles of S1 and S2 were reversed: S2 experienced alternating periods of continuous cartoons and contingent withdrawal/re-presentation, while S1 experienced the yoked, noncontingent withdrawal/re-presentation operations during the same alternate periods.

Figure 2 shows the results. (The curves are slightly retouched in places where the pen left too fine a line for photographic reproduction.) In either session, the subject undergoing contingent withdrawal/re-presentation of the cartoons for thumbsucking came promptly under the control of this contingency. The subject who experienced yoked withdrawal/re-presentation under the same schedule at the same time, but only randomly associated

with his thumbsucking, showed no obvious effect. However, the observer did note a transitory exception to this pattern in S1 during Session 2. In the previous session, S1 had been subjected to contingent withdrawal/re-presentation for thumbsucking. When S1 was subjected to a random withdrawal/re-presentation of the cartoons (yoked to S2) during the first Control period of Session 2, he removed his thumb from his mouth quite frequently; but he replaced it almost immediately each time. This operation was closely correlated to the withdrawal operations (contingent upon the thumbsucking of S2). It did not appreciably reduce the amount of cumulative thumbsucking, and therefore is barely discernible in Figure 2. During subsequent Control periods of Session 2, this pattern of response virtually disappeared.

Hence, contingent withdrawal/re-presentation of the cartoons appears to weaken the thumbsucking response during periods when it is in effect; but random withdrawal/re-presentation operations of the same frequency, extent, and timing do not appreciably affect a thumbsucking response occurring at the same time.

No claims are made about the generality of this effect. The Ss numbered three; all were boys; and all were chosen because of their unusually high rate of thumbsucking in nursery school settings. Hence, they are not a random sample of young thumbsuckers.

---

1 The reliability of the two observers in recording thumbsucking was checked by having both observers record the thumbsucking of a single S on separate recorders during the second of the three preliminary sessions. Their records, when superimposed, were virtually identical, implying near-100% reliability. This technique for assessing reliability was suggested by Goldiamond (1962).

Effects of adult social reinforcement on child behavior [1]

FLORENCE R. HARRIS, MONTROSE M. WOLF, AND DONALD M. BAER

There is general agreement among educators that one of the primary functions of a nursery school is to foster in each child social behaviors that contribute toward more pleasant and productive living for all. However, there is no similar consensus as to precisely how this

From *Young Children* (formerly *The Journal of Nursery Education*), 1964, **20** (1), 8–17. Reprinted by permission of the National Association for the Education of Young Children.

1 This investigation was supported in part by Public Health Service Research Grants MH-02232 and MH-02208, from the National Institute of Mental Health.

objective is to be attained. Many writers subscribe to practices based on a combination of psychoanalytic theory and client-centered therapy principles, usually referred to as a mental hygiene approach. Yet there are considerable variation and vagueness in procedures recommended, particularly those dealing with such problem behaviors as the child's hitting people, breaking valuable things, or withdrawing from both people and things. Read (1955), for example, recommends accepting the child's feelings, verbalizing them for him, and draining them off through vigorous activities. Landreth (1942) advises keeping adult contacts with the child at a minimum based on his needs, backing up verbal suggestions by an implicit assumption that the suggestion will be carried out and, when in doubt, doing nothing unless the child's physical safety is involved. In addition to some of the above precepts, Taylor (1954) counsels parents and teachers to support both desirable and undesirable behaviors and to give nonemotional punishment. According to Standing (1959), Montessori advocates that teachers pursue a process of nonintervention, following careful preparation of a specified environment aimed at "canalizing the energy" and developing "inner command." Nonintervention does not preclude the "minimum dose" of instruction and correction.

Using some combination of such guidance precepts, teachers have reported success in helping some nursery school children who showed problem behaviors; but sometimes adherence to the same teaching principles has not been helpful in modifying the behavior of concern. Indeed, it is usually not at all clear what conditions and principles may or may not have been operative. All of these precepts have in common the adult behaviors of approaching and attending to a child. Therefore, it seemed to the staff of the Laboratory Preschool at the University of Washington that a first step in developing possible explicit criteria for judging when and when not to attend was to study the precise effects that adult attention can have on some problem behaviors.

This paper presents an account of the procedures and results of five such studies. Two groups of normal nursery school children provided the subjects studied. One group enrolled twelve three-year-olds and the other, sixteen four-year-olds. The two teachers of the younger group and the three teachers of the older group conducted the studies as they carried out their regular teaching duties. The general methodology of these studies was developed in the course of dealing with a particularly pressing problem behavior shown by one child at the beginning of the school year. It is worth considering this case before describing the procedures which evolved from it.

The study dealt with a three-year-old girl who had regressed to an excessive amount of crawling (Harris, Johnston, Kelley, and Wolf, 1964). By "excessive" is meant that after three weeks of school she was spending most of her morning crawling or in a crouched position with her face hidden. The parents reported that for some months the behavior had been occurring whenever they took her to visit or when friends came to their home. The teachers had used the conventional techniques, as outlined above, for building the child's "security."

Observations recorded in the third week at school showed, however, that more than 80% of the child's time was spent in off-feet positions. The records also showed that the crawling behavior frequently drew the attention of teachers. On-feet behaviors, such as standing and walking, which occurred infrequently, seldom drew such notice.

A program was instituted in which the teachers no longer attended to the child whenever she was crawling or crouching, but gave her continuous warm attention as long as she was engaging in behavior in which she was standing, running, or walking. Initially the only upright behaviors that the teachers were able to attend to occurred when the child pulled herself almost to her feet in order to hang up or take down her coat from her locker, and when she pulled herself up to wash her hands in the wash basin. Within a week of the initiation of the new attention-giving procedure, the child acquired a close-to-normal pattern of on-feet behavior.

In order to see whether the change from off- to on-feet behavior was related to the differential attention given by the teachers, they reversed their procedure, making attention once again contingent only upon crawling and other off-feet behavior. They waited for occasions of such off-feet behavior to "reinforce" with attention, while not attending to any on-feet behavior. By the second day the child had reverted to her old pattern of play and locomotion. The observational records showed the child was off her feet 80% of the class session.

To see whether on-feet behavior could be re-established, the teachers again reversed their procedure, giving attention to the child only when she was engaging in behaviors involving upright positions. On-feet behavior rose markedly during the first session. By the fourth day, the child again spent about 62% of the time on her feet.

Once the child was not spending the greater portion of her day crawling about, she quickly became a well-integrated member of the group. Evidently she already had well-developed social play skills.

As a result of this demonstration that either walking or crawling could be maintained and that the child's responses depended largely upon the teachers' attending behaviors, the teachers began a series of further experimental analyses of the relationship between teacher attention and nursery school child behavior.

PROCEDURES

A specified set of procedures common to the next studies was followed. First, a child showing problem behavior was selected and records were secured. An observer recorded all of the child's behavior, the environmental conditions under which it occurred, and its immediate consequences under conventional teacher guidance. This was done throughout the 2½-hour school session, daily, and for several days. The records gave detailed pictures of the behavior under study. In each case, it became apparent that the problem behavior almost always succeeded in attracting adult attention.

As soon as these records, technically termed "baseline" records, of the typical behavior of the child and teachers were obtained, teachers instituted a program of systematically giving differential attention to the child. When the undesired behavior occurred, they did not in any way attend to him, but remained absorbed in one of the many necessary activities of teachers with other children or with equipment. If the behavior occurred while a teacher was attending to the child, she at once turned to another child or task in a matter-of-fact and nonrejecting manner. Concurrently, teachers gave immediate attention to other behaviors of the child which were considered to be more desirable than the problem behavior. The net effect of these procedures was that the child could gain a great deal of adult attention if he refrained from engaging in "problem behavior." If under this regime of differential attention the problem behavior diminished to a stable low level at which it was no longer considered a problem, a second procedure was inaugurated to check out the functional relationship between changes in the child's behavior and the guidance procedures followed.

The second procedure was simply to reverse the first procedure. That is, when the problem behavior occurred, the teacher went immediately to the child and gave him her full, solicitous attention. If the behavior stopped, she turned to other children and tasks, remaining thus occupied until the behavior recurred. In effect, one sure way for the child to secure adult attention was to exhibit the problem behavior. This procedure was used to secure reasonably reliable information on whether the teachers' special program had indeed brought about the changes noted in the child's behavior. If adult attention was the critical factor in maintaining the behavior, the problem behavior should recur in stable form under these conditions. If it did so, this was evidence that adult attention was, technically speaking, a positive social reinforcer for the child's behavior.

The final stage of the study was, of course, to return to procedures in which attention was given at once and continuously for behaviors considered desirable. Concurrently, adult attention was again withheld or withdrawn as an immediate consequence of the problem behavior. As the problem disappeared and appropriate behaviors increased, the intense program of differential adult attention was gradually diminished until the child was receiving attention at times and in amounts normal for the teachers in the group. However, attention was given only on occasions of desirable behavior, and never (or very seldom) for the undesirable behavior.

CRYING AND WHINING

Following the above procedures, a study was conducted on a four-year-old boy who cried a great deal after mild frustrations (Hart, Allen, Buell, Harris, and Wolf, 1964). This child averaged about eight full-fledged crying episodes each school morning. The baseline observations showed that this crying behavior consistently brought attention from the teachers, in the form of going to him and showing solicitous concern. During the following days, this behavior was simply ignored. (The only exceptions to this were to have been incidents in which the child had hurt himself considerably and was judged to have genuine grounds for crying. Naturally, his hurts were to be attended to. Such incidents, however, did not occur.) Ten days of ignoring the outcries, but giving approving attention for verbal and self-help behaviors, produced a steady weakening of the crying response to a nearly zero level. In the final five days of the interval, only one crying response was recorded. The number of crying episodes on successive days is graphed in cumulative form in Figure 1.

During the next ten days, crying was again reinforced whenever it occurred, the teachers attending to the boy on these occasions without fail. At first, it was necessary to give attention for mere grimaces that might follow a bump. The daily crying episodes quickly rose to a rate almost as high as formerly. A second ten-day period of ignoring the outcries again produced a quick weakening of the response to a near-zero level, as is apparent in the figure. Crying remained at this low level thereafter, according to the informal judgment of the teachers.

The same procedures were used in another study of "operant crying" of a four-year-old boy, with the same general results.

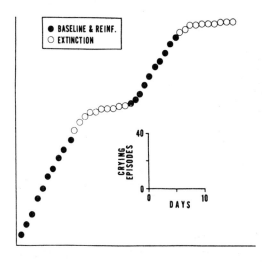

Figure 1. *Cumulative record of the daily number of crying episodes.*

ISOLATE PLAY

Two studies involved children who exhibited markedly solitary play behavior. Extremely little of their morning at nursery school was spent in any interaction with other children. Instead, these children typically played alone in a quiet area of the school room or the play yard, or interacted only with the teachers. For present purposes, both of these response patterns will be called "isolate play." Systematic observation showed that isolate play usually attracted or maintained the attention of a teacher, whereas social play with other children did so comparatively seldom.

A plan was initiated in which the teacher was to attend regularly if the child approached other children and interacted with them. On the other hand, the teacher was not to attend to the child so long as he engaged in solitary play. To begin with, attention was given when the child merely stood nearby, watching other children; then, when he played beside another child; and finally, only when he interacted with the other child. Teachers had to take special precautions that their attending behaviors did not result in drawing the child away from children and into interaction solely with the teacher. Two techniques were found particularly effective. The teacher directed her

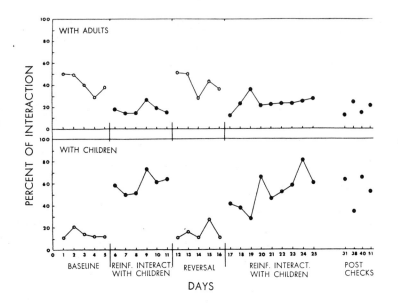

Figure 2. Daily percentages of time spent in social interaction with adults and with children during approximately two hours of each morning session.

looks and comments to the other child or children, including the subject only as a participant in the play project. For example, "That's a big building you three boys are making; Bill and Tom and Jim (subject) are all working hard." Accessory materials were also kept at hand so that the teacher could bring a relevant item for the subject to add to the play: "Here's another plate for your tea party, Ann." In both isolate cases this new routine for giving adult attention produced the desired result: Isolate play declined markedly in strength while social play increased two- or threefold.

After about a week of the above procedure, the consequences of nonisolate and isolate play were reversed. The teachers no longer attended to the child's interactions with other children, but instead gave continuous attention to the child when he was alone. Within a week, or less, isolate play became the dominant form of activity in both cases.

The former contingencies were then reinstated: The teachers attended to social interactions by the child, and ignored isolate play as completely as they could. Again, isolate play declined sharply while social interaction increased as before. The results of one of these studies (Allen, Hart, Buell, Harris, and Wolf, 1964) are summarized in Figure 2.

Figure 2 shows the changes in behavior of a 4½-year-old girl under the different guidance conditions. The graph shows the percentage of play time that she spent in interaction with other children and the percentage of time spent with an adult. The remainder of her time was spent alone. It is apparent that only about 15% of this child's play time was spent in social play as long as the teachers attended primarily to her solitary play. But interacting behaviors rose to about 60% of total play time when the teachers attended only to her social play. At the same time, her interactions solely with teachers, not being reinforced, fell from their usual 40% of the child's play time to about 20%. These were considered reasonable percentages for this nursery school child. During Days 17 through 25 the schedule of adult reinforcement of social play was gradually reduced to the usual amount of attention, given at the usual irregular intervals. Nevertheless, the social behavior maintained its strength, evidently becoming largely self-maintaining.

After Day 25, the teachers took care not to attend too often to the child when she was alone, but otherwise planned no special contingencies for attending. Four checks were made at later dates to see if the pattern of social behavior persisted. It is apparent (Figure 2, Post Checks) that the change was durable, at least until Day 51. Further checks were not possible because of the termination of the school year.

A parallel study, of a three-year-old isolate boy,[2] yielded similar results showing the same pattern of rapid behavioral change in response to changing contingencies for adult attention. In the case of this boy, post checks were made on three days during the early months of the school following the summer vacation period. The data showed that on those days his interaction with children averaged 55% of his play time. Apparently his social play was well established. Teachers reported that throughout the remainder of the year he continued to develop ease and skills in playing with his peers.

The immediate shifts in these children's play behavior may be partly due to the fact that they had already developed skills readily adapted to play with peers at school. Similar studies in progress are showing that, for some children, development of social play behaviors may require much longer periods of reinforcement.

EXCESSIVE PASSIVITY

A fifth case[3] involved a boy noted for his thoroughgoing lack of any sort of vigorous play activity. The teachers reported that this child consistently stood quietly about the play yard while other children ran, rode tricycles, and climbed on special climbing frames, trees, fences, and playhouses. Teachers also reported that they frequently attempted to encourage

him, through suggestions or invitations, to engage in the more vigorous forms of play available. Teachers expressed concern over his apparent lack of strength and motor skills. It was decided to select a particular form of active play to attempt to strengthen. A wooden frame with ladders and platforms, called a climbing frame, was chosen as the vehicle for establishing this activity. The teachers attended at first to the child's mere proximity to the frame. As he came closer, they progressed to attending only to his touching it, climbing up a little, and finally to extensive climbing. Technically, this was reinforcement of successive approximations to climbing behavior. Figure 3 shows the results of nine days of this procedure, compared to a baseline of the preceding nine days. In this figure, black bars represent climbing on the climbing frame, and white bars represent climbing on any other equipment in the play yard. The height of the bars shows the percentage of the child's play time spent in such activities. It is clear that during the baseline period less than 10% of the child's time was spent in any sort of climbing

2 Margaret K. Johnston, Susan C. Kelley, Florence R. Harris, M. M. Wolf, and D. M. Baer. Effects of positive social reinforcement on isolate behavior of a nursery school child. Unpublished manuscript.
3 Margaret K. Johnston, Susan C. Kelley, Florence R. Harris, and M. M. Wolf. An application of reinforcement principles to development of motor skills of a young child. Unpublished manuscript.

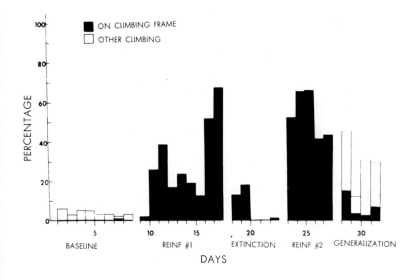

Figure 3. Daily percentages of time spent in using a climbing-frame apparatus. Open bars indicate time spent in climbing on other equipment.

activity, but that during the course of reinforcement with pleased adult attention for climbing on the frame, this behavior greatly increased, finally exceeding 50% of the child's morning. (Climbing on other objects was not scored during this period.) There then followed five days during which the teachers ignored any climbing on the frame, but attended to all other appropriate activities. The rate of climbing on the frame promptly fell virtually to zero, though the child climbed on other apparatus and was consistently given attention for this. Another five days of reinforcement of use of the climbing frame immediately restored the climbing-frame behavior to a high stable level, always in excess of 40% of the boy's play time. After this, the teachers began an intermittent program of reinforcement for climbing on any other suitable objects, as well as vigorous active play of all sorts, in an effort to generalize the increased vigorous activity. Frame-climbing weakened considerably, being largely replaced by other climbing activities, which were now scored again as data. Activities such as tricycle-riding and running were not systematically recorded due to difficulties in reliably scoring them. It is clear from the data obtained, however, that climbing activities were thoroughly generalized by this final procedure. Checks made the following school year in another play yard indicated that vigorous climbing had become a stable part of his behavior repertoire.

SUMMARY AND DISCUSSION

The above studies systematically examined effects of adult attention on some problem behaviors of normal preschool children. The findings in each case clearly indicated that for these children adult attention was a strong positive reinforcer. That is, the behavior which was immediately followed by a teacher's giving the child attention rose rapidly to a high rate, and the rate fell markedly when adult attention was withheld from that behavior and concurrently given to an incompatible behavior. While it seems reasonable that for most young children adult attention may be a positive reinforcer, it is also conceivable that for some children adult attention may be a

negative reinforcer. That is, the rate of a behavior may decrease when it is immediately followed by the attention of an adult, and rise again as soon as the adult withdraws. Actually, for a few children observed at the preschool, it has been thought that adult attention was a negative reinforcer. This seemed to be true, for instance, in the case of the climbing-frame child. Before the study was initiated, the teachers spent several weeks attempting to make themselves positively reinforcing to the child. This they did by staying at a little distance from him and avoiding attending directly to him until he came to them for something. At first, his approaches were only for routine help, such as buttoning his coat. On each of these occasions they took care to be smilingly friendly and helpful. In time, he began making approaches of other kinds, for instance, to show a toy. Finally, when a teacher approached him and commented with interest on what he was doing, he continued his play instead of stopping, hitting out, or running off. However, since his play remained lethargic and sedentary, it was decided that special measures were necessary to help him progress more rapidly. It was the use and effects of these special measures that constituted the study. Clearly, however, adult attention must be or become positively reinforcing to a child before it can be successfully used to help him achieve more desirably effective behaviors.

Studies such as those reported here seem to imply that teachers may help many children rapidly through systematic programming of their adult social reinforcements. However, further research in this area seems necessary. Some of our own studies now in progress suggest that guidance on the basis of reinforcement principles may perhaps bring rapidly into use only behaviors which are already available within the repertory of the child. If the desired behavior requires skills not yet in the child's repertory, then the process of developing those skills from such behaviors as the child has may require weeks or months. For example, a four-year-old child who could verbalize but who very rarely spoke was helped to speak freely within several days. On the other hand, a child of the same age who had never verbalized required a lengthy shaping process that involved reinforcing first any vocalization, and then gradually more appropriate sounds and combinations of sounds. The latter study was still incomplete at the close of a year of work. The time required to develop social behaviors in isolate children has likewise varied considerably, presumably for the same reasons.

Although the teachers conducted these studies in the course of carrying out their regular teaching duties, personnel in excess of the usual number were necessary. The laboratory school was staffed with one teacher to no more than six children, making it possible to assign to one teacher the role of principal "reinforcer teacher" in a study. This teacher was responsible for giving the child immediate attention whenever he behaved in specified ways. In addition, observers were hired and trained to record the behavior of each child studied. Each observer kept a record in ten-second intervals of his subject's behavior throughout each morning at school. Only with such staffing could reinforcement contingencies be precisely and consistently administered and their effects recorded.

Unless the effects are recorded, it is easy to make incorrect judgments about them. Two instances illustrate such fallibility. A boy in the laboratory preschool frequently pinched adults. Attempts by the teachers to ignore the behavior proved ineffective, since the pinches were hard enough to produce at least an involuntary startle. Teachers next decided to try to develop a substitute behavior. They selected patting as a logical substitute. Whenever the child reached toward a teacher, she attempted to forestall a pinch by saying, "Pat, Davey," sometimes adding, "Not pinch," and then strongly approving his patting, when it occurred. Patting behavior increased rapidly to a high level. The teachers agreed that they had indeed succeeded in reducing the pinching behavior through substituting patting. Then they were shown the recorded data. It showed clearly that although patting behavior was

indeed high, pinching behavior continued at the previous level. Apparently, the teachers were so focused on the rise in patting behavior that, without the objective data, they would have erroneously concluded that development of a substitute behavior was in this case a successful technique. A second example illustrates a different, but equally undesirable, kind of erroneous assumption. A preschool child who had to wear glasses (Wolf, Risley, and Mees, 1964[4]) developed a pattern of throwing them two or three times per day. Since this proved expensive, it was decided that the attendants should put him in his room for ten minutes following each glasses-throw. When the attendants were asked a few days later how the procedure was working, they said that the glasses-throwing had not diminished at all. A check of the records, however, showed that there was actually a marked decrease. The throwing dropped to zero within five days. Presumably, the additional effort involved in carrying out the procedure had given the attendants an exaggerated impression of the rate of the behavior. Recorded data, therefore, seem essential to accurate objective assessments of what has occurred.

The findings in the studies presented here accord generally with results of laboratory research on social development reviewed in this journal by Horowitz (1963). The importance of social reinforcement was also noted by Bandura (1963) in his investigations of imitation. Gallwey[5] has replicated the study of an isolate child discussed here, with results "clearly confirmatory of the effectiveness of the technique." Further studies in school situations that can combine the function of research with that of service seem highly desirable.

---

4 Pages 187–193 of this volume.
5 Mary Gallwey, Director of the Nursery School, Washington State University, Pullman, Washington, personal communication.

A new treatment of constipation by conditioning: A preliminary report

C. QUARTI AND J. RENAUD[1]

INTRODUCTION

Today, constipation is one of the most wide-spread functional disorders. Its varied causes include irregularity of alimentary habits, functional disorders of the gallbladder or—more often—the psychosomatic correlates of certain modes of contemporary living, as in the case of city dwellers who lead lives which are physically sedentary yet subject to continual stress. Whatever its cause, constipation is basically a disorder of intestinal motility, presenting in a variety of forms: spastic, paretic, or as an irregularity in the alternation of the phases of contraction and relaxation in the intestinal muscle.

The consequences of constipation are as different as their causes and all are to be deplored. The "maladie des laxatifs" may be considered as the least serious. It occurs following a long period, during which the patient exhausts the pharmacopoeia, passing from one group of laxatives to another. As laxatives are substituted and doses are increased, the process of elimination becomes progressively artificial, deviating more and more from the normal physiologic pattern, due to exhaustion of the liver cells, irritation of the gall bladder or interference with the reflex system of intestinal motility.

Treatment of constipation therefore calls for a therapy aimed at the cause rather than the symptom. It should make use of the natural resources of the organism, avoiding the use of any medication which, because of the complexity of the mechanism of defecation in its temporal sequence, may exert an untimely pharmacological action. The goal of treatment should be to restore the normal physiological functioning of the mechanism of defecation, not by artificially stimulating defecation, but by re-educating the intestinal motility and helping it regain its own harmony.

PHYSIOLOGICAL BASIS OF DEFECATION

To facilitate the presentation of the techniques to be utilized in our method of re-education, a brief physiological account seems to be in order.

Movements of the alimentary canal, responsible for the transfer of the contents from the esophagus through the stomach, small intestines, and finally to the anus, are under the co-ordinated control of the nervous system. The prerequisites for a normal passage are:

(a) Adequate food intake, both quantitatively and qualitatively. This food intake is, in itself, an important stimulant for intestinal motility. The rate of passage also depends on the state of fluidity and viscosity of the intestinal contents, which in turn depend on the type of foods consumed (bringing us to the psychological implications of alimentary habits), the intestinal juices and bile (the flow of the latter being under the reflex control of the nervous system).

(b) Well co-ordinated intestinal movements. Three types of intestinal movements are responsible for the progression of the intestinal contents, namely: segmentary, pendular and peristaltic. The first two are attributed to intrinsic nervous reflexes and are modified by extrinsic sympathetic and vagal activity. Peristalsis is produced by extrinsic nervous impulses; it is a mass reflex response that may encompass the entire length of the intestines, and is dependent upon the co-ordinated action of certain medullary centers and abdomino-pelvic autonomic pathways.

The average time for the passage of chyme from the stomach to the anus is about 24

From C. M. Franks (Ed.), *Conditioning Techniques in Clinical Practice and Research.* New York: Springer Publishing Company, Inc., 1964. Pp. 219—227.

1 Translated and adapted by Moneim A. El-Meligi.

hours. Serious irritation of the gastric mucosa produces a "mass reflex" represented by an active peristaltic wave which reduces the duration to a few minutes. The stimulus for this reflex is the entry of food into the stomach, which explains the healthy habit of having the first bowel movement in the morning after breakfast, thereby evacuating the digestive products of the previous day.

(c) The act of defecation begins with the passage of feces across the pelvirectal flexure where local sphincter-like thickening of the circular muscle fibres exists. The sphincter presumably relaxes and feces enter the rectum, whose lumen immediately reacts by slight constriction or dilatation, depending on the size of the fecal mass, so as to produce an active resistance which will now be the stimulus for the final explusive movements. Distention of the rectum by sudden entry of feces gives rise to a perineal sensation, often agreeable, and a conscious desire to defecate. If this desire is acceded to, a co-ordinated reflex is set up, emptying every part of the bowel from the middle of the transverse colon to the anus; the diaphragm descends, the glottis is closed, the abdominal muscles and levator ani contract, waves of peristalsis pass over the distal part of the colon, the sphincter ani are relaxed and the feces are evacuated through the narrow anal canal. The reflex centers for defecation are situated in the medulla and in the spinal cord corresponding to the sacral segments 2, 3, and 4.

NEUROPHYSIOLOGICAL CHANGES IN CONSTIPATION

The rectum initially presents the physiological phenomenon of adaptation, which is also the ultimate end of all physiopathological changes in constipation. It ceases to respond to the presence of the fecal mass in its lumen, either due to paretic relaxation of the rectal wall instead of maintaining an active resistance to the pressure exerted by the feces, or to failure of the pressure and stretch receptors to respond to their specific stimulus. On the other hand, the phenomenon of adaptation may take place normally in instances of refrain from defecation, when circumstances are unfavorable at the moment the desire is experienced. In this way, certain modes of existence, serving only to increase these unfavorable conditions, become a common cause of constipation. The resulting rectal stasis sets up the colo-colic reflex producing reflex inhibition of intestinal motility and peristalsis. The vicious circle, characteristic of chronic constipation, is thereby established.

RESTORATION OF NORMAL PHYSIOLOGICAL RHYTHM TO THE INTESTINAL PASSAGE

The physiological rhythm of the bowel motions should first be obtained, at which point the vicious circle will be interrupted. Laxatives may succeed in overcoming rectal inertia, once in a while, by strong stimulation reaching above the threshold of its wall receptors.

The afferent component of the defecation reflex is associated with a special conscious sensation, "the desire to defecate." This characteristic indicates the exact moment at which the reflex commences, and aids in the physiologic timing of any therapeutic procedure.

According to the laws of conditioning of the nervous system, it is possible to establish almost any reflex at will, including that of defecation. Conditioning consists of subordinating acts and signals. In other words, if a neutral stimulus or signal is repeatedly applied a few seconds before the basic unconditioned stimulus which elicits a precise organic reaction, the initially neutral stimulus will finally replace the unconditioned stimulus and will *of itself* elicit the reaction. The reaction becomes conditioned to the neutral stimulus which will therefore be called a conditioned stimulus. Almost any stimulus, suitably employed, may become a conditioned stimulus, viz. internal or external afferent impulses, the conscious or physiological notion of time or even the disappearance of a stimulus.

Conditioned reflexes may be simple or chain-like, with overlapping of one reflex with the other, since the acquired conditional quality may be transferred from one stimulus to the next, giving rise to conditioning of the 1st, 2nd, 3rd order and so forth. This process is known by Soviet scientists as summation.

The conditioned reflex depends for its appearance on the formation of new functional connections in the central nervous system in accordance with precise laws, of which the following are of interest to us:

(a) For a conditioned stimulus to retain its new properties, it should be reinforced periodically by following it with the basic unconditioned stimulus.

(b) A conditioned stimulus repeated without reinforcement will, after a variable interval of time, lead to weakening and, finally, extinction of the conditioned reflex. However, extinction is never complete because the pathway will always remain.

(c) Under similar experimental conditions, visceral conditioned responses develop more rapidly and are more lasting than responses conditioned within other systems. This phenomenon is attributed to the functional differences existing between the corresponding visceral or cortical sensory areas of the brain. Recording the action potentials evoked by sensory stimulation of both areas shows that, in the former, the potential persists much longer even after cessation of the stimulation.

(d) Though all sensory stimuli reach the cerebral cortex few are retained, the rest are ignored. It can therefore be assumed that, in the same manner, selection is made from different stimuli sharing the same sensory field. This capacity to make a selection is a function of the affect, and the process which leads to it is called motivation. The totality of motivations ranges in intensity from the very instinctive act to the highest intellectual activity. Instinctive behavior is produced by an essential "primitive" affective stimulus; and the more behavior becomes emotionally-free, i.e., intellectualized, the less pronounced becomes the participation of the affective quality. Nevertheless, all mental acts comprise an affective component; the more marked this component is, viz. motivation, the more rapid and lasting the conditioning will be. In other words, the more emotionally charged is the material to be learned, the more the learning process is effective.

The neurophysiological basis for the above is as follows:

It is known that the same association areas and fibres in the frontal lobes permit the transmission and spread of the emotional charge to the corresponding areas in the brain with which they are functionally synergistic. Therefore, the frontal lobes produce a certain "quantum" of energy comprising an intellectual and an affective component, the ratio of which will depend on the functional associations engaged at the moment of production of this energy.

There exist two pathways for the reflexion of the cortico-subcortical afferents. The first is essentially cortico-thalamic; a given sensory stimulation takes place through intra-cortical associations, produced by the impulses received through the diffuse thalamic system. This implies very little, if any, of a vegetative, affective or "primitive" type of response. The second is more complex; in addition to the preceding pattern we have the regions that play a paramount role in the emotional life, namely, the limbic system. This system, apart from the functional characteristics mentioned above, is closely related to the hypothalamus and, through it, to the neurovegetative expressions of affectivity, its primitive or instinctive aspects. This implies also the participation of the reticular alerting system which brings about the massive intervention of *cortical activity*. When stimulated, the activating effect of both the hypothalamus and the reticular formation is so great that the reappearance of the extinguished conditioned reflexes could be brought about without further reinforcement and sometimes could even be sustained several months.

(e) Finally, there is the role played by electric stimulation in methods of training. According to certain authors, the most minor electric shock serves as a necessary reinforcement for obtaining rapid and durable associations. The mechanism by which this phenomenon is produced is yet unknown. It may be due either to the emotional charge contained in the defense reflex provoked by the shock, or to an inherent power in the electricity itself. The only evidence available in this respect is from the experiments of Vinogradova and Sokolov who demonstrated that the response evoked by a new stimulus differs from that produced by the same stimulus associated with an electric shock.

RE-EDUCATION OF THE MECHANISM OF DEFECATION USING THE LAWS OF CONDITIONING

Because of an awareness of the act of defecation, the subject is conscious of the moment at which the defecation reflex is set up. The stimulus that elicits this reflex is the passage of the fecal mass through the pelvi-rectal flexure or, in the case of chronically constipated subjects, the stimulation of the wall of the rectum. We are going to designate this stimulation the absolute or unconditioned stimulus and we will associate with it a signal or conditioned stimulus.

Since defecation is accompanied by a mass reflex in the colon, associating the conditioned stimulus with the sensation of defecation will also mean associating the colic reflex with the conditioned stimulus. Repetition of the conditioned stimulus in association with the unconditioned stimulus would make it possible, after a certain period of time, for the former alone to elicit not only the defecation mechanism but also the accompanying reflex colonic contractions.

The conditioned stimulus should have a slight affective quality and, if possible, be of a pleasant nature lest sympathetic reactions interfere with the elicited processes. It is also thought useful to utilize electrical means of stimulation because of the empirical importance of this modality in conditioning.

The apparatus used is transistorized and generates a current modifiable so as to provoke a sensation which is almost pleasant. The subject is stimulated by two electrodes which are applied on each side of the lumbar spine and secured on the abdomen by a strap. The apparatus is visible to the subject and has a switch which permits him to change the intensity of stimulation at will. In practice, individual differences in sensitivity and resistance of the skin are very wide.

The subject to be re-educated continues to take his usual laxatives so as to produce one bowel movement per day. As he goes to the toilet he puts on the apparatus, starts operating it prior to defecation and stops the electric stimulation as soon as his evacuation is terminated. Should the desire continue, and should evacuation reoccur while still on the toilet,

stimulation should be resumed each time. Since the characteristics of the stimulation maintain an affective state that we may call "pre-emotional awakening," it is very important that the subject thinks of the association taking place within him. An association is thus facilitated between the conditioned stimulus and the evacuation reflex.

Gradually the subject should reduce the quantity of laxatives until eventually he will no longer take any and will go to the toilet even without having the desire to defecate. Once conditioning has been established, which generally happens after 20 to 30 applications, the electrical stimulation alone produces defecation according to the individual rhythm of digestion.

The second step is for the subject to utilize the principle of vertical synthesis, going to the toilet every day at a given hour (preferably after breakfast in order to benefit from the morning gastro-colic response). Thus, one gets conditioning of the second order, the chosen hour becomes the conditioned stimulus and finally the patient can dispense with the apparatus altogether.

It is advisable in periods of nervous or physical stress to reinforce the reflex by resuming the use of the apparatus for a few days. In principle, a normally developed subject can practice his own re-education without special guidance; in practice it is preferable that the overall management be the responsibility of the treating physician. The physician is best able to assess progress, supervise the tapering off of laxatives and determine the moment when re-education has been accomplished.

The following are three illustrative case reports:

Case 1

An unconstipated subject used as a control. The object of this experiment is to demonstrate the instigation of defecation by electric stimulation in a healthy woman of 38 years. Her intestinal passage was normal apart from ordinary irregularities and transitory periods of constipation which had never necessitated the use of laxatives. During the first ten applications daily evacuations took place at all times, though never in the morning. On the morning of the eleventh day, as the subject was manipulating the apparatus to prepare the electrodes, she was suddenly seized by quite intense tenesmus and straining. The feeling was not distinct enough to lead her to the toilet, but a feeling of heaviness and of intestinal movements persisted until her attention was diverted by another activity.

From the 20th day the subject decided to try one application without having any desire to defecate, in the morning and on an empty stomach. The preliminary operations (preparation of the saline solution to moisten the electrodes, fixing the belt, and so forth) were sufficient to trigger a pressing need, followed by normal defecation. After twelve days the subject had conditioned herself to evacuate at a fixed hour. A few days later, the process of vertical synthesis having been extended, seeing the apparatus, or even hearing or pronouncing its name, would be sufficient to elicit the sensation of the need to defecate. Naturally, her voluntary inhibition could control these phenomena, which we point out here only for their physiological importance. It should be noted that the technique was also effective during her periods of transitory constipation.

Case 2

M. M., a young woman of 34 years, suffering from dysmenorrhea and migraine, of a nervous temperament but otherwise quite balanced. Occasional periods of constipation appeared to be principally related to her mode of living, her menstrual cycle and her emotional state. She did not go spontaneously to the toilet except when her daily life imposed on her a physical and nervous hyperactivity. This occurred at a regular rate of three to four times per week.

During this period of conditioning she could, thanks to nightly laxatives, evacuate, on the average, of once every two days. After a week, a sort of "reverse" conditioning took place, the apparatus becoming indispensable to her. On the one hand, in spite of her absent-mindedness, she would never leave it at home when she went out all day; on the other hand, should she feel the need to go to the toilet under circumstances that made it impossible to use the apparatus, this circumstance would immediately cut off the need.

After 21 days, either seeing the instrument or just talking about it would make her feel some intestinal movements, but without distinctive need. On the 26th day, following a bulky movement on the previous day, we advised her to try the method without feeling the need to defecate. She had some mild abdominal pains, passed a great deal of flatus and experienced a sensation of "evacuation" but no bowel movement.

The following day a very positive result ensued without any desire to defecate. She described the event as follows: . . . "after about thirty seconds of electric stimulation, without any effort on my behalf, and without preliminary sensations of any sort, defecation happened precipitously." Since then positive results were obtained each day.

Case 3

M. R., a woman of 36 years, suffering since she was 30 from hepatic insufficiency which severely restricted her diet and intake of laxatives and certain other medicines. Moreover, she had megacolon. She managed to go to the toilet about twice per week through the effects of mucilages. Being a simple-minded woman, she could not relate to us precise physical or psychic phenomena other than the fact that, after only eight days, she had already cut down by half the dose of laxatives necessary for a normal evacuation. To avoid irregularity in the progress of the treatment we waited 30 days before encouraging her to go to the toilet and administer the stimulation without a desire to defecate. She had had her mucilage the previous evening. The result was very positive.

Later, among the trials with or without laxative, some failed and some succeeded. The ultimate result of all these more or less successful trials was that the patient was able to go regularly to the toilet three or four times per week, without laxatives but always with the apparatus. For reasons which could not be readily ascertained it was not possible to establish second order conditioning in her case.

CONCLUSION

We have thus demonstrated that the principles of conditioning may be practically applied in the treatment of constipation. Bowel evacuation represents but one among the many activities of the human organism which can be conditioned. In man, such conditioning is easily brought about without a complicated apparatus. The present method is of significance for several reasons: it is convenient, easy and simple; the principle of "visceral re-education" may be extended to a wide variety of other diseases of a largely functional nature; it helps us to understand some of the mechanisms which govern our physiological existence. Finally, it is suggested that the general approach represents a most important medical attitude: confidence in the mechanisms of re-adaptation and in the fundamental tendency to revert to normal functioning that is inherent in every living organism.

Reduction in rate of multiple tics by free operant conditioning methods

BEATRICE H. BARRETT

The experimental investigation of neuromuscular tics has probably been most limited by difficulties in developing sensitive and reliable behavioral measurement techniques. The closest approximation to an experimental study of tics, by Yates (1958), was based on a patient's records of her ability to reproduce her tic symptoms. Yates did not attempt to obtain objective records or measurement of the patient's tics.

The method of free operant conditioning, originally developed by Skinner (1938) to study animal behavior and later modified by Lindsley (1956) to study the behavior of chronic psychotics, has provided precise techniques of behavioral measurement and control. These techniques have been extended to the investigation of such pathological behaviors as vocal hallucinatory episodes (Lindsley, 1959, 1960, 1961b), pressure of speech (Shearn, *et al.*, 1961), and stuttering (Flanagan, *et al.*, 1958). By the application of free operant techniques, Ferster (Ferster and DeMyer, 1961) succeeded in expanding the very limited behavioral repertories of two autistic children, and Brady and Lind (1961) performed an experimental analysis with therapeutic results in a patient with hysterical blindness.

The basic datum of the free operant method is the frequency of a specific and reliably defined response within a controlled experimental environment. The method is most readily applied, therefore, in cases where changes in the rate of a repeated movement are of primary concern. The present report describes an application of free operant methods to the control of multiple neuromuscular tics.

METHOD

Patient

The patient in this experiment was a 38-year-old veteran, hospitalized in the Neurology Service of a local Veterans Administration hospital. His extensive multiple tics started approximately 14 years ago, during his term of duty in the armed services. Although a medical discharge was available to him, the patient chose to continue in the service, eventually serving overseas, until regular discharge. Since then he has been employed as an accountant by a single firm.

From *Journal of Nervous and Mental Disease*, 1962, **135**, 187–195.

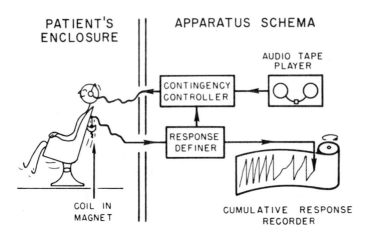

Figure 1. Schema of apparatus used to pick up, automatically record, and program the contingent consequences of multiple tics.

An interview prior to the experiment revealed that the patient knew of no traumatic experience preceding the abrupt onset of tics. He told of awakening during the night with a choking sensation accompanied by a momentary inability to breathe or swallow. He recalled this as a frightening experience and was puzzled by the subsequent development of tics. Within a few months, spasmodic movements had developed in much of his body. At the time of this experiment, his major movements included contractions of neck, shoulder, chest, and abdominal muscles, head nodding, bilateral eye blinking, opening of the mouth, and other comparatively mild facial movements.[1] The patient complained of difficulty in swallowing, hence of slow ingestion. His clear, intelligent speech was marked only occasionally by barely noticeable hesitation.

In recent years the patient was not fully aware of the presence of his tics. On occasion, when he thought himself relatively free of them, his wife reported that there was no reduction in his twitching. The patient did feel, however, that his movements were reduced in frequency while he was playing his saxophone in a local band on weekends. His greatest concern was the extent to which his tics made him conspicuous to strangers and limited his business advancement. In general, little was known of the patient's personal history.

The patient had undergone psychological counseling for a number of months and had received pharmacological treatment which included a variety of tranquilizing and muscle-relaxing drugs. Neither treatment had afforded symptomatic relief. The patient displayed no outstanding symptoms of psychopathology. His tics were considered symptomatic of an extrapyramidal system disturbance and untreatable by conventional methods.

Since he had experienced no success with other methods, the patient was highly motivated to participate in this experiment. Although he was soon discharged to return to work in a neighboring state, he voluntarily rehospitalized himself two months later for continuation of the experiment.

Arrangement of Apparatus

Patient's enclosure: A quiet, well ventilated room with observation facilities was equipped with a comfortable swivel-tilt armchair, an ashtray, a set of comfortable earphones which the patient wore throughout all experimental sessions, and a Grass EEG console (see Figure 1).

Operandum: A large U-shaped magnet, securely attached to the outside of the chair

---

1 Some of the patient's movements were so strong that, when he was seated in a chair on casters, they caused slight rolling.

back, served as a convenient device for summating multiple tics. Although the swivel arc of the chair was restricted and the chair's casters removed, its tilt was freely operative. An induction coil rested in a "nest" of electrical tape strung between the poles of the magnet.[2] Slack in the tape was adjusted so that when the patient was seated in the chair his most noticeable spasmodic movements, regardless of locus or amplitude, created a slight movement of the coil in the magnetic field.

Response definition and recording: The current induced in the moving coil was amplified by one channel of an EEG recorder to operate a sensitive relay. The operations of this relay were directly recorded as tics. The duration and amplitude of the recorded tics were determined by setting the amplifier gain so that each strong and obvious tic would operate the response relay and cumulative response recorder. After initial selection, this amplifier gain was held constant throughout the experiment.

Response-Contingent Events

In free operant conditioning, the frequency of a response is altered by programing particular consequences contingent upon the emission of that response. Generally this method has been used to generate steady rates of responding or to increase the frequency of a given response. When *reduction* in the frequency of a symptom is desired, the event contingent upon symptom occurrence may be 1) the removal of a positive stimulus or 2) the presentation of an aversive stimulus. In this experiment, both types of tic-contingent events were used.

By the use of a tape recorder, a positive stimulus (music) could be removed or an aversive stimulus (noise) presented when a tic occurred. Pulses from the response relay were transmitted through a timer to a circuit which controlled the tape recorder output to the patient's earphones (see schema in Figure 1). All recording and controlling equipment was located in a nearby room.

Music: In order to maximize the patient's interest, the music used in the experiment was selected by the patient himself from the hospital's music library. Boredom and satiation were minimized by using several selections with no repetitions.

The contingency arrangement was programed so that each tic produced a 1.5 second interruption of music. If the patient did not tic for at least 1.5 seconds, he could hear the music until it was automatically interrupted by the next tic. In effect, this schedule differentially reinforced time intervals between tics of 1.5 seconds or more.[3]

Noise: Azrin (1958) found that responses could be eliminated by making the presentation of white noise contingent upon their occurrence; and Flanagan, Goldiamond and Azrin (1958) successfully reduced chronic stuttering by presentation of a stutter-produced loud tone. In the present experiment a tape loop of white noise (60 db) was used as a tic-produced aversive stimulus.

The contingency was arranged so that each tic produced 1.5 seconds of noise over the patient's earphones. When the patient was tic-free for at least 1.5 seconds, the noise was automatically interrupted and did not recur until the next tic.

Contingency Testing

As a control measure to test the effect of the contingencies described above, periods of continuous music and continuous noise were used. This amounted to removal of the contingency requirement which, in the case of music, more nearly approximated the conditions of music therapy.

Self-Control

The effects of music and noise were compared with the patient's own efforts to con-

---

2 Michael J. Malone, M.D., offered the general idea of the "tic chair" and magnetic pickup.

3 In technical terms, this schedule is a time contingent crf drl of 1.5 seconds with an unlimited hold (Ferster and Skinner, 1957).

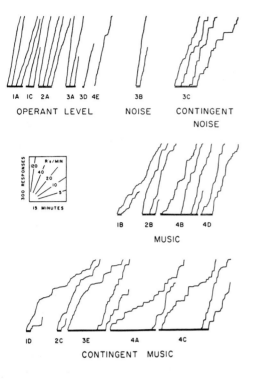

OPERANT LEVEL   NOISE   CONTINGENT NOISE

MUSIC

CONTINGENT MUSIC

Figure 2. Cumulative response records of the first four experimental sessions showing changes in tic rate under conditions of tic-contingent noise and tic-contingent interruption of music and control runs of both noise and music without the contingency requirement. The experimental sessions are numbered and the sequence of conditions within each session identified by letters. Double bars connect all immediately successive curves under designated conditions. Breaks in double bars indicate a change of conditions.

For example, the first four pen excursions labeled 1A were continuously recorded tics during a 26-minute period at the start of the first session to get an operant level. Without interruption, the 1B curves follow, showing 27 minutes of tics under continuous music. The two curves labeled 1C record a return to the operant level for 10 minutes, followed immediately by the 1D period of 34 minutes with each tic producing interruption of the music. The 2A curves show operant level rates at the start of session 2, followed by 25 minutes of continuous music (2B), then 21 minutes of tic-contingent interruption of music (2C), and so on. The same identification system is used in Figure 4 for sessions 7 and 8.

trol his tics. A signal light (60 watt bulb) was introduced and the patient was instructed to control his tics by his most frequently used methods for as long as the light was on.

Experimental Sessions

The patient was informed that we would be studying the effects of various conditions on his tic rate. He had selected a lasting supply of music tapes with the understanding that he would hear them at least some of the time during the experiment. He was instructed to make himself comfortable and to remain seated in the chair, with earphones on, throughout the sessions. Aside from previously mentioned instructions concerning the signal light, no further explanation was given. The experimental room was closed, and recording was begun. Experimental conditions were changed without interruption by adjusting the controlling equipment. The duration of sessions varied from two to three hours depending on meal schedules and other hospital routines. No attempt was made to set up predetermined time intervals for each experimental condition. With a few exceptions due to time limits, each condition was run long enough to show its maximal effect when compared with the normal tic rate or operant level.

RESULTS

Cumulative records of the first four sessions showing the effects of music and noise on tic rate are shown in Figure 2. These sessions were conducted during a 48-hour period prior to the patient's discharge. The remaining sessions were held two months later when the patient voluntarily rehospitalized himself for continuation of the experiment.

To facilitate comparison of tic rates under the various experimental conditions, the continuous records in all figures have been telescoped and grouped. The steeper the slope of the curves, the higher the tic rate. Rate estimates may be made by reference to the grid showing rates for representative slopes.

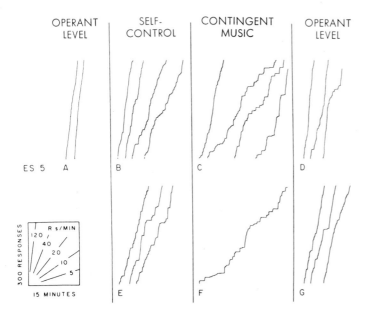

OPERANT LEVEL	SELF-CONTROL	CONTINGENT MUSIC	OPERANT LEVEL

ES 5   A   B   C   D

R s/MIN
120
40
20
10
5

300 RESPONSES

15 MINUTES   E   F   G

Figure 3. A continuous cumulative record of the fifth experimental session showing rate changes under sustained self-control compared with the greater reduction under tic-produced interruption of music. The sequence of conditions is indicated by letters.

Operant level determinations: The patient's normal tic rate (operant level) ranged between 64 and 116 tics per minute (tpm), with some decrease in the short run at 4E during the last session in Figure 2. No diurnal variations in tic rate were noted. Although sessions were run during various hours of the day and evening to capitalize on limited time, neither fatigue nor hunger affected tic rate or response to experimental conditions.[4]

Effects of noise: There was a very slight increase in the tic rate during a brief seven-minute period when continuous white noise (60 db) was played ("noise" in Figure 2). However, when made tic-contingent, noise reduced the tic rate to about 40 tpm ("contingent noise" in Figure 2). The long tic-free intervals toward the end of the contingent noise period may have been due to dozing which the patient later reported. Because of its apparent soporific effect, noise was not used further.

Effects of music: Continuous music ("music" in Figure 2) reduced the tic rate about as much as did contingent noise (40 tpm). However, when each tic interrupted the music ("contingent music"), the rate was lowered to 15 to

30 tpm. During every period of contingent music, the effect of the contingency was an additional reduction of 40 to 50 per cent in tic rate. After the first session there was no overlap between the range of rates under continuous music and under tic-contingent interruption of music. The differential magnitude of these effects on this patient thus requires no statistical test.

The fact that contingent music produced a greater reduction in rate of ticing than did continuous music appears to be the result of longer, more frequent tic-free periods when the contingency was in effect. The improbability of fatigue effects is indicated by a comparison of the 4A rate under contingent music obtained at the start of a morning session with the 1D, 2C, and 3E rates under this condition recorded at the end of the three previous sessions.

Effects of self-control: The tic-reducing effect of contingent music is compared with the patient's sustained efforts of self-control in Figure 3 (fifth session). In response to instructions and a signal light, the patient reduced

4 Sessions 2, 4, and 8 were run in the morning and terminated for the patient's lunch; sessions 1 and 3 occurred in the afternoon; sessions 5 and 7 were conducted in the evening.

his tic rate to 50 to 60 per minute. This rate is only slightly higher than that previously obtained with contingent noise and non-contingent music. Under the condition of tic-contingent interruption of music, however, rates were considerably lower, ranging from 20 to 35 per minute.[5] Again there was no overlap between the range of rates under the three conditions (operant level, self-control, and contingent music). Note the initial rapid tic rate at the beginning of the C period of contingent music. This increase in rate following a period of self-control (B) parallels what clinicians have observed in tiqueurs (Wechsler, 1952). It appears that this effect was strong enough to counteract temporarily the effect of the contingent music (C).

In addition to the differential effects on tic rate of self-control and the music contingency condition, there was also a difference in the patient's general behavior topography. In the B period of self-control, the patient was observed to engage in headholding and general prolonged contraction. In contrast, during the E period of self-control, he engaged in relaxed tapping with finger or foot and occasional singing. This new form of behavior was first observed as the patient accompanied contingent music in the C period.

These differences in behavior topography shown during the B and E periods of self-control may account for the longer tic-free intervals in E than in B. They may also explain the differential response to contingent music in C and F. In other words, it appeared that the patient used two different methods of reducing his tics and that these two methods had different effects on subsequent tic reduction under contingent music. During B, self-control was effected by a generalized rigid contraction which was followed in C by an initial increase in rate despite the availability of contingent music. In contrast, during E self-control was achieved through release methods with the subsequent rapid and marked rate reduction under contingent music (F).

Reliability of the effect of contingent music: The previously described data from six experimental sessions showed that tic-contingent interruption of music reduced the patient's tic rate far more than did non-contingent music, tic-produced white noise, or the patient's efforts at self-control. During those sessions, the patient had approximately six

---

5 This differential effect was reproduced repeatedly in session 6, which is not shown here.

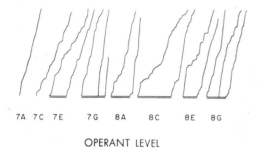

7A 7C 7E   7G   8A   8C   8E 8G

OPERANT LEVEL

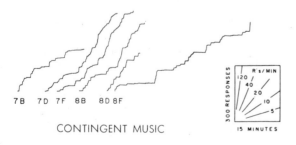

7B 7D 7F 8B   8D 8F

CONTINGENT MUSIC

Figure 4. *Records of sessions 7 and 8 demonstrating reproducibility of the marked tic-reducing effect of tic-contingent interruption of music in six replications. Letters designate the sequence of conditions within numbered sessions.*

hours' exposure to contingent music. Following a two-month interruption of the experiment, the reliability of the tic-reducing effect of contingent music was subjected to empirical test by a series of replications on the same patient.[6] The result of alternating operant level control periods (7A, 7C, 7E, and 7G; and 8A, 8C, 8E, and 8G) with periods of tic-produced interruption of music (7B, 7D, and 7F; and 8B, 8D, and 8F) are shown in Figure 4. The effect of contingent music on tic-free intervals was dramatically and reliably demonstrated by reductions of from 55 to 85 per cent below the operant rate on each of these six replications.

The tic-reducing effect of contingent music was more immediate and prolonged than in earlier sessions. Tic-free intervals were, for the most part, considerably longer and more frequent than previously, and only brief bursts of tics occurred with high local rate. The patient expressed irritation at the end of session 8 because he had wanted to hear the remainder of a jazz concert being played during 8F (the period with lowest tic rate: nine per minute). He commented that he was concentrating on the musical ideas and became annoyed when his brief bursts of tics interrupted it. During most of the 44-minute 8F period of contingent music he was observed to be almost motionless as he listened to the music.

The pattern of tic-free intervals followed by brief intervals of heightened local rate which developed in response to contingent music appeared to generalize to the operant ticing rate as early as session 4. If this was a true generalization, it may have therapeutic implications. On the other hand, it may simply represent a minor shift of unknown nature in the tic rate. Because of possible operandum unreliability (discussed below), the most valid comparisons should be limited to the differential effects of self-control, non-contingent music, and contingent music relative to the operant tic rate.

Intrasession decrease in operant level rate did appear with regularity during the last two sessions (Figure 4). Operant tic rates 7C, 7E, 8C, and 8E, which were recorded between periods of contingent music, showed somewhat longer tic-free intervals than those

recorded at the beginning of these sessions (7A and 8A) or those recorded at the end of these sessions (7G and 8G). The reasons for this decrease are far from clear, but the decrease may have something to do with attention. The patient reported that during these sessions he was anticipating more music and knew he would not hear it if he had many tics.

DISCUSSION

The results of this experiment clearly demonstrate that non-contingent music and tic-contingent white noise reduced the tic rate to a level comparable with that produced by self-control. A far more powerful reduction was produced by tic-contingent interruption of music.

In evaluating the differential control of tic rate shown in these data and the possible extensions of the basic method to other symptoms for either therapeutic or research purposes, the most pertinent consideration is the design of the operandum, the device which permits the symptom to operate a switch (Skinner, 1962). Two major requirements of a good operandum are the reliability of its operation and the specificity of the response class which actuates it.[7] The fragile tape arrangement of our crude operandum does not insure reliable operation for continued general application. It is not stable enough to maintain accurate calibration during repeated use. A more stable operandum might have permanently fixed pickups, preferably embedded in upholstery in different areas of a chair.

Although a chair operandum provided a relatively comfortable situation for the patient, it did restrict his motility more than might

---

6 Both Claude Bernard, in 1865, and Murray Sidman, in 1961, have pointed out that the most convincing test of reliability of an "effect" is the demonstration of its reproducibility in a series of replications.

7 Ferster (1953) has discussed in some detail the general requirements of an accurate operandum (manipulandum). This device, which is manipulated by the subject's behavior, also defines the response being conditioned or attenuated. It is the point of contact between the subject and the automatic recording equipment. For these reasons its operating characteristics are of utmost importance.

be desired. Moreover, it was not specific to tic movements alone. A more tic-specific operandum would be operated solely by tic movements. Improved specificity of tic measurement without restrictions on motility might be obtained by pickups placed at the loci of various tics which would be telemetered by transmitters worn on the patient's belt or in a pocket (Hefferline, 1962). The patient could then engage in routine daily activities while effects of interest are continuously recorded.

Once the operandum requirements have been refined, therapeutic effects can be more reliably evaluated. The use of tic-contingent interruption of music could be extended in time or otherwise modified. For example, the duration of the tic-free interval necessary to produce music could be progressively lengthened. With remote recording, the long term effects of an appropriate contingency arrangement could be evaluated by furnishing the patient with a portable contingency controller to plug into his home radio or television set for relief of his symptom. The contingencies for music and noise, already demonstrated to be effective, could be combined in a multiple contingency whereby each tic would bring 1.5 seconds of noise and pauses greater than 1.5 seconds would bring music, until the next tic impulse simultaneously interrupted the music and restored the white noise.

The observed behavior changes offered as possible explanations for differential tic rates recorded under self-control could be objectively measured to evaluate the interaction between symptomatic and non-symptomatic responses. For example, if operanda had been provided for simultaneously recording the patient's finger-tapping and singing, it might have been possible to show an inverse relationship between the rate of vocalizing and finger-drumming and the tic rate. In addition, experiments could be run to deter-

mine whether tic movements may be diminished or even eliminated by differentially reinforcing another more circumscribed and more socially acceptable motor response which serves the same discharge function as tics.

A free operant conditioning analogy to the negative practice technique used by Yates (1960) could be readily investigated by positively reinforcing the patient for each tic. If this variation of the method is therapeutic, positive reinforcement of the symptom should be followed by reduction in the operant tic rate.

The general aspects of the pickup and continuous recording system described here provide a method for direct and objective behavioral measurement of motor symptom frequency which would be useful in studying the effects of drugs, the influence of attention, and variations in tic rate during diagnostic or therapeutic interviews.

SUMMARY

A method for continuous automatic recording of the rate of multiple tics has been used in a demonstration of differential control of tic rate by free operant conditioning procedures.

The results showed that the multiple tics of a neurological patient, previously refractory to pharmacological and psychological therapies, could be reduced in rate by self-control, by tic-produced white noise, and by continuous music. The most dramatic, rapid, and reliable reduction resulted from tic-produced interruption of music. The power of tic-contingent environmental consequences in controlling this patient's symptom was shown, and suggestions were offered for extending and refining the basic method for more definitive investigations of this and other motor disturbances.

Treatment of persistent enuresis with the electric buzzer

IAN G. WICKES

The treatment of enuresis has largely defeated physicians in the past. Some have readily acknowledged this and have pinned their faith on the child growing out of it. Others have used numerous drugs with varying success; since there is a tendency towards spontaneous improvement, and since inert pills are partly effective by suggestion, it has been difficult to assess what specific effect, if any, a particular drug possesses. Psychiatrists have tended to attribute the disorder to infantile regression and have sought, by child guidance techniques, to readjust the child's interpersonal relationships; they have turned a blind eye to the symptom itself, a wise move since it so seldom disappears with such therapy. Nevertheless there is a widespread belief that enuresis is purely psychogenic, a belief which is illustrated by a common mis-spelling 'eneuresis' —as if the condition were a neurosis. Undoubtedly nervous factors influence enuresis (as with epilepsy and asthma) but it is equally true that the cure of bedwetting will often greatly improve the child's emotional state, indicating that the anxiety is secondary, in part at least.

The treatment of enuresis was revolutionized when it was discovered by chance that an apparatus for signalling to the parents that their child had a wet bed and needed changing also had the property of training the child to become dry. Pfaundler (1904) used a quilted pad for the purpose, Mowrer (1938) improved the apparatus by including a relay, and Seiger (1946) first described a metal and rubber pad that could be dried. Subsequently Davidson and Douglass (1950) reported 20 cases in deprived children with 15 cures; Seiger (1952) reported a series of 106 cases, 94 becoming dry for two months or longer, in the majority of cases after less than one month's treatment. Geppert (1953) reported a series of 42 cases with 38 successes using a similar method. Crosby (1950) used the conditioning method but instead of a bell or buzzer he used electrodes attached to the genitalia and loin so that at the start of micturition 'a stimulus,

capable of variation to any devised intensity, is applied to the patient'. His results were successful in 52 out of 58 cases.

In view of the intractable nature of enuresis the above results seem almost too good to be true. It is certainly surprising that the medical profession has not adopted the method to any extent in Great Britain, but commercial firms have exploited the treatment on a large scale offering it direct to the public without the supervision of a physician. Only one small series (in deprived children) has been reported and occasional letters (Gillison, 1956) have appeared in the medical press supporting the method. In some quarters there is considerable resistance to it as evidenced by the reply in the *British Medical Journal* (1957) in which the writer, after describing many largely ineffective and blunderbuss remedies, goes on to refer to the conditioning method as 'rather a crude type of therapy'! Since ignorance and prejudice envelop the subject it seemed desirable to collect a series of persistent intractable enuretics to observe how they responded to this form of treatment.

THE APPARATUS AND ITS USE

One of the reasons why this treatment has not been popular amongst doctors is because of the lack of availability of sets. For some years one firm has been hiring sets for a sum which far exceeds that which the average hospital patient can afford. Recently another manufacturer has begun to produce one which sells at less than half that sum. I have been fortunate in that the father of a former patient has been producing efficient sets which have been sold at less than one-fifth the cost of hiring. Furthermore, through the generosity of the Chamberlain Foundation, I have been able to lend a similar set free of charge to those parents who were unable to buy one.

From *Archives of Disease in Childhood*, 1958, **33**, 160–164.

The apparatus consists of an alarm unit containing a buzzer, light, relay and 6-volt battery together with two flexible leads that can be clipped on to two fine metallic rectangular gauze mats about 16 x 20 in. The mats are best secured on the bed by slipping each into a pocket obtained by sewing a pillowcase to a drawsheet along its three closed sides to make a double open-ended pocket. The child, preferably devoid of pyjama trousers, lies above the linen sandwich containing the mats. The alarm unit stands on a table or chair close to the bed and is switched on at bed time. The alarm is actuated when the circuit is completed by urine that has soaked through the layers to reach the lower of the two mats. Occasionally a 'dry ring' is obtained if the mats inadvertently touch (frayed ends of wire may traverse the intervening material) or if the patient sweats profusely. Conversely, the alarm may fail to sound if a clip becomes dislodged by a restless sleeper. Normally, however, a teaspoonful of urine will suffice to start the buzzer and this, by awakening the child, will bring an end to micturition and will eventually, in favourable cases, prevent the act starting at all. The size of the wet patch indicates how quickly the child has awakened. In a typical response the size of the patches diminishes as the training takes effect but sometimes the child is such a heavy sleeper that all the patches remain large because he is not awakened by the buzzer (another member of the family may have to switch it off). In such cases a louder bell can be plugged into the set or dexamphetamine can be prescribed as well but these additional measures are seldom required. When the alarm sounds and the child awakens he is instructed to switch it off, get up and finish passing urine. In very bad cases it is desirable to re-set the apparatus using a dry drawsheet ensemble but in the majority one alarm per night is sufficient.

THE SERIES

In the past five years over 500 enuretic children have been referred to my out-patient clinics. Many of them have responded to simple forms of therapy and many others have recovered spontaneously but gradually a hard core of resistant cases accumulated. They were treated with the electric buzzer, the only criteria for selection being that they were old enough, sufficiently severe, and resistant to other forms of therapy. There were only nine omissions from a consecutive series of 109 cases selected for treatment and provided with an apparatus: in four the parents refused to report progress, in two the children (aged 10 and 12) refused to use the apparatus, in two the parents were too stupid to be able to work it and in one the boy stopped wetting before the set was put into use.

The series therefore consists of 100 persistently enuretic children consecutively supplied and treated with a conditioning apparatus. It is important to emphasize that inclusion was by enrolment rather than by completion of treatment. Since the successes are usually rapid, a better rate of cure could have been obtained by discarding those in whom the treatment is incomplete.

Age

There has been a tendency to provide older children with this treatment partly because they have usually resisted many others and partly because they are more likely to cooperate. A few young ones have been included, usually because they had inherited a set after an older sibling had completed treatment. In general, however, the use of an apparatus under the age of 7 has not been recommended and it will be seen from Table 1 that 74 fall within the 7–13 bracket, 14 being younger and 12 older than this group.

Sex

There is general agreement that males predominate in any series of enuretic children and this has been the case here. Only 19% were girls.

Onset

In the vast majority enuresis had been present since birth and the longest dry spells

Table 1. *Age at start of treatment and sex.*

Age in Years	Total	5 – 7	– 9	– 11	– 13	– 15	– 17	17+
Male	81	12	18	19	22	7	2	1
Female	19	2	4	8	3	2	–	–
Total	100	14	22	27	25	9	2	1

(if any) before treatment had seldom exceeded one week. In five cases enuresis had begun, after a long period of dryness, at the age of 4 years or older; in two others it had been very infrequent until the age of 5. Four mothers stated that there had been a dry spell at least six months long between the ages of 1 and 3 years—a difficult fact to explain. Two boys had been dry for four and five months respectively after treatment with a conditioning apparatus obtained elsewhere; they were therefore relapses but entered this series as new cases because their parents could not afford to hire a second apparatus.

Family History

For the purpose of this enquiry, enuresis was regarded as having been present if bed-wetting had occurred above the age of 5 years. A positive history in a close relative (parent or sibling) was obtained in 47 cases (one or both parents in 30, one or more siblings in 17, parent and sibling in ten). The history relating to enuresis in the patients' parents was not complete in 18 cases but in six a more distant blood relative had been affected. A negative history in near relatives was obtained in 35 cases with complete records but in 22 of these it was positive in more distant relatives (aunts, uncles and first cousins). These findings indicate that about 50% of cases have a positive family history and a further 30% have blood relatives affected by the disorder.

Intelligence

In this series the great majority were of average intelligence. Eight were above, nine were below and one was educationally subnormal.

Nervous State

Parents were asked if the child had any other nervous troubles. In 30 they were absent and in 70 they were present, being very severe in five. (In an unselected series of children starting school 50% were stated to be nervous, but this is a younger age group.)

Investigations

All the children were medically examined and their urine tested. Twenty-eight of the first 50 cases in the series and 17 of the second 50 had been fully investigated by means of micturating cysto-urethrograms, cysto-urethro-scopy, pyelography, etc. This falling off in zeal for investigation was due to a change of policy whereby latterly only failures were investigated. In two cases this was refused.

Previous Treatment

Almost every patient had failed to respond to weeks or months of drug therapy which had extended for over one year in 29 and was continuous for five years in one. Three were referred from child guidance clinics and one other had failed to respond to that kind of treatment. One successful case had previously attended a faith healer for many months. As already stated, two had relapsed following this form of therapy.

Table 2. *Early response correlated with severity of enuresis.*

Total No. Wet Nights During 3rd Month	Total	Severity of Enuresis Before Treatment (Approximate Proportion of Wet Nights)			Group	
		<50%	50% – 75%	75% – 100%	Charity	Private
Nil	44	5	15	24	25	19
1 – 3	10	2	1	7	6	4
4 – 6	14	2	3	9	10	4
7+	17	1	3	13	12	5
Abandoned	7	1	3	3	5	2
Not known	8	2	2	4	4	4
Total	100	13	27	60	62	38

Table 3. *Late results correlated with early response.*

Total No. Wet Nights During 3rd Month After Starting Treatment	Total	Final Assessment (4 mth. – 2 yr.)			
		Dry	Occasion-ally Wet	Improved	Failed
Nil	44	38	5	—	1
1 – 3	10	7	3	—	—
4 – 6	14	3	5	4	2
7+	17	1	1	3	12
Abandoned	7	—	—	—	7
Not known	8	1	1	2	4
Total	100	50	15	9	26

RESULTS

It soon became apparent that successful cases usually responded rapidly. This led us to use the total number of wet nights during the third month as a criterion of early response which subsequently proved to be a reliable index of the final outcome.

In Table 2 the early response is correlated with the frequency of wetting when treatment was first started. Infrequent wetting means that the training effect is seldom applied. Hence children who were wet appreciably less than 50% were not treated in this way and those in this group did rather less well than the average. In the worst group the results are also suboptimal because concealed within it were several children who were wet more than once each night and hence had further to go to become dry. The best results

were therefore obtained in the group with 50 to 75% wet nights at the outset, for 59% had fewer than four wet nights in the third month compared with 54% and 50% in the other two groups.

Also in Table 2 a distinction is made between those who bought an apparatus and those who borrowed one free of charge. The latter group included many with very low social standards which perhaps explains why they achieved less good results. Taking all the cases which were wet fewer than four times during the third month, there were 23 out of 38 (60%) who bought their own sets compared with 31 out of 62 (50%) who borrowed one.

In Table 3 the late results are correlated with early response. The successful 65 cases have been followed up for a period ranging from four months to well over one year; it exceeded six months in 43 cases of which 15 were followed up for more than one year.

Of the 50 cases finally classified as 'dry', 38 became completely dry before the third month of treatment began, whereas only one was ultimately cured when the number of wet nights in the third month exceeded seven.

In addition to the 50 dry cases, 15 children have been classed as 'occasionally wet'. They had on an average one or two wet nights per month after treatment was completed. As might be expected, the early response tended to be less rapid in this group.

The nine classified as 'improved' each showed a marked reduction in the amount of wetting but at the final assessment there was still appreciable wetting. Thus one child was wet 19 times during the first week of treatment but steadily improved so that in the 32nd week he was only wet twice.

Eighteen of the failures failed to respond appreciably. One responded at first but then relapsed and continued to wet frequently; he lived in a very poor home and had no bed of his own. To these failures must be added seven in whom the treatment was abandoned before the end of the third month, making a total of 26 failures.

Younger children did slightly better than older ones, the average age of the successful cases being 9 years compared with 11 years for the 26 failures.

There were too few children of below average intelligence from whom to draw definite conclusions but the impression has been gained that those with lower intelligence respond less rapidly.

Relapses

There were nine cases in which relapses requiring a refresher course occurred and eight responded rapidly and completely. One had been completely dry for nine months before relapsing. No doubt as further time passes other relapses will require treatment. In most cases the relapse was clearly related to an infection, fatigue or anxiety over examinations at school. Even some of the children classified as 'dry' experienced an isolated wet night in such circumstances but they were very rare.

PATTERN OF RESPONSE

The mechanism of the treatment is clearly one of training; in a favourable case the number of wet nights steadily diminishes and at the same time the size of the wet patch gets smaller indicating that the child is waking up more quickly. This is well illustrated by the following typical case history:

L.C., a boy aged 11 years, had never had a dry night all his life. He was of average intelligence, not nervous, a restless sleeper; his maternal grandmother, mother and brother had all been bedwetters. Drug therapy had not helped him. His response was as follows:

Weeks	Wet Nights	Size of Patch
1st	7 (twice one night)	3 large
2nd	4	All small
3rd	2	Both small
4th	1	Small

The set was then removed from his bed and he has been followed up for eight months but has never since been wet. Occasionally he has to get up in the night to pass urine.

Some children find that they have to get up at night in order to keep dry but as their confidence increases the necessity diminishes. If, however, they are ill or tired they may fail to do so and wet the bed. Forty-one successful cases replied to a questionnaire which revealed that 27 never got up in the night, eight occasionally did and six usually or always did. Some parents who were enuretic in childhood still had to get up to micturate each night indicating that nocturnal frequency persisted.

FAILURES

It would be tedious to give details of all the failures. Probably lack of cooperation is the commonest cause; thus of the eight in whom no detailed reports for the first three months were available, four were failures. Parents were usually to blame and in a few cases treatment was started in hospital in an effort to avoid this. In one case treatment had to be abandoned because the county M.O.H. forbade us to treat him in the residential home where he lived because a psychiatrist advised against this form of therapy and recommended an alarm clock instead! One juvenile delinquent was responding well in hospital but absconded before treatment was completed because he learned that he was wanted by the police. Two mothers were definitely psychotic. Very heavy sleepers were not awakened but this was sometimes overcome by administering dexamphetamine for a time as well. In one case this failed and so did vibrators attached to his forehead; perhaps an electric shock would have roused him but it was not considered justifiable. Some were awakened but failed to be trained so that the number of wet nights did not diminish though the bed was less soaking. In three cases an initial response was followed by a return to the original frequency suggesting an active resistance to the treatment, probably emotionally determined. We aimed at keeping the child on the set until four consecutive dry weeks had been achieved but one educationally subnormal girl aged 13 refused to use it for more than one week and a boy complained that the neighbours heard the buzzer and he resented the publicity that this entailed.

CONCLUSION

The fact that a favourable response was rapidly obtained in 65 out of 100 severe enuretics speaks for itself. The marked improvement in the mental outlook of these cases was most gratifying. Several parents reported that their children were happier and more confident now that their enuresis had been eliminated. It is clear that a great deal of the associated anxiety was secondary to the enuresis and disappeared with it. There can be no doubt that psychological aetiological factors have been greatly exaggerated in this disorder, though they certainly play a part in aggravating it. Probably they are of the same degree of importance in enuresis as in asthma, migraine and epilepsy, disorders, incidentally, with which it is frequently associated. In my opinion it is fully justifiable and very rewarding to tackle the symptom directly by the conditioning method, a triumph for therapeutic behaviourism.

SUMMARY

One hundred intractable severe persistent enuretics have been treated by the conditioning method.

There were 81 boys and 19 girls aged 5–17 years.

Fifty responded rapidly and completely, 15 dried up almost completely, nine improved markedly but slowly and 26 were failures.

The pattern of response and the reasons for failure are described.

A positive family history was obtained in 47 and more distant relatives were enuretic in a further 28 cases but the records were not all complete.

Successful cases frequently showed definite improvement emotionally. The importance of psychological factors in causing enuresis of this type has been greatly exaggerated.

Relapses were mainly provoked by infections, sometimes by fatigue and anxiety.

Geriatric behavioral prosthetics

Human behavior is a functional relationship between a person and a specific social or mechanical environment. If the behavior is deficient, we can alter either the individual or the environment in order to produce effective behavior. Most previous attempts to restore behavioral efficiency by retraining, punish-

From R. Kastenbaum (Ed.), *New Thoughts on Old Age.* New York: Springer Publishing Company, Inc., 1964. Pp. 41–60.

ment, or physiological treatment have focused on only one side of this relation, the deficient individual. This approach implies that normal individuals can function in all currently existing social environments, that deficient individuals can be normalized, and that there are ordinarily no deficient environments. Scientists have only recently directly focused on the environmental side of deficient behavior functions and on the design of specialized or *prosthetic environments* to restore competent performance.

Prosthetic environments are not new, however. For centuries specialized environments have supported or reinforced the behavior of infants and children. Special foods, feeding devices, bedding, furniture, and clothing for infants are commonplace. Special entertainments — toys, primary colors, simple books, music, games — have been less clearly recognized in their behavioral role of reinforcers designed particularly for children. All of these are provided by society in expectation of the services the child will provide as an adult.

More recently, prosthetic environments have been extended to the physically handicapped. Blind persons use Braille books, noise-making canes, seeing-eye dogs, and specially designed houses. Paraplegic veterans of war have specially designed homes provided by a grateful public for relatively brief service to society.

But what of the aged, veterans of an entire lifetime of social service? Are they provided with special environments designed to support their behavior at its maximum? Are we using their behavior most efficiently?

To prolong health, physicians offer aging persons a wide range of physiological prosthetics, from vitamins and hormones to increased oxygen utilization, for their internal environment. Beyond providing eyeglasses, hearing aids, dentures, cribs, and crutches, however, science has done little to modify the external mechanical and social environments of the aged. The skills of current behavioral science, and free-operant conditioning in particular, can provide more than compound lenses, audio amplifiers, and mechanical restraint and support. Behavioral engineers can design prosthetic environments to support the behavior of the aged as crutches support their weight.

In this chapter, I will offer suggestions, developed from the methods and discoveries of free-operant conditioning, for developing geriatric prosthetic environments.[1]

In *free-operant conditioning* the frequency of performance of an act is altered by locating and arranging suitable consequences (reinforcement). The person being conditioned is at all times free to make the response and receive the arranged consequences, or to make other responses. By isolating the individual within an appropriate enclosure, the behavior specialist can empirically — rather than merely statistically — control all environmental events which can affect the behavior he is studying. The behavioral response and any environmental manipulations whose effects on the response are being studied can be automatically and continuously recorded. This environmental control and automatic, continuous recording mark the method as a laboratory natural science, comparable to modern chemistry, physics, and biology.

Free-operant methods are suited to behavioral geriatrics for several reasons.[2] Concentrating on *motivational aspects*, or consequences, of behavior, free-operant conditioning alters the *immediate environment* to generate and maintain behavior. The sensitivity of the methods to subtle changes in such aspects of the person's performance as response rate, efficiency, and perseverance makes these methods appropriate to the study of *single individuals*. Because the sensitivity does not decrease with very long periods of application with the same individual, reliable *longitudinal studies* are possible. Free-operant conditioning methods for the analysis of functional and dynamic relationships between individuals and both their *social and nonsocial environments* can produce separate measures of mechanical dexterity, intellectual functioning, and social adjustment.

---

1 Suggestions for designing prosthetic environments for the behavior of retarded persons have also been made recently (Lindsley, 1963b).

2 These reasons also make free-operant methods especially appropriate to a wide range of clinical behavioral problems. For a discussion of applications of the method to psychotherapy see Lindsley (1963c).

Free-operant principles and techniques may provide behavioral geriatrics with 1) a fresh theoretical approach; 2) laboratory description, prognosis, and evaluation; 3) design of prosthetic environments; and 4) individualized prosthetic prescriptions. Although I know of no free-operant experiments on the aged, and research in our laboratory with senile psychotics has not been extensive, preliminary suggestions can be well supported by the results of extensive experiments on the behavior of psychotic, neurotic, and mentally retarded individuals, whose behavioral deficits are usually as debilitating and challenging as those of aged persons.[3]

A FRESH THEORETICAL APPROACH

Free-operant conditioning principles can provide a highly relevant approach for increasing the efficiency of ward management and patient care routines. In this new approach, ward attendants do not perform custodial tasks. They are instead trained to act as behavioral engineers in arranging appropriate behavioral programs and reinforcements, so that the patients themselves maintain their ward and their persons.[4] Most important in this application of free-operant methods are 1) precise behavioral description; 2) functional definition of stimulus, response, and reinforcement; and 3) attention to behavioral processes.

Precise behavioral description facilitates communication between behavioral engineer and ward supervisor. It not only focuses attention on the actual behavioral movement which is occurring at either too high or too low a rate, but also permits observing and counting the response and directly reinforcing it with suitable consequences.

Functional definition of stimulus, response, and reinforcement focuses the attention of the nurse or attendant on the relationship between the behavior she is attempting to manage and her management procedures. When she realizes that an event may be a stimulus for one patient but not for another, and that a second event may be reinforcing to one patient but punishing to still another, then she recognizes the full complexity of human behavior and in

behavioral management no longer makes errors based upon misplaced empathy and generalization. For example, the socially deprived patients found in large hospitals may be rewarded by any attention from the nurse, even scolding for misbehavior. Consequently, a patient will continue to do the thing for which he was scolded in attempts to obtain the social contacts from the nurse, even though the nurse designed the topography of these contacts as punishment for what the patient was doing.

Attention to the behavioral processes of positive reinforcement, extinction, satiation, and mild punishment has proven extremely useful in engineering a ward for maximal behavioral accomplishment. Ayllon and Michael (1959[5]) successfully trained ward nurses to increase patients' self feeding by talking to patients only when they fed themselves. Ayllon (1963[6]) also trained nurses to satiate a towel hoarder by filling her room with towels, and to punish the wearing of extra clothing by letting a patient eat only when she was below a certain weight with her clothes on.

Important for generating maximal behavior on a geriatric ward is the early establishment of a conditioned general reinforcer, or token, which must be used to purchase all items and opportunities of importance and reinforcing value to the patients. The ward tokens are used by the attendants and the nurses to reinforce appropriate behavior. The patients can then use the tokens to purchase personal articles, cigarettes, afternoon naps, television and record playing time, talks with chaplains and volunteers, and all other events of value and importance to them. The patients will readily perform custodial duties on their ward in

---

3 For an excellent review of these experiments see Rachman (1962).

4 Research scientists suggesting new approaches for managing patients often overlook the crucial administrative problem of recruiting and training personnel. It is a good idea, but if it works who will put it into practice? An excellent source of behavioral engineers who could train and supervise attendants and nurses in these new prosthetic procedures would be Special Educators. Their current training, motivation, and philosophy are ideal for operant prosthetic methods. A few graduate courses and some ward experience under the supervision of an expert should make Special Educators into excellent Prosthetic Behavioral Engineers.

5 Pages 177−187 of this volume.

6 Pages 170−176 of this volume.

order to earn the tokens. Ayllon has successfully used tokens in this way in managing a ward of chronic psychotic patients.[7]

High on the list of types of behavior that it is desirable to generate in a geriatric patient are very mild physical exercise and sunbathing. The patient is immediately reinforced with a token for each exercise period and for small daily gains in his exercise achievement. Such exercise, shaped very gradually and watched carefully by the ward physician, can do much to restore physical health and well-being to a geriatric patient.

LABORATORY DESCRIPTION, PROGNOSIS, AND EVALUATION

Free-operant conditioning methods can be used to develop a behavior research laboratory for the accurate measurement and description of behavior deficits found in the aged. Inglis (1962) has found that psychometric tests are almost useless in these applications and recommends that experimental methods be applied to geriatric problems.

Over the past 10 years, we have clearly demonstrated that a free-operant conditioning laboratory is useful in describing, prognosticating, and evaluating psychoses (Lindsley, 1960, 1962b). In brief, our laboratory consists of several small experimental rooms which provide controlled environments for automatically recording behavioral deficits. Patients are brought to the rooms by a technician and permitted to behave freely in them for a period of time long enough to determine accurately the presence and degree of certain behavioral deficits.

The rooms differ from one another only in the equipment necessary for measuring different behavioral deficits. One room, for example, may have a chair and a wall panel with a single knob on it. Pulling the knob is reinforced by the illumination of a television screen mounted in the panel. The rate at which a patient pulls the knob indicates the reinforcing power of the narrative material presented to him via the television system. The material televised can be standard commercial broadcasts, specialized programs recorded on audio-visual tape, or a family visitor seated in front of a closed-circuit television camera in another part of the laboratory. In this room, the differential reinforcing value of audio-visual narrative reinforcers can be objectively determined by the continuous, automatic, cumulative records of knob-pulling. Similar rooms have been developed for recording behaviors as disparate as hallucinating and pacing in chronic psychotics, social deficits, and a patient's interest in his psychotherapist or visitor (Cohen, 1962;[8] Lindsley, 1961c, 1962a, 1962b).

Fully automatic programming of stimuli and recording of responses insure completely objective measurement. Technicians who do not differentially involve themselves with the data handle the patients and equipment and therefore do not introduce complicating observer bias. Furthermore, longitudinal studies are not disrupted when technicians are changed. Because there is no observer bias, cross-hospital and cross-cultural comparisons can be made. Because a fully controlled environment and automatic recording dispense with observer ratings, longitudinal studies can be conducted without the loss of observer sensitivity which occurs with closely repeated ratings (Lindsley, 1956). With automatic programming and recording, verbal instructions can be used or not. This opportunity to dispense with verbal instructions permits analysis of their effects and consequently more specific behavioral analysis, as well as the study of nonverbal patients. Free-operant methods thus provide prognostic data and reliable, valid behavioral measures which can be included in case histories even more confidently than blood pressure and blood cell count, which usually involve observer bias.

Long-term laboratory measures of the type and degree of behavioral deficits of individual patients permit exact evaluation of the effects of therapeutic variables on each patient's behavior. The behavioral effects of medications, as well as the effects of such social variables as ward reassignments, home visits, and deaths in the family, can be readily determined.

---

7 T. Ayllon, personal communication.

8 Pages 98–103 of this volume.

Since records are available on each patient, objective, high quality behavioral research can be conducted by physicians in charge of medication by occasionally referring a patient to the behavior laboratory for a current evaluation. Therapeutic dosage can be accurately adjusted to the deficit and drug-response of each patient. Individualized behavioral treatment can then be conducted with the same precision with which individualized physiological treatment is now conducted in well-staffed general hospitals.

DESIGN OF PROSTHETIC ENVIRONMENTS

There is little hope of retarding the aging process at this time, but we can reduce its behavioral debilitation by designing environments which compensate for or support the specific behavioral deficits of each aged person.[9] Because we will not actually alter the deficits, but merely provide an environment in which the deficits are less debilitating, these environments cannot be considered purely therapeutic. Therapeutic environments generate some behavior which is maintained when the patient is returned to the normal or general social environment. Therapeutic environments are essentially training or retraining centers for the generation of behavioral skills which maintain themselves once the patient has left the therapeutic environment. Prosthetic environments, however, must operate continually in order to decrease the debilitation resulting from the behavioral deficit. Eyeglasses are prosthetic devices for deficient vision, hearing aids for deficient hearing, and crutches and wheel chairs for deficient locomotion.

To describe suggestions for geriatric prosthetic environments as accurately as possible, I will use the analytical categories of the laboratory behavioral scientist: 1) discriminative stimuli; 2) response devices; 3) reinforcers; and 4) reinforcement schedules. The number of different types of special stimuli and devices required for prosthesis in each of these categories must be determined by the analysis of each aged individual. The types of environmental alteration required to support aged behavior cannot be determined until the number, degree, and range of behavioral deficits are determined. It may be that a given prosthetic device can be used to prosthetize more than one type of behavioral deficit. Adequately detailed analysis may also show that a single behavioral deficit can be prosthetized by more than one device. In these cases, the most economic and most general devices would be selected first.

My suggestions for the design of specific prosthetic environments for aged individuals are certainly not exhaustive. They are only suggestions for the direction of future research, examples of the kinds of things we should try in searching for new prosthetic devices. The range of prosthetic devices is limited only by the creativity and ingenuity of the investigator and the time and funds at his disposal. His time and funds are, in turn, limited only by society's interest in providing devices for restoring effective behavior to its older citizens.

Geriatric Discriminative Stimuli

The environmental events which signal when a response is appropriate and when it should not be made are extremely important in controlling behavior. Traffic lights are a familiar example. These colored lights are useful discriminative stimuli to a person with normal color vision, much less useful to a color-blind person, and of no use to a totally blind person. The geriatric patient may well have behavioral deficits which, like blindness, limit the range of discriminative stimuli in the normal environment which can control his behavior. The full and exact nature of geriatric behavioral deficits has not yet been determined.

The *intensity and size of discriminative stimuli* for the aged have received some prosthetic

---

9 The American Psychiatric Association (1959) conducted a survey on the care of patients over 65 in public mental hospitals and gleaned the following suggestions for improving the design of geriatric facilities: tilted bathroom mirrors for wheelchair patients; better lighting with no glare; ramps and short stair risers; guardrails, hold-bars, and non-skid floors; draft-free radiant heat; higher chairs to eliminate stooping to sit; facilities for daytime naps; and work, recreational, and social activities geared to the physical abilities of the patients.

attention. Eyeglasses have been developed for amplifying and correcting visual responses. Hearing aids have been developed for amplifying sounds to serve as discriminative stimuli for people whose hearing is deficient. Touch, smell, and taste amplifiers have not yet been developed, probably because our basic knowledge of these senses is more limited.

Simple and dramatic patterns, long durations, and higher intensities of stimulation should be investigated, for we can increase the intensity of the environmental stimulus when prosthetic amplifiers are not available.[10] It is amazing, for example, that although we give children books with large type, we force elderly people with deficient vision to use heavy eyeglasses or hand magnifying lenses to read normal-size type. We might find that even with large type, certain aged persons with deficient vision develop headaches or become nervous while reading. If we provided Braille or "talking books" for these individuals, we might find an increase in their usefulness to us and to themselves.

Multiple sense displays should be investigated in attempts to design geriatric discriminative stimuli. While an older person might not respond appropriately to a loud sound alone or to a bright light alone, he might respond appropriately to a simultaneous combination of loud sound and bright light. A normal person under the high control of a small portion of his environment is much more likely to respond to a multiple sense display than to a single sense display in the rest of his environment. Similarly, an aged person with generally weakened attention might respond more appropriately to a multiple sense display.

Expanded auditory and visual narrative stimuli should also be investigated. Melrose (1962) has found that many aged persons who cannot understand normal speech can understand expanded speech. Expanded speech does not differ in intensity or tone from normal speech. It is just spread out more in time, being truly slower. Melrose's finding suggests that old people cannot integrate rapidly presented information. It is the frequency of the *words*, not the frequency of the sounds, which they cannot integrate. This suggests that the visual discriminative response to a pictorial drama might also be deficient when the drama is presented at the normal rate. By using videotape recording systems to expand visual materials, we might restore understanding of and interest in visual narration to many aged people. The possibility of using expanded auditory and visual materials as reinforcing stimuli is discussed below.

Response-controlled discriminative stimulation should be tried as a prosthetic device for geriatric patients who appear to have intermittent attention. If a patient is periodically unresponsive to stimulation, the stimuli which occur during these "dead" periods in his attention may as well not be presented. To him the world has missing portions, as if a normal person were watching a movie and periodically the projector lens was covered for brief periods of time while the narration continued. There would be many important portions of the movie narration to which he would have no opportunity to respond.

Response-controlled stimulation permits the narration to move along in time only when the patient is responding to it. If the patient does not respond to a given stimulus, the next stimulus is not presented. Rather, it is stored until the patient responds again. The stimulus can be stored either by stopping the tape or film or by running a small continuous loop in which the last narrative event responded to is repeated. When the patient becomes attentive again and the next response is made, the narration continues. With this technique, the "dead" portions in the patient's attention would merely increase the total presentation time without removing portions of the narration.

Response-controlled stimulation could, of course, be used for nonnarrative discriminative stimuli such as signal lights, as well as for more complicated and more socially relevant narrative forms of stimulation. Many other modifications of discriminative stimuli should be tried in attempts to prosthetize discrimination deficits in the aged. The examples given are merely suggestions of what can be done in this field.

---

10 I have been told that Lord Amulree of University College Hospital, London, arranged for stronger odors to be added to utility gas so that aged persons with decreased senses of smell would know when the gas heaters had blown out and would not be asphyxiated.

Geriatric Response Devices

The design of prosthetic response devices for geriatric patients is a wide-open field. Innumerable response force amplifiers are available for normal persons. Most hand tools, for example, amplify response force. Hammers increase the force of manual pounding by extending the leverage of the arm; wrenches, the force of finger grip. In a sense, most modern machinery is designed to increase the force or accuracy of normal human action.

Response force amplifiers should be provided for old people with extremely weak motor responses. Geriatric environments should contain a much wider range of response force amplifiers than the fully automated factory or fully electrified home. Why, for example, must the aged open their own doors in hospitals when supermarket and garage doors are opened electronically?

For elderly people with feeble voices, the force of speech could be amplified by throat microphones and transistorized amplifiers. Such a simple device might greatly facilitate communication between older persons.

Wide response topographies should be provided so that palsied movements and inaccurate placement of hands and fingers would not be disabling. An individual with extreme palsy, for example, could operate a telephone with push buttons, instead of the normal dial arrangement, if the buttons were far enough apart and required enough pressure so they could not be accidentally pushed by a shaking hand. The voice-operated telephones in the Bell system design will, of course, completely prosthetize dialing deficits.

The standard electrical typewriter, sensitive to the slightest touch, is an example of a device which maximizes the efficiency of a normal person for whom accuracy and placement are no problem, but which is probably the most poorly designed typewriter for operation by an older person. The older person would make many errors of placement, and in trembling would jam the sensitive machine by depressing two keys simultaneously.

Rate switches, which operate only when repeatedly pressed above a certain rate, would be useful in maintaining high constant attention from aged persons with intermittent or weak attention. Most complicated and dangerous manufacturing machinery previously was operated by single-throw hand switches. The machine operated as long as the switch stayed in the "down" position. An inattentive operator could mash his fingers or cut off his arm. Stationary switches of this sort were found to be too dangerous even for normal individuals. They were replaced with spring-loaded switches which require continuous force in order for the machine to operate. Foot switches which must be continually depressed by the operator have greatly reduced industrial accidents, because when the operator turns away or leaves the machine, he takes his foot off the control switch and the machine stops.

An even higher degree of attention could be demanded by using a switch which had to be pressed repeatedly at a high rate in order for the machine to operate. A high rate of pressing demands closer attention than does continual depression of a switch. Impulse shorteners in the circuits of operant conditioning response levers are used for this purpose. Remember that a sleeping, dozing, or even dead person could operate a spring-loaded switch and its connected machinery by the weight of his inactive body. A switch that must be continually pressed should reduce the accident hazards of machine operation for many older persons with mild attention disorders. When their attention drifted so that they failed to press the switch at the required rate, the machine would automatically stop.

Response feedback systems should be developed so that response location errors can be corrected before they actually occur. For example, if an older person could not always control his fingers, he could be prevented from pushing a wrong button or placing his finger at the edge of a saw by a loud tone which sounded whenever his finger was moving away from the appropriate response location. Such response feedback systems could greatly compensate for a reduced kinesthetic ability. In effect, they would substitute for the deficient afferent input from the aged limbs which once guided the hands so accurately.

If a little time, money, and thought were applied to the problem, I am sure that a wide range of imaginative and successful devices could be developed for helping aged persons overcome their fairly obvious response deficits.

Geriatric Reinforcers

The generally low interest or motivation of the aged is very familiar. The elderly person appears capable of behaving but has lost his "will to live." We assume that he is able to respond, because on occasional brief instants he "lights up" and behaves appropriately. Rather than interpreting brief periods of appropriate behavior as normal episodes or phases in the aging process, we usually attribute them to special circumstances which temporarily increase motivation.

In precise behavioral terms, this means either that the reinforcers currently programmed in his immediate environment are no longer adequate or that the old person has simply lost the ability to be reinforced. The difference is of great importance and should be tested experimentally by attempting to reinforce his behavior with a wide range of events.

Individualized historical reinforcers. We should look closely at a geriatric patient's rare moments of high behavioral rate. Is some unusual, more appropriate reinforcer operating —something from the past—an old song, an old food, an old friend? If parts of such individualized historical reinforcers were recorded and presented on audio tape or closed-circuit television, an old person might perform regularly at high rates to hear and see them.

Expanded narrative reinforcers. Melrose's recent research (1962) suggests another possibility. If an aged person can comprehend expanded speech but not speech presented at a normal rate, he might be reinforced by expanded music and narrative themes, when the same themes presented at the normal rates would not be reinforcing. In seeking more adequate reinforcers for aged persons, we should explore music, movies, and video tapes expanded in both the audio and visual dimensions; for example, video tapes could be used to expand visits from family and friends.

Casual observation of music preferences of different generations supports this notion. Today's oldster, who prefers the waltz, did the turkey trot as a youth. Today's middle-ager prefers ballads and ballroom tempos, but did the Charleston or big-apple in high school and college. Today's teenage twister may also be waltzing a few decades from now. The perennial reinforcing value of the waltz to older persons may be due to their need for a slower, more expanded auditory reinforcer. Conversely, the high interest of youngsters in the chipmunk-singing, sound effects records suggests that very young children might be more reinforced by compressed music presented at extremely high rates.

If appropriate historical or expanded reinforcers could be located for each àged individual, newer and more generally available events might even be conditioned to the idiosyncratic reinforcers—that is, the adequate but idiosyncratic reinforcers might be used to develop or restore value to the general conditioned reinforcers currently used in society. By gradual shaping and conditioning, an old person could be given a new interest in contemporary life.

Long-range personal reinforcers, such as education, development of a skill, or the building of a reputation, would have little value for an old person. Each step in the development of skill or reputation would have little conditioned reinforcement value, since it would merely be a step on a stairway which an old person could hardly hope to scale completely. He might reasonably ask, "Build a skill for what? To die tomorrow?"

A child is almost completely under the control of the immediate environment because he has not yet acquired long-range personal reinforcers. An old person may be solely at the mercy of the immediate environment, not only because of severe recent memory loss, but because long-range personal reinforcers are made impotent by brief and uncertain life expectancy. This dependence of both old people and children on immediate personal reinforcers may be why aged persons are often described as "childish."

Long-range social reinforcers which would be of value to society no matter when the older person died might be more useful with the aged. The conditioned reinforcement would be the contribution to the next generation. However, the development of this type of reinforcer would be extremely complicated, would require the participation of the members of society at large, and would still have to be conditioned to immediate personal reinforcers.

Extremely powerful, immediate personal reinforcers might be located. We should try highly compelling expanded musical and visual narrations, exciting foods, costly and beautiful clothing, and so forth. Reinforcers of this nature are costly, but they might generate such high rates of behavior in aged persons that their high dollar cost would be compensated by savings in medical care and ward management.

Geriatric Reinforcement Schedules

In most social situations, reinforcement occurs intermittently (Ferster, 1958b). Not all responses are immediately reinforced; only a small portion are followed by a reinforcing episode. Nevertheless, in normal individuals, responding continues at high, predictable rates which are presumably maintained by conditioned reinforcement from the occasionally reinforced responses. In our long-term experiments with psychotic children and adults, however, we have found many patients who are unable to maintain high rates of responding on intermittent schedules of reinforcement, even when adequate reinforcers are used (Lindsley, 1960). These deficits in responding for intermittent reinforcement are probably attributable to deficits in recent memory and in formation of conditioned reinforcement.

It is very possible that many geriatric patients will also prove unable to maintain high rates of responding on intermittent schedules and will have to be kept on regular reinforcement contingencies in which every response is immediately followed with a reinforcing episode. Other patients may have to be reinforced on conjugate programs in which the intensity of a continuously available reinforcer is a direct function of the response rate. Conjugate reinforcement permits the use of narrative social reinforcers and appears to go deeper into sleep, anesthesia, infancy, and psychosis than

does episodic reinforcement (Lindsley, 1957, 1961a; Lindsley, et al., 1961). Conjugate reinforcement may also go deeper into aging and generate behavior in geriatric patients who would not behave on any episodic schedule of reinforcement.

INDIVIDUALIZED PROSTHETIC PRESCRIPTIONS

If a geriatric hospital were equipped with a behavior laboratory, each aged patient could visit the laboratory upon admission. His specific behavioral deficits would be measured, and prosthetic stimuli, responses, reinforcers, and reinforcement schedules prescribed. The laboratory would determine the patient's current learning ability and assess the extent to which his current behavioral repertoire could be used in place of newly acquired responses.[11]

In our own laboratory, we found that 90% of our involutional psychotics, 85% of our chronic psychotics, and only 65% of our retarded children had deficits in acquiring new discriminations and differentiations (Barrett and Lindsley, 1962; Lindsley, 1958).[12] The severe deficits in current learning ability in involutional and chronic psychotic patients were surprising, since many of these patients had large repertoires of complex behavior which they could emit at a moment's notice. Laboratory measurements proved, however, that their current learning abilities in a novel situation were extremely deficient. These patients had apparently acquired their complicated behavioral repertoires prior to developing their severe learning deficits.

Clearly, the fact that a complicated response can be emitted appropriately is no indication that a new response of equal complexity can be acquired. Retarded children with learning deficits since birth have had no opportunity to acquire complicated repertoires. Therefore, since they never exhibit complex behaviors,

---

11 Barrett (1963) has recently stressed the need for individualized prosthetic prescriptions based upon laboratory behavioral measurement for use in designing and selecting different programs of instruction for retarded children.

12 For a conclusive review of the experimental literature on learning deficits in elderly patients, see Inglis (1958).

casual observation of their behavior is not as misleading in predicting current learning ability as it is with psychotics or the aged. Furthermore, some involutional psychotics are very skillful at "covering up" their severe current learning deficits. In brain damaged patients, less skillful attempts at "covering up" are well known.

These data suggest that we may find severe current learning deficits more frequent among older people than in retarded individuals. These data also suggest that current learning deficits will be very difficult to ascertain by sampling current behavioral repertoires or by ward observations. Moreover, with geriatric patients we should expect general reinforcers to be less adequate because of the historical aging of appropriate reinforcers and because of the need for reinforcer expansion.

There is little doubt that each aged individual can and should have his current behavioral abilities and deficits measured in the laboratory so that an individualized prosthetic environment could be prescribed to support his particular behavioral deficits. Possibly, the patient could be assigned to a ward specializing in patients with similar, but not necessarily the same, patterns of behavioral deficits. On the other hand, we may find wards that are more efficiently designed to cover a wide range of deficits. On these vertically organized wards, the more skillful patients could act as leaders and programmers for their more deficient peers. In hospitals with a vertical ward design, patients with similar deficits could be assigned similar roles about the hospital, but on different wards.

THEORIES OF AGING

It is my opinion that theories of behavioral deviation in the grand or inclusive sense are academic luxuries unless they help us prevent or reduce the behavior pathology, or make it less debilitating. Nevertheless, there are people who insist that theories are not only useful but necessary. To validate their own position, they attribute theories to those researchers who actively state that they have none. The important points seem to be how inclusive and general theories are, how strongly they are held, and whether they are descriptive or explanatory.

The developmental theory of aging presented by Kastenbaum (1964) is an explanatory theory. It attempts to explain how and why aging develops as a small part of a larger general process in the behavior of man. This general developmental process is assumed to be found in both the ontogenetic development of the infant and in perception. The same process is found reversed or in regression in the delusions of the psychotic and in the deterioration of the aged. In this sense, the inclusive property of this explanatory theory is historically related to the schools of philosophy which attempted to describe all things by the simplest possible set of laws or statements.

In contrast, I find the disengagement theory presented by Cumming (1964) more descriptive than explanatory. She describes the process of aging as disengagement with society and the dilemma of the aged whose behavior is no longer supported by society. In my terms, disengagement means mostly the abrupt cessation of reinforcement, or extinction.

My own approach to aging is even more finely descriptive than Cumming's disengagement theory and might be described as a descriptive multiple cause-deficit-repair theory of aging. In other words, the aged person has an accumulation of behavioral deficits in all areas, each patient with his own pattern of multiple deficits. In physiological deterioration of the aged, there is rarely a single cause of organic debility, although one specific debility may be more outstanding at a given moment in time than the others. Similarly, we may locate syndromes or patterns of specific behavioral deficits which later will be related to deterioration of specific behavioral function, and most older people have suffered so many traumas, periods of disease, abuse, and poor environments, that most will have several measurable deficits in differing degrees, and each specific deficit will undoubtedly have multiple causes.

Also, as with organic illness, there undoubtedly is more than one way of treating a specific behavioral deficit. Therefore, we face not only multiple causation and multiple deficit, but multiple treatment, in both organic and behavioral medicine. In general, we now use the term *old age* whenever performance becomes less efficient without any known disruptive factor other than time and practice.

When specific geriatric behavioral deficits have been accurately measured and prosthetized, a fuller experimental analysis may permit the development of explanatory theories of specific deficit syndromes. Involved in the development of these explanatory or etiologic theories will be the experimental induction or catalysis of geriatric deficits and symptoms. I know of only one experiment of this sort which has been conducted to date. Cameron (1941) placed senile patients in dark rooms and was able to catalyze or induce senile nocturnal delirium. This experiment showed that senile nocturnal delirium was not due to fatigue at the end of the day as had been previously supposed, but was due to the darkness which also came at the end of the day. Further research in which the environmental variables which precipitate and control geriatric behavioral deficits are isolated will do much to produce useful explanatory sub-theories of aging.

CONTINUITY OF AGING

Even though the severe deficits characteristic of aging do not show up until very late in life, the process of aging might develop much earlier. The behavioral debilities produced by this continuous process of aging may not appear because there are ample devices available for middle-aged persons to use in prosthetizing their milder behavioral deficits. For example, our recent memory may become poorer either because our ability to remember simply decreases with age or because our storage system becomes filled or overloaded. The older we become, however, the more we use prosthetic devices such as notebooks, address books, the telephone information operator, and mnemonic devices. The young executive relies on his accurate recent memory, but the older and still highly productive executive relies heavily on his young secretary. It may be that it is only when he loses his secretary that he loses his "recent memory."

In other words, the age at which we see marked, severe behavioral deficits in older persons may only be the point at which appropriate prosthetic devices are no longer available. In this sense, forced retirement or "disengagement" may not only deprive a man of necessary reinforcement, but rob him of his prosthetic devices at the time they are most needed. A justification of retirement by comparing his productive efficiency before and after retirement would therefore erroneously self-validate itself unless reinforcement and prosthetic devices were equated in each condition.

SOCIAL NEGLECT OF THE AGED

The problem of the aged has only recently become a major one. This is not only because more people are living to an older age because of the marked success of organic medicine, but because our more urban and complicated society provides situations in which the deficits of the aged are more debilitating. The increased complexity of the behavioral tasks required of modern society members is displacing not only the less skillful aged, but also the less skillful middle-aged person.

Since our aged citizens are less able to produce in this more complicated society, they have fewer reinforcers for the rest of society and will suffer greater social neglect. They have nothing with which to reinforce social attention from either their peers or the rest of society.

Even patients with organic illnesses may have social responses with which to reinforce their attendants, nurses, physicians, and family visitors. The plucky words and weak smile of the organically ill patient are extremely strong reinforcement to a nurse or visitor.

An infant has little behavior with which to acquire reinforcing objects to distribute among his family, but people are so constituted that the gurgle, smile, and primitive movements of an infant are strong social reinforcers for adults. The infant also promises genetic and cultural immortality to the adults who contribute to his genetic constitution or cultural education and training. These genetic and cultural immortality factors are also strong social reinforcers.

The retarded individual, although he has little future and does not promise much genetic or cultural immortality, has much behavior which is very similar to the infant's and therefore provides society with social reinforcers to satisfy what might be called "maternal instinct." The smile or caress of a retarded child is a strong social reinforcer for those who attend him or visit him. This is probably why the retarded have always been fairly well treated by society and considered the "children of God" or the "holy innocents."

The psychotic, of course, has fared less well. And this may be because his behavior is not only less rewarding to normal adults, but in many cases is socially aversive. It is a strong attendant who can withstand the verbal onslaught of a sensitive paranoid who criticizes and verbally attacks the attendant's weakest spot. This aversive behavior of the psychotic, coupled with his inability to be a productive member of society, may be why the psychotic has been for centuries maligned, rejected, and considered "possessed by the devil." Family visits to chronic psychotics are much less frequent than visits to the mentally retarded. It is much more difficult to maintain volunteer groups to assist in the care of psychotics than it is to maintain those to care for the retarded. And again, among a group of chronic psychotics it is the laughing, joking, pleasant patient—the classic hebephrenic—who receives the most attention on the ward and is the most welcome at hospital parties and home visits.

And so with the aged, the patient with laugh wrinkles, a full head of white hair, and clean white dentures receives more attention and is more reinforcing to attendants and family than the tragic oldster with a scowl, vertical worry wrinkles, a toothless smile, and skin lesions. The aged person whose countenance and behavior present aversive stimuli to other individuals is bound to be avoided and neglected. When he also has behavioral deficiencies, so that he no longer can produce in society or reinforce us with pleasant conversation, he becomes extremely aversive and subject to severe social neglect.

A realistic approach to the social neglect of the psychotic and the aged would accept the fact that they are just too aversive for us to expect highly motivated social response to them from normal middle-aged individuals. Rather than spend a great deal of time and money trying to talk people into overcoming this aversion in charitable attempts to help the psychotic and aged, it may be more economical to remove the source of aversion.

Psychotic and aged patients could be made much less aversive by cosmetic attention. Also, if prosthetic devices were developed which would permit them to communicate with normal people and produce positive, though limited, products for the use of society, they would become much more reinforcing to normal individuals and suffer much less neglect. By permanently removing the aversive causes of social neglect, this approach would be more lasting than the current attempts to reduce social neglect by repeated compensatory verbal appeals and the generation of guilt in others.

CONCLUSION

Since 1953, more than 100 applications of free-operant methods to human behavioral pathology have been published. Continuing, systematic investigations are being conducted in psychoses, mental retardation, neurological disorders, and neurosis. These experiments have demonstrated that free-operant principles and methods have wide applicability in social and behavioral research.

The method shows promise for analyzing and prosthetizing geriatric behavioral deficits. The time and money spent in developing behavioral prosthetics should be more than compensated by reduced management costs as more aged patients are made capable of caring for themselves and their peers. A properly engineered geriatric hospital maximally utilizing the behavior of the patients, should require little more than supervisory non-geriatric labor.

At this time, no systematic applications of operant methods to geriatric behavior have been made. However, the method is ready and the hour is late. Organic medicine has shown great progress in keeping our bodies alive well past the point where behavioral medicine is able to keep our bodies behaving appropriately.

7

MODIFICATION
OF SEVERE BEHAVIOR DISORDERS

The term "psychotic" has been applied to individuals whose behavior severely departs from conventional forms. The bizarre nature of the behaviors involved presents one of the most dramatic and potentially one of the most rewarding areas of challenge to the ingenuity and skills of the behavioral technician or engineer. The present section includes several attempts to manipulate directly some of the more extreme forms of inappropriate behavior. As will be seen, such efforts have already involved manipulation of behaviors usually regarded as symptomatic of a deep, underlying disorder. The ease with which this manipulation is accomplished should bring into serious question the entire notion that behavior is merely a symptom or expression of a disorder occurring at a different level.

Like the investigations included in section 6, the work presented in this section does not rely on assumptions or speculations as to the ultimate or original causes of the maladaptive behavior. Such causes are as difficult to determine with any assurance as they are to manipulate effectively. Rather than attributing behavior to some unknown or underlying cause, or to a diagnostic category, the major attempt has been to secure effective control of the variables which are actually maintaining the behavior. However, the fact that direct changes in behavior do result from specific alteration of the environment lends strong encouragement to those who would see similar processes involved in the generation of the original deficit.

Ayllon's work with psychotic patients illustrates several techniques, among them two instances of the use of access to food as a reinforcer. In one instance the withdrawal of food is used to eliminate stealing of food, and in the other access to food is employed to increase the patient's tendency to remove excess clothing. Since the emotional component of many psychotic conditions is commonly emphasized, it is interesting to note the apparently uncomplicated alteration of specifically "emotional" behaviors incident to the major behavioral changes.

The concept "behavioral engineer," as the term is used by Ayllon and Michael, has arisen from the effectiveness of these new techniques. While their article illustrates a variety of behavioral engineering techniques as applied by hospital nursing personnel to a variety of disorders, it also points up the effects on behavior of the more commonplace aspects of the patient's environment, such as the social attention of nurses and aides. Whatever the merit of the doctrine of tender loving care, human sympathy and concern may obviously be directed toward better ends than creating and maintaining many of the very behaviors which lead to continued incarceration in a mental institution.

A question which frequently arises is whether or not behavior generated in a laboratory or institutional setting will be maintained when the patient returns to the "outside world." Since, in most cases, it was the noninstitutional environment which provided the conditions leading to the production of the undesirable behavior, exposure to these same conditions will most likely reinstate this behavior. Thus, the environment to which the patient will return must be reformed if the behavioral change is to survive beyond the setting in which the newer behavioral repertoire has been established.

Some of the principles which determine whether or not a particular behavior will survive in new situations are considered in the article by Isaacs, Thomas and Goldiamond. The two cases reported differ in the degree to which the newly reinstated verbal behavior of the patients generalized to conditions outside the therapeutic situation. The difference allows the authors to contrast the two instances in terms of the stimulus conditions surrounding the therapy given in each case and to emphasize the importance of the setting under which behavioral changes are initiated and maintained.

The use of individuals to provide a connecting link between the original and the new setting is shown in the work of Wolf, Risley and Mees. Since the conditions necessary to maintain a child's newly acquired behaviors must ultimately involve the parents, the parents are brought into the institution to insure that the child's new behavior will occur and be reinforced in their presence, as well as in the presence of the ward attendants and therapists. This practice not only allows the child to, in effect, take a part of the institutional environment home with him, but also makes the parents available for training in the techniques which will maintain the child's adaptive behaviors.

Most of all, the articles in this section present explicit techniques whose effectiveness can be measured objectively. Too often, in the past, therapy has proceeded toward ill-defined goals by using vaguely stated techniques. This practice allows for no real criteria of effectiveness. On the other hand, a technology which deals explicitly with behavior, because it specifies its goals and procedures exactly, has the self-corrective features usually associated with physical science. Since behavioral change can be measured objectively, the procedures can be continually adjusted until the desired change in behavior actually occurs. These advantages should, at last, enable therapists to build up an easily transmitted, thoroughly tested body of techniques for the treatment of severe behavioral disorders.

Intensive treatment of psychotic behaviour by stimulus satiation and food reinforcement

TEODORO AYLLON

INTRODUCTION

Until recently, the effective control of behaviour was limited to the animal laboratory. The extension of this control to human behaviour was made when Lindsley successfully adapted the methodology of operant conditioning to the study of psychotic behaviour (Lindsley, 1956). Following Lindsley's point of departure other investigators have shown that, in its essentials, the behaviour of mentally defective individuals (Orlando and Bijou,

From *Behaviour Research and Therapy*, 1963, 1, 53−61.

1960), stutterers (Flanagan, Goldiamond, and Azrin, 1958), mental patients (Hutchinson and Azrin, 1961), autistic (Ferster and DeMyer, 1961), and normal children (Bijou, 1961; Azrin and Lindsley, 1956) is subject to the same controls.

Despite the obvious implications of this research for applied settings there has been a conspicuous lag between the research findings and their application. The greatest limitation to the direct application of laboratory principles has been the absence of control over the subjects' environment. Recently, however, a series of applications in a regulated psychiatric setting has clearly demonstrated the possibilities of behavioural modification (Ayllon and Michael, 1959;[1] Ayllon and Haughton, 1962). Some of the behaviour studied has included repetitive and highly stereotyped responses such as complaining, pacing, refusal to eat, hoarding and many others.

What follows is a demonstration of behaviour techniques for the intensive individual treatment of psychotic behaviour. Specific pathological behaviour patterns of a single patient were treated by manipulating the patient's environment.

The Experimental Ward and Control over the Reinforcement

This investigation was conducted in a mental hospital ward, the characteristics of which have been described elsewhere (Ayllon and Haughton, 1962). Briefly, this was a female ward to which only authorized personnel were allowed access. The ward staff was made up of psychiatric nurses and untrained aides who carried out the environmental manipulations under the direction of the experimenter. Using a time-sample technique, patients were observed daily every 30 minutes from 7.00 a.m. to 11.00 p.m.

The dining room was the only place where food was available and entrance to the dining room could be regulated. Water was freely available at a drinking fountain on the ward. None of the patients had ground passes or jobs outside the ward.

Subject

The patient was a 47-year-old female patient diagnosed as a chronic schizophrenic. The patient had been hospitalized for 9 years. Upon studying the patient's behaviour on the ward, it became apparent that the nursing staff[2] spent considerable time caring for her. In particular, there were three aspects of her behaviour which seemed to defy solution. The first was stealing food. The second was the hoarding of the ward's towels in her room. The third undesirable aspect of her behaviour consisted in her wearing excessive clothing, e.g. a half-dozen dresses, several pairs of stockings, sweaters, and so on.

In order to modify the patient's behaviour systematically, each of these three types of behaviour (stealing food, hoarding, and excessive dressing) was treated separately.

EXPERIMENT I

Control of Stealing Food by Food Withdrawal

The patient had weighed over 250 pounds for many years. She ate the usual tray of food served to all patients, but, in addition, she stole food from the food counter and from other patients. Because the medical staff regarded her excessive weight as detrimental to her health, a special diet had been prescribed for her. However, the patient refused to diet and continued stealing food. In an effort to discourage the patient from stealing, the ward nurses had spent considerable time trying to persuade her to stop stealing food. As a last resort, the nurses would force her to return the stolen food.

To determine the extent of food stealing, nurses were instructed to record all behaviour associated with eating in the dining room. This record, taken for nearly a month, showed that the patient stole food during two thirds of all meals.

---

1 Pages 177–187 of this volume.
2 As used in this paper, 'nurse' is a generic term including all those who actually work on the ward (attendants, aides, psychiatric and registered nurses).

Procedure

The traditional methods previously used to stop the patient from stealing food were discontinued. No longer were persuasion, coaxing, or coercion used.

The patient was assigned to a table in the dining room, and no other patients were allowed to sit with her. Nurses removed the patient from the dining room when she approached a table other than her own, or when she picked up unauthorized food from the dining room counter. In effect, this procedure resulted in the patient missing a meal whenever she attempted to steal food.

Results

Figure 1 shows that when withdrawal of positive reinforcement (i.e. meal) was made dependent upon the patient's 'stealing', this response was eliminated in two weeks. Because the patient no longer stole food, she ate only the diet prescribed for her. The effective control of the stealing response is also indicated by the gradual reduction in the patient's body weight. At no time during the patient's 9 years of hospitalization had she weighed less than 230 pounds. At the conclusion of this treatment her weight stabilized at 180 pounds or 17 per cent loss from her original weight. At this time, the patient's physical condition was regarded as excellent.

Discussion

A principle used in the laboratory shows that the strength of a response may be weakened by the removal of positive reinforcement following the response (Ferster, 1958a). In this case, the response was food-stealing and the reinforcer was access to meals. When the patient stole food she was removed from the dining room and missed her meal.

After one year of this treatment, two occasions of food stealing occurred. The first occasion, occurring after one year of not stealing food, took the nurses by surprise and, therefore the patient 'got away' with it. The second occasion occurred shortly thereafter. This time, however, the controlling consequences were in force. The patient missed that meal and did not steal again to the conclusion of this investigation.

Because the patient was not informed or warned of the consequences that followed stealing, the nurses regarded the procedure as unlikely to have much effect on the patient's behaviour. The implicit belief that verbal instructions are indispensable for learning is part of present day psychiatric lore. In keeping with this notion, prior to this behaviour treatment, the nurses had tried to persuade the patient to co-operate in dieting. Because there were strong medical reasons for her losing weight, the patient's refusal to follow a prescribed diet was regarded as further evidence of her mental illness.

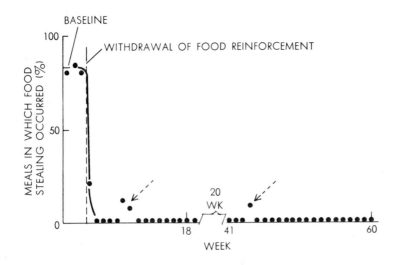

Figure 1. A response, food stealing, is eliminated when it results in the withdrawal of food reinforcement. The dotted arrows indicate the rare occasions when food stealing occurred. For purposes of presentation a segment comprising 20 weeks during which no stealing occurred is not included.

Control of One Form of Hoarding Behaviour Through Stimulus Satiation

During the 9 years of hospitalization, the patient collected large numbers of towels and stored them in her room. Although many efforts had been made to discourage hoarding, this behaviour continued unaltered. The only recourse for the nursing staff was to take away the patient's towels about twice a week.

To determine the degree of hoarding behaviour, the towels in her room were counted three times a week, when the patient was not in her room. This count showed that the number of towels kept in her room ranged from 19 to 29 despite the fact that during this time the nurses continued recovering their towel supply from the patient's room.

Procedure

The routine removal of the towels from the patient's room was discontinued. Instead, a programme of stimulus satiation was carried out by the nurses. Intermittently, throughout the day, the nurses took a towel to the patient when she was in her room and simply handed it to her without any comment. The first week she was given an average of 7 towels daily, and by the third week this number was increased to 60.

Results

The technique of satiation eliminated the towel hoarding. Figure 2 shows the mean number of towels per count found in the patient's room. When the number of towels kept in her room reached the 625 mark, she started taking a few of them out. Thereafter, no more towels were given to her. During the next 12 months the mean number of towels found in her room was 1.5 per week.

Discussion

The procedure used to reduce the amount of towel hoarding bears resemblance to satiation of a reinforcer. A reinforcer loses its effect when an excessive amount of that reinforcer is made available. Accordingly, the response maintained by that reinforcer is weakened. In this application, the towels constituted the reinforcing stimuli. When the number of towels in her room reached 625, continuing to give her towels seemed to make their collection aversive. The patient then proceeded to rid herself of the towels until she had virtually none.

During the first few weeks of satiation, the patient was observed patting her cheeks with a few towels, apparently enjoying them. Later, the patient was observed spending much of her time folding and stacking the approximately 600 towels in her room. A variety of remarks were made by the patient regarding receipt of towels. All verbal statements made by the patient were recorded by the nurse. The following represent typical remarks made

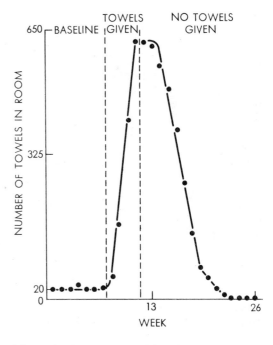

Figure 2. A response, towel hoarding, is eliminated when the patient is given towels in excess. When the number of towels reaches 625 the patient starts to discard them. She continues to do so until the number found in her room averages 1.5 compared to the previous 20 towels per week.

during this experiment. First week: As the nurse entered the patient's room carrying a towel, the patient would smile and say, "Oh, you found it for me, thank you". Second week: When the number of towels given to patient increased rapidly, she told the nurses, "Don't give me no more towels. I've got enough". Third week: "Take them towels away. . . . I can't sit here all night and fold towels". Fourth and fifth weeks: "Get these dirty towels out of here". Sixth week: After she had started taking the towels out of her room, she remarked to the nurse, "I can't drag any more of these towels, I just can't do it".

The quality of these remarks suggests that the initial effect of giving towels to the patient was reinforcing. However as the towels increased they ceased to be reinforcing, and presumably became aversive.

The ward nurses, who had undergone a three year training in psychiatric nursing, found it difficult to reconcile the procedure in this experiment with their psychiatric orientation. Most nurses subscribed to the popular psychiatric view which regards hoarding behaviour as a reflection of a deep 'need' for love and security. Presumably, no 'real' behavioural change was possible without meeting the patient's 'needs' first. Even after the patient discontinued hoarding towels in her room, some nurses predicted that the change would not last and that worse behaviour would replace it. Using a time-sampling technique the patient was under continuous observation for over a year after the termination of the satiation programme. Not once during this period did the patient return to hoarding towels. Furthermore, no other behaviour problem replaced hoarding.

EXPERIMENT III

Control of an Additional Form of Hoarding Through Food Reinforcement

Shortly after the patient had been admitted to the hospital she wore an excessive amount of clothing which included several sweaters, shawls, dresses, undergarments and stockings. The clothing also included sheets and towels wrapped around her body, and a turban-like head-dress made up of several towels. In addition, the patient carried two to three cups on one hand while holding a bundle of miscellaneous clothing, and a large purse on the other.

To determine the amount of clothing worn by the patient, she was weighed before each meal over a period of two weeks. By subtracting her actual body weight from that recorded when she was dressed, the weight of her clothing was obtained.

Procedure

The response required for reinforcement was stepping on a scale and meeting a predetermined weight. The requirement for reinforcement consisted of meeting a single weight (i.e. her body weight plus a specified number of pounds of clothing). Initially she was given an allowance of 23 pounds over her current body weight. This allowance represented a 2 pound reduction from her usual clothing weight. When the patient exceeded the weight requirement, the nurse stated in a matter-of-fact manner, "Sorry, you weigh too much, you'll have to weigh less". Failure to meet the required weight resulted in the patient missing the meal at which she was being weighed. Sometimes, in an effort to meet the requirement, the patient discarded more clothing than she was required. When this occurred the requirement was adjusted at the next weighing-time to correspond to the limit set by the patient on the preceding occasion.

Results

When food reinforcement is made dependent upon the removal of superfluous clothing the response increases in frequency. Figure 3 shows that the patient gradually shed her clothing to meet the more demanding weight requirement until she dressed normally. At the conclusion of this experiment her clothes weighed 3 pounds compared to the 25 pounds she wore before this treatment.

Some verbal shaping was done in order to encourage the patient to leave the cups and bundles she carried with her. Nurses stopped her at the dining room and said, "Sorry, no things are allowed in the dining room". No mention of clothing or specific items was made to avoid focusing undue attention upon them. Within a week, the patient typically stepped on the scale without her bundle and assorted objects. When her weight was over the limit, the patient was informed that she weighed "too much". She then proceeded to take off a few clothes, stepped on the scale again, and upon meeting the weight requirement, gained access to the dining room.

Discussion

According to the principle of reinforcement a class of responses is strengthened when it is followed by reinforcement. A reinforcer is such when it results in a response increase. In this application the removal of excessive clothing constituted the response and the reinforcer was food (i.e. access to meals). When the patient met the weight requirement she was reinforced by being given access to meals.

At the start of this experiment, the patient missed a few meals because she failed to meet the weight requirement, but soon thereafter she gradually discarded her superfluous clothing. First, she left behind odd items she had carried in her arms, such as bundles, cups and handbags. Next she took off the elaborate headgear and assorted "capes" or shawls she had worn over her shoulders. Although she had worn 18 pairs of stockings at one time, she eventually shed these also.

During the initial part of this experiment, the patient showed some emotional behaviour, e.g. crying, shouting and throwing chairs around. Because nurses were instructed to "ignore" this emotional behaviour, the patient obtained no sympathy or attention from them. The withholding of social reinforcement for emotional behaviour quickly led to its elimination.

At the conclusion of this behaviour treatment, the patient typically stepped on the scale wearing a dress, undergarments, a pair of stockings and a pair of light shoes. One of the behavioural changes concomitant with the

current environmental manipulation was that as the patient began dressing normally she started to participate in small social events in the hospital. This was particularly new to the patient as she had previously remained seclusive spending most of the time in her room.

About this time the patient's parents came to visit her and insisted on taking her home for a visit. This was the first time during the patient's 9 years of hospitalization that her parents had asked to take her out. They remarked that previously they had not been interested in taking her out because the patient's excessive dressing in addition to her weight made her look like a "circus freak".

CONCLUSIONS

The research presented here was conducted under nearly ideal conditions. The variables

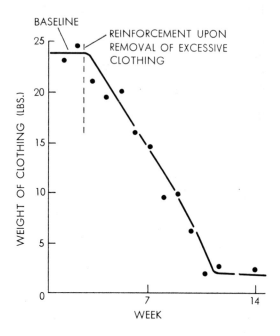

Figure 3. A response, excessive dressing, is eliminated when food reinforcement is made dependent upon removal of superfluous clothing. Once the weight of the clothing worn by the patient drops to 3 pounds it remains stable.

manipulated (i.e. towels and food) were under full experimental control. Using a time-sample technique the patient was observed daily every 30 minutes from 7.00 a.m. to 11.00 p.m. Nurses and aides carried out these observations which were later analysed in terms of gross behaviour categories. These observations were in force for over a year during which time these three experiments were conducted. The results of these observations indicate that none of the three pathological behaviour patterns (i.e. food stealing, hoarding and excessive dressing) exhibited by the patient were replaced by any undesirable behaviour.

The patient displayed some emotional behaviour in each experiment, but each time it subsided when social reinforcement (i.e. attention) was not forthcoming. The patient did not become violent or seclusive as a consequence of these experiments. Instead, she became socially more accessible to patients and staff. She did not achieve a great deal of social success but she did begin to participate actively in social functions.

A frequent problem encountered in mental hospitals is overeating. In general this problem is solved by prescribing a reduction diet. Many patients, however, refuse to take a reduction diet and continue overeating. When confronted with this behaviour, psychiatric workers generally resort to two types of explanations.

One explanation of overeating points out that only with the active and sincere co-operation of the patient can weight reduction be accomplished. When the patient refuses to co-operate he is regarded as showing more signs of mental illness and all hopes of eliminating overeating come to an end.

Another type of explanation holds that overeating is not the behaviour to be concerned with. Instead, attention is focused on the psychological 'needs' of the patient. These 'needs' are said to be the cause of the observable behaviour, overeating. Therefore the emphasis is on the removal of the cause and not on the symptom or behaviour itself. Whatever theoretical merit these explanations may have, it is unfortunate that they fail to suggest practical ways of treating the behaviour itself. As a consequence, the patient continues to overeat often to the detriment of his health.

The current psychiatric emphasis on the resolution of the mental conflict that is presumably at the basis of the symptoms, is perhaps misplaced. What seems to have been forgotten is that behaviour problems such as those reported here, prevent the patient from being considered for discharge not only by the hospital personnel but also by the patient's relatives. Indeed, as far as the patient's relatives are concerned, the index of improvement or deterioration is the readily observable behaviour and not a detailed account of the mechanics of the mental apparatus.

Many individuals are admitted to mental hospitals because of one or more specific behaviour difficulties and not always because of a generalized 'mental' disturbance. For example, an individual may go into a mental hospital because he has refused to eat for several days, or because he talks to himself incessantly. If the goal of therapy were behavioural rehabilitation, these problems would be treated and normal eating and normal talking reinstated. However, the current emphasis in psychotherapy is on 'mental-conflict resolution' and little or no attention is given to dealing directly with the behavioural problems which prevent the patient from returning to the community.

The psychiatric nurse as a behavioral engineer

TEODORO AYLLON AND JACK MICHAEL

The behavior which leads to a person's admission to a mental hospital often involves danger to himself or others, withdrawal from normal social functions, or a dramatic change from his usual mode of behaving. The professional staff of the psychiatric hospital directs its major efforts toward the discovery of the flaw in the patient's mental apparatus which presumably underlies his disturbing and dangerous behavior. Following the medical paradigm, it is presumed that once the basic disfunction has been properly identified the appropriate treatment will be undertaken and the various manifestations of the disfunction will disappear.

While diagnosis is being made and during subsequent treatment, the patient is under the daily care of the psychiatric nurses[1] in the ward. There, he often exhibits annoying and disrupting behavior which is usually regarded as a further manifestation of his basic difficulty. This behavior is sometimes identical with that which led to his admission; but at other times it seems to originate and develop within the hospital setting. Although it is still regarded as a reflection of his basic problem, this disruptive behavior may become so persistent that it engages the full energies of the nurses, and postpones, sometimes permanently, any effort on their part to deal with the so-called basic problem.

Disrupting behaviors usually consist in the patient's failure to engage in activities which are considered normal and necessary; or his persistent engagement in activities that are harmful to himself or other patients, or disrupting in other ways. For example, failures to eat, dress, bathe, interact socially with other patients, and walk without being led are invariably disruptive. Hoarding various objects, hitting, pinching, spitting on other patients, constant attention-seeking actions with respect to the nurses, upsetting chairs in the day-room, scraping paint from the walls, breaking windows, stuffing paper in the mouth and ears, walking on haunches or while in a squatting position are disruptive when they occur frequently and persistently.

At present, no systematic approach to such problems is available to the nurses. A psychodynamic interpretation is often given by psychiatrists and psychologists; and, for that matter, the nurses sometimes construct "depth" interpretations themselves. These interpretations seldom suggest any specific remedial actions to the nurses, who then have no other recourse than to act on the basis of common sense, or to take advantage of the physical therapy in vogue. From the point of view of modern behavior theory, such strong behaviors, or behavioral deficits, may be considered the result of events occurring in the patient's immediate or historical environment rather than the manifestations of his mental disorder. The present research represents an attempt to discover and manipulate some of these environmental variables for the purpose of modifying the problem behavior.

RESEARCH SETTING

The research was carried out at the Saskatchewan Hospital, Weyburn, Saskatchewan, Canada. It is a psychiatric hospital with approximately 1500 patients. Its most relevant features in terms of the present experiment are:

1. The nurses are trained as psychiatric nurses in a 3-year program.

2. They are responsible for the patients in their wards and enjoy a high degree of autonomy with respect to the treatment of a patient. The psychiatrists in the hospital function as advisers to the nursing staff. This means that psychiatrists do not give orders, but simply offer advice upon request from the psychiatric nurses.

3. The nurses administer incoming and outgoing mail for the patients, visitor traffic, ground passes, paroles, and even discharge,

From *Journal of the Experimental Analysis of Behavior*, 1959, **2**, 323–334.

1 As used in this paper, "psychiatric nurse" is a generic term including all those who actually work on the ward (aides, psychiatric nurses, and registered nurses).

although the last is often carried out after consultation with a psychiatrist. The nurses also conduct group therapy under the supervision of the psychiatric staff.

The official position of the senior author, hereafter referred to as E, was that of a clinical psychologist, who designed and supervised operant-conditioning "therapy" as applied by the nurses. Once his advice had been accepted, the nurses were responsible for carrying out the procedures specified by E. It was the privilege of the nurses to discontinue any treatment when they believed it was no longer necessary, when they were unable to implement it because of lack of staff, or when other ward difficulties made the treatment impossible. Whenever termination became necessary, E was given appropriate notice.

SUBJECTS

The subjects used in this investigation were all patients in the hospital. Of the total 19 patients, 14 had been classified as schizophrenic and 5 as mentally defective. Except for one female patient who was resident for only 7 months, all patients had been hospitalized for several years. Each subject presented a persistent behavior problem for which he had been referred to E by the nursing staff. None of the Ss was presently receiving psychotherapy, electroconvulsive therapy, or any kind of individual treatment.

The behaviors which were studied do not represent the most serious problems encountered in a typical psychiatric hospital. They were selected mainly because their persistence allowed them to survive several attempts at altering them.

PROCEDURE

Prior to a systematic observational study of the patient's behavior the nurses were asked about the kind and frequency of naturally occurring reinforcement obtained by the patient, the duration and frequency of the problem behavior, and the possibility of controlling the reinforcement. Next, a period of systematic observation of each patient was undertaken prior to treatment. This was done to obtain objective information on the frequency of the behavior that was a problem to the nurses, and to determine what other behaviors were emitted by the patient.

Depending on the type of behavior, two methods were used for recording it. If the behavior involved interaction with a nurse, it was recorded every time it occurred. Entering the nurses' office, and eating regular meals are examples of such behavior.

Behavior which did not naturally involve contact with the nurse was recorded by a time-sampling technique. The nurse who was in charge of the program was supplied with a mimeographed record form. She sought out the patient at regular intervals; and without interaction with him, she recorded the behavior taking place at that time. She did not actually describe the behavior occurring, but rather classified it in terms of a pre-established trichotomy: (a) the undesirable behavior; (b) incompatible behavior which could ultimately displace the undesirable behavior; and (c) incompatible behavior which was not considered shapeable, such as sleeping, eating, and dressing. (Although these latter acts are certainly susceptible to the influence of reinforcement, they were regarded as neutral behaviors in the present research.) The period of observation varied from 1 to 3 minutes. After making an observation, the nurse resumed her regular ward activities until the next interval was reached, whereupon she again sought out the patient. Except for one patient, who was observed every 15 minutes, such observations were made every 30 minutes.

The relevant aspect of the data obtained by the time-check recording is the proportion of the total number of observations (excluding observations of neutral behavior) during which the patient was engaging in the behavior being altered. This will be called the relative frequency of the behavior. As an example, on the first day of the program of extinction for psychotic talk in the case of Helen (see below), 17 nonneutral behaviors were recorded. Of these, nine were classed as psychotic talk and eight as sensible talk; the relative frequency of psychotic talk was 0.53.

Although it would have been desirable, a

long pretreatment period of observation was precluded by the newness of this approach and the necessity of obtaining the voluntary co-operation of the nurses.

After the pretreatment study had been completed, E instructed the ward nurses in the specific program that was to be carried out. In all cases the instruction was given at ward meetings and usually involved the cooperation of only two shifts, the 7 a.m. to 3 p.m., and 3 p.m. to 11 p.m., since the patients were usually asleep during the 11 p.m. to 7 a.m. shift.

The pretreatment studies indicated that what maintained undesirable behavior in most of the patients was the attention or social approval of the nurses toward that behavior. Therefore, the emphasis in instructing the nursing staff was on the operation of giving or withholding social reinforcement contingent upon a desired class of behavior. What follows illustrates the tenor of E's somewhat informal instructions to the nurses. "Reinforcement is something you do for or with a patient, for example, offering candy or a cigarette. Any way you convey attention to the patient is reinforcing. Patients may be reinforced if you answer their questions, talk to them, or let them know by your reaction that you are aware of their presence. The common-sense expression 'pay no attention' is perhaps closest to what must be done to discourage the patient's behavior. When we say 'do not reinforce a behavior,' we are actually saying 'ignore the behavior and act deaf and blind whenever it occurs.'"

When reinforcement was given on a fixed-interval basis, the nurse was instructed to observe the patient for about 1 to 3 minutes at regular intervals, just as in the pretreatment observation period. If desirable behavior was occurring at the time of observation, she would reinforce it; if not, she would go on about her duties and check again after the next interval had passed. Strictly speaking, this is fixed interval with a limited-hold contingency (Ferster and Skinner, 1957). During a program of extinction the nurse checked as above; however, instead of reinforcing the patient when he exhibited the behavior being altered, she simply recorded it and continued her other work. Except for specific directions for two patients, the nurses were not given instructions on the operation of aversive control.

The programs requiring time-sample observations started after breakfast (around 9 a.m.) and ended at bedtime (around 9 p.m.), and were usually carried out by only one of the 6 to 12 nurses on each shift. Because of the daily shift changes, the monthly ward rotations, and a systematic effort to give everyone experience at this new duty, no patient's program was followed by any one nurse for any considerable length of time. Nineteen, as a minimum, different nurses were involved in carrying out each patient's program. Over 100 different nurses participated in the entire research project.

Most social ward activities took place in the dayroom, which was a large living room containing a television set, card tables, magazines, and games. It was here that reinforcement was given for social behaviors toward patients, and for nonsocial behaviors which were strengthened to compete with undesirable behaviors. The fact that the research was carried out in five wards distributed far from each other in a four-floor building made it impossible for E to observe all the nurses involved in the research at any one time. Because of the constant change in nursing personnel, most of E's time was spent in instructing new people in the routines of the programs. In addition, since E did not train the nurses extensively, he observed them, often without their knowledge, and supervised them in record keeping, administering reinforcement, extinction, etc. That the nurses performed effectively when E was absent can be at least partially determined by the ultimate results.

RESULTS

The results will be summarized in terms of the type of behavior problem and the operations used in altering the behavior. In general, the time required to change a specific behavior ranged from 6 to 11 weeks. The operations were in force for 24 hours a day, 7 days a week.

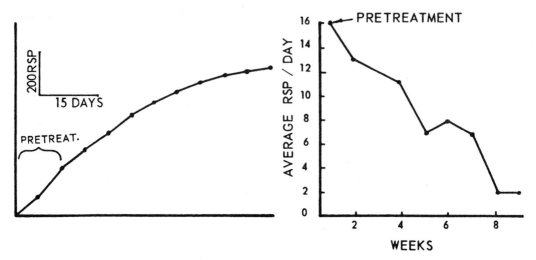

Figure 1. *Extinction of the response "entering the nurses' office"; a. cumulative record, b. conventional record.*

Strong Behavior Treated by Extinction, or Extinction Combined with Reinforcement for Incompatible Behavior

In the five cases treated with this program, the reinforcer was the attention of the nurses; and the withholding of this reinforcer resulted in the expected decline in frequency. The changes occurring in three of the behavior problems, scrubbing the floor, spending too much time in the bathroom, and one of the two cases of entering the nurses' offices, were not complicated by uncontrollable variables. Lucille's case is presented in detail as representative of these three. The interpretation of the changes occurring in the other two behavior problems, entering the nurses' offices, and psychotic verbal behavior, is not so clearcut. Helen's case illustrates this point. For details concerning the cases not discussed in this paper, see Ayllon (1959).

Lucille. Lucille's frequent visits to the nurses' office interrupted and interfered with their work. She had been doing this for 2 years. During this time, she had been told that she was not expected to spend her time in the nurses' office. Frequently, she was taken by the hand or pushed back bodily into the ward.

Because the patient was classified as mentally defective, the nurses had resigned themselves to tolerating her behavior. As one of the nurses put it, "It's difficult to tell her anything because she can't understand—she's too dumb."

The following instructions were given to the nurses: "During this program the patient must not be given reinforcement (attention) for entering the nurses' office. Tally every time she enters the office."

The pretreatment study indicated that she entered the office on an average of 16 times a day. As Figure 1b shows, the average frequency was down to two entries per day by the seventh week of extinction, and the program was terminated. Figure 1a shows the same data plotted cumulatively.

Helen. This patient's psychotic talk had persisted for at least 3 years. It had become so annoying during the last 4 months prior to treatment that other patients had on several occasions beaten her in an effort to keep her quiet. She was described by one of the psychiatrists as a "delusional" patient who "feels she must push her troubles onto somebody else, and by doing this she feels she is free." Her conversation centered around her illegitimate child and the men she claimed were constantly pursuing her. It was the nurses'

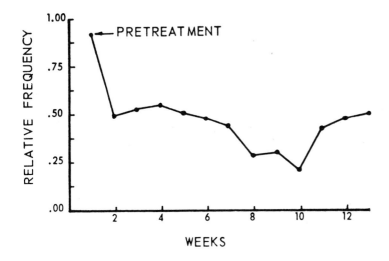

Figure 2. *Extinction of psychotic talk.*

impression that the patient had "nothing else to talk about."

A 5-day pretreatment observation of the patient was made at 30-minute intervals to compare the relative frequencies of psychotic and sensible content in her talk. Some of the nurses reported that, previously, when the patient started her psychotic talk, they listened to her in an effort to get at the "roots of her problem." A few nurses stated that they did not listen to what she was saying but simply nodded and remarked, "Yes, I understand," or some such comment, the purpose of which was to steer the patient's conversation onto some other topic. These reports suggested that the psychotic talk was being maintained by the nurses' reaction to it. While it is recognized that a distinction between psychotic and normal talk is somewhat arbitrary, this case was included in the research because of its value as a problem involving primarily verbal behavior.

The following instructions were given to the nurses: "During this program the patient must not be given reinforcement (attention) for her psychotic talk (about her illegitimate child and the men chasing her). Check the patient every 30 minutes, and (a) tally for psychotic talk; and (b) reinforce (and tally) sensible talk. If another patient fights with her, avoid making an issue of it. Simply stop the other patient from hurting her, but do so with a matter-of-fact attitude."

The 5-day observation period resulted in a relative frequency of psychotic talk of 0.91. During treatment (Figure 2), the relative frequency dropped to less than 0.25; but, later on, it rose to a value exceeded only by the pretreatment level. The sudden increase in the patient's psychotic talk in the ninth week probably occurred because the patient had been talking to a social worker, who, unknown to the nurses, had been reinforcing her psychotic talk. The reinforcement obtained from the social worker appeared to generalize to her interaction with other patients and nurses. The patient herself told one of the nurses, "Well you're not listening to me. I'll have to go and see Miss _____ (the social worker) again, 'cause she told me that if she would listen to my past she could help me."

In addition to the reinforcement attributable to the social worker, two other instances of bootleg reinforcement came to light. One instance occurred when a hospital employee came to visit the ward, and, another, when volunteer ladies came to entertain the patients. These occasions were impossible to control, and indicate some of the difficulties of long-term control over verbal behavior.

It is of interest to note that since the reinforcement program began, the patient has not been attacked by the other patients and is only rarely abused verbally. These improvements were commented upon by the nurses, who were nevertheless somewhat disappointed. On the basis of the improvement shown in verbal behavior, the nurses had expected a dramatic over-all change which did not occur.

Strong Behavior Treated by Strengthening Incompatible Behavior

This case represented an attempt to control violent behavior by strengthening an incompatible class of responses, and to recondition normal social approaches while the violence was under control. The first phase was quite successful; but errors in strategy plagued the last half of the program, and it was terminated by the nurses because the patient became more violent.

The immediate reason for referral was that the patient, Dotty, had become increasingly violent over the last 5 years, and recently attacked several patients and hospital personnel without any apparent reason. Since admission and up to the present, she had received many electroconvulsive-therapy treatments aimed at reducing this violence, with little or no success. In 1947, a physician recommended her as a good case for psychosurgery. In December of the same year, she attempted to strangle her mother who was visiting her at the time. In July 1948, the patient had a leucotomy. The situation had recently become so serious that at the least suspicious move on her part the nurses would put her in the seclusion room. She spent from 3 to 12 hours daily in that room.

A 5-day pretreatment study, at 15-minute intervals, indicated that one of the nonviolent behaviors exhibited fairly often was "being on the floor" in the dayroom. The response included lying, squatting, kneeling, and sitting on the floor. Strengthening this class of responses would control the violence and, at the same time, permit the emotional behavior of other patients and nurses toward her to extinguish. To strengthen the patient's own social behavior, her approaches to the nurses were to be reinforced. The response "approach to nurse" was defined as spontaneous requests, questions or comments made by the patient to the nurse. Ultimately, the plan was to discontinue reinforcing being on the floor once the patient-nurse social interaction appeared some-

what normal. Presumably, this would have further increased the probability of approach to the nurses.

For the duration of the program, continuous social reinforcement was to be available for her approach to the nurses. Social reinforcement was to be available for the first 4 weeks only, on a fixed interval of 15 minutes, contingent on the response being on the floor. For the last 4 weeks, social reinforcement was to be withheld for being on the floor.

The following instructions were given to the nurses for the first 4 weeks of the program: "Reinforce (and tally) her approaches to you every time they occur. Check the patient every 15 minutes, and reinforce (and tally) the behavior being on the floor."

From the fifth week on the instructions were modified as follows: "Continue reinforcing (and tallying) her approaches to you every time they occur. Check the patient every 15 minutes, and tally but do not reinforce the behavior being on the floor."

During the period of reinforcement, as shown in Figure 3, the relative frequency of the response being on the floor increased from the pretreatment level of less than 0.10 to a value of 0.21. During the succeeding 4 weeks of extinction, the frequency of being on the floor returned to the pretreatment level.

It was clear that being on the floor was incompatible with the fighting behavior and that the latter could be controlled by reinforcing the former. During the period of reinforcement for being on the floor, she attacked a patient once; but during the period of extinction, she made eight attacks on others. Her approaches to nurses increased over-all during the 4 weeks of reinforcement, but they decreased during the last 4 weeks, even though they were still being reinforced. This decrease paralleled the decrease in being on the floor. While being on the floor was undergoing extinction, attacks on the patients and nurses increased in frequency, and the nurses decided to return to the practice of restraining the patient. The program was terminated at this point.

The patient's failure to make the transition from being on the floor to approaching the nurses suggests that the latter response was poorly chosen. It was relatively incompatible with being on the floor. This meant that a previously reinforced response would have to be extinguished before the transition was possible, and this, too, was poor strategy with a violent patient.

Weak Behavior Strengthened by Escape and Avoidance Conditioning

Two female patients generally refused to eat unless aided by the nurses. One, Janet, had to be forcefully taken to the dining room, where she would permit the nurses to spoon-feed her. The other patient, Mary, was spoon-fed in a room adjacent to the dining room. Both patients had little social contact with others and were reported to be relatively indifferent to attention by the nurses. Both were also reported to care only for the neat and clean appearance of their clothing. Mary had been at the hospital for 7 months, and Janet had been there for 28 years. These two patients were in different wards and apparently did not know each other.

The program involved a combination of escape and avoidance conditioning, with food spilling as the aversive stimulus. All spoon-feeding was to be accompanied by some food spilling which the patient could escape by feeding herself after the first spilling, or avoid by

feeding herself the entire meal. Social reinforcement was to be given contingent on feeding herself.

It was hoped that once self-feeding began to occur with some regularity, it would come under the control of environmental variables which maintain this behavior in most people, such as convenience, social stimulation at meal time, etc. In both cases, the program ultimately resulted in complete self-feeding, which now has been maintained for over 10 months. Janet's behavior change was complicated by a history of religious fasting, and her change took a little longer. Mary's case will be given here in detail.

The following instructions were given to the nurses: "Continue spoonfeeding the patient; but from now on, do it in such a careless way that the patient will have a few drops of food fall on her dress. Be sure not to overdo the food dropping, since what we want to convey to the patient is that it is difficult to spoonfeed a grown-up person, and not that we are mean to her. What we expect is that the patient will find it difficult to depend on your skill to feed her. You will still be feeding her, but you will simply be less efficient in doing a good job of it. As the patient likes having her clothes clean, she will have to choose between feeding herself and keeping her clothes clean, or being

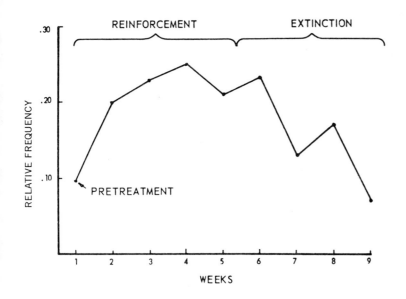

Figure 3. *Reinforcement and subsequent extinction of the response "being on the floor."*

fed by others and risking getting her clothes soiled. Whenever she eats on her own, be sure to stay with her for a while (3 minutes is enough), talking to her, or simply being seated with her. We do this to reinforce her eating on her own. In the experience of the patient, people become nicer when she eats on her own."

During the 8-day pretreatment study, the patient ate 5 meals on her own, was spoonfed 12, and refused to eat 7. Her weight at this time was 99 pounds. Her typical reaction to the schedule was as follows: the nurse would start spoonfeeding her; but after one or two "good" spoonfuls, the nurse would carelessly drop some food on her dress. This was continued until either the patient requested the spoon, or the nurse continued spoonfeeding her the entire meal. The behaviors the patient adopted included (a) reaching for the spoon after a few drops had fallen on her dress; (b) eating completely on her own; (c) closing her mouth so that spoonfeeding was terminated; or (d) being spoonfed the entire meal. Upon starting the schedule, the most frequent of all these alternatives was the first; but after a while, the patient ate on her own immediately. The relevant data are shown in Figure 4. On the 12th day, the patient ate all three meals on her own for the first time. Four meals were refused out of the last 24: one meal was missed because she stated she didn't like "liver" and the other

three because she said she was not hungry. Her weight when she left the hospital was 120 pounds, a gain of 21 pounds over her pretreatment weight.

Mary's relapse in the fifth week, after she had been eating well for 2 weeks, was quite unexpected. No reasonable explanation is suggested by a study of her daily records; but, after she had been spoonfed several meals in a row, the rumor developed that someone had informed the patient that the food spilling was not accidental. In any event, the failure to feed herself lasted only about 5 days.

Since the patient's hospital admission had been based on her refusal to eat, accompanied by statements that the food was poisoned, the success of the program led to her discharge. It is to be noted that although nothing was done to deal directly with her claims that the food was poisoned, these statements dropped out of her repertoire as she began to eat on her own.

Strong Behavior Weakened Through a Combination of Extinction for Social Attention and Stimulus Satiation

For 5 years, several mentally defective patients in the same ward, Harry, Joe, Tom, and Mac, had collected papers, rubbish, and magazines and carried these around with them inside their clothing next to their body. The

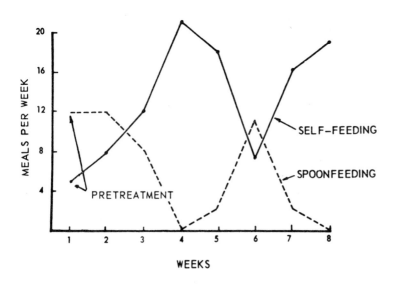

Figure 4. Escape and avoidance conditioning of self-feeding.

most serious offender was Harry, whose hoarding resulted in skin rashes. He carried so much trash and so persistently that for the last 5 years the nurses routinely "dejunked" him several times during the day and before he went to bed.

An analysis of the situation indicated that the patient's hoarding behavior was probably maintained by the attention he derived because of it and by the actual scarcity of printed matter. There were few papers or magazines in the ward. Some were brought in occasionally; but since they were often torn up and quickly disappeared, the nurses did not bring them in very often.

It was expected that flooding the ward with magazines would decrease the hoarding behavior after the paradigm of satiation. Similarly, the availability of many magazines was expected to result in their being the major object of hoarding. The latter would facilitate an easier measurement of this behavior.

In addition, social reinforcement was to be withheld for hoarding magazines and rubbish. The results for all patients were essentially similar: a gradual decrease in hoarding. After 9 weeks of satiation and extinction, the program was terminated, since hoarding was no longer a problem. This improvement has been maintained for the last 6 months.

The following instructions were given to the nurses: "During this program the patients Harry, Mac, Joe, and Tom must not be given reinforcement (attention) for hoarding. There will be a full supply of magazines in the dayroom. Every night, after all patients have gone to bed, replenish the magazine supply in the dayroom. Every night while the patients are in bed, check their clothes to record the amount of hoarding. Do not, however, take their hoarding from them."

The original plan was to count the number of magazines in the patients' clothing after they had gone to bed. This is, in fact, the dependent variable shown in Figure 5 for Joe, Tom, and Mac. The recording for Harry had to be changed, however; after 4 days of the program, he no longer carried the rubbish or magazines in his clothing. Instead, he kept a stack of magazines on his lap while he was sitting in the dayroom. The number of magazines in his stack was counted when he left the dayroom for supper, and this is the dependent variable shown for Harry in Figure 5. (Mac was out of the ward for 3 weeks because of illness.)

Prior to the program, one of the nurses questioned the possibility and even advisability of changing Harry's behavior. Her argument was that "behavior has its roots in the personality of the individual. The fact that he hoards so much indicates that Harry has a strong need for security. I don't see how we are going to

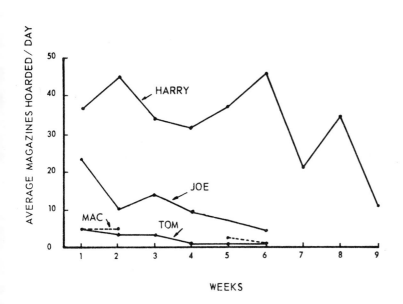

Figure 5. *Satiation and extinction of two forms of magazine hoarding.*

change this need, and I also wonder if it is a good thing to do that." This was a point of view commonly encountered, especially regarding relatively nonverbal patients.

It would seem in this case that Harry transferred his security needs from hoarding rubbish and magazines to sitting in the dayroom and looking at magazines, especially during T.V. commercials. The transfer occurred with no apparent signs of discomfort on his part.

Other Cases

Combinations of extinction, reinforcement, and avoidance programs were set up for three patients; in two of these the problem behavior was eliminated in only a few weeks. The program of the third patient was followed for 20 days and then terminated since he had shown no changes by that time. An interpretation of the outcome of each of these programs is rendered questionable by the number of controlling variables involved and the nature of the changes.

The pretreatment study of four additional patients showed that the problem behavior of three of them did not occur often enough to justify carrying through a program; and in the fourth case, no easily controllable variables were available and, again, no program was undertaken.

DISCUSSION

On the basis of this work, further research along the same lines is now under way (see Ayllon, 1963[2]). The present results are presented in this preliminary form in the hopes that they will provide encouragement to those who are in a position to conduct similar research. Therefore, it will be useful to mention a few other aspects of this work.

A major problem concerns the use of nurses as experimental assistants as well as substitutes for the recording and programming apparatus of the laboratory. There is no question as to the greater reliability of the ordinary laboratory component. In large part, however, the nurses' failures in carrying out E's instructions were unsystematic with respect to the results obtained, and although undesirable, they do not by any means render this kind of work uninterpretable. Systematic errors in observation can be reduced to some extent by dealing with response classes that are relatively easily identified. But, of course, this problem will become more serious as efforts are made to alter more subtle aspects of behavior. Perhaps the only solution is to be dissatisfied with one's techniques and principles until the behavioral changes are so obvious as to render statistical analysis superfluous.

Another question concerns the acceptability of this approach to the hospital staff. The nurses and psychiatrists who were familiar with the "reinforcement programs," as they were called, were given questionnaires and interviews to determine their attitudes toward this work. The results indicate a mildly favorable reception in general, with some enthusiastic support from both nurses and psychiatrists.

Regarding time actually spent in carrying out the programs, it might seem unreasonable to expect the already overworked nurse to devote 2 or 3 minutes every half-hour to observation and recording. However, this is only about 40 minutes of an 8-hour shift; and, besides, much of her work stems from patients' behavior problems, the elimination of which would make the 40 minutes an excellent investment of time.

Two sources of possible misunderstanding between E and nurses should be pointed out. First, when nurses were asked about the sort of problems they had in the ward, if no dramatic behaviors, such as attempts at suicide, or violent acts, had been recently reported, they often denied having any problems. Problems also went unrecognized because they were considered unsolvable. For example, since most nurses attributed the behavior of a patient to his diagnosis or age, little or no effort was made to discover and manipulate possibly relevant environmental variables.

Second, even after a behavior had been modified, it was not uncommon to hear nurses remark, "We've changed her behavior. So what? She's still psychotic." It seemed that once a persistent problem behavior was elimi-

---

2 Pages 170–176 of this volume.

nated, its previous importance was forgotten and other undesirable aspects of the patient's repertoire were assumed to be the most important ones. In general, their specific expectations were unclear or unverbalized, and they tended to be somewhat dissatisfied with any change less than total "cure."

Finally, an objection often raised against this approach is that the behavior changes may be only temporary. However, permanent elimi-nation of ward behavior problems requires a permanent elimination of the environmental variables that shape them up and maintain them. The clinical belief that a favorable behavioral change, if properly accomplished, will be permanent probably rests on a faulty evaluation of the role of environmental variables in controlling behavior. Certainly, it is not based on any actual accomplishments in the field of mental health.

Application of operant conditioning procedures to the behaviour problems of an autistic child

MONTROSE M. WOLF, TODD RISLEY, AND HAYDEN MEES

INTRODUCTION

During the past few decades an experimental analysis of behaviour has produced several powerful and reliable techniques for controlling behaviour (Holland and Skinner, 1961). Although these procedures were originally established with lower organisms, they are increasingly being applied in areas concerned with human behaviour (Ayllon and Michael, 1959;[1] Baer, 1962a;[2] Bijou, 1963; Ferster, 1961; Isaacs, Thomas, and Goldiamond, 1960;[3] Lindsley, 1962b; Williams, 1959; Zimmerman and Zimmerman, 1962[4]). Even so, techniques developed for dealing with specific human anomalies are limited.

This case study is an example of the application of behavioural principles to psychopathology. We developed techniques for dealing with the behaviour problems of a hospitalized pre-school autistic boy. Each of the techniques was derived from procedures developed and studied in experimental laboratories, such as handshaping, extinction, food deprivation, time-out from positive reinforcement, and discrimination training.

Dicky, the subject, was 3½ years old when the study began. He is the son of middle socio-economic class parents and has one younger and two older apparently normal female siblings.

From hospital records it appears that Dicky progressed normally till his ninth month, when cataracts were discovered in the lenses of both eyes. At this time severe temper tantrums and sleeping problems began to develop. During his second year he had a series of eye operations which culminated with the removal of his occluded lenses. This made wearing of glasses necessary. For more than a year his parents tried, and failed, to make Dicky wear glasses. During this time Dicky was seen by a variety of specialists who diagnosed him, variously, as mentally retarded, diffuse and locally brain-damaged, and psychotic, with the possibility of such additional anomalies as phenylpyruvic oligophenia and hyperthyroidism. One recommendation was that he be placed in an institution for the retarded since his prognosis was so poor.

Dicky did not eat normally and lacked normal social and verbal repertoires. His tantrums included self-destructive behaviours such as head-banging, face-slapping, hair-pulling and face-scratching. His mother reported that after a severe tantrum "he was a mess, all

From *Behaviour Research and Therapy*, 1964, 1, 305–312.
1 Pages 177–187 of this volume.
2 Pages 127–130 of this volume.
3 Pages 115–127 of this volume.
4 Pages 94–96 of this volume.

black and blue and bleeding." He would not sleep at night, forcing one or both parents to remain by his bed. Sedatives, tranquilizers, and restraints were tried, without success.

He was admitted to a children's mental hospital with the diagnosis of childhood schizophrenia at the age of three. After three months of hospitalization the terminal report stated that there was some improvement in his schizophrenic condition but no progress in the wearing of glasses. A few months later his ophthalmologist predicted that unless Dicky began wearing glasses within the next six months he would permanently lose his macular vision. At this point the authors were invited in as consultants by the hospital staff for the purpose of training Dicky to wear glasses.

After observing a 20 min interaction between Dicky and his mother, a period occupied by almost continuous tantrums, we recommended that he be readmitted to the hospital in order to separate him from his mother temporarily and to deal with his disruptive behaviours, while training him to wear glasses.

Our prescribed operations were carried out by the attendants and the parents both on the ward and in the home. In addition to general comments we carefully specified behaviours and environmental events to be recorded on Dicky's chart and in notes from the parents. As the specific events to be recorded were highly distinctive and co-operation by the attendants and parents was good, the data presented probably reflect actual events to a large but undetermined degree.

By manipulating the consequences of the behaviours, we concurrently developed techniques for dealing with Dicky's tantrums, sleeping and eating problems, for establishing the wearing of glasses, and appropriate verbal and social behaviour.

PROCEDURES, RESULTS AND DISCUSSION

Temper Tantrums

There is some evidence that temper tantrums will succumb to extinction (Williams, 1959). However, under ward conditions, with personnel untrained in these procedures, it was far

from certain that extinction would be reliably carried out. So the prescribed procedure was a combination of mild punishment and extinction. Dicky was placed in his room contingent upon each tantrum, the door remaining closed until the tantrum behaviour ceased. Each occurrence was to be noted on his chart.

Such a procedure, although initially involving social contacts and thus possible reinforcement at the onset of a tantrum, eliminated the possibility of continuous contact throughout the undesired behaviour. This procedure also provided for differential reinforcement of non-tantrum behaviour by the door being opened contingent upon such behaviour. Such a contingency, involving the removal of all social reinforcers for a period of time, resembles Ferster and Appel's (1961) use of a time-out from positive reinforcement as an aversive stimulus.

A cumulative record showing the frequency with which Dicky was placed in his room for tantrums and self-destructive behaviour is presented in the upper graph of Figure 1. The curve is, however, partially artifactual. The record shows a constant rate of being placed in his room for tantrums during the first four months, indicating a lack of change in behaviour during this period which was contradictory to casual observation.

Several variables, each involving a sacrifice of experimental rigor, contributed to this discrepancy:

(1) When Dicky was first admitted he whined, cried, slapped himself frequently. The attendant was therefore instructed to place him in his room only when he was engaging in two or more of these behaviours simultaneously. As Dicky's behaviour improved, the attendants lowered the original criterion finally to include any atavism. Since the authors believed this was to the distinct advantage of the child, the criterion change was encouraged.

(2) During the first few weeks the attendants' records contained reports of elaborate explanations offered Dicky as he was escorted to his room, and of tender, practically tearful apologies and fondling after the door was reopened. This pattern evolved to a perfunctory trip to the room with the door simply being reopened

at the end of the tantrum, presenting a ward going on much as before.

(3) By the beginning of the third month, tantrums lasting less than five minutes began to occur frequently, creating the likelihood that the trip to the room would become a socially reinforcing event. A minimum time of ten minutes in the room was therefore imposed.

(4) Dicky's contact with his family and home progressively increased during this time. The major changes are indicated in the tantrum curve.

At (a) Dicky's parents were permitted their first one-hour visit. Subsequently they made several scheduled visits a week, during which an attendant observed and instructed them in their handling of Dicky.

At (b) the father put Dicky to bed on the ward for the first time.

At (c) Dicky began wearing his glasses.
At (d) the mother put Dicky to bed on the ward for the first time.
Midway between (d) and (e) Dicky began short home visits accompanied by the attendant.
At (e) Dicky spent his first night at home.
At (f) Dicky spent a second night at home.
After (f) he spent an average of three nights a week at home, increasing to five nights a week during the final month.

Some estimate of the decreasing severity of the tantrums is indicated in the middle cumulative record of Figure 1. Each step represents a tantrum, either during the day or at bedtime, involving head-banging, hair-pulling, or face-scratching. Such severe self-destructive behaviour remained near zero after the first two and a half months. The remainder of the tantrum record consists of face-slapping, whining, and crying.

Conditions for handling tantrums at the home were made comparable to those on the ward. The attendants coached the parents to deal with Dicky's tantrums by putting him in his room both on the ward and at home. The descriptions of the parents' behaviour by the attendants and by the parents themselves indicated that this training was effective.

Bedtime Problems

The bedtime problem was handled in a manner similar to the tantrums. Dicky was bathed at a regular hour each night, cuddled for a short time, put to bed, and left with the door open. If he got up, he was told to go back to bed or the door would be closed. If he remained up, the door was closed. The door was reopened after a short time, or if a tantrum occurred, after it subsided. He was told again to get in his bed. If he stayed in bed the door was left open. Each door-closing at bedtime was recorded.

The lower graph in Figure 1 shows cumulative bedtime door-closings. The door was closed several times during the first five nights. The resulting tantrums were quite violent, one series totalling more than an hour. On the sixth night the attendant tucked Dicky in and said goodnight. Dicky remained in bed and

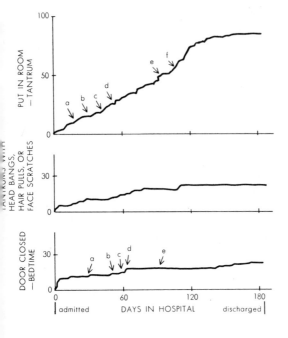

Figure 1. *Three cumulative records showing the effects of extinction and mild punishment (time-out from positive reinforcement) upon the tantrums, severe self-destructive episodes, and bedtime problems of a hospitalized pre-school autistic boy.*

soon went to sleep. Bedtime was seldom a problem again.

At (a) the father first put Dicky to bed on the ward.

At (b) the mother first put him to bed.

From (b) to (e) the parents put Dicky to bed once or twice a week.

At (c) and (d) the parents had to shut the door.

At (e) Dicky spent his first night at home. For a few weeks prior to this, he had been making short home visits accompanied by an attendant. Several days prior to (e) he was taken home in the evening, and after a few minutes of play, went through the routine of getting ready for bed with his siblings. The attendant then brought him back to the ward and put him to bed. Since this trial run was successful, he was sent home to spend the night several days later at (e). He was bathed and put in bed. After about thirty minutes he was heard humming to himself. The mother started to go in to Dicky but the attendant dissuaded her. Fifteen minutes later, Dicky was asleep.

Over the next three months, until his release from the hospital, Dicky spent a progressively greater proportion of his nights at home. One night a week an attendant went along to observe both Dicky and his parents.

The four times the door had to be shut after point (e) all occurred at home. These may have been the result of a certain amount of reshaping by the parents during a period when Dicky had chronic diarrhoea.

Wearing Glasses

Shaping (Skinner, 1953) was the basic procedure used to get Dicky to wear his glasses. Our shaper, an attendant, was instructed to spend two or three twenty-minute sessions each day, with the subject in the subject's room.

During the first several sessions a conditioned reinforcer was established by having the clicks of a toy noisemaker followed by Dicky's receiving small bites of candy or fruit. The click soon became a discriminative stimulus and after each click Dicky would go to the bowl where the reinforcers were placed.

Since Dicky had worn the prescription glasses for a few seconds on at least one occasion and had not left them on, it was assumed that wearing them was not immediately reinforcing. The glasses might even have been mildly aversive, since they would drastically change all visual stimuli, as well as force the eyes into greater accommodation. Also, glasses with the full prescription had been paired in the past with attempts to physically force glasses-wearing.

For these reasons we decided not to begin with the actual prescription glasses. Instead, several empty glasses frames were placed around the room and Dicky was reinforced for picking them up, holding them, and carrying them about. Slowly, by successive approximations, he was reinforced for bringing the frames closer to his eyes.

The original plan was, after he was wearing the lensless frames, to introduce plain glass and then prescription lenses in three steps of progressing severity. This was not the actual sequence of events, however, since our shaper met with considerable difficulty in getting Dicky to wear the glassless frames in the proper manner, i.e. with the ear pieces over instead of under the ears and the eye openings in line with the eyes. Furthermore, it was impossible to help place the frames correctly since Dicky became upset when anyone touched any part of his head.

The slow progress was probably attributable to two factors. First, the attendant, although co-operative, was inexperienced and imprecise with the shaping procedure. Secondly, due to the reluctance of the ward staff to deprive the child of food we began with reinforcers such as candy and fruit. It soon became obvious, however, that, at least for this child, these were rather weak reinforcers.

After the first two weeks we attempted to increase deprivational control by using breakfast as a shaping session, bites of breakfast now being dependent upon approximations to the wearing of glasses. Two weeks later we added to the glasses larger adult ear pieces and a "roll bar" which would go over the top of his head and guide the ear pieces up and over the ears.

At the end of the fifth week Dicky was still not wearing the ear frames appropriately; so the authors, who had not previously spent any time shaping the subject themselves, spent the major portion of a day directing the shaping procedure.

A second bar was added to the back of the glasses. Now, they fit like a cap and would not slide off readily. As usual the breakfast session was not particularly effective. Lunch was also used as a session, but still there was no progress.

Later, at approximately two o'clock that afternoon, we had a third session. Dicky had received very little to eat all day, just a few pieces of dry cereal, and was most interested in the ice cream we brought to the session. We also decided to try the full prescription lenses. At the beginning of the session it was quite obvious that our reinforcers were much more powerful than earlier in the day. He carried the glasses at all times, often putting them up to his face, although not in the desired manner. However, since there was a great deal of the approximate kind of behaviour it was easy to differentially reinforce the two aspects of wearing we wanted, placing the ear pieces straight over the ears, and looking through the lenses. At the end of approximately thirty minutes Dicky was holding the ear pieces properly over his ears, and the nose piece at the tip of his nose. He was looking through the lenses at such objects as a ring, a clicker, etc., that were displayed in the hopes of maintaining his looking behaviour. After this, progress was rapid and he was soon wearing his glasses continuously during the meal sessions in his room.

After wearing the glasses was established in these sessions, it could be maintained with other, less manipulable reinforcers. For example, the attendant would tell Dicky, "Put your glasses on and let's go for a walk." Dicky was usually required to wear the glasses during meals, snacks, automobile rides, walks, outdoor play, etc. If he removed the glasses, the activity was terminated.

The progress of glasses-wearing is presented cumulatively in the upper graph of Figure 2. At the time of Dicky's release from the hospital he had worn the glasses for more than 600 hours and was wearing them about 12 hours a day.

Throwing of Glasses

The lower cumulative record in Figure 2

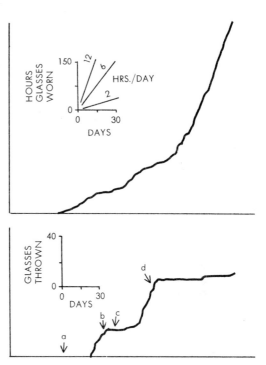

Figure 2. *Two cumulative records showing the effects of positive reinforcement (bites of meals, etc.) upon glasses-wearing and the effects of extinction and mild punishment (time-out from positive reinforcement) upon the glasses-throwing of a hospitalized autistic boy.*

depicts the course of a problem that grew out of wearing glasses, namely, throwing the glasses. Wearing the glasses began at (a). Two weeks later Dicky threw his glasses for the first time. A week later he began throwing them approximately twice a day. Although this in itself was not a serious behaviour problem, it was moderately expensive due to breakage, and there was the danger that, once home, it would be reinforced by the mother's ineffectual fussing and thereby increase the frequency of throwing to a degree incompatible with wearing the glasses. We therefore attempted to develop a technique to control it. Beginning at (b) Dicky was put in his room for ten minutes following each glasses-throw, or if a tantrum developed, until it ceased. Throwing the glasses decreased to zero in five days. At (c) the conditions were reversed: he was no longer to be put in his room for throws. After about three weeks the rate of throwing the glasses resumed its earlier high level. At (d) he was again put in his room for throwing his glasses, and six days later the rate reached and remained near zero.

Verbal Behaviour

After the wearing of glasses was established we developed a technique for generating a verbal repertoire. The technique also aimed at maintaining the wearing of glasses and reinforcing visual attending. Like the glasses training, the verbal training consisted of sessions in which an attendant administered food reinforcers. Initially, we tried candy and fruit but these were unsuccessful. Only when we began using breakfast and lunch as training sessions did we have rapid and dramatic effects.

Dicky had no socially appropriate verbal behaviour and, according to his parents, neither his verbal nor non-verbal behaviour was under their verbal control. However, Dicky was far from mute. He had some long and complex verbal chains such as songs (*Chicago*, for example) and occasionally he would mimic quite clearly, but the mimicking could not be evoked under normal conditions.

Our training began with the attendant presenting, one at a time, five pictures (a Santa Claus, a cat etc.). The attendant would say, "This is a cat", "Now, say cat", and so on, until Dicky mimicked her, whereupon she would say, "Good", or "That's right" and give him a bite of his meal. After several more days of differential reinforcement the attendant gradually omitted saying the word first and Dicky would usually say the word in the presence of each picture without a prompt. In three weeks he did this in the presence of about ten pictures. We then progressed to picture books, common household objects, and finally to remote events, for example, "Where are you going tonight?", "What did you do outside?"

The more powerful food reinforcers were evidently necessary for initial strengthening, but weaker conditioned reinforcers, such as adult attention and approval, were effective for maintaining and expanding the original repertoire. The parents, although reluctant at first, were trained by the attendant to use the same technique at home. They have expanded his repertoire to include, for instance, the correct usage of personal pronouns, and Dicky now initiates requests and comments without adult prompting. However, his present verbal behaviour is by no means comparable to that of a normal five-year-old child.

Dicky's ability to mimic entire phrases and sentences was apparently crucial to the rapid progress in verbal training. The authors' current work with other children indicates that without this mimicking behaviour a long and arduous handshaping procedure would have been necessary to establish responses of the required topography (words, phrases, and sentences) prior to the discrimination training described above.

Eating Problems

During those meals which Dicky ate with the rest of the children in the dining room, he would not use silverware, would snatch food from the other children's plates and would throw food around the room. We attempted to deal with these behaviours by having the attendant remove Dicky's plate for a few minutes whenever he ate with his fingers and, after a warning, remove Dicky from the dining room (and the remainder of his meal) whenever he would throw food or take food from others' plates. Dicky spent an average of 55 per cent of the mealtime inappropriately eating with his fingers. During one meal his plate was removed several times, and he was told to use his spoon. After this, and in all subsequent meals he used a spoon for all appropriate foods. It was only necessary to warn Dicky and send him from the dining room a few times to completely eliminate food-stealing and food-throwing.

Probably as the result of being consistently paired with the aversive consequence of being put in his room, such verbal stimuli as "No", "Stop that", or "If you do that again you'll have to go to your room", came to suppress much undesirable non-verbal behaviour. This type of control also seems important for normal child development.

According to a report from the mother six months after the child's return home, Dicky continues to wear his glasses, does not have tantrums, has no sleeping problems, is becoming increasingly verbal, and is a new source of joy to the members of his family.

Experimental manipulation of autistic behaviors and generalization into the home

TODD RISLEY AND MONTROSE M. WOLF

In a study reported by Wolf, Risley and Mees (1964[1]) describing the procedures used to instate normal behaviors in an institutionalized autistic child, we collected no systematic data in two important areas—the establishment of speech, and the training of the parents to work with their own child. In recent work we have explicitly investigated these two areas. I will report here on one of the subsequent children with whom we have worked, using operant conditioning procedures.

This is a six-year-old autistic child, who exhibited bizarre mannerisms and echolalia, and was withdrawn and inactive with no appropriate verbal behavior. The child lived at home and was brought to the Developmental Psychology Laboratory at the University of Washington in a state of mild food deprivation each weekday by his mother.

SPEECH TRAINING

Using bites of ice cream as a reinforcer, appropriate mimicking, then naming of pictures, and then appropriate phrases and sentences were established in these daily sessions. In the first session the subject was reinforced for imitating the word "ice cream." The experimenter said the word several times a minute. Since the child would occasionally echo novel sounds, within the first minute he repeated "ice cream." The experimenter then said "very good" and gave him a bite of ice cream. The mimicking of this word occurred at a low, stable rate throughout the session (from start to point a in Figure 1). However, the pairing of the words "very good" with the reinforcer served to establish a high rate of the subject saying "very good, very good" (Figure 1). This paradigm of increasing the probability that the subject will produce a sound, simply by pairing that sound with reinforcement, perhaps is functional in maintaining the subject's echolalia.

In the next session, beginning at point a in Figure 1, a picture of a train was introduced and the word "train" was repeated by the experimenter. The subject mimicked this novel word once and was reinforced. After a long delay during which the subject began repeating "ice cream, ice cream" and tantruming, he again mimicked "train." After this, the rate of mimicking the word rapidly increased.

At point b in Figure 1, three other words (flower, car, and airplane) were introduced. The subject mimicked each word appropriately the *first* time it was presented and at each further presentation. Thus, in slightly more than an hour we had established the general behavior class of appropriate mimicking.

From point b to point c in Figure 1, pictures of a train, flower, car, and airplane were held out one at a time, and the subject was required to look at each picture before the experimenter said the name. The subject quickly began attending to the pictures, which indicated that the experimenter's *saying* the word (which was discriminative for the subject to mimic it and be reinforced) had become a reinforcer.

Paper read at American Psychological Association, Los Angeles, September, 1964.

1 Pages 187–193 of this volume.

Just before point c in Figure 1 the experimenter began delaying naming the picture, requiring a longer period of attending by the subject. This was to increase the probability that the subject would name the picture instead of mimicking the experimenter. At point c the subject began to tantrum during an especially long delay. The experimenter merely sat quietly holding the picture toward the subject. The tantrum gradually subsided, and the subject again attended to the picture—and promptly named it. After this he named the picture with increasing speed with each presentation.

At point d the picture of the airplane was reintroduced. The subject immediately said "car." The experimenter said "No, *airplane*." The subject mimicked "airplane" and correctly named the picture on the next presentation. The other two pictures were then reintroduced and the subject correctly named each after a single prompting. After this he correctly named the four pictures when each was presented. Thus, in an additional hour, the general behavior class of naming objects was established.

After a high rate of naming the four pictures had been established, the procedures were altered to experimentally isolate the function of the contingent delivery of the ice cream. At the first arrow in Figure 2 the ice cream was given randomly, which resulted in only an occasional bite immediately following naming one of the pictures. At the second arrow the ice cream was again given only contingent upon naming the pictures. Throughout these reversals, the experimenter continued to say "very good" contingent upon naming the pictures.

The random delivery of ice cream resulted in an immediate decrease in the rate of naming from 7.5 to 3.1 responses per minute. As the random reinforcement procedure continued, the rate gradually declined further to

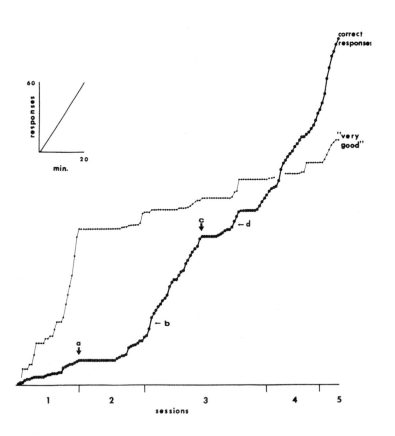

Figure 1. A cumulative record of S1's initial acquisition of appropriate verbal behavior. The heavy line represents correct imitations or naming. The fine line represents S1's frequency of repeating the verbal reinforcer. From the start to point a, S1 was reinforced for mimicking 'ice cream.' At point a, a picture of a train was introduced and S1 was reinforced for mimicking 'train.' At point b, 3 other pictures were introduced and S1 was reinforced for mimicking the names of each. At point c, S1 was reinforced for naming rather than mimicking one of the pictures. At point d, the other 3 pictures were again introduced and S1 was reinforced for correctly naming each.

1.9 responses per minute. When the contingent delivery of ice cream was resumed, the rate rapidly increased to 9.8 responses per minute. This reversal demonstrates that the *contingent* delivery of the ice cream, rather than other variables in the situation, served to maintain the naming behavior. After this reversal, more complex phrases and sentences were established in the experimental sessions.

After appropriate mimicking had been established in the experimental sessions, mimicking could be used to instigate appropriate verbal behavior in other situations. For example, opening the doors to and from the experimental room was used to reinforce the comment, "out (or in) the door." The experimenter would say "out the door," the subject would mimic this, and the door would be opened. After several trials on succeeding days, the experimenter began fading out his verbal prompt, only saying "out the—," and the subject continued to say "out the door." This fading progressed until the experimenter would only put his hand on the doorknob and look at the subject, and the subject would say "out the door." The experimenter then faded in the question "Where are you going?" first by mumbling it softly as they approached the door and then increasing the volume on succeeding trials. If the subject mimicked the question, the experimenter would repeat the question at a lower volume and follow it with a prompt for the appropriate response: "Where are you going? Out —" This would usually generate the appropriate response "Out the door." The prompt "Out —" was then faded until the subject would respond to the closed door and the question "Where are you going?" with the statement "Out the door."

This same procedure was used to establish appropriate answers to the question "Where are you going?" in each of the steps of going to and from the experimental room: "Up the stairs. In the door. Down the hall. In the room. Out the door. Down the hall. Out the door. Down the stairs. In the car." In each case, the reinforcer was simply being allowed to proceed out the door, down the hall, etc.

This technique of giving a prompt for the subject to imitate and then fading out the prompt was used to establish appropriate responses to many other questions such as:

"What's your name?" "My name is (name)."
"What do you want?" "I want some ice cream."
"Hello, (name)." "Hello, Mr. Risley."

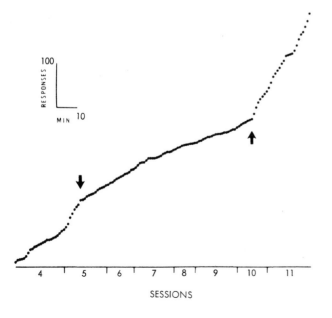

Figure 2. A cumulative record showing the effects of delivering the food reinforcement non-contingent on naming pictures. At the first arrow the food reinforcers were randomly presented. At the second arrow the food reinforcers were again made contingent upon correctly naming pictures. Each dot represents a 1 min. period.

Since new responses were established more quickly to each new question, the subject apparently began to discriminate the subtle stimuli of inflection and volume as cues for which phrases to mimic.

PARENT TRAINING

The mother had periodically observed these sessions from behind a one-way screen. After the child was brought to the point where the imitative paradigm was effective in establishing new verbal behavior, the mother was trained to take over the job of rehabilitating her child.

First she was given the relatively easy task of teaching the child to put puzzles together. A series of large plywood puzzles each with four or five isolated figures were used. Sessions were held in the home in the late afternoon, with bites of ice cream as the reinforcer. The mother was instructed on the general procedure and coached by the experimenter during the first session. After this the experimenter would observe occasional sessions. The mother recorded the number of puzzle pieces completed and total time of each session.

During the initial sessions the mother expressed concern that the stated goal of the child putting all the pieces in the puzzle (without assistance) for each bite of ice cream, was an impossible one. She commented that the only way she was getting him to do *anything* was by continuously prompting and assisting him. Therefore, after the sixth session she was instructed to stop all urging and assistance and to do nothing except to reinforce each successful fitting of a puzzle piece. The rate then began to increase. At the first arrow in Figure 3, the mother was instructed to reinforce every other response. When the rate had increased markedly with this fixed-ratio 2 schedule, the mother was instructed to lean out the schedule still more. At the second arrow the final schedule, of a reinforcer only contingent upon assembling the complete puzzle, was begun.

The next puzzle (number 2 in Figure 3) was started with this reinforcement schedule. The mother assisted the child only for the first few pieces and then stopped on her own initiative. The rate steadily increased from session to session.

The third puzzle (number 3 in Figure 3) was introduced with no assistance as were the fourth, fifth, sixth, and seventh puzzles. By the seventh puzzle (number 7 in Figure 3) the child's behavior showed almost no decrement

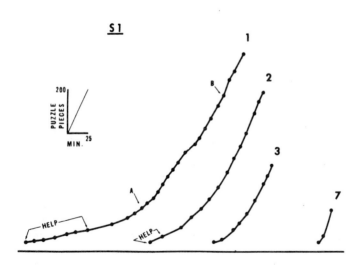

Figure 3. *Cumulative records of successive improvement in S1's rate of assembling a series of puzzles in sessions at home. Each number indicates the ordinal position of each puzzle in the series. Each dot indicates the end of a daily session. The periods labeled 'help' indicate where S1's mother assisted in placing the puzzle pieces. At A an FR2 schedule of reinforcement was begun. Reinforcement frequency was gradually decreased until, at point B and on all subsequent puzzles, a reinforcer was given only contingent upon completing a puzzle (FR or 5).*

when a new puzzle was introduced, and a new puzzle could be assembled nearly as fast as an old one. At about this time the child also began fitting puzzles together by himself during play.

Through this experience the mother learned to rely on the reinforcer, rather than urging or prompting, to increase the child's behavior. She. learned that the procedure was effective in establishing general classes of behavior in addition to those specific behaviors which were reinforced. And she learned that the effects of the procedures would generalize to new tasks and new situations.

The mother was then given a series of pictures, and, using the same procedures as had been used in the experimental sessions, she began teaching the child to recognize and name pictures. She would introduce new pictures when he was consistently naming all the pictures used during that session. A picture was considered learned when the child correctly named it the first time it was presented, three days in a row. Then it would be retired until ten subsequent pictures had been learned, at which time it would be re-presented to test for recall. Initially, two sessions a day were run with separate pictures for each session. With one set of pictures the reinforcer was praise ("That's right. Very good.") and a bite of ice cream. Only praise was used with the other set.

While praise alone was an effective reinforcer (dashed line in Figure 4), praise plus ice cream resulted in a 50 per cent greater rate of learning (solid line in Figure 4). However, words learned under both conditions were equally well recalled (bar graph in Figure 4).

After this evaluation was made, only the sessions with ice cream were continued. The child learned approximately one new word per session with this reinforcer (dotted line in Figure 4).

In addition to simply expanding his naming vocabulary, this procedure was designed to establish the general skill of attending to small differences in printed matter which is a step in preparing him for academic materials.

Concurrent with these procedures, the parents had been recording instances of stereotyped chanting which had characterized much of the child's verbal behavior. The child would repeat a word over and over with increasing volume which would terminate in shrieks and crying. The parents could "turn off" this sequence at any point by simply attending to the child.

For example, the child, standing by the couch, would repeat "sit down, sit down," etc., which would terminate when the parents responded in any way ["Yes, (name)"; "O.K., sit down"; "You can sit down if you want to"; "Be quiet."].

Instead of reinforcing this behavior, the child was sent to his room contingent upon the shrieking and crying. This decreased the occurrences of the shrieking (solid line in Figure 5), but did not affect the rate of the stereotyped chanting (dotted line in Figure 5).

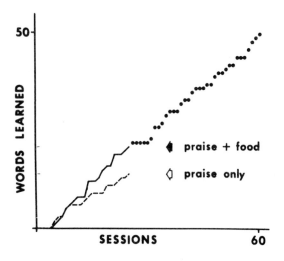

Figure 4. Records of the number of pictures learned and recalled in daily sessions at home under two reinforcement conditions. A picture was considered learned when S1 named it when it was first presented in three successive sessions. A picture was considered recalled when S1 named it when it was first re-presented after 10 subsequent pictures had been learned.

It was decided to change the form of these occurrences, rather than attempt to eliminate them, as there were elements of appropriate social behavior in these occurrences.

The parents were instructed to turn away from the child on these occasions. One parent (the father) would then call out the name of the other parent ("Mommy") and the child would mimic this, at which point the other parent (the mother) would reinforce the imitation by attending to the child and saying, "Yes, (name)?" The first parent would then say a complete sentence ("I want to sit down, please.") which the child would mimic. The other parent would again reinforce the imitation by responding accordingly, "Oh, you want to sit down. Well, you can sit down right here." On subsequent occasions the verbal prompts were faded out and the parents would withhold reinforcement by looking away until the child called their names and would wait while looking at the child until the complete sentence was emitted before responding to his request.

This procedure was begun at the arrow in Figure 5. The stereotyped chanting soon decreased to zero, as the child began to initiate more appropriate requests such as "Mommy, I want to sit down, please."

The explicitness and effectiveness of operant conditioning procedures enables parents to contribute significantly to the rehabilitation of their deviant children with only a minimum of training. Of the seven sets of parents with which we have attempted similar programs, all have been effective and all are now conducting the major part of the rehabilitation of their children.

It is apparent that the child's initial echolalic behavior was crucial to the rapid establishment of appropriate verbal behavior. Other work by the present authors and others (Sherman, 1964) indicates that it is much more difficult to establish a mimicking repertoire in a mute individual than to bring already present mimicking behavior under the control of appropriate discriminative stimuli, as was done in this study.

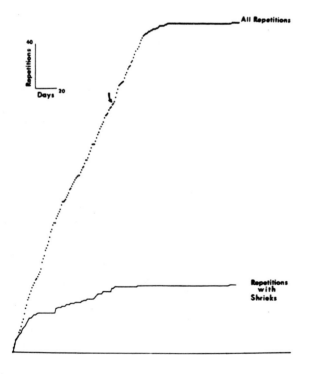

Figure 5. A cumulative record of the frequency of S1's stereotyped chanting at home. At the arrow S1's parents began establishing appropriate behaviors incompatible with chanting.

Application of operant conditioning
to reinstate verbal behavior in psychotics

WAYNE ISAACS, JAMES THOMAS, AND ISRAEL GOLDIAMOND

In operant conditioning, behavior is controlled by explicitly arranging the consequences of the response, the explicit consequence being termed reinforcement. For example, a lever-press by a rat activates a mechanism which releases food. If the rat has been deprived of food, lever-pressing responses will increase in frequency. If this relationship between food and response holds only when a light is on, the organism may discriminate between light on and light off, that is, there will be no lever-pressing responses when the light is turned off, but turning it on will occasion such responses. From this simple case, extensions can be made to more complicated cases which may involve control of schedules of reinforcement. These procedures have recently been extended to the study of psychopharmacology (Dews, 1958b), controlled production of stomach ulcers (Brady, 1958b), obtaining psycho-physical curves from pigeons (Blough, 1958), conditioning cooperative behavior in children (Azrin and Lindsley, 1956), programming machines which teach academic subjects (Skinner, 1958), analyzing the effects of noise on human behavior (Azrin, 1958), and decreasing stuttering (Flanagan, et al., 1958) to mention a few examples.

The following account is a preliminary report of the use of operant conditioning to reinstate verbal behavior in two hospitalized mute psychotics. Patient A, classified as a catatonic schizophrenic, 40, became completely mute almost immediately upon commitment 19 years ago. He was recorded as withdrawn and exhibiting little psychomotor activity. Patient B, classified as schizophrenic, mixed type, with catatonic features predominating, was 43, and was committed after a psychotic break in 1942, when he was combative. He completely stopped verbalizing 14 years ago. Each S was handled by a different E (experimenter). The E's were ignorant of each other's activities until pressed to report their cases. This study covers the period prior to such report.

CASE HISTORIES

Patient A

The S was brought to a group therapy session with other chronic schizophrenics (who were verbal), but he sat in the position in which he was placed and continued the withdrawal behaviors which characterized him. He remained impassive and stared ahead even when cigarettes, which other members accepted, were offered to him and were waved before his face. At one session, when E removed cigarettes from his pocket, a package of chewing gum accidentally fell out. The S's eyes moved toward the gum and then returned to their usual position. This response was chosen by E as one with which he would start to work, using the method of successive approximation (Keller and Schoenfeld, 1950). (This method finds use where E desires to produce responses which are not present in the current repertoire of the organism and which are considerably removed from those which are available. The E then attempts to "shape" the available behaviors into the desired form, capitalizing upon both the variability and regularity of successive behaviors. The shaping process involves the reinforcement of those parts of a selected response which are successively in the desired direction and the nonreinforcement of those which are not. For example, a pigeon may be initially reinforced when it moves its head. When this movement occurs regularly, only an upward movement may be reinforced, with downward movement not reinforced. The pigeon may now stretch its neck, with this movement reinforced. Eventually the pigeon may be trained to peck at a disc which was initially high above its head and at which it would normally never peck. In the case of the psychotic under discussion, the succession was eye movement,

From *Journal of Speech and Hearing Disorders*, 1960, **25**, 8–12.

which brought into play occasional facial movements, including those of the mouth, lip movements, vocalizations, word utterance, and finally, verbal behavior.)

The S met individually with E three times a week. Group sessions also continued. The following sequence of procedures was introduced in the private sessions. Although the weeks are numbered consecutively, they did not follow at regular intervals since other duties kept E from seeing S every week.

Weeks 1, 2. A stick of gum was held before S's face, and E waited until S's eyes moved toward it. When this response occurred, E as a consequence gave him the gum. By the end of the second week, response probability in the presence of the gum was increased to such an extent that S's eyes moved toward the gum as soon as it was held up.

Weeks 3, 4. The E now held the gum before S, waiting until he noticed movement in S's lips before giving it to him. Toward the end of the first session of the third week, a lip movement spontaneously occurred, which E promptly reinforced. By the end of this week, both lip movement and eye movement occurred when the gum was held up. The E then withheld giving S the gum until S spontaneously made a vocalization, at which time E gave S the gum. By the end of this week, holding up the gum readily occasioned eye movement toward it, lip movement, and a vocalization resembling a croak.

Weeks 5, 6. The E held up the gum, and said, 'Say *gum, gum*,' repeating these words each time S vocalized. Giving S the gum was made contingent upon vocalizations increasingly approximating *gum*. At the sixth session (at the end of Week 6), when E said, 'Say *gum, gum*,' S suddenly said, 'Gum, please.' This response was accompanied by reinstatement of other responses of this class, that is, S answered questions regarding his name and age.

Thereafter, he responded to questions by E both in individual sessions and in group sessions, but answered no one else. Responses to the discriminative stimuli of the room generalized to E on the ward; he greeted E on

two occasions in the group room. He read from signs in E's office upon request by E.

Since the response now seemed to be under the strong stimulus control of E, *the person*, attempt was made to generalize the stimulus to other people. Accordingly, a nurse was brought into the private room; S smiled at her. After a month, he began answering her questions. Later, when he brought his coat to a volunteer worker on the ward, she interpreted the gesture as a desire to go outdoors and conducted him there. Upon informing E of the incident, she was instructed to obey S only as a consequence of explicit verbal requests by him. The S thereafter vocalized requests. These instructions have now been given to other hospital personnel, and S regularly initiates verbal requests when nonverbal requests have no reinforcing consequences. Upon being taken to the commissary, he said, 'Ping pong,' to the volunteer worker and played a game with her. Other patients, visitors, and members of hospital-society-at-large continue, however, to interpret nonverbal requests and to reinforce them by obeying S.

Patient B

This patient, with a combative history prior to mutism, habitually lay on a bench in the day room in the same position, rising only for meals and for bed. Weekly visits were begun by E and an attendant. During these visits, E urged S to attend group therapy sessions which were being held elsewhere in the hospital. The E offered S chewing gum. This was not accepted during the first two visits, but was accepted on the third visit and thereafter. On the sixth visit, E made receipt of the gum contingent upon S's going to the group room and so informed S. The S then altered his posture to look at E and accompanied him to the group room, where he seated himself in a chair and was given the gum. Thereafter, he came to this room when the attendants called for him.

Group Sessions 1–4. Gum reinforcement was provided for coming to the first two weekly sessions, but starting with the third, it was made contingent upon S's participation in the announced group activity. The group (whose other members were verbal) was arranged in a semicircle. The E announced that each S would, when his turn came, give the name of an animal. The E immediately provided gum to each S who did so. The S did not respond and skipped his turn three times around. The same response occurred during the fourth session.

Group Session 5. The activity announced was drawing a person; E provided paper and colored chalk and visited each S in turn to examine the paper. The S had drawn a stick figure and was reinforced with gum. Two of the other patients, spontaneously and without prior prompting by E, asked to see the drawing and complimented S. Attendants reported that on the following day, S, when introduced to two ward visitors, smiled and said, 'I'm glad to see you.' The incident was followed by no particular explicit consequences.

Group Session 6. The announced activity was to give the name of a city or town in Illinois. The S, in his turn, said, 'Chicago.' He was reinforced by E, who gave him chewing gum, and again two members of the group congratulated him for responding. Thereafter, he responded whenever his turn came.

After the tenth session in the group, gum reinforcement was discontinued. The S has continued to respond vocally in the situations in which he was reinforced by E but not in others. He never initiates conversations, but he will answer various direct questions in the *group sessions*. He will not, however, respond vocally to questions asked *on the ward*, even when put by E.

DISCUSSION

Both S's came from special therapy wards of patients selected because of depressed verbal behavior and long stay in the hospital; tranquilizing drugs were not used. The extent to which reinstatement of verbal behavior was related to the special treatment offered the patients in the special wards set up for them cannot readily be assayed. Among the special treatments accorded them were group therapy sessions. Nevertheless, the similarities between the pattern of reacquisition of verbal behavior by the patients and the patterns of learning encountered in laboratory studies suggest that the conditioning procedures themselves were involved in the reinstatement of verbal behavior.

In the case of Patient A, the speaking response itself was gradually shaped. The anatomical relation between the muscles of chewing and speaking probably had some part in E's effectiveness. When a word was finally produced, the response was reinstated along with other response members of its class, which had not been reinforced. The economy of this process is apparent, since it eliminates the necessity of getting S to produce *every* desired response in order to increase his repertoire. In this case, E concentrated on one verbal response, and in reinstating it, reinstated verbal responses in general. On the stimulus side, when the response came under the stimulus control of E, the stimulus could be generalized to other members of E's class of discriminative *stimuli*, namely, people. This may have relevance for the clinical inference of the importance for future interpersonal relations of prior identification with some person. In the case of Patient B, the stimulus control involved a *given setting*, the rooms where he had been reinforced. The discrimination of E in one case, and not in the other, may be explained in terms of the establishment of operant discrimination, which also involves extinction (Keller and Schoenfeld, 1950). Operant discrimination is established when a response in the presence of S^D, a discriminative stimulus, is reinforced, and a response in the presence of S^Δ, a stimulus other than S^D, is not. After some time, the response will occur when S^D is presented, but not when S^Δ is presented; the response discriminates S^D from S^Δ, it having been extinguished when S^Δ was presented. In the case of Patient A, E was with S on the ward, in the group room, and privately. Reinforcement occurred in all occasions. But S was on the ward (and other rooms) without E, and therefore without reinforcement for those responses which were occasioned by the ward and which only E reinforced. Hence, these responses would extinguish in the ward alone, but would continue in the presence of E, defining discrimination of E from other stimuli. In the case of Patient B, this process may have been delayed by the fact that E and the other patients reinforced only in a specific room. It will be recalled that attendants rather than E brought S to the group room.

Interestingly, in the group sessions, when Patient B emitted the responses which E reinforced, other psychotic patients also reinforced Patient B. They were thereby responding, on the occasion of S's responses (discriminative stimuli for them), in the same way that E did. The term *identification*, used as a label here, shares some behavioral referents with the term as used in the preceding paragraph and might be explained behaviorally in terms of the *generalized reinforcer* (Skinner, 1953). These behaviors by the patients are similar to behaviors reported in client-centered group sessions, where clients increase in reflective behaviors as counseling progresses, and in psychoanalytic group sessions, where patients increasingly make analytic interpretations of each other. Here, the patients are also behaving like the therapist. While this parallel lends itself to the facetious thought that operant group sessions may produce operant conditioners, it does suggest that psychotics are behaving, with regard to responses by the major source of reinforcement in the group, according to the same laws which govern such group behaviors of non-hospitalized S's.

The various diagnostic labels applied to psychotics are based to a considerable extent upon differences between responses considered abnormal, for example, hallucinations, delusions of persecution, and the like. The therapeutic process is accordingly at times seen in terms of eliminating the abnormal behaviors or states. Experimental laboratory work indicates that it is often extremely difficult to *eliminate* behavior; extinction is extremely difficult where the schedule of reinforcement has been a variable interval schedule (Ferster and Skinner, 1957), that is, reinforcement has been irregular, as it is in most of our behaviors. Such behaviors persist for considerable periods without reinforcement. Experimental laboratory work has provided us quite readily with procedures to *increase* responses. In the case of psychotics, this would suggest focusing attention on whatever *normal* behaviors S has; an appropriate operant, no matter how small or insignificant, even if it is confined to an eye movement, may possibly be raised to greater probability, and shaped to normal behavior (Goldiamond, 1958b). Stated otherwise, abnormal behaviors and normal behaviors can be viewed as reciprocally related, and psychotics as exhibiting considerable abnormal behavior, or little normal behavior. Normal behavior probability can be increased by decreasing probability of abnormal behaviors, or abnormal behaviors can be decreased by the controlled increase of normal behaviors. This preliminary report suggests that a plan of attack based upon the latter approach may be worth further investigation.

SUMMARY

Verbal behavior was reinstated in two psychotics, classified as schizophrenics, who had been mute for 19 and 14 years. The procedures utilized involved application of operant conditioning. The relationship of such procedures, based on controlled laboratory investigations with men and animals, to procedures based on clinical practice with human patients was discussed and was considered as directing our attention to shaping and increasing the probability of what normal behaviors the psychotic possesses.

8

PHYSIOLOGICAL AND CHEMICAL MODIFICATION OF BEHAVIOR

Evidence as old as the discovery of fermentation has engendered belief in the potency of the effect of chemical agents on behavior, and knowledge of the electrical properties of behavior dates from Galvani's work, now a century and a half past. If present knowledge does not yet reach the more exotic predictions of science fiction, it is not because of lack of activity of interested scientists.

The past thirty years have seen a prolific rise in the sophistication of instruments and techniques for the exploration of the biological basis of man's behavior. It is difficult to predict the time or the manner of intimate contact between specialized areas of physical biology and the study of human behavior, but the substantial contribution such knowledge will provide can be presaged in a general way. That profound progress in the control of human behavior will be effected by increasingly refined physiological agents can be surmised from the present wide use of pharmaceuticals in and out of mental hospitals. Although there has been some objection to these procedures, practical recognition of the physiological basis of behavior has been given by every individual who has purchased a tranquilizer, a stimulant, or a cocktail.

The two papers included in this section can no more than suggest the future course of events linking physical biology to human behavior. The first article, by Russell, reviews many of the methods of biochemical intervention currently used in the study of behavior. He has extended the term "lesion" to encompass not only the usual technique of severing tracts or ablating small areas of the brain, but to the alteration of the normal biochemical chain of events which are likely to be correlated with behavioral changes. While indicating the tentative nature of the present state of the art, Russell has convincingly demonstrated the vitality of these techniques and their relevance to the study of behavior.

Since its discovery by Olds and Milner in 1954, electrical self-stimulation of the brain has been investigated in numerous species in the animal laboratory. The effect, which has been repeated many times, is essentially that minute electrical shocks delivered to discrete portions of the brain will act as reinforcement (or punishment) in much the same fashion as food to a hungry animal. Behavior which produces such stimulation may be maintained for hours. The extrapolation of this knowledge by Heath to a therapeutic situation with humans provides a fascinating account. Certainly refined techniques and localization may be expected to be profitably extended to help other forms of neuropsychiatric patients, and, at the same time, these extensions may provide some interesting leads back into the animal laboratory.

If the present section is no more than provocative, it will have served its purpose of illustrating some of the rather profound effects which physiological variables can have on behavior.

Effects of "biochemical lesions" on behavior

ROGER W. RUSSELL

INTRODUCTION

Wherever we turn in our study of biological mechanisms we find chemical changes taking place. Collectively these biochemical events constitute an organism's metabolism. The basic assumption of this paper is that the behavior patterns of living organisms are correlated, directly or indirectly, with these biochemical or metabolic events. One way of testing this assumption is to observe the behavior of organisms in which the normal course of these events has been altered. Interference with specific aspects of biochemical system is frequently referred to as producing a "biochemical lesion" (Essig, *et al.*, 1950; Peterson, 1949); it has the effect of altering intermediary metabolism. The objective of this paper is to present a systematic view of the kinds of research in which such "lesions" are being employed in a search for biochemical correlates of behavior.

Experimental and clinical studies of the effects of chemical agents on behavior are by no means new. The use of drugs to induce sleep, to deaden the perception of pain, to produce hallucinations and to affect behavior in numerous other ways is centuries old. More recently research has shown that nutritional deficiencies may lead to changes of behavior and that unusual behavior patterns may be associated with inherited abnormalities of a biochemical nature. The vast majority of these studies has been based upon research designs in which the independent variable has been the presence in some degree of a chemical agent and the dependent variables, measures of behavior. With developments in modern biochemistry and pharmacology we are coming to know much more about the modes of action of chemical agents in the body; how they affect intermediary metabolism. With such knowledge the traditional research design can be altered. The chemical agent now becomes a means of producing a "biochemical lesion"; the presence of a "lesion" in some degree is the independent variable and may be correlated with concomitant changes in measures of be-

havior, which constitute the dependent variables. Hypotheses tested are stated in terms of relations between biochemical events and behavior rather than in terms of relations between chemical agents and behavior. We are thus brought considerably closer to the goal of our search for biochemical correlates of behavior.

Of course much of our progress toward this goal depends upon developments in biochemistry and pharmacology. I was very discouraged some years ago in discussing my interest in this field with a well-known biochemist to be told that I should come back in a hundred years when biochemistry might have the information I needed to start my research. But more recently, I have been told by an equally well-known expert that he is looking to refinements in the techniques of the behavioral sciences to help in the search for ways in which chemical agents act in the body. The point is that research in our present field of interest is dependent upon advance in our allied sciences, but that collaborative attacks on mutual problems are likely to lead to earlier successes.

PRODUCTION OF "BIOCHEMICAL LESIONS"

There are four general ways in which "biochemical lesions" are produced for our present purposes. In certain instances there is evidence that they are hereditary in origin and, in infrahuman animals, may be bred for selectivity. Comparisons of individuals or strains with and without a particular "lesion" may reveal differences in behavior associated with the "lesion."

The other three methods involve more immediate experimental control of the "lesion." They are based upon techniques for altering the velocities at which specific biochemical events take place. The first involves interference with enzyme activity. The surprising rapidity with which biochemical events norm-

From *Acta Psychologica*, 1958, **14**, 281–294.

ally take place in the body is made possible by the presence of organic catalysts "enzymes." A number of selective inhibitors have been discovered which alter specified enzyme activity levels. By selectively reducing these activity levels relations between particular biochemical events and behavior may be studied.

The second of these experimental methods of affecting intermediary metabolism involves altering the concentration of the substrate upon which an enzyme acts. According to the law of mass action, the velocity of a chemical reaction is proportional to the concentrations of the reacting substances. This law holds for biochemical reactions, for, within a given time, a specified amount of enzyme will act upon a larger percentage of its substrate when that substrate is dilute than when it is concentrated. Therefore, by altering the concentration of the substrate the velocity of a particular biochemical event can be changed and the concomitant effects on behavior observed.

The third experimental method is based upon the fact that biochemical reactions are affected by changes in the temperature of their environments in much the same way as chemical reactions generally are influenced by such changes, velocity being proportional to temperature. The limiting factor at the high end of this relation is the susceptibility of enzymes to destruction by heat beyond body temperature. Later in this paper I will describe studies in which metabolism has been altered by varying temperature experimentally in order to observe the effects on behavior.

INHERITED METABOLIC VARIATIONS

For many years it has been known that inherited metabolic variations occur in man. Although this knowledge is at present confined to a series of rather anomalous examples, recent developments in human biochemical genetics (Haldane, 1954; Harris, 1955; Penrose, 1954) suggest that new discoveries may soon provide research materials of considerable value to those searching for biochemical correlates of behavior. Even today better use could be made of those instances in which inherited "biochemical lesions" can be identified. It is for these reasons that I wish to call attention to the use of inherited metabolic variations as materials for studying the particular problems with which we are presently concerned.

Variations Affecting Complex Behavior Patterns

Some fifty-five years ago Garrod (1902, 1923), an English physician, advanced the rather simple hypothesis that inherited metabolic variations observable in man were understandable if it were assumed that in each case the body failed to carry out one particular step in normal metabolism. This failure could be accounted for in terms of a congenital absence of the enzyme required for the biochemical step affected. Since this suggestion was made, it has been possible to isolate in a few instances the nature of the particular "biochemical lesion" involved. In these instances detailed studies of behavior could be very informative; as it is we can make only very general statements of the relations involved. Let me give an illustration.

There are three closely related disorders which are frequently cited as examples of inherited biochemical lesions: phenylketonuria, alkaptonuria, and tyrosinosis. I shall not go into the chemistry of these three conditions except to indicate how very specific these particular lesions are:

"It is probable that they represent failures to carry out three quite distinct steps in the metabolic chain by which the benzine ring of the aromatic ammino-acids is normally broken down in the body." (Harris, 1955).

How does the behavior of persons suffering from these conditions differ from the normal? All individuals diagnosed as phenylketonurics have been found to have some degree of intellectual impairment, being typically at the level of imbecility. Their general behavior is good-tempered, cooperative and friendly, those I have seen in hospital wards being entirely amenable to clinical and research treatments. One very noticeable behavioral feature is a constant and marked accentuation of reflexes, often associated with hyperkinesis

(Harris, 1955; Penrose, 1954). Very recent studies (Homer and Streamer, 1956; Woolf, et al., 1955) have indicated that, with a proper diet, this biochemical abnormality can be treated successfully. To quote the results of one study (Woolf, et al., 1955) involving three patients, "the rate of increase of mental age of all three rose markedly on the diet, their I.Q.'s have risen, and they may reach educable levels." Our interest here is in the fact that altering a very specific biochemical abnormality leads so directly to significant changes in behavior.

Information on the behavior of persons with either alkaptonuria or tyrosinosis is much more limited. Garrod (1902) in one of his early reports refers to the former condition as "harmless and usually congenital and lifelong." Its most notable clinical features are somatic rather than behavioral in nature. There appears to be only one authenticated case of tyrosinosis (Mendes, 1932) and this patient's symptoms suggest other complications. However, the clinical records available indicate that he was able to engage in various kinds of light work, some of a skilled nature, and to adjust satisfactorily to his social environment.

The "biochemical lesions" characterizing these three conditions are distinct, but all very intimately involved in the same metabolic chain. Yet, as I have pointed out, one is associated with very significant changes of behavior and the others not.

Variations Affecting Sensory Processes

There are some exciting studies ahead for those who are interested in the effects of inherited metabolic variations on sensory events rather than on more complex behavior patterns of the kind just considered. Haldane (1954) has suggested:

"There is no doubt that many of the congenital anomalies of human sensation have a biochemical basis, and certain fairly obvious speculations can be made as to the biochemistry of color-blindness, night blindness, and day blindness."

At the present time the best documented example comes from studies of taste sensitivity to a particular class of chemical substances, the thioureas (Harris, 1955). Tests of taste thresholds for these substances divide individuals into essentially two groups: those to whom the substance is extremely bitter and those to whom it is practically tasteless. There is evidence that this dichotomy is largely determined genetically, possibly as a simple Mendelian character. The exact nature of the biochemical variations underlying the dichotomy is not yet known, although there is some suggestion that it may be correlated with a difference in thyroid response.

Again let me emphasize that our knowledge of inherited metabolic variations is still extremely limited. However, as new discoveries are made research material will become available which can add considerably to our understanding of biochemical correlates of behavior, providing behavior, as well as the genetic and biochemical aspects of the material, is thoroughly analyzed.

ALTERATION OF ENZYME ACTIVITY

A second method of influencing biochemical events, and thereby altering intermediary metabolism, is by interfering with the normal activity of enzymes which control the velocities of these events. This can be accomplished by the use of selective inhibitors. During the past several years we have been using this method in our laboratory and I would like to describe our results to illustrate the method in use.

Effects of General Interference with Intermediary Metabolism

Normal functioning of the nervous system depends upon an entire chain of biochemical events, among which is the synthesis of acetycholine (ACh). ACh plays its vital role as long as it is present in small quantities; beyond certain concentrations its effects are to paralyse nerve transmission. This means that, during the normal functioning of nerves, ACh must not accumulate. Existing at the proper places and in adequate amounts is an enzyme, cholinesterase (ChE), which hydrolyses ACh and inactivates it very rapidly after its release. The activity level of ChE may be reduced by certain selective inhibitors, anticholinesterases, thus preventing ACh from being inactivated at the normal rate. Since behavior depends upon neural activity, we would expect such alterations in biochemical events to be reflected in changes of behavior.

Research in our laboratory[1] was designed to study the differential effects of chronic reductions in brain ChE activity on a wide variety of behavior patterns. Rats were used as subjects. The experimental groups were fed, in their diet or orally, standardized concentrations of an organophosphorus compound[2] which maintained brain ChE activity at consistently reduced levels during the entire period of each experiment. Since there is a large margin of safety in the amount of ChE normally present in the brain it is possible to reduce ChE activity drastically before pathological signs appear. In our experiments we were careful not to carry reductions to this level. Our research design enabled us to compare performances of experimental animals with controls whose brain ChE activity remained at its normal level.

In an extensive preliminary investigation involving a variety of test situations and different forms of motivation, we found that the experimental animals were slower in eliminating responses which had been learned previously but were no longer adequate, less efficient in serial problem solving, and less efficient in adjusting to stresses imposed by the environment. In other behavior patterns—including locomotion, simple learning, instrumental conditioning and visual discrimination—their performances did not differ significantly from those of control animals. We have followed these leads in a series of more intensive experiments and have substantiated the earlier results. We believe that our results are of interest in three main regards.

First, they show that reduction in ChE activity, within the range of normal to the level when pathological signs appear, is associated with differential effects on behavior, some aspects of behavior being affected significantly and others not.

Second, when behavior is affected it appears to pass through four phases as ChE activity is reduced. From 60 to 100 per cent activity no significant effects have been observed. There is a suggestion in our data that between 40 and 60 per cent activity the behavior may show a phase of heightened efficiency. Discussions with Professors Rosenzweig and Krech (Krech, et al., 1954; 1956) have indicated that their observations also suggest the existence of such a phase. Further reduction is associated with a rapid loss in efficiency, which might for convenience be referred to as a phase of "behavioral toxicity." The fourth and final phase is characterized by signs of bodily toxicity, ending in convulsions and death.

Third, those aspects of behavior which are affected appear to be important in the animal's adjustment to changes in its environment. In many instances adaptive behavior requires the extinction of old behavior patterns and the formation of new. Under such circumstances speed of extinction may well be the pacemaker step in the series of adaptive behavior changes. Our experiments have shown that this pacemaker step, at least under certain circumstances, is related to brain ChE activity in such a way that high activity is associated with more rapid extinction. If this reasoning is valid, it leads to conclusions similar to those of Krech, Rosenzweig and Bennett (1956) that "a high ChE level is associated with an ability to maintain a probabilistic response pattern, while a low ChE level is associated with a more thorough concomitment to the dominant stimulus."

Effects of Local Interference with Intermediary Metabolism

These studies are examples of investigations in which the "biochemical lesion" has been produced without experimental control over the site in the body at which the "lesion" occurs. However, since a particular biochemical event may occur solely or predominantly in a particular organ or tissue, the site of the "lesion" may in fact be limited. For example, the "true"

1 Carried out by the author in collaboration with Dr. R. H. J. Watson, Dr. Amelia Banks and Mrs. M. Frankenhaeuser, and supported by the Medical Research Council.

2 OO-diethyl-S-ethylmercaptoethanol-thiophosphate ("systox").

ChE with which we have been concerned in our own studies is predominantly associated with nervous tissue and erythrocytes. It is also distinguished from other nervous system enzymes by the specificity of its action on ACh and by its sensitivity to selective inhibitors (Davison, 1955). In addition to such natural localizations of "biochemical lesion," it is important for certain experimental purposes that the investigator be able to select the site of the "lesion." Relations between biochemical events and behavior may well depend not only on the events themselves but also on the locale in which they occur. A number of different techniques have been used and others are being developed to allow experimental control of this kind.

For example, the action of a chemical agent on a particular organ can be segregated to some extent by injecting the agent into an afferent blood vessel of that organ. It has been demonstrated that, when this technique is used, the effects of the agent on behavior depends upon the site of the injection (Freedman and Himwich, 1949). The technique is well illustrated in a series of experiments (Aprison, *et al.*, 1954; Essig, *et al.*, 1950; Freedman and Himwich, 1949) in which injection of an anticholinesterase drug into the right common carotid artery of several species of animals produced asymmetric "biochemical lesions" clearly discernible when ChE activity levels of the frontal cortex and caudate nucleus on both sides of the brain were compared. The "lesions" were reversible and were observed to induce temporary circling movements analogous to behavior previously obtained by extirpation or by electrical stimulation of these specific cerebral areas.

Another technique allows injection of drugs directly into the ventricular system of the brains of unanaesthetized animals through a permanently implanted cannula (Feldberg and Sherwood, 1953). The use of this technique has led to very interesting results which have been summarized by Feldberg and Sherwood (1954) as follows:

"The fact that, from the ventricular system, a variety of effects on the motor or sensory side, or both, can be elicited with different drugs suggests that anatomical localization alone may not be sufficient for interpreting neural mechanisms and integration, but that consideration must be given to the pharmacological sensitivity and specificity of central synapses."

Recently I have seen work in progress at several laboratories aimed at developing new techniques for microinjection which will permit the production of specific "biochemical lesions" with at least a primary focus in very restricted sites in the nervous system. With these developments should come clarification of the question as to whether relations between biochemical events and behavior depend only on the events themselves or on their occurrence at particular localities in the body.

CHANGES IN CONCENTRATION OF SUBSTRATE

Alterations in the concentrations of substrates involved in biochemical events have also been demonstrated to be correlated with changes in behavior. Some of the most fully documented relations of this kind are found in research on sensory processes. For instance, vitamin A, which is an important constituent in the photo-chemical cycle of vision, is related selectively to certain aspects of visual perception. Deficiency in vitamin A affects brightness but not color discrimination (Russell and Younger, 1943; Russell and Walton, 1942).

More complex aspects of behavior may also be affected selectively by changes in the concentrations of essential substrates. For example, one series of studies (Peterson, 1949) has shown that raising the concentration of ACh by local applications made unilaterally to motor areas of the cerebral cortex of rats may change handedness, a habit of long standing. Injection of ACh and other chemical agents directly into the ventricles of the brain, thus changing substrate concentrations, has been shown to be reflected in a variety of behavior patterns (Feldberg and Sherwood, 1954).

Less localized variations in concentrations of other elements in the substrate may also be associated with changes of behavior. In a recent series of studies (Khairy, *et al.*, 1957; Knöpfelmacher, *et al.*, 1956) we have found that, prior to the onset of polyneuritis, thiamine deficiency is associated with exaggerated reactions during exposure of the subject to situations involving a conflict between responses, while having no significant effects upon a number of other forms of behavior, e.g., locomotion, simple learning and instrumental conditioning. Thiamine is a constituent of a co-enzyme important to the metabolism of carbohydrates in the nervous system. Inadequacies in the concentration of thiamine result in alterations of biochemical events which appear to be reflected initially in selective changes of behavior and later in typical bodily symptoms.

TEMPERATURE EFFECTS

The velocities of biochemical events are also influenced by the temperature of the environment in which they occur, tending within limits to change proportionally as temperature changes. Technical problems arise when this method of altering biochemical events is used, particularly with subjects whose body temperature is regulated internally.

Local Temperature Changes at Body Surfaces

Local heating or cooling of particular body surface areas is relatively easy. Presumably such temperature changes affect local biochemical events in the regions underlying the treated area. Several studies (Mackworth, 1950, 1953; Russell, 1957; Weitz, 1941, 1942) have shown how pressure, pain, vibratory and kinesthetic sensitivities may diminish when local skin temperatures rise or fall beyond an optimal range between 20° and 40°C. More complex behavior, e.g., skilled tracking performance, which depends at least in part upon such sensitivities, shows similar changes.

The task of discovering the events which intervene between temperature changes and variations in sensitivity is difficult. One theoretical model has been suggested which may be illustrative of the direction our thinking will take in the future. This model (Weitz, 1942) hypothesizes that

". . . a stimulus impinges upon a cutaneous receptor and there sets up a chemical reaction which in turn gives rise to the neural impulse leading to the mediation of a sensation."

Investigators have found that histamine is released when painful stimuli are applied to the skin, and it has been suggested that this synthesis of histamine may be the chemical reaction underlying pain sensitivity. Histamine when released may, under certain circumstances, be destroyed by an enzyme, histaminase. The effects of changes in temperature may be to alter the velocity with which histamine is synthesized or destroyed, or perhaps to affect the velocities of these processes differentially. Changes in these biochemical events might then be reflected in the observed changes in pain thresholds as temperature varies. Models of this kind are helpful, not only in suggesting new research approaches, but also in integrating our thinking regarding biochemical correlates of behavior.

General Changes in Deep Body Temperature

It would be particularly interesting if deep body temperatures could be altered, thus affecting biochemical events which cannot be reached by temperature changes at the body surface. Techniques for altering deep body temperature are available and have been used in observing the effects on various behavior patterns of altering general metabolism, although I know of no studies involving deep body temperature changes in a particular, isolated area. Brief descriptions of three studies will illustrate the application of this general approach to the type of problem in which we are presently interested.

The first (Hoagland, 1933) was concerned with the perception of time by human subjects. Judgments of short durations of time were made while deep body temperature was increased by diothermy treatment over a range of 3.2°C. above normal. Analysis of these time judgments showed that they varied with the internal body temperature and, although they might differ in any one subject from day to day, the effect of changes in temperature remained constant. The results suggested "that judgments of short duration may depend immediately on the velocity of a particular continuous chemical reaction (clock) in the nervous system . . ."

Wider variations in deep body temperature can, of course, be achieved when infrahuman animals serve as subjects. Analyses of the temperature characteristics of different aspects of behavior should help considerably in discovering their biochemical correlates. This approach is illustrated in an experiment designed to study the effects of alterations in body temperature on properties of convulsive seizures in rats (Toman and Swineyard, 1948). The three main stages of the convulsive behavior — seizure threshold, seizure duration and post seizure recovery — varied differentially with changes of deep body temperature, which "would seem to indicate a difference in the fundamental chemical processes underlying these three functions . . ."

The third study to which I would like to refer was carried out in our own laboratory (Andjus, et al., 1955, 1956). We were concerned with the aftereffects of very drastic reductions in general metabolism on learning and retention. Techniques had just been developed for reanimating rats subjected to extreme hypothermia (Andjus, 1951), with deep body temperature maintained below +15°C, for as long as 70 minutes. Such treatment results in complete arrest of heart beat, circulation, and respiration. It also suppresses electrical activity in the brain and in our animals cerebral activity may have been arrested for as long as 1½ to 2 hours. Our experimental design contained a control and two experimental groups of animals, the deep body temperature of animals in one of the latter groups being reduced to between 13.4 and 18.5°C. and that of the other to between 0° and +1°C. The effects of these drastic reductions on metabolism were most striking, for, as you might expect, no behavior could be elicited while the animals were so severely hypothermic. However, the aftereffects of this experience were perhaps even more dramatic. We failed to find evidence that arrest of these vital metabolic processes as a result of hypothermia produced any very serious effects on behavior once an animal had been successfully reanimated. An impairment in learning was noted, but it was small and temporary.

"BIOCHEMICAL LESIONS" OF THE ENDOCRINE SYSTEM

The examples I have given have been concerned primarily with "biochemical lesions" in the nervous system, and it would be a serious omission to close this discussion without reference to another great coordinating system in the body, the endocrine glands — variations of which we would expect to be reflected directly or indirectly in changes of behavior. During the past few years there has been a revival of interest in the ways in which the secretions of these glands, "hormones," act in affecting brain function and behavior. Hormones ". . . are endogenously produced drugs regulating the internal environment of the cells and modifying many aspects of behavior" (Hoagland, 1957). It is known that, in some instances, these hormones exert their influences on behavior indirectly, by affecting the functioning of the central nervous system. For example, certain hormones from the adrenal gland have a regulatory influence on the excitability of the brain, which in turn affects behavioral processes. In other instances, e.g., sex behavior, it is apparent that certain hormones are essential to the initiation and maintenance of behavior patterns, although little is yet known of the relations between the hormone action and neural functioning.

Much of our information regarding the roles played by hormones in behavior comes from studies involving "biochemical lesions" of the endocrine system, produced experimentally or appearing spontaneously. It can be taken for granted that further research of this kind will lead to significant advances in our knowledge of the biochemical correlates of behavior.

CONCLUSION

I hope this presentation has been sufficiently systematic to give a reasonably clear view of certain types of evidence which, I believe, support the basic validity of our assumption that behavior has its biochemical correlates. On the other hand, it would be unfortunate if, by emphasizing the influences of biochemical events on behavior, I have seemed to support a sort of push-button, slot-machine psychology —a psychology in which the brilliance of our personality, the intelligence of our actions and the success of our interpersonal relations depend solely on swallowing the proper tablets. It is not reasonable that this should be the case. Some forms of behavior are linked more directly to their biochemical correlates than others. Where the linkage is direct, changes in biochemical events are reflected in specific changes in behavior. But where the linkage is diffuse, changes in biochemical events may affect a variety of behavior patterns. In this latter instance a particular biochemical state may facilitate change of behavior, but the actual change may not occur without learning or the application of some other psychological procedure for altering behavior. I suspect that this is what is meant when chlorpromazine, reserpine and other tranquillizing drugs are described as "facilitating psychotherapy" (Ayd, 1957).

Despite the considerable number of examples of both specific and diffuse relations between biochemical events and behavior, it is quite correct to say that our general knowledge of the biochemical correlates of behavior is still very primitive. We have little knowledge of the processes by which biochemical events are, to use a recent phrase (Grenell, 1957), "transduced into general behavior patterns." Present theoretical models purporting to describe these processes are couched in terms of diffuse physiological mechanisms, metabolic events in specific regions of the brain, synaptic transmission, and molecular shifts and interactions in nerve cell membranes. A decision as to which, if any, of these models is adequate awaits much more information than we now possess. This information can only be obtained by research which includes among its approaches systematic observations of the effects of "biochemical lesions" on behavior.

Electrical self-stimulation of the brain in man

ROBERT G. HEATH

At a symposium concerning depth electrode studies in animals and man in New Orleans in 1952, the Tulane investigators described (and illustrated with films of patients treated between 1950–1952) a pleasurable response with stimulation of specific regions of the brain (Heath, 1954; Heath, et al., 1954). The pleasurable response to stimulation of some deep regions of the brain, first observed with electrical stimulation to the septal region, has proved a consistent finding in continuing studies (Heath, 1955, 1958; Heath and Mickle, 1960). Since 1952 we have reported various aspects of the phenomenon including demonstration of relief of physical pain by stimulation to this pleasure-yielding area of the brain (Heath, et al., 1954).

With the introduction of ingenious techniques for self-stimulation by Olds (1960, 1962; Olds and Milner, 1954; Olds and Olds, 1964), the need to depend largely upon verbal reports of the subjective response was eliminated and it was possible to study apparent reward and aversive areas of the brain in animals. Subjective data, of course, were lacking in the animal studies.

During the last few years the Tulane researchers have incorporated and modified some animal intracranial self-stimulation (ICSS) methods for human investigation, permitting extension of the pleasurable phenomenon studies in man. An ICSS study recently published (Bishop, et al., 1963) was designed to explore human behavior under strict laboratory conditions of the type characteristically employed in animal studies. A

From American Journal of Psychiatry, 1963, 120, 571–577.

study has also been described in which a patient was equipped with a small portable self-stimulator with 3 buttons, permitting delivery of electrical stimuli of fixed parameters to any one of 3 brain sites (Heath, 1964). The primary motivation in these studies, as in all depth electrode studies in man at Tulane, was therapeutic (Heath, 1954; Heath, et al., 1954).

Study of reward areas in the brain of man, including use of induced reward for therapeutic purposes, is extensive and complex. This presentation will focus on a description of the subjective responses of two patients treated by the self-stimulation technique. Their reports provide information concerning the reasons for repeated ICSS—information that is not available from animal studies.

MATERIAL AND METHODS

Two patients were used in the study. Patient No. B-7, age 28, with a diagnosis of narcolepsy and cataplexy, had failed to respond to conventional treatments. He had electrodes implanted by the method developed in our laboratory (Becker, et al., 1954, 1957) into 14 predetermined brain regions and fixed to remain in exact position for prolonged study. These small silver ball electrodes (most of those used in this study consisted of 3 leads each separated by 2 mm.) were placed into the right anterior and posterior septal region, left anterior and posterior septal region, right anterior hypothalamus, mid-line mesencephalic tegmentum, left anterior and posterior hippocampus, left anterior and posterior caudate nucleus and over the right frontal cortex, right and left mid-temporal cortex, and left anterior temporal cortex.

Patient No. B-10, age 25, a psychomotor epileptic with episodic brief periods of impulsive behavior uncontrolled with the usual treatments, had 51 leads implanted into 17 brain sites: left and right centromedian, left caudate nucleus, right ventricle, left and right hippocampus, mid-line mesencephalic tegmentum, left and right septal region, left amygdaloid nucleus, left paraolfactory area, and over the left and right temporal cortex, left and right occipital cortex, and left and right frontal cortex. Twenty-four leads were of stainless

steel .003 inch in diameter coated with Teflon; 27 were the small silver ball type electrode.

ICSS studies were not initiated until a minimal period of 6 months following operation, assuring elimination of any variables introduced by operative trauma, e.g., edema, anesthetic effects.

Stimuli were delivered from a specially constructed transistorized self-contained unit which was worn on the patient's belt. The unit generated a pre-set train of bi-directional stimulus pulses each time that one of the 3 control buttons was depressed. Each button directed the pulse train to a different electrode pair permitting the operator a possible selection of cerebral sites. A mechanical counter was coupled to each button to record the total number of stimuli directed toward a given area. An internal timer limited each pulse train to 0.5 second for each depression, thereby prohibiting the operator from obtaining continuous stimuli merely by keeping the button depressed. An additional feature of the unit provided 3 separate level potentiometers to give wide-range control of stimuli for each electrode pair. . . .

Studies conducted on the two patients differed somewhat because of therapeutic considerations. For studies with Patient No. B-7, the narcoleptic, the 3 buttons of the unit were attached to electrodes in the septal region, hippocampus, and mesencephalic tegmentum, and he was free to stimulate any of these sites as he chose. The patient wore the stimulator for a period of 17 weeks. Before he was equipped with the unit, baseline data concerning the time he spent sleeping during an arbitrary 6-hour period each day were charted by specified ward personnel. These data were later compared with sleeping time following attachment of the unit. This study was basically therapeutic (treatment results will be presented elsewhere) but from the experimental design we were able to obtain considerable subjective data regarding the effects of ICSS to several regions of the brain.

With Patient No. B-10, the psychomotor epileptic, a number of different experimental designs were employed to investigate the effects of ICSS. For illustrative purposes, the results of one study are presented herein as background for a description of the subjective responses. In the first part of the study a total of 17 different cerebral regions were stimulated. They were selected at random, the unit design permitting 3 sites to be hooked up at any one time. Each electrode was made available to the patient for stimulation for a minimal period of 2 hours. Various combinations of 3 sites were arranged. The purpose in making stimulation to different combinations of sites available was based on well-documented animal studies which indicate that rate of stimulation at a given site will vary somewhat depending upon the site stimulated beforehand. Data are presented in terms of the hourly stimulation to a given site as recorded with the automatic counter of the unit. Additionally, the same site of the brain was attached to different buttons to determine if the patient would relate a response to a given button. He reported, however, a consistent response to stimulation of a given electrode regardless of the button to which it was attached.

In the second part of the study the 3 sites of the brain which the subject had elected to stimulate most frequently during the first part of the study were compared over a 6-hour period.

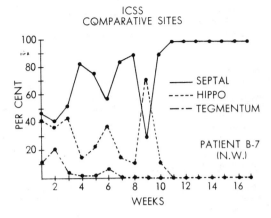

Figure 1. *Comparative sites, ICSS. Frequency of stimulation to various intracranial sites expressed in percentages in patient with narcolepsy and cataplexy.*

RESULTS

Patient No. B-7

After randomly exploring the effects of stimulation with presses of each of the 3 buttons, Patient No. B-7 almost exclusively pressed the septal button (Figure 1).

Stimulation to the mesencephalic tegmentum resulted in a prompt alerting, but was quite aversive. The patient, complaining of intense discomfort and looking fearful, requested that the stimulus not be repeated. To make certain that the region was not stimulated, he ingeniously modified a hair pin to fit under the button which directed a pulse train to the mesencephalic tegmentum so it could not be depressed.

Hippocampal stimulation was mildly rewarding.

Stimulation to the septal region was the most rewarding of the stimulations and, additionally, it alerted the patient, thereby combatting the narcolepsy. By virtue of his ability to control symptoms with the stimulator, he was employed part-time, while wearing the unit, as an entertainer in a night club.

The patient's narcolepsy was severe. He would move from an alert state into a deep sleep in the matter of a second. Recognizing that button pressing promptly awakened him, fellow patients and friends occasionally resorted to pushing the button if he fell asleep so rapidly that he was unable to stimulate himself.

The patient, in explaining why he pressed the septal button with such frequency, stated that the feeling was "good"; it was as if he were building up to a sexual orgasm. He reported that he was unable to achieve the orgastic end point, however, explaining that his frequent, sometimes frantic, pushing of the button was an attempt to reach the end point. This futile effort was frustrating at times and described by him on these occasions as a "nervous feeling."

Patient No. B-10

Studies conducted on the psychomotor epileptic patient were more varied and provided more information concerning subjective responses. The average number of button presses per hour for various regions of the

Table 1. *ICSS in man: reward (?) sites.*

Region Stimulated	Average/Hour	Subjective Response
L. Centromedian	488.8	Partial memory recall; anger and frustration
R. P. Septal	394.9	"Feel great"; sexual thoughts; elimination of "bad" thoughts
L. Caudate	373.0	Cool taste; "like it OK"
Mesenceph. Teg.	280.0	"Drunk feeling"; "happy button"; elimination of "bad" thoughts
A. Amygdala	257.9	Indifferent feeling; somewhat pleasant, but feeling not intense
P. Amygdala	224.0	Moderately rewarding; increase of current requested

Table 2. *ICSS in man: aversive sites.*

Region Stimulated	Average/Hour	Subjective Response
R. Hippocampus	1.77	Strongly aversive; "feel sick all over"
L. Paraolfactory	0.36	Moderately aversive
R. Parietal Cortex	0.50	
R. Frontal Cortex	0.00	No significant subjective response
R. Occipital Cortex	0.00	
R. Temporal Cortex	0.00	

brain is listed in Tables 1 and 2. Regions of the brain are listed in order of the frequency with which they were selectively stimulated by the subject. A summary of the principal subjective feelings is given.

The button most frequently pushed provided a stimulus to the centromedian thalamus. This stimulus did not, however, induce the most pleasurable response; in fact, it induced irritability. The subject reported that he was almost able to recall a memory during this stimulation, but he could not quite grasp it. The frequent self-stimulations were an endeavor to bring this elusive memory into clear focus.

The patient most consistently reported pleasurable feelings with stimulation to two electrodes in the septal region and one in the mesencephalic tegmentum. With the pleasurable response to septal stimuli, he frequently produced associations in the sexual area. Actual content varied considerably, but regardless of his baseline emotional state and the subject under discussion in the room, the stimulation was accompanied by the patient's introduction of a sexual subject, usually with a broad grin. When questioned about this, he would say, "I don't know why that came to mind—I just happened to think of it." The "happy feelings"

with mesencephalic stimulation were not accompanied by sexual thoughts.

Patient No. B-10 also described as "good," but somewhat less in pleasurable-yielding quality, stimuli to two sites, the amygdaloid nucleus and the caudate nucleus. Several other septal electrodes and one other electrode in the amygdaloid nucleus were stimulated a moderate number of times. His reports concerning these stimulations suggested a lesser magnitude of pleasurable response, but definitely not an unpleasant feeling.

Minimal positive response was obtained with stimulation of several other septal electrodes. The most aversive response ("sick feeling") was obtained with stimulation to one hippocampal electrode and one lead in the paraolfactory area. With stimulation of the latter lead, he complained of light flashes, apparently due to spread to the optic nerve, and of general discomfort.

No consistent changes, either significantly aversive or rewarding, were displayed with stimulation to any of 12 cortical leads dispersed widely over the cortical surface, including the frontal, temporal, occipital, and parietal lobes.

In the second part of the study the 3 electrodes which were stimulated most during the first phase of the study were attached to the 3 buttons. The sites of these electrodes were the centromedian thalamus, the septal region, and the mesencephalic tegmentum. Data indicated that the combination of sites available influenced the number of times that a given region of the brain was stimulated (Figure 2). When coupled with the subjective reports, the data also suggested that the overall state of the subject at a given moment was an influential determinant for selecting the region to be stimulated. For example, the centromedian thalamus was stimulated up to 1,100 times per hour when in combination with relatively inactive sites of stimulation and only a maximum of 290 times per hour when in combination with two other highly rewarding areas, the septal region and the mesencephalic tegmentum.

The patient noted that the frustration and anger resulting from stimulation of the centromedian thalamus was alleviated with stimulation to the septal region and to the mesencephalic tegmentum. As Figure 2 indicates, the patient during the first two hours stimulated the centromedian thalamus most frequently. This was associated with discomfort in his attempt to recapture a fleeting memory. He reported that stimulation of the other areas relieved this discomfort. There was little activity during the next two hours. Toward the end of the study, in the 5th and 6th hours, stimulation to septal and tegmental leads increased. During the 5th hour, the mesencephalic tegmentum was stimulated most frequently; during the 6th hour, the septal lead was stimulated most frequently. The patient evolved a pattern coupling the stimulus to the centromedian thalamus (which stirred his curiosity concerning the memory) with stimuli to the more pleasurable areas to lessen the feeling of frustration.[1]

DISCUSSION

Changes in parameters of stimuli to a given region of the brain, including current intensity, wave form, pulse width, and frequency, in many instances altered the patients' responses. This has similarly been reported with animal ICSS.

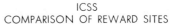

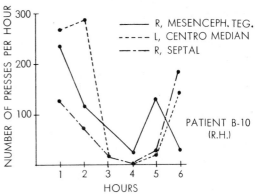

Figure 2. *Comparison of frequency of stimulation to reward sites in the brain of patient with psychomotor epilepsy.*

Information acquired from the patients' reporting of their reasons for button pressing indicates that all ICSS is not solely for pleasure. The highest rate of button pressing occurred with Patient No. B-7 when he was somewhat frustrated in his pleasurable pursuit and as he attempted to achieve an orgastic end point. In Patient No. B-10 the highest rate of button pressing also occurred with frustration, but of a different type, evolving with attempts to bring into focus a vague memory that ICSS had evoked. The subject's emotional state in this instance built into strong anger. It was interesting that the patient would button press to

1 When the paper was presented, it was here that the 16 mm. sound film was shown. Clinical effects of stimulation to a variety of deep regions of the brain, as summarized herein, were demonstrated.

In the last sequence of the film, Patient No. B-10, the psychomotor epileptic, was stimulated in the septal region during a period when he was exhibiting agitated, violent psychotic behavior. The stimulus was introduced without his knowledge. Almost instantly his behavioral state changed from one of disorganization, rage, and persecution to one of happiness and mild euphoria. He described the beginning of a sexual motive state. He was unable, when questioned directly, to explain the sudden shift in his feelings and thoughts. This sequence of film was presented to demonstrate a phenomenon which appears to be consistent and which has been repeated in a large number of patients in our laboratories. This phenomenon is the ability to obliterate immediately painful emergency emotional feelings in a human subject through introduction of a pleasurable state by physical or chemical techniques.

stimulate the region within the centromedian thalamus for a prolonged period, but at a slower rate when buttons providing more pleasurable septal and tegmental stimulation were also available. Depression of the septal button, with resultant pleasant feelings, alleviated the painful emergency state, according to the subject's report, and thereby provided him comfort to pursue his quest for the fleeting memory.

With septal stimulation in other patients, as well as the two subjects discussed here, a sexual motive state has frequently been induced in association with the pleasurable response. This sexual state has not developed in association with pleasurable feelings during stimulation to other regions. The consistent observation of a relation between sexual feelings and stimulation to the septal region has been described by MacLean in monkey experiments (1959). These reports, in part, answer questions raised by Galambos (1961) regarding ICSS when he asked, "What motivates these animals to do such unheard-of things? Is it some exquisite pleasure they receive, as several students of the problem staunchly contend, or the feeling of utter and complete well-being as others claim?".

The ICSS techniques represent one of several methodologies that the Tulane researchers have used in man to investigate the pleasurable phenomenon associated with certain types of cerebral activity. These studies complement early subcortical electrical stimulation studies (Heath, 1954; Heath, et al., 1954). The pleasurable response has also been induced in man with introduction of certain chemicals into specific deep brain regions (Heath, 1964; Heath and deBalbian Verster, 1961; Heath and Founds, 1960). It is noteworthy that intense pleasurable responses induced with chemical stimulation of the brain occurred when a high amplitude spindling type of recording was set up in the septal region.

The observation that introduction of a stimulus which induces pleasure immediately eliminates painful emergency states is quite consistent. If our psychodynamic formulations are correct, this basic observation may have widespread implication for the development of therapeutic methods to alter favorably disordered behavior.

SUMMARY

Studies are described of two human patients under treatment with ICSS. Their subjective reports in association with stimulation to reward areas of the brain are presented. The data indicate that patients will stimulate regions of the brain at a high frequency for reasons other than to obtain a pleasurable response. These data extend information obtained from ICSS in animals.

9

MODIFICATION OF BEHAVIOR
IN INDUSTRY AND ADVERTISING

When an attempt is made to modify the responses of the criminal or the psychotic, or other behaviors generally considered deviant, there are usually few complaints. However, when the object of the behavioral study becomes the control of responses considered normal (obviously more like our own), we are faced with a different reception. The husband and wife sitting at home watching television may well be influenced to buy Brand X as opposed to Y or to buy one style of apparel in preference to another. If this process of control is arrived at by chance, there will be very few who will raise their voices in protest. However, when it becomes apparent that research is being conducted to determine exactly how buying can be controlled more effectively or how more work can be obtained from an employee, there is often a different reaction. People are not as willing to condone research leading toward deliberate and precise manipulation as they are to condone the results of accident or more crude attempts, especially when applied to *their* behavior.

The articles contained in this section, which represent control in such everyday settings—industry and advertising—are good examples of the kinds of control which can be applied to normal behavior. The first is a delightful, speculative extrapolation of laboratory findings to human behavior on the production lines in our factories. Aldis offers a number of interesting suggestions designed to heighten productivity by introducing elements of uncertainty in both the magnitude and the frequency of reinforcement.

Although programmed instruction was originally intended primarily for use in our schools, industry and the military are today among its most enthusiastic endorsers. The comparative study, by Hughes and McNamara, of programmed and conventional instruction accounts for some of this enthusiasm. Since industry is comprised of profit-making organizations, it is not surprising that the primary criterion stressed in considering one method of training personnel as opposed to another is simply efficiency. The results of this study can be considered typical of others done in industrial settings, both in terms of the proved efficiency of programmed methods, and in terms of the trainees' response to an evaluative questionnaire at the end of the training period.

The final article, by Lindsley, describes an ingenious behavioral measure of the viewing of television material. One of the most attractive features of his technique is the extent to which the looking response by the viewers is externalized. Thus, the method shows exactly how attractive a commercial is by measuring how hard the consumer will work to look at it. Also, the only reinforcement utilized is the advertising copy itself, rather than money or some inadvertently applied social reinforcer such as pleasing the copy tester. Perhaps the most important aspect of the article, however, is simply that it demonstrates the almost unlimited applied possibilities of operant behavioral analysis and techniques.

Of pigeons and men

OWEN ALDIS

"Man's best friend," proclaimed an ancient sage, "is the dog." But our canine friend is increasingly taking a back seat to the pigeon, whose thoughtful guidance of psychologists has led to many highly significant insights into the behavior of people. Today we can thank pigeons (and their human experimenters) for such innovations as the teaching machines which have attracted so much national interest.

But the pigeons' efforts go on. They peck away under the inquiring gaze of the experimental psychologist who has begun to wonder whether their simple behavior patterns do not contain some useful intimations about why workers — human workers — behave as they do under various wage-incentive schemes. It is disconcerting — or encouraging, depending on how you look at it — that the results of these studies with pigeons do not apply only to birds. They have been validated under comparable laboratory conditions for a wide range of higher species, including chimpanzees, human children, and human adults in controlled (i.e., non-work) situations.

Now I realize that the intimations about worker behavior to be discussed here are still wholly speculative. I know that generalizing about the reactions of a relatively low form of animal life and applying these generalizations to a real-life human situation like work is bound to be dangerous. I also realize full well that labor unions might wax indignant if they ever thought that their members were to be manipulated as cavalierly as have been our pigeons.

I should like to suggest, however, that it might be foolish for both labor and management to prejudge my conclusions as farfetched, and as utterly lacking in practical implications that could not only improve production rates but make working much more interesting and exciting. And, in the meantime, can't we all have some fun, and just enjoy the pigeons for their own sake? (But we had better forget Clarence Day's ironic proposal, made back in 1936, that someday we ought to develop animals to run machines.) . . .[1]

Now if we do some thinking about some of the implications of our laboratory findings about how pigeons respond to various wage schedules, what suggestions might we have for managements to consider?

QUICK PAYMENTS [IMMEDIATE REINFORCEMENT]

The first generalization we can make is that organisms . . . like to receive immediate rewards for work accomplishment. If this, upon further experiment, turns out to be the best way of motivating human workers, would this not outweigh the conveniences of bookkeeping that are inherent in the regular salary schedules now increasingly in vogue in business?

Thus, one pointed suggestion for improving prevailing wage systems would be to conduct experiments with plans that reward the individual immediately upon completion of his task. Experiments have also indicated that even a small delay in rewarding destroys a certain amount of working incentive. Just consider how much motivation is lost when a man works for a week and then has to stand in a pay line for his reward.

It would be fairly simple to design a test situation for a typical factory — although it might seem at first glance to be so bizarre as to be amusing. Let us take, for example, a worker whose job consists of installing a taillight on an automobile as it passes along the assembly line. We might attach a small device similar to a taximeter to the machine the worker employs. This device would ring a bell after the man has made a sufficient number of responses and the amount he has earned would flash before him. Under a setup like this, he might have to be pulled away from the line for a coffee break. It certainly would be more dif-

From *Harvard Business Review*, 1961, July — August, 59 — 63.

1 Or maybe we ought not to forget it. See, for example, section 10, pages 238 — 256. (Ed.)

ficult for him to imagine that he could "make up" lost time than it would be if the money he was earning or not earning was kept in the abstract until later in the week.

Now, granted, this is a rather crude experiment and would offer all sorts of complications if it were installed throughout a factory. But, if we knew that workers did in fact work harder when they had before them a running total of how much money they have earned, it might indeed be the basis for the creation of a more workable system that could be easily installed. Then, too, even a crude system might work quite well in less developed countries where workers are less conditioned to the pay customs established in this country.[2]

USE OF PIECE RATES [RATIO SCHEDULES]

As we have seen from the experiments run on pigeons, the fixed-rate schedule of payments is superior to the fixed-interval schedule in motivating workers. Thus, the second suggestion I would make is that businessmen would do well to re-evaluate their attitude toward piece-rate systems. Where there are no compelling reasons against changing from a routine salary schedule to a piece-rate system, employers at least should experiment and find out whether or not workers would respond favorably to a change.

The possible advantages are obvious. Slacking off during the early phases of the interval seems to be a natural inclination of any organism. From what we have observed in our pigeon experiments, the birds seem just as much in the mood for a coffee break early in the pay period as any civil servant.

This innate tendency to dawdle under fixed-interval schedules may account for the considerable amount of supervision that is required when regular wages are paid. Supervision carries with it a veiled threat of discipline; hence it is implicitly negative and likely to breed hostility in the worker. Thus, any wage system that can cut down supervision should improve worker morale. If, at the same time, this system increases worker productivity, what more can management ask? That is the case for piece rates.

But if piece-rate pay in experimental studies of behavior is so clearly superior to non-piece-rate systems, why has American industry turned increasingly away from piece rates? There are three major influences which seem to account for this trend and will support the pay schedules of most businesses today. Specifically:

(1) With increased mechanization and automation, output in many industries is determined by the level of operation of machines, not of workers. And in some less automated plants it is necessary that there be careful control over what is put into a particular part of the system, so that surpluses in specific components do not occur. Piece-rate pay would make such control less possible. Thus, in many industries, piece rates would be inapplicable and perhaps even unfair to willing workers.

(2) Whenever technological innovations increase worker efficiency in some parts of a plant and not in others, gross inequities result between the piece-rate pay of individual workers. Even when new production standards are set and agreed on both by labor and management, inequities still seem to crop up. In such situations, both parties have often been eager to switch over to non-piece-rate systems. The resultant improvement in worker morale and production has frequently been regarded as a sign of the latter system's greater motivating power. Our experiments suggest that a renewed effort to straighten out inequities in the piece-rate system might, over the long run, have been more effective.

(3) The third factor influencing the abandonment of piece-rate systems has been the establishment of "group norms" among workers that determine the pace at which they work.

In view of these and other complicating factors, it is hardly surprising that no clear-cut answers can be given to questions about the relative advantages of piece rates as compared to other systems. There are too many variables at work. Variations in worker efficiency, under any form of wage system, are often enormous among individual plants and localities. And, so,

2 For instance, in parts of Asia and Africa, workers are often paid on the spot for each wheelbarrow load of dirt transported. And when Hillary climbed Mt. Everest, he was forced to carry extra baggage in the form of sacks of coins which were used to pay the native bearers at the end of each day's climb. Otherwise they refused to work!

the form of wage system itself is no magic panacea for increasing worker productivity. For this reason, the experimental studies now emerging from the laboratories may prove useful in isolating and weighing the influence of the different variables at work.

MORE RANDOMIZATION
[VARIABLE RATIO SCHEDULES]

The size of the used-car lots in Reno and Las Vegas are testaments to the power of the variable-ratio form of payment. And in our tests with pigeons, we have discovered that variable schedules produce higher rates of response than do comparable fixed schedules. Furthermore, the pigeons tend to sustain these higher rates of response in a constant and reliable fashion. Surely such findings should be of interest to wage incentive-plan strategists. With some thought it should be fairly easy to design pay systems which would be just as fair as today's plans but considerably more exciting for the worker concerned.

Take the annual Christmas bonus as an example. In many instances, this "surprise" gift has become nothing more than a ritualized annual salary supplement which everybody expects. Therefore, its incentive-building value is largely lost. Now suppose that the total bonus were distributed at irregular intervals throughout the year and in small sums dependent upon the amount of work done. Wouldn't the workers find their urge to work increased?

Then, too, there is another approach which can be taken to the matter of stimulating workers. So far I have been discussing only situations in which an individual receives the same amount of food, water, or money per task performance. But our pigeon studies have told us that the incentive value of many systems of reinforcement depends not only on variations in the frequency of payment, but also upon variations in the amount of payment. Gambling offers a notable case in point; it might be profitable to gamble if we won every time, but it would certainly be a lot less fun. The same emotional reliance on uncertainty heightens our interest in fishing and golfing, and almost all spectator sports. Why should we not try to heighten interest in work by introducing elements of uncertainty as to the amount of reward that will be received for accomplishing a task?

What response could we expect if we set up an experiment in one corner of a factory where workers would be paid, say, $1 for producing each of the first three units, then on the fourth unit be given a chance to collect $2 or nothing, depending on some random chance factor? Would these workers perform more efficiently than those receiving the regular rates? If so, how long would this keep up before the excitement departed?

Suppose we set up another pay experiment like this. A contest is organized whereby a worker's number is pulled out of a hat each week. How much he wins depends on how much work he has performed that week. For each unit (or groups of units) by which his production that week exceeds some agreed-on standard, his winnings would go up geometrically. In other words, this system would operate much like a pari mutuel, but the worker buys a higher valued ticket by sheer hard labor. How well would this system work? It would be worth conducting some experiments to find out.

Of course, many people will object to this as outright gambling. But a great deal of apparently respectable behavior in the business world is actually gambling. Consider the stock market's operations, or the activities of the bank loan officer who risks money with a questionable borrower, trusting that the higher interest rate he is charging will cover the risk. We live in an uncertain world in which we are all willy-nilly gamblers of sorts. If such wage systems hurt nobody and improve worker interest in getting the job done, where is the immorality?

CONCLUSION

Most of us fully realize that a large proportion of all workers hold jobs that are boring and repetitive and that these employees are motivated to work not by positive rewards but by various oblique forms of threat. One important problem for the future is that of learning how to make jobs so interesting that threats can be held to a minimum. The challenge is to motivate men by positive rewards rather than by punishments or threats of punishments. . . .

Thus the promise of newer methods of wage payments which rely on more immediate rewards, on piece-rate pay, and greater randomization does not lie only in the increase in productivity that might follow. The greater promise is that such experiments may lead to happier workers as well.

A comparative study of programed and conventional instruction in industry

J. L. HUGHES AND W. J. McNAMARA

Studies of automated teaching or programed instruction (PI) in schools, colleges, and the Armed Forces (Lumsdaine and Glaser, 1960) have shown that this technique has considerable promise in terms of reducing training time and teaching more effectively. At the time of writing this article, no comparable studies had been reported on the use of PI with industrial employees. Because of the implications of PI for industrial training programs, a research project was undertaken to evaluate its feasibility and effectiveness in an industrial training situation by means of experiments at technical employee training centers of a large company. This article will describe the first experiment completed under this project, which compared the learning achievement of employee classes taught by PI in the form of programed textbooks with that of classes taught by conventional classroom instruction. The reactions of the experimental classes to the use of PI were also obtained.

PROCEDURE

In March 1960, a team composed of a training center instructor and a psychologist was formed to prepare programed textbooks for the introductory section of a 16-week course on the IBM 7070 Data Processing System given to computer service men at a company training center.

By September, five programed textbooks containing 719 frames were completed. These frames covered the first 15 hours of conventional classroom presentation. This amount of class time would be equivalent to 5 weeks of a 3-hour college course. The topics covered were the names and functions of units of the 7070, bit coding, data flow, types of computer words, and the program step. To test the effectiveness of PI in teaching this type of material, the following experiment was designed:

Two classes ($n = 42$) which reported to the training center during September 1960, were designated the control classes. They were taught the introductory material of the course by two different instructors using the conventional classroom method (lecture-discussion). This instruction covered a period of four mornings and totaled 15 hours, 3 hours on the first morning and 4 hours on each of the remaining three mornings. The afternoons of each day were spent on another phase of 7070 training. On the fifth morning, these classes were administered a comprehensive 2-hour achievement test consisting of 88 completion and multiple-choice items. This test was prepared by the program writing team with the cooperation of several training center instructors. A new test was necessary because no satisfactory objective test of sufficient length was available for the part of the course taught by PI.

Six classes ($n = 70$) made up the experimental group. Two of these classes reported for training each month from October through December 1960. They were instructed solely by means of programed textbooks, which were

From *Journal of Applied Psychology*, 1961, **45**, 225–231.

substituted for the lectures and discussions of the introductory part of the course.

The classroom time allotted for programed texts was reduced to 11 hours spread over a 3-day period, with 3 hours on the first day and 4 hours on each of the last 2 days. This reduction in classroom presentation time was based on fairly conservative estimates of the time needed for the trainees to complete the programed texts. The trainees were also permitted to take the programed texts home with them for evening study.

The class instructors were directed to act as if the programed textbooks were part of the regular classroom procedure in order to minimize any possible Hawthorne effect. It was never mentioned to the students that they were participating in an experiment. The instructors confined their role to stating at the beginning of the first class period that this section of the course would be taught by five self-explanatory programed textbooks. They then passed out the first programed text. The third and fifth texts were passed out at the beginning of the second and third days of the experiment, respectively. The second and fourth texts were given to the trainees during the first and second classroom periods, respectively, after they had finished the texts passed out at the beginning of the period.

The reason for deliberately pacing the completion of the five programed texts over the 3-day period in this manner was to assure better administrative control. This experimental design, however, prevented the faster students from finishing all of the texts before the third day, and did not permit the direct measurement of the full saving in presentation time possible under PI.

After passing out the texts at the beginning of each class period, the instructors retired to the back of the classroom and confined their activities to recording the number of frames that each trainee completed in class. They were also instructed to answer as briefly as possible the questions asked by trainees. A record was kept of all questions asked.

The experimental classes also took the same comprehensive achievement test on the day following the completion of their instruction. In addition, they anonymously completed a Student Questionnaire asking them to evaluate PI. The questionnaire consisted of five items with five-point descriptive scales measuring the effectiveness, difficulty, and acceptability of PI, and three open-ended questions asking for any general comments and any aspects of PI particularly liked or disliked.

The control and experimental groups were run consecutively rather than concurrently in order to reduce any contamination of results. Since members of both classes starting each month at the training center might come from the same company field office and might also room together, it was decided to eliminate the possibility that study materials would be exchanged by control and experimental trainees during evening study periods.

To avoid interference with the administration of the company training center, no attempt was made to assign trainees to class by random procedures. Instead, men were assigned to classes as they were reported available for training by their office managers in the field. In planning the experiment, it was anticipated that analysis of covariance procedures would make it possible to control on background variables which differed for the control and experimental groups and were correlated with achievement test scores.

In order to test the comparability of the control and experimental groups on various background data, such as age, educational level, total months of experience, and previous computer experience, data were collected by means of an Education and Experience Questionnaire. It should be noted that these groups generally consisted of well-selected, highly motivated men who had originally been carefully screened for employment and who had satisfactory work records with the company. A company developed test of reasoning ability—Programer Aptitude Test (PAT)—was also administered. The significance of differences on these variables for the control and experimental groups and correlations of these variables with achievement test scores were calculated.

RESULTS

The subject matter covered in these experiments took 15 hours of classroom time to present by the conventional lecture-discussion

Table 1. *Comparison of control and experimental groups on background and aptitude test variables.*

Variable		Control (n = 42)	Experimental (n = 70)	with Achievement Test Score Control	with Achievement Test Score Experimental
Age	M	28.8	29.3	−.070	−.025
	SD	5.7	5.4		
Education (% attended college)		26	46*	.107	.145
Total months	M	62.3	63.1	−.077	.066
experience	SD	57.2	38.8**		
Percent with previous computer experience		38	43	.212	.362***
Programer	M	51.2	58.2***	.313*	.333***
Aptitude Test	SD	12.0	8.5**		

*Significant at .05 level by *t* test. For education and previous computer experience, the product moment coefficients were computed using 2 and 1 as scale values for the independent variable.
**Significant at the .02 level by *F* test.
***Significant at the .01 level by *t* test.

Table 2. *Analysis of covariance of aptitude test (X) and achievement test (Y) scores for control and experimental groups.*

Sums of Squares and Sums of Cross-Products:

	Control Group (n = 42)	Experimental Group (n = 70)	Within Groups	Between Groups	Total (n = 112)
Σx^2	6062	5008	11070	1280	12350
Σxy	1165	786	1951	1645	3596
Σy^2	2284	1115	3399	2114	5513

Partition of Sums of Squares of Residuals:

Source of Variation	SS of Residuals	df	MS	F
Between adj. group means	1411	1	1411	
Within common slope	3055	109	28	50.39*
Between slopes	3	1	3	
Within slopes	3052	108	28	.107
Total	4466	110		

Adjustment of Achievement Test Means:

Group	Observed Mean $\overline{X}_i$	Observed Mean $\overline{Y}_i$	Adjusted Y Mean $\overline{Y}_i - b_w(\overline{X}_i - X_t)^a$
Control	51.2	86.2	86.9
Experimental	58.2	95.1	94.7
Total	55.6	91.8	

$^a b_w$ = common within-groups slope = 1,951/11,070 = .176.
*Significant at .01 level of confidence.

method. The same information was covered in 11 hours by programed textbooks, a saving of 4 hours or 27% in classroom presentation time.

In response to an item on the Student Questionnaire, 60% of the experimental class reported that PI required less home study than the conventional classroom method. Twenty-four percent reported spending the same amount of home study under both methods, and 16% stated that PI required more home study. These results indicated that the total reduction in study time achieved by the use of programed texts was actually more for most of the students than indicated in this experiment, which measured only the reduction in classroom presentation time.

It should also be remembered that the amount of classroom presentation time for the experimental group was arbitrarily fixed to effect a conservative savings in classroom time. Because the programed textbooks were taken out of class by the trainees, records of the actual time needed for completing the five texts could not be maintained. From the instructors' records of the number of frames that each trainee completed in class, however, it was possible to derive some estimates of individual differences in the time required to complete the program. A mean completion time per frame was calculated for each trainee. On the basis of these figures, the mean completion time per frame for the entire group was calculated to be 49 seconds and the standard deviation, 9 seconds. For the total 719-frame program, it was therefore estimated that the mean completion time was 9.8 hours and the standard deviation, 1.8 hours. Individual differences in estimated completion time ranged from 7.2 to 15.3 hours. Thus, the mean completion time was 1.2 hours less than the 11 classroom hours allotted for PI in this experiment, and there were large individual differences in completion times. This finding suggested that even greater savings in instruction time would be possible for most trainees if they used instruction on an individual basis. Because of the experimental design used, these savings could not be directly measured in the present experiment.

A comparison of the aptitude test scores and background variables for the control and experimental groups and their correlations with the achievement test scores are given in Table 1. Of all the background variables, only the PAT scores showed a significant difference between the two groups and had a significant relationship with achievement test scores. The hypothesis that both groups were drawn from the same population on reasoning ability was rejected at the .05 level. The hypothesis of no relationship between reasoning ability and achievement test scores was rejected at the .05 and .01 levels for the control and experimental groups, respectively. Analysis of covariance was used to test the significance of differences in residual achievement test scores after eliminating the effect of PAT scores on achievement.

Table 2 shows the results obtained from the analysis of covariance (Walker and Lev, 1953). The null hypothesis of no difference between the control and experimental group regression slopes was accepted ($F = .107$). The null hypothesis of no differences in residual achievement test scores between experimental and control groups was rejected by F test at the .01 level of confidence ($F = 50.39$). Thus, the obtained differences in achievement test scores could not be wholly attributed to differences in aptitude test scores (PAT).

On the achievement test scores, the control group had a mean of 86.2 and a standard deviation of 7.4. The experimental group had a mean of 95.1 and a standard deviation of 4.0. When the achievement test scores were adjusted for the effect of PAT test scores, the control and experimental group means became 86.9 and 94.7, respectively (Table 2). The difference in adjusted means was 7.8, only slightly less than the difference of 8.9 in the unadjusted means.

The standard deviations of the adjusted achievement test scores for the control and experimental groups were 7.0 and 3.8, respectively. An F test of homogeneity of variance rejected the hypothesis at the .02 level that both samples were from populations with the same variance. Thus, the difference in adjusted achievement test means between the two groups could have been accounted for by a difference in variance between the groups (Edwards, 1950). It was also noted that the difference in achievement variance was paralleled by a difference in reasoning ability variance as measured by the PAT (Table 1).

In order to remove the possible effect of the initial difference in reasoning ability variance on achievement variance, control and experimental groups matched for PAT scores were set up. This resulted in reducing the number in each group to 34 cases. The achievement test means and standard deviations for these matched samples were 86.7 and 7.3 for the control group, and 93.9 and 4.6 for the experimental group. The differences in means and standard deviations were found to be significant at the .01 and .02 levels, respectively, by t test for matched groups. Therefore, the higher mean and lower variance in achievement for the experimental group did not appear to be due either to differences in reasoning ability level or variability, but rather to the different teaching method used.

Distributions of the adjusted achievement test scores for the control and experimental groups are given in Table 3. The distribution for the experimental group indicates a concentration of scores at the upper score levels. If a score of 95 or above is adopted as an indication of mastery of the subject matter taught, it can be seen that the experimental group had 67% at this level or above, compared to only 12% for the control group. The PI group thus had more than five times as many trainees at the highest achievement level.

On the Student Questionnaire administered anonymously to the six experimental classes, the replies of the trainees were very favorable to PI (Table 4). Of the total group of 70 men, 87% liked PI more than conventional instruction, and 83% said they would prefer using it in future IBM courses. Only 6% liked PI less than conventional instruction, and 13% would have some objections to using it in future courses. A possible reason for the size of the latter negative response was the impression of some students that PI would completely replace the use of instructors and class discussions in future courses.

It was interesting to note that practically all of the trainees realized the advantages of PI over conventional instruction. All of the group (100%) stated before taking the examination that PI was more effective than conventional instruction, and 93% also found

Table 3. *Distributions of adjusted achievement test scores for control and experimental groups.*

Adjusted Achievement Score Level	Control Group (n = 42)		Experimental Group (n = 70)	
	N	%	N	%
95 and above	5	12	47	67
90-94	14	33	15	22
85-89	9	22	5	7
80-84	7	17	3	4
75-79	5	12		
70-74	1	2		
65-69	1	2		
Mean	86.9		94.7	
Standard Deviation	7.0		3.8	

it less difficult. None of the trainees found PI more difficult than the present instruction method.

The Student Questionnaire also provided the trainees with several open-ended questions asking what they particularly liked or disliked about PI. In their responses, 69 of the 70 trainees mentioned some aspect of PI which they liked. A content analysis indicated that the most frequently liked aspects of PI were its effectiveness as an instruction method (46 comments); certain characteristics of the method itself, such as the repetition of important points, the gradual and logical sequence of presentation, the way it maintained the student's attention and concentration (23 comments); and the ability to proceed at one's individual rate (10 comments). It appeared from these comments that, through their own experience with PI, the trainees themselves recognized a number of the advantages usually ascribed to it.

In response to the question on what they particularly disliked, 40 of the 70 trainees wrote in a number of comments, but no single comment was made by many individuals. For example, there was criticism of the need to turn pages constantly (8 comments), the amount of repetition and written responses required (6 comments), the amount of time allotted for studying the materials (7 comments), and the absence of an instructor and

Table 4. *Summary of student questionnaire responses for experimental classes (n = 70).*

Compared to the regular classroom instruction in other company courses you have taken:	Scale Category[a]				
	PI Much Less	PI Less	PI Same	PI Somewhat More	PI Much More
1. How do you like the programed instruction (PI) method?	3%	3%	7%	24%	63%
2. How difficult was it to learn using the programed instruction (PI) method?	62	31	7		
3. How much home study does the programed instruction (PI) method require?	24	36	24	13	3
4. How well has the programed instruction (PI) method taught you the material covered?				21	79
	Strongly Object	Some Objections	Don't Care	Some Preference	Strongly Prefer
5. In future company courses you may take, would you like to see the programed instruction (PI) method used in place of the regular classroom method?		13	4	37	46

[a]For each question, the form had a five-point descriptive scale containing very unfavorable to very favorable statements about PI. To save space, these statements have not been completely reproduced here.

class discussion (5 comments). Another criticism made by 7 trainees was the failure of the PI textbook used in this experiment to provide adequate summaries or outlines of the topics covered to aid in reviewing the material.

Forty-nine trainees responded to another question asking for additional comments, but most of these remarks merely amplified the positive or negative comments reported above. Of most interest were the 14 comments recommending the use of PI in other courses. Of these, however, 8 trainees qualified this recommendation by stating that PI should not be used for extended periods without some type of instructor contact or classroom discussion.

DISCUSSION

The results of this experiment using PI in an industrial training situation corroborated the positive findings found by other investigators in studies of PI in schools, colleges, and the Armed Forces (Lumsdaine and Glaser, 1960). They indicated the reduction in training time and the improvement in learning achievement possible through the use of PI in industrial training.

These findings suggested several applications to industrial training programs which promise important economies. One is the reduction in the number of days that employees need to spend at central company training centers learning a given course. This reduction can be translated immediately into savings in the direct daily living expenses and salaries of these trainees and eventually into reductions of other educational and administrative costs.

A second application is the possibility of greater decentralization of training by enabling employees to be trained in basic courses at local field offices or other locations rather than in a central company training center. Since the trainee works individually on PI materials, an educational package can be prepared for distribution to these field locations. The possible economies in this method of instruction can be easily seen.

In addition to savings in training costs, another promising result of PI is the possibility of better trained employees. At present, there appears to be no reason why PI cannot be applied to substantial portions of technical, manufacturing, clerical, sales, and management training courses now given to company employees. Although the effect of better trained personnel cannot always be measured directly, it is obviously a major factor in improving industrial efficiency.

Some important qualifications regarding the use of PI for industrial training are suggested, however, by the analysis of trainee responses to the Student Questionnaire (Table 4). While these responses were generally very favorable, the write-in comments on particularly disliked aspects of PI suggested a number of areas where potential trainee dissatisfaction could impair the effectiveness of a training program using PI. These comments concerned the frequency of page turning, the boredom of too much repetition and writing-in of responses, and the feeling of not having enough time to go through the programed textbook. Although these comments were made relatively infrequently in this experiment, the areas mentioned must be kept in mind in planning to use PI in industrial training. Fortunately, much of the page turning can be eliminated by improvements already under way in programed text format, rote repetition can be minimized by the preparation of more stimulating programs, and reasonable time limits can be determined by preliminary tryouts of programed materials.

Further trainee dissatisfaction with PI could arise from failure to integrate it properly with other instructional techniques. It must be remembered that PI is not a panacea for all training ills. While 87% of the trainees in this experiment expressed a liking for PI, there were comments that too much PI without breaks for class discussion, laboratory, or other instructor contact at intervals would, in their opinion, become boring. Anyone concerned with using PI in industrial training must therefore carefully plan how to use it in limited amounts to supplement existing educational procedures rather than to replace them completely. It is anticipated that future research in PI will furnish suggestions on how this may best be done.

SUMMARY

Programed textbooks containing 719 frames were prepared covering the introductory 15 hours of a 16-week course for trainees in a 7070 Data Processing System servicing course. Achievement test scores for six experimental classes ($n = 70$) who used these programed texts were compared with those of two control classes ($n = 42$) taught by the lecture-discussion method. Significant gains in achievement and reduction of training time were found for the experimental classes. Student reaction to programed instruction as measured by a questionnaire was found to be favorable.

A behavioral measure of television viewing

OGDEN R. LINDSLEY

If a television commercial is to induce purchase, it must first induce looking and listening. The only efficient commercials are those that are seen and heard by the prospective purchaser. How can an advertiser insure that his commercials will be thus perceived?

He may predict consumer viewing and listening on the basis of his past experience with other consumers and other commercials. Telephone interviews and receiver tuning can provide helpful feedback. But telephone interviews suffer the inaccuracies of recall; and tuned receivers mean not that the message was perceived, but only that it could have been. And since these are measures of previously used copy, they tell the advertiser when he has

From *Journal of Advertising Research*, 1962, **2**, 2–12.

erred but do not insure him against error. For such insurance he must *pre*test, and for accurate pretest methods he has lately turned to the behavioral sciences.

Pretests based on experimental psychological methods are more objective than raw past experience. Using a representative sample of the consumer population, a pretest can compare two media bearing the same message, or two different messages in the same medium. The best techniques evaluate the commercial by recording the consumer's immediate response to it without inverviews, without recall, and without pausing. If the response is continuously recorded, it can be used to correct parts of the copy in order to induce sustained perceptual response.

One such behavioral measure has been obtained by the Lazarsfeld Program Analyzer (Peterman, 1940) in which the subject registers pleasure or displeasure by turning knobs. Another, recently reported by Hess and Polt (1960), is of the viewer's pupil. Pupil dilation was assumed to indicate pleasure, if incoming light were held constant, and was photographed with an infrared camera.

The present report describes a more precise behavioral measure which has grown out of the operant conditioning methods developed during the past 30 years by B. F. Skinner (1959). These methods have been widely applied in the pharmaceutical industry to predict the effects of drugs, and more recently in the classroom to program instruction by "teaching machines."

Our technique shows how rewarding a commercial is to the consumer by measuring how hard he will work to look at it. The measure is continuous, immediate, objective, and sensitive. It avoids most of the validity problems inherent in verbal or recall methods.

We will describe this new copy testing technique against a background of the history of operant conditioning. Some sample results will be shown and other applications of the technique suggested.

BACKGROUND

Operant Conditioning Methods

A response which involves little effort and can be emitted by the subject faster than he can make decisions is chosen to be the "operant." By selecting a simple response, physiological fatigue is ruled out of the experimental data and behavior can be analyzed in very fine units. Such would not be the case with responses such as writing down words, talking, or operating a complicated apparatus. One response often used in human behavioral analysis is the pressing of a small switch (requiring no more than 300 grams of force through a distance of two centimeters). It may be thought of as the sharply pointed fulcrum on a chemical balance. The more delicate and sharp the response, the more finely can the behavior be measured.

The response is defined by its consequences. These later events may be rewards or punishments. If pushing a button produces a candy bar, then button-pushing is called the candy response. If button-pushing produces cigarettes, it is called the cigarette response. If it illuminates a television receiver screen, it is called the television-viewing response.

Almost anyone can press a button several times a second. When his responses are recorded on a moving paper graph, the record permits behavioral analysis in units shorter than the time it takes to make most gross responses. Thus operant conditioners have a behavioral yardstick with measurement units finer than the behavioral processes which they wish to measure. High behavioral "resolution" is achieved, since operant methods are sensitive to very slight and subtle behavioral changes which occur in fractions of a second.

Since we are concerned only with measuring the *rate* of the response, a special technique of recording it has been developed. Recording paper moves continuously at 30 centimeters (almost 12 inches) per hour. Each response is indicated on the passing record by an upward movement of the recording pen. Thus the slope of the resulting graph indicates the rate of responding, and the original record can be fully interpreted without further analysis.

Laboratory scientists seek to control so much of the experimental environment that they need not resort to statistical analysis to determine the significance of the effects of the variables studied. In operant conditioning, this control takes the form of an experimental room which prevents variables other than those being studied from subtly altering the behavior of the subjects and thus putting unwanted "noise" into the data. Automatic programing presents all stimuli and experimental variables to the subject, thus eliminating the possibility of the experimenter's biasing the data by unconscious manipulation of the variables. Automatic recording similarly prevents experimenter bias in collecting data. Automatic equipment also saves money: one technician can monitor many subjects at once.

This environmental control, besides eliminating extra-experimental variables and experimenter bias, also permits recording the effects of experimental variables with such accuracy that conclusions can often be reached from single subjects. Usually the research design insures that each individual serves as his own control by presenting and removing the experimental variable several times within a single experimental session. Strong individual differences revealed in this manner can later be used to predict the behavior of single subjects or groups.

Studies of the Looking Response

By making five-second durations of projected Kodachrome slide images contingent on an operant response, we have been able to show wide individual differences among chronic psychotics and normal individuals responding to different pictorial themes (Skinner, Solomon, and Lindsley, 1954; Lindsley, 1956). For example, male homosexuals responded at higher rates for male nude pictures presented as reinforcement than they did for female nude pictures.

Holland (1957, 1958[1]) instructed Navy enlisted men to observe as many deflections of the pointer on a dial as they could. They were seated in a dark enclosure, with a key which produced a .07-second illumination of the dial each time it was pressed. The men pressed the key at rates as high as 120 per minute to light up the dial, showing that the opportunity to observe the dial was reinforcing to them.

It has been suggested by Jeffrey (1955) and Bijou and Sturges (1959) and shown by Baer (1960) that children will respond to prevent sound movies from being totally withdrawn for five-second periods of time. This technique is called a Hefferline escape-avoidance schedule of reinforcement. In our laboratories since 1959 we have had children and adults respond on conjugate reinforcement schedules in order to produce the sound or picture of sound movies.

Conjugate Reinforcement

In conjugate reinforcement the intensity of a continuously available reinforcing stimulus varies directly and immediately with the rate of response (Lindsley, Hobika, and Etsten, 1961). This schedule permits a more direct, immediate, and finer-grained analysis of the moment-to-moment changes in the value of a reinforcing stimulus than the episodic schedules of reinforcement which were previously used by operant conditioners (Ferster and Skinner, 1957).

By making brief, slight reductions in the intensity of a loud, aversive tone conjugately contingent upon pressing a switch, we were able to generate high, stable rates of response which were sensitive to intermediate levels of awareness and which could be used to induce behavior during sleep and thereby to evaluate the depth of sleep (Lindsley, 1957). Similar use of conjugate reinforcement revealed subtle changes in level of consciousness and produced unconscious responding in subjects under surgical anesthesia and in EST-produced coma (Lindsley, Hobika, and Etsten, 1961; Lindsley and Conran, 1962).

Music, movies, or television must be continuously available to have maximal reinforcing power. Episodic presentation of these reinforcers greatly decreases their reward value. Five-second bursts of a Beethoven symphony are more a musical recognition test than an evaluation of the reinforcing effect of the music. Short bursts of Beethoven provide no chance for the music to reach its maximal reinforcing effect through the development of emotional responses.

Gradual approach or withdrawal of stimuli often enhances their reward value. Abrupt presentation of views of the human body produces responses in the opposite sex as unemo-

---

1 Pages 53–64 of this volume.

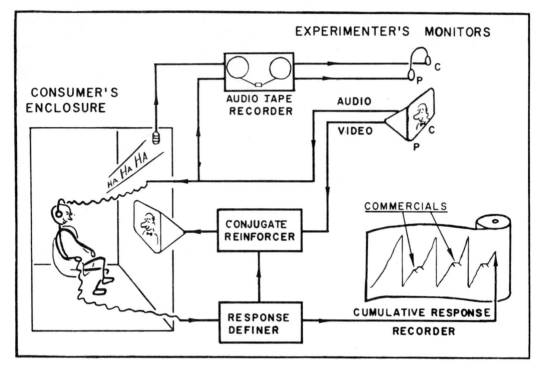

Figure 1. *A schematic diagram of the experimental room.*

tional as those of an anatomy class. In contrast, the gradual revelation of anatomical areas produces a much greater reinforcing effect of a vague, sexual nature. If an anatomy professor slowly and gradually revealed female anatomical structures on a chart, he would probably be expelled for "improper" presentation of his subject matter!

METHOD

The *consumer's enclosure* is schematically diagrammed, along with the other important apparatus components, in Figure 1. The enclosure can be any comfortably air-conditioned room which isolates the experimental consumer from other individuals and unwanted variables which might disturb his viewing behavior. Our experimental rooms are painted blue and are equipped with comfortable chairs for the viewer. Mounted in the wall approximately six feet from the viewer is the television receiver, whose brightness the consumer controls. The consumer can hold in either hand a small switch which produces a brief (less than 0.5 second), slight increase in the brightness of the television image. Even if the switch is held down, only this brief period of illumination is permitted. The *response definer* converts each press of the switch to an electrical pulse which operates the *conjugate reinforcer*. Thus, high rates of responding (above 60 per minute) keep the picture brightly illuminated for comfortable viewing; intermediate rates of responding keep the picture at dimmer levels; and during periods of no responding the picture tube is dark.

The audio part of the television program is continuously presented to the consumer through comfortable earphones. Earphones are used so that his vocal responses (e.g., laughing) can be recorded by a microphone within the room without also picking up the responses of the television audience.

The *experimenter's monitors* consist of earphones, one (labeled "P" in Figure 1) through which the experimenter can hear the audio part of the television program and another (labeled

"C") through which he can hear the vocal responses of the consumer. The experimenter also has a television receiver equipped with a monitoring switch so that he may view either the program the consumer has an opportunity to see or the image on the consumer's receiver produced by his responses. The use of these monitors permits the experimenter to check when the consumer is not responding to see if it is because the set is out of tune or because the consumer is not interested in looking at a clear image.

Consumer's operant response rate is recorded on the *cumulative response recorder* (diagrammed in Figure 1 and described above). The slope of the line on these records indicates the rate of pressing the switch and the brightness of the consumer's receiver. These records provide a direct measure of the consumer's moment-to-moment interest, or desire to work for the video portion of the television program. In other words, they are records of his looking responses. The experimenter can indicate anything of interest on these records by pressing a switch which moves the pen to the right and downward, making a "hatch" mark on the record. In the figures in this article these hatch marks indicate the beginning and end of commercials appearing in a television program. If the experimenter wishes, he can also write on the cumulative response record any changes in program content, etc.

Consumer's vocal responses are recorded through the microphone in the consumer's enclosure onto one channel of a *stereophonic tape recorder*. At the end of the program additional responses are obtained from the consumer by having him fill out a questionnaire and by interviewing him. However, these questionnaire and interview results suffer from recall bias, even though the recall is almost immediate. Our data have shown that the results of these interviews are by no means as accurate, subtle, or sensitive to moment-to-moment changes in viewing behavior as is the directly recorded operant response.

Copy content is recorded on the second channel of the stereophonic tape recorder. It is also possible to record the video content on a video tape recorder. These records of copy content can then be compared with the cumulative response record and the consumer's vocal response record for moment-to-moment analysis.

We pay the subjects to attend. This payment in no way interacts with the subject's viewing behavior since it is not contingent upon viewing responses but merely on his attendance.

The subject can be placed in the enclosure with absolutely no prior instructions, nor indeed any knowledge of the English language. The response is learned almost immediately. There is no possibility of distorting the subject's responses by instructions, since there are no instructions. To use infants as young as

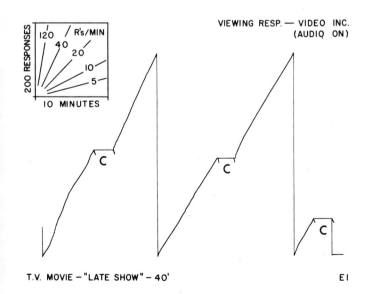

VIEWING RESP. — VIDEO INC.
(AUDIO ON)

200 RESPONSES

120 / R's/MIN
40
20
10
5

10 MINUTES

C

C

C

T.V. MOVIE – "LATE SHOW" – 40'

E I

Figure 2. How one man viewed the late show and its commercials (C).

four months, for example, one need only substitute a crib for the chair, and a panel that the infant can kick for the hand switch used by adults. One copy testing session was run with a seven-year-old boy for six hours without interruption. The type of experimental consumer selected is determined by the nature of the product and the market rather than by the copy testing technique.

RESULTS

Figure 2 is a cumulative response record of a 40-year-old male adult's viewing behavior for a re-run Hollywood film on the Late Show. Sound was on continuously. The looking responses are recorded on the graph. Three commercials are shown (labeled "C"). Note that no looking responses occurred during the commercials. It is important to realize that since the consumer did not leave his chair, these interruptions in the looking behavior produced by the commercials cannot be attributed to an opportunity to visit the kitchen or bathroom. The commercials simply were not worth the operant looking responses required to view them. With this consumer the video channel of these commercials was wasted. The Late Show's audience is probably larger than that of most radio programs, but for this part, these commercials might just as well have been presented on radio.

Good commercials should induce both looking and listening responses. Had we used a two-response situation, in which both looking and listening responses were required of the consumer, it may well have been that the consumer would not even have listened to the commercial but would only have spot-checked it with his listening response to make sure the movie had not yet begun again.

Note that the movie produced a high, even rate (30 to 50 responses per minute) of looking responses with continuous audio presentation. We find that movies generally produce more looking behavior than do programs developed expressly for television, perhaps because so many television producers and performers were trained in radio and have not yet learned to take full advantage of the video portion of television programs.

Analysis of a Program

Figure 3 presents the cumulative viewing response record for the first 40 minutes of a Du Pont Show of the Week, "Laughter U.S.A.," shown Sunday, September 17, 1961, over WBZ-TV, Boston, at 10 P.M. The subject was a 28-year-old woman with a high school education, married, with one child. Her husband was a machinist.

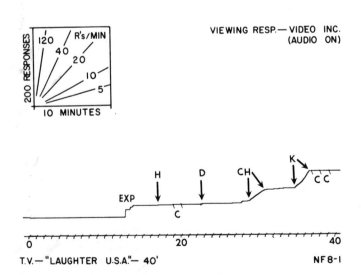

Figure 3. How a young woman viewed a Du Pont Show of the Week.

Note that very few looking responses occurred. At "EXP" the experimenter entered the consumer's enclosure and rapidly pressed the switch ten times to insure that the apparatus was working and to give the consumer a "demonstration." She made a few looking responses after this but did not brighten the screen again until she heard Bob Hope over the audio and took a brief look (labeled "H"). She did not watch the commercial (first "C"), but when she heard Jimmy Durante start to sing "Ink, a-dink a dee," she took another brief look at the video (labeled "D").

For about two minutes her viewing behavior was sustained by Charlie Chaplin ("CH" in the figure). She took four more brief looks, but did not continuously view the show again until the Keystone Cops came on ("K" in the figure). Two more commercials were not observed.

The analysis of this single record suggests that the commercials did not generate looking behavior and that the show itself was not suitable for television. Since it did not generate looking behavior, it might as well have been broadcast on radio. Note that most of the looking behavior was produced by actors who had prior experience in silent films (Chaplin and the Keystone Cops), not by performers originally on radio (Hope and Durante).

Figure 4 contains the last 20 minutes of "Laughter U.S.A.," followed by the 11 P.M. news and weather, for this same consumer. It is a continuation of the record shown in Figure 3. To be sure that "Laughter U.S.A." was at least functioning as an audio show for this consumer, we changed the experimental circuit so that the video channel was on continually while the consumer had to press the switch in order to increase the intensity of the audio channel. Note that when she had an opportunity to see the show continuously she pressed the switch to hear it. However, she did not bother to listen to the commercials, even when they were visually presented. At the arrow marked "P" she listened to Jack Paar.

When the news came on, the circuit was changed back again so that the sound was on continually while responding produced the television picture. She watched all the news report except the commercials. The commercial marked with only one hatch (marked "CS") was a spot commercial which caused a very brief interruption in looking behavior. At "B" she refrained from watching while the baseball scores were given, but when the football scores were given immediately afterward (at "F") she watched the football playing scenes. She did not look at the next commercial until (at "D") the sound track mentioned "and look at these lovely dresses," at which point she pressed the button to get a brief look. She followed by watching the whole weather report but looked at only a small portion of the last of its three commercials.

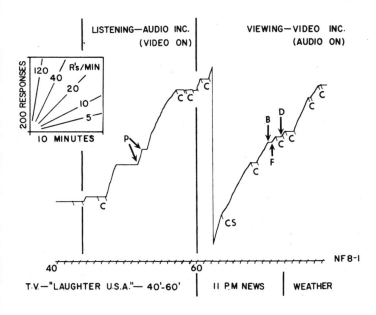

Figure 4. *Same woman's later viewing of Du Pont Show, news and weather report.*

Analysis of a Commercial

Figure 5 is a continuation of Figure 4. At the beginning of the figure the Alka-Seltzer commercial was shown. The expanded record of this commercial, which was recorded on another instrument running at twice the speed, is shown above the response record. At the point marked "23" the sound track said "and 23 mechanical men," whereupon the consumer looked at the commercial. The sound track of the whole commercial generated looking behavior in this woman only at that point; at all other points the video portion was wasted. The rest of the record is clear evidence that the consumer was neither fatigued nor bored, for she continued to watch the "Late Show" with a high, even rate of looking responses except during the commercials (labeled "C"). The record shown in Figure 5 provided a control for possible satiation, boredom, and fatigue effects. Therefore, the low rates of looking response shown in Figure 3 must be attributed to low visual interest.

OTHER APPLICATIONS

The effects of different commercials on listening or looking responses can be compared easily. It is also possible to *select an appropriate program for a given commercial.* Perhaps, if a program commands very great viewing interest, trips to the kitchen and bathroom will be forced into the time of a moderately good commercial, reducing the advertising exposure more than if the commercial had been placed in a weaker program. Of course, if the program is too weak, the consumer will probably not tune in at all.

Interprogram comparisons are possible using this technique. As shown in Figure 2, "Laughter U.S.A." was not as powerful a television program as the movie shown in Figure 5. These data were available immediately after the program was shown and could have been provided by copy testing prior to the presentation of the program. Critics' reports and interviews conducted later supported this experimental record, which suggested the program was more properly a radio show.

Accurate selection of media would be facilitated with this technique. If a taped or filmed program produced listening responses but not looking responses, it clearly would be most efficiently presented over the radio medium.

Description of consumer targets should become more and more precise as individually significant and sensitive looking and listening behavior is recorded and grouped into similar categories. Many investigators have already shown that men and women have very different viewing habits. As more precise copy testing techniques are developed, the consumer popu-

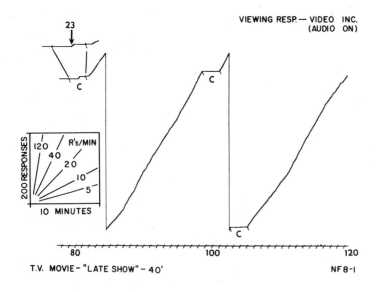

VIEWING RESP. — VIDEO INC.
(AUDIO ON)

200 RESPONSES

120 R's/MIN
40 20
10
5

10 MINUTES

80   100   120

T.V. MOVIE—"LATE SHOW"—40'   NF 8-1

Figure 5. Same woman's later viewing of late show and commercials (C).

lation will probably be broken down into a small number of subtypes with particular viewing and listening habits. Being able to describe the viewer subtypes and to predict their viewing responses should be useful in the selection and design of advertising media and messages.

Choice of technical procedures for producing commercials can be pretested by comparing the viewing responses under various technical procedures. For example, taped versus filmed commercials could be compared for ability to produce looking responses. A decision as to whether to use lyrics or not in background music could also be made in this fashion. Since the purpose of this paper is to describe this new method rather than to encompass all of its possible applications, these few suggestions for further application should suffice.

OTHER RESEARCH METHODS

The Audience Concepts Committee of the Advertising Research Foundation recently published a report clarifying the issues involved in measuring the effectiveness of advertising through media (Banks, *et al.*, 1961). This committee concluded that the perceptive response to advertising is the most logical and convenient point to make comparisons between different media. It is clear that accumulated practical experience does not predict advertising consumer response accurately; experience must be supplemented by pretests. The copy tester must decide whether to use an older research method which, despite its well-known limitations, provides a large body of data to fall back upon, or whether to try newer, more objective devices which promise more accurate predictions, but lack norms.

Telephone and personal interview techniques are limited by the errors involved in human memory and recall. Moreover, the unconscious motivations of the consumer and his social interaction with his peers between the advertising exposure and the time of interview alter his interview response. A happily married man may be unable to take his eyes away from a screen displaying a scantily clothed young lady, but in an interview be unable to describe his interest in that commercial.

Television receiver operation and tuning informa-tion is objective and reliable, but by itself indicates only that there was an opportunity for one or more individuals to observe. It does not objectively record the viewing response. Individuals who have such automatic recording equipment in their homes may show sample inclusion bias: they turn on their sets to watch programs they would like the country to watch, rather than programs which they themselves would be more rewarded for observing (Dailey and Stahl, 1962).

The methods above measure consumer response to copy which has already been aired. They are of little help in preventing the waste of costly air time on untested copy. The objective methods described below, however, can pretest copy experimentally, do not include errors of memory and recall because they provide immediate measures of advertising response, and produce relatively continuous measurement, permitting a fine-grain analysis of copy content so that the poor parts of a copy can be cut and portions which produce more viewing behavior inserted. In this way, these measures can be used to monitor continuously the design and construction of efficient advertising copy.

Pupillary dilation, recorded by an infrared camera as a measure of pleasure (Hess and Polt, 1960), is affected by variables other than the content of the advertising copy. The amount of light falling on the eye must be controlled, as well as emotional stimulation and drugs which alter pupillary dilation. Also, the method is costly since the pupillary dilation measures must be taken from motion picture film which the copy tester must observe frame by frame. McCann-Erickson is now investigating the practicality of this method for copy testing.

Eyeball focusing information can also be obtained with the Hess-Polt technique. The focusing of the eyes indicates how long the particular portions of advertising copy are looked at. Head movement disturbances could readily be ruled out by using a head positioning device with a biting board, or by superimposing the pattern of focus and the copy when a major shift occurred. It would also be possible to affix the copy to the head or to control the copy by head movements with servo mechanisms. More disturbing than the head movements is the realization that focusing the eyes on a part of advertising copy for a long period of time is not necessarily an indication that this part of the copy was preferred to other parts. It could well be, for example, that this part of the copy was simply more puzzling than other parts (Leavitt, 1961).

Objective reports of pleasure and displeasure, provided by a subject's turning one knob to indicate pleasure and another knob to indicate displeasure while viewing advertising copy, were developed by Lazarsfeld (Peterman, 1940) as a program analyzer for CBS. Recently modified by Marquis for Screen Gems, this is not a direct behavioral measurement device. The reinforcement to the experimental consumer for turning the knobs and registering his pleasure or displeasure is not provided by the advertising copy itself. Rather, it may be some social reinforcer involved with trying to please the copy tester, or perhaps a feeling that if the knobs are not continually adjusted and readjusted, payment will be withheld. Furthermore, it is possible for an experimental consumer to be pleased while he unconsciously turns the displeasure knob. In other words, the reward for busily adjusting the knobs is money or social approval. The rewarding value of the advertising copy is not directly and irreversibly related to the knob turning response. Even if pleasure and displeasure were accurately measured by this device, the data could not be considered conclusive, for pleasure does not always indicate reward value. People will stare, for example, at scenes such as automobile accidents, ugly sores, or deformed persons, which produce displeasure.

DISCUSSION

The operant viewing response described in this report can be thought of as giving the experimental consumer an additional, artificial pupil over which he has volitional control. With operant procedures, the looking response is externalized. The reinforcement for this response is the advertising copy itself. If the advertising copy is important to the experimental consumer he must respond in order to view it. There is no way for him to view the copy without recording his viewing.

Some additional points concerning copy testing with this new technique are discussed below.

Increasing response cost, by increasing the amount of force required to press the response switch or by increasing the rate of response required to illuminate fully the television screen, serves to adjust the sensitivity of the technique. Only strongly reinforcing aspects of advertising copy would be viewed when a high response cost was required. By increasing response cost, it is possible to take a commercial which produces stable and continuous viewing responses when response cost is low and determine which parts of the commercial have the most reinforcing value for viewing behavior. For example, the contents of the television programs shown in Figures 1 and 5 could be analyzed by increasing the response costs. This procedure is similar to increasing the degree of amplification on a cathode ray oscilloscope when it indicates a continuous voltage for different conditions. Similarly, if particular copy does not produce viewing responses from a particular subject, it is possible to reduce the response cost to the point where some viewing occurs. Thus, by adjusting response cost upward or downward it is possible to analyze experimentally the separate parts of copy which otherwise are either totally ignored or continuously viewed.

Sample inclusion bias may occur if an experimental consumer behaves differently when he is in an advertising research sample than when he is not. This has been suggested by many critics of advertising research techniques (most recently, Dailey and Stahl, 1962). The method described in this report has minimal sample inclusion bias for two reasons. The first is that it is very difficult for individuals to "fake" the looking response. If the advertising copy has truly compelling visual interest, it is more reinforcing for the experimental consumer to look at the visual content than to refrain from responding in order to get the delayed social reinforcement of "fooling" the advertising researcher. The second reason is that after 10 to 20 minutes of operating the switch to view the television screen, the response becomes unconscious. This is shown by increased rates of pressing when the actual program becomes dim or hazy, or when an image on the screen is hidden by some other object. In other words, the pressing of the switch gets to be as much of a looking response as focusing the eye or bending the head. When a character on the screen goes behind a fence or building, for example, there is an increased rate of response as the experimental consumer tries to "follow" the individual behind the fence by increasing his looking response rate.

Individual versus group prediction. It is important to note that the ability of this method to predict the viewing behavior of single individuals is a distinct advantage in copy testing. Since sales responses are emitted by single individuals, it may be better to sell a hundred individuals fully than to sell a million partially. With this method it should be possible to predict how many individuals will be fully exposed to the advertising message. If different items in advertising copy produce viewing responses from different individuals, rather than having to choose among types of individuals to stimulate, it is possible to redesign the copy to include two or more viewing stimuli simultaneously. That is, by the summation of individually specific viewing stimuli, advertising copy can be experimentally constructed so that it will simultaneously and continuously maintain the viewing behavior of individuals with widely different viewing tastes. Only when a stimulus is reinforcing to one type of individual, and at the same time aversive to another type, would it be difficult to summate viewing stimuli in order to produce efficient advertising exposure for a heterogeneous population.

There is no limit to the number of experimental consumers whose looking and listening behavior can be experimentally recorded and analyzed at the same time for the same copy. Any number of experimental enclosures can be operated simultaneously.

Ideal copy testing steps. Ideally, the advertising copy selector should follow this procedure:

1. Characteristics of prospects should be determined from the nature of the product, its costs, prior sales response, and the manufacturer's recommendations.
2. A vehicle or program to carry the commercial should be selected for exposure to the maximum number of prospects.
3. After initial advertising copy is prepared

by the usual creative and empirical procedures, it should be subjected to copy testing. This copy testing would insure maximal exposure efficiency, and would involve: (a) testing the program for optimal reinforcing value on experimental consumers selected to represent the prospect group; (b) testing the commercial for its reinforcement of the experimental consumers' viewing responses; (c) analyzing and correcting the advertising copy so that it will continuously maintain the viewing behavior of all viewing subtypes of the prospect group; (d) matching the viewing responses of the commercial to those of the program vehicle to insure that the vehicle does not rob the commercial of viewing behavior.

4. At this stage, since the rewritten copy is maximally efficient in producing viewing responses from all members of the prospect group and is also correctly matched to its vehicle, the first general distribution of the commercial could be safely undertaken.

5. When the advertising copy has been exposed to prospects long enough for sales responses to occur, it would be appropriate to correlate the advertising exposure with sales response. Since the advertising exposure is previously tested and modified for maximal efficiency, one could expect higher correlations with sales response than are usually obtained.

CONCLUSIONS

A modification of operant conditioning techniques and conjugate reinforcement has provided an extremely sensitive device for measuring and predicting consumer response to advertising.

The method directly measures viewing behavior and can be used to evaluate television programs and commercials. The records are sensitive to subtle individual differences among consumers, as well as to small details in the content of the message. Operant viewing responses appear to be closer to the ARF Audience Concepts Committee recommendation for copy testing by directly measuring advertising perception than any other available copy testing technique.

10

THE USE OF ANIMALS TO PERFORM
TYPICALLY HUMAN TASKS

Man down through the ages has relied upon animals to aid him in his efforts to cope with his environment. He has used animals to help him hunt his food, till his crops, and guard his home. Man has ridden animals into war, followed them when he was blind, and trained them to entertain him. Although, in general, we as humans recognize the service animals have rendered us, we still do not fully realize the extent to which the capabilities of animals might be used to our advantage. Not everyone, however, has overlooked this potential, and today, more than ever before, a scientific technology of behavior is at hand that allows man to control the behavior of animals to an extent far beyond his once purely speculative dreams.

All three of the articles included in this section can be classified as concept formation studies. In the first, by Herrnstein and Loveland, pigeons learn the concept "person." The last two papers, by Verhave and Cumming, give applications of this ability of the pigeon to form fairly complex visual concepts. In each, pigeons learn to distinguish between "good" and "bad" pharmaceutical capsules and diodes, in preparation for potential jobs as efficient inspectors on assembly lines.

Although for various reasons the pigeons were not accepted by management as suitable employees, these studies point up the tremendous potential lying in the ability of simple organisms to perform tasks too complex for machines and too simple and monotonous for humans. Once we eagerly left back-breaking physical tasks to animals better suited to perform them; today we might hope that animals will be allowed to relieve us of some of the more odious "intellectual" tasks on which the capabilities of human beings for extremely complex judgments and decisions are wasted.

Complex visual concept in the pigeon

R. J. HERRNSTEIN AND D. H. LOVELAND

It is well known that animals can use one or a few distinguishing features to discriminate stimuli such as simple visual arrays differing in size, shape, or color. In the experiment described here, however, pigeons were trained to detect human beings in photographs, a class of visual stimuli so diverse that it precludes simple characterization.

Five male racing (homing) pigeons between 1 and 2 years of age were obtained from a local breeder. Apart from the likelihood that they had been housed in outdoor coops, nothing was known about their past histories. All five were given approximately the same training and all performed similarly.

The pigeons were first fed on a minimal diet until their weights fell 20 percent. They were then fed enough food to maintain them at the reduced weights. Once a day each bird was placed in a box containing a hinged switch mounted on a wall next to a 5 cm by 5 cm translucent plate and a feeding device. During the first few sessions, the pigeons were trained to eat from the feeding device each time it was operated, when food was made available for approximately 3 seconds. Next, the pigeons were taught to peck at the hinged switch to trigger the feeder. At first, every peck at the switch operated the feeder, but, after two sessions, the procedure was changed so that pecks were effective only once a minute, on the average. An intermittent schedule of reward of this type produced relatively steady behavior, with little satiation of hunger. As a final stage in the preliminary training the pigeons were taught that only when the translucent plate next to the switch was illuminated with a uniform white light were pecks effective, but still only intermittently. When the plate was dark, pecks were entirely ineffective. The illumination changed randomly in time, averaging a change a minute, with the sole reservation that the onset of illumination could not take place within 15 seconds of the occurrence of a peck. In just a few sessions, the pigeons learned to peck when the plate was lit and not to peck when it was dark.

In the terminal procedure, the plate was illuminated throughout each session with projections of 35-mm color slides from a projector that housed 81 slides and that could be advanced by an electrical pulse. Over 1200 unselected slides obtained from private and commercial sources were available. Before each session, the projector was loaded with 80 or 81 different photographs of natural settings, including countryside, cities, expanses of water, lawn, meadow, and so on. For any one session, approximately half the photographs contained at least one human being; the remainder contained no human beings – in the experimenter's best judgment. In no other systematic way did the two sets of slides appear to differ. Many slides contained human beings partly obscured by intervening objects: trees, automobiles, window frames, and so on. The people were distributed throughout the pictures: in the center or to one side or the other, near the top or the bottom, close up or distant. Some slides contained a single person; others contained groups of various sizes. The people themselves varied in appearance: they were clothed, seminude, or nude; adults or children; men or women; sitting, standing, or lying; black, white, or yellow. Lighting and coloration varied: some slides were dark, others light; some had either reddish or bluish tints, and so on.

With the difference that pictures containing people now meant an opportunity to feed and that pictures without people meant no such opportunity, the procedure remained unchanged. Each day the slides themselves, and also the random sequence of positive slides (that is, containing a person) and negative slides (without people), were changed for each pigeon. Many slides were used again in later sessions, but never in the order with other slides in which they had appeared earlier. The pigeons had no opportunity, therefore, to learn groups of particular slides or sequences of positives and negatives in general.

From *Science*, 23 October 1964, **146**, 549 – 551.

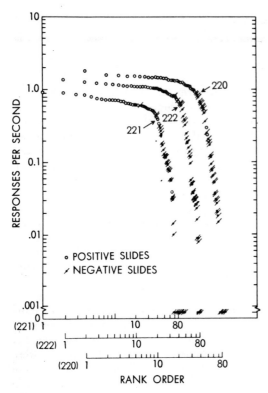

Figure 1. *Rate of pecking in the presence of each picture as a function of the rank order of the rate, on logarithmic coordinates; 35-mm color transparencies were used. Open circles represent pictures containing people; closed circles pierced by a line, pictures without people. A 1-day session is shown for each of three pigeons, with the abscissas displaced as indicated.*

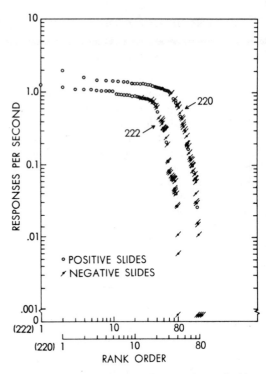

Figure 2. *One-day sessions for two pigeons looking at black and white pictures.*

The first test for a concept based on the image of a human being is simply whether a pigeon pecks at different rates in the presence of positive and negative slides. By this criterion, all five pigeons showed some grasp of the concept within seven to ten sessions with the pictures, but performances continued to improve with training over a period of months. Figure 1 shows a typical day's performance, with 80 or 81 totally new slides, by three pigeons after approximately 70 sessions of training. The rate of pecking in the presence of each slide was calculated. The rates were then ranked, and are plotted against their ranks on log-log coordinates. The three functions are displaced along the abscissa to facilitate inspection. Slides

containing at least part of a person appear as open circles; slides without people, as closed circles pierced by a line. The evidence for a concept is incontrovertible: the probability of obtaining by chance a set of ranks with such a degree of separation between positives and negatives is exceedingly small. The performances of the two pigeons not shown here were equally convincing.

Although the pigeons were undoubtedly responding to something closely associated with people in the pictures, it remains to be shown that it was the visual array that we would ourselves call a person. It could be that the results arose from some trivial and unsuspected visual clue in the slides, or from some nonvisual property of the procedure. To check the possibility of some correlation between the presence of a human being and color distribution in the slides, a set of slides was reproduced in black and white. Figure 2 shows the results obtained for two pigeons with black and white slides.

Despite a slight deterioration in discrimination, the behavior was still unmistakably selective. To test the possibility that the pigeons were reacting to some nonvisual aspect of the procedure, a session was conducted in which half the positive slides were treated as if they were negative and half the negative slides as if they were positive. That is to say, the apparatus had a 50:50 chance of producing the wrong consequence when the pigeon pecked. Even under these contingencies, the pigeons reacted to the presence or absence of people. Numerous other simple tests have been performed, all suggesting that the pigeons were, in fact, looking for, and reacting to, images of people.

Additional evidence for the existence of the concept "person" lies in the nature of the errors made by the pigeons. For example, the pigeons sometimes failed to peck when the human being was severely obscured, and they occasionally pecked when the picture contained objects frequently associated with people, such as automobiles, boats, and houses. Both types of errors diminished greatly as training progressed. There were also, of course, a few errors that defied simple explanation.

The most plausible conclusion to be drawn from these results is not that the pigeons were taught the general concept "person" but that they were taught the particular features of the procedure, such as learning to eat from the feeder, learning how and when to peck at the disk, and, perhaps, learning to look at two-dimensional arrays. The speed with which their performances improved, coupled with the complexity and variety of even the first slides used, strongly suggests that they entered the experiment with the concept already formed. Whether the pigeons had learned the concept before they were subjected to the experiments, or whether they are in some way innately endowed with it, the present experiment does not reveal.

It has been the practice of most psychologists to use human beings to study conceptualization. The use of categories, which is the mark of a concept, is not only most evident in human behavior, but most easily explored in a creature that can talk. But no one would question the idea that animals can learn rules for sorting, and that they can generalize the rules to some extent, so that new objects are also sorted more or less correctly. Even in the study of instinctive behavior with animals low in the phyletic scale, there is abundant evidence for sorting and generalizing.

There has been reluctance to assume that the sorting done by human beings is of the same nature as that done by animals. Given the large difference in degree between the concepts of man and animals, a difference in kind has long seemed plausible. Man obviously sorts with pinpoint accuracy over classes involving indefinitely large membership and bewildering complexity ("even numbers," "elm trees," "grammatical sentences") and picks out new instances with ease and rapidity. Animals, on the other hand, have seemed to form concepts built on only limited critical properties ("red spot on the beak," "left turn in the maze") and have seemed hard-put to pick out new instances. The technical vocabulary itself suggests a basic difference: a human being is said to "conceptualize" or "abstract" when he sorts; an animal, to "discriminate." But, unless there is something extraordinary about the conceptual capacities of pigeons, our findings show that an animal readily forms a broad and complex concept when placed in a situation that demands one.

The pigeon as a quality-control inspector[1,2]

THOM VERHAVE

Many of the operations involved in the quality-control inspection of commercial products consist of monotonous checking jobs performed by human operators. In addition to monotony, these, usually visual, inspection jobs have several other characteristics in common: (1) they require little if any manual skill or dexterity, (2) they require good visual acuity, (3) they require a capacity for color vision, and (4) they are extremely difficult to automate. There is, however, an organic device which has the following favorable properties: (1) an average life span of 10 to 15 years (Levi, 1963), (2) an extreme flexibility in adjusting to its environment as well as an enormous learning ability (Smee, 1850; Ferster and Skinner, 1957), (3) a visual acuity as good as the human eye (Reese, 1964), and (4) color vision (Reese, 1964). The price for one such device is only (approximately) $1.50; its name: *Columba livia domestica*, or the pigeon. Because of the characteristics listed above it is quite feasible to train pigeons to do all the visual checking operations involved in commercial manufacture. What follows is a brief account of an exploratory attempt to put the above suggestion into actual practice (Verhave, 1959a[3]).

In July of 1955 I was employed as a "psychopharmacologist" at one of the larger pharmaceutical companies. The main purpose of the laboratory was to develop and evaluate techniques for the experimental analysis of the effects of drugs on the behavior of animals.

Sometime, probably early in 1958, I finally took the tour of the plant which is mandatory for all new employees. During the all-day tour of the extensive research and manufacturing facilities I ran into the (gelatin) drug-capsule facilities. The capsules are manufactured by several very large and extremely complex machines, which together have a maximum production capacity of approximately 20 million capsules per day. All of the capsules, which are made in a large variety of sizes and colors, are visually inspected. This job was done by a contingent of about seventy women. After inspection the capsules go to other machines which fill them automatically with the appropriate pharmaceuticals.

The capsules are inspected in batches. The number of "caps" in a batch depends on the size of the capsules: the larger the capsule size, the smaller the number in a batch to be inspected. All of the capsules in a particular batch are of the same shape, size, and color. A big reservoir with a funnel drops the capsules at a fixed rate onto a moving belt. The inspector, or "capsule sorter," as she is called, is located in front of the moving belt, which is illuminated from underneath. She "pattern-scans" the capsules as they move by and picks up and throws out all "skags." A skag may be discarded because it is off-color, has a piece of gelatin sticking out, has a dent in it, or is what is known as a "double-cap skag."

The double-cap skag is particularly problematic. When the capsule comes to the capsule sorter, it is already closed by putting its two halves, a cap and a body, together. This step is performed by the production machine. Sometimes, however, during transportation or in storage, a second cap is put on top of an already capped capsule (a cap and body may vibrate apart and a loose cap may then slide over the body of another, already capped capsule). These double-cap skags produce problems later on in the filling machine. The double-cap skag is also one of the more difficult types to spot.

The sorters (all female) are paid off on a group-bonus schedule employing "error cost." After the inspection of a batch is completed, a supervisor (usually also female) scoops a ladle full of inspected capsules out of the barrel in which they were collected. The types of

---

Written for *Control of Human Behavior*. Printed by permission of author.

1 Opinions and conclusions contained in this article are those of the author. They are not to be construed as necessarily reflecting the views or the endorsement of either the pharmaceutical industry or any pigeon.

2 I am indebted to John E. Owen, my former collaborator, for a critical reading of this paper, which saved me from many errors due to faulty memory.

3 Pages 32–42 of this volume.

skag defects are categorized, and the inspector can allow up to three or four of the more minor imperfections per sample before a batch is rejected. However, if she finds more than the allowed number of skags in the sample ladled from the batch, the inspector has to re-inspect the entire batch of capsules. She is thus likely to reduce her bonus pay for the day since it depends partially on her own inspection output.

To come back to the main story: seeing these women and their simple, monotonous task and knowing about Skinner's "Pigeons in a Pelican" (1960, 1965), I said to myself, "A pigeon can do that!" Some time later, I mentioned my birdbrain idea to a friend and fellow scientist in the Physiochemistry Department who also supervised the Electronics Shop which supported the Research Division. He almost fell out of his chair and choked in a fit of laughter. However, after the joke had worn off, we talked more seriously about my odd notion, especially after I told him about project ORCON[4] (Skinner, 1960, 1965). Eventually the Director of Research and I talked about it. It happened that my suggestion had arrived at an opportune time. The company had recently spent a considerable sum of money on a machine, constructed by an outside engineering firm, designed to inspect automatically for double-cap skags. It did not work. After some deliberation the Director of Research gave me permission to build a demonstration and try-out setup. With the able help and splendid cooperation of the instrument-shop people under the direction of my friend of the Physiochemistry Department, a demonstration apparatus was built.

While the apparatus was being designed and built, I had plenty of opportunity to consider varying aspects of the discrimination-training problems with which I would be faced. The first decision to be made was which particular "skag" problem to tackle first. I obtained samples of capsules of different colors and sizes. It was tempting to tackle the most troublesome problem first: the double-cap skag involving small capsules of colorless and transparent gelatin. On the actual inspection line these were the most difficult to spot. After playing around with different ways of presenting these capsules to a pigeon behind a modified pigeon key, a simple solution to the double-cap problem was discovered by accident. One of the minor problems to be solved was the lighting of the capsules presented behind the key. I discovered that, by shining a narrow beam of light at the proper angle on a three-dimensional transparent curved surface, one obtains a focal point of light inside the object. (The tops and bottoms of all capsules are either round or oval.) In the case of a double-cap skag, one gets two clearly distinct focal points in slightly different positions. So, even in the case of the transparent double-cap capsule, all a pigeon had to do was to discriminate between one versus two bright spots of light inside the curious objects behind his key![5]

For the purpose of working out the details of the actual training and work procedure, however, I decided to take the simplest discrimination problem possible. I chose a simple color discrimination: white versus red capsules. Two naïve birds were selected for inspection duty. For one bird the red capsules were arbitrarily defined as skags (S^Δ). For the other birds, the white capsules were given the same status.

As is clear from Figure 1, there were two pigeon keys. One key was actually a small transparent window; the other was opaque. The capsules could be brought into view behind the transparent key one by one at a maximum rate of about two per second. After a preliminary training phase, the birds were run as follows: A single peck on the weakly illuminated opaque key would, first, momentarily (0.5 sec.) turn off the light behind the transparent key and, second, weakly illuminate this window-key to an extent insufficient to see much of the capsule in place behind it.

Next, a single peck on the weakly lit window-key would turn on a bright and narrow beam of light which clearly illuminated the capsule. The capsules were individually mounted in small and hollow rubber bottlestops glued onto the metal plates of the endless belt (see Figure 1). If the bird now pecked three more times on the window-key with the new illuminated cap-

---

4 From the words "organic control."
5 The opaque, single color, double-cap skag may still be a difficult discrimination problem, even for a pigeon.

sule exposed to view, a brief tone would sound. Next came the moment of decision. If the capsule exposed to view was judged to be a skag, the bird was required to make two more pecks on the window-key. This would (1) turn off the beam of light illuminating the capsule, (2) move up the next capsule, and (3) produce food by way of the automatic hopper on a fixed-percentage basis (usually 100 per cent). However, if the capsule was considered to be acceptable, the bird indicated this by changing over to the opaque key. A peck on this key would also (1) turn off the beam of light behind the window-key, and (2) move up the next capsule. It would not, however, produce food reinforcement.

A bird, then, determined his own inspection rate. A peck on the opaque key would initiate an inspection cycle. However, reinforcement came only after making the appropriate number of pecks on the window-key when a true skag was presented. Skags occurred rarely; they made up 10 per cent of all the capsules on the belt. Wrong pecks, either false alarms or misses, did not get reinforced, and produced a blackout (Ferster, 1954) of 30 seconds. The results were very encouraging: both birds inspected on a 99 per cent correct basis within one week of daily discrimination training. The Director of the Pharmacology Division, my immediate superior, who had watched the entire project with serious misgiving since its inception, was delighted. In his immediate enthusiasm he called the Director of Research, who came over for a look. One week later the vice-presidents as well as the president of the company had been given a demonstration. Everyone, including my immediate associates and co-workers, was greatly excited. The situation, as Skinner had previously discovered (Skinner, 1960), was a great source for jokes. There was talk about a new company subsidiary: "Inspection, Inc.!" (Company slogan: "It's for the birds!")

There were also some sobering thoughts, however. One of them concerned the staggering problem of the logistics involved in getting pigeons to inspect as many as 20 million separate objects each day. Although this problem did not seem insoluble to me, the details of the various possible approaches to a solution were never worked out.

After the company president had watched my feathered pupils perform, he congratulated me on my achievement. I was subsequently informed that serious consideration would be given to the further use and development of the method. I was also told that I could expect

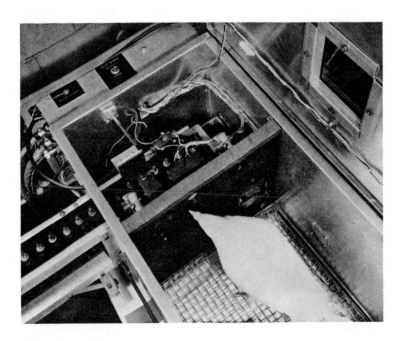

Figure 1. A quality-control inspector at an "assembly-line" station.

a visit from the Chairman of the Board and his brother, both elder statesmen of the company, who made all final policy decisions of importance. During their brief visit to the laboratory, one of them raised the question of possible adverse publicity. What about the Humane Society? More important, suppose salesmen from other pharmaceutical houses should tell doctors not to buy any of our company's products: "Who would trust medicine inspected by pigeons?!" I suggested that the use of pigeons was incidental and that, for example, one could use hawks just as well; after all, what's better than a hawk's eye? This suggestion produced a wan smile.

Furthermore, the competition could well choose to ignore the mechanical details of the situation and exploit the more distasteful but imaginary possibilities. Even though the birds would only see the capsules at a distance through a window, the first mental picture[6] is usually one of a pigeon "manually" (proboscically?) sorting capsules, a thought no doubt repulsive to many people, especially to those who already have an aversion to birds as such.

After a brief stay, and a polite pat on the back, my distinguished visitors left.

Three weeks went by without any further word from HUM.[7] I concluded that probably meant that my pigeons were finished. I was right. Sometime later I was so informed. Through the grapevine I learned that the Board of Directors had voted 13 to 1 not to continue to explore the use of animals for quality-control inspection. The one "yes" vote presumably came from the Director of Research who initially had given me the green light for the preliminary demonstration.

There is one further amusing tale to the story: the company did try to patent my inspection method. The poor lawyer assigned to the case almost developed a nervous breakdown. It turned out to be "unpatentable" because, as the lawyers of the patent office put it (so succinctly), the method involved "a mental process" which is unpatentable in principle.[8] I tried to pin my lawyer friends down on what they meant by a "mental process." I suggested that the pigeon was merely an organic computer. However, I got nowhere. Lawyers apparently want no part of either physicalism or behaviorism.

So much as far as my own story is concerned. My efforts stimulated another exploratory attempt by my friend Dr. William Cumming of Columbia University who trained pigeons to inspect diodes.[9]

One problem not yet touched on deserves some discussion. In the demonstration apparatus the capsules were coded as to whether they were acceptable or not. In this way the automatic programing (relay) circuit could set up and enforce the appropriate discriminatory behavior of the birds. However, on an actual inspection line, this aspect of the training procedure could no longer be maintained. There would be no way of knowing which capsules are skags except by actual inspection. Consequently on a real inspection line there would be no way of knowing when to reward or not to reward the animal inspector! As a result, due to the lack of differential reward, the animal's discriminations would rapidly deteriorate.[10] There are two solutions.

The first solution would involve the use of known skags. A certain percentage of the capsules inspected would consist of such labeled duds and be used to check up on the discriminatory behavior of the birds. This is similar to the use of catch-tests in human psychophysical experiments. This solution to the problem of guaranteeing that the animal inspector conforms to the values of his human employers makes it necessary to determine what minimum percentage of the objects inspected have to be planted skags in order to keep the inspecting behavior at an acceptable level of reliability.[11]

However, this general solution is expensive and awkward. The on-line inspection equipment would need special machinery to insert

---

6 If a behaviorist may be excused for using such illegitimate terms. . . .

7 HUM: Higher-Up-Management (Verhave, 1961).

8 On this point, I may refer the reader to a recent article in *Science* (1965) by J. H. Munster, Jr., and Justin C. Smith.

9 See pages 246–256 of this volume.

10 Skinner, in his Second World War project to train pigeons to home missiles, did not face this problem. His birds were meant to "extinguish" after a brief period of duty.

11 This question was investigated experimentally by Dr. Cumming.

in a random manner a fixed percentage of "stool-pigeon skags" and, after inspection, to remove them again automatically for later re-use. The slightest observable difference be-tween the "planted" objects and the other ones would lead to the development of a conditional discrimination (Lashley, 1938) and reintroduce the problem one set out to solve initially.

The second solution is simpler from a purely mechanical point of view. It also is of more theoretical or philosophical interest. Briefly, it would involve the use of a minimum of two animals to simultaneously inspect each object. Initially, each animal would be trained to in-spect capsules by using a training apparatus such as the one I had already constructed. In this apparatus all the skags would be labeled beforehand.

After the desired discriminatory perform-ance is well established the two birds would be moved to the on-line inspection situation. From then on the birds would only be rewarded if they *both* agreed on whether a particular object was a skag or not. Such an "agreement contingency" would most likely be quite ade-quate to maintain the desired behavior. There is, of course, the possibility that both birds would indeed, once in a while, agree to treat a skag as an acceptable object. However, the probability of this happening for any particular object on a particular inspection trial is the product of the error frequencies (the proba-bility of such an error) of both birds. If, therefore, each bird independently has an error frequency as high as 1 out of 100, the probability of both birds being "wrong" but still rewarded would be 1 out of 10,000! Hook-ing additional animals into the agreement con-tingency circuit would make the possibility of the development of a "multiple folly"[12] very unlikely.

The solution is of some philosophical in-terest because it causes the pigeon observers to act according to Charles Pierce's pragmatic theory of truth (1878): "The opinion which is fated to be ultimately agreed to by all who investigate, is what is meant by the truth, and the object represented in this opinion is real." (pp. 56–57). It also appears to me that the agreement contingency provides a basic para-digm for the experimental analysis of social behavior, a *terra incognita* so far hardly even explored by systematic experimental investiga-tion (Verhave, 1965).[13]

In conclusion, let me point out that the idea of using trained animals for the tasks formerly performed by *homo sapiens* is very old indeed. Since antiquity man has domesticated many animals. It seems an obvious development to apply our modern knowledge of behavioral analysis to the task of training some of our animal companions for the performance of various sophisticated tasks (Clarke, 1958; Herrnstein, 1965).

The obstacle in the way of such developments is not our ignorance of behavior—though it is still large—but mainly, it seems, the obstinate belief of man in his intellectual superiority over other creatures as well as his generalized fear of the imagined consequences of novel developments.

---

12 "*Folie à deux, trois, ... n.*"
13 For examples of such research with humans, see pages 97–113 of this volume.

A bird's eye glimpse of men and machines

WILLIAM W. CUMMING

"*Plato having defined man to be a two-legged animal without feathers, Diogenes plucked a cock and brought it into the Academy, and said, 'This is Plato's man.' On which account this addition was made to the definition,—'With broad flat nails.'*"
Diogenes Laertius, *Diogenes*, ca. A.D. 200.

Most of us have little difficulty in telling the difference between men and birds, even *au* *naturel*, for avian nature is more than feather deep. Some of us have more difficulty telling when the unique capacities of the human or-ganism are largely wasted in trivial perform-ances that lower organisms are perfectly capa-ble of mastering and better able than we to

---

Written for *Control of Human Behavior*. Printed by permis-sion of author.

tolerate. Although, in the past, Diogenes' bird has had different homes within the Academy, it now frequently resides in the laboratory of the experimental psychologist. In its latest capacity it has taught us a good deal about the similarities and differences between man and his co-members of the animal kingdom. From it we are also beginning to learn when to send a bird to do a bird's job.

The particular narrative recounted here is a case in point. It begins with an industrial problem which either men or machines could, if called upon, handle with ease, although their ability to do so is hardly a matter of pride. Furthermore, the economics of the manufacturing situation forces us to recognize the enormous waste involved when a complex instrument or organism is employed on an insignificant task.

PLANNING THE STUDY

To call this work an experiment might offend the scientific purist, for it was really more of a pilot study or demonstration. It began casually enough during a pleasant holiday conversation with an engineer from a large industrial concern which was beginning to explore the possibility of automating some of its manufacturing facilities. The engineer was amused, and more than somewhat concerned, by some of the problems automation raised. He spoke of a machine which he had just helped to design and install. The machine accepted component parts at one end and assembled them into finished products which emerged from the other end. It did an excellent job at a considerably higher rate of speed than the previously used assembly line which had relied on human operators to manually assemble the same product. It was far more economical, and the finished items showed fewer defects and less variability than those which had previously been produced. However, although the machine operated perfectly so long as the component parts which it assembled contained no defects, it was unable to accept deviant parts without stopping and acting as if it had a chicken bone in the throat. Much of the time it remained idle while mechanics swarmed over its intestinal tract. When the assembly had been done by human operators, a part which did

not fit properly was given several taps with a hammer or cast aside, so that it created no difficulty.

The number of ways in which a component part could be defective was almost infinite. An automatic sensor could have been built, at some expense, which would detect some kinds of defects before the parts entered the machine. But to build an automatic inspection station versatile enough to detect all possible defects was a difficult and frightfully costly prospect. The alternative was to retain the workers, who had previously assembled the product, for inspection of the parts. This alternative, of course, would take all of the economy out of automation.

Seized by a whimsey, I suggested to the engineer that either a machine or a human being might be wasted on such a simple task. Even a relatively simple animal could look at a part and see that it was bent. Since I was most familiar with pigeons, I used them to illustrate the advantage of using animals in such an inspection system. I pointed out that their initial cost was very low—less than five dollars for the very best—that they eat very little, and can be maintained for a matter of pennies a day. They are small, requiring only a cubic foot or so of living space, and appear to require little, if any, sleep. I told him of records I had seen in which pigeons had worked continuously, not only for hours and days, but even for weeks and months without stopping. Pigeons have a relatively long life span, and I reported on the performance of several I had used which were over 15 years old at the time of experimentation. The pigeon's visual system is remarkably good, perhaps as good as that of humans. To duplicate such an eyeball and its associated nervous system in an electromechanical system would involve enormous expense.

The engineer chortled some over the prospect of running an inspection station for "chicken feed." He asked some questions about the variety of defects which a single bird could be expected to sort. The matter was clearly one of concept formation, and I agreed that little was known, but I believed that there was every expectation that a bird could be trained to detect a wide variety of defects. We did not yet have available Herrnstein and Loveland's

(1964) study of visual concept formation in the pigeon,[1] but I did tell him a little about Skinner's (1960) experiments using pigeons in a missile guidance system.

The conversation drifted to other topics, but apparently the discussion had intrigued him, for a week or so later he called to ask for more details. His company,[2] it developed, wanted to know if I could provide a demonstration of the feasibility of animal inspection systems. Although I was reluctant to devote valuable laboratory space and time to the project, I was by this time sufficiently ego-involved to consider the project seriously. We needed some apparatus which the company agreed to build and a small sum to pay an assistant[3] to run the experiment.

The company raised several problems for consideration before the apparatus could be designed. The first problem concerned the selection of the parts to be inspected. This I left entirely to the company and its engineers, and they decided to have the animals inspect the paint cover on small electronic parts called diodes. These parts have the shape of a top hat with a wire protruding from the top and another from the bottom. Exclusive of the wires, they are 7 mm. in height, 7 mm. in diameter, and 10 mm. across the rim around the bottom of the diodes (the brim of the hat).

These parts are normally painted black, but the paint cover can be scratched, as often happens inadvertently during manufacture, or the painting machine can fail in such a way that either paint is applied only to a portion of the diode or not at all. In actual practice, insufficient paint cover constituted a small problem for the company and one for which they were not likely to inspect. They felt, however, that, since it was a problem in which a large number of different defects were possible, it provided some test of the pigeon's capacity for concept formation. The scratches could be on the brim, on the side, or on the top of the diode, and could vary considerably in magnitude.

The second problem which the company raised was more interesting, since it went to the heart of the industrial inspection problem. In my description of an animal inspection system, I had pointed out that a pigeon would be rewarded, or reinforced, for correct inspections and given a small punishment for errors. While that is all very fine in the laboratory of an experimental psychologist, on an assembly line one would not know beforehand whether or not the part being inspected was good or defective. To know would require that the parts be inspected before they came to the pigeon, giving the pigeon the status of a fifth wheel.

The answer to this question was that the animal need not be reinforced or punished for every inspection. To do so would make the pigeon not only unnecessary, but unhungry. A great deal of experimental data shows that an animal will continue to discriminate correctly even though only a small proportion of his responses are reinforced. Therefore, the condition of only a small fraction of the parts going by the pigeon would need to be known. For these known, or *coded,* parts the pigeon would be reinforced for correctly identifying a bad part. The vast majority of parts, the condition of which would be unknown, would be sorted simply because the pigeon could not discriminate between a coded bad part and an uncoded bad part. On an actual assembly line the coding could be done invisibly, as, for example, by magnetizing the part. A coded good part could be magnetized with the north pole up, while a coded bad part could be magnetized with the north pole down. Uncoded parts would not, of course, be magnetized. In the demonstration experiment, the condition of all parts would be known, but some would be treated as coded and some as uncoded to test the system and imitate actual operating conditions.

Conceptually, the proposed demonstration experiment was extremely simple. The birds were to be trained to peck at a window when a bad part was presented behind it by reinforcing such a response with grain. Responding to a good part would not only be unreinforced (extinguished) but would be mildly punished.

---

1 See pages 239–241 of this volume.

2 The sponsoring organization has requested that it not be identified. Without its aid in the form of funds, equipment, and engineering time, however, this study would not have been possible.

3 Michael Leffand served throughout the summer of 1959 as research assistant on this project.

We would begin with a discrimination which was relatively easy: between a completely unpainted part and a fully painted one. As the experiment went on, the difficulty of the discrimination would be increased, and the probability of reinforcement would be decreased until the birds were making the most difficult discrimination and were being tested with coded parts only a small fraction of the time.

The company was apparently satisfied with this proposed design, and negotiations were completed. Several months later the finished apparatus was installed in the laboratory and experimentation began.

Figure 1. Sketch of the animal chamber on the mock assembly line. The round key was added to the chamber after the second week of the experiment.

THE MOCK ASSEMBLY LINE STATION

The completed apparatus imitated, insofar as the pigeon was concerned, an assembly line which passed the parts along before the bird. Figure 1 gives a view of this apparatus. The diodes were held upright in fixtures spaced along the circumference of a rotating circular table. This table carried the diodes as they would be carried along an actual assembly line. The diode to be inspected was placed in a brightly lit stage where it rotated behind a transparent Plexiglass window. If the pigeon found fault with the diode, he pecked on this window, which also served as a recording mechanism for such responses.

Directly beneath this window-key the pigeon had access to a solenoid-operated grain hopper which lit up when food became available. The interior of the cage was illuminated through a translucent panel.

Ninety degrees to the pigeon's left was an operator's control panel (not shown in Figure 1). It permitted a human operator to insert a diode into the fixture immediately before him and to push a button on the panel, indicating whether the part was good or bad, and whether it was to be considered coded or uncoded. In addition, the operator could control the duration of food hopper reinforcement and the duration of blackout for punishment. The operator could also present a new part to the pigeon by rotating the table to the next position.

THE EXPERIMENTAL PROGRAM

Four White Carneaux pigeons between five and seven years of age were used as subjects. For the first several weeks after their arrival in the laboratory they were given unrestricted access to food, grit, and water, and were weighed daily. Feeding was then limited to three grams of grain daily (although grit and water were continuously available) until the weights were reduced to 80 per cent of their value under conditions of *ad libitum* feeding. Thereafter each bird was given enough grain at the conclusion of a daily experimental session to bring his weight back to the 80 per cent value.

The initial training consisted of placing a bird in a standard laboratory experimental enclosure which was similar to the animal cage of the mock assembly line. The animal was trained to eat from the food magazine by presenting it intermittently (about once each minute) until hopper activation caused the bird to immediately approach and eat. Shaping of the key-pecking response was then accomplished by first presenting food for turning toward the key, then for approaching it, and, finally, for pecking. Once the key-pecking response was established, the bird was allowed

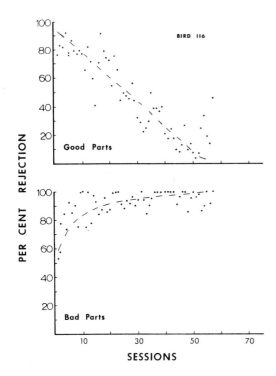

Figure 2. *Per cent of good parts (upper panel) and bad parts (lower panel) rejected by response to the window-key during the course of the experiment for Bird 116.*

to obtain its entire daily ration on each of several days by pecking the key and receiving a three-second period of access to grain as reinforcement.

Each bird was then placed in the chamber on the mock assembly line with an unpainted diode behind the window-key. Only a small number of additional shaping reinforcements were required to establish the key-pecking response in this slightly altered environment. As soon as the animal readily pecked at the square window to obtain food, discrimination training was begun. Pecks at the window in the presence of an unpainted diode were reinforced with grain, while responses to the window-key when a fully painted diode was present resulted in a short blackout of all illumination within the cage and behind the window-key. At the end of each reinforcement or blackout a new diode, either painted or

unpainted, was cycled into position behind the window-key. If the bird refrained from pecking at the key for a period of five seconds when an unpainted part was being presented, it was punished with a blackout of all illumination in the cage. Other experimental work has demonstrated that such blackouts are mildly aversive to pigeons. Refraining from responding in the presence of a painted part resulted in the cycling of the rotating table to present a new part for a new trial. No grain was presented, although the blackout which an incorrect response would have produced was avoided.

It should be noted that this procedure provided food reinforcement for responding to bad diodes, while no grain was given for allowing a good diode to go by. However, after a few sessions of discrimination training, the cycling of the apparatus itself came to constitute a reinforcement since often the new part was defective and thus was a cue for responding and subsequent reinforcement. It is a well-established fact that such cues come to function as secondary reinforcers. Thus, although not followed by food, a correct acceptance response was reinforced with the cycling of the assembly line.

During the early stages of the experiment, in which the discrimination between painted and completely unpainted parts was being formed, all parts were treated as coded so that maximum feedback of information was provided for each response and for each failure to respond.

The study continued until somewhat prematurely terminated after approximately 60 one-hour sessions had been given each bird. During this time: (1) the discrimination was made gradually more difficult by introducing diodes with progressively smaller defects; (2) the percentage of bad parts passing the assembly line was progressively reduced from 50 per cent to about 8 per cent; (3) uncoded parts were introduced and gradually increased in number; (4) the procedure was revised by the introduction of a second ("accept") key; and (5) the number of responses required on the window-key for the rejection of a part was increased. Although these changes were taking place concurrently, they will be discussed separately below.

THE ACQUISITION
OF INSPECTION BEHAVIOR

All four pigeons learned to inspect under the conditions of the experiment, although individual differences were noted. It is impossible in a short space to present all of the data, but enough can be shown to exhibit both the regularities found in the behavior of all of the subjects and some of the interesting departures from regularity which some of the individual birds' data show. It must be remembered in examining the acquisition data that alterations were introduced from day to day in the difficulty of the discrimination, the duration of the blackouts, the relative proportions of good and bad parts and of coded and uncoded parts, the use of one or two keys, the number of responses on the window-key required for rejection, and so forth. The problem of presenting these changes in any meaningful way in a short time seemed insuperable, so that the curves must be interpreted as occurring during a learning situation similar to that which might be found with human subjects in an industrial situation. Both the regularities found in the curves and some of the apparent "noise" must be attributed to the fact that this was an instructional situation rather than a strict experimental one.

Figure 2 shows the per cent rejection of good and bad parts for Bird 116. All but one of the birds show a similar curve with the rejection rate of good parts declining steadily during the study and rejection rate for bad parts increasing initially and then remaining at a steady high percentage with some perturbations when a shift was made from one class of defects to a more difficult one. Indeed, the rise in the rejection of good parts at the very end of the experiment for this bird occurred immediately after the introduction of a new and more difficult variety of defect. If the data from the other birds are any guide, that curve would have rapidly fallen to the asymptote which it seemed to be approaching earlier. This bird was considerably slower than the others in its rate of inspection so that, not only did it inspect fewer parts per hourly session, but it had therefore proceeded more slowly than the others through the progression of defects.

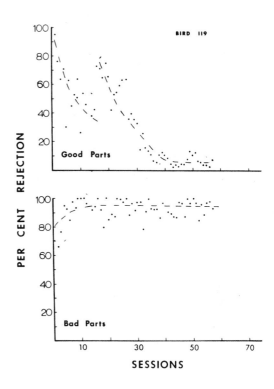

Figure 3. *Per cent of good parts (upper panel) and bad parts (lower panel) rejected by response to the window-key during the course of the experiment for Bird 119.*

A somewhat deviant acquisition function was shown by Bird 119 (Figure 3) whose performance in accepting good parts suddenly deteriorated at about session 15. This was attributed to an overrapid progression to more difficult defects. The bird was returned to simpler inspections after which its performance recovered, and it proceeded normally through the rest of the experiment.

Data from these and the other two birds led us to believe that the animals could be expected to reject perhaps 5 per cent of the good parts with which they were presented, while rejecting over 98 per cent of the bad parts. This performance might well improve with more cautious experimental procedures (as some of the important parameters of the situation were investigated) and could certainly be improved by requiring that each part be inspected by a succession of birds in series on the inspection line. It is even possible that some of the rejec-

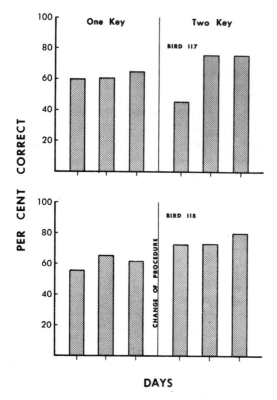

Figure 4. *Per cent correct inspections of the last three days of the one-key procedure and on the first three days following the installation of the auxiliary "accept" key. Data are for the two birds on which this procedure was first tried.*

tion of good parts was the result of dust on the key or on the part itself, although some care was taken to prevent this. Inaccuracies from any such source might be eliminated by special design of the apparatus in any actual application.

ONE RESPONSE OR TWO?

During the first several weeks of acquisition, only the window-key through which the birds inspected the diodes was present in the cage and available for responding. The experiment was run very much in the style of a standard discrimination experiment in which a response was reinforced in the presence of one stimulus class (bad diodes) and mildly punished in the presence of another stimulus class (good

diodes). While evidence of discriminative control by the diodes was unmistakably present in the behavior of all birds, they continued to make a fairly large number of errors, usually by rejecting good diodes. In the presence of a bad diode the birds responded rapidly and vigorously, while they responded more slowly and somewhat more weakly in the presence of a good diode. It appeared as if the bird had a good deal of difficulty restraining itself from responding. Further, the requirement that the bird wait out the presence of a good diode acted to slow the inspection process considerably.

It was therefore decided to alter the procedure for two of the subjects by installing a round translucent key next to the window-key (see Figure 1). Responses on the round key cycled the part being viewed past the window-key and presented a new part for inspection, provided that the part being viewed was not a coded bad part. In that case, a response to this new auxiliary key produced a blackout which was followed by the cycling of the table. Thus, the new key allowed the bird to accept a part without waiting out the cycle time. The only consequence of the acceptance response, other than the operation of the assembly line, was blackout punishment for incorrectly responding to a bad diode. No food reinforcements were ever given for correct responses on the round key.

Nevertheless, the round key response was quickly acquired by both of the subjects with which this procedure was tried. Furthermore, their accuracy in inspection rapidly increased thereafter as shown in Figure 4. Because of its demonstrated efficacy, the two-response procedure was then instituted with the remaining two subjects and the entire latter part of the study was conducted with all birds by requiring either a reject response or an accept response upon each presentation of a part for inspection. It is not clear that the ultimate accuracy of the one-key procedure would have been lower than that for the two-key procedure, but accuracy certainly improved at a much more rapid rate when an alternative response was available. The birds were also able to inspect at a much higher rate when they did not have to wait out the cycle time of the apparatus.

The two-key procedure did not solve all problems, however. Several weeks after its introduction it became clear that some of the diode rejections were the result of accidental responding on the window-key while examining the diode. Thereafter, a fixed number of responses on the window-key was required for the rejection of the diode (a fixed ratio schedule). This ratio was adjusted from time to time to accommodate each bird's behavior. For two of the birds a fixed ratio of five responses was sufficient to prevent accidental rejections while for the other two the requirement was finally set at ten responses.[4]

RATE OF INSPECTION

Initially, the rate of inspection was essentially paced by the experimenter who had control of the cycle time, or time during which parts remained before the bird if it failed to respond. With the institution of the two-key procedure, the bird itself cycled the parts past the inspection window by pecking either the window-key or the round key. In this latter mode of operation the rate of inspection was, to a large extent, controlled by the bird itself. A bird could work slowly, taking a good deal of time for observing each part, or could work rapidly, making quick "decisions" about whether a part was good or bad.

It is obvious that the rate at which a bird inspects under such circumstances has a good deal to do with the feasibility of animal inspection. A curve typical of the acquisition curves of inspection rate is shown in Figure 5. Three of the birds worked at about the rate shown in the figure, ending the experiment handling about 1000 parts per experimental hour (including reinforcement and blackout time). Bird 116 worked more slowly, seldom inspecting more than 600 parts per hour and sometimes inspecting less than 200 in the same time period. Since the accuracy of the inspections did not seem to be related to the rate at which the birds worked, a fast, accurate bird clearly would be preferred to a slow, accurate one. In all cases both the rate of inspection and inspection accuracy seemed to be still improving at the time the experiment was concluded.

It should be noted parenthetically that neither noise nor visual stimuli from the world outside the chamber appeared to distract the

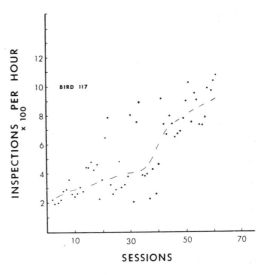

Figure 5. *Number of inspections during the daily experimental hour for Bird 117.*

animals during a session. During the latter part of the experiment, construction was begun on a new building adjacent to the laboratory. Neither the blasting nor the noise of excavation equipment stopped the pigeons, nor did it decrease their accuracy. Further, although two of the birds worked with a transparent cage door, frequent visitors to the laboratory appeared to be unnoticed unless they approached to within a foot or so of the animal.

MAGNITUDE OF DEFECT

At the beginning of the study the company provided us with diodes which had been separated into categories by the company engineers so that each category represented, to them, a different magnitude of defect. The categories, with some interpretation of the meaning of each category, were:

Class Six: diodes entirely lacking in paint cover.

Class Five: diodes painted on one side only (50 per cent cover).

Class Four: diodes with unpainted spots averaging about 4 mm. in diameter.

Class Three: diodes with unpainted spots averaging about 2.5 mm. in diameter. (During

---

4 Only one response was required for acceptance.

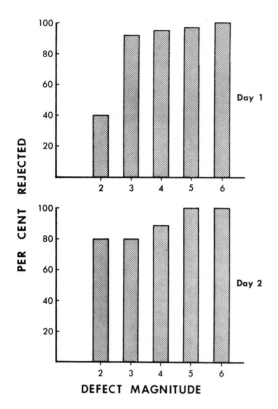

Day 1

Day 2

DEFECT MAGNITUDE

PER CENT REJECTED

Figure 6. Per cent rejection of defects as a function of defect magnitude on the two days of testing. Data are from all four birds.

the experiment it was found necessary to divide Class Three into Two sub-classes: Class Three-A in which the spots were located on the body of the diodes, and Class Three-B in which the spots were located on the rim.)

Class Two: diodes with unpainted spots averaging about 1 mm. in diameter.

Class One: diodes with spots and scratches smaller than 0.5 mm. in diameter which were considered by the company's engineers to be of low probability of detection by human inspectors unless they were closely observing each diode.

In addition to these classes of defective parts, there was, of course, an additional class consisting of fully painted, or good parts.

As we shall point out later, the experiment was terminated by the sponsor before it was finished. Since the plan of experimentation

consisted of beginning with Class Six defective parts and proceeding to each succeeding class of smaller defects as mastery was achieved, insufficient time was available to obtain data on all of these classes of defects. Extensive training was given only through Class Three, although measures were later taken of the birds' ability to reject Class Two diodes.

At the conclusion of approximately 60 hours of training, when the experiment was about to be concluded, the birds' ability to inspect and reject defects ranging from Class Two through Class Six was tested on two successive days. Prior to this time, only one class of defect had been presented during a particular session, but during these test sessions the defect magnitude, whenever a defective part was presented, was randomized. The results are presented in Figure 6 and show that on the first day of testing the animals rejected about 40 per cent of the Class Two defects which they had not previously seen, while the ability to reject all less difficult defects remained high. On the second day of testing, the birds rejected about 80 per cent of the Class Two defects, but some impairment was noted of their ability to reject Class Three diodes.

Throughout the course of the experiment, whenever the birds advanced to a more difficult discrimination, their performance was temporarily set back for defect magnitudes which they had previously mastered. The rapid improvement when Class Two diodes were introduced suggests that they would have quickly mastered that magnitude of defect. It should be noted that the data in Figure 6 are averages for all four birds. Several of the subjects did much better than these averages indicate, since two of the birds had not by this time mastered the rejection of Class Three defects. It is possible that, were animals ever actually used for inspection, a selection procedure for those animals with best performance and most rapid discrimination learning could considerably improve the picture presented here.

HOW MANY PARTS SHOULD BE CODED?

Prior to the conclusion of the study, a brief attempt was made to determine the optimal percentage of coded bad parts (the parts for which the reinforcement was possible). In the brief time available only suggestive results could be obtained. Holding the percentage of coded good parts and uncoded bad parts constant at two per cent each, the percentage of coded bad parts was varied from one to six per cent. With as many as six per cent coded bad parts the birds gained weight much too rapidly, while with as few as one per cent the behavior tended to extinguish. It is certainly possible that, with extended training, behavior could have been maintained with as few as one per cent coded bad parts or even fewer. At the stage of training at which this pilot work was done, optimal balance between satiation and extinction seemed to lie between two and three per cent.

LENGTH OF WORK DAY

Throughout the experiment, each experimental session, for practical reasons, was limited to one hour. As a very last step, several sessions were run with two of the birds in which this period was increased to four hours in order to determine the effects of prolonging session length. The data from these sessions, in terms of per cent correct inspections and rate of inspection, are shown hour by hour for these lengthened sessions in Figure 7. It is clear that performance did not deteriorate during the lengthened sessions. One of the birds tended to improve greatly over the length of the session. There is certainly no evidence of fatigue.

It would have been of great interest to try even longer sessions, but two factors prevented this. First, we had been directed by the sponsor to terminate the experiment as rapidly as possible, and, more important, while the bird did not fatigue, the assistant who was manually running the experiment found it impossible to continue at the bird's rate for more than four hours at a time. He reported his own subjective feeling that for a human operator to examine these diodes for four hours caused the head to reel and the eyes to swim.

During the entire length of the two four-hour periods of inspection, Bird 119 inspected almost 6000 diodes and failed to detect defects in only four cases. The warm-up effect shown

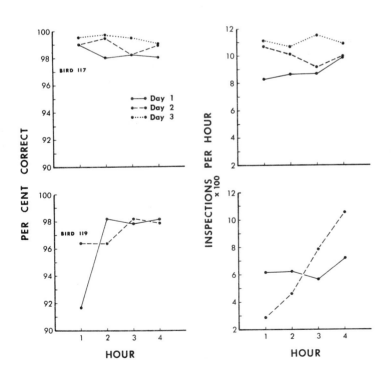

Figure 7. Inspection accuracy (left) and rate (right) during the course of several days of testing with four-hour sessions for Birds 117 (upper curves) and 119 (lower curves).

by this bird was entirely due to a tendency to reject good diodes early in the session. During Bird 117's second session, it averaged only one per cent errors during the entire session while inspecting at a rate of more than 1000 inspections per hour. There is no reason to suspect that performance would have deteriorated quickly had the session been longer than four hours.

CONCLUSION

The termination of the experiment occurred with some abruptness when support was withdrawn by the sponsoring organization. While all of the training which we had planned for the pilot work had not been completed, the acquisition phase was hurriedly finished and short experiments on the importance of defect magnitude, session length, and optimal proportion of coded bad parts were squeezed into the last weeks. The major aim of the project had at least been realized. There seemed little doubt that birds could be trained to sort or inspect with good accuracy and at a respectable rate. Other matters were only details of this larger picture.

The success which we enjoyed, brief as the experimental time was, probably contributed to the sudden demise of the experimental program. Reports of progress had been relayed to the sponsoring organization and these were circulated within the company. What had been a "far out" project rapidly became a matter for executive decision. The practical decision was quick and forceful: no use of the procedure could be made within the company.

There are many reasons for hesitation about the introduction of animal inspection into an industry, and one or more of these may have contributed to this action. Animals represent a whole new technology for organizations not already prepared to undertake the humane care and feeding required. There are the animal lovers to think of—a vocal lot even when it can be demonstrated, as in this case, that the animals loved their work. Then there is the matter of organized labor and its reaction to such an innovation. And, of course, there is the consumer on whom the industry depends. What would his reaction be? The buyer of products is known to be a fickle organism and not so easily manipulated as the industrious pigeon.

Birds can be trained to review products, but not—so far—to render judgments on policy. Perhaps this is a failing shared by experimental psychologists as well. For whatever reason, the experiment was ended by management decision, and the action may well have been a wise one. The fact that a technique works is only one of the factors which executives must weigh.

Plato's "man" may never emerge from the Academy. Although he is not human he has demonstrated a dignity and potential usefulness of his own. Beyond his scientific utility as an experimental organism is his potential economic usefulness. Through his ability to perform some of man's more simple tasks, the humble pigeon may be capable of freeing man from many kinds of triviality and routine. This is a capacity to which a modern Diogenes might give some thought.

FALLACIES IN THE INTERPRETATION AND CONTROL OF BEHAVIOR

m

11

FALLACIES IN INTERPRETATION

Of all natural phenomena, man's own behavior has been subject to some of the strangest and most varied explanations. "Reasons" for our behavior have been given by astrologists, phrenologists, palmists, common-sense philosophers, and shamans. Today, in an age when science has offered so much, we have come to it seeking answers formerly supplied by nonscientific disciplines. And, because truly scientific explanations have proved so effective in many fields, we tend to accept uncritically any explanation merely labeled "scientific." It is important, therefore, to examine closely the assumptions underlying presumably scientific statements about human nature and the exact meaning, ramifications, and not only plausible but common consequences of such statements in our colleges, courts, industries, and institutions for the mentally ill.

The first paper included in this section shows that vague, general statements which could be true about almost anyone were accepted by college students as having special, individual meaning for themselves. Furthermore, the test interpreters were praised for their exceptional insight. Research such as this suggests the possible existence of a self-maintaining cycle of error, in which the individual accepts statements about himself, and the interpreter is reinforced by the individual's acceptance and praise. Thus the acceptance and survival of personality interpretations may have little dependence on their specificity or accuracy.

As part of this trend toward the "scientific," there has been, since World War II, an increasing emphasis on the importance of psychological measuring devices. Applicants for positions in industry, the armed forces, and various other government jobs, as well as students desiring entrance to college, are all thoroughly tested on their "adjustment" as well as their "intelligence." Unfortunately, however, there is no direct measure of either, and the validity of the tests and especially the questionnaires has long been doubted. It was thus not surprising that Azrin, Holz and Goldiamond, in testing a questionnaire designed to measure fear in combat, found that responses to the questionnaire seemed to be more a measure of the impression the examinee thought this answer would make on the examiner than of any actual fear felt by the examinee.

Another setting in which psychology, because it is labeled a "science," is called upon for assistance is our courts. The papers by Jeffery and Leifer both point up the symbiosis existing between psychologists and the courts, the psychologists assisting the courts by making decisions for which they, in fact, have no special qualifications, and the courts reinforcing the psychologists by designating them both "scientific" and "expert."

When one realizes that all of these areas—clinical diagnosis, personality evaluation, and assignment of legal responsibility—have far-reaching effects on the lives of many individuals, the need for a more honest evaluation of the present capabilities of psychology and psychologists becomes striking. Although psychologists should not abandon their attempts to be of assistance in any area, there is an obvious need for careful evaluation of the "scientific" techniques they may develop.

Student acceptance of generalized personality interpretations

ROGER E. ULRICH, THOMAS J. STACHNIK, N. RANSDELL STAINTON

Previous investigators (Carter, 1963) have been concerned with how individuals react to personality interpretations which are based on information obtained from personality tests. Since "virtually every psychological trait can be observed to some degree in everyone" (Forer, 1949), it is possible that such interpretations may be given in terms so general that they could apply to almost anyone. The following study was conducted in an attempt to discover the degree of acceptance of vague, generalized personality interpretations, presumably derived from personality tests, and to determine whether the "prestige" of the person making the interpretation is related to acceptance.

PROCEDURE

Two experiments were performed involving 136 students from three educational psychology classes plus 79 other Ss. In the first experiment ($N = 57$), the instructor of the class administered both the Bell Adjustment Inventory and the House-Tree-Person (HTP) test. The students were told by the instructor that he would score and interpret each of their tests and return the interpretations to them at a later date. About a week later each student was given an interpretation with his or her name on it. All interpretations returned were identical, but the statements were arranged in a different order. The students were then asked to read and think about the interpretations carefully and to rate them as follows:

A.   Rate the interpretation of your personality according to the following scale: I feel that the interpretation was:
   Excellent Good Average Poor Very Poor
   B. Please make any additional comments about the test interpretation that you feel would be appropriate.

In the second experiment members of two classes (total $N = 79$) were given instructions for administering the tests to one other person, e.g., a roommate, neighbor, etc. Both the tests and the personality interpretations were the same as those used in Exp. I. The students were not to reveal to their Ss that they were part of an experiment. They were simply to state that they were studying personality testing and needed an S for practice. Ss were to be given the tests, and several days later they were to be given the interpretation. Ss were then to be instructed to rate the interpretation. The method of rating was similar to that of the first experiment.

The following interpretation, adapted from Forer (1949, p. 120), was used in both experiments.

You have a strong need for other people to like you and for them to admire you. You have a tendency to be critical of yourself. You have a great deal of unused capacity which you have not turned to your advantage. While you have some personality weaknesses, you are generally able to compensate for them. Your sexual adjustment has presented some problems for you. Disciplined and controlled on the outside, you tend to be worrisome and insecure inside. At times you have serious doubts as to whether you have made the right decision or done the right thing. You prefer a certain amount of change and variety and become dissatisfied when hemmed in by restrictions and limitations. You pride yourself as being an independent thinker and do not accept others' opinions without satisfactory proof. You have found it unwise to be too frank in revealing yourself to others. At times you are extroverted, affable, sociable, while at other times you are introverted, wary, and reserved. Some of your aspirations tend to be pretty unrealistic.

RESULTS

It is evident from the data that Ss for the most part accepted the interpretations. Table 1

From *Psychological Reports*, 1963, **13**, 831–834.

Table 1. *Ratings of personality interpretations.*

	Total	Excellent	Good	Average	Poor	Very Poor
Psychologist's Interpretations						
	57	27	26	3	1	0
Student's Interpretations						
	79	29	30	15	5	0

shows the students' ratings of the test interpretation for the first experiment. Fifty-three of the 57 students rated the interpretation as good or excellent. Row 2 gives the students' ratings of the test interpretations for the second experiment. Fifty-nine of the 79 students rated the interpretation as good or excellent in spite of the fact that these interpretations were given by admittedly inexperienced students! Chi-square tests significant at the .001 level indicate that in both experiments the ratings given the interpretations were higher than chance expectancy.

Other data obtained were the comments of Ss concerning the validity as well as the helpfulness of the interpretation. Several examples were chosen which are indicative of the opinions and reactions of the majority of Ss. The following statements were taken directly from the students' papers.

1. I feel that you have done a fine job with the material which you had to work with. I agree with almost all your statements and think they answer the problems I may have.
2. On the nose! Very good. I wish you had said more, but what you did mention was all true without a doubt. I wish you could go further into this personality sometime.
3. The results have brought out several points which have worried me because I was not sure if I had imagined these to be personality traits of mine. Tests like this could be valuable to an individual in helping him to solve some of his own problems.
4. I believe this interpretation applies to me individually, as there are too many facets which fit me too well to be a generalization.
5. The interpretation is surprisingly accurate and specific in description. I shall take note of many of the things said.
6. I feel that the interpretation does apply to

me individually. For the first time things that I have been vaguely aware of have been put into concise and constructive statements which I would like to use as a plan for improving myself.
7. It appears to me that the results of this test are unbelievably close to the truth. For a short test of this type, I was expecting large generalizations for results, but this was not the case; and I give all the credit to the examiner whose conclusions were well calculated.

The first three statements were written by the group of Ss who were given the test and interpretation by a professional psychologist. The last four statements were written by those Ss given the test and interpretation by students. These results indicate not only that Ss were "taken in" by the interpretation, but also that Ss were very likely to praise highly the examiner on his conclusions.

DISCUSSION

The principal finding is that the majority of the people tested accepted a personality interpretation stated in general terms as an accurate description of their own personalities without being aware that the same interpretation could be applied to almost anyone.

A previous study (Forer, 1949) demonstrated the same phenomenon and suggested that the probability of acceptance of the interpretation was increased when it was made by a prestigeful person, i.e., a psychologist. However, in the present study the interpretations made by inexperienced students were as readily accepted as those made by a professional psychologist. The mean ratings given the student and psychologist interpretations were 4.05 and 4.38, respectively ($t = .21$, n.s.). This in part indicates the awe with which personality tests *per se* are viewed by the naive student or others of comparable test sophistication.

Furthermore, the fact that some of the students did praise the interpretation demonstrates that individuals accepting a general interpretation as an accurate description of their personality are very likely to praise the examiner. It has been noted that approval can serve as a reinforcement (Skinner, 1953), thereby increasing the probability that the approved behavior will recur. It thus follows that in a counseling setting such reinforcement might cause the examiner to continue to make this type of vague, general interpretation. When the counselor has given a test and is interpreting its results, general statements used by him are perhaps reinforced by statements of praise similar to those observed in the present experiment, although neither the client nor the counselor is capable of verbalizing the contingency which has caused such a situation to occur.

Response bias in questionnaire reports

NATHAN H. AZRIN, WILLIAM HOLZ, AND ISRAEL GOLDIAMOND

If one defines psychology as the study of behavior, the direct measurement of behavior appears to be a minimal prerequisite to further analysis. Several alternatives to a direct measurement of behavior are commonly practiced. One such indirect method defines and measures the behavior in terms of the effect of that behavior upon the environment. For example, the measurement of reaction time typically is based upon the moment of closure of an electric switch or push-button. The simple fact of closure of the push-button does not guarantee that the movement of any one finger be involved since any finger or even the palm, wrist, arm, or leg might just as easily have been used. Such ambiguities in interpretation are easily overcome, and the experimenter can easily confirm his interpretation of the switch closure by occasionally or continuously observing the behavior directly.

A second alternative to direct behavioral observation is the interview or questionnaire procedure. Here the experimenter typically does not have any simple means of direct behavioral observation. Rather, the subject himself is expected to observe his own behavior and to describe it at some future date. The subject's reports usually cannot be evaluated by direct observation of the behavior being reported as was true of closing of the switch. The problem is often enhanced by the fact that the behavior being reported upon is basically unobservable by the experimenter by its very nature. This is true for the so-called "subjective reactions" as when an individual states that he feels hostile or afraid. In addition, it is quite likely that a report of one's own behavior will be modified considerably by the audience or experimenter to whom the report is being made. Other factors such as social acceptability may also be involved. The reply to the question "Did you cheat?" would probably be different if the interviewer were a classmate than if he were an instructor. For whatever the ultimate reasons may be, the individual being questioned may have a pre-existing tendency or bias in admitting to some statements and not to others. The present study was performed in order to study the influence of such response biases upon the reports of behavior obtained through a questionnaire.

A well-known study by Shaffer (1947) deals with the reports of combat flyers of their fears in combat. The reports had been obtained from these flyers by means of a questionnaire some 2 months following the termination of their combat experiences. This study has been widely interpreted as demonstrating that some behavioral reactions such as "soiling one's pants" are more indicative of fear in combat than are behavioral reactions such as "feeling nervous and tense." In order to evaluate the validity of

From *Journal of Consulting Psychology*, 1961, **25**, 324–326.

Table 1. *Reported symptoms of combat fear of 160 college students.*

During Combat Missions Did You Feel:	% of Students Stating "Often" or "Sometimes"
That your muscles were very tense	72
A pounding heart and rapid pulse	71
"Butterflies" in the stomach	67
Dryness of the throat or mouth	67
"Nervous perspiration" or "cold sweat"	61
Sense of unreality that this couldn't be happening to you	49
Easily irritated, angry, or "sore"	43
Need to urinate very frequently	42
Trembling	39
Unable to concentrate	36
Sick to the stomach	34
Right after a mission, unable to remember details of what happened	32
Confused or rattled	28
Weak or faint	25
That you have wet or soiled your pants	11

this interpretation, 160 college freshmen and sophomores, including males and females, in five separate psychology and sociology classes were given a questionnaire. This questionnaire contained the same 15 "symptoms" reported in the original investigation by Shaffer. All of the questionnaires had the following directions:

Imagine that you are a combat flyer who has flown many missions over enemy territory. Your commanding officer gives you the questionnaire below and tells you to fill it in. Fill in the answers keeping in mind what your commanding officer expects you to have felt.

Two forms of the questionnaire were used, however; half of each class of students received one form and half received the other form. One form stated after the first sentence:

You have been extremely frightened on all of your missions and have experienced each of the symptoms below on every flight.

The other form stated:

You have never been frightened on any of your missions and have not experienced each of the symptoms below on every flight.

One half of the students are thereby told that they have never experienced any of the listed symptoms, whereas the other half are told they have experienced all of the symptoms. Further, all students were instructed by the questionnaire to answer in terms of what is expected, regardless of what behavior is presumed to have occurred.

RESULTS AND DISCUSSION

Table 1 presents the percentage of students who chose each symptom as occurring "often" or "sometimes." It will be recalled that the students had been told that all symptoms were experienced equally often. The only basis for checking some symptoms more than others was the specific instruction to keep in mind what answers are expected. Had there been no predisposition or response bias toward some symptoms, one should expect all symptoms to have been selected equally often. Certainly, no particular rank ordering of the symptoms should have emerged. The results of Table 1 demonstrate that the selection of symptoms does not follow a random distribution. Some symptoms were selected as much as six times as often as others.

Spearman rank-order correlations were performed to determine the consistency of this response bias among the students. It was found that the rank-order of symptoms for males correlated with that of females with $\rho = .88$. Similarly, the rank-order correlation of symptoms was .95 between those students who were told that they had experienced all the symptoms and those who were told that they had not experienced the symptoms. This high degree of similarity demonstrates that the response bias toward certain symptoms exists regardless of whether or not the symptom was alleged to occur.

In order to determine whether the same response bias might have affected the reports of the combat flyers, a Spearman rank-order correlation was performed between the symptoms reported by the flyers and those reported by the students. It was found that the rank orders of the responses were highly similar ($\rho = .89$) between the students and the flyers. Nor was this relationship reduced for those students who were told that they had not experienced the symptoms ($\rho = .94$) as compared with those who were told that they had experienced all of the symptoms ($\rho = .90$). The statistical stability of this response bias is evidenced by the degree to which the rank-order in each classroom of students was correlated with the rank-order reported by the combat flyers: $\rho = .70, .82, .85, .90,$ and $.92$.

The response pattern obtained from the students by means of the questionnaire is almost completely predictable on the basis of response bias. Therefore, it is quite likely that the same type of response bias operated on the combat flyers. Any conclusions concerning the actual symptoms must await study by a method that provides for a more direct and objective measurement.

The present findings may well be considered for their implications for the use of interview and questionnaire methods in general. Unless an objective and direct means of measurement is available, the questionnaire responses may be independent of the behavior being studied.

A definitive method of determining the validity of the reports is the direct and objective measurement of the behavior being reported. Once such a direct measure is available, however, the very need for questionnaire reports is eliminated.

The psychologist as an expert witness on the issue of insanity

RAY JEFFERY

Recent discussions of psychology and law have been concerned with certification, privileged communication, and the like, but there are little data on the subject of the psychologist as an expert on criminal cases involving the issue of insanity.

The Code of Ethics urges psychologists to behave in a responsible manner with regard to interpretation of test data. The author is aware of the fact that the interpretation of many psychological tests and reports is open to differences of opinion, that they are by no means settled issues, and that considerable research is currently going on in the area.

Nevertheless, some psychologists have behaved in the courtroom as though the issues were settled. They have made assertions that do not have the blessings of the entire professional psychological community, and these assertions have brought court opprobrium to them, and perhaps to the psychologist in general. On one occasion, following such testimony, the presiding judge literally threw a deck of projective cards onto the floor. The defense attorney then requested that the court record show that the judge had expressed his feelings toward the testimony of this expert witness, to which the judge replied that the record would also show that he (the judge) was going even further in that he was throwing out all of the testimony of this psychologist. Quite obviously, testimony which can arouse such a reaction in a reputable court of law is, or should be, of concern to psychologists interested in the contribution they can make to society, and in the role of their professional image in the acceptance or rejection of such contributions. The data to be presented were gathered in the District Court of the District of Columbia, and the impression created in the court was that the psychologists were not poor representatives of their profession, since in the words of the Government attorney, they

From *American Psychologist*, 1964, **19**, 838–843.

were men "with more degrees than a thermometer."

The testimony may also serve the function of providing psychologists who rely on projective tests with information on how such evaluations may be treated by an opposing and often hostile attorney, or how they may be interpreted in a court of law which permits cross-examination of witnesses, including expert witnesses.

The writer is a sociologist who recently was a coinvestigator on a National Institute of Mental Health project concerning the operation of the insanity defense in the District of Columbia. He had occasion to observe psychologists in the courtroom, and to examine in detail court transcripts of over 25 cases in which insanity was an issue. Testimony by psychologists was given in 2 of the cases, relevant excerpts from which are presented below. The other trials involved psychiatric testimony exclusively.

The writer is not an expert on personality assessment and diagnosis, and he will leave it to the psychological community to evaluate the testimony herein presented. It should be noted that the transcripts become public records open for public inspection. As will be evident from these transcripts, attorneys have available such public records as research reports on psychological tests — and may read them, even if psychologists do not. This is in contrast to hospital hearings, where the records are private and confidential.

UNITED STATES V. KENT[1]

Psychologist A: Defense

Psychologist A testified that she had administered the following tests to Kent: the Wechsler Memory Scale, the Bender-Gestalt, the Rorschach, the Thematic Apperception Test, the House-Tree-Person Test, and the Szondi Test. From this evidence she diagnosed the defendant as schizophrenic, chronic undifferentiated type, characterized by abnormal thoughts, difficulty with emotional control, deficient in common-sense judgment, and lacking in close relationships with other people. She considered these as indicative of psychosis, and that the crimes of housebreaking, robbery, and rape,
of which the defendant was accused, were products of the mental disease.

Cross-Examination by Government

Q[uestion]. What did the House-Tree-Person Test reveal?

A[nswer]. The major finding was a feeling of withdrawal, running away from reality, feelings of rejection by women.

Q. And the results of the Szondi?

A. This showed a passive, depressed person who withdrew from the world of reality, with an inability to relate to others.

Q. Wasn't the Szondi Test made up around 1900, or the early 1900 period? And wasn't it made up of a number of pictures of Europeans who were acutely psychotic?

A. Yes, that is true.

Q. And this tells you something about his personality?

A. Yes, you can tell something about the person from his responses to the photos.

Q. And the House-Tree-Person Test — you handed the defendant Kent a pencil and a blank piece of paper, is that right, Doctor?

A. That is correct.

Q. And you asked him to draw a house?

A. Yes.

Q. And what did this tell you about Kent?

A. The absence of a door, and the bars on the windows, indicated he saw the house as a jail, not a home. Also, you will notice it is a side view of the house; he was making it inaccessible.

Q. Isn't it normal to draw a side view of a house? You didn't ask him to draw a front view, did you?

A. No.

Q. And those bars on the window — could they have been Venetian blinds and not bars? Who called them bars, you or Kent?

A. I did.

Q. Did you ask him what they were?

A. No.

Q. What else did the drawing reveal about Kent?

---

1 Criminal No. 798–61, District Court for the District of Columbia.

A. The line in front of the house runs from left to right. This indicates a need for security.

Q. This line indicates insecurity! Could it also indicate the contour of the landscape, like a lawn or something?

A. This is not the interpretation I gave it.

Q. And the chimney—what does it indicate?

A. You will notice the chimney is dark. This indicates disturbed sexual feelings. The smoke indicates inner daydreaming.

Q. Did I understand you correctly? Did you say dark chimneys indicate disturbed sex feelings?

A. Yes.

Q. You then asked Kent to draw a tree. Why?

A. We have discovered that a person often expresses feelings about himself that are on a subconscious level when he draws a tree.

Q. And what does this drawing indicate about Kent's personality?

A. The defendant said it was a sequoia, 1500 years old, and that it was diseased. This indicates a feeling of self-depreciation. Also, the tree has no leaves and it leans to the left. This indicates a lack of contact with the outside world—the absence of leaves.

Q. Don't trees lose their leaves in winter, Doctor? If you look out the window now, in Washington, do you see leaves on the trees? Perhaps the defendant was drawing a picture of a tree without leaves, as they appear in the winter.

A. The important thing is, however, why did the defendant select this particular tree. He was stripped of leaves, of emotions.

Q. You then asked him to draw a person?

A. Yes.

Q. And he drew this picture of a male?

A. Yes.

Q. And what does this drawing indicate about Kent?

A. The man appears to be running. This indicates anxiety, agitation. He is running, you will notice, to the left. This indicates running away from the environment. If he had been running to the right this would indicate entering the environment.

Q. How about the hands?

A. The sharp fingers may indicate hostility.

Q. Anything else?

A. The head and the body appear to be separated by a dark collar, and the neck is long. This indicates a split between intellect and emotion. The dark hair, dark tie, dark shoes, and dark buckle indicate anxiety about sexual problems.

Q. You then asked Kent to draw a person of the opposite sex. What did this picture indicate?

A. The dark piercing eyes indicated a feeling of rejection by women, hostility toward women.

Q. Are you familiar with the occasion upon which a Veterans Administration psychologist gave this House-Tree-Person Test to 50 psychotics, and then gave 50 normal subjects the same test, and then had a group of psychologists rate them?

A. No, I am not familiar with that research.

Psychologist B: Defense

Psychologist B testified that he administered the Wechsler-Bellevue, the Graham Kendall, the Rorschach, and the Symonds Picture Story Tests. He also testified that he had diagnosed the defendant as schizophrenic, undifferentiated type, and that mental illness had produced the alleged crimes.

Cross-Examination by Government

Q. Did you administer the Szondi Test, Doctor?

A. No. I don't happen to think much of it. The test assumes a schizophrenic looks a certain way, and we have evidence this isn't so.

Q. What responses did you receive from Kent on the Rorschach, the ink-blot test?

A. Wolf, butterfly, vagina, pelvis, bats, buttocks, etc.

Q. And from this you concluded the defendant was schizophrenic?

A. Yes, that and other things.

Q. You gave him the Wechsler Adult Scale?

A. Yes.

Q. On the word-information part of the test, the word "temperature" appears. What question did you ask the defendant?

A. At what temperature does water boil.

Q. You gave him a zero. Why?

A. Because he answered 190° and that is the wrong answer. The right answer is 212° F.

Q. What question did you ask about the Iliad?

A. I am not sure; I believe I asked him to identify the Iliad or who wrote the Iliad.

Q. And he answered "Aristotle"?

A. Yes.

Q. And you scored him zero?

A. That's correct.

Q. Now you asked the defendant to define blood vessels, did you not?

A. Yes.

Q. And his answer was capillaries and veins. You scored him zero. Why? Aren't capillaries and veins blood vessels?

A. I don't know. The norms don't consider that answer acceptable.

Q. What norms?

A. You see, these tests are scored on the basis of norms secured by administering the test to thousands of people.

Q. On the comprehension section you asked Kent: "If you found a sealed, addressed, stamped envelope on the street, what would you do with it?" and he answered "Turn it in." Why did you give him a 1? Why not a 2?

A. Because of the norms. A 2-answer would require more—something like "Mail it" or "Take it to the post office."

Q. You asked Kent: "What does the phrase 'Strike when the iron is hot' mean?" What was his answer?

A. "Strike when it is best to strike." I gave him a zero.

Q. Why? Doesn't "Strike when the iron is hot" mean to strike when the opportunity presents itself?

A. In terms of the norms it is not an acceptable answer.

Q. You asked Kent: "What is similar about the eye and the ear?" and he said "They are organs." You gave him a 1. Why?

A. Because a 2-answer is more precise, such as "organs of perception."

Q. You asked him: "What is winter?" and he stated "A season of the year." You gave him a 1—why not a 2? Isn't winter a season of the year, Doctor?

A. Well, again it is a matter of the norms. A 2-answer would include a "cold season of the year."

Q. You asked him: "What is a slice?" and he said "to cut." What is wrong with that? You gave him a 1.

A. A 2-answer would include "to slice thin" or "cut into thin pieces."

Q. You asked him to define "conceal" and he said "to get rid of." What score did you give him?

A. A zero.

Q. You asked him to define "sentence" and he said: "A group of words, as a noun and a verb." Why did you give him a 1?

A. A 2-answer would include the notion that a sentence expresses an idea.

Q. You asked him "What is a sanctuary?" and he said "Protection." Why did you give him a 1?

A. According to the norms, a 2-answer includes the notion of a place or a building.

Q. You asked Kent to define "calamity," and he said "a bad thing." You gave him a zero. Isn't a calamity a bad thing, Doctor?

A. Bad is not an acceptable answer in terms of the norms.

Psychologist C: Defense

The witness testified he administered the Wechsler Intelligence Scale, the Rorschach, the Human Figure Drawing, the Kohn, the Porteus Maze, and the Thematic Apperception Tests.

Cross-Examination by Government

Q. You asked the defendant to draw a human figure?

A. Yes.

Q. And this is the figure he drew for you? What does it indicate to you about his personality?

A. You will note this is a rear view of a male. This is very rare, statistically. It indicates hiding guilt feelings, or turning away from reality.

Q. And this drawing of a female figure, does it indicate anything to you; and, if so, what?

A. It indicates hostility towards women on the part of the subject. The pose, the hands on the hips, the hard-looking face, the stern expression.

Q. Anything else?

A. The size of the ears indicates a paranoid outlook, or hallucinations. Also, the absence of feet indicates feelings of insecurity.

Q. On the Wechsler, you asked him: "What would you do if you found a sealed, addressed, stamped envelope?" and he answered: "Open it and find out who it belongs to. I will show you I know right from wrong." [This is the same subject who answered "Turn it in" to the previous psychologist.]

Psychologist D: Defense

Psychologist D testified he saw the subject once at jail or the receiving home for an hour and a half; that he administered the Rorschach and started the Human Figure Drawing Test. The testing was interrupted when the defendant's father was announced, and Kent became very upset, highly emotional.

He diagnosed the defendant as schizophrenic, undifferentiated type. He thought productivity existed; that is, the schizophrenia produced the housebreakings, robberies, and rapes. The test showed severe thinking disturbance, an inability to control impulses, and disturbed sexual feelings.

Cross-Examination by Government

Q. Why did you see the defendant Kent?

A. Because of a call from Mr. Arens.

Q. Are you a member of the Washington School of Psychiatry?

A. No.

Q. The defendant made one drawing for you, right, Doctor?

A. Yes, that is right.

Q. After the announced arrival of his father?

A. Yes.

Q. Do you use the House-Tree-Person Test?

A. Never.

Q. Does it have validity?

A. Yes.

Q. Do you use the Szondi?

A. Five or six times.

Q. When did you stop using it?

A. At the fifth administration, about nine years ago.

Q. What does this drawing that Kent made for another psychologist indicate to you?

A. The transparency of the picture—that is, seeing through the figure to something beneath —suggests pathology.

Q. Do you usually use an extensive battery of tests before reaching a diagnosis?

A. Yes.

Q. Do you usually arrive at the diagnosis on the basis of one Rorschach administered twice within an hour?

A. Frequently.

Q. What else in the drawing is significant psychologically?

A. The irregularity or sketchiness of the lines may suggest tension and anxiety. The attention paid to details—to the belt-bow-tie, and pockets—indicate a little-boy-like quality about the defendant.

Q. Is it significant that the figure is running to the left, and not to the right?

A. To some people, yes. I don't place any significance on it.

Q. What about this drawing, made by Kent for another psychologist? What is significant about it?

A. The minimization of the breasts and the three lines across the genital area indicate tension in the sexual area. Breasts are symbolic of motherhood and early infant experiences. By minimizing the breasts the defendant indicates he has not received the satisfaction from women he had hoped to.

Q. Now, I will show you the picture Kent drew for you on September 9, 1961. What is significant about it?

A. The overemphasis of the breasts indicates how upset the defendant was because his father had been announced.

Q. You showed the defendant a series of Rorschach cards, right? And what responses did you get to Card 1, Card 2, etc.?

A. Cat, flying bird, a house, people, crab, wolf, pinchers, wings, clouds, blood, "like a vagina," menstrual blood, buckets, hip-bones, breast, apes, butterflies, jet airplane.

Q. On the basis of these responses, you concluded the defendant was a schizophrenic?

A. Yes.

UNITED STATES V. JENKINS[2]

Psychologist A: Defense

Psychologist A testified that he had administered the following tests to the defendant: Wechsler Adult Intelligence Scale, Bender-Gestalt, Rorschach, and Szondi. The IQ rating was 74, a dull normal.

Direct Examination by Defense

Q. Why do you give these tests?

A. To get at personality functioning—to get a sample of behavior. It is assumed that the sample is representative of how a person deals with other life situations.

COURT. Do you say you can conclude that a person is suffering from schizophrenia from answers to a Rorschach?

A. Yes. For example, if somebody looked at this card and described it as a church with a steeple with three men standing there and the Virgin Mary descending, with the Devil hiding behind the house, I would feel confident in thinking that person is suffering from disordered thinking.

Q. As a result of your tests, what is your diagnosis?

A. Schizophrenia.

Q. And productivity?

A. I cannot fail to see how a man's mental condition is unrelated to his behavior. I would expect there is a relationship, yes. I cannot say definitely that one thing is a product of another.

Cross-Examination by Government

Q. Doctor, do you agree with this statement: "It is well established that psychiatrists and psychologists freely concede there is no absolute accuracy and reliability of tests in the measurement of intelligence."

A. I do not agree.

Q. How about this statement: "Two persons of substantially the same mental capacity may test with materially different scores or rating depending on education, training, environment, etc."

A. Well, environment includes so much that I would think this would affect the performance on intelligence tests.

Q. You can tell from responses to Rorschach cards what his personality is like?

A. From a global picture.

Q. What response did he give to Card 4?

A. He saw a frog.

Q. And what significance do you attach to this answer, Doctor?

A. This is not the response normal people give. People often see two boots.

Q. And Card 5?

A. He saw a butterfly. This is a perfectly acceptable response. Many normal people see butterflies in this card.

Q. Card 6?

A. He said: "Don't see nothing—don't look like nothing."

Q. What things about the defendant's responses to the Rorschach led you to your diagnosis of schizophrenia?

A. The poor quality of his responses, the lack of seeing other kinds of responses, more typical responses you would expect from an adult.

Q. You also administered the Draw-a-Person test?

A. Yes.

Q. And what did it indicate?

A. The defendant drew the figure on the upper left-hand corner of the page. This indicated explosive feelings, insecurity, in a sense, holding onto the edges of the paper. This indicates anxiety and insecurity.

Q. What if he had placed the drawing in the middle of the page—what would that indicate?

A. It would mean he is a little less insecure.

Q. Do you believe in free will?

A. I believe it means complete control over one's actions and thoughts. I believe one's environment and heredity affect one's ability to exercise choice. Man has ability to make choices, but this is affected by other factors.

Q. Do you come from the so-called behavioristic school?

A. No, I am an eclectic.

Q. Do you believe all crime is a product of mental illness?

---

2 Criminal No. 614–59, District Court for the District of Columbia.

A. No.

Q. Any category of crimes?

A. I would expect bizarre crimes are often a product of mental illness.

Q. On the Wechsler, you asked him, "What color is the flag?" What did the defendant answer?

A. He answered, "Red, white, blue" — a 1, or perfect score. The test is scored 1-0.

Q. The second question?

A. "What shape is a ball?" He answered, "Round" — a 1 response.

Q. The fifth question?

A. "What does rubber come from?" His answer was "wood." I gave him a zero.

Q. Why a zero — aren't trees wood?

A. Yes, but it doesn't follow that rubber comes from wood.

COURT. You know where we get wood other than trees?

A. No.

[Other questions, similar to Kent material used, not recorded here because of repetition.]

Q. Why do you use pictures of insane people on the Szondi? Why not normal subjects?

A. We know penicillin works; we don't know why it works. It's the same thing here. We know that certain kinds of tests work; we don't understand why they work.

Q. You stated he was a chronic, undifferentiated schizophrenic. Can he also be an undifferentiated psychotic?

A. No. Undifferentiated psychosis is not a recognized classification.

Q. Do you know whether or not these schizophrenia symptoms were in remission on June 10, 1959?

A. No, I do not.

Q. You cannot state an opinion as to whether or not the schizophrenia caused the crime?

A. Yes, that is right.

Psychologist B: Defense

This psychologist testified that she gave one part of the Szondi Test. She made a diagnosis of schizophrenia on the basis of the increase in the IQ scores.

Direct Examination by Defense

Q. What background factors confirmed your diagnosis of schizophrenia?

A. He was a withdrawn person who had few friends. He didn't associate with other children. He couldn't control his behavior.

Cross-Examination by Government

Q. What do you mean by adequate controls?

A. When the tensions build up in him to a state of anxiety, anger, frustration, his emotions explode into behavior over which he has no control.

Q. Do you believe in free will?

A. That is a philosophic, not a psychological, problem. Free will is an arbitrary, sudden explosion without cause. I don't believe that. If I am free to choose, why is it I choose one thing and you choose another? It is because of the structure of the nervous system, and the influence of the environment.

Q. You believe in God?

A. Yes, certainly.

Court. You believe in free will, don't you?

A. I believe I can make a free choice, based on what I am.

Court. Any individual is free to make a choice, isn't he?

A. Yes.

Q. Why did you use photographs of mentally ill persons — why not normal persons?

A. Because photographs of mentally ill persons are supposed to accentuate the needs or drives or deprivations or frustrations that human beings experience. Normal people have managed to resolve their frustrations. I don't know why it works. It is something underneath. It is difficult to explain and understand. Doctors use digitalis for heart disease without knowing why it acts as it does.

[On questioning concerning the Szondi Test, the witness testified that a psychologist could diagnose illness by the pictures a subject selected as those he liked or disliked. At this point the judge threw the cards down. At a Bench conference the defense attorney asked: "May the record reflect that after the last question the Court slammed the cards down?"]

Court. The record may reflect it but the record may show I am throwing it all out. That will take care of that session.

The psychiatrist and tests of criminal responsibility

RONALD LEIFER

The primary tests of criminal responsibility in this country are based on two well-known rules, the McNaughten Rule[1] and the Durham Decision.[2] The effect of both of these rules has been to thrust the psychiatrist into increasing courtroom prominence as an expert witness in cases of challenged responsibility. Although these rules have been criticized on various grounds the psychiatrist's capacity as an expert witness has, with few exceptions (Szasz, 1957), been taken for granted. The purpose of this essay is to demonstrate that psychiatric testimony fails to meet certain scientific standards on two grounds: First, in the case of the McNaughten Rule, it answers questions put in ordinary language by ordinary means; second, in the case of the Durham Rule, it serves the same ethical function as the jury, namely the ascription of responsibility.

In Western society, prior to the seventeenth century, the guilt of an accused criminal was often determined by tests which were believed to express the will of God, and punishment was prescribed according to a prevalent principle, such as the Law of Talion. In 1724, Judge Tracey formulated the "wild beast" test according to which an offender was not held responsible for his actions if he could not distinguish good from evil more than a wild beast.[3] This test held that it was the function of reason that distinguished man from beast. In 1760, the terms "right and wrong" were substituted for "good and evil" (Sobeloff, 1958). Like the wild beast test, the McNaughten Rule, which was formulated in England in 1843, also used a cognitive criterion for the determination of responsibility. McNaughten's acquittal on the grounds of insanity provoked a debate in Parliament which was answered by the judges of England; in that answer were embodied the rules of responsibility which bear McNaughten's name:

"the jurors ought to be told in all cases that every man is to be presumed to be sane and to *possess a sufficient degree of reason to be responsible* for his crimes, until the contrary be proved to their satisfaction: and that, to establish a defense on the grounds of insanity, it must be clearly proved that at the time of committing the act, the party accused was labouring under such *defect of reason* from disease of the mind, as to not *know* the nature and quality of the act he was doing; or if he did *know* it that he did not *know* that what he was doing was wrong." (Weihofen, 1933, p. 28, italics added).

This rule forms the basis of tests for criminal responsibility in the large majority of states in this country.

The McNaughten Rule *asserts* that responsibility is a function of the intellect: Reason is aligned with responsibility, and defect of reason is aligned with nonresponsibility. The key to the determination hinges on an evaluation of the "intellect" of the accused, specifically on whether he *knows* the nature and quality of his act and whether he *knows* that what he was doing was wrong. The job of the psychiatric expert witness is to aid the court in making this determination. For the psychiatrist to be considered an expert, he must have special skills or special knowledge which enable him to determine whether or not "Mr. Jones knows x," for which the "right and wrong" test offers specific instances.

Much like the medical pathologist or internist, the psychiatrist is considered to be a scientific expert, whose special province is the mind and the personality. Thus, it is thought that the psychiatrist has special skills and tools which enable him to penetrate the mind much as the toxicologist has special skills and tools for examining the blood. The basis for this view is the ancient notion, derived from the Greeks, that the mind is resident in the body, much like the blood, and has as its

From *American Psychologist*, 1964, **19**, 825 – 830.

1 McNaughten's Case, 10 Cl. & Fin. 200, 8 Eng. Rep. 718 (1843).

2 Durham v. United States, U.S. App. D.C. 214 F.2d 862 (1954).

3 Rex v. Arnold, 16 How. St. Tr. 695 (1724).

defining properties knowing and reasoning which occur in a private stream of consciousness. However, there are differences between the psychiatrist and the toxicologist.

First, the determination that "Mr. Jones knows x" is an ordinary determination which most people make every day of their lives. Every day teachers determine whether their students know their work, employers determine whether their workers know their jobs, and mothers determine whether children know their manners. Such judgments do not require special skills. The difficulty in making the determination does not depend on skill, but rather depends on the seriousness of the consequences of the judgment. The more serious the consequences, the more the need is felt to justify them and the greater will be the tendency to enlarge the inquiry and to enlist the assistance of experts or arbitrators. In contrast, the toxicologist's determination of blood arsenic, for instance, requires the use of special bioanalytic tools, which requires special skills.

Second, the judgment of whether or not "Mr. Jones knows x" is an ordinary one precisely because it is based on a knowledge of language usage, which most people possess. On the other hand, the judgment about the blood level of arsenic is based on the understanding of the specialized subjects of chemistry and physiology. Some elaboration on these points will clarify the manner in which the psychiatrist makes a determination about another person's knowledge.

The applicability of the verb "to know" is based on an evaluation of the behavior of the person in question, but contrary to common belief, it is not the case that we infer behind that behavior to a private sphere of events, the mind. Rather, our evaluation of another person's knowledge is a commentary *about* his behavior, in the same way that to judge an object useful is not to remark about an additional property such as weight or shape, but to comment about its properties in relation to a certain purpose we have for them. This point has been well clarified by modern philosophers such as Ryle (1949) and Ayer (1956), and is insufficiently attended to by those who would understand psychiatric operations. Thus, we consider that a man knows geography if he can tell us the characteristics of various regions; and we can judge that a man knows what he has done if he can tell us the details, history, purposes, and consequences of his actions. We can only tell whether a man "knows" by applying conventional standards which link behavior and language. Conversely, there are conventional standards which govern the use of the phrase "He does not know." These criteria for the use of language do not require a special knowledge of language (for if it did the philologist or the philosopher would be the true expert here) nor a special knowledge of human nature. Some special techniques might be required for eliciting the behavior on which a judgment is based, i.e., asking the proper questions, but interviewing is not a skill which the psychiatrist monopolizes. A skillful lawyer, detective, or personnel manager, among others, may be equally skillful in interviewing. Although this skill requires verbal techniques beyond those used in ordinary conversation, they are techniques which are employed in a variety of occupations.[4]

It should be obvious that the determination of the proposition "Mr. Jones knows x" is easy at the extremes. If when asked about the nature and quality of his act, Mr. Jones continually replies with irrelevant and disconnected phrases, we would consider him not to know the nature and quality of the act in question. Of course, considering what may lie ahead for him, he could be lying or faking, but the determination of this is an equally ordinary task. On the other hand, if he could give a detailed, coherent account of his actions, including their history and purposes, we would consider, *by convention*, that he knew their nature and quality.[5] It is in the middle ground that this determination is difficult; not because

4 The nontechnical task associated with the McNaughten Rule has received some mention. Thus, Davidson (1952) states: "A simple way of finding out is to ask the offender whether he now thinks his act is right or wrong." (p. 7). And Roche (1958) writes: "It must be apparent that the only direct way one can determine whether the accused has 'knowledge' of right and wrong is to place the question to him." (p. 19). However, this has never been considered a major criticism of the courtroom function of the psychiatrist. In fact, psychiatrists usually treat their task as a medical matter simply because they have medical training; then they proceed to criticize the remoteness of the legal tests from the "truths" of medical science.

5 The terms "nature" and "quality" are equally as ordinary as the term "knowledge," and their application is similarly a matter of the use of ordinary language.

of a borderline mental state, but because the rules of the language game are imprecise and ambiguous. When we add the ambiguous terms "right and wrong" and "nature and quality" to the middle ground of "knowing," we have created linguistic difficulties which no scientific technique or theory can overcome.

The fundamental linguistic ambiguity of this test is one basis of the court's burden in ascribing responsibility (Szasz, 1956), and has led to the employment of psychiatric "experts" to aid in the determination.[6] The use of a "scientific expert" to aid in the determination of responsibility eases the burden of the court by giving the impression that the determination rests on a scientifically determined fact rather than on an ambiguous matter of semantics. It thus disguises and distracts us from the fact that the courts have to justify life and death decisions on the basis of arbitrary and ambiguous criteria and provides what appears to be a scientific justification for the court's decision. Psychiatrists have been all too eager to testify, and why not?—they have everything to gain and nothing to lose by it. In exchange for helping the court out of its difficulty, the psychiatrist's own claim to scientific status is underwritten by the courts.[7] And there are no risks. For since there are no explicit conventions describing the conditions under which "he does know" or "does not know" would be appropriate judgments, the psychiatrist is free to formulate his own rules. These rules are usually underwritten primarily by the psychiatrist's credentials rather than by an explicit method. It is the fact that the psychiatrist is using his personal judgment, and not that psychiatry is a young or inexact science, that explains the notorious disagreements between psychiatrists in courtroom procedures. These difficulties have been recognized by psychiatrists who have criticized the McNaughten Rule since its inception. In two recent polls, more than 85% of the psychiatrists questioned disapproved of this test (Guttmacher and Weihofen, 1952, p. 408). Philip Roche (1958, p. 407) states:

"The tests of responsibility as expressed in the McNaughten Rule . . . are untenable propositions within the discipline of scientific medical psychology."

Gregory Zilboorg (1949) goes further:

"To force a psychiatrist to talk in terms of the ability to distinguish between right and wrong and of legal responsibility is—let us admit it openly and frankly—to force him to violate the Hippocratic Oath, even to violate the oath he takes as a witness to tell the truth and nothing but the truth, to force him to perjure himself for the sake of justice."

The fact that psychiatrists have willingly testified and continue to testify in tests of responsibility in spite of these criticisms and hazards can be explained by the social advantages, in terms of money, prestige, and power, that accrue to psychiatrists and to the institution of psychiatry as a result of this activity.

Psychiatrists, having willingly engaged in a task for which they were admittedly ill suited, set about to alter the task (Group for the Advancement of Psychiatry, 1954). The first revision of the McNaughten Rule occurred in the 1869 Pike case in New Hampshire.[8] The most famous of these reformulations is the Durham Decision of 1954 (see Footnote 2) which adopts the principle of the New Hampshire ruling. The essence of this ruling is that an accused criminal will not be held responsible if his criminal act was the product of a mental disease or defect, which is made a matter of fact for the jury to decide.

This change has several implications. It acknowledges a voluble psychiatric assertion that the intentionality of human actions is not a function of the intellect alone, but rather of a complex of interrelated cognitive, emotional, and unconscious factors.[9] The Durham Deci-

---

6 Cf. Hess and Thomas (1963) who state: "Our conclusion was that the issue of the defendant's competency to be tried was most frequently raised not on the basis of the defendant's mental status but rather was employed as a means of handling situations and solving problems for which there seemed to be no other recourse under the law." (p. 714).

7 This must be considered in the light of the fact that, in its youth, psychiatry had difficulty in achieving acceptance both within medicine and outside of it. The opportunity to gain status by performing an important sociolegal function was not without its advantages.

8 State v. Pike, 49 N.H. 399 (1869).

9 This widely held view can by no means be taken as scientific fact. For a discussion of this problem see Nagel (1959).

sion thus changes the legal definition of responsibility from a competent intellect to a well-integrated personality. *This is to assume that the McNaughten ruling was an erroneous characterization of human nature rather than a criterion for the ascription of legal responsibility, and betrays the psychiatric tendency to redefine all human events in its own terms.* By bringing the test for criminal responsibility up to date with psychiatric theory, it was assumed that the ascription of responsibility was made more scientific. In fact, however, ascriptions of any sort, although they may be based on a consideration of facts, are themselves neither facts nor scientific principles; rather, they are human actions similar to "giving" or "bestowing" and as such are neither true nor false, and, therefore, cannot be considered to be scientific (Hart, 1960).[10] The ascription of responsibility on the basis of mental health is no more scientific than the ascription of responsibility on the basis of personal wealth. The primary effect of the Durham Decision is to make the psychiatrist more comfortable with his testimony; he may now speak with the widest latitude, in his own parlance, using his own theories.[11]

Psychiatrists frankly admit this advantage and promote it, although they define it as primarily for the advantage of the court, whom they feel can now legitimately receive all of the information the psychiatrist is capable of giving. The absurdity of this euphemism is that it is the rare jurist or juror who can understand what the psychiatrist has to tell him (Wiseman, 1961). This "technicalization" of psychiatric testimony has resulted in the paradox that although one of the purposes of the Durham Decision is to insure that the moral decision is made by the jury rather than the expert, the facts on which that decision is to be based are so technical that the jury must hear the psychiatrist's conclusion as to whether the act was a product of mental disease or not, which is equivalent to an opinion about responsibility. Far from making their own decision the jury can only agree or disagree with one of two psychiatrists, each of whom presents technical language which the jury cannot understand. Thus, it tends to be the psychiatrist, rather than the facts, that influences the jury; the effect is that the moral decision is placed more firmly in the hands of the psychiatrist, although more subtly.

Underlying the Durham Decision is the belief that the concept of mental illness is scientifically valid. Paradoxically, at the same time that Durham-like rules are becoming increasingly popular, serious objections are being raised about the scientific validity of psychoanalytic theory (Nagel, 1959) and the concept of mental illness (Becker, 1962; Szasz, 1961b). It is implicit in the Durham Decision that mental illness is a fact of very much the same type as a fractured leg or pneumonia. This is false, the diagnosis of mental illness is ascriptive and *implies* nonresponsibility. Forensic psychiatrists err on this crucial point. Guttmacher (1963), for example, admits this implication but does not recognize its significance. He states:

"There are various factors . . . , which may greatly limit this freedom of choice, chief among which are levels of intelligence and the presence or absence of what we denominate mental disease."

The point of this discussion is to show that mental disease is not an independent variable which is inversely related to the dependent variable of free choice, but it is *by definition* inversely related to it. The relationship is tautological and not factual. Since responsibility is *by definition* a function of intention, it logically follows that responsibility is definitionally related to the diagnosis of mental illness. Since the diagnosis of mental illness is considered to be a fact on which the psychiatrist is expert, then his conclusion that an act is the product of mental illness *logically* implies lack of intention and, thus, lack of responsibility.

---

10 This is why the question of whether there is such a thing as free choice is an improper question (Guttmacher, 1963). Choice, like intention, is *ascribed* to (and not described of) a human action according to the circumstances of that action; whether or not it *should* be ascribed in a given circumstance is a moral question since the answer partly depends on the desirability of the consequences of such an ascription.

11 This change is similar to other instances of giving special concessions to those with "dirty" jobs, e.g., an arrangement whereby an executioner can avoid a face-to-face confrontation with his victim. The reciprocal relationship between law and psychiatry, where the law underwrites psychiatry and is then influenced by it, also has its counterpart in groups being influenced by agencies to whom they have delegated power, e.g., a government being "run" by a police force which has been charged with keeping the security.

The determination of mental illness *logically* implies lack of intention determination similar to that with which the court is charged. In order to demonstrate this I must comment on the concept of responsibility (Szasz, 1961a).

The court is charged with determining the responsibility of the defendant in two senses. First, it must determine whether the accused is *descriptively* responsible for the crime with which he is charged. This is essentially a matter of determining and proving the fact that the accused acted in such a way as to bring about certain consequences. Thus, we may say that X is responsible for the death of Y because he pulled the trigger of the gun which discharged a bullet into Y's heart. The determination of this question outside a court of law may be considered to be a genuine scientific question, since it deals with the verification or falsification of two facts which are held to be causally connected. It is important to note that psychiatric expert testimony is not utilized to aid the court in this determination, but other medical experts, such as toxicologists or pathologists, may be called upon. This demonstrates the functional difference between scientific determinations such as the blood level of arsenic, and nonscientific ascriptions such as the diagnosis of mental illness. Second, the court must *ascribe* responsibility, that is to say, it must determine whether or not the defendant shall be punished. This is essentially decided on the basis of "defeating" circumstances, that is to say, circumstances in addition to the fact of the crime which provide a basis for excusing the crime. Descriptive and ascriptive responsibility are thus independent, and a man may be descriptively responsible in that it is proven that he did, in fact kill Y, but responsibility may not be ascribed in that additional facts demonstrate the act to be an accident which could not have been prevented by more prudent action. The primary defenses in cases of homicide are provided by *facts* which are held to demonstrate self-defense, mental disease, or an accident. Each of these defeats the ascription of responsibility. For instance, the fact that Y first came at X with a knife would demonstrate that the excusing condition of self-defense was applicable. This is a fact in addition to the descriptive fact of the crime which would negate the ascription of

responsibility. Or, it might be established as a fact that X believed that Y was a part of an elaborate plot to execute him; this belief might be considered to be a delusion which is a symptom of a mental disease on the basis of which X might be judged not responsible for his act. To put it another way, criminal responsibility is ascribed if (*a*) descriptive responsibility is proven and (*b*) it is not demonstrated that there are facts which indicate self-defense, accident, or mental illness.

Mental illness is held to defeat the ascription of responsibility because it is commonly believed to be a fact which is inversely correlated with intention. *However, neither "intention" nor "mental disease" are facts, but are ascriptive terms like "responsibility."* Responsibility is ascribed unless defeating circumstances can be demonstrated which indicate, for instance, accident or self-defense. Intention is ascribed to an action unless defeating circumstances can be demonstrated, for instance, accident or coercion. Mental health is ascribed unless defeating circumstances can be demonstrated, for instance, delusions or hallucinations. It is thus a logical error to consider mental disease to be a fact which is inversely correlated with intention, since mental disease is not a fact but is, like intention, ascribed on the basis of facts. *It is thus the facts that defeat the ascription of mental health that form the genuine but cryptic basis for defeating intention and, thus, criminal responsibility.* What kinds of facts are these?

The determination that a defendant has mental illness is based on certain facts about his behavior, usually (sometimes by law) excluding the crime for which he is being tried, and is therefore, let us be clear, *not an additional fact, but a name for a class of facts* (Szasz, 1961c). For instance, the diagnosis "paranoid personality" is a name designating a type of individual who tends to demonstrate suspiciousness, ideas of reference, or ideas of persecution. Three characteristics of the designation "mental illness" deserve to be mentioned. First, it is a name which is applied only to negatively valued behavior. It therefore registers a covert disapproval of, and is an ethical judgment about, certain forms of behavior (Szasz, 1961b). Second, while we tend to give conventional explanations for "reasonable" behavior, we tend to explain "unreasonable" behavior with unconventional explanations; socially acceptable actions are explained in terms of purposes, justifications, or rules, and unacceptable actions tend to be explained in terms of causes. Thus, the ordinary act of getting married might be explained in terms of "wanting a family," or "following custom," or "being in love." However, the more deviant behavior of the homosexual bachelor tends to be explained in terms of antecedent physical or psychosocial causes. The reasons for using causal explanations for unconventional behavior are complex. One reason is that conventional explanations do not fit; no conventional explanation can be given for a woman running stark naked through the streets simply because it is not a conventional act. Freud's attribution of psychic determinism to human behavior is based upon observations of accidents, slips, and other behavioral mishaps; these events are considered "accidents" precisely because no conventional explanations can be offered for them in terms of purposes or conventions. Thus the relationship between causal explanations and unconventional actions. Another explanation is the deep-rooted Judeo-Christian belief that man does not freely choose evil or illness; thus, Eve was influenced by the Devil, Adam was influenced by Eve, and their descendants have been influenced by a succession of malevolent factors from demons to instincts to twisted molecules to mental disease. Third, since mentally ill behavior is explained causally, it cannot be considered to be free. The diagnosis of mental illness illegitimates any consideration of intention. But intention is not a fact which is discoverable; it is a designation for certain types of behavior which do not exhibit features which are defeating to the ascription of intention. *In psychiatry, the characteristic of behavior which negates its intentional nature and qualifies it for the designation "illness" is precisely that it is unconventional; that is to say, no acceptable conventional explanations can be offered by the actor. It is therefore a history of unconventional behavior of a socially disruptive nature which defeats the ascription of both mental health and intention.* The diagnosis of mental illness logically implies the absence of choice or intention because they are both defeated by the same kinds of facts.

Here we have a hidden paradox which undermines the autonomy of the courts in ascribing responsibility. For the diagnosis of mental illness, which is supposed to be a "fact" which excludes intent, is itself a judgment that implies that certain kinds of undesirable behavior shall not be considered intentional. The determination of intention and responsibility are supposed to be judgments for the court to make, but we can now see that the psychiatrist actually makes them tacitly. The dilemma has a curious twist. The formulation of the notion of mental illness is based on the idea that only that behavior which is in some way maladaptive, deviant, and undesirable shall be included, and that behavior is considered to be determined, and thus, not to be free. The criminal who displays undesirable behavior during his lifetime, or prior to his crime, is thus more likely to be excused for his crime than the man who has led an exemplary life.

In the light of this discussion we may conjecture about why psychiatrists play such a large role in the determination of criminal responsibility. Certainly the theoretical position of most contemporary psychiatrists is offered as justification for this activity. Whether or not this position is erroneous will hopefully be decided after a vigorous consideration of arguments and evidence. In any case, there are compelling social factors which favor the perpetuation of the current point of view. The ethical question, "Ought this man be punished?" is an extremely difficult one to answer with convincing justifications. In their difficulty in solving this vital question, the courts have turned to "experts" for help, and psychiatrists, in all good faith, have been willing and eager to perform the task. Thus, a mutually beneficial partnership was established between law and psychiatry, in which, in return for their help with a difficult problem, psychiatrists were rewarded with a change in rules which made their task conform more closely with their own professional identity. Any challenge to the psychiatrist's status as an expert is not likely to be well received by either psychiatry or the law—for psychiatrists would have to abdicate from a favored function and the law would be forced into the painful search for its own formulae and justifications for the ascription of criminal responsibility.

12

FALLACIES IN CONTROL

While it is certainly to the advantage of both layman and behavioral scientist to accept the facts of behavior control, it is also to the advantage of both to be aware of fallacies concerning such control. Either of two instances involving control might appropriately be termed fallacious: any situation in which (1) certain procedures allegedly produce certain behavioral results when, in fact, these results do not occur, and (2) an explanation of behavior is sufficiently lacking in parsimony as to seriously disguise the nature of the controlling variables.

The first three of the following articles fall into the first category. In discussing subliminal perception, Goldiamond notes that the furor over the use of this technique in advertising was due largely to a misunderstanding of perceptual processes, and that the arbitrary, reflexive manipulation of the supposedly hapless consumer was a gross exaggeration.

The study, by Azrin, *et al.*, on the control of the content of conversation began as an attempt to replicate earlier work by Verplanck in which the frequency with which statements of opinion occurred was manipulated by selective reinforcement. In this replication, the authors encountered immense procedural difficulties, results that were a function of the experimenters' expectations, and even evidence of data falsification. The authors do not conclude that control over verbal behavior through reinforcement is impossible, but that the effectiveness of experimental procedures used in attempts to control casual conversation is open to serious question. The study serves as a warning that our enthusiasm for applying operant conditioning procedures to new settings must be tempered by the same careful definition of the response and tight experimental control that characterize research in the laboratory.

As with subliminal perception, the case for effective learning during sleep has been built largely by novelists and other laymen quite divorced from the objective study of human behavior. However, while enthusiasm for subliminal perception has apparently waned, the advocates of sleep learning are still very much in evidence, and a number of current magazines typically carry an advertisement encouraging the reader to send for records or tapes in order to "experiment" with sleep learning. The report by Emmons and Simon is a careful evaluation of sleep learning in a tightly controlled setting. It produced no evidence whatever that learning can occur during sleep.

The article by Orne and Evans on hypnosis is directed at the second type of fallacious control—situations in which control does exist, but where the nature of the controlling variables has been obscured. The authors attempt to determine if the degree of control which occurs under hypnosis actually exceeds the amount of control already existing in any situation: Are a prior procedure and internal state called "hypnosis" *necessary* to account for positive responses to suggestions of hallucinations, analgesia, or antisocial behavior? As yet, there are no known physiological changes occurring under hypnosis which cannot be duplicated by mere suggestion to nonhypnotized subjects. Furthermore, a survey of research in hypnosis shows that the reported effects usually involve getting a subject *not* to see, feel, or fear something, rather than enabling him to make perceptual discriminations or perform other feats which cannot be accomplished by non-hypnotized subjects. The most relevant evidence is the rapidly accumulating data which suggest that nonhypnotized subjects, when exhorted to do their very best on a task, not only duplicate but even exceed the performance of their hypnotized counterparts.

Statement on subliminal advertising

ISRAEL GOLDIAMOND

Regarding the current controversy on subliminal advertising and related phenomena, I believe the hysteria which currently exists is unwarranted. It is unwarranted because, in my opinion, it arises from a misunderstanding of the scientific issues involved. The notion of subliminal perception has arisen out of data obtained in the experimental laboratories of psychophysics. It can best be understood in reference to the data and methods of laboratories of experimental behavior.

My main conclusions regarding the issue of subliminal projection and advertising are the following:

1. Rather than protesting against the alleged invasion of privacy of our homes by the subliminal advertisers, those of us who are concerned with obnoxious advertising on TV might welcome this occurrence. It would be welcome because it can render obnoxious advertising *less* effective. If the advertiser wishes to reduce the force of his message and to reduce its effectiveness, I can think of few better ways for him to do so than by blanket use of this procedure.

2. By the same token, those advertisers who have an honest claim upon our attention are advised to examine this procedure with great care, since it can render their advertising less effective.

These two conclusions are based on the following statements, which have considerable research backing in experimental psychology:

1. Sensitivity depends upon stimulus magnitude. Generally, the less intense the stimulus, the less the response to it. This holds whether the stimulus is a visual, auditory, tactile, or any other sensory stimulus. Intensity is related to duration in vision, by a law stating that within certain limits (and these hold for subliminal advertising phenomena) intensity times duration is a constant. Thus, a stimulus can be made equally less visible by cutting its intensity in half while keeping it on the same amount of time, or by cutting its time in half and keeping the intensity the same as it was before. Stated otherwise, we can make a poster less visible by presenting it very quickly or by presenting it very dimly. On this basis, anyone who believes that a message which is hardly audible is more effective than a message which is fully audible should state over and over to himself one thousand times: "A dull, faded campaign poster which has been out in the sun and can hardly be seen is a more effective votegetter than a brand new poster just off the printing press."

2. Effects of the stimulus on behavior. The hysteria over subliminal advertising may rest upon a further misunderstanding concerning

Submitted at the request of the State of New Jersey Commission on Subliminal Projection, April 8, 1959.

the nature of the relationship between the stimulus and the response. There are at least two kinds of stimuli. First, there are certain sensory stimuli which serve to evoke reactions in us. This is the kind of stimulus that Pavlov dealt with in his experiments. He placed a piece of meat before a dog, who salivated upon sight of it. A tone was then sounded just before the presentation of the meat, and after a number of presentations the tone alone produced salivation. This, of course, is classical conditioning.

Generally, the effects of this type of conditioning have been over-emphasized in regard to human and animal behavior. Few stimuli that we come across extract responses from us in this way. Whereas the tone elicits salivation from the dog whether the dog "wills" it or not, there is nothing in the sign "Buy Kellogg's Corn Flakes" which makes me buy Kellogg's Corn Flakes and controls my buying behavior in the same way that a tone controls the dog's salivation behavior. There is nothing about a parking meter which makes me put a nickel into it in the same way that a steak makes my mouth water. A choice steak may make me salivate, but the parking meter and the box of corn flakes don't make me do anything. They merely provide an opportunity for me to behave in a certain way, if there are sufficient other reasons for me to do so. If there is a strike of policemen on a given day, it is doubtful that hitherto effective parking meters will collect many nickels. In other words, behavior in the presence of a parking meter and a sign urging me to buy Kellogg's Corn Flakes is not elicited by those stimuli as in the case of the beef steak, but is related to the consequences of the behavior. That is, the behavior will be controlled by what happens afterwards, or by a prior history of such consequences. The training procedures for the two types of responses are quite different.

The Pavlovian situation is considered as generally referring to emotional responses, that is, to responses in which the autonomic nervous system is primarily involved. You can condition salivation, maybe skin resistance, and other such activities using the Pavlovian method. It is also possible to condition such motor behaviors as finger-flexion this way, but the restriction generally holds. To govern most other behaviors in which the motor as-

pects of the central nervous system are primarily involved—such responses as opening doors, buying packages, shaking hands, walking, talking, voting, in other words, the vast majority of behaviors of concern to us—we must concern ourselves with control of the consequences of such behavior. This type of control has been systematically explored in the United States by psychologists and educators, among the major names being Thorndike and Keller at Columbia, and Skinner at Harvard.

Thus, children go to school because the consequences are different if they go or do not go. If they do not go to school, the truant officer may get after them. The preferred situation is that they go to school because if they do not go they will not learn the things being taught there, or will not meet their friends. In either event, going to school is governed by its consequences. Similarly, buying behavior is governed by its consequences. After a while many of these behaviors become habitual, that is we engage in them upon the presentation of certain stimuli which may be the "alarm clock" for the behavior. Nevertheless, no matter how habitual the behavior is, if the consequences are altered, the behaviors will in time also alter. As Ogden Nash once stated:

"I could live my life in ease and insouciance, Were it not for making a living which is rather a nuisance."

If they stopped paying me for coming to work, this nice ingrained habit I have might quickly vanish.

Accordingly, if a person had been trained in the past to clench his fist and raise it over his head yelling "Tovarish!" every time a picture of Khrushchev was flashed on the screen, then in the presence of the kind of audience which provided the desirable consequences for such behavior he might continue to do so whenever Khrushchev's picture appeared on that screen. He might do this to the extent that he could see the picture, that is. If he could hardly see the picture he might not respond, or if the picture were so dim that he might confuse it with that Enemy of the People, Malenkov, he also might not engage in this behavior.

The Sunday *Times* has suggested that subliminal advertising might be used to influence voting. Conceivably, I would vote for Faubus if he were running against Khrushchev. I can think of few other circumstances which would impel me to vote for him. If he were running against your own Governor Meyner, I would not vote for him. And, if a radio subliminally whispered: "Vote for Faubus" in my ear one thousand times a day, I would still not vote for him under these conditions. If he were running against Khrushchev, fearful for the consequences for myself and my children, I might vote for Faubus rather than for Khrushchev or Malenkov, but it would not take subliminal stimulation to induce me to do so.

3. Regarding experimental findings that people can accurately discriminate stimuli which are presented so faintly (or quickly) that people report not being able to perceive them, or findings that people can otherwise be affected by such faint stimuli, these findings can be explained on highly technical grounds which have little to do with the issue at hand. The technical grounds are considered in differing detail in the two articles attached (Goldiamond, 1958a, 1958c). Basically, they report a change in methodology and in approach over the past five years that tends rather overwhelmingly to alter conceptualization in this area of science. The general public is, however, proceeding on the assumptions of the psychology of fifty years ago. Unfortunately, these statements can also be made about many psychological investigations in perception. Progress is seldom even, and it often happens that advances in one area of a science are not immediately communicated to other areas, even to investigators applying techniques of those areas.

What use can the advertiser make of this procedure? If he delivers a five minute spiel, I can turn him off. But if he throws in a frame advertising his product for every hundred frames of show, I can not turn him off without turning the program off. If *"Bouvez Coca Cola"* appears in the middle of a Hamlet soliloquy, this is precisely what I may do. The advertiser runs this risk, as well as the risk that I will miss seeing the advertisement at all, since I may be blinking at the time, or have my set too low to catch the advertisement, but not too low for the show.

To summarize, the hysteria over subliminal projection rests upon two misunderstandings:

1. The confusion over the effects of the stimulus upon behavior. It is assumed that the stimulus which governs buying behavior is of the Pavlovian kind, when actually it is a discriminative stimulus of the kind technically called an operant discriminative stimulus.

2. The confusion over the effects of diminishing the stimulus. Making the stimulus less visible so that we are not conscious of it does not make it enter the Unconscious or the Subconscious. Rather, it tends to make it less visible or audible. In short, the advertiser may be saving me the trouble of turning him down, when he does so himself. With many advertisements, this would be, to quote another poet, "a consummation/Devoutly to be wish'd."

Regarding the use which subliminal projection may have, when one considers it in light of the difficulties raised, one may question its effectiveness, rather than its ethics.

Many years ago, when the X-ray was first announced, the legislature of one of our eastern states passed a bill forbidding the use of X-ray machines in public theatres, on the grounds that they might be used by unscrupulous men to peer through women's clothes. One can imagine the hysteria involved in this misunderstanding of this advance in science. Today, a misunderstanding of science is leading to hysteria over subliminal perception. I find it difficult to be alarmed over subliminal perception. I would suggest that, compared to the X-ray which has had a lasting impact, the impact of subliminal projection upon us may be as faint as the images it presents.

The control of the content of conversation through reinforcement

NATHAN H. AZRIN, WILLIAM HOLZ, ROGER E. ULRICH, AND ISRAEL GOLDIAMOND

The present study is an attempt to replicate an investigation by Verplanck (1955). In that investigation, psychology students were reported as able to exert strong control over the casual conversations of other people by selectively reinforcing a certain type of opinion-statement and extinguishing all other types of statements. To produce reinforcement, the student E paraphrased or agreed with each opinion of the S. Conversely, to produce extinction, the student E openly disagreed with the opinions or simply said nothing. Each S was studied for 30 minutes. For some groups of Ss, 10 minutes of extinction was preceded and followed by 10 minutes of reinforcement. For other groups, a 10-minute period of reinforcement was preceded and followed by 10 minutes of extinction.

The results of this experiment were quite dramatic. Within this brief 30-minute period, "All Ss increased their rate of stating opinions, regardless of the topic of conversation, its setting, or S's particular relationship with the E." (Verplanck, 1955, p. 673).

From the theoretical view, this study is one of the very few successful attempts to reinforce human verbal behavior in a free-operant situation. From a more practical view, this study seemed ideal as a laboratory exercise for a class of college graduate students. No special laboratory apparatus was needed other than a clock or watch which permitted the students to record the number of opinions and statements at 1-minute intervals. No laboratory space was needed because the experiment had been conducted in informal settings, such as a cafeteria or dormitory, or even over a telephone. Other advantages were the brief period of time required (30 minutes) and the apparent simplicity of the procedure. For example, after adequate instruction, "Of the 17 students who undertook the experiment, all were able to collect one or two sets of data as the design demanded." (Verplanck, 1955, p. 669).

CLASS EXPERIMENT I

Unlike the original study, a class composed of graduate students rather than undergraduates was used here. Of the 16 students, 11 either majored or minored in psychology. Before replicating this experiment, these students had received intensive instruction in the principles of operant conditioning, and had been tested on their knowledge. Further, each student read Verplanck's original study and was examined on his knowledge of it, and the procedure was discussed and rehearsed in detail in class. Two procedures were used. Half of the students conducted 10 minutes of extinction followed by 10 minutes of reinforcement, which was followed by another 10 minutes of extinction. The other half of the students reversed the procedure: reinforcement – extinction – reinforcement. Reinforcement consisted of the student E's agreement with the opinions of the subject. Extinction consisted of saying nothing. As in the original study, the student Es were instructed to say nothing at any time other than when agreeing with expressed opinions.

The results here were quite similar to those of the original study. Out of 15 students, 14 reported a higher frequency of opinions during the reinforcement period than during extinction. An application of the test by Wilcoxin for paired replicates[1] to these results showed that they were statistically significant well below the .0001 level. As was also true of the original study, the frequency of statements other than opinions did not change greatly.

Except for one student who could not complete the experiment, none of the students reported any difficulty either in conducting the

From *Journal of the Experimental Analysis of Behavior,* 1961, **4**, 25 – 30.

1 This test was used in all statistical comparisons in this paper.

experiment, defining the responses, scoring the behavior, or obtaining the expected results. However, the one student reported that he was unable to maintain a conversation without actively participating in the conversation, although such participation clearly violated the prescribed procedure. Also, he found it difficult to categorize the conversation into opinion vs. statements while simultaneously attending to his watch for purposes of timing. After six attempts, this one student reported that he was unable to complete the experiment according to the required procedure. After class discussion of his difficulties, eight of the other students stated that they had had similar difficulties, previously unmentioned, and were thereby forced to deviate appreciably from the stated procedure. The most frequently stated difficulties were: (1) the *S* walked out during extinction; (2) the *E* was forced to actively participate by nodding, smiling, or asking questions; (3) the *S* was aware of the recording; (4) *E* made errors in timing; and, finally, (5) *E* became too interested in the subject of conversation to concentrate on the recording of opinions.

During this class discussion, one student mentioned that he had taken a tape recording of his own experiment. A second student was therefore assigned to analyze the tape to determine the reliability of the recording. After several attempts, this second observer reported that he could not discriminate between the reinforcement and extinction periods, since the *E* had been actively participating throughout. A comparison of the frequency of opinions and statements between the two observers revealed little or no correspondence.

Because of this apparent difficulty in categorizing verbal behavior as an opinion or a statement, the following study was conducted.[2] A 30-minute tape recording was taken of a conversation in which the speaker knew that his opinions and statements were being recorded. Five students from this same class, including the original *E*, then listened to the recording individually and recorded the numbers of opinions and statements made. To minimize errors in timing, the five observers noted the behavior in terms of 5-minute rather than 1-minute intervals.

Figure 1 presents the number of opinions

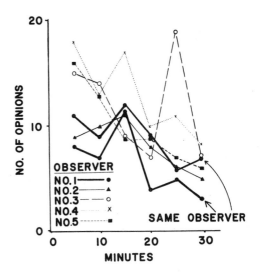

Figure 1. Number of opinions identified by each of five observers listening to the same tape. Observer No. 1 (heavy lines) listened to the conversation a second time after an interval of 2 hours.

recorded by the five observers. It shows that during each 5-minute interval, the number of opinions differed greatly among observers. The minimum and maximum is in a ratio of about 2 to 1 for each 5-minute period. More surprising is the difference found between the *E*'s original scoring and his own later scoring from the tape recording only 2 hours later. (See dark lines in Figure 1.)

CLASS EXPERIMENT II

The many difficulties reported by the first class in replicating the original experiment, as well as the surprising lack of reliability in identifying the responses, might be interpreted simply as differences in the types of students used. A second class was therefore given the same experiment, but was not given the original article to read. Furthermore, they were not told that the study had ever been done before. As in the original study by Verplanck, this class was composed largely of undergraduates who had been instructed and tested on the

---

2 Mr. R. Teague assisted in the collection of the data for this aspect of the study.

principles of reinforcement. The procedure followed for this second class was the same as that followed in the previous class. There were successive 10-minute periods of reinforcement — extinction — reinforcement. However, extinction was defined as disagreement rather than as silence. Verplanck had found that disagreement was as effective as silence in decreasing the response, and the present results support these findings. Of the 12 students who completed the study, 11 found that disagreement (described as extinction) produced a lower frequency of opinions than did agreement (described as reinforcement). This difference was again statistically significant at below the .001 level. Again, the students reported no serious difficulty.

These results pose somewhat of a dilemma. Despite seemingly great unreliability in identifying an opinion, and despite the numerous difficulties the first class of students mentioned, agreement with opinions is reported almost unanimously to produce a higher frequency of opinions than does silence or disagreement with the opinions. The procedure also seems to work as well for undergraduates as for graduate students.

CLASS EXPERIMENT III

An analysis of the results of the previous classes revealed some apparent relationship between the student's understanding of reinforcement principles and his reported results. For example, those students who were frequently absent from class and who revealed relatively little knowledge of reinforcement on their class exams usually reported relatively little effect of reinforcement upon opinions. At least two reasons might account for this failure: either these students did not follow the appropriate procedure, or they had no firm expectations about the results. To evaluate this second possibility, a third class of undergraduates was assigned to the same experiment. This class had not read the original article. Half of the students conducted consecutive 10-minute periods of reinforcement — extinction — reinforcement, and the other half conducted periods of extinction — reinforcement — extinction. Again, reinforcement consisted

of agreeing with each opinion, whereas extinction consisted of silence. This experiment was conducted during and after classroom instruction on the principles of reinforcement. The results were virtually the same as those in the previous class: 44 out of 47 students reported a greater frequency of opinions during reinforcement than during extinction ($P<.001$). One month later, following classroom discussion of emotions, essentially the same experiment was assigned to these students except that periods of disagreement were used instead of periods of silence. Verplanck had found that silence and disagreement were functionally identical in producing a decrease of opinions. However, the effect of disagreement was discussed in the present class in terms of catharsis rather than in terms of extinction, as in Verplanck's class and in the second class of the present experiment. The students were told that catharsis is the release of emotion, and that such release could be obtained by agreeing with an individual, so that a relative state of tranquility followed in which there was little reason for stating strong opinions. Conversely, disagreement was described as preventing catharsis, so that an increase of emotionally charged opinions followed. These comments about catharsis were intended to produce a bias toward obtaining an increase in the frequency of opinions rather than the decrease that was reported by Verplanck and that was obtained in the previous class in the present study.

Figure 2 compares the mean number of opinions reported by the students of this third class with the number reported by the students of the second class under the two sets of response bias. According to Figure 2, the procedure of disagreement produced an increase of opinions when identified as catharsis but a decrease when identified as extinction. Statistically, the difference in the number of opinions between agreement and disagreement for each class, as well as the difference between the two disagreement periods, is significant at well below the .001 level. Allegedly, the procedure of disagreeing with the subjects' opinions was the same for both classes. Therefore, the actual procedures used appeared to be almost irrelevant for obtaining the above changes in opinions. Rather, the same procedures of disagreeing with opinions have resulted in diametrically opposite effects because of the response bias given to the experimenters.

It will be recalled that the first class of graduate students had reluctantly admitted to various procedural difficulties. By coincidence, a student was enrolled in this third class who was also employed as a research assistant in a psychology laboratory. This student employee was assigned to question the other students informally and outside of class as to how they had conducted their experiments. The other students had no knowledge of this arrangement. Out of 19 students questioned, consisting of almost one-half of the class, 12 stated that they fabricated part or all of the data. This admission of "dry-running" was readily made when the student was asked by the employee, "I'm having trouble with my experiment; can you tell me how you did yours?" Five of the remaining seven students questioned stated that they had deviated greatly from the prescribed procedure. Only two out of nineteen students stated that they had followed the prescribed procedure. Consequently, an attempt at an exact replication seemed pointless, since the data reports themselves were probably fabricated.

Granted that students may not be competent investigators, the question still remained whether or not more experienced investigators could demonstrate the control of casual conversation by reinforcement. The study was therefore repeated by four experienced investigators. Each of these four investigators had (1) advanced pyschology training—a Ph.D. or M.A.; (2) skill in shaping animal behavior; (3) a healthy respect for negative results; and (4) practice in defining opinions. Verplanck (personal communication) considers these four criteria as essential in guaranteeing the success of the reinforcement procedure. In order to maximize the likelihood of success, a sequence of agreement—disagreement—agreement was used to avoid the expected difficulties in maintaining silence. Out of 12 attempts, not one of the four Es could complete his experiment. It may be recalled that the procedure requires that the E restrict himself to agreement (or disagreement) of opinions, and stipulates no questions, statements, nods, smiles, or other types of interaction. The reason for forbidding

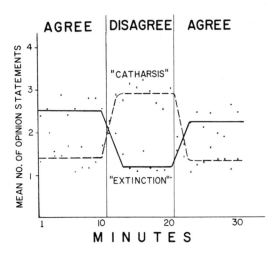

Figure 2. *The effect of the expectations of experimenters upon the results obtained. One group of Es (dotted line) was told that disagreement was expected to produce an increase because of catharsis. The other group of Es (solid line) was told that disagreement (the same procedure) would produce a decrease of opinion.*

such behavior proved to be obvious: E's reaction, however subtle, could often be seen to exert profound but uncontrolled effects upon the conversation of the subject. In the absence of any reaction by the four Es, however, all of the twelve Ss terminated the conversation within 10 minutes by leaving the room where the conversation was taking place.

The above results indicate that the successful reinforcement of opinions by student experimenters in casual conversation seems open to serious question. Out of a sincere attempt to produce such reinforcement, procedural difficulties emerged, also unreliability in identifying the response, results that were a function of E's expectations, and, finally, evidence of extensive falsification of the data. These findings have implications for the conduct of research in operant conditioning. Operant-conditioning procedures have generally been characterized by a high degree of control. In order to avoid unreliability, the response is usually defined very simply and precisely. In order to ensure proper programming of the procedure, automatic apparatus is used.

Printed records of the responses are also obtained by automatic means to eliminate bias from the *E*'s expectations. These and other precautions have been used, not because of any inherent fascination with "artificial" situations or with complex equipment, but because empirical considerations have demanded such control. The importance of extending the procedures of operant conditioning to "real-life" situations should not be allowed to override the elementary considerations of experimental control.

It would be incorrect to conclude from this study that control over verbal behavior through reinforcement is not possible. Indeed, the existence of such control seems demonstrated by the degree to which the reports of the experimenters could be modified. Certainly, if the situation could be structured in such a manner that the *E* is not expected or required to speak, there would seem to be a reasonable basis for selective reinforcement. However, the present findings indicate that different procedures will be needed before free-operant conditioning can be validly extended to the control of casual conversation. More important, these findings emphasize the necessity of objective programming and recording in the study of verbal conditioning. In the absence of such objectivity, the results of studies in verbal conditioning may be more of a reflection of the experimenter's expectations and theories than of the subject's behavior.

The non-recall of material presented during sleep

WILLIAM H. EMMONS AND CHARLES W. SIMON

The possibility of people being able to learn during sleep has attracted considerable interest, particularly in popular novels and science fiction stories. For example, sleep-learning occupied a central position in the educational process in Huxley's *Brave New World*. Devices have been placed on the market for people to "painlessly" increase their knowledge. At one time an international airline installed a device on its airplanes whereby people could "learn" the language of the country that they were going to visit while they were asleep en route to it. One does not need to exercise his imagination very much before he can see the great potential applications of sleep-learning for increasing knowledge or even for instilling new opinions and attitudes. Because of its great practical as well as theoretical importance, a number of experiments have been conducted to determine whether it is possible to learn while asleep. Some of these studies have actually indicated that people do learn while asleep, but they have all been limited in one important respect. That is, the subjects may not actually have been asleep when the material to be learned was presented to them. If in fact they were not asleep, or were only in a drowsy state, the conclusions of these previous studies would be invalidated. To run a valid experiment on sleep learning, therefore, some objective information is necessary in order to determine the condition of sleep of the subject when the training material is actually presented to him. The present experimenters sought to meet this problem with the use of an electroencephalograph. An electroencephalograph is a device which records brain waves by placing electrodes in various places on a person's head. The resulting recordings are called electroencephalograms (EEGs), and are classified into several different types. Previous research has indicated that one type, which is known as the alpha pattern, is absent when a person is asleep. This was the criterion of sleep adopted in the present experiment; that is, when a subject did not show alpha patterns he was judged to be asleep. The present experiment, then, offers an effective experimental test of the hypothesis that people can learn while they are asleep.

Adapted by the authors from *American Journal of Psychology*, 1956, **69**, 76–81.

Subjects

Nine men were used as experimental subjects, and a group of 113 men were used as control subjects.

Apparatus

The experimental subjects slept in clean, comfortable beds in three separate soundproof, air-conditioned, electrically shielded booths. Electrodes were placed on the head in such a manner that no discomfort was suffered. The EEGs were automatically recorded, and the learning material was played from tape recorders through loudspeakers placed in the booths. The loudness-level was such that the material could be heard clearly, but not great enough to disturb a soundly sleeping subject. A two-way intercommunication system allowed the experimenter to communicate with the subjects.

The use made of the control subjects will be discussed under the section entitled Results.

Criterion of Sleep

The EEG of each subject was continuously recorded, so that at all times during the experiment it was possible to tell when the subject was asleep by his lack of alpha patterns. The training material was played only when alpha patterns were absent (thus when the subjects were actually asleep) for 30 seconds prior to and during presentation of the training material.

Training Material

A list of 50 one-syllable nouns was used in the experiment. Ten of these nouns were presented to the experimental subjects while they were asleep.

Learning Procedure

The experimental subjects retired between 10 – 12 P.M. Before going to sleep they were given the following instructions.

We are going to play a list of words to you while you sleep. We want you to learn them. If you should awaken during the night, say your name and booth number. If you should awaken and hear anything say all of the words that you heard.

No attempt was made to play the list of nouns until one hour after the final instructions had been given. If the EEG indicated that the subject was asleep and no alpha pattern had been present for the previous 30 seconds, a recording of irrelevant material was played; then if the subject still showed no signs of awakening, the list of ten nouns was played. It was immediately turned off if there was any reason to doubt that the subject was still asleep. In some instances the subject would tend to awaken each time the irrelevant material was played. In these cases the loudness was progressively diminished until it no longer awakened him, although it was never reduced below a previously determined minimum level of intelligibility. The material was played to each subject as many times as possible. If the subject tended to awaken easily, the material was turned off long enough to allow him to go into a deep sleep. The number of times each subject awoke and whatever he said at these times were recorded. Due to the necessity of turning off the material when the subject showed signs of awakening, it was not possible to present each word an equal number of times. It seemed safe, however, to assume that the procedure was a random one, and an examination of the number of times each word was presented supported this assumption.

Testing Procedure

Upon awakening in the morning and before leaving his booth, each subject was asked to write down any words he had heard or thought he had heard during the night. The papers were collected and the subjects were then presented with the total list of 50 nouns from which the 10 training words had been selected. The subjects were instructed to read every word on the list and to select the 10 words that were played during the night. This was Test 1. Upon completing their selections the subjects were allowed to dress and wash, after which they were given the list of 50 words a second time and again instructed to select the 10 words played during the night. They were instructed that they could either choose the same words they selected the first time or they could change their selections, whichever they wished. This was Test 2.

The subjects then returned to their booths and the list was played through once at the minimal loudness at which it had been played during the night. If the subjects could correctly identify the words under these conditions, then it may be assumed that presentation of the words while the subjects were asleep was sufficiently loud and clear to be received by them. The subjects were asked to repeat each word as it was played. *Every* word was correctly repeated by all subjects.

RESULTS AND DISCUSSION

The control subjects were never exposed to the experimental situation. They were used only to determine the number of times that a noun is selected when subjects are merely guessing. To determine this, the 113 control subjects were presented with the list of 50 nouns mentioned previously. They were told that the experimenter had arbitrarily designated 10 of these 50 nouns as correct. They were also told that their task was to attempt, by means of extrasensory perception (telepathy), to guess which of the ten nouns were correct. Thus, the frequency with which each noun was guessed by subjects who did not have the nouns presented to them during sleep could be determined. If it could be shown that the experimental subjects could correctly identify more of the ten nouns that were presented to them during sleep than could the control subjects who had never had the nouns presented to them, then it could be concluded that the experimental subjects learned the ten nouns while they were asleep.

The results of this experiment, however, gave no evidence that material could be recalled after being presented a number of times during sleep. When they attempted to identify the ten words that were presented during

sleep the experimental group's performance was essentially the same as that of the control group on both the first and second test.

One might argue, however, that the reason that the experimental subjects did not learn was that the number of times that they were exposed to the words during sleep was insufficient. However, it was found that the average number of repetitions of the words for all experimental subjects was 46.3. Presumably this number of repetitions is sufficient for sleep-learning to show up if it would at all.

One suggestion was that negative findings in sleep-learning studies may be due to the fact that the subjects were in too deep a level of sleep during the presentation of the material. In the present study an analysis was made of the EEG records obtained during the presentation periods in accordance with several sleep-level categories. It was found that no material was presented while the subjects were wide awake, 1.2% of the material was presented in the deep drowsy state, 15.9% was presented in the transition state where sleep begins, 57.3% occurred in light sleep, 22.2% in deep sleep, and 3.4% in very deep sleep. It is unlikely that the negative results in this study are due to too deep a sleep-level at the time of stimulus presentation since 74.4% of the repetitions occurred at the borderline and lighter levels of sleep.

The importance of continuous EEG monitoring while presenting the test material in sleep-learning studies is shown by the fact that material could be played on the average of only 2.4 minutes without the subject's showing some signs of awakening. Although this interval may increase after an additional period of adjustment to the experimental situation the subjects in this study were already experienced, having previously spent one or more nights in the laboratory under similar conditions.

SUMMARY

A list of 10 one-syllable nouns were repeated as many times as possible to an experimental group of 9 subjects during an 8-hour sleeping period. A continuous EEG recording during the presentation of the training material was used to determine the sleep-level, and the material was turned off as soon as there were indications that the subjects were awakening.

The results indicated that the experimental subjects' performance was essentially the same as the control group in selecting the words on the training list from a list of 50 words. It was concluded that material presented a number of times during sleep cannot be recalled at a later time, and therefore the present experiment presented no evidence of sleep-learning.

This is another excellent example of the importance of adequate experimental controls. Previous studies of sleep-learning failed to provide a satisfactory answer because they did not use a satisfactory criterion to determine when subjects were actually asleep. This problem was solved in the present study through the use of the electroencephalograph. Thus the fond hope of science fiction writers and others who have sought a "painless" technique of learning is found to be lacking in experimental support.

Social control in the psychological experiment: Antisocial behavior and hypnosis

MARTIN T. ORNE AND FREDERICK J. EVANS

SOCIAL CONTROL IN THE PSYCHOLOGICAL EXPERIMENT

There has been increasing awareness by behavioral scientists that the subject in an experimental investigation is not a passive entity. Experimental evidence (Orne, 1959; Orne and Scheibe, 1964) has demonstrated that the subject takes an active role in interpreting the nature of the investigation and makes implicit assumptions about the hypotheses being investigated which influence his performance in the experimental situation. Nor is an experimenter free from the influence of his own investment in the hypotheses he is investigating. In a series of studies Rosenthal has shown that experimenters who have different hypotheses about the outcome of a particular experiment may obtain results which are congruent with their hypotheses (for example, Rosenthal, 1964; Rosenthal and Fode, 1963). Such studies imply that it is necessary to consider the particular nature of the special interpersonal interaction which exists between the subject and the experimenter in psychological experiments.

Orne (1962a, 1962b) has emphasized that the experimental context legitimizes a very broad range of behavioral requests. Subjects have implicit faith that experimenters are responsible people, that they will not be asked to carry out tasks which are devoid of meaning, and that regardless of appearances they will not be permitted to suffer any harm because of obvious social sanctions.

In a series of informal experiments in our laboratory, it has been impossible to devise a task which the subject perceives as completely "meaningless" within the context of an experiment. For example, subjects were confronted with a stack of paper, each page containing rows of random digits. The experimenter instructed subjects to continue adding the rows of numbers successively, and after accurately completing each page, to tear it into a minimum of 32 pieces. Although subjects were given no reason to justify the task, they continued this apparently meaningless endeavor beyond the tolerance limits of the experimenters (Orne, 1962b).

Frank (1944) has reported some informal experiments in which subjects continued meaningless and impossible tasks, including trying to balance a marble on a small steel ball and transferring spilled mercury to a small bottle with a wooden paddle, even when an assistant tried to prevent them from trying to complete

From *Journal of Personality and Social Psychology*, 1965, 1, 189–200.

the tasks. No justification was given for performing the tasks other than that it was an experiment.

In the same study, Frank also reported that subjects continued eating several unsavory, unsalted soda crackers for time periods in excess of what would seem reasonable for such an unpleasant task, and longer than subjects who were told they could stop eating them as soon as they wished. Shor (1962) has reported that subjects were willing to accept extremely high levels of electric shock when requested to select a level of intensity which was as high as they could tolerate for experimental purposes. Milgram (1963) has shown that subjects continue to administer what they believe are extremely high levels of electric shock, exceeding apparently dangerous levels, to another "subject" in the context of a learning experiment.

The limits of boredom, tolerance, pain, and fatigue which are accepted as reasonable requests within an experimental situation seem extremely broad. However, the actual range of social and behavioral control legitimized by the special contract implicit in the subject's agreement to participate in a psychological experiment has received few explicit tests.

ANTISOCIAL BEHAVIOR AND HYPNOSIS

It is generally considered that a hypnotized subject relinquishes considerable social and behavioral control to the hypnotist. A subject frequently reports that he felt compelled to carry out the commands of the hypnotist; that he could not resist the suggestions made by the hypnotist. This apparent increase in the amount of social control relinquished by the hypnotized subject to the hypnotist has raised the unresolved question whether a subject can be compelled, under hypnosis, to perform apparently antisocial acts or behavior which is perceived as injurious and dangerous to self or others. Estabrooks (1943), Rowland (1939), Weitzenhoffer (1949), Wells (1941), Wolberg (1945), and Young (1952) have stated that, provided adequate techniques are used, hypnotized subjects may be compelled to carry out apparently antisocial actions, while Erickson (1939), Meares (1960), and Schilder and Kauders (1927) have disagreed with this

viewpoint. The extensive literature presenting the conflicting viewpoints has been reviewed elsewhere (Barber, 1961; Orne, 1962a; Weitzenhoffer, 1953). The present investigation is concerned with two studies frequently cited as evidence that hypnosis can be used to induce antisocial behavior.

Rowland (1939)

Two deeply hypnotized subjects were asked to reach through the window of a box and pick up a large, active, diamondback rattlesnake. This request was rationalized to them by suggesting that the snake was a coil of rope. One hypnotized subject immediately complied, but was prevented from handling the snake by a pane of invisible glass. The other subject came out of the hypnotic state and refused to continue with the experiment. Another two hypnotized subjects attempted to grasp the snake, even when no attempt was made to delude them about what it was. Similarly, two hypnotized subjects were requested to throw concentrated sulphuric acid, which they had been told was very dangerous, at the face of an assistant. The two subjects complied with this request.

"By way of control, forty-two persons, of every age and degree of sophistication, were asked to come to the laboratory and pick up the snake. . . . With one exception all the persons were not only badly frightened at the appearance of the snake, but would not come close to the box . . ." (p. 116).

Young (1952)

In a replication of Rowland's study, Young asked eight deeply hypnotized subjects to carry out similar tasks. Young reported,

"The results show that seven of the eight subjects would enter into a situation which unhypnotized observers shrank from, the subjects carrying out suggestions to handle snakes and throw nitric acid under conditions from which they themselves recoiled in the waking state." (p. 405).

One major aim of the present study was to confirm these results by replicating in exact detail the procedures outlined by Young (1952). It is apparent from the accounts of both Rowland and Young that strong pressure was placed upon the hypnotized subjects to comply with the requested antisocial acts. However, Rowland did not exert similar pressure to comply when testing the independent, informal waking control group, nor did Young confront his hypnotized subjects with the same type of pressure in the subsequent waking condition. Consequently, it is doubtful if the informal controls used by these investigators provide any answer to the fundamental question being considered: does the degree of social control which occurs under hypnosis actually exceed the amount of social and behavioral control already existing in the experimental situation?

SOCIAL CONTROL, ANTISOCIAL BEHAVIOR, AND HYPNOSIS

The basic question may be formally stated: does the degree of social and behavioral control under hypnosis exceed that which is legitimized by the special social and behavioral control implicit in the experimental situation?

In order to determine that subjects have indeed been compelled to carry out any actions which they would not have carried out without the intervention of hypnosis it must be shown that:

1. Subjects in hypnosis carry out actions which are not performed by nonhypnotized control subjects.

2. Control subjects must be treated in an identical fashion to hypnotized subjects; both in regard to explicit instructions as well as implicit cues.

If these actions are to be designated as antisocial or self-destructive it must be shown that they are perceived as such by the subjects, i.e., truly dangerous or harmful to themselves or others. The implicit cues are of crucial importance. A subject is aware of certain realities imposed by the experimental situation. It is as clear to a subject as it is to any scientist that no reputable investigator can risk injuring a subject during the course of an experiment. A subject knows that an experimenter will outline in advance any possible specific and deliberate danger which could be associated with his actual participation in a study. Consequently, any requested behavior which appears to a subject to be dangerous at face value may be reinterpreted in the context of a laboratory situation. In spite of the apparent objective danger of a task it may nonetheless be perceived to be harmless because the subject realizes that necessary precautions will be taken to avoid possible injury to him. If an apparently dangerous task is requested of a subject during an experiment the subject's compliance, or refusal, may depend on whether he perceives that he is expected, or is not expected, to carry out the task. It is particularly vital in an experiment which depends on a contrived situation to determine what the subject, in different groups, perceives about the experimental situation and what is implicitly communicated to the subject within different groups.

Even though the experimenter is extremely careful to treat all groups alike, subtle and unintentional cues may be differentially communicated by him to subjects in different experimental groups, particularly when the experimenter knows to which experimental group a specific subject belongs. These experimenter influences on results have been demonstrated in both animal (Rosenthal and Lawson, 1963) and human research (Rosenthal and Fode, 1963).

It is essential, therefore, that the nonhypnotized control groups and the hypnotized subjects are treated in an identical manner. The real-simulating hypnosis model described by Orne (1959, 1962a, 1962b) provides one method of making reasonably sure that experimental and control subjects are treated alike. With this procedure both hypnotized and control group subjects are run "blind" by an experimenter, because he is not informed, and cannot readily detect, which subjects are hypnotized, and which subjects are awake but simulating hypnosis. The procedure has similar aims to those of the "blind" designs used in the evaluation of new drugs in psychopharmacology.

The real-simulator design has been adopted as the main control procedure in the present study. If both real and simulating subjects carry out behavior which is apparently antisocial or self-destructive, it would seem inappropriate to conclude that the hypnotized group was compelled to carry out these actions because of the use of hypnosis: rather, the behavior of both groups could be interpreted more parsimoniously as an appropriate response to the existing cues in the experimental situation.

In addition to the use of the crucial simulating control group, the content of social and behavioral control existing within the experimental situation was explored by including a normal waking control group. This independent waking control group was treated, as far as possible, in the same way as the hypnotized and simulating groups. An attempt was also made to demonstrate that it is possible to communicate to a subject that he should fail to carry out the apparently dangerous acts. The procedure adopted was the same as our understanding of the informal controls used by Rowland (1939). In addition, each hypnotized subject was retested in the waking condition, as his own control, similar to the control procedure of Young (1952). A parallel procedure using subjects with no previous experience with hypnosis was used as an additional waking control group.

lators. Each simulating subject was told that he was participating in research investigating the nature of hypnosis, but he was not told that the study involved allegedly antisocial behavior. He was told that his task was to try to fool an experienced hypnotist, in an experimental setting, by pretending to be deeply hypnotized. Even though he would probably not experience or produce any real hypnotic response, he was to act as if things were happening just as the hypnotist said they would. Although the hypnotist was described as an authority on the subject, it was stressed that it was possible, though very difficult, for the subject to fool the hypnotist.

No special training or instruction about how to simulate was given to the subjects in this group, nor were they told what phenomena would be involved in the experimental session. However, each simulator had individually watched a good hypnotic subject being hypnotized, demonstrating motor and challenge suggestions, simple positive hallucinations, amnesia, and posthypnotic suggestion.

Additional control groups. Six subjects, who did not meet the criteria for either good hypnotic subjects or simulators, formed one of the additional control groups. The remaining two control groups contained subjects recruited from the student population who did not know the experiment also involved hypnosis.

PROCEDURE[1]

Selection of Subjects[2]

Hypnosis group. Several volunteer undergraduate students were individually tested for susceptibility to hypnosis. After at least two hour-long screening sessions, six subjects were selected to participate in the study as the real hypnosis group. These subjects could readily achieve deep somnambulistic hypnosis manifesting such typical phenomena as catalepsy and rigidities, positive and negative hallucinations, posthypnotic suggestions, and complete posthypnotic amnesia.

Simulating hypnosis group. Another six subjects who showed no hypnotic responses during at least two extensive, individual hypnotic induction sessions participated in the study as simu-

1 Several procedural details have been deposited with the American Documentation Institute. This material contains additional detail about selection of subjects, choice of a venomous reptile, the effects of the nitric acid on the coin and safety procedures protecting the subject, description of the procedure for substituting the colored solution for the acid, and a scale diagram of the apparatus. Order Document No. 8203 from ADI Auxiliary Publications Project, Photoduplication Service, Library of Congress, Washington, D.C. 20540. Remit in advance $1.25 for microfilm or $1.25 for photocopies and make checks payable to: Chief, Photoduplication Service, Library of Congress.
2 One experimenter (FJE), who selected subjects, trained simulators, was assistant and observer during the study, subsequently confirmed that hypnotized subjects were amnesic for the session, that simulators experienced no real effects of the hypnotic induction and suggestions, and conducted postexperimental inquiries. The second experimenter (MTO) induced hypnosis for the main session, conducted the five groups in the experimental procedure, and at the completion of each subject's experimental participation, conducted a further independent inquiry after being informed which were real and simulating subjects.

Experimental Procedure

The experiment follows the procedure described by Young (1952) as closely as possible.[3]

Hypnosis was induced in a room adjacent to the experimental room. After the induction of hypnosis the subject was led, with eyes closed, into the experimental room and seated in front of a large wooden box which stood on a table.

The box was divided into two compartments by a removable partition. The subject could easily reach into the front compartment through a window. A sheet of plate glass could be raised or lowered silently across the window, sliding along felted grooves. The compartment was illuminated by two concealed lights, so that no light was reflected directly onto the surface of the glass. The two lights were the only source of illumination in the room. From the position of the subject it was not possible to detect the presence of the glass.[4]

Behavior Requested of the Subject

Inanimate objects. The hypnotist suggested that the subject would have an irresistible urge to do whatever the hypnotist told him. The subject was then asked to open his eyes, to reach into the compartment, to pick up and identify objects he saw there, and to place them in a bag held by the hypnotist. A two-shilling coin, then a piece of chalk, were placed in the compartment. All subjects identified and removed these objects.

Harmless reptiles. The subject was then told that a harmless, live reptile would be placed into the compartment. A thick-tailed gecko lizard (*Gymnodactylus milii*) was placed in the compartment. When the lizard had been removed, a thin, 14-inch long, harmless, green tree snake (*Ahaetulla punctulatus*) was lowered into the compartment.

The remaining three activities described below objectively appeared to be dangerous or harmful, either to the subject himself, or to a third person present in the room.

Venomous snake. An assistant wearing long, thick, X-ray gloves placed a 14-inch long venomous snake into the compartment. The rep-tile, popularly known as the red-bellied black snake (*Pseudechis porphyriacus*), is generally considered to be one of the two most venomous snakes found in Australia, capable of inflicting a mortal wound if the victim is not treated immediately upon being bitten.

The hypnotist asked the subject to pick up the snake carefully about its middle, and place it in the bag. Unknown to the subject, the glass screen had been lowered silently across the window. If an attempt was made to grasp the reptile, the subject struck his hand firmly against the glass.

Coin in acid. The screen, and the snake, were removed. The subject then watched the hypnotist pour fuming concentrated nitric acid (15 molar) in a small, shallow, Pyrex glass beaker. After watching the acid actively dissolve a copper-alloy half-penny coin for approximately a minute, the subject was asked to remove the coin from the beaker as quickly as possible with his bare hand, and then to plunge both hand and coin into a nearby basin of soapy lukewarm water.

Throwing acid. The experimenter stood between the subject and the box as he carefully washed the subject's hand. While the subject was distracted, the acid was replaced with an identical beaker containing a harmless, colored

---

3 We are indebted to P. C. Young for his kindness in providing an unpublished manuscript describing apparatus and procedure in detail and for clarifying further details in private communications.

4 The invisibility of the glass was attested by the following: (*a*) Inability of the experimenters to detect if the glass was in position unless they had prior knowledge of its position. (*b*) The witness and bruised knuckles of several members of the Department of Psychology whose curiosity got the better of them. (*c*) The expressed concern of a graduate student when watching a subject reach for the snake. Although he knew about the glass screen, and although he had been watching closely, he did not see the screen being lowered. (*d*) Only one subject in a subsequent inquiry reported detecting the glass. This happened because of the forgetfulness of the experimenters who failed to clean the window before this particular subject was tested. Most subjects expressed spontaneous surprise if, and when, they discovered the glass in their attempts to grab the snake, often making exploratory movements across the surface of the window.

Elizabeth Erickson (1962) has argued that visual acuity may increase under hypnosis; hence, hypnotized subjects would detect the presence of the glass. This hypothesis would be relevant if clear-cut differences were found between the hypnotized group and other crucial groups in the willingness to comply with requests to perform the antisocial activities.

solution which was the same color as the acid. The subject was similarly distracted if he did not remove the coin, so that changing the solution was not observed.

The central partition in the box was removed, exposing the assistant who had been responsible for recruiting and training the subject, sitting at the opposite end of the open-ended box. The hypnotist suggested assertively that the subject was very angry with the assistant for placing him into the unpleasant situation of the experiment. The subject was told he felt so angry that he would have an irresistible urge to throw the acid firmly into the face of the assistant and authoritatively told to pick up the acid and throw it.

Postexperimental Interview

The subject was taken back into the adjoining room, and hypnosis was terminated. Comprehensive interviews were conducted with each subject to allow him to express his subjective reactions to the experiment, and his thoughts and comments about the experiment. Appropriate questions were asked to establish that the subject had remained amnesic throughout the experimental session, or, in the case of simulators, to confirm that no trance effects occurred during the experiment.

Treatment of Experimental Groups

The procedure has been outlined as it was encountered by the subjects in the hypnosis group. The hypnotized group of subjects was subsequently retested in the waking state, while still amnesic for the hypnosis session, and an additional four groups were tested.

For clarity of exposition a detailed statement of the aims of testing each group will be presented below in the Results section. General modifications in the experimental procedures for the respective waking control groups will be quite apparent. The procedures outlined above were followed either exactly, or as approximately as the nature of the specific groups would allow. The major difference between groups was the manner and attitude of the experimenter, and the subtle means whereby

expectations of compliance or noncompliance with the apparently antisocial actions were conveyed. Differences in the approach of the experimenter, in terms of the aims and purpose of each group, will be discussed as the results for each group are being presented.

There was, of course, no difference in the treatment of the hypnotized subjects and simulating subjects because the hypnotist remained unaware of the subgroup membership of these subjects throughout the experiment.

RESULTS

The number of subjects in each group who attempted to comply with the requested tasks is summarized in Table 1. A detailed analysis of the responses of each subject within the various groups is presented in Table 2, together with ratings of the degree of subjective involvement in the tasks. The latter ratings were made by the assistant who was aware of the group membership of hypnotized and simulating subjects, and must be interpreted accordingly.[5]

---

5 The data presented in Tables 1 and 2 are not amenable to further statistical analysis. There is a partial experimental dependence of the tasks because of the way in which they were, of necessity, presented to the subject. Consequently, neither treating each antisocial action as a separate activity, nor the alternative of tabulating the number of acts actually attempted by each subject, is a valid method of treating the data statistically. Even if either alternative were possible, the analysis of frequency data, preferably by exact probability procedures, requires the determination of the expected frequencies of occurrence. Hypothetical expected frequencies of *six* subjects in any group successfully attempting each act could be defended as readily as hypothetical expected frequencies of *no* subject in any particular group attempting each act. Even the statistical determination of expected frequencies from marginal entries has limited merit in groups of this size, for this would impose a level of precision on the data which is not warranted, as well as limiting the possibility of finding statistically significant differences. However, this does not reflect upon the size of the groups, for the experimental rationale is such that the *mere occurrence* of apparently antisocial behavior is significant if it occurs in the crucial simulating control group. The aim of the study is, in a real sense, to demonstrate the truth of the null hypothesis: to demonstrate that specially designed groups do not differ in their propensity to respond in a defined manner.

Table 1. *Frequency of attempts to carry out apparently antisocial acts.*

Group[a]	Grasp Harmless Reptiles[b]	Grasp Venomous Snake	Take Coin from Acid	Throw Acid at Assistant
1. Real Hypnosis	5	5	5	5
1a. Retest Real, as Waking Control (Young)	X	2	3	2
2. Waking Control: Press for Fail (Rowland)	6	3	1	1
3. Simulating Hypnosis	6	6	6	6
4. Waking Compliance Control	5	3	5	5
5. Waking Control: Eliminate "Shaping" Procedures	X	2	3	2

[a]Six subjects in each group; see text for description of groups.
[b]Includes small lizard and harmless snake. Two subjects refused both. Eliminated from procedure in waking retest of Group 1a and Group 5.

REPLICATION OF RESULTS OF ROWLAND (1939) AND OF YOUNG (1952)

Real Hypnosis: Group 1

Treatment. The hypnotist told the subject that he had an irresistible urge to carry out easily and readily all suggestions given to him. Each activity was preceded by a firm statement—"I want you to . . . ." The apparent dangers in the venomous reptile and acid situations were stressed. The experimenter conveyed by his verbal tone and nonverbal manner and attitude that he expected compliance. Further pressure and persuasion were adopted if the subject showed hesitancy about carrying out any of the activities.

After the experimental tasks were completed, hypnosis was terminated. A careful evaluation of the validity of the suggested complete amnesia for the session was made, and depth of hypnosis was checked by testing a posthypnotic suggestion administered by the hypnotist at the completion of the experimental tasks.

Results. Five of the six hypnotized subjects carried out all of the suggested activities.[6] The major result of the earlier studies of Rowland (1939) and Young (1952) was thus replicated: hypnotized subjects will carry out apparently antisocial and injurious activities such as handling dangerous reptiles and concentrated acid.

HYPNOSIS SUBJECTS RETESTED AS OWN CONTROL (YOUNG, 1952): GROUP 1

Treatment. The five subjects in the real hypnosis group who had carried out the actions returned the following day. Each subject was asked, in the waking state, whether he would be willing to carry out the suggested activities involving the snake and acid. This was the control measure carried out by Young (1952). Although the verbal content of the request implied the possibility of compliance, it was conveyed by the experimenter's general manner and nonverbal behavior that compliance with the request was not necessarily expected.

Results. As found by Young (1952), and as expected in the present study, subjects generally refused to carry out the actions in the waking state, even though they had been quite willing to carry them out in the hypnotic condition. However, two subjects could be persuaded to attempt to pick up the venomous snake and to throw the acid at the assistant.

6 The remaining subject became emotionally disturbed at the sight of the harmless lizard and it was not possible to administer the remaining tasks. As the subject had passed the selection criteria, it was decided not to replace her. It is noted that she was one of the two hypnotic-group subjects whose previous experience with the experimenters was minimal, and it is possible that the interpersonal relationships existing were not as strongly developed as with other subjects.

Another subject removed the coin from the acid.

Amnesia for the previous day's hypnotic experience was again confirmed, and was then removed. Subjects reported that under hypnosis they felt more passive, were not particularly concerned with the consequences of their actions or what safeguards existed, and generally were less disturbed by the situation than they were in the waking state. The subjects who attempted any of the activities claimed they were much more hesitant in the waking state than they had been in the previous hypnotic state. These reported differences were consistent with the observer's ratings of such differences between the two performances, summarized in Table 2.

Waking Control Used by Rowland (1939): Group 2

Treatment. As far as could be ascertained, the six subjects in this group were treated similarly to the informal control group in Rowland's (1939) study.

The experimenter implicitly communicated the expectation that the subject would refuse to carry out the requested activities. The apparent danger was stressed at least as much as it was with subjects in other groups. The request to carry out the various actions was phrased more in the form of a question of whether he would be willing to comply with such obviously dangerous actions. However, persuasion and pressure were applied if a subject refused to carry out any activity, although not as insistently as for subjects in the hypnotized and simulating groups.

Results. Three of the six subjects in this group attempted to pick up the snake, but only one of them attempted to take the coin from the acid, and throw the acid at the assistant, both after considerable hesitation. It had been expected that subjects in this group would refuse to carry out the activities.[7] Some subjects could be persuaded to carry out the tasks. It appears that either the experimenter could not refrain from being more insistent than Rowland, or the psychological experiment is more institutionalized for University

of Sydney students in 1960 than it was for University of Tulsa students in 1939.

Summary of Attempted Replication of Studies of Rowland (1939) and Young (1952)

The results obtained from the three groups reported in the present study are in substantial agreement with the findings reported by Rowland and by Young. Their results, as far as comparisons are relevant, have been confirmed, and their procedure has been replicated successfully.

LIMITS OF SOCIAL AND BEHAVIORAL CONTROL IN THE EXPERIMENTAL SITUATION

Rowland and Young concluded from their data that hypnosis was instrumental in producing antisocial and dangerous behavior which could not be elicited otherwise. However, these results cannot answer the fundamental question of whether the apparently antisocial behavior elicited under hypnosis *exceeds* the limits of behavior which may be legitimized by the experimental situation per se. To answer this question, it is necessary to test whether the request to carry out the apparently antisocial and self-injurious acts exceeds the limits of social and behavioral control implicitly existing in the experimental situation.

Simulators: Group 3

Treatment. Because the experimenter did not know whether he was testing a hypnotized or a simulating subject at any time, both the hypnotized and simulating groups of subjects were treated alike, and were exposed to the

---

7 It was frequently noted in the records made by the assistant that the experimenter exerted more pressure with subjects in the three control groups in which noncompliance was predicted than our understanding of the parallel procedures of Rowland and Young warranted. The excessive persuasion was not intended: we do not know if this accounted for the unpredicted successful attempts in these groups.

Table 2. *Analysis of attempts to carry out apparently antisocial acts for each subject.*

Group and Subject	Sex	Grasp Harmless Reptiles[a]	Grasp Venomous Snake[b]	Take Coin from Acid[b,c]	Throw Acid at Assistant[b,d]
1. Real Hypnosis					
JB	F	Yes	Yes (H)	Yes (H)	Yes (A, T)
YM	F	Yes	Yes	Yes (A)	Yes (A, T)
GP	M	Yes	Yes	Yes	Yes (T)
CW	F	Yes	Yes	Yes	Yes
EB[e]	F	No	—	—	—
SM	F	Yes	Yes	Yes (U)	Yes
1a. Retest Real Hypnosis Subjects in Waking State (Young Control)[f]					
JB	F	—	No	No	No
YM	F	—	No	Yes (H)	Yes (A, T)
GP	M	—	No	Yes (H)	No
CW	F	—	Yes (H)	Yes (H)	Yes (A, T)
EB[e]	F	—	—	—	—
SM	F	—	Yes	No	No
2. Waking Control: Press for Failure (Rowland Control)					
RF	M	Yes	Yes	Yes	Yes (H, V)
JF	F	Yes	Yes (A)	No	No
DF	M	Yes	No	No	No
PH	M	Yes	Yes (H)	No	No
HH	F	Yes	No	No	No
EC	F	Yes	No	No	No
3. Simulating Hypnosis					
KM	F	Yes	Yes (H)	Yes (A, U)	Yes (V)
RW	F	Yes	Yes	Yes	Yes (T)
ST	F	Yes	Yes	Yes (H, U)	Yes (A, T)
JJ	M	Yes	Yes	Yes	Yes (V)
MF	M	Yes	Yes (H)	Yes (H, U)	Yes (H)
AT	M	Yes	Yes	Yes (H, U)	Yes (V)
4. Waking Compliance Control					
FP	F	No	No	No	No
JM	F	Yes	No	Yes (H)	Yes (H)
RS	M	Yes	No	Yes (A)	Yes (H)
PP	M	Yes	Yes (H)	Yes	Yes
AL	M	Yes	Yes	Yes	Yes (V)
FJ	M	Yes	Yes	Yes (A)	Yes (V)
5. Waking Control: Elimination of "Shaping" Procedures					
IR	F	—	Yes (H)	Yes	Yes (H)
NG	M	—	No	Yes (H)	No
RM	M	—	Yes	Yes (H)	Yes
RE	M	—	No	No	No
MA	F	—	No	No	No
CR	F	—	Yes (?)[g]	No	No

Note.— Yes = attempt to carry out requested activity; No = refused to carry out requested activity.
[a] Gecko lizard and harmless snake. Procedures omitted for Groups 1a and 5 (see text).
[b] H = hesitant in attempting task; A = agitation and emotional involvement markedly apparent.
[c] U = unsuccessful in removing coin, but attempted to extent of placing fingers in acid.
[d] T = tentative throw, hardly splashing assistant; V = violent throw, for example, hurling solution and container.
[e] Subject almost hysterical at sight of lizard; remaining activities omitted. Counted failure (see Footnote 6).
[f] Hypnosis-group subjects retested.
[g] Subject reported detecting glass screen at end of experiment (see Footnote 4).

same demand characteristics concerning compliance with the experimenter's requests. Consequently, compliance with the requests of the experimenter by the simulators would indicate that the requested behavior is within the limits of what they perceived as legitimate and reasonable within the experimental context. Such a result would demonstrate that the present tasks do not provide a test of whether hypnosis can be used to compel the subject to carry out antisocial behavior.

Results. All six subjects who were simulating hypnosis attempted to comply with the apparently antisocial and injurious activities requested of them. They objectively attempted to carry out the various tasks at least as readily as the subjects who were actually hypnotized.

Qualitatively, it appeared that the simulators were more hesitant than the hypnotized subjects about grasping the snake, less successful in their attempts to remove the coin from the acid, but more violent and less hesitant about throwing the acid solution at the assistant[8] (see Table 2).

Waking Compliance Control: Group 4

Treatment. There are special motivational aspects involved when a subject simulates hypnosis which are not present when a subject is actually hypnotized. A simulator is motivated by two special features: he must attempt to please one experimenter by striving to deceive a second experimenter. It is possible that these special motivations may increase the range of social and behavioral control implicit within the unique type of experimental situation which exists for the simulating subject.

In an attempt to evaluate this possibility, an additional set of six subjects served as the usual type of control group. They were told that they were a normal waking control group in a study employing hypnotized subjects. As far as possible, they were treated identically to the hypnosis and the simulating groups; the experimenter's manner conveyed an expectation that subjects would comply with his requests. This group differs from the informal controls employed by Rowland (see Group 2 above) in that these subjects were treated as

formal experimental subjects and compliance with the requests was taken for granted, whereas such pressure was not applied in Group 2, described above, or by Rowland. *Results.* Five subjects attempted to carry out the two tasks involving the acid, but two of these subjects refused to handle the venomous snake. The performance of this group was only slightly inferior to that of the hypnotized and simulating groups. It would appear that consideration of the special motivations which existed for subjects simulating hypnosis is not necessarily essential to account for the present results.

Elimination of "Shaping" Procedures: Group 5

Treatment. It is possible that the preliminary tasks, taking inanimate objects from the compartment and handling harmless reptiles, could operate as a type of "shaping" or "conditioning" procedure, gradually leading the subject to tasks which in themselves look frightening, but in the context of the "shaping" procedure lose much of their fearsome potency.

A separate waking control group was conducted without the preliminary harmless tasks. These subjects were asked to participate in a psychological experiment, but they were not told that they were controls in a study involving hypnosis. Apart from the elimination of the innocuous tasks, the procedure was essentially the same as for Group 2. Unfortunately, the pressure exerted to gain compliance was generally greater than it was for Group 2.[9]

---

8 For example, some simulators (and some members of Group 4 below) hurled both solution *and container* at the assistant. In comparison the hypnosis group, though throwing the solution, sometimes failed to splash the assistant with it. These subjective differences were observed by the assistant who was aware of the group membership of the subjects.

9 There was some confusion between the two experimenters when subjects in this group were being tested. While the experimenter was testing some subjects in this group, the relevant question was seen as to whether expectation of failure could be as readily communicated with and without the preliminary "shaping" procedures, in which it was predicted the results would be similar to Group 2. For other subjects the question was implicitly seen as whether subjects would comply as readily with the tasks when the innocuous tasks were eliminated

Results. Two subjects attempted to handle the snake and to throw the acid, and a third subject attempted to take the coin from the acid. The results are somewhat equivocal, but it appears that the "shaping" procedure employed is not an essential determinant of subsequent behavior.

Informal Controls

A number of colleagues were informally shown the experimental tasks. These faculty members were treated in a fashion similar to the treatment of the control group used by Rowland (1939).

They invariably refused to carry out even the least objectionable of these three tasks, the removal of the penny from the nitric acid. The fellow faculty members who were asked to perform these tasks could not be pressured or persuaded in any way to undertake them. It is significant that their behavior was identical to that of Rowland's informal control group.

Two aspects appear relevant in interpreting these informal observations:

1. The faculty members were not in a formal experimental situation.

2. A different role relationship existed between faculty members and the experimenters compared to that existing between subjects and experimenters. These differences emphasize the importance of the special contexts provided by the combined subject-experimenter relationship and the nature of the experimental situation in terms of the willingness of the subjects to carry out the experimental tasks.

Postexperimental Inquiry

With few exceptions, subjects who attempted to carry out the requested activities reported in the postexperimental inquiry that they felt quite safe in the experimental situation. Though they reported feeling rather uncertain about the tasks, and reported strong emotional reactions to the repugnant activities, the subjects reported that they were quite convinced that they would not be harmed *because* the context was an experimental one, presumably being conducted by responsible experimenters. All subjects appeared to assume that some form of safety precautions had been taken during the experiment. Although no subject reported suspecting the presence of a glass screen, subjects felt that the snake had either been milked of its venom or defanged. Some felt that the solution was not really acid, even when they plunged their hand into it; others suspected the assistant could duck in time to avoid the acid; or the glass screen would be in place again (having previously discovered its presence during the procedure with the snake); or perhaps the assistant would even plunge himself into a nearby tub of water; or in one case, that the assistant was not actually there — it was an illusion produced by a complex arrangement of mirrors.

DISCUSSION

1. No conclusions can be drawn from the present investigation about the potential use of hypnosis to induce antisocial behavior. However, the study clarifies conclusions which may be drawn from two previous studies. After replicating the studies by Rowland (1939) and Young (1952) and confirming their results, it has been shown that similar apparently antisocial behavior can be elicited in control groups treated in an identical fashion to a group of hypnotized subjects. The apparently antisocial actions were also carried out successfully by subjects who were not hypnotized, indicating that the tasks are within the broad range of activities which are perceived as legitimized by the nature of the situation: they were requests made by experimenters, viewed by subjects as responsible scientists, in the context of a psychological experiment.

2. The present study is essentially methodological, demonstrating experimental condi-

compared to the ease of gaining compliance when they were included. It was predicted from this viewpoint that results would be similar to Group 4, and even the simulating subjects, Group 3. Clearly two separate groups should have been tested. It is certain that some subjects within this group were treated quite differently from others. The confusion was not recognized until after the completion of the study, and it is not known to what extent the equivocal results are concordant with the differing expectations that were undoubtedly induced. The results for the group are reported only for the sake of completeness.

tions which are necessary to investigate the antisocial hypothesis. The burden of demonstrating the production of antisocial behavior by hypnotic techniques lies with the investigator, who must demonstrate that the so-called antisocial behavior does exceed that which is legitimized by the experimental situation and that the behavior is perceived by the subject as truly dangerous or antisocial. It is our belief that it may not be possible to test the antisocial question in an experimental setting because of the problems of finding tasks which are not seen as legitimized by the experimental context.

3. It may seem surprising that the waking control group subjects who were pressed to comply with the apparently dangerous behavior were quite willing to follow the experimenter's commands. This confirms the anecdotal evidence reported above from our own laboratory: we still have not found an aspect of behavior which is sufficiently safe to request of a subject, and which a subject will refuse to carry out if the expectation of compliance is communicated to him. In the present study the experimenter could virtually predetermine the nature of the resulting behavior by deciding in advance whether he would *consciously*, but subtly, communicate to a subject an expectation either of failure or of compliance. Such a result is concordant with other findings (for example, Rosenthal, 1964) showing the relative ease with which an experimenter *may* nonconsciously bias the results of a study by subtly communicating his own expectations and hypotheses.

Failure to gain compliance with hypnotized subjects would indicate inadequate replication of the exact details of Young's investigation.

Because the experimenter is unaware of the group membership of real and simulating subjects outcome-bias should not differentially affect performance of subjects in these two crucial groups. It is partly because of the problem of outcome-bias that simulating subjects are included as the crucial control group.

4. The purpose of the simulating group was to examine whether the chosen behavior exceeded the limits of behavior legitimized by the special nature of the experimental context. The waking control subjects (Group 4) also complied with the requested activities, and in this sense the simulating subjects were not essential to demonstrate that the alleged antisocial actions were within the realm of what subjects accept as reasonable requests in the experimental situation. However, the simulating group of subjects cannot be eliminated from future investigations of this type. It is not always possible to determine whether waking control subjects have been treated differently from the nonhypnotized subjects, even though an experimenter is not aware of such differential treatment.

5. The present investigation demonstrates the misleading conclusions that may be drawn when casual, informal "control" groups, of the type employed by Rowland (1939) and Young (1952), form the basis for evaluating experimental performance. It cautions against making untested assumptions about the way in which subjects will behave in an experimental situation, or making assumptions about what aspects of behavior are within the repertoire of the subjects, however reasonable these assumptions may appear, when subjects are participating in the social phenomenon known as "the psychological experiment."

IMPLICATIONS OF BEHAVIOR CONTROL

w

13

CONCERN OVER THE CONTROL OF HUMAN BEHAVIOR

Man's increasing power to control other men has raised many important questions concerning "ethics," "values," "freedom," and "power," to name but a few areas. The main problem at this stage, however, is to sift out the important issues from the trivial and to derive workable answers. The following papers help both to clarify some of the issues and problems surrounding the control of human behavior and to provide some tentative solutions.

Many of these issues and concerns are aired in the exchange between Rogers and Skinner. The central issue discussed by the participants—and one that frequently appears in such discussions—is what usually is called the question of "values." To what purpose should behavior control be used? Rogers contends that "values" emerge from the individual's "freedom of choice," a realm unavailable to science. Hence, contends Rogers, the determination of "values"—of the ends to which we should apply our science—lies forever outside the scope of science. Skinner, in rebuttal, points out that the scientific view of man does not allow for such exceptions, and that "choice" and the resulting, or determining, "values" are, like other behavior, a function of man's biology and his environment. Since biology and environment lie within the realm of science, "choice" and "values" must also be accessible to scientific inquiry. Thus, claims Skinner, the science which produces techniques of control has also the wherewithal to determine the uses to which these techniques may be put.

Krasner, viewing this point from the role of the clinician, concurs with Skinner. Too often the control exerted by clinicians is ignored, and ignoring this control will not cause it to disappear. Rather, we should apply scientific means to determine the "values" to which clinicians should adhere in treating patients.

Another question discussed by Rogers and Skinner is the question of power—the possibility that the power given by behavioral control will be abused. Although Skinner suspects that the power of the science of behavior control may be self-limiting, he admits that the possibility of misuse is indeed present and alarming. Rogers stresses this point still further. Krasner, in addition, offers some practical, although temporary, measures which can be taken immediately by scientists involved in behavior control.

Skinner, in his presentation, points out that the public is prone to grouping the scientific control of behavior with Machiavellian and other aversive techniques of control which have long been in use. The clamor over brainwashing provides a good example. Many see the brainwashing cell as the natural end of the "psychological" control of behavior. Yet, as Farber, Harlow and West point out, the mysterious effects of brainwashing can be traced to the all too familiar results of internment and physical discomfort or pain. These aversive measures are by no means new, and have little in common with the techniques proposed by such behavioral scientists as Skinner and his associates.

In short, there is much to suggest that the scientific control of behavior will supply its own aims and limits, and that our past experience with aversive control may have little in common with the techniques and aims advanced in this collection.

Some issues concerning the control of human behavior: A symposium

CARL R. ROGERS AND B. F. SKINNER

I – SKINNER

Science is steadily increasing our power to influence, change, mold—in a word, control—human behavior. It has extended our "understanding" (whatever that may be) so that we deal more successfully with people in nonscientific ways, but it has also identified conditions or variables which can be used to predict and control behavior in a new, and increasingly rigorous, technology. The broad disciplines of government and economics offer examples of this, but there is special cogency in those contributions of anthropology, sociology, and psychology which deal with individual behavior. Carl Rogers has listed some of the achievements to date in a recent paper (1956). Those of his examples which show or imply the control of the single organism are primarily due, as we should expect, to psychology. It is the experimental study of behavior which carries us beyond awkward or inaccessible "principles," "factors," and so on, to variables which can be directly manipulated.

It is also, and for more or less the same reasons, the conception of human behavior emerging from an experimental analysis which most directly challenges traditional views. Psychologists themselves often do not seem to be aware of how far they have moved in this direction. But the change is not passing unnoticed by others. Until only recently it was customary to deny the possibility of a rigorous science of human behavior by arguing, either that a lawful science was impossible because that a lawful science was impossible because

man was a free agent, or that merely statistical predictions would always leave room for personal freedom. But those who used to take this line have become most vociferous in expressing their alarm at the way these obstacles are being surmounted.

Now, the control of human behavior has always been unpopular. Any undisguised effort to control usually arouses emotional reactions. We hesitate to admit, even to ourselves, that we are engaged in control, and we may refuse to control, even when this would be helpful, for fear of criticism. Those who have explicitly avowed an interest in control have been roughly treated by history. Machiavelli is the great prototype. As Macaulay said of him, "Out of his surname they coined an epithet for a knave and out of his Christian name a synonym for the devil." There were obvious reasons. The control that Machiavelli analyzed and recommended, like most political control, used techniques that were aversive to the controllee. The threats and punishments of the bully, like those of the government operating on the same plan, are not designed—whatever their success—to endear themselves to those who are controlled. Even when the techniques themselves are not aversive, control is usually exercised for the selfish purposes of the controller and, hence, has indirectly punishing effects upon others.

Man's natural inclination to revolt against selfish control has been exploited to good

From *Science*, 1956, **124**, 1057–1066.

purpose in what we call the philosophy and literature of democracy. The doctrine of the rights of man has been effective in arousing individuals to concerted action against governmental and religious tyranny. The literature which has had this effect has greatly extended the number of terms in our language which express reactions to the control of men. But the ubiquity and ease of expression of this attitude spells trouble for any science which may give birth to a powerful technology of behavior. Intelligent men and women, dominated by the humanistic philosophy of the past two centuries, cannot view with equanimity what Andrew Hacker has called "the specter of predictable man" (1954). Even the statistical or actuarial prediction of human events, such as the number of fatalities to be expected on a holiday weekend, strikes many people as uncanny and evil, while the prediction and control of individual behavior is regarded as little less than the work of the devil. I am not so much concerned here with the political or economic consequences for psychology, although research following certain channels may well suffer harmful effects. We ourselves, as intelligent men and women, and as exponents of Western thought, share these attitudes. They have already interfered with the free exercise of a scientific analysis, and their influence threatens to assume more serious proportions.

Three broad areas of human behavior supply good examples. The first of these —*personal control*—may be taken to include person-to-person relationships in the family, among friends, in social and work groups, and in counseling and psychotherapy. Other fields are *education* and *government*. A few examples from each will show how nonscientific preconceptions are affecting our current thinking about human behavior.

Personal Control

People living together in groups come to control one another with a technique which is not inappropriately called "ethical." When an individual behaves in a fashion acceptable to the group, he receives admiration, approval, affection, and many other reinforcements which increase the likelihood that he will continue to behave in that fashion. When his behavior is not acceptable, he is criticized, censured, blamed, or otherwise punished. In the first case the group calls him "good"; in the second, "bad." This practice is so thoroughly ingrained in our culture that we often fail to see that it is a technique of control. Yet we are almost always engaged in such control, even though the reinforcements and punishments are often subtle.

The practice of admiration is an important part of a culture, because behavior which is otherwise inclined to be weak can be set up and maintained with its help. The individual is especially likely to be praised, admired, or loved when he acts for the group in the face of great danger, for example, or sacrifices himself or his possessions, or submits to prolonged hardship, or suffers martyrdom. These actions are not admirable in any absolute sense, but they require admiration if they are to be strong. Similarly, we admire people who behave in original or exceptional ways, not because such behavior is itself admirable, but because we do not know how to encourage original or exceptional behavior in any other way. The group acclaims independent, unaided behavior in part because it is easier to reinforce than to help.

As long as this technique of control is misunderstood, we cannot judge correctly an environment in which there is less need for heroism, hardship, or independent action. We are likely to argue that such an environment is itself less admirable or produces less admirable people. In the old days, for example, young scholars often lived in undesirable quarters, ate unappetizing or inadequate food, performed unprofitable tasks for a living or to pay for necessary books and materials or publication. Older scholars and other members of the group offered compensating reinforcement in the form of approval and admiration for these sacrifices. When the modern graduate student receives a generous scholarship, enjoys good living conditions, and has his research and publication subsidized, the grounds for evaluation seem to be pulled from under us. Such a student no longer *needs* admiration to carry him over a series of obstacles (no matter how much he may need it for other reasons), and, in missing certain familiar objects of admiration, we are likely to conclude that such *conditions* are less admirable. Obstacles to scholarly work may serve as a useful measure of motivation—and we may go wrong unless some substitute is found—but we can scarcely defend a deliberate harassment of the student for this purpose. The productivity of any set of conditions can be evaluated only when we have freed ourselves of the attitudes which have been generated in us as members of an ethical group.

A similar difficulty arises from our use of punishment in the form of censure or blame. The concept of responsibility and the related concepts of foreknowledge and choice are used to justify techniques of control using punishment. Was So-and-So aware of the probable consequences of his action, and was the action deliberate? If so, we are justified in punishing him. But what does this mean? It appears to be a question concerning the efficacy of the contingent relations between behavior and punishing consequences. We punish behavior because it is objectionable to us or the group, but in a minor refinement of rather recent origin we have come to withhold punishment when it cannot be expected to have any effect. If the objectionable consequences of an act were accidental and not likely to occur again, there is no point in punishing. We say that the individual was not "aware of the consequences of his action" or that the consequences were not "intentional." If the action could not have been avoided—if the individual "had no choice"—punishment is also withheld, as it is if the individual is incapable of being changed by punishment because he is of "unsound mind." In all these cases—different as they are—the individual is held "not responsible" and goes unpunished.

Just as we say that it is "not fair" to punish a man for something he could not help doing, so we call it "unfair" when one is rewarded beyond his due or for something he could not help doing. In other words, we also object to wasting *reinforcers* where they are not needed or will do no good. We make the same point with the words *just* and *right*. Thus we have no right to punish the irresponsible, and a man has no right to reinforcers he does not earn or deserve. But concepts of choice, responsibility, justice, and so on, provide a most inadequate analysis of efficient reinforcing and punishing contingencies because they carry a heavy semantic cargo of a quite different sort, which obscures any attempt to clarify controlling practices or to improve techniques. In particular, they fail to prepare us for techniques based on other than aversive techniques of control. Most people would object to forcing prisoners to serve as subjects of dangerous medical experiments, but few object when they are induced to serve by the offer of return privileges—even when the reinforcing effect of these privileges has been created by forcible deprivation. In the traditional scheme the right to refuse guarantees the individual against coercion or an unfair bargain. But to what extent *can* a prisoner refuse under such circumstances?

We need not go so far afield to make the point. We can observe our own attitude toward personal freedom in the way we resent any interference with what we want to do. Suppose we want to buy a car of a particular sort. Then we may object, for example, if our wife urges us to buy a less expensive model and to put the difference into a new refrigerator. Or we may resent it if our neighbor questions our need for such a car or our ability to' pay for it. We would certainly resent it if it were illegal to buy such a car (remember Prohibition); and if we find we cannot actually afford it, we may resent governmental control of the price through tariffs and taxes. We resent it if we discover that we cannot get the car because the manufacturer is holding the model in deliberately short supply in order to push a model we do not want. In all this we assert our democratic right to buy the car of our choice. We are well prepared to do so and to resent any restriction on our freedom.

But why do we not ask *why* it is the car of our choice and resent the forces which made it so? Perhaps our favorite toy as a child was a car, of a very different model, but nevertheless bearing the name of the car we now want. Perhaps our favorite TV program is sponsored by the manufacturer of that car. Perhaps we have seen pictures of many beautiful or prestigeful persons driving it—in pleasant or glamorous places. Perhaps the car has been designed with respect to our motivational patterns: the device on the hood is a phallic symbol; or the horsepower has been stepped up to please our competitive spirit in enabling us to pass other cars swiftly (or, as the advertisements say, "safely"). The concept of freedom that has emerged as part of the cultural practice of our group makes little or no provision for recognizing or dealing with these kinds of control. Concepts like "responsibility" and "rights" are scarcely applicable. We are prepared to deal with coercive measures, but we have no traditional recourse with respect to other measures which in the long run (and especially with the help of science) may be much more powerful and dangerous.

Education

The techniques of education were once frankly aversive. The teacher was usually older and stronger than his pupils and was able to "make them learn." This meant that they were not actually taught but were surrounded by a threatening world from which they could escape only by learning. Usually they were left to their own resources in discovering how to do so. Claude Coleman has published a grimly amusing reminder of these older practices (1953). He tells of a schoolteacher who published a careful account of his services during 51 years of teaching, during which he administered: ". . . 911,527 blows with a cane; 124,010 with a rod; 20,989 with a ruler; 136,715 with the hand; 10,295 over the mouth; 7,905 boxes on the ear; [and] 1,115,800 slaps on the head. . . ."

Progressive education was a humanitarian effort to substitute positive reinforcement for such aversive measures, but in the search for useful human values in the classroom it has never fully replaced the variables it abandoned. Viewed as a branch of behavioral technology, education remains relatively inefficient. We supplement it, and rationalize it, by admiring the pupil who learns *for himself;* and we often attribute the learning process, or knowledge itself, to something *inside* the individual. We admire behavior which seems to have inner sources. Thus we admire one who *recites* a poem more than one who simply *reads* it. We admire one who *knows* the answer more than one who *knows where to look it up.* We admire the *writer* rather than the *reader.* We admire the arithmetician who can do a problem in his head rather than with a slide rule or calculating machine, or in "original" ways rather than by a strict application of rules. In general we feel that any aid or "crutch"—except those aids to which we are now thoroughly accustomed—reduces the credit due. In Plato's *Phaedrus,* Thamus, the king, attacks the invention of the alphabet on similar grounds! He is afraid "it will produce forgetfulness in the minds of those who learn to use it, because they will not practice their memories. . . ." In other words, he holds it more admirable to remember than to use a memorandum. He also objects that pupils "will read many things without instruction. . . [and] will therefore seem to know many things when they are for the most part ignorant." In the same vein we are today sometimes contemptuous of book learning, but, as educators, we can scarcely afford to adopt this view without reservation.

By admiring the student for knowledge and blaming him for ignorance, we escape some of the responsibility of teaching him. We resist any analysis of the educational process which threatens the notion of inner wisdom or questions the contention that the fault of ignorance lies with the student. More powerful techniques which bring about the same changes in behavior by manipulating *external* variables are decried as brainwashing or thought control. We are quite unprepared to judge *effective* educational measures. As long as only a few pupils learn much of what is taught, we do not worry about uniformity or regimentation. We do not fear the feeble technique; but we should view with dismay a system under which every student learned everything listed in a syllabus—although such a condition is far from unthinkable. Similarly, we do not fear a system which is so defective that the student must *work* for an education; but we are loath to give credit for anything learned without effort—although this could well be taken as an ideal result—and we flatly refuse to give credit if the student already knows what a school teaches.

A world in which people are wise and good without trying, without "having to be," without "choosing to be," could conceivably be a far better world for everyone. In such a world we should not have to "give anyone credit"—we should not need to admire anyone—for being wise and good. From our present point of view we cannot believe that such a world would be admirable. We do not even permit ourselves to imagine what it would be like.

Government

Government has always been the special field of aversive control. The state is frequently defined in terms of the power to punish, and jurisprudence leans heavily upon the associated notion of personal responsibility. Yet it is becoming increasingly difficult to reconcile current practice and theory with these earlier views. In criminology, for example, there is a strong tendency to drop the notion of responsibility in favor of some such alternative as capacity or controllability. But no matter how strongly the facts, or even practical expedience, support such a change, it is difficult to make the change in a legal system designed on a different plan. When governments resort to other techniques (for example, positive reinforcement), the concept of responsibility is no longer relevant and the theory of government is no longer applicable.

The conflict is illustrated by two decisions of the Supreme Court in the 1930's which dealt with, and disagreed on, the definition of control or coercion (Freund, *et al.*, 1954, p. 233). The Agricultural Adjustment Act proposed that the Secretary of Agriculture make "rental or benefit payments" to those farmers who agreed to reduce production. The government agreed that the Act would be unconstitutional if the farmer had been *compelled* to reduce production but was not, since he was merely *invited* to do so. Justice Roberts expressed the contrary majority view of the court that "The power to confer or withhold unlimited benefits is the power to coerce or destroy." This recognition of positive reinforcement was withdrawn a few years later in another case in which Justice Cardozo (Freund, *et al.*, 1954, p. 244) wrote "To hold that motive or temptation is equivalent to coercion is to plunge the law in endless difficulties." We may agree with him, without implying that the proposition is therefore wrong. Sooner or later the law must be prepared to deal with all possible techniques of governmental control.

The uneasiness with which we view government (in the broadest possible sense) when it does not use punishment is shown by the reception of my utopian novel, *Walden Two* (Skinner, 1948b). This was essentially a proposal to apply a behavioral technology to the construction of a workable, effective, and productive pattern of government. It was greeted with wrathful violence. *Life* magazine called it "a travesty on the good life," and "a menace . . . a triumph of mortmain or the dead hand not envisaged since the days of Sparta . . . a slur upon a name, a corruption of an impulse." Joseph Wood Krutch devoted a substantial part of his book, *The Measure of Man* (1954), to attacking my views and those of the protagonist, Frazier, in the same vein, and Morris Viteles has recently criticized the book in a similar manner in *Science* (1955). Perhaps the reaction is best expressed in a quotation from *The Quest for Utopia* by Negley and Patrick (1952):

"Halfway through this contemporary utopia, the reader may feel sure, as we did, that this is a beautifully ironic satire on what has been called 'behavioral engineering.' The longer one stays in this better world of the psychologist, however, the plainer it becomes that the inspiration is not satiric, but messianic. This is indeed the behaviorally engineered society, and while it was to be expected that sooner or later the principle of psychological conditioning would be made the basis of a serious construction of utopia—Brown anticipated it in *Limanora*—yet not even the effective satire of Huxley is adequate preparation for the shocking horror of the idea when positively presented. Of all the dictatorships espoused by utopists, this is the most profound, and incipient dictators might well find in this utopia a guidebook of political practice."

One would scarcely guess that the authors are talking about a world in which there is food, clothing, and shelter for all, where everyone chooses his own work and works on the average only 4 hours a day, where music and the arts flourish, where personal relationships develop under the most favorable circumstances, where education prepares every child for the social and intellectual life which lies before him, where—in short—people are truly happy, secure, productive, creative, and forward-looking. What is wrong with it? Only one thing: someone "planned it that way." If these critics had come upon a society in some remote corner of the world which boasted similar advantages, they would undoubtedly have hailed it as providing a pattern we all might well follow—provided that it was clearly the result of a natural process of cultural evolution. Any evidence that intelligence had been used in arriving at this version of the good life would, in their eyes, be a serious flaw. No matter if the planner of *Walden Two* diverts none of the proceeds of the community to his own use, no matter if he has no current control or is, indeed, unknown to most of the other members of the community (he planned that, too), somewhere back of it all he occupies the position of prime mover. And this, to the child of the democratic tradition, spoils it all.

The dangers inherent in the control of human behavior are very real. The possibility of the misuse of scientific knowledge must always be faced. We cannot escape by denying the power of a science of behavior or arresting its development. It is no help to cling to familiar philosophies of human behavior simply because they are more reassuring. As I have pointed out elsewhere (Skinner, 1955), the new techniques emerging from a science of behavior must be subject to the explicit countercontrol which has already been applied to earlier and cruder forms. Brute force and deception, for example, are now fairly generally suppressed by ethical practices and by explicit governmental and religious agencies. A similar countercontrol of scientific knowledge in the interests of the group is a feasible and promising possibility. Although we cannot say how devious the course of its evolution may be, a cultural pattern of control and countercontrol will presumably emerge which will be most widely supported because it is most widely reinforcing.

If we cannot foresee all the details of this (as we obviously cannot), it is important to remember that this is true of the critics of science as well. The dire consequences of new techniques of control, the hidden menace in original cultural designs—these need some proof. It is only another example of my present point that the need for proof is so often overlooked. Man has got himself into some pretty fixes, and it is easy to believe that he will do so again. But there is a more optimistic possibility. The slow growth of the method of science, now for the first time being applied to human affairs, *may* mean a new and exciting phase of human life to which historical analogies will not apply and in which earlier political slogans will not be appropriate. If we are to use the knowledge that a science of behavior is now making available with any hope of success, we must look at human nature as it is brought into focus through the methods of science rather than as it has been presented to us in a series of historical accidents.

If the advent of a powerful science of behavior causes trouble, it will not be because science itself is inimical to human welfare but because older conceptions have not yielded easily or gracefully. We expect resistance to new techniques of control from those who have heavy investments in the old, but we have no reason to help them preserve a series of principles that are not ends in themselves but rather outmoded means to an end. What is needed is a new conception of human behavior which is compatible with the implications of a scientific analysis. All men control and are controlled. The question of government in the broadest possible sense is not how freedom is to be preserved but what kinds of control are to be used and to what ends. Control must be analyzed and considered in its proper proportions. No one, I am sure, wishes to develop new master-slave relationships or bend the will of the people to despotic rulers in new ways. These are patterns of control appropriate to a world without science. They may well be the first to go when the experimental analysis of behavior comes into its own in the design of cultural practices.

II – ROGERS

There are, I believe, a number of matters in connection with this important topic on which the authors of this article, and probably a large majority of psychologists, are in agreement. These matters then are not issues as far as we are concerned, and I should like to mention them briefly in order to put them to one side.

Points of Agreement

I am sure we agree that men — as individuals and as societies — have always endeavored to understand, predict, influence, and control human behavior — their own behavior and that of others.

I believe we agree that the behavioral sciences are making and will continue to make increasingly rapid progress in the understanding of behavior, and that as a consequence the capacity to predict and to control behavior is developing with equal rapidity.

I believe we agree that to deny these advances, or to claim that man's behavior cannot be a field of science, is unrealistic. Even though this is not an issue for us, we should recognize that many intelligent men still hold strongly to the view that the actions of men are free in some sense such that scientific knowledge of man's behavior is impossible. Thus Reinhold Niebuhr, the noted theologian, heaps scorn on the concept of psychology as a science of man's behavior and even says, "In any event, no scientific investigation of past behavior can become the basis of predictions of future behavior." (1955, p. 47). So, while this is not an issue for psychologists, we should at least notice in passing that it is an issue for many people.

I believe we are in agreement that the tremendous potential power of a science which permits the prediction and control of behavior may be misused, and that the possibility of such misuse constitutes a serious threat.

Consequently Skinner and I are in agreement that the whole question of the scientific control of human behavior is a matter with which psychologists and the general public should concern themselves. As Robert Oppenheimer told the American Psychological Association last year (1956a) the problems that psychologists will pose for society by their growing ability to control behavior will be much more grave than the problems posed by the ability of physicists to control the reactions of

matter. I am not sure whether psychologists generally recognize this. My impression is that by and large they hold a laissez-faire attitude. Obviously Skinner and I do not hold this laissez-faire view, or we would not have written this article.

Points of Issue

With these several points of basic and important agreement, are there then any issues that remain on which there are differences? I believe there are. They can be stated very briefly: Who will be controlled? Who will exercise control? What type of control will be exercised? Most important of all, toward what end or what purpose, or in the pursuit of what value, will control be exercised?

It is on questions of this sort that there exist ambiguities, misunderstandings, and probably deep differences. These differences exist among psychologists, among members of the general public in this country, and among various world cultures. Without any hope of achieving a final resolution of these questions, we can, I believe, put these issues in clearer form.

Some Meanings

To avoid ambiguity and faulty communication, I would like to clarify the meanings of some of the terms we are using.

Behavioral science is a term that might be defined from several angles but in the context of this discussion it refers primarily to knowledge that the existence of certain describable conditions in the human being and/or in his environment is followed by certain describable consequences in his actions.

Prediction means the prior identification of behaviors which then occur. Because it is important in some things I wish to say later, I would point out that one may predict a highly specific behavior, such as an eye blink, or one may predict a class of behaviors. One might correctly predict "avoidant behavior," for example, without being able to specify whether the individual will run away or simply close his eyes.

The word *control* is a very slippery one, which can be used with any one of several meanings. I would like to specify three that seem most important for our present purposes. *Control* may mean: (i) The setting of conditions by B for A, A having no voice in the matter, such that certain predictable behaviors then occur in A. I refer to this as external control. (ii) The setting of conditions by B for A, A giving some degree of consent to these conditions, such that certain predictable behaviors then occur in A. I refer to this as the influence of B on A. (iii) The setting of conditions by A such that certain predictable behaviors then occur in himself. I refer to this as internal control. It will be noted that Skinner lumps together the first two meanings, external control and influence, under the concept of control. I find this confusing.

Usual Concept of Control of Human Behavior

With the underbrush thus cleared away (I hope), let us review very briefly the various elements that are involved in the usual concept of the control of human behavior as mediated by the behavioral sciences. I am drawing here on the previous writings of Skinner, on his present statements, on the writings of others who have considered in either friendly or antagonistic fashion the meanings that would be involved in such control. I have not excluded the science fiction writers, as reported recently by Vandenburg (1956), since they often show an awareness of the issues involved, even though the methods described are as yet fictional. These then are the elements that seem common to these different concepts of the application of science to human behavior.

1. There must first be some sort of decision about goals. Usually desirable goals are assumed, but sometimes, as in George Orwell's book *1984*, the goal that is selected is an aggrandizement of individual power with which most of us would disagree. In a recent paper Skinner suggests that one possible set of goals to be assigned to the behavioral technology is this: "Let men be happy, informed, skillful, well-behaved and productive." (1955–1956[1]).

In the first draft of his part of this article, which he was kind enough to show me, he did not mention such definite goals as these, but desired "improved" educational practices, "wiser" use of knowledge in government, and the like. In the final version of his article he avoids even these value-laden terms, and his implicit goal is the very general one that scientific control of behavior is desirable, because it would perhaps bring "a far better world for everyone."

Thus the first step in thinking about the control of human behavior is the choice of goals, whether specific or general. It is necessary to come to terms in some way with the issue, "For what purpose?"

2. A second element is that, whether the end selected is highly specific or is a very general one such as wanting "a better world," we proceed by the methods of science to discover the means to these ends. We continue through further experimentation and investigation to discover more effective means. The method of science is self-correcting in thus arriving at increasingly effective ways of achieving the purpose we have in mind.

3. The third aspect of such control is that as the conditions or methods are discovered by which to reach the goal, some person or some group establishes these conditions and uses these methods, having in one way or another obtained the power to do so.

4. The fourth element is the exposure of individuals to the prescribed conditions, and this leads, with a high degree of probability, to behavior which is in line with the goals desired. Individuals are now happy, if that has been the goal, or well-behaved, or submissive, or whatever it has been decided to make them.

5. The fifth element is that if the process I have described is put in motion then there is a continuing social organization which will continue to produce the types of behavior that have been valued.

Some Flaws

Are there any flaws in this way of viewing the control of human behavior? I believe there

----

1 Pages 11–20 of this volume.

are. In fact the only element in this description with which I find myself in agreement is the second. It seems to me quite incontrovertibly true that the scientific method is an excellent way to discover the means by which to achieve our goals. Beyond that, I feel many sharp differences, which I will try to spell out.

I believe that in Skinner's presentation here and in his previous writings, there is a serious underestimation of the problem of power. To hope that the power which is being made available by the behavioral sciences will be exercised by the scientists, or by a benevolent group, seems to me a hope little supported by either recent or distant history. It seems far more likely that behavioral scientists, holding their present attitudes, will be in the position of the German rocket scientists specializing in guided missiles. First they worked devotedly for Hitler to destroy the U.S.S.R. and the United States. Now, depending on who captured them, they work devotedly for the U.S.S.R. in the interest of destroying the United States, or devotedly for the United States in the interest of destroying the U.S.S.R. If behavioral scientists are concerned solely with advancing their science, it seems most probable that they will serve the purposes of whatever individual or group has the power.

But the major flaw I see in this review of what is involved in the scientific control of human behavior is the denial, misunderstanding, or gross underestimation of the place of ends, goals or values in their relationship to science. This error (as it seems to me) has so many implications that I would like to devote some space to it.

Ends and Values in Relation to Science

In sharp contradiction to some views that have been advanced, I would like to propose a two-pronged thesis: (i) In any scientific endeavor—whether "pure" or applied science—there is a prior subjective choice of the purpose or value which that scientific work is perceived as serving. (ii) This subjective value choice which brings that scientific endeavor into being must always lie outside of that endeavor and can never become a part of the science involved in that endeavor.

Let me illustrate the first point from Skinner himself. It is clear that in his earlier writing (1955–1956) it is recognized that a prior value choice is necessary, and it is specified as the goal that men are to become happy, well-behaved, productive, and so on. I am pleased that Skinner has retreated from the goals he then chose, because to me they seem to be stultifying values. I can only feel that he was choosing these goals for others, not for himself. I would hate to see Skinner become "well-behaved," as that term would be defined for him by behavioral scientists. His recent article in the *American Psychologist* (1956) shows that he certainly does not want to be "productive" as that value is defined by most psychologists. And the most awful fate I can imagine for him would be to have him constantly "happy." It is the fact that he is very unhappy about many things which makes me prize him.

In the first draft of his part of this article, he also included such prior value choices, saying for example, "We must decide how we are to use the knowledge which a science of human behavior is now making available." Now he has dropped all mention of such choices, and if I understand him correctly, he believes that science can proceed without them. He has suggested this view in another recent paper, stating that "We must continue to experiment in cultural design . . . testing the consequences as we go. Eventually the practices which make for the greatest biological and psychological strength of the group will presumably survive" (Skinner, 1955, p. 549).

I would point out, however, that to choose to experiment is a value choice. Even to move in the direction of perfectly random experimentation is a value choice. To test the consequences of an experiment is possible only if we have first made a subjective choice of a criterion value. And implicit in his statement is a valuing of biological and psychological strength. So even when trying to avoid such choice, it seems inescapable that a prior subjective value choice is necessary for any scientific endeavor, or for any application of scientific knowledge.

I wish to make it clear that I am not saying that values cannot be included as a subject of science. It is not true that science deals only with certain classes of "facts" and that these classes do not include values. It is a bit more complex than that, as a simple illustration or two may make clear.

If I value knowledge of the "three R's" as a goal of education, the methods of science can give me increasingly accurate information on how this goal may be achieved. If I value problem-solving ability as a goal of education, the scientific method can give me the same kind of help.

Now, if I wish to determine whether problem-solving ability is "better" than knowledge of the three R's, then scientific method can also study those two values but *only*—and this is very important—in terms of some other value which I have subjectively chosen. I may value college success. Then I can determine whether problem-solving ability or knowledge of the three R's is most closely associated with that value. I may value personal integration or vocational success or responsible citizenship. I can determine whether problem-solving ability or knowledge of the three R's is "better" for achieving any one of these values. But the value or purpose that gives meaning to a particular scientific endeavor must always lie outside of that endeavor.

Although our concern in this symposium is largely with applied science, what I have been saying seems equally true of so-called "pure" science. In pure science the usual prior subjective value choice is the discovery of truth. But this is a subjective choice, and science can never say whether it is the best choice, save in the light of some other value. Geneticists in the U.S.S.R., for example, had to make a subjective choice of whether it was better to pursue truth or to discover facts which upheld a governmental dogma. Which choice is "better"? We could make a scientific investigation of those alternatives but only in the light of some other subjectively chosen value. If, for example, we value the survival of a culture, then we could begin to investigate with the methods of science the question of whether pursuit of truth or support of governmental dogma is most closely associated with cultural survival.

My point then is that any endeavor in science, pure or applied, is carried on in the pursuit of a purpose or value that is subjectively chosen by persons. It is important that

this choice be made explicit, since the particular value which is being sought can never be tested or evaluated, confirmed or denied, by the scientific endeavor to which it gives birth. The initial purpose or value always and necessarily lies outside the scope of the scientific effort which it sets in motion.

Among other things this means that if we choose some particular goal or series of goals for human beings and then set out on a large scale to control human behavior to the end of achieving those goals, we are locked in the rigidity of our initial choice, because such a scientific endeavor can never transcend itself to select new goals. Only subjective human persons can do that. Thus if we chose as our goal the state of happiness for human beings (a goal deservedly ridiculed by Aldous Huxley in *Brave New World*), and if we involved all of society in a successful scientific program by which people became happy, we would be locked in a colossal rigidity in which no one would be free to question this goal, because our scientific operations could not transcend themselves to question their guiding purposes. And without laboring this point, I would remark that colossal rigidity, whether in dinosaurs, or dictatorships, has a very poor record of evolutionary survival.

If, however, a part of our scheme is to set free some "planners" who do not have to be happy, who are not controlled, and who are therefore free to choose other values, this has several meanings. It means that the purpose we have chosen as our goal is not a sufficient and a satisfying one for human beings but must be supplemented. It also means that if it is necessary to set up an elite group which is free, then this shows all too clearly that the great majority are only the slaves—no matter by what high-sounding name we call them—of those who select the goals.

Perhaps, however, the thought is that a continuing scientific endeavor will evolve its own goals; that the initial findings will alter the directions, and subsequent findings will alter them still further, and that science somehow develops its own purpose. Although he does not clearly say so, this appears to be the pattern Skinner has in mind. It is surely a reasonable description, but it overlooks one element in this continuing development, which is that subjective personal choice enters in at every point at which the direction changes. The findings of a science, the results of an experiment, do not and never can tell us what next scientific purpose to pursue. Even in the purest of science, the scientist must decide what the findings mean and must subjectively choose what next step will be most profitable in the pursuit of his purpose. And if we are speaking of the application of scientific knowledge, then it is distressingly clear that the increasing scientific knowledge of the structure of the atom carries with it no necessary choice as to the purpose to which this knowledge will be put. This is a subjective personal choice which must be made by many individuals.

Thus I return to the proposition with which I began this section of my remarks — and which I now repeat in different words. Science has its meaning as the objective pursuit of a purpose which has been subjectively chosen by a person or persons. This purpose or value can never be investigated by the particular scientific experiment or investigation to which it has given birth and meaning. Consequently, any discussion of the control of human beings by the behavioral sciences must first and most deeply concern itself with the subjectively chosen purposes which such an application of science is intended to implement.

Is the Situation Hopeless?

The thoughtful reader may recognize that, although my remarks up to this point have introduced some modifications in the conception of the processes by which human behavior will be controlled, these remarks may have made such control seem, if anything, even more inevitable. We might sum it up this way: Behavioral science is clearly moving forward; the increasing power for control which it gives will be held by someone or some group; such an individual or group will surely choose the values or goals to be achieved; and most of us will then be increasingly controlled by means so subtle that we will not even be aware of them as controls. Thus, whether a council of wise psychologists (if this is not a contradiction in terms), or a Stalin, or a Big Brother has the power, and whether the goal is happiness,

or productivity, or resolution of the Oedipus complex, or submission, or love of Big Brother, we will inevitably find ourselves moving toward the chosen goal and probably thinking that we ourselves desire it. Thus, if this line of reasoning is correct, it appears that some form of *Walden Two* or of *1984* (and at a deep philosophic level they seem indistinguishable) is coming. The fact that it would surely arrive piecemeal, rather than all at once, does not greatly change the fundamental issues. In any event, as Skinner has indicated in his writings, we would then look back upon the concepts of human freedom, the capacity for choice, the responsibility for choice, and the worth of the human individual as historical curiosities which once existed by cultural accident as values in a prescientific civilization.

I believe that any person observant of trends must regard something like the foregoing sequence as a real possibility. It is not simply a fantasy. Something of that sort may even be the most likely future. But is it an inevitable future? I want to devote the remainder of my remarks to an alternative possibility.

Alternative Set of Values

Suppose we start with a set of ends, values, purposes, quite different from the type of goals we have been considering. Suppose we do this quite openly, setting them forth as a possible value choice to be accepted or rejected. Suppose we select a set of values that focuses on fluid elements of process rather than static attributes. We might then value: man as a process of becoming, as a process of achieving worth and dignity through the development of his potentialities; the individual human being as a self-actualizing process, moving on to more challenging and enriching experiences; the process by which the individual creatively adapts to an ever-new and changing world; the process by which knowledge transcends itself, as, for example, the theory of relativity transcended Newtonian physics, itself to be transcended in some future day by a new perception.

If we select values such as these we turn to our science and technology of behavior with a very different set of questions. We will want to know such things as these: Can science aid in the discovery of new modes of richly rewarding living? more meaningful and satisfying modes of interpersonal relationships? Can science inform us on how the human race can become a more intelligent participant in its own evolution — its physical, psychological and social evolution? Can science inform us on ways of releasing the creative capacity of individuals, which seems so necessary if we are to survive in this fantastically expanding atomic age? Oppenheimer has pointed out (1956b) that knowledge, which used to double in millennia or centuries, now doubles in a generation or a decade. It appears that we must discover the utmost in release of creativity if we are to be able to adapt effectively. In short, can science discover the methods by which man can most readily become a continually developing and self-transcending process, in his behavior, his thinking, his knowledge? Can science predict and release an essentially "unpredictable" freedom?

It is one of the virtues of science as a method that it is as able to advance and implement goals and purposes of this sort as it is to serve static values, such as states of being well-informed, happy, obedient. Indeed we have some evidence of this.

Small Example

I will perhaps be forgiven if I document some of the possibilities along this line by turning to psychotherapy, the field I know best.

Psychotherapy, as Meerloo (1955) and others have pointed out, can be one of the most subtle tools for the control of A by B. The therapist can subtly mold individuals in imitation of himself. He can cause an individual to become a submissive and conforming being. When certain therapeutic principles are used in extreme fashion, we call it brainwashing, an instance of the disintegration of the personality and a reformulation of the person along lines desired by the controlling individual. So the principles of therapy can be used as an effective means of external control of human personality and behavior. Can psychotherapy be anything else?

Here I find the developments going on in client-centered psychotherapy (Rogers, 1951) an exciting hint of what a behavioral science can do in achieving the kinds of values I have stated. Quite aside from being a somewhat new orientation in psychotherapy, this development has important implications regarding the relation of a behavioral science to the control of human behavior. Let me describe our experience as it relates to the issues of this discussion.

In client-centered therapy, we are deeply engaged in the prediction and influencing of behavior, or even the control of behavior. As therapists we institute certain attitudinal conditions, and the client has relatively little voice in the establishment of these conditions. We predict that if these conditions are instituted, certain behavioral consequences will ensue in the client. Up to this point this is largely external control, no different from what Skinner has described, and no different from what I have discussed in the preceding sections of this article. But here the similarity ceases.

The conditions we have chosen to establish predict such behavioral consequences as these: that the client will become self-directing, less rigid, more open to the evidence of his senses, better organized and integrated, more similar to the ideal which he has chosen for himself. In other words, we have established by external control conditions which we predict will be followed by internal control by the individual, in pursuit of internally chosen goals. We have set the conditions which predict various classes of behaviors — self-directing behaviors, sensitivity to realities within and without, flexible adaptiveness — which are by their very nature unpredictable in their specifics. Our recent research (Rogers and Dymond, 1954) indicates that our predictions are to a significant degree corroborated, and our commitment to the scientific method causes us to believe that more effective means of achieving these goals may be realized.

Research exists in other fields — industry, education, group dynamics — which seems to support our own findings. I believe it may be conservatively stated that scientific progress has been made in identifying those conditions in an interpersonal relationship which, if they exist in B, are followed in A by greater maturity in behavior, less dependence on others, an increase in expressiveness as a person, an increase in variability, flexibility and effectiveness of adaptation, an increase in self-responsibility and self-direction. And, quite in contrast to the concern expressed by some, we do not find that the creatively adaptive behavior which results from such self-directed variability of expression is a "happy accident" which occurs in "chaos." Rather, the individual who is open to his experience, and self-directing, is harmonious not chaotic, ingenious rather than random, as he orders his responses imaginatively toward the achievement of his own purposes. His creative actions are no more a "happy accident" than was Einstein's development of the theory of relativity.

Thus we find ourselves in fundamental agreement with John Dewey's statement: "Science has made its way by releasing, not by suppressing, the elements of variation, of invention and innovation, of novel creation in individuals." (Ratner, 1939, p. 359). Progress in personal life and in group living is, we believe, made in the same way.

Possible Concept of the Control of Human Behavior

It is quite clear that the point of view I am expressing is in sharp contrast to the usual conception of the relationship of the behavioral sciences to the control of human behavior. In order to make this contrast even more blunt, I will state this possibility in paragraphs parallel to those used before.

1) It is possible for us to choose to value man as a self-actualizing process of becoming; to value creativity, and the process by which knowledge becomes self-transcending.

2) We can proceed, by the methods of science, to discover the conditions which necessarily precede these processes and, through continuing experimentation, to discover better means of achieving these purposes.

3) It is possible for individuals or groups to set these conditions, with a minimum of power or control. According to present knowledge, the only authority necessary is the authority to establish certain qualities of interpersonal relationship.

4) Exposed to these conditions, present knowledge suggests that individuals become more self-responsible, make progress in self-actualization, become more flexible, and become more creatively adaptive.

5) Thus such an initial choice would inaugurate the beginnings of a social system or subsystem in which values, knowledge, adaptive skills, and even the concept of science would be continually changing and self-transcending. The emphasis would be upon man as a process of becoming.

I believe it is clear that such a view as I have been describing does not lead to any definable utopia. It would be impossible to predict its final outcome. It involves a step-by-step development, based on a continuing subjective choice of purposes, which are implemented by the behavioral sciences. It is the direction of the "open society," as that term has been defined by Popper (1945), where individuals carry responsibility for personal decisions. It is at the opposite pole from his concept of the closed society, of which *Walden Two* would be an example.

I trust it is also evident that the whole emphasis is on process, not on end-states of being. I am suggesting that it is by choosing to value certain qualitative elements of the process of becoming that we can find a pathway toward the open society.

The Choice

It is my hope that we have helped to clarify the range of choice which will lie before us and our children in regard to the behavioral sciences. We can choose to use our growing knowledge to enslave people in ways never dreamed of before, depersonalizing them, controlling them by means so carefully selected that they will perhaps never be aware of their loss of personhood. We can choose to utilize our scientific knowledge to make men happy, well-behaved, and productive, as Skinner earlier suggested. Or we can insure that each person learns all the syllabus which we select and set before him, as Skinner now suggests. Or at the other end of the spectrum or choice we can choose to use the behavioral sciences in ways which will free, not control; which will bring about constructive variability, not conformity; which will develop creativity, not contentment; which will facilitate each person in his self-directed process of becoming; which will aid individuals, groups, and even the concept of science to become self-transcending in freshly adaptive ways of meeting life and its problems. The choice is up to us, and, the human race being what it is, we are likely to stumble about, making at times some nearly disastrous value choices and at other times highly constructive ones.

I am aware that to some, this setting forth of a choice is unrealistic, because a choice of values is regarded as not possible. Skinner has stated:

"Man's vaunted creative powers . . . his capacity to choose and our right to hold him responsible for his choice—none of these is conspicuous in this new self-portrait (provided by science). Man, we once believed, was free to express himself in art, music, and literature, to inquire into nature, to seek salvation in his own way. He could initiate action and make spontaneous and capricious changes of course. . . . But science insists that action is initiated by forces impinging upon the individual, and that caprice is only another name for behavior for which we have not yet found a cause." (1955–1956, pp. 52–53).

I can understand this point of view, but I believe that it avoids looking at the great paradox of behavioral science. Behavior, when it is examined scientifically, is surely best understood as determined by prior causation. This is one great fact of science. But responsible personal choice, which is the most essential element in being a person, which is the core experience in psychotherapy, which exists prior to any scientific endeavor, is an equally prominent fact in our lives. To deny the experience of responsible choice is, to me, as restricted a view as to deny the possibility of a behavioral science. That these two important elements of our experience appear to be in contradiction has perhaps the same significance as the contradiction between the wave theory and the corpuscular theory of light, both of which can be shown to be true, even though incompatible. We cannot profitably deny our subjective life, any more than we can deny the objective description of that life.

In conclusion then, it is my contention that science cannot come into being without a personal choice of the values we wish to achieve. And these values we choose to implement will forever lie outside of the science which implements them; the goals we select, the purposes we wish to follow, must always be outside of the science which achieves them. To me this has the encouraging meaning that the human person, with his capacity of subjective choice, can and will always exist, separate from and prior to any of his scientific undertakings. Unless as individuals and groups we choose to relinquish our capacity of subjective choice, we will always remain persons, not simply pawns of a self-created science.

III—SKINNER

I cannot quite agree that the practice of science *requires* a prior decision about goals or a prior choice of values. The metallurgist can study the properties of steel and the engineer can design a bridge without raising the question of whether a bridge is to be built. But such questions are certainly frequently raised and tentatively answered. Rogers wants to call the answers "subjective choices of values." To me, such an expression suggests that we have had to abandon more rigorous scientific practices in order to talk about our own behavior. In the experimental analysis of other organisms I would use other terms, and I shall try to do so here. Any list of values is a list of reinforcers—conditioned or otherwise. We are so constituted that under certain circumstances food, water, sexual contact, and so on, will make any behavior which produces them more likely to occur again. Other things may acquire this power. We do not need to say that an organism chooses to eat rather than to starve. If you answer that it is a very different thing when a man chooses to starve, I am only too happy to agree. If it were not so, we should have cleared up the question of choice long ago. An organism can be reinforced by—can be made to "choose"—almost any given state of affairs.

Rogers is concerned with choices that involve multiple and usually conflicting consequences. I have dealt with some of these elsewhere (Skinner, 1953) in an analysis of self-control. Shall I eat these delicious strawberries today if I will then suffer an annoying rash tomorrow? The decision I am to make used to be assigned to the province of ethics. But we are now studying similar combinations of positive and negative consequences, as well as collateral conditions which affect the result in a laboratory. Even a pigeon can be taught some measure of self-control! And this work helps us to understand the operation of certain formulas—among them value judgments —which folk-wisdom, religion, and psychotherapy have advanced in the interests of self-discipline. The observable effect of any statement of value is to alter the relative effectiveness of reinforcers. We may no longer enjoy the strawberries for thinking about the rash. If rashes are made sufficiently shameful, illegal, sinful, maladjusted, or unwise, we may glow with satisfaction as we push the strawberries aside in a grandiose avoidance response which would bring a smile to the lips of Murray Sidman.

People behave in ways which, as we say, conform to ethical, governmental, or religious patterns because they are reinforced for doing so. The resulting behavior may have far-reaching consequences for the survival of the pattern to which it conforms. And whether we like it or not, survival is the ultimate criterion. This is where, it seems to me, science can help —not in choosing a goal, but in enabling us to predict the survival value of cultural practices. Man has too long tried to get the kind of world he wants by glorifying some brand of immediate reinforcement. As science points up more and more of the remoter consequences, he may begin to work to strengthen behavior, not in a slavish devotion to a chosen value, but with respect to the ultimate survival of mankind. Do not ask me why I want mankind to survive. I can tell you why only in the sense in which the physiologist can tell you why I want to breathe. Once the relation between a given step and the survival of my group has been pointed out, I will take that step. And it is the business of science to point out just such relations.

The values I have occasionally recommended (and Rogers has not led me to recant) are transitional. Other things being equal, I am betting on the group whose practices make for healthy, happy, secure, productive, and creative people. And I insist that the values recommended by Rogers are transitional, too, for I can ask him the same kind of question. Man as a process of becoming—*what?* Self-actualization—for what? Inner control is no more a goal than external.

What Rogers seems to me to be proposing both here and elsewhere (Rogers, 1956), is this: Let us use our increasing power of control to create individuals who will not need and perhaps will no longer respond to control. Let us solve the problem of our power by renouncing it. At first blush this seems as implausible as a benevolent despot. Yet power has occasionally been foresworn. A nation has burned its Reichstag, rich men have given away their wealth, beautiful women have become ugly hermits in the desert, and psychotherapists have become nondirective. When this happens, I look to other possible reinforcements for a plausible explanation. A people relinquish democratic power when a tyrant promises them the earth. Rich men give away wealth to escape the accusing finger of their fellowmen. A woman destroys her beauty in the hope of salvation. And a psychotherapist relinquishes control because he can thus help his client more effectively.

The solution that Rogers is suggesting is thus understandable. But is he correctly interpreting the result? What evidence is there that a client ever becomes truly *self*-directing? What evidence is there that he ever makes a truly *inner* choice of ideal or goal? Even though the therapist does not do the choosing, even though he encourages "self-actualization"—he is not out of control as long as he holds himself ready to step in when occasion demands— when, for example, the client chooses the goal of becoming a more accomplished liar or murdering his boss. But supposing the therapist does withdraw completely or is no longer necessary—what about all the other forces acting upon the client? Is the self-chosen goal independent of his early ethical and religious training? of the folk-wisdom of his group? of the opinions and attitudes of others who are important to him? Surely not. The therapeutic situation is only a small part of the world of the client. From the therapist's point of view it may appear to be possible to relinquish control. But the control passes not to a "self," but to forces in other parts of the client's world. The solution of the therapist's problem of power cannot be *our* solution, for we must consider *all* the forces acting upon the individual.

The child who must be prodded and nagged is something less than a fully developed human being. We want to see him hurrying to his appointment, not because each step is taken in response to verbal reminders from his mother, but because certain temporal contingencies, in which dawdling has been punished and hurrying reinforced, have worked a change in his behavior. Call this a state of better organization, a greater sensitivity to reality, or what you will. The plain fact is that the child passes from a temporary verbal control exercised by his parents to control by certain inexorable features of the environment. I should suppose that something of the same sort happens in successful psychotherapy. Rogers seems to me to be saying this: Let us put an end, as quickly as possible, to any pattern of master-and-slave, to any direct obedience to command, to the submissive following of suggestions. Let the individual be free to adjust himself to more rewarding features of the world about him. In the end, let his teachers and counselors "wither away," like the Marxist state. I not only agree with this as a useful ideal, I have constructed a fanciful world to demonstrate its advantages. It saddens me to hear Rogers say that "at a deep philosophic level" *Walden Two* and George Orwell's *1984* "seem indistinguishable." They could scarcely be more unlike—at any level. The book *1984* is a picture of immediate aversive control for vicious selfish purposes. The founder of *Walden Two*, on the other hand, has built a community in which neither he nor any other person exerts any *current* control. His achievement lay in his original *plan*, and when he boasts of this ("It is enough to satisfy

the thirstiest tyrant") we do not fear him but only pity him for his weakness.

Another critic of *Walden Two*, Andrew Hacker (1955), has discussed this point in considering the bearing of mass conditioning upon the liberal notion of autonomous man. In drawing certain parallels between the Grand Inquisition passage in Dostoevsky's *Brothers Karamazov*, Huxley's *Brave New World*, and *Walden Two*, he attempts to set up a distinction to be drawn in any society between conditioners and conditioned. He assumes that "the conditioner can be said to be autonomous in the traditional liberal sense." But then he notes: "Of course the conditioner has been conditioned. But he has not been conditioned by the conscious manipulation of another *person*." But how does this affect the resulting behavior? Can we not soon forget the origins of the "artificial" diamond which is identical with the real thing? Whether it is an "accidental" cultural pattern, such as is said to have produced the founder of *Walden Two*, or the engineered environment which is about to produce his successors, we are dealing with sets of conditions generating human behavior which will ultimately be measured by their contribution to the strength of the group. We look to the future, not the past, for the test of "goodness" or acceptability.

If we are worthy of our democratic heritage we shall, of course, be ready to resist any tyrannical use of science for immediate or selfish purposes. But if we value the achievements and goals of democracy we must not refuse to apply science to the design and construction of cultural patterns, even though we may then find ourselves in some sense in the position of controllers. Fear of control, generalized beyond any warrant, has led to a misinterpretation of valid practices and the blind rejection of intelligent planning for a better way of life. In terms which I trust Rogers will approve, in conquering this fear we shall become more mature and better organized and shall, thus, more fully actualize ourselves as human beings.

Behavior control and social responsibility

LEONARD KRASNER

In recent years, research in psychotherapy has increasingly focused on investigations which could be interpreted as being part of a broad psychology of behavior control (Bandura, 1961; Frank, 1961; Kanfer, 1961; Krasner, 1958, 1961; Salzinger, 1959; Skinner, 1953). The essential element of behavior control studies is the influence, persuasion, and manipulation of human behavior. Two broad categories of controlling techniques have been utilized. The first can be termed the "social reinforcement" process, namely, those techniques which utilize the behavior of the examiner and structure of the interview situation as a means of influencing behavior. These include studies of psychotherapy, hypnosis, operant conditioning, attitude influence, placebos, and brainwashing. A second category of influence techniques involves the use of physical devices or drugs, such as tranquillizers, brain stimulation, sensory deprivation, or teaching machines. Both categories of investigation have in common the development of techniques for enhancing the effectiveness of the control or manipulation of individual behavior. Many investigators in this field have been influenced by Skinnerian behaviorism with its emphasis on environmental control and shaping of behavior (Skinner, 1953). Although there is as yet no direct evidence on this point, it is hypothesized that the social reinforcement type of influence is more effective than physical devices because the subject is less likely to be aware of them and thus is —more likely to respond to them.

It is in the field of psychotherapy that the issues of the *moral* and *ethical implications* of behavior control first arose as a relevant problem. Psychotherapy involves the direct application of the findings of behavior control (Krasner, 1961). A professionally trained individual uses a variety of techniques to change, modify, or direct the behavior of another person. It differs from brainwashing in the implied assent given by the patient to this manipulation. This view of the therapist as a manipulator of behavior is one that arouses considerable opposition from many therapists who deny that they are actively involved in controlling behavior. This is perhaps best expressed by Rogers, both in his debate with Skinner (Rogers and Skinner, 1956[1]) and in his article on "Persons or Science" (1955). In this latter paper, he goes into the dangers of control and deplores the tendency toward social control implicit in the results of the kinds of studies discussed in this paper. His attitude is that therapy is a process which is "intensely personal, highly subjective in its inwardness, and dependent entirely on the relationship of two individuals, each of whom is an experiencing media." Rogers contends that:

"Therapists recognize — usually intuitively — that any advance in therapy, any fresh knowledge of it, any significant new hypothesis in regard to it, must come from the experience of the therapists and clients, and can never come from science."

He feels that there is a danger in science which may lead toward manipulation of people, and cites as examples of this the attempts to apply laws of learning to control people through advertisements and propaganda. Skinner's *Walden Two* (1948b) is cited as a psychologist's picture of paradise:

"A paradise of manipulation in which the extent to which one can be a person is greatly reduced unless one can be a member of the ruling council."

This point of view can be best summarized as Rogers does, as follows:

"What I will do with the knowledge gained through scientific method — whether I will use it to understand, enhance, enrich, or use it to control, manipulate, and destroy — is a matter of subjective choices depending upon the values which have personal meaning for me."

Yet in another paper (Rogers and Skinner, 1956) even Rogers is willing to concede that:

From *American Psychologist*, 1964, **17**, 199–204.
1 Pages 301–316 of this volume.

"In client-centered therapy, we are deeply engaged in the prediction and influencing of behavior, or even the control of behavior. As therapists, we institute certain attitudinal conditions, and the client has relatively little voice in the establishment of these conditions. We predict that if these conditions are instituted, certain behavioral consequences will ensue in the client."

The "anti-control" view is also well presented in a series of papers by Jourard (1959, 1961). He contends that manipulation will have harmful effects both on the patient and on the therapist. Jourard (1959) contends that:

"'Behavioristic' approaches to counseling and psychotherapy, while rightly acknowledging a man's susceptibility to manipulation by another, ignore the possibly deleterious impact of such manipulation on the whole man and, moreover, on the would-be manipulator himself — whereas the essential factor in the psychotherapeutic situation is a loving, honest and spontaneous relationship between the therapist and the patient."

In contrast, a "behavioristic" viewpoint might argue that apparent spontaneity on the therapist's part may very well be the most effective means of manipulating behavior. The therapist is an individual programed by his training into a fairly effective behavior control machine. Most likely the machine is most effective when it least appears like a machine.

Despite the views of Rogers and of other therapists, the evidence seems quite strong that psychotherapy as a social reinforcement process is part of a broader psychology of behavior control in which the therapist is actively influencing the behavior, attitudinal and value system of the patient (Krasner, 1961). Further, recent research has begun to put the therapist back into the therapy situation insofar as studying his personality and other personal attributes, including his value system. Marmor (1961) points out that psychoanalysis, as well as other types of psychotherapy, involves the communication of the therapist's implicit values and behavioral characteristics. Marmor's conviction is that:

"Whether or not the analyst is *consciously*

'tempted to act as a teacher, model, and ideal' to his patients, he *inevitably* does so to a greater or lesser extent; and this is a central aspect of the psychoanalytic process."

One of the reasons for denial on the part of therapists that they control behavior, or that they even desire to do so, is that such control would raise many moral, ethical, and legal problems, which the therapist is not prepared to handle. Thus, therapists are put in the paradoxical position of saying to the patient, "we will change your behavior, but we do not really want to change your behavior." Generally, science fiction is more willing to come to grips with some of the basic issues involved than is the professional therapist (Vandenberg, 1956).

Yet, we cannot avoid facing the issue of values. In fact, psychology is in the process of having a strong revival of interest in values. Recognition of the need for concern with the *ethics* or *moral values* of the therapist is implicit in an increasing number of articles (May, 1953; Papanek, 1958; Patterson, 1958; Rotter, 1961; Watson, 1958; Whitehorn, 1959). For example, May (1953) points out that the progress of psychoanalysis in the last decade can be judged by the increasing recognition that it is an illusion for the analyst to suppose that he can avoid value judgments. He feels that this recognition is explicit in the writings of Fromm and Horney and implicit in the works of Fromm-Reichman, Kubie, Alexander, and French. May cites a statement of J. McV. Hunt, who says ". . . I have reluctantly come to the conclusion that the scientist cannot avoid the value assumptions merely by deciding to do so." Hunt concludes, and May agrees, that values do belong to the subject material of science and must be taken into account in devising measuring instruments of behavioral or situational change. The study of Rosenthal (1955) on changes in "moral values" following psychotherapy is an illustration. Patients who are rated as "improved" changed significantly in their performance on a value test in the direction of values held by their therapists in sex, aggression, and authority, whereas unimproved patients tended to become less like their therapists in these values.

Lowe (1959) points out some of the ethical

dilemmas involved insofar as the therapist is concerned, with possible conflicts over four sets of values. After reviewing value systems in four different categories, called naturalism, culturism, humanism, theism, Lowe concludes that "there is no single professional standard to which the psychologist's values can conform." The dilemma for the psychologist, as he sees it, is that if *one* set of values is to become absolute, psychology would cease to be a science and would become a social movement. However, he feels that psychologists cannot, on the other hand, do research without intending it to serve a particular value orientation. His suggestion is that value orientations be dealt with as objectively as possible, and that each area in psychology become more fully aware of the implications of its efforts. Further, since value orientations are in such conflict that at this point they are unresolvable, each therapist must understand his own values and those of others.

There have been infrequent attempts to measure attitudes of therapists, but most of these have been in terms of attitudes to therapy rather than attitudes to the broader implications of their social role (Shaffer, 1953). There have certainly been investigations of personality variables of the therapist, or psychologist, or psychiatrist (Holt and Luborsky, 1958; Kelley and Fiske, 1951), but these have been generally oriented toward traditional personality variables rather than value attitudes. Shaffer (1953), for example, found in his analysis of objective versus intuitive psychologists, that the differences are not in terms of personality but in terms of attitudes toward role. Skinner (Rogers and Skinner, 1956), who was among the first to call attention to the ethical problems inherent in a psychology of behavior control, has pointed out that an important reinforcement for the therapist himself is his success in manipulating human behavior.

While the issue of behavior control first arose in regard to psychotherapy, it is now far broader and covers other areas such as operant conditioning, teaching machines, hypnosis, sensory deprivation, subliminal stimulation, and similar studies. There is considerable public interest, concern, and misunderstanding about the range and power of psychological findings.

How does a "psychology of behavior control" differ from the science of psychology? The differences are subtle, but important. A science of psychology seeks to determine the lawful relationships in behavior. The orientation of a "psychology of behavior control" is that these lawful relationships are to be used to deliberately influence, control, or change behavior. This implies a manipulator or controller, and with it an ethical and value system of the controller. As we learn more about human behavior, it is increasingly obvious that it is controllable by various techniques. Does this mean that we, as psychologists, researchers, or even therapists, *at this point* could modify somebody's behavior in any way we wanted? The answer is no, primarily because research into the techniques of control thus far is at the elementary stage. Science moves at a very rapid pace, however, and now is the time to concern ourselves with this problem before basic knowledge about the techniques overwhelms us.

The obvious analogy is with the atomic physicists, who have been very concerned about the application of their scientific findings. Of course, many of the comments from the physical scientists have come *since* the dropping of the first atom bomb. The concern of the psychologist must come before the techniques of behavior control are fully developed. *Public* concern is more readily discernible at this point as shown by popular articles (Brecher and Brecher, 1961) and the cries of indignation some years back when subliminal stimulation was a going fad.

Carl Rogers has recently been quoted as saying that:

"To hope that the power which is being made available by the behavioral sciences will be exercised by the scientists, or by a benevolent group, seems to me to be a hope little supported by either recent or distant history. It seems far more likely that behavioral scientists, holding their present attitudes, will be in the position of the German rocket scientists specializing in guided missiles. . . . If behavioral scientists are concerned solely with advancing their science, it seems most probable that they will serve the purpose of whatever group has the power." (Brecher and Brecher, 1961).

This rather pessimistic quotation is from a popular article in a recent issue of *Harper's* magazine. The authors cite this and other research, particularly the work of Olds on brain stimulation, as evidence for deep concern about the role of the behavioral scientist. In what is perhaps an overdramatization of the situation, yet one which may legitimately express lay concern, they conclude that:

"New methods of controlling behavior now emerging from the laboratory may soon add an awe-inspiring power to enslave us all with our own engineered consent."

Oppenheimer (1956a), in comparing the responsibility of the physicist with that of the psychologist, makes the cogent point that:

"The psychologist can hardly do anything without realizing that for him the acquisition of knowledge opens up the most terrifying prospects of controlling what people do and how they think and how they behave and how they feel."

We can approach the problem of social responsibility by asking three basic questions:

1. Is human behavior controllable? Overwhelming experimental evidence in fields of motivation, conditioning, and personality development indicates that this is true.

2. If so, is it desirable or wise for psychologists to continue research in these fields? Psychologists have no choice but to continue their research. The findings can be used just as meaningfully to help man as to hinder him. Further, methods of counter control can be developed. The danger is *not* in the research findings but in their potential misuse.

3. What safeguards can be incorporated into this type of research? The answer to this is the crux of the psychologist's dilemma. First, a code of ethics such as that of the APA is a good first step, but certainly not enough. An ethical code merely says that the psychologist will not deliberately misuse his findings. It does not go into the more basic question of the psychologist or behavior controller's value system. If we see him as one who is in a position to change or modify others' behavior, this implies a value decision as to what is "good behavior," what is "mental health," and what is desirable adjustment. To deny control is to do a disservice and, in effect, to hide one's head in the sand like the proverbial ostrich. The fact that the behavior controllers are professional individuals is no guarantee that behavior control will not be misused. We have only to turn to the role of German physicians in medical atrocities as evidence of misuse by a supposedly professional group.

Berg (1954) goes into one aspect of the ethical and value problem in discussing principles that should guide the use of human subjects in psychological research. His concern with the problem is an outgrowth of the "barbarous medical experiments" performed on human subjects by Nazi physicians in the name of science. These German physicians were not mere tools, but were leaders in their profession. Berg suggests that future research using human subjects adhere to the principles of "consent," "confidence," and "standard procedure." He cites the basic principles governing permissible government experiments laid down at the Nuremberg trials. These are relevant for future discussion of the kinds of behavior permissible, or not permissible, to behavior controllers.

Basically, they are similar to the principles that Roe (1959) pointed out, namely, that *awareness* is a major ingredient in defense against manipulation. Roe makes pertinent comments in stressing the need for man to be aware of himself and the world around him:

"Awareness of our own needs and attitudes is our most effective instrument for maintaining our own integrity and control over our own reactions."

Roe contends that the psychologist's role in changing society should be an active one. She cites a talk by Halpern who reported a survey which showed that an overwhelming number of our young psychologists were interested only in the practice of therapy. Halpern is quoted as follows:

"It seems to me that there is something a bit amiss with a group of scientists who are so overwhelmingly service oriented and who, recognizing that life adjustment has been increasingly complex and difficult, offer to cure the ills resulting from the present state of affairs, but do little or nothing to help society learn how best to meet their interpersonal, emotional and social problems so that the present seemingly all-pervasive disturbances may be avoided."

A somewhat similar view is expressed by Cattell (1948), who also calls for research into ethical values and feels that moral laws can be derived from psychological and physiological investigation of living matter. He does not accept the viewpoint, which he attributes to a majority of psychologists and most laymen, that ethical values lie outside the realm of science. Creegan (1958) also concerns himself with the need for scientific investigation of ethical problems. In comparing the responsibility of the psychologist with that of the atomic physicist he points out that:

"Psychology does not produce nuclear warheads, nor does it produce the apocalyptic birds which may take them to a selected target, but psychology is concerned with human decisions. . . . The greatest power in the world is the power of rational decision. Atomic physics deals with the release of great forces, but answers to ethical questions may be the decisive ones for the future of humanity."

Creegan further goes into questions of whether force and hidden persuasion ought to be used for a good cause. Once we have committed ourselves on economic, social, and religious problems, how should we go about implementing our ideals? How does the psychologist define "the good life"? Does the psychologist constitute an ethical elite? Creegan points out that at present it is the physicist who communicates with the public about moral problems, rather than the psychologist. Muller (1958) also feels that values are a legitimate source of scientific investigation. He disagrees with those who say that man's values are determined by a higher authority outside of himself or those who say that values are a private matter. But Muller is a biologist, not a psychologist.

The attacks on psychological investigators of behavior control are often quite unfair.

For example, Krutch (1954) is highly critical of the implications of Skinner's *Walden Two* because of a fear that social control will pass into the hands of experimentalists who are not concerned with moral issues. Yet it is often these experimenters who are most concerned with value problems and who are in a position to approach on an objective basis the whole question of moral and value issues.

We would suggest two major steps be taken at this point. The first is to develop techniques of approaching experimentally the basic problem of social and ethical issues involved in behavior control. One initial approach would be to investigate the attitudes and fantasies of experimenters and therapists toward their own role as behavior controllers in studies in which the effectiveness of their influence can be readily tested. As an example, in our laboratory we are presently devising ways of measuring attitudes toward mental health, "the good life," and applications of science. Fantasy behavior will be elicited in response to special stimuli and reports of role perception and role reaction will be obtained from therapists and from experimenters in psychotherapy, verbal conditioning, and other behavior controlling experiments. The attitude measures will be associated with behavioral ratings of these "controllers" and subject responsivity to them. These studies are undertaken within a framework of investigating the variables that go into resisting influence situations.

A second major step in dealing with this problem is communication between the general public and the research investigators. In this field, particularly, researchers must keep in contact with each other. Any kind of research which is kept secret, such as work in sensory deprivation, is to be deplored. Furthermore, it is the psychologist-researcher who should undertake the task of contact with the public rather than leaving it to sensationalists and popularizers.

In summary, behavior control represents a relatively new, important, and very useful development in psychological research. It also may be horribly misused unless the psychologist is constantly alert to what is taking place in society and unless he is active in investigating and controlling the social uses of behavior control.

Brainwashing, conditioning and DDD (debility, dependency, and dread)

I. E. FARBER, HARRY F. HARLOW, AND LOUIS JOLYON WEST

Few aspects of Communism have been more puzzling and disturbing to the Western world than the widely publicized collaboration, conversion, and self-denunciation in individuals —communist and noncommunist, innocent and guilty alike—who have suffered Communist imprisonment. Such behavior in persons whose intelligence, integrity, or patriotism can scarcely be doubted has suggested to many a mysterious power or knowledge that enables Communists to manipulate the thoughts and actions of others in a manner ordinarily reserved to characters in the more lurid sorts of science fiction. Accordingly, such terms as "brainwashing," "thought control," "menticide," and so on, have been applied to the process or product of this manipulation. To lend some degree of scientific respectability to such concepts, attempts have been made (Meerloo, 1954; Santucci and Winokur, 1955) to relate them to the psychiatric implications of Pavlovian conditioning procedures.

While these speculations have an undeniable romantic appeal, more sober analyses (Bauer, 1956; Biderman, 1956; Hinkle and Wolff, 1956) of factors influencing the behavior of prisoners under Communist control indicate that they are neither mysterious nor indicative of any unusual amount of psychiatric sophistication on the part of Communists. Indeed, considering the extraordinary degree of control the Communists maintain over the physical and social environments of their prisoners, it is rather surprising that their efforts to indoctrinate and convert have not been more successful. Contrary to the views of some writers in popular media, the record indicates that most American prisoners in Korea, for instance, showed remarkable "sales resistance," even under profound duress.

It is a fact that the Communist Chinese in Korea achieved considerable success in stimulating cooperative behavior in a large number of United Nations prisoners of war through a combination of threats, propaganda, group pressures, and group manipulation. By Segal's criteria, 15 per cent of American army prisoners cooperated unduly. And if it can be considered that it was every man's duty to exercise active resistance to the enemy and his propaganda during the period of captivity, then fully 95 per cent failed to meet the most stringent criteria for commendable behavior (Segal, 1956; Communist Interrogation . . ., 1956). Nevertheless, the Chinese induced only 21 American prisoners to remain under Communism (Pasley, 1955), and it is doubtful whether all these were truly "converted." Most authorities agree that despite occasional lapses the vast majority of American prisoners of war performed well and honorably. As the Secretary of Defense's advisory committee on POW's has reported, "the record seems fine indeed" (POW: The Fight . . ., 1955).

In the light of these findings, a complete analysis would concentrate more heavily on the factors that enabled the large majority of POW's to resist in some degree. However, it is not with these phenomena that the present discussion is primarily concerned. Rather, we wish to discuss the basis for the success of techniques whereby false confessions, self-denunciations, and participation in propaganda activities were brought about. The Communists made special efforts to elicit these behaviors in flying personnel, particularly with regard to confessions of participation in bacteriological warfare. After their world-wide propaganda campaign went into high gear with accusations of "germ warfare" in Korea, beginning on February 21, 1952, a vigorous policy of coercive pressure was applied to a large number of American flying personnel captured during the Korean conflict. As a result, a number of flyers from the Air Force and Marine Corps signed false confessions of bacteriological warfare and participated to various extents in enemy propaganda activities. A detailed account of those events may

From *Sociometry*, 1957, **20**, 271 – 283. Reprinted by permission of the American Sociological Association.

be found elsewhere (West, 1956; Communist Interrogation . . ., 1956).

The objective intensity of noxious stimulation, injury, disease, malnutrition, deprivation, sleeplessness, fatigue, isolation, and threat suffered by many prisoners for a greater or lesser period was extreme. There were few, if any, who were not subjected to some of these conditions. Accounts of observations and experiments related to these various types of stress are now appearing in the literature in increasing number (Lilly, 1956; Group for the Advancement of Psychiatry, 1956). The present discussion is concerned with the theoretical analysis of the psychological states and processes resulting from such objective conditions of stress.

DDD

Although the specific components of these states varv in intensity and pattern, in the case of the prisoner of war they contain at least three important elements: debility, dependency, and dread. They refer to the fact that individuals subjected to the kinds of environmental conditions listed above have reduced viability, are helplessly dependent on their captors for the satisfaction of many basic needs, and experience the emotional and motivational reactions of intense fear and anxiety. These components are separable, but it is evident that they also interact. Consequently it seems appropriate as well as convenient to conceive of these states and processes as though they were an entity or syndrome including debility, dependency, and dread, to be referred to as DDD. Among the POW's pressured by the Chinese Communists, the DDD syndrome in its full-blown form constituted a state of discomfort that was well-nigh intolerable.

Debility was induced by semistarvation, fatigue, and disease. Chronic physical pain was a common feature. Loss of energy and inability to resist minor abuse, combined with lack of proper facilities for the maintenance of personal hygiene, led to inanition and a sense of terrible weariness and weakness.

Dependency, produced by the prolonged deprivation of many of the factors, such as sleep and food, needed to maintain sanity and life itself, was made more poignant by occasional unpredictable brief respites, reminding the prisoner that it was possible for the captor to relieve the misery if he wished. If an individual was placed in prolonged isolation, as was so often the case with flyers pressed to confess to the bacteriological warfare charges, the deprivation of ordinary social stimulation and relations markedly strengthened the dependency. Although we shall not dwell on this aspect of the situation, the effectiveness of Communist methods was undoubtedly greatly enhanced by their control of the means for satisfying nuclear social needs for recognition, status, communication, and so on. The captors' condemnation and misunderstanding of American social values, in connection with the withdrawal of accustomed social supports, e.g., reliable sources of information and communication with others as a means of testing reality and of appraising moral standards, played a significant part in the dependency relationship.

Dread is the most expressive term to indicate the chronic fear the Communists attempted to induce. Fear of death, fear of pain, fear of nonrepatriation, fear of deformity or permanent disability through neglect or inadequate medical treatment, fear of Communist violence against loved ones at home, and even fear of one's own inability to satisfy the demands of insatiable interrogators—these and many other nagging despairs constituted the final component of the DDD syndrome (Biderman, 1956).

The interrelations of these factors, carefully contrived and nurtured by the Communists, were of great importance in determining the total effect of DDD. Although there were some individuals who acceded to the demands of their captors fairly early in the game, it is clear that the Chinese realized the importance of preparing the resistant prisoner, through DDD, for the long, drawn-out process designed to bring about the desired goal—complete compliance.

Before considering in greater detail the specific mechanisms underlying the role of DDD in accomplishing this aim, three prefatory comments are in order. First, the present analysis lays no claim to comprehensiveness. It deals with only a few aspects of

DDD occurring under certain conditions. We believe these aspects to be important, but they are not all that is important. In this connection, the present paper may be considered as an elaboration of portions of the comprehensive discussion of Communist "thought reform" by Hinkle and Wolff (1956). It is gratifying that our conclusions, arrived at independently and on somewhat more theoretical grounds, are essentially in agreement with theirs.

Secondly, our use of the terminology of learning theory, broadly conceived, and our use of concepts derived from conditioning does not imply that we consider learning theory uniquely competent to explain the effects of *DDD*. On the other hand, we do consider factors influencing behavior in *DDD* to have something in common with factors affecting behavior in learning situations generally, and, therefore, that it may be worth while attempting to analyze some aspects of behavior associated with *DDD* in terms of principles of classical and instrumental conditioning. But, as an eminent conditioning theorist has recently noted (Spence, 1956), the view that principles derived from conditioning might apply to more complex behavior does not at all imply that complex behavior can be explained solely in terms of the variables affecting conditioning. In this instance, it is particularly doubtful that the procedures used to influence the behavior of prisoners under Communism derived from the methods of Pavlov, or that the prisoners' reactions are generally understandable in purely Pavlovian terms. On the contrary, to the extent that such concepts apply at all, selective or instrumental (Thorndikean) learning was a more prominent feature than classical (Pavlovian) conditioning. Certainly, only limited aspects of the behavior of prisoners under Communism bear any resemblance to the generalized inhibitory or excitatory states characterizing some of Pavlov's dogs (Pavlov, 1941).

Finally, we should beware of the "psychologist's error." Although some of the behavior of prisoners under Communism may be susceptible to analysis in terms of learning and conditioning principles, it does not follow that the application of these principles by Communist captors was deliberate and self-conscious. Animal trainers and side-show barkers are often extremely competent manipulators of behavior; this does not mean they are comparative or social psychologists.

DDD, SELF-PERCEPTION, AND THINKING

By providing a radically changed context *DDD* might be expected to produce new responses that actively compete or interfere with wonted behavior. It may also produce a condition of markedly reduced responsiveness, not unlike the generalized inhibitory states described by Pavlov (1941) and Liddell (1944), due to the reduced or monotonous stimulation associated with isolation and confinement, or to reduced energy, or to the frustration of previously successful techniques for achieving goals. Whenever individuals show extremely selective responsiveness to only a few situational elements, or become generally unresponsive, there is a disruption of the orderliness, i.e., sequence and arrangement of experienced events, the process underlying time spanning and long-term perspective. By disorganizing the perception of those experiential continuities constituting the self-concept and impoverishing the basis for judging self-consistency, *DDD* affects one's habitual ways of looking at and dealing with oneself.

This effect, which has elsewhere been related to the collapse of certain ego functions (Strassman, *et al.*, 1956), bears an interesting resemblance to some aspects of the postlobotomy syndrome. The latter, too, is characterized by apathy and the disturbance of the self-concept or self-regarding tendency (Robinson and Freeman, 1954). The frequency and degree of flattened affect and self-deprecation in the confessions of prisoners under Communism have probably been over-estimated, but to the extent they have occurred, the observed behavior has much in common with that of some brain-damaged individuals.

Closely related to the foregoing consequence of *DDD* is a disturbance of association and a concreteness of thinking similar to that sometimes seen in schizophrenia. The retention of recent experiences and habit patterns may be impaired, with consequent regression, i.e., primitivization, in language, thought, and those integrative and mediating symbolic processes essential to reasoning and foresight. Conditioning performance in human subjects is impaired by some kinds of symbolic activity, and conversely, the impoverishment of thinking may increase susceptibility to arbitrary and unsubtle training procedures (cf. Dollard and Miller, 1950) leading to relatively automatic and uncritical imitative responses. This susceptibility may be further enhanced by anxiety and emotionality (Farber, *et al.*, 1957; Spence and Farber, 1953; Taylor, 1951).[1]

REINFORCEMENT OF SOCIAL COMMUNICATION

On the assumption that conditioning principles apply in part to the behavior of prisoners of war, it is important to analyze further the nature of the conditioned stimuli and the responses elicited by them. Careful consideration would seem to indicate that the situation contains features both of selective or instrumental learning and of classical conditioning (Spence, 1956). The instrumental (i.e., Thorndikean rather than Pavlovian) aspect is emphasized by the fact that an individual must acquire a particular set of responses in order to bring about a reinforcing state of affairs. It is our thesis that an alleviation in the state of *DDD* provides the reinforcement for much of the behavior desired by the enemy. In other words, *DDD* does not, in and of itself, produce the desired behavior. *DDD* merely provides the occasion for the selective reinforcement of certain modes of response.

The role of *DDD* in the reinforcement process depends on the fact that it is not constant. Instead, it may be assumed to fluctuate in time, partly as a result of spontaneous psychophysiological processes, and partly as a result of deliberate manipulations designed to maintain its intermittent nature (Biderman, 1956), thus preventing its fall to a baseline of permanent depression and hopelessness. Those individuals who were reduced to complete apathy undoubtedly represented failures from the point of view of their Communist captors.

At the risk of considerable oversimplification, one may conceive of two consequences of the occasional mitigation of *DDD*. First is the conditioning of the "expectancy" that *DDD* will be alleviated. (This constitutes the actual classically conditioned anticipatory goal response.) Relief, whether due to spontaneous factors or deliberate manipulations, is intermittent, temporary, and unpredictable. Far from weakening the expectancy of relief, however, this tends to maintain the expectancy and renders it less susceptible to extinction. In nontechnical terms, this process serves to keep hope alive, permitting some degree of adaptive behavior, and inhibiting self-destructive tendencies, which would frustrate the enemy's purpose.

This aspect of the learning process throws some light on the frequent practice in Communist prisons of having prisoners "punish themselves." Thus, a captive might be instructed to stand or kneel in a certain position until he should decide to cooperate. This emphasis on the self-inflicted nature of the prisoner's punishment, and his ability to mitigate his condition "voluntarily," is clearly calculated to increase the intensity of expectancies of the possibility of relief. At the same time, it is evident that the prisoner's belief that he actually exercises control is delusory, so far as the objective facts are concerned, since the captor may select any behavior he chooses as the condition for relieving a prisoner's distress.

The alleviation of *DDD* at the time of occurrence of the desired behavior leads to the second consequence—the learning of instrumental acts. This is not so difficult to arrange as one might suppose and is certainly not the result of any mysterious power of the manipulator. Very often, the desired behavior is verbal

---

1 These assumptions do not imply a negative correlation between intelligence and conditioning in normal subjects, nor better conditioning in feeble-minded or brain-damaged subjects than in normal individuals. The empirical evidence does not support any such views. The suggested effect of impoverished thinking relates only to that produced by debility, isolation, and such factors. One may speculate, in this connection, on the relation between this putative effect of *DDD* and the kinds of hypersuggestibility and automatism reported among primitive peoples suffering from prolonged physical stress and privation. Whether these symptoms result from some state of hyperconditionability is a moot question. Arctic hysteria and latah, for instance, are presumably dissociative and therefore hysteroid in nature (West, in press), and the relation between hysteria and conditioning is as yet uncertain (Eysenck, 1955; Farber, *et al.*, 1957; Franks, 1956). Thus it is not possible at present to identify the effects of *DDD* with any particular psychiatric state.

in nature. Verbal behavior is in a general way already strongly conditioned to *DDD* in all human adults. One learns from infancy to use verbal behavior as a means of relieving or avoiding many of the components of *DDD*. And, as the foregoing discussion indicates, the aperiodic and unpredictable nature of the selective reward of particular language responses may be one of its chief strengths. If one may extrapolate from the results of numerous laboratory experiments, this is the very procedure calculated to produce the maximum number of responses and also to make them highly resistant to extinction, even in the absence of rewards (Skinner, 1938).

The nature of the rewards used needs no elaboration. Relief of hunger, fatigue, isolation, or pain, even temporarily, serves as an automatic reward. Even the verbal and empty promise of alleviation of *DDD* leads to appropriate anticipatory goal responses, keeping hope alive. Paradoxically, interrogation, harangues, threats, and contumely may also have a rewarding aspect, so great is the acquired reinforcement value of social communication and speech, under conditions of isolation, dependency, and physical debility.

Since the habits of social communication associated with *DDD* are initially strong, and are further strengthened by selective reinforcement, it is not strange that prisoners often show considerable social responsiveness in the presence of their captors. Despite the impoverishment of the self-concept and primitivization of thinking referred to earlier, prisoners could enjoy in some degree a much needed social relationship in the interrogation and indoctrination situations. It may be hypothesized that some prisoners became the victims of the very socialization process that under ordinary circumstances is regarded as a desirable and, indeed, essential aspect of civilized living. It is of interest in this connection to record the finding of Lifton (1954), who explicitly noted among a group of repatriated prisoners who had most aggressively resisted collaboration with the Communists, a large portion of individuals with significant antisocial tendencies. We do not suggest that collaboration and confession by prisoners under Communism are signs of desirable social attitudes. We do suggest that socialization training facilitates the tendency to engage in social communication, even with a recognized enemy, particularly under conditions in which the behavior is reinforced by the satisfaction of powerful drives while at the same time interfering or inhibitory tendencies are markedly reduced.

There are some analogies between the condition of an individual under such circumstances and that of a hypnotized subject. The hypnotized subject also tends to respond automatically, especially to verbal stimuli, to be greatly influenced by the attitude of the hypnotist, and to be highly selective in his social responsiveness. Furthermore, there is general agreement regarding the susceptibility of most normal individuals to hypnosis, except in the case of strong deliberate resistance. Under conditions of *DDD*, the possibility of resistance over a very long period may be vanishingly small. As soon as resistance appears, the intensity of *DDD* can be increased, thus at one and the same time punishing resistance and increasing the influence of the reward when relief occurs. It must be remembered that the strengthening effects of rewards — in this instance the alleviation of an intensely unpleasant emotional state — are fundamentally automatic. They occur because of the kind of nervous system we have, and not in any essential way because of the mediation of conscious thought processes.

RETENTION OF PRISON EXPERIENCES AND BEHAVIOR

What is the aftermath of such experiences? The evidence clearly indicates that, except in the case of organic brain damage such as might result from avitaminosis, the behavior of the typical returnee from Communist prisons is "normal," in the special and important sense that he behaves in a manner that would be predicted on the basis of ordinary laws of behavior. There is not the slightest evidence for the necessity of postulating new or unknown factors or conditions. This does not mean the experience of imprisonment leaves no trace. Such a circumstance would in itself be abnormal, i.e., inconsistent with the known principles of behavior. In terms of normative criteria, many ex-prisoners are more than ordinarily anxious, defensive, dependent, suspicious, insecure. Pressed to explain any possibly discreditable acts, they often exhibit a very considerable degree of hesitancy, vagueness, paramnesia, and rationalization. In a word, they behave exactly as one would expect of any individual required to explain and defend his behavior, many determinants of which he is not aware.

Most returnees remember a great deal of what occurred during their imprisonment. They do not remember everything and may be unable to give a very clear account of their own behavior. Some behavior may appear as strange and inexplicable to the person concerned as to anyone else. The explanation of whatever impairment of memory occurs may be found in the laws of forgetting, deriving from both clinic and laboratory. There is no need to expatiate here on the role of repression in forgetting when the material to be recalled elicits anxiety and guilt. But it may be useful to note briefly some of the factors that would influence retention even in the absence of these emotions.

In an earlier section, it was pointed out that the state of *DDD* produces responses that actively compete with ordinary responses to environmental stimuli. By the same process, the comforting and familiar stimuli of home and friends are associated with a wholly different set of responses from those produced by *DDD*. The changed context may actively inhibit recall of the prison experiences. This phenomenon is nothing more than the familiar psychological explanation of forgetting in terms of associative interference.

Among the most important of these competing responses are the affective ones. The returnee simply does not feel as he did as a prisoner. He may be able to talk about how he felt, although this too offers difficulties because our terminology for describing emotional states is woefully inadequate and vague (Dollard and Miller, 1950), but he does not currently respond affectively in the same way. Similarly, the familiar stimuli of home reinstate different verbal responses, both overt and implicit, that affect recall. The returnee feels different, talks differently, and thinks differently than he did in the former context. Since, like all of us, he is unaware of many of the cues to his former behavior (as well as his current behavior), it is as useless to ask him to explain his earlier reactions as it is to ask a person why he once disliked olives or is for the moment unable to recall the name of an old acquaintance.

The particular reactions and attitudes constituting patriotism, bravery, loyalty, and so on, depend on the appearance of particular cues, symbolic or other. Such qualities are tendencies to respond positively or negatively, in varying degrees and combinations, in the presence of certain combinations of cues. From this point of view, unwonted reactions occurring under *DDD* do not represent a different attitude; rather, the habitual attitude does not appear because the appropriate cues have been removed. Back home in the presence of adequate cues, the returnee tends to act and feel as he did prior to imprisonment.

Finally, one must consider the effect on retention of the adequacy of the original impression. Occasionally the returnee does not remember much because he did not observe much. The impoverished stimulation, impaired responsiveness, reduced symbolic activity, and disorganization of time-spanning characteristic of *DDD* reduce the clarity and strength of impressions at the time of the original experience, and thus decrease ability to recall.

In the light of all these factors, whose pejorative influence on retention is well known by students of human learning, it is clearly to be expected that the recall of returnees would be something less than complete and wholly accurate as regards their actual prison experiences and behavior.

RESISTANCE TO EFFECTS OF *DDD*

Despite our opinion that the most undesirable effects of *DDD* are not necessarily permanent, or, given appropriate social conditions after repatriation, even particularly long-lived, the general picture of *DDD* presented in the foregoing discussion is rather gloomy. This is in part because we have emphasized its stressful aspects rather than the considerable resources most persons can muster to oppose them. The many environmental, social, and motivational variables that produce resistance to these effects have not been discussed, but their potency should certainly not be underestimated. As we have observed earlier, the resistance of American prisoners under Communism, in the face of the objective circumstances detailed above, was in most instances notable, and in some nothing less than heroic.

It is evident that there are great individual differences in susceptibility to *DDD* even under conditions in which the level of *DDD* itself could reasonably be regarded as constant, i.e., not a differential factor. To state the point somewhat differently, there are unquestionably a number of variables, whose values differ from person to person, affecting the degree of resistance to the effects of *DDD*. The question may then be raised whether the potency of these variables might not be increased in any given individual. We believe they can.

The statement, "Every man has his breaking point," contains a germ of truth, but like other bromides, is liable to misinterpretation. It does not mean the "breaking point" is fixed for any given individual, so that nothing can affect it. Such a view is scientifically indefensible, if not meaningless, since it implies that some kinds of behavior are unlawful, i.e., not affected by variations in any kinds of antecedent conditions. Furthermore, the term "breaking point" is itself misleading. Susceptibility to *DDD* or any other stressful condition is not an all-or-none affair. We are discussing behavior, and behavior varies in degree and in kind. It may be possible to define "breaking" in the manner that one defines a right or wrong response in arithmetic, but it should be recognized that such a definition would be arbitrary at best and of doubtful conceptual significance. As Biderman (1956) has pointed out, a prisoner's physical and moral strength may be sapped by Communist coercive methods to a degree that resistance appears insignificant. But, however feeble his performance, motivation to resist usually persists and shows itself as circumstances permit.

It is not the purpose of the present discussion to consider all the possible personal or social variables of which resistance to the effects of *DDD* may be a function, or indeed to consider any of them in detail. We mention two, not because they are necessarily of particular importance, but because they throw further light on the nature of the *DDD* state. First, there is the factor of physical health. Other things equal, there is probably a negative relation between degree of physical health and vigor on the one hand and susceptibility to *DDD* on the other. Debility can be postponed longer, dependency fought against, and the self-concept maintained more easily if bodily well-being obtains. Second, there is the factor of initial or chronic anxiety. No matter what anxiety is due to, the higher the anxiety level, the greater is the possibility of rewarding behavior by its momentary reduction. Contrariwise, a low level of initial anxiety should retard the growth of the "dread" component of *DDD*, and at least indirectly affect some of its antecedents, e.g., the reactivity to pain (Wolff and Wolf, 1952).

Thus, techniques for promoting health and decreasing anxiety in those who may become prisoners are probably of great importance. Nevertheless, one should not expect factors such as these to block the effects of *DDD* indefinitely. Physical health, for instance, may be of utmost value over a short haul, e.g., during early interrogation. But on a long-term basis it may be relatively insignificant. Health can be broken down by a determined and informed enemy in a very short time. And although a healthy individual can better resist the effects of debilitating variables, there is no evidence that, once illness and physical debility occur, previously healthy individuals can tolerate this condition better than those who might have become habituated to it. In some cases, indeed, the reverse might obtain.

A somewhat similar reservation may be expressed concerning procedures calculated to reduce initial anxiety, i.e., training individuals to be generally nonanxious. The fear component of *DDD*, unlike neurotic anxiety or neurotic fears (phobias), is quite realistic for the most part. Realistic fears are not easily extinguishable and, if they were, the desirability of extinguishing such fears is not altogether certain. For instance, fear of punishment for displaying hostility toward one's captors is adaptive. Wolf and Ripley (1947) quote one prisoner of the Japanese in World War II in this regard: "I had to make a conscious effort not to resent things because I realized that my bones are brittle."

On the other hand, certain anticipatory fears may be modified through training procedures. Alleviation of unrealistic fears of the unknown (through accurate indoctrination regarding enemy methods) undoubtedly improves the ability of the individual to deal with those fears that are realistic. It may make it possible for him to admit his fear to himself, as a reasonable and expected reaction, thus modifying its influence as a covert force toward compliance. Furthermore, an expectation of the probable psychophysiological effects of stress may rob them of some of their "shock" value. Finally, a certain amount of transfer may be expected from stressful training experiences in which adaptive modalities have been learned, thus permitting the prisoner to conceptualize his current stressful experience in terms of previous (and at least partly successful) transactions under stress.

Still, it would be foolish to disregard the fact that some of the elements of *DDD* represent a pathological organic state, some consequences of which are probably innately determined. To the extent this is true, one cannot expect to achieve a great degree of prophylactic success in regard to the effects of *DDD*, any more than one can reasonably expect at the present state of knowledge to prevent some of the undesirable consequences of lobotomy.

Though many of the behavioral consequences of *DDD* are not innately determined, the conditioning of certain types of responses desired by the enemy may eventually occur, even in the face of superlative resistance. One of the conclusions that may legitimately be drawn from the present analysis of the circumstances of imprisonment under Communism is that, if a prisoner's state of *DDD* reaches a truly extreme degree of severity (and it cannot now be predicted whose ability to resist will be the most effective in combating *DDD*), and *if he lives* he probably cannot be expected to resist indefinitely. This prediction does not require the assumption that Communists have mysterious powers, or that their prisoners are subjected to some strange process of "brainwashing" negating the effects of their previous training and attitudes. It is based, rather, on the assumption that under the physical, social, and emotional conditions of extreme *DDD*, some degree of ultimate compliance may be considered a natural consequence of the operation of ordinary principles of human behavior.

SUMMARY

Although the behavior of some prisoners under Communism, including collaboration, conversion, and self-denunciation, appears to suggest that Communists are able to "brainwash" their prisoners in a mysterious way, a consideration of the physical, emotional, and social conditions of the prisoner in conjunction with the ordinary principles of human behavior reveals that such behavior may be readily explained. The state of the prisoner may be described in terms of the concepts of debility, dependency, and dread (*DDD*), and some of the behavioral principles explaining the effects of the *DDD* state derive from learning and conditioning phenomena.

It is assumed that *DDD* operates in part to produce a generalized state of hyporesponsiveness, disrupting time-spanning processes and disorganizing the self-concept. Another consequence of *DDD* is the impairment of symbolic processes, perhaps rendering the prisoner susceptible to relatively simple conditioning techniques. The intermittent nature of *DDD* leads both to the expectancy of relief (i.e., hope) and to the reinforcement of specific kinds of verbal behavior. The latter effect is facilitated by the fact that social communication is already strongly conditioned to cues such as those produced by *DDD*, as a result of normal socialization training.

The typical prisoner returnee exhibits no extraordinary peculiarities of memory. The degree of forgetting of prison experiences is such as would be expected as a result of the inhibition of anxiety-producing thoughts (repression), change of situational context during recall, and the inadequacies of original impressions during imprisonment.

Resistance to the undesirable consequences of *DDD* is a matter of degree and may be modified by such factors as physical health and level of initial anxiety. Nevertheless, factors such as these cannot reasonably be expected to provide more than temporary respite. Through various defenses, a prisoner may postpone the development of extreme *DDD* for a long time, perhaps indefinitely. But if a prisoner's state of *DDD* is extreme, and if he lives, he probably cannot resist indefinitely. Far from furnishing proof of the operation of some unnatural process of "brainwashing," this eventuality is a predictable consequence of the operation of laws of normal human behavior.

14
THE FUTURE OF BEHAVIOR CONTROL

This collection has attempted to present, through examples and discussion, a picture of the scientific control of human behavior as it exists today. Yet, as both protagonists and antagonists would agree, it is the future of the control of human behavior that will prove most interesting.

In the future, we can certainly hope and, in fact, expect that the knowledge provided by the behavioral sciences will increase at its present rate. Likewise, we can anticipate an increase in the range and refinement of techniques for the application of this knowledge to the behavior of human beings.

Yet techniques which modify the behavior of individuals, although their contribution may be impressive, are often simply more efficient representatives of the same, remedial attempts we make today. Techniques which reform the deviant behavior of psychotics remain a patchwork system which can make no real headway as long as child rearing and other social practices which produce psychotic behavior flourish throughout our society. Likewise, programmed instruction and improvements in course design seem relatively impotent when molded into an educational system built upon aversive control. Controlling the aggressive behavior of individual members, or even of groups in our society, is dwarfed beside a system of international politics that reinforces or otherwise maintains aggressive behavior and more often than not punishes trends toward cooperative, nonaggressive international responses.

Many examples could be cited, but it is evident that the most striking aspect of the future of behavior control lies in its application to what Skinner calls the "design of cultures." Thus it seems appropriate to end this collection with his discussion of the role of science and the scientist in cultural design.

In this final selection, Skinner points out that cultural design is not new, but that, until now, it has been operating primarily on guesswork. Cultural practices have also included an enormous collection of impedimenta, some of which are necessary to prop up our present incomplete system, and some of which are superstitious. With the application of science to cultural design, Skinner expects much of the guesswork to be eliminated and much of the impedimenta to fall away.

Skinner also stresses that, in the scientific design of cultures, the scientist does not stand aloof from his society on an Olympus of behavioral technology. Rather, he "also is the product of a genetic endowment and an environmental history. He also is controlled by the culture or cultures to which he belongs." The reciprocity of the relationship between the "controller" and the "controlled" is one of the most frequently overlooked, and one of the most important, facets of behavior control. When it is kept in mind, many of the more forbidding aspects of the control of human behavior, particularly on the cultural level, are minimized.

It has long been a maxim that, in achieving social reform, good intentions are not enough. The methods used in the past have varied in their effectiveness. However, now that we can see the advent of the scientific design of cultures, we can at least hope that the future of behavior control and, indeed, the future of human society will fulfill the hopes of the wildest of social dreamers.

The design of cultures

B. F. SKINNER

Anyone who undertakes to improve cultural practices by applying a scientific analysis of human behavior is likely to be told that improvement involves a value judgment beyond the pale of his science and that he is exemplifying objectionable values by proposing to meddle in human affairs and infringe on human freedoms. Scientists themselves often accept this standard contention of Western philosophy, even though it implies that there is a kind of wisdom which is mysteriously denied to them and even though the behavioral scientists among them would be hard pressed to give an empirical account of such wisdom or to discover its sources.

The proposition gains unwarranted strength from the fact that it appears to champion the natural against the artificial. Man is a product of nature, the argument runs, but societies are contrived by men. Man is the measure of all things, and our plans for him—our customs and institutions—will succeed only if they allow for his nature. To this it might be answered that man is more than an immutable product of biological processes; he is a psychological entity, and as such also largely man-made. His cause may be as contrived as society's and possibly as weak. He is, nevertheless, an individual, and his defenders are individuals, too, who may borrow zeal in his defense from their own role in the great conflict between the one and the many. To side with the individual against the state, to take a specific example, is reassuringly to defend one's own, even though it might be answered that mankind has won its battles only because individual men have lost theirs.

These are merely answers in kind, which can no doubt be met with plausible rejoinders. The disputing of values is not only possible, it is interminable. To escape from it we must get outside the system. We can do this by developing an empirical account of the behavior of both protagonists. All objections to cultural design, like design itself, are forms of human behavior and may be studied as such. It is possible that a plausible account of the design of cultures will allay our traditional anxieties and prepare the way for the effective use of man's intelligence in the construction of his own future.

It is reasonable to hope that a scientific analysis will some day satisfactorily explain how cultural practices arise and are transmitted and how they affect those who engage in them, possibly to further the survival of the practices themselves or at least to contribute to their successors. Such an analysis will embrace the fact that men talk about their cultures and sometimes change them. Changing a culture is itself a cultural practice, and we must know as much as possible about it if we are to question it intelligently. Under what circumstances do men redesign—or, to use a discredited term, reform—their way of life? What is the nature of their behavior in doing so? Is the deliberate manipulation of a culture a threat to the very essence of man or, at the other extreme, an unfathomed source of strength for the culture which encourages it?

From *Daedalus,* Summer, 1961, 534–546. Published by the American Academy of Arts and Sciences, 280 Newton Street, Brookline Station, Boston, Massachusetts. Also from H. Hoagland and R. W. Burhoe (Eds.), *Evolution and Man's Progress.* New York: Columbia University Press, 1962. Pp. 124–136.

We need not go into the details of a scientific account of behavior to see how it bears on this issue. Its contribution must, however, be distinguished from any help to be drawn from historical analogy or the extrapolation of historical trends or cycles, as well as from interpretations based on sociological principles or structures. Such an account must make contact with biology, on the one hand, but serve in an interpretation of social phenomena, on the other. If it is to yield a satisfactory analysis of the design and implementation of social practices, it must be free of a particular defect. Evolutionary theory, especially in its appeal to the notion of survival, suffered for a long time from circularity. It was not satisfying to argue that forms of life which had survived must therefore have had survival value and had survived because of it. A similar weakness is inherent in psychologies based on adjustment or adaptation. It is not satisfying to argue that a man adapts to a new environment because of his intelligence and emotional stability if these are then defined in terms of capacities to adapt. It is true that organisms usually develop in directions which maximize, phylogenetically, the survival of the species and, ontogenetically, the adjustment of the individual; but the mechanisms responsible for both kinds of change need to be explained without recourse to the selective effect of their consequences.

In biology this is now being done. Genetics clarifies and supports evolutionary theory with new kinds of facts, and in doing so eliminates the circularity in the concept of survival. A comparable step in the study of human behavior is to analyze the mechanisms of human action apart from their contribution to personal and cultural adjustment. It is not enough to point out that a given form of behavior is advantageous to the individual or that a cultural practice strengthens the group. We must explain the origin and the perpetuation of both behavior and practice.

A scientific analysis which satisfies these conditions confines itself to individual organisms rather than statistical constructs or interacting groups of organisms, even in the study of social behavior. Its basic datum is the probability of the occurrence of the observable events we call behavior (or of inferred events having the same dimensions). The probability of behavior is accounted for by appeal to the genetic endowment of the organism and its past and present environments, described wholly in the language of physics and biology. The laboratory techniques of such an analysis, and their technological applications, emphasize the prediction and control of behavior via the manipulation of variables. Validation is found primarily in the success with which the subject matter can be controlled.

An example of how such an analysis differs from its predecessors is conveniently at hand. An important group of variables which modify behavior have to do with the consequences of action. *Rewards* and *punishments* are variables of this sort, though rather inadequately identified by those terms. We are interested in the fact (apart from any theory which explains it) that by arranging certain consequences—that is, by making certain kinds of events *contingent upon behavior*—we achieve a high degree of experimental control. Our present understanding of the so-called "contingencies of reinforcement" is undoubtedly incomplete, but it nevertheless permits us to construct new forms of behavior, to bring behavior under the control of new aspects of the environment, and to maintain it under such control for long periods of time—and all of this often with surprising ease. Extrapolation to less rigorously controlled samples of behavior outside the laboratory has already led to promising technological developments.

But the importance of the principle is embarrassing. Almost any instance of human behavior involves contingencies of reinforcement, and those who have been alerted to their significance by laboratory studies often seem fanatical in pointing them out. Yet behavior *is* important mainly because of its consequences. We may more readily accept this fact if we recall the ubiquity of the concept of purpose. The experimental study of reinforcing contingencies is nothing more than a nonteleological analysis of the *directed effects* of behavior, of relations which have traditionally been described as purpose. By manipulating contingencies of reinforcement in ways which conform to standard practices in the physical sciences, we study and use them without appealing to final causes.

We can put this reinterpretation of purpose

to immediate use, for it bears on a confusion between the phylogenetic and the ontogenetic development of behavior which has clouded our thinking about the origin and growth of cultures. Contingencies of reinforcement are similar to what we might call contingencies of survival. Inherited patterns of behavior must have been selected by their contributions to survival in ways which are not unlike those in which the behavior of the individual is selected or shaped by its reinforcing consequences. Both processes exemplify adaptation or adjustment, but very different mechanisms must be involved.

The evolution of inherited forms of behavior is as plausible as the evolution of any function of the organism when the environment can be regarded as reasonably stable. The internal environment satisfies this requirement, and a genetic endowment of behavior related to the internal economy—say, peristalsis or sneezing—is usually accepted without question. The external environment is much less stable from generation to generation, but some kinds of responses to it are also plausibly explained by evolutionary selection. The genetic mechanisms are presumably similar to those which account for other functions. But environments change, and any process which permits an organism to modify its behavior is then important. The structures which permit modification must have evolved when organisms were being selected by their survival in novel environments.

Although the mechanisms which permit modification of behavior are inherited, learned behavior does not emerge from, and is not an extension of, the unlearned behavior of the individual. The organism does not simply refine or extend a genetic behavioral endowment to make it more effective or more inclusive. Instead, it develops collateral behavior, which must be distinguished from an inherited response system even when both serve similar functions. It is important to remember this when considering social behavior. In spite of certain intriguing analogies, it is not likely that the social institutions of man are founded on or that they emerged from the instinctive patterns of animal societies. They are the achievements of individuals, modifying their behavior as inherited mechanisms permit. The co-ordinated activities of the anthill or beehive operate on

very different principles from those of a family, a large company, or a great city. The two kinds of social behavior must have developed through different processes, and they are maintained in force for different reasons.

To take a specific example, verbal behavior is not a refinement upon instinctive cries of alarm, distress, and so on, even though the reinforcing contingencies in the one case are analogous to the conditions of survival in the other. Both may be said to serve similar adaptive functions, but the mechanisms involved in acquiring verbal behavior clearly set it apart from instinctive responses. The innate vocal endowment of an organism is indeed particularly refractory to modification, most if not all verbal responses being modifications of a nonspecific behavioral endowment.

In general, the evolution of man has emphasized modifiability rather than the transmission of specific forms of behavior. Inherited verbal or other social responses are fragmentary and trivial. By far the greater part of behavior develops in the individual through processes of conditioning, given a normal biological endowment. Man becomes a social creature only because other men are important parts of his environment. The behavior of a child born into a flourishing society is shaped and maintained by variables, most of which are arranged by other people. These social variables compose the "culture" in which the child lives, and they shape his behavior in conformity with that culture, usually in such a way that he in turn tends to perpetutate it. The behavioral processes present no special problems. Nevertheless, a satisfactory account calls for some explanation of how a social environment can have arisen from nonsocial precursors. This may seem to raise the hoary question of the origin of society, but we have no need to reconstruct an actual historical event or even a speculative beginning, such as a social compact from which conclusions about the nature of society can be drawn. We have only to show that a social environment could have emerged from nonsocial conditions. As in explaining the origin of life, we cannot discover an actual historical event but must be satisfied with a demonstration that certain structures with their associated functions could have arisen under plausible conditions.

The emergence of a given form of social behavior from nonsocial antecedents is exemplified by imitation. Inherited imitative behavior is hard to demonstrate. The parrot may possibly owe its distinction only to an inherited capacity to be reinforced by the production of imitative sounds. In any case, an inherited repertoire of imitative behavior in man is insignificant, compared with the product of certain powerful contingencies of reinforcement which establish and maintain behaving-as-others-behave. For example, if organism *A* sees organism *B* running in obvious alarm, *A* will probably avoid aversive consequences by running in the same direction. Or, if *A* sees *B* picking and eating ripe berries, *A* will probably be reinforced for approaching the same berry patch. Thousands of instances of this sort compose a general contingency providing for the reinforcement of doing-as-others-do. In this sense, behavior exemplifying imitation is acquired, yet it is practically inevitable whenever two or more organisms live in contact with one another. The essential conditions are not in themselves social.

Most social behavior, however, arises from social antecedents. Transmission is more important than social invention. Unlike the origin of cultural practices, their transmission need not be a matter for speculation, since the process can be observed. Deliberate transmission (that is, transmission achieved because of practices which have been reinforced by their consequences) is not needed. For example, some practices are perpetuated as the members of a group are severally replaced. If *A* has already developed specific controlling behavior with respect to *B*, depending partly upon incidental characteristics of *B*'s behavior, he may impose the same control on a new individual, *C*, who might not himself have generated just the same practices in *A*. A mother who has shaped the vocal responses of her first baby into a primitive verbal repertoire may bring already established contingencies to bear on a second child. A leader who has acquired aversive controlling practices in his interactions with a submissive follower may take by storm a second follower even though, without this preparation, the leader-follower relation might have been reversed in the second case. Overlapping group membership is, of course, only one factor contributing to manners, customs, folkways, and other abiding features of a social environment.

These simple examples are offered not as solutions to important problems but to illustrate an approach to the analysis of social behavior and to the design of a culture. A special kind of social behavior emerges when *A* responds in a definite way *because of the effect on the behavior of B*. We must consider the importance of *B* to *A* as well as of *A* to *B*. For example, when *A* sees *B* looking into a store window, he is likely to be reinforced if he looks too, as in the example of the berry patch. But if his looking is important to *B*, or to a third person who controls *B*, a change may take place in *B*'s behavior. *B* may look into the window in order to induce *A* to do the same. The carnival shill plays on the behavior of prospective customers in this way. *B*'s behavior is no longer controlled by what is seen in the window but (directly or indirectly) by the effect of that behavior on *A*. (The original contingencies for *A* break down: the window may not now be "worth looking into.") Action taken by *A* because of its effect on the behavior of *B* may be called "personal control." An important subdivision is verbal behavior, the properties of which derive from the fact that reinforcements are mediated by other organisms (Skinner, 1957b). Another subdivision is cultural design.

In analyzing any social episode from this point of view a complete account must be given of the behaviors of both parties as they contribute to the origin and maintenance of the behavior of each other. For example, in analyzing a verbal episode, we must account for both speaker and listener. This is seldom done in the case of nonverbal personal control. In noticing how the master controls the slave or the employer the worker, we commonly overlook reciprocal effects and, by considering action in one direction only, are led to regard control as exploitation, or at least the gaining of a one-sided advantage; but the control is actually mutual. The slave controls the master as completely as the master the slave, in the sense that the techniques of punishment employed by the master have been selected by the slave's behavior in submitting to them. This does not mean that the notion of exploitation is meaningless or that we may not appropriately ask,

Cui bono? In doing so, however, we go beyond the account of the social episode itself and consider certain long-term effects which are clearly related to the question of value judgments. A comparable consideration arises in the analysis of any behavior which alters a cultural practice.

We may not be satisfied with an explanation of the behavior of two parties in a social interaction. The slaves in a quarry cutting stone for a pyramid work to escape punishment or death, and the rising pyramid is sufficiently reinforcing to the reigning Pharaoh to induce him to devote part of his wealth to maintaining the forces which punish or kill. An employer pays sufficient wages to induce men to work for him, and the products of their labor reimburse him, let us say, with a great deal to spare. These are on-going social systems, but in thus analyzing them we may not have taken everything into account. The system may be altered by outsiders in whom sympathy with, or fear of, the lot of the slave or exploited worker may be generated. More important, perhaps, is the possibility that the system may not actually be in equilibrium. It may breed changes which lead to its destruction. Control through punishment may lead to increasing viciousness, with an eventual loss of the support of those needed to maintain it; and the increasing poverty of the worker and the resulting increase in the economic power of the employer may also lead to countercontrolling action.

A culture which raises the question of collateral or deferred effects is most likely to discover and adopt practices which will survive or, as conditions change, will lead to modifications which in turn will survive. This is an important step in cultural design, but it is not easily taken. Long-term consequences are usually not obvious, and there is little inducement to pay any attention to them. We may admire a man who submits to aversive stimulation for the sake of later reinforcement or who eschews immediate reinforcement to avoid later punishment, but the contingencies which lead him to be "reasonable" in this sense (our admiration is part of them) are by no means overpowering. It has taken civilized societies a long time to invent the verbal devices — the precepts of morals and ethics — which successfully promote such an outcome. Ultimate advantages seem to be

particularly easy to overlook in the control of behavior, where a quick though slight advantage may have undue weight. Thus, although we boast that the birch rod has been abandoned, most school children are still under aversive control — not because punishment is more effective in the long run, but because it yields immediate results. It is easier for the teacher to control the student by threatening punishment than by using positive reinforcement with its deferred, though more powerful, effects.

A culture which has become sensitive to the long-term consequences of its measures is usually supported by a literature or philosophy which includes a set of statements expressing the relations between measures and consequences. To the cultural designer, these statements function as prescriptions for effective action; to the members of the group, they are important variables furthering effective self-management. (To both, and to the neutral observer, they are sometimes said to "justify" a measure, but this may mean nothing more than strengthening the measure by classifying it with certain kinds of events characteristically called "good" or "right.") Thus, a government may induce its citizens to submit to the hardship and tragedy of war by picturing a future in which the world is made safe for democracy or free of Communism, or to a program of austerity by pointing to economic changes which will eventually lead to an abundance of good things for all. In so doing, it strengthens certain behavior on the part of its citizens which is essential to its purposes, and the resulting gain in power reinforces the government's own concern for deferred effects and its efforts to formulate them.

The scientific study of behavior underlines the collateral effects of controlling practices and reveals unstable features of a given interaction which may lead to long-deferred consequences. It may dictate effective remedial or preventive measures. It does not do this, however, by taking the scientist out of the causal stream. The scientist also is the product of a genetic endowment and an environmental history. He also is controlled by the culture or cultures to which he belongs. Doing-something-about-human-behavior is a kind of social action and its products and by-products must be understood accordingly.

A reciprocal relationship between the knower and the known, common to all the sciences, is important here. A laboratory for the study of behavior contains many devices for controlling the environment and for recording and analyzing the behavior of organisms. With the help of these devices and their associated techniques, we change the behavior of an organism in various ways, with considerable precision. *But note that the organism changes our behavior in quite as precise a fashion.* Our apparatus was designed by the organism we study, for it was the organism which led us to choose a particular manipulandum, particular categories of stimulation, particular modes of reinforcement, and so on, and to record particular aspects of its behavior. Measures which were successful were for that reason reinforcing and have been retained, while others have been, as we say, extinguished. The verbal behavior with which we analyze our data has been shaped in a similar way: order and consistency emerged to reinforce certain practices which were adopted, while other practices suffered extinction and were abandoned. (All scientific techniques, as well as scientific knowledge itself, are generated in this way. A cyclotron is "designed" by the particles it is to control, and a theory is written by the particles it is to explain, as the behavior of these particles shapes the nonverbal and verbal behavior of the scientist.)

A similarly reciprocal effect is involved in social action, especially in cultural design. Governmental, religious, economic, educational, and therapeutic institutions have been analyzed in many ways—for example, as systems which exalt such entities as sovereignty, virtue, utility, wisdom, and health. There is a considerable advantage in considering these institutions simply as behavioral technologies. Each one uses an identifiable set of techniques for the control of human behavior, distinguished by the variables manipulated. The discovery and invention of such techniques and their later abandonment or continued use—in short, their evolution—are, or should be, a part of the history of technology. The issues they raise, particularly with respect to the behavior of the discoverer or inventor, are characteristic of technology in general.

Both physical and behavioral technologies have shown progress or improvement in the sense that new practices have been discovered or invented and tested and that some of them have survived because their effects were reinforcing. Men have found better ways, not only to dye a cloth or build a bridge, but to govern, teach, and employ. The conditions under which all such practices originate range from sheer accident to the extremely complex behaviors called thinking (Skinner, 1953). The conditions under which they are tested and selected are equally diverse. Certain immediate personal advantages may well have been the only important variables in the behavior of the primitive inventors of both physical and cultural devices. But the elaboration of moral and ethical practices has reduced the importance of personal aggrandizement. The honorific reinforcements with which society encourages action for the common weal, as well as the sanctions it applies to selfish behavior, generate a relatively disinterested creativity. Even in the field of personal control, improvements may be proposed, not for immediate exploitation, but —as by religious leaders, benevolent rulers, political philosophers, and educators—for "the good of all."

Only an analysis of moral and ethical practices will clarify the behavior of the cultural designer at this stage. He has faced a special difficulty in the fact that it is easier to demonstrate the right way to build a bridge than the right way to treat one's fellowmen (the difference reducing to the immediacy and clarity of the results). The cultural inventor, even though relatively disinterested, has found it necessary to appeal for support to secular or divine authorities, supposedly inviolable philosophical premises, and even to military persuasion. Nothing of the sort has been needed for the greater part of physical technology. The wheel was not propagated by the sword or by promises of salvation—it made its own way. Cultural practices have survived or fallen only in part because of their effect on the strength of the group, and those which have survived are usually burdened with unnecessary impedimenta. By association, the current designer is handicapped by the fact that men look behind any cultural invention for irrelevant, ingenuous, or threatening forces.

There is another step in physical technology, however, which must have a parallel in cultural design. The practical application of scientific knowledge shows a new kind of disinterestedness. The scientist is usually concerned with the control of nature apart from his personal aggrandizement. He is perhaps not wholly "pure," but he seeks control mainly for its own sake or for the sake of furthering other scientific activity. There are practical as well as ethical reasons for this: as technology becomes more complex, for example, the scientist himself is less and less able to pursue the practical implications of his work. There is very little personal reimbursement for the most profitable ideas of modern science. As a result, a new idea may yield immediate technological improvements without bringing the scientist under suspicion of plotting a personal coup. But social technology has not yet reached this stage. A disinterested consideration of cultural practices from which suggestions for improvement may emerge is still often regarded as impossible. This is the price we pay for the fact that men (1) have so often improved their control of other men for purposes of exploitation, (2) have had to bolster their social practices with spurious justifications, and (3) have so seldom shared the attitudes of the basic scientist.

Most people would subscribe to the proposition that there is no value judgment involved in deciding how to build an atomic bomb, but would reject the proposition that there is none involved in deciding to build one. The most significant difference here may be that the scientific practices which guide the designer of the bomb are clear, while those which guide the designer of the culture which builds a bomb are not. We cannot predict the success or failure of a cultural invention with the same accuracy as we do that of a physical invention. It is for this reason that we are said to resort to value judgments in the second case. What we resort to is guessing. It is only in this sense that value judgments take up where science leaves off. When we can design small social interactions and, possibly, whole cultures with the confidence we bring to physical technology, the question of value will not be raised.

So far, men have designed their cultures largely by guesswork, including some very lucky hits; but we are not far from a stage of knowledge in which this can be changed. The change does not require that we be able to describe some distant state of mankind toward which we are moving or "deciding" to move. Early physical technology could not have foreseen the modern world, though it led to it. Progress and improvement are local changes. We better ourselves and our world as we go.

We change our cultural practices because it is in our nature as men to be reinforced in certain ways. This is not an infallible guide. It could, indeed, lead to fatal mistakes. For example, we have developed sanitation and medical science to escape from aversive events associated with illness and death, yet a new virus could conceivably arise to wipe out everyone except those to whom chronic illness and filth had granted immunity. On the present evidence, our decision in favor of sanitation and medicine seems to make for survival, but in the light of unforeseeable developments we may in time look back upon it as having had no survival value.

From time to time, men have sought to reassure themselves about the future by characterizing progress as the working out of some such principle as the general will, universal or collective reason, or the greatest good. Such a principle, if valid, would seem to guarantee an inevitable, if devious, improvement in the human condition. No such principle is clearly supported by a scientific analysis of human behavior. Yet the nature of man tells us something. Just as an ultimate genetic effect cannot be reached if immediate effects are not beneficial, so we must look only to the immediate consequences of behavior for modifications in a cultural pattern. Nevertheless, cultural inventions have created current conditions which have at least a probabilistic connection with future consequences. It is easy to say that men work for pleasure and to avoid pain, as the hedonists would have it. These are, indeed, powerful principles; but in affecting the day-to-day behavior of men, they have led to the construction of cultural devices which extend the range of both pleasure and pain almost beyond recognition. It is the same man, biologically speaking, who acts selfishly or for the good of the group, and it is the same man who, as a disinterested scientist, will make human behavior vastly more effective through cultural invention.

REFERENCES

A

Adams, J. A. Vigilance in the detection of low-intensity visual stimuli. *J. exp. Psychol.*, **1956**, *52*, 204–208.

Allen, K. Eileen, Hart, Betty M., Buell, Joan S., Harris, Florence R., & Wolf, M. M. Effects of social reinforcement on isolate behavior of a nursery school child. *Child Develpm.*, **1964**, *35*, 511–518.

American Psychiatric Association. Report on patients over 65 in public mental hospitals. **1959**.

Andjus, R. K. Sur la possibilité de réanimer le rat adulte refroidi jusqu'à proximité du point de congélation. *C. R. Acad. Sci.*, Paris: **1951**, *232*, 1591–1593.

Andjus, R. K., Knöpfelmacher, F., Russell, R. W., & Smith, A. U. Effects of hypothermia on behavior. *Nature*, **1955**, *176*, 1015–1016.

Andjus, R. K., Knöpfelmacher, F., Russell, R. W., & Smith, A. U. Some effects of severe hypothermia on learning and retention. *Quart. J. exp. Psychol.*, **1956**, *8*, 15–23.

Aprison, M. H., Nathan, P., & Himwich, H. E. A study of the relationship between asymmetric acetylcholinesterase activities in rabbit brain and three behavioral patterns. *Science*, **1954**, *119*, 158.

Argyle, M. *The scientific study of social behavior.* London: Methuen, **1957**.

Ayd, F. J. A critique of chlorpromazine and reserpine therapy. In H. E. Himwich (Ed.), *Tranquilizing drugs.* Washington: Amer. Ass. Adv. Sci., **1957**. Pp. 173–181.

Ayer, A. J. *The problem of knowledge.* Edinburgh: Pelican Books, **1956**.

Ayllon, T. The application of reinforcement theory toward behavior problems. Unpublished doctoral dissertation. U. of Houston, **1959**.

Ayllon, T. Intensive treatment of psychotic behavior by stimulus satiation and food reinforcement. *Behav. Res. Ther.*, **1963**, *1*, 53–61.

Ayllon, T., & Azrin, N. H. Reinforcement and instructions with mental patients. *J. exp. Anal. Behav.*, **1964**, *7*, 327–331.

Ayllon, T., & Haughton, E. Control of the behavior of schizophrenic patients by food. *J. exp. Anal. Behav.*, **1962**, *5*, 343–352.

Ayllon, T., & Michael, J. The psychiatric nurse as a behavioral engineer. *J. exp. Anal. Behav.*, **1959**, *2*, 323–334.

Azrin, N. H. Some effects of two intermittent schedules of immediate and non-immediate punishment. *J. Psychol.*, **1956**, *42*, 3–21.

Azrin, N. H. Some effects of noise on human behavior. *J. exp. Anal. Behav.*, **1958**, *1*, 183–200.

Azrin, N. H., & Lindsley, O. R. The reinforcement of cooperation between children. *J. abnorm. soc. Psychol.*, **1956**, *52*, 100–102.

B

Baer, D. M. Escape and avoidance responses of preschool children to two schedules of reinforcement withdrawal. *J. exp. Anal. Behav.*, **1960**, *3*, 155–159.

Baer, D. M. The effect of withdrawal of positive reinforcement on an extinguishing response in young children. *Child Develpm.*, **1961**, *32*, 67–74.

Baer, D. M. Laboratory control of thumbsucking by withdrawal and re-presentation of reinforcement. *J. exp. Anal. Behav.*, **1962a**, *5*, 525–528.

Baer, D. M. A technique of social reinforcement for the study of child behavior: Behavior avoiding reinforcement withdrawal. *Child Develpm.*, **1962b**, *33*, 847–858.

Bakan, P. Discrimination decrement as a function of time in a prolonged vigil. *J. exp. Psychol.*, **1955**, *50*, 387–390.

Bandura, A. Psychotherapy as a learning process. *Psychol. Bull.*, **1961**, *58*, 143–159.

Bandura, A. The role of imitation in personality development. *J. nursery Educ.*, **1963**, *18*, 207–215.

Bandura, A., & Huston, Aletha C. Identification as a process of incidental learning. *J. abnorm. soc. Psychol.*, **1961**, *63*, 311–318.

Banks, S., et al. *Toward better media comparisons.* New York: Advertising Res. Found., **1961**.

Barber, T. X. Antisocial and criminal acts induced by "hypnosis": A review of experimental and clinical findings. *Arch. gen. Psychiat.*, **1961**, *5*, 301–312.

Barrett, Beatrice H. Reduction in rate of multiple tics by free operant conditioning methods. *J. nerv. ment. Dis.*, **1962**, *135*, 187–195.

Barrett, Beatrice H. Programmed instruction and retarded behavior. Paper read at Amer. Ass. Ment. Defic., Portland, Ore., May, **1963**.

Barrett, Beatrice H., & Lindsley, O. R. Deficits in acquisition of operant discrimination and differentiation shown by institutionalized retarded children. *Amer. J. ment. Defic.*, **1962**, *67*, 424–436.

Bartlett, S. C., Beinert, R. L., & Graham, J. R. Study of visual fatigue and efficiency in radar observation. Rome Air Development Center Tech. Rep. RADC 55–100, **1955**.

Bauer, R. A. Brainwashing—psychology or demonology? Paper read at Amer. Psychol. Ass., September, **1956**.

Becker, E. *The birth and death of meaning.* New York: Free Press of Glencoe, **1962**.

Becker, H. C., Founds, W. L., Peacock, S. M., Jr., Heath, R. G., & Llewellyn, R. C. Improvements in the techniques for implanting subcortical electrodes in man by a stereotaxic method. In R. G. Heath, *et al.* (Eds.), *Studies in schizophrenia.* Cambridge: Harvard U. Press, **1954**. Pp. 565–570.

Becker, H. C., Founds, W. L., Peacock, S. M., Jr., Heath, R. G., Llewellyn, R. C., & Mickle, W. A. A roentgenographic stereotaxic technique for implanting and maintaining electrodes in the brain of man. *Electroenceph. clin. Neurophysiol.*, **1957**, *9*, 533–543.

Berg, I. A. The use of human subjects in psychological research. *Amer. Psychologist*, **1954**, *9*, 108–111.

Bernard, C. (1865) *An introduction to the study of experimental medicine.* New York: Dover, 1957.

Biderman, A. D. Communist techniques of coercive interrogation. Air Force Personnel and Training Res. Center Dev. Rep. TN–56–132, Lackland Air Force Base, Texas, **1956**.

Bijou, S. W. Patterns of reinforcement and resistance to extinction in young children. *Child Develpm.*, **1957**, *28*, 47–54.

Bijou, S. W. A child study laboratory on wheels. *Child Develpm.*, **1958**, *29*, 425–427.

Bijou, S. W. Discrimination performance as a baseline for individual analysis of young children. *Child Develpm.*, **1961**, *32*, 163–170.

Bijou, S. W. Theory and research in mental (developmental) retardation. *Psychol. Rec.*, **1963**, *13*, 95–110.

Bijou, S. W., & Orlando, R. Rapid development of multiple-schedule performances with retarded children. *J. exp. Anal. Behav.*, **1961**, *4*, 7–16.

Bijou, S. W., & Sturges, P. T. Positive reinforcers for experimental studies with children—consumables and manipulatables. *Child Develpm.*, **1959**, *30*, 151–170.

Bishop. M. P., Elder, S. T., & Heath, R. G. Intracranial self-stimulation in man. *Science*, **1963**, *140*, 394–396.

Blough, D. S. A method of obtaining psychophysical thresholds from the pigeon. *J. exp. Anal. Behav.*, **1958**, *1*, 31–44.

Bohr, N. H. D. *Atomic theory and the description of nature.* New York: Macmillan, **1934**.

Brady, J. P., & Lind, D. L. Experimental analysis of hysterical blindness. *Arch. gen. Psychiat.*, **1961**, *4*, 331–339.

Brady, J. V. Extinction of a conditioned "fear" response as a function of reinforcement schedules for competitive behavior. *J. Psychol.*, **1955**, *40*, 25–34.

Brady, J. V. Assessment of drug effects on emotional behavior. *Science*, **1956**, *123*, 1033–1034.

Brady, J. V. The paleocortex and behavioral motivation. In H. F. Harlow, & C. N. Woolsey (Eds.), *Biological and biochemical bases of behavior.* Madison: U. of Wisconsin Press, **1958a**. Pp. 193–235.

Brady, J. V. Ulcers in "executive" monkeys. *Sci. Amer.*, **1958b**, *199* (4), 95–100.

Brady, J. V., & Hunt, H. F. An experimental approach to the analysis of emotional behavior. *J. Psychol.*, **1955**, *40*, 313–324.

Brady, J. V., & Nauta, W. J. H. Subcortical mechanisms in emotional behavior: The duration of effective changes following septal and habnular lesions in the albino rat. *J. comp. physiol. Psychol.*, **1955**, *48*, 412–420.

Brecher, Ruth, & Brecher, E. The happiest creatures on earth? *Harper's*, **1961**, *222*, 85–90.

Brit. med. J. Enuresis in children. 27 April **1957**, 1017–1018.

Broadbent, D. E. Classical conditioning and human watch-keeping. *Psychol. Rev.*, **1953**, *60*, 331–339.

C

Caldwell, B. McD. An evaluation of psychological effects of sex hormone administration in aged women. 2. Results of therapy after eighteen months. *J. Gerontol.*, **1954**, *9*, 168–174.

Cameron, D. E. Studies in senile nocturnal delirium. *Psychiat. Quart.*, **1941**, *15*, 47–53.

Cameron, D. E. Impairment of the retention phase of remembering. *Psychiat. Quart.*, **1943**, *17*, 395–404.

Carter, N. Need correlates of gullibility. *J. abnorm. soc. Psychol.*, **1963**, *66*, 84–87.

Cassirer, E. *Determinismus und Indeterminismus in der modernen Physik.* Göteborg: Elanders Boktryckeri Aktiebolag, **1937**.

Cattell, R. B. Ethics and the social sciences. *Amer. Psychologist,* **1948,** *3,* 193–198.

Clarke, A. C. Our dumb colleagues. *Harper's,* **1958,** *216,* 32–33.

Cohen, D. J. Justin and his peers: An experimental analysis of a child's social world. *Child Develpm.,* **1962,** *33,* 697–717.

Coleman, C. The hickory stick. *Bull. Amer. Ass. univ. Professors,* **1953,** *39,* 457–473.

Communist interrogation, indoctrination and exploitation of American military and civilian prisoners. In *Hearings before the Permanent Subcommittee on Investigations of the Committee on Government Operations, U.S. Senate, 84th Congress, 2nd Session.* Washington, D.C.: U.S. Government Printing Office, **1956.**

Creegan, R. F. Concerning professional ethics. *Amer. Psychologist,* **1958,** *13,* 272–275.

Crosby, N. D. Essential enuresis: Successful treatment based on physiological concepts. *Med. J. Aust.,* **1950,** *372,* 533–542.

Cumming, E. Further thoughts on the theory of disengagement. In R. Kastenbaum (Ed.), *New thoughts on old age.* New York: Springer, **1964.** Pp. 3–18.

D

Dailey, J., & Stahl, B. Their opinion really counts. *TV Guide,* **1962,** *10* (28), 6–9.

Davidson, H. A. *Forensic psychiatry.* New York: Ronald Press, **1952.**

Davidson, J. R., & Douglass, E. Nocturnal enuresis: A special treatment. *Brit. med. J.,* 10 June **1950,** 1345–1347.

Davison, A. N. Return of cholinesterase activity in the rat after inhibition by organophosphorus compounds. 2. A comparative study of true and pseudo cholinesterase. *Biochem. J.,* **1955,** *60,* 339–346.

Day, C. *After all.* New York: Knopf, **1936.**

Deese, J. Some problems in the theory of vigilance. *Psychol. Rev.,* **1955,** *62,* 359–368.

Deese, J., & Ormond, E. Studies of detectability during continuous visual search. Wright Air Development Center Tech. Rep. WADC 53–8, **1953.**

Descartes, R. Discours de la méthode. **(1637)** In E. Gilson (Ed.), Paris: Librarie Philosophique J. Vrin, 1947.

Dews, P. B. Analysis of effects of psychopharmacological agents in behavioral terms. *Federat. Proc.,* **1958a,** *17,* 1024–1030.

Dews, P. B. The effects of chlorpromazine and promazine on performance on a mixed schedule of reinforcement. *J. exp. Anal. Behav.,* **1958b,** *1,* 73–82.

Dollard, J., & Miller, N. E. *Personality and psychotherapy.* New York: McGraw-Hill, **1950.**

E

Edwards, A. L. *Experimental design in psychological research.* New York: Rinehart, **1950.**

Ellis, N. R., Barnett, C. D., & Pryer, M. W. Operant behavior in mental defectives: Exploratory studies. *J. exp. Anal. Behav.,* **1960,** *3,* 63–69.

Erickson, Elizabeth M. Observations concerning alterations in hypnosis of visual functions. *Amer. J. clin. Hyp.,* **1962,** *5,* 131–134.

Erickson, M. H. An experimental investigation of the possible anti-social use of hypnosis. *Psychiat.,* **1939,** *2,* 391–414.

Essig, C. F., Hampson, J. L., McCauley, A., & Himwich, H. E. An experimental analysis of biochemically induced forced circling behavior. *J. Neurophysiol.,* **1950,** *13,* 269–275.

Estabrooks, G. H. *Hypnotism.* New York: Dutton, **1943.**

Estes, W. K., & Skinner, B. F. Some quantitative properties of anxiety. *J. exp. Psychol.,* **1941,** *29,* 390–400.

Eysenck, H. J. Cortical inhibition, figural after effect, and theory of personality. *J. abnorm. soc. Psychol.,* **1955,** *51,* 94–106.

Eysenck, H. J. (Ed.) *Behavior therapy and the neuroses.* New York: Pergamon, **1960.**

F

Farber, I. E., Spence, K. W., & Bechtoldt, H. P. Emotionality, introversion-extraversion, and conditioning. Paper read at Midwest Psychol. Ass., May, **1957.**

Feldberg, W., & Sherwood, S. L. A permanent cannula for intraventricular injections in cats. *J. Physiol.,* **1953,** *120,* 3–4P.

Feldberg, W., & Sherwood, S. L. Injections of drugs into the lateral ventricle of the cat. *J. Physiol.,* **1954,** *123,* 148–167.

Fenichel, O. *The psychoanalytic theory of the neuroses.* New York: Norton, **1945.**

Ferster, C. B. The use of the free operant in the analysis of behavior. *Psychol. Bull.,* **1953,** *50,* 263–274.

Ferster, C. B. Use of the black-out in the investigation of temporal discrimination in fixed-interval reinforcement. *J. exp. Psychol.,* **1954,** *47,* 69–74.

Ferster, C. B. Withdrawal of positive reinforcement as punishment. *Science,* **1957,** *126,* 509.

Ferster, C. B. Control of behavior in chimpanzees and pigeons by time out from positive reinforcement. *Psychol. Monogr.,* **1958a,** *72,* 1–38.

Ferster, C. B. Reinforcement and punishment in the control of human behavior by social agencies. *Psychiat. res. Rep.*, **1958b**, *10*, 101–118.

Ferster, C. B. Positive reinforcement and behavioral defects of autistic children. *Child Develpm.*, **1961**, *32*, 437–456.

Ferster, C. B., & Appel, J. B. Punishment of S responding in match to sample by time out from positive reinforcement. *J. exp. Anal. Behav.*, **1961**, *4*, 45–56.

Ferster, C. B., & DeMyer, M. K. The development of performances in autistic children in an automatically controlled environment. *J. chron. Dis.*, **1961**, *13*, 312–345.

Ferster, C. B., & DeMyer, M. K. A method of experimental analysis of the behavior of autistic children. *Amer. J. Orthopsychiat.*, **1962**, *32*, 89–98.

Ferster, C. B., Nurnberger, J. I., & Levitt, E. B. The control of eating. *J. Mathetics*, **1962**, *1*, 87–109.

Ferster, C. B., & Skinner, B. F. *Schedules of reinforcement.* New York: Appleton-Century-Crofts, **1957**.

Flanagan, B., Goldiamond, I., & Azrin, N. H. Operant stuttering: The control of stuttering behavior through response-contingent consequences. *J. exp. Anal. Behav.*, **1958**, *1*, 173–177.

Forer, B. R. The fallacy of personal validation: A classroom demonstration of gullibility. *J. abnorm. soc. Psychol.*, **1949**, *44*, 118–123.

Frank, J. D. Experimental studies of personal pressure and resistance: I. Experimental production of resistance. *J. gen. Psychol.*, **1944**, *30*, 23–41.

Frank, J. D. *Persuasion and healing: A comparative study of psychotherapy.* Baltimore: Johns Hopkins Press, **1961**.

Frank, P. *Das Kausalgesetz und seine Grenzen.* Vienna: Springer, **1932**.

Franks, C. M. Conditioning and personality: A study of normal and neurotic subjects. *J. abnorm. soc. Psychol.*, **1956**, *52*, 143–150.

Fraser, D. C. The relation between angle of display and performance in a prolonged visual task. *Quart. J. exp. Psychol.*, **1950**, *2*, 176–181.

Freedman, A. M., & Himwich, H. E., DFP: Site of injection and variation in response. *Amer. J. Physiol.*, **1949**, *156*, 125–128.

Freund, P. A., et al. *Constitutional law: Cases and other problems.* Vol. 1. Boston: Little, Brown, **1954**.

G

Galambos, R. Neurophysiological studies on learning and motivation. *Federat. Proc.*, **1961**, *20*, 603–608.

Garnett, R. W., & Klingman, W. O. Cytochrome C: Effects of intravenous administration on presenile, senile and arteriosclerotic cerebral states. *Amer. J. Psychiat.*, **1959**, *106*, 697–702.

Garrod, A. E. Incidence of alkaptonuria. *Lancet*, **1902**, *2*, 1616–1620.

Garrod, A. E. *Inborn errors of metabolism.* Oxford: U. Press, **1923**.

Geppert, T. V. Management of nocturnal enuresis by conditioned response. *J. Amer. med. Ass.*, **1953**, *152*, 381–383.

Gillison, T. H. Enuresis. *Brit. med. J.*, 19 May **1956**, 1174–1175.

Goldiamond, I. Indicators of perception: I. Subliminal perception, subception, unconscious perception; an analysis in terms of psychophysical indicator methodology. *Psychol. Bull.*, **1958a**, *55*, 373–411.

Goldiamond, I. Research which can be done in a mental hospital. Address delivered to Ill. State Mental Hospitals Conf., Giant City State Park, Ill., **1958b**.

Goldiamond, I. Some recent contributions of experimental psychology to psychopathology: Contributions from psychophysics. Paper read at Midwest Psychol. Ass., Detroit, **1958c**.

Goldiamond, I. The maintenance of ongoing fluent verbal behavior and stuttering. *J. Mathetics*, **1962**, *1* (2), 57–95.

Goldiamond, I. Justified and unjustified alarm over behavioral control. In O. Milton (Ed.), *Behavior disorders: Perspectives and trends.* Philadelphia: Lippincott, **1965a**.

Goldiamond, I. Stuttering and fluency as manipulable operant response classes. In L. Krasner, & L. P. Ullman (Eds.), *Research in behavior modification: New developments and implications.* New York: Holt, **1965b**.

Goldiamond, I. Perception, language, and conceptualization rules. In B. Kleinmuntz (Ed.), *Cognition symposium: Problem solving.* New York: Wiley, **1966**.

Goldiamond, I., Dyrud, J., & Miller, M. Practice as research in professional psychology. *Canadian Psychologist*, January, **1965**.

Grenell, R. G. Considerations regarding metabolic factors in the action of chlorpromazine. In H. E. Himwich (Ed.), *Tranquilizing drugs.* Washington: Amer. Ass. Adv. Sci., **1957**. Pp. 61–71.

Grosslight, J. H., Hall, J. F., & Scott, W. Reinforcement schedules in habit reversal—a confirmation. *J. exp. Psychol.*, **1954**, *48*, 173–174.

Group for the Advancement of Psychiatry. *Criminal responsibility and psychiatric expert testimony.* (Rep. No. 26) New York: GAP Publication Office, **1954**.

Group for the Advancement of Psychiatry. *Symposium No. 3. Factors used to increase the susceptibility of individuals to forceful indoctrination: Observations and experiments.* New York: GAP Publication Office, **1956**.

Guttmacher, M. S. What can the psychiatrist contribute to the issue of criminal responsibility? *J. nerv. ment. Dis.*, **1963,** *136,* 103–117.

Guttmacher, M. S., & Weihofen, H. *Psychiatry and the law.* New York: Norton, **1952.**

H

Hacker, A. The specter of predictable man. *Antioch Rev.,* **1954,** *14,* 195–207.

Hacker, A. Dostoevsky's disciples: Man and sheep in political theory. *J. Politics,* **1955,** *17,* 590–613.

Haldane, J. B. S. *The biochemistry of genetics.* London: Allen & Unwin, **1954.**

Harris, Florence R., Johnston, Margaret K., Kelley, C. Susan, & Wolf, M. M. Effects of positive social reinforcement on regressed crawling of a nursery school child. *J. educ. Psychol.,* **1964,** *55,* 35–41.

Harris, H. *An introduction to human biochemical genetics.* London: Cambridge U. Press, **1955.**

Hart, Betty M., Allen, K. Eileen, Buell, Joan S., Harris, Florence R., & Wolf, M. M. Effects of social reinforcement on operant crying. *J. exp. child Psychol.,* **1964,** *1,* 145–153.

Hart, H. L. A. The ascription of responsibility and rights. In A. Flew (Ed.), *Logic and language.* (1st series) Oxford: Basil Blackwell, **1960.**

Harwood, C. T., & Mason, J. W. *J. clin. Endocrinology and Metabolism,* **1952,** *12,* 519 (sic).

Heath, R. G. The theoretical framework for a multidisciplinary approach to human behavior. In R. G. Heath, *et al.* (Eds.), *Studies in schizophrenia.* Cambridge: Harvard U. Press, **1954,** Pp. 9–56.

Heath, R. G. Correlations between levels of psychological awareness and physiological activity in the central nervous system. *Psychosom. Med.,* **1955,** *17,* 383–395.

Heath, R. G. Correlation of electrical recordings from cortical and subcortical regions of the brain with abnormal behavior in human subjects. *Confinia Neurol.,* **1958,** *18,* 305–315.

Heath, R. G. In R. G. Heath (Ed.), *The role of pleasure in behavior.* New York: Hoeber, **1964.**

Heath, R. G., & deBalbian Verster, F. Effects of chemical stimulation to discrete brain areas. *Amer. J. Psychiat.,* **1961,** *117,* 980–990.

Heath, R. G., & Founds, W. L., Jr. A perfusion cannula for intracerebral microinjections. *Electroenceph. clin. Neurophysiol.,* **1960,** *12,* 930–932.

Heath, R. G., Leach, B. E., Monroe, R. R., Mickle, W. A., & Strohmeyer, R. B. Immediate chemical and behavioral effects with stimulation of chronically implanted electrodes in Rhesus monkeys and in patients. In R. G. Heath, *et al.* (Eds.), *Studies in schizophrenia.* Cambridge: Harvard U. Press, **1954.** Pp. 555–564.

Heath, R. G., & Mickle, W. A. Evaluation of seven years' experience with depth electrode studies in human patients. In E. R. Ramey, & D. S. O'Doherty (Eds.), *Electrical studies on the unanesthetized brain.* New York: Hoeber, **1960.** Pp. 214–247.

Hefferline, R. F. Learning theory and clinical psychology—an eventual symbiosis? In A. J. Bachrach (Ed.), *Experimental foundations of clinical psychology.* New York: Basic Books, **1962.** Pp. 92–138.

Hefferline, R. F., Keenan, B., & Harford, R. A. Escape and avoidance conditioning in human subjects without their observation of the response. *Science,* **1959,** *130,* 1338–1339.

Hempel, C. G., & Oppenheim, P. Studies in the logic of explanation. *Phil. Sci.,* **1948,** *15,* 135–175.

Herrnstein, R. J. In defense of bird brains. *Atlantic Monthly,* **1965,** *216,* 101–104.

Herrnstein, R. J., & Loveland, D. H. Complex visual concept in the pigeon. *Science,* **1964,** *146,* 549–551.

Herrnstein, R. J., & Sidman, M. Avoidance conditioning as a factor in the effects of unavoidable shocks on food-reinforced behavior. *J. comp. physiol. Psychol.,* **1958,** *51,* 380–385.

Hess, E. H., & Polt, J. M. Pupil size as related to interest value of visual stimuli. *Science,* **1960,** *132,* 349–350.

Hess, J. H., & Thomas, H. E. Incompetency to stand trial. *Amer. J. Psychiat.,* **1963,** *119,* 713–720.

Hilgard, E. R. *Theories of learning.* New York: Appleton-Century-Crofts, **1948.**

Hingtgen, J. N., Sanders, B. M., & DeMyer, M. K. Shaping cooperative responses in early childhood schizophrenics. In L. Ullmann, & L. Krasner, (Eds.), *Case studies in behavior modification.* New York: Holt, **1965.** Pp. 130–138.

Hinkle, L. E., & Wolff, H. G. Communist interrogation and indoctrination of "enemies of the state." *Arch. Neurol. Psychiat.,* **1956,** *76,* 115–174.

Hively, W. An exploratory investigation of an apparatus for studying and teaching visual discrimination, using preschool children. In A. A. Lumsdaine, & R. Glaser (Eds.), *Teaching machines and programmed learning.* Washington: Dept. of Audio-Visual Instruction, National Education Ass., **1960.** Pp. 247–256.

Hoagland, H. The physiological control of judgments of duration: Evidence for a chemical clock. *J. gen. Psychol.,* **1933,** *9,* 267–287.

Hoagland, H. (Ed.) *Hormones, train function and behavior.* New York: Academic Press, **1957.**

Holland, J. G. Technique for behavioral analysis of human observing. *Science,* **1957,** *125,* 348–350.

Holland, J. G. Human vigilance. *Science,* **1958,** *128,* 61–67.

Holland, J. G., & Skinner, B. F. *The analysis of behavior.* New York: McGraw-Hill, **1961.**

Holt, R. R., & Luborsky, L. *Personality patterns of psychiatrists.* New York: Basic Books, **1958.**

Holz, W. C., & Azrin, N. H. A comparison of several

procedures for eliminating behavior. *J. exp. Anal. Behav.*, **1963**, *6*, 399–406.

Homer, S. A., & Streamer, C. W. Effect of a phenylalanine restricted diet on patients with phenylketonuria. *J. Amer. med. Ass.*, **1956**, *161*, 1628–1630.

Homme, L. E., & Glaser, R. Relationships between programmed textbook and teaching machines. In E. Galanter (Ed.), *Automatic teaching.* New York: Wiley, **1959**. Pp. 103–107.

Horowitz, Frances D. Social reinforcement effects on child behavior. *J. nursery Educ.*, **1963**, *18*, 276–284.

Hovland, C. I. A "communication analysis" of concept learning. *Psychol. Rev.*, **1952**, 59, 461–472.

Hovland, C. I. A set of flower designs for experiments in concept formation. *Amer. J. Psychol.*, **1953**, *66*, 140–142.

Hunt, H. F., & Brady, J. V. Some effects of electroconvulsive shock on a conditioned emotional response. *J. comp. physiol. Psychol.*, **1951**, *44*, 88–98.

Hunter, W. S. *Human Behavior.* **(1919)** In Chicago: U. of Chicago Press, 1928.

Hutchinson, R. R., & Azrin, N. H. Conditioning of mental hospital patients to fixed-ratio schedules of reinforcement. *J. exp. Anal. Behav.*, **1961, 4**, 87–95.

I

Inglis, J. Psychological investigation of cognitive deficit in elderly psychiatric patients. *Psychol. Bull.*, **1958**, *54*, 197–214.

Inglis, J. Psychological practice in geriatric problems. *J. ment. Sci.*, **1962**, *108*, 669–674.

Isaacs, W., Thomas, J., & Goldiamond, I. Application of operant conditioning to reinstate verbal behavior in psychotics. *J. speech hearing Dis.*, **1960**, *25*, 8–12.

J

Jeans, J. *Physics and philosophy.* Oxford: Cambridge U. Press, **1945**.

Jeffrey, W. E. New technique for motivating and reinforcing children. *Science*, **1955**, *121*, 371.

Jourard, S. I-thou relationship versus manipulation in counseling and psychotherapy. *J. indiv. Psychol.*, **1959**, *15*, 174–179.

Jourard, S. On the problem of reinforcement by the psychotherapist of healthy behavior in the patient. In F. J. Shaw (Ed.), *Behavioristic approaches to counseling and psychotherapy: A Southeastern Psychological Association symposium.* University: U. of Ala. Press, **1961**.

K

Kanfer, F. H. Comments on learning in psychotherapy. *Psychol. Rep.*, **1961**, *9*, 681–699.

Kastenbaum, R. Is old age the end of development? In R. Kastenbaum (Ed.), *New thoughts on old age.* New York: Springer, **1964**. Pp. 61–71.

Keller, F. S., & Schoenfeld, W. N. *Principles of psychology.* New York: Appleton-Century-Crofts, **1950**.

Kelly, E. L., & Fiske, D. W. *The prediction of performance in clinical psychology.* Ann Arbor: U. of Mich. Press, **1951**.

Khairy, M., Russell, R. W., & Yudkin, J. Some effects of thiamine deficiency and reduced caloric intake on avoidance training and on reactions to conflict. *Quart. J. exp. Psychol.*, **1957**, *9*, 190–205.

Knöpfelmacher, F., Khairy, M., Russell, R. W., & Yudkin, J. Some effects of thiamine deficiency and reduced caloric intake on "behavior under stress" and on learning. *Quart J. exp. Psychol.*, **1956**, *8*, 54–65.

Köhler, W. *Gestalt psychology: An introduction to new concepts in modern psychology.* New York: Liveright, **1947**.

Krasner, L. Studies of the conditioning of verbal behavior. *Psychol. Bull.*, **1958**, *55*, 148–170.

Krasner, L. The therapist as a social reinforcement machine. Paper presented at second Conf. on Res. in Psychother. Chapel Hill: U. of N.C., May, **1961**.

Krech, D., Rosenzweig, M. R., & Bennett, E. L. Dimensions of discrimination and level of cholinesterase activity in the cerebral cortex of the rat. *J. comp. physiol. Psychol.*, **1956**, *49*, 261–268.

Krech, D., Rosenzweig, M. R., Bennett, E. L., & Krueckel, B. Enzyme concentrations in the brain and adjustive behavior-patterns. *Science*, **1954**, *120*, 994–996.

Krutch, J. W. *The measure of man.* New York: Bobbs-Merrill, **1954**.

L

Landreth, Catherine. *Education of the young child.* New York: Wiley, **1942**.

Lashley, K. S. Conditional reactions in the rat. *J. Psychol.*, **1938**, *6*, 311–324.

Leavitt, C. Intrigue in advertising—the motivating effects of visual organization. In *Proceedings: Seventh annual conference.* New York: Advertising Res. Found., **1961**.

Levi, W. M. *The pigeon.* (revised ed.) Sumter, S.C.: Levi Publishing Co., **1963**.

Liddell, H. S. Conditioned reflex methods and experimental neurosis. In J. McV. Hunt (Ed.), *Personality and the behavior disorders.* New York: Ronald Press, **1944**.

Lifton, R. J. Home by ship: Reaction patterns of American prisoners of war repatriated from North Korea. *Amer. J. Psychiat.*, **1954**, *110*, 732–739.

Lilly, J. C. Effects of physical restraint and of reduction of ordinary levels of physical stimuli on intact, healthy persons. In Group for the Advancement of Psychiatry, *Symposium No. 2. Illustrative strategies for research on psychopathology in mental health.* New York: GAP Publication Office, **1956.**

Lindsley, O. R. Operant conditioning methods applied to research in chronic schizophrenia. *Psychiat. res. Rep.*, **1956,** *5*, 118–139.

Lindsley, O. R. Operant behavior during sleep: A measure of depth of sleep. *Science,* **1957,** *126*, 1290–1291.

Lindsley, O. R. Analysis of operant discrimination and differentiation in chronic psychotics. Paper read at East. Psychol. Ass., Atlantic City, April, **1958.**

Lindsley, O. R. Reduction in rate of vocal psychotic symptoms by differential positive reinforcement. *J. exp. Anal. Behav.*, **1959,** *2*, 269.

Lindsley, O. R. Characteristics of the behavior of chronic psychotics as revealed by free-operant conditioning methods. *Dis. nerv. System,* **1960,** *21*, 66–78.

Lindsley, O. R. Conjugate reinforcement. Paper read at Amer. Psychol. Ass., New York, September, **1961a.**

Lindsley, O. R. Direct measurement and functional definition of vocal hallucinatory symptoms in chronic psychosis. Paper read at Third World Congress of Psychiat., Montreal, Canada, June, **1961b.**

Lindsley, O. R. **(1961c)** Experimental analysis of co-operation and competition. In T. Verhave (Ed.), *The experimental analysis of behavior: Selected readings.* New York: Appleton-Century-Crofts, 1965.

Lindsley, O. R. Direct behavioral analysis of psychotherapy sessions by conjugately programed closed-circuit television. Paper read at Amer. Psychol. Ass., St. Louis, **1962a.**

Lindsley, O. R. Operant conditioning methods in diagnosis. In J. H. Nodine, & J. H. Moyer (Eds.), *Psychosomatic medicine: The first Hahnemann symposium.* Philadelphia: Lea & Febiger, **1962b.** Pp. 41–54.

Lindsley, O. R. Direct measurement and functional definition of vocal hallucinatory symptoms. *J. nerv. ment. Dis.*, **1963a,** *136*, 293–297.

Lindsley, O. R. Direct measurement and prosthesis of retarded behavior. Paper read at Boston U., Dept. of Spec. Educ., March, **1963b.**

Lindsley, O. R. Free-operant conditioning and psychotherapy. In J. H. Masserman (Ed.), *Current psychiatric therapies.* Vol. 3. New York: Grune & Stratton, **1963c.** Pp. 47–56.

Lindsley, O. R., & Conran, P. Operant behavior during EST: A measure of depth of coma. *Dis. nerv. System,* **1962,** *23*, 407–409.

Lindsley, O. R., Hobika, J. H., & Etsten, B. E.

Operant behavior during anesthesia recovery: A continuous and objective method. *Anesthesiology,* **1961,** *22*, 937–946.

Lowe, C. M. Value orientations: An ethical dilemma. *Amer. Psychologist,* **1959,** *14*, 687–693.

Lumsdaine, A. A., & Glaser, R. *Teaching machines and programmed learning.* Washington: Natl. Educ. Ass., **1960.**

Lundin, R. W. *Personality: An experimental approach.* New York: Macmillan, **1961.**

M

Mackworth, N. H. The breakdown of vigilance during prolonged visual search. *Quart. J. exp. Psychol.*, **1948,** *1*, 6–21.

Mackworth, N. H. *Researches on the measurement of human performance.* [Med. Res. Council (British) Spec. Rep. Ser. No. 268] London: H. M. Stationery Office, **1950.**

Mackworth, N. H. Finger numbness in very cold winds. *J. appl. Psychol.*, **1953,** *5*, 533–543.

MacLean, P. D., Robinson, B. W., & Ploog, D. W. Experiments on localization of genital function in the brain. *Trans. Amer. neurol. Ass.*, **1959,** *84*, 105–109.

Marmor, J. Psychoanalytic therapy as an educational process: Common denominators in the therapeutic approaches of different psychoanalytic "schools." Paper presented to the Acad. of Psychoanal., Chicago, May, **1961.**

Mason, J. W., Brady, J. V., & Sidman, M. Plasma 17-hydroxycorticosteroid levels and conditioned behavior in the Rhesus monkey. *Endocrinology,* **1957,** *60*, 741–752.

May, R. Historical and philosophical presuppositions for understanding therapy. In O. H. Mowrer (Ed.), *Psychotherapy theory and research.* New York: Ronald Press, **1953.**

Meares, A. *A system of medical hypnosis.* Philadelphia: Saunders, **1960.**

Meerloo, J. A. M. Pavlovian strategy as a weapon of menticide. *Amer. J. Psychiat.*, **1954,** *110*, 809–813.

Meerloo, J. A. M. Medication into submission; danger of therapeutic coercion. *J. nerv. ment. Dis.*, **1955,** *122*, 353–360.

Melrose, J. Research in the hearing of the aged. Paper read at Natl. Ass. Music Ther., Cambridge, Mass., October, **1962.**

Mendes, G. A new error of tyrosine metabolism: Tyrosinosis. *Biochem. J.*, **1932,** *26*, 917.

Milgram, S. Behavioral study of obedience. *J. abnorm. soc. Psychol.*, **1963,** *67*, 371–378.

Mowrer, O. H. Apparatus for the study and treatment of enuresis. *Amer. J. Psychol.*, **1938,** *51*, 163–165.

Mowrer, O. H. *Learning theory and personality dynamics.* New York: Ronald Press, **1950.**

Muller, H. J. Human values in relation to evolution. *Science,* **1958,** *127,* 625 – 629.

Munster, J. H., Jr., & Smith, J. C. The care and feeding of intellectual property. *Science,* **1965,** *148,* 739 – 743.

N

Nagel, E. Methodological issues in psychoanalytic theory. In S. Hook (Ed.), *Psychoanalysis, scientific method and philosophy.* New York: Grove Press, **1959.**

Negley, G., & Patrick, J. M. *The quest for utopia.* New York: Schuman, **1952.**

Nicely, Patricia E., & Miller, G. A. Some effects of unequal spatial distribution on the detectability of radar targets. *J. exp. Psychol.,* **1957,** *53,* 195 – 198.

Niebuhr, R. *The self and the dramas of history.* New York: Scribners, **1955.**

O

Olds, J. Approach-avoidance dissociations in rat brain. *Amer. J. Physiol.,* **1960,** *199,* 965 – 968.

Olds, J. Hypothalamic substrates of reward. *Physiol. Rev.,* **1962,** *42,* 554 – 604.

Olds, J., & Milner, P. Positive reinforcement produced by electrical stimulation of septal area and other regions of rat brain. *J. comp. physiol. Psychol.,* **1954,** *47,* 419 – 427.

Olds, J., & Olds, M. E. In R. G. Heath (Ed.), *The role of pleasure in behavior.* New York: Hoeber, **1964.**

Oppenheimer, J. R. Analogy in science. *Amer. Psychologist,* **1956a,** *11,* 127 – 135.

Oppenheimer, J. R. Science and our times. *Roosevelt U. occasional Papers,* **1956b,** No. 2.

Orlando, R., & Bijou, S. W. Single and multiple schedules of reinforcement in developmentally retarded children. *J. exp. Anal. Behav.,* **1960,** *3,* 339 – 348.

Orne, M. T. The nature of hypnosis: Artifact and essence. *J. abnorm. soc. Psychol.,* **1959,** *58,* 277 – 299.

Orne, M. T. Antisocial behavior and hypnosis: Problems of control and validation in empirical studies. In G. H. Estabrooks (Ed.), *Hypnosis: Current problems.* New York: Harper & Row, **1962a.** Pp. 137 – 192.

Orne, M. T. On the social psychology of the psychological experiment: With particular reference to demand characteristics and their implications. *Amer. Psychologist,* **1962b,** *17,* 776 – 783.

Orne, M. T., & Scheibe, K. E. The contribution of nondeprivation factors in the production of sensory deprivation effects: The psychology of the "panic button." *J. abnorm. soc. Psychol.,* **1964,** *68,* 3 – 12.

Osipova, V. N. Speed of formation of the associated reflex in school children. *Novoye v Reflexologii i Fiziologii nervnoy Systemy,* **1926,** *2,* 218 – 234.

P

Palermo, D. S. Thumbsucking: A learned response. *Pediatr.,* **1956,** *17,* 392 – 399.

Papanek, H. Ethical values in psychotherapy. *J. indiv. Psychol.,* **1958,** *14,* 160 – 166.

Pasley, V. *21 stayed.* New York: American Book – Stratford Press, **1955.**

Patterson, C. H. The place of values in counseling and psychotherapy. *J. counsel. Psychol.,* **1958,** *5,* 216 – 223.

Pavlov, I. P. *Conditioned reflexes and psychiatry.* (Translated by W. H. Gantt). (2nd ed.) New York: International U. Press, **1941.**

Penrose, L. S. *The biology of mental defect.* London: Sidgwick & Jackson, **1954.**

Perin, C. T. The effect of delayed reinforcement upon the differentiation of bar responses in white rats. *J. exp. Psychol.,* **1943,** *32,* 95 – 109.

Peterman, J. N. The program analyzer, a new technique in studying liked and disliked items in radio programs. *J. appl. Psychol.,* **1940,** *24.*

Peterson, G. M. Changes in handedness in the rat from the local application of acetylcholine to the cerebral cortex. *J. comp. physiol. Psychol.,* **1949,** *42,* 404 – 412.

Petrunkevitch, A. The controversy of faith versus reason. *Amer. Scientist,* **1945,** *33,* 189 – 193 & 201.

Pfaundler, M. *Verhandlungen Gesellschaft Kinderheilkunde,* **1904,** *21,* 219.

Pierce, C. (1878) How to make our ideas clear. In M. R. Cohen (Ed.), *Chance, love and logic.* New York: Harcourt, Brace, 1923.

Popper, K. R. *The open society and its enemies.* London: Rutledge & Kegan Paul, **1945.**

POW: The fight continues after the battle. In *Report of the Secretary of Defense's Advisory Committee on Prisoners of War.* Washington, D.C.: U.S. Government Printing Office, **1955.**

Premack, D. Toward empirical behavior laws: I. Positive reinforcement. *Psychol. Rev.,* **1959,** *66,* 219 – 233.

Pressey, S. L. Simple apparatus which gives tests and scores and teaches. *Sch. and Soc.,* **1926,** *23,* 373 – 376.

R

Rachman, S. Learning theory and child psychology: Therapeutic possibilities. *J. child Psychol. Psychiat.,* **1962,** *3,* 149 – 163.

Ratner, J. (Ed.) *Intelligence in the modern world: John Dewey's philosophy.* New York: Modern Library, **1939.**

Razran, G. H. S. Conditioned responses in children. *Arch. Psychol.*, **1933**, *23* (148), 33–81.

Read, Katherine H. *The nursery school.* (2nd ed.) Philadelphia: Saunders, **1955**.

Reese, E. P. *Experiments in operant behavior.* New York: Appleton-Century-Crofts, **1964**.

Reid, L. S. The development of noncontinuity behavior through continuity learning. *J. exp. Psychol.*, **1953**, *46*, 107–112.

Roberts, E. Thumb and finger-sucking in relation to feeding in early infancy. *Amer. J. Dis. Child.*, **1944**, *68*, 7–8.

Robinson, F. P. *Effective study.* New York: Harper, **1946**.

Robinson, M. F., & Freeman, W. *Psychosurgery and the self.* New York: Grune and Stratton, **1954**.

Roche, P. Q. *The criminal mind.* New York: Farrar, Straus, & Cudahy, **1958**.

Roe, Anne Man's forgotten weapon. *Amer. Psychologist,* **1959**, *14*, 261–266.

Rogers, C. R. *Client-centered therapy.* Boston: Houghton Mifflin, **1951**.

Rogers, C. R. Persons or science: A philosophical question. *Amer. Psychologist,* **1955**, *10*, 267–278.

Rogers, C. R. Implications of recent advances in prediction and control of behavior. *Teachers coll. Rec.*, **1956**, *57*, 316–322.

Rogers, C. R., & Dymond, R. (Eds.) *Psychotherapy and personality change.* Chicago: U. of Chicago Press, **1954**.

Rogers, C. R., & Skinner, B. F. Some issues concerning the control of human behavior: A symposium. *Science,* **1956**, *124*, 1057–1066.

Rosenthal, D. Changes in some moral values following psychotherapy. *J. consult. Psychol.*, **1955**, *19*, 431–436.

Rosenthal, R. Experimenter outcome-orientation and the results of the psychological experiment. *Psychol. Bull.*, **1964**, *61*, 405–412.

Rosenthal, R., & Fode, K. L. Psychology of the scientist: V. Three experiments in experimenter bias. *Psychol. Rep.*, **1963**, *12*, 491–511.

Rosenthal, R., & Lawson, R. A longitudinal study of the effects of experimenter bias on the operant learning of laboratory rats. *J. psychiat. Res.*, **1963**, *2*, 61–72.

Rotter, J. B. Psychotherapy. *Annu. Rev. Psychol.*, **1961**, *11*, 318–414.

Rowland, L. W. Will hypnotized persons try to harm themselves or others? *J. abnorm. soc. Psychol.*, **1939**, *34*, 114–117.

Russell, R. W. Effects of variations in ambient temperature on certain measures of tracking skill and sensory sensitivity. U.S. Army Med. Res. Lab. Rep. No. 300, **1957**.

Russell, R. W., & Walton, W. E. The effects of avitaminosis-A on visual discrimination in the rat: Gross effects on color discrimination. *J. genet. Psychol.*, **1942**, *61*, 327–333.

Russell, R. W., & Younger, J. The effects of avitaminosis-A on visual intensity difference thresholds in the rat. *J. exp. Psychol.*, **1943**, *32*, 507–512.

Ryle, G. *The concept of mind.* New York: Barnes & Noble, **1949**.

S

Salzinger, K. Experimental manipulation of verbal behavior: A review. *J. gen. Psychol.*, **1959**, *61*, 65–94.

Santucci, P. S., & Winokur, G. Brainwashing as a factor in psychiatric illness. *Arch. Neurol. Psychiat.*, **1955**, *74*, 11–16.

Schilder, P., & Kauders, O. Hypnosis. (Translated by S. Rothenberg) *Nerv. men. Dis. monogr. Ser.*, **1927**, No. 46.

Schlick, M. *Problems of ethics.* New York: Prentice-Hall, **1939**.

Schoenfeld, W. N. An experimental approach to anxiety, escape and avoidance behavior. In P. H. Hoch, & J. Zubin (Eds.), *Anxiety.* New York: Grune and Stratton, **1950**. Pp. 70–99.

Schrödinger, E. *What is life?* New York: Macmillan, **1945**.

Segal, I. X. Materials for the study of conditioned salivary reflexes in oligophrenics. *Zh. Nevropatologii,* **1929**, *22*, 625–632.

Segal, J. Factors related to the collaboration and resistance behavior of U.S. Army PW's in Korea. Tech. Rep. 33, Human Resources Res. Office, George Washington U., Washington, D.C., **1956**.

Seiger, H. W. Practical urine or wet diaper signal. *J. Pediatr.*, **1946**, *28*, 733–736.

Seiger, H. W. Treatment of essential enuresis. *J. Pediatr.*, **1952**, *40*, 738–749.

Shaffer, L. F. Fear and courage in aerial combat. *J. consult. Psychol.*, **1947**, *11*, 137–143.

Shaffer, L. F. Of whose reality I cannot doubt. *Amer. Psychologist,* **1953**, *8*, 608–623.

Shastin, N. R. Unconditioned and conditioned reflexes in myxedema. *Medico-biologichesky Zh.*, **1930**, *6*, 470–482.

Shearn, D., Sprague, R. L., & Rosenzweig, S. A method for the analysis and control of speech rate. *J. exp. Anal. Behav.*, **1961**, *4*, 197–201.

Sherman, J. Reinstatement of verbal behavior in mute psychotics. Unpublished doctoral dissertation, U. of Washington, **1964**.

Shor, R. E. Physiological effects of painful stimulation during hypnotic analgesia under conditions designed to minimize anxiety. *Int. J. clin. exp. Hyp.*, **1962**, *10*, 183–202.

Sidman, M. Avoidance conditioning with brief shock and no exteroceptive warning signal. *Science,* **1953a**, *118*, 157–158.

Sidman, M. Two temporal parameters of the maintenance of avoidance behavior by the white rat. *J. comp. physiol. Psychol.*, **1953b**, *46*, 253–261.

Sidman, M. Drug-behavior interaction. *Ann. N. Y. Acad. Sci.*, **1956a**, *65*, 282–302.

Sidman, M. Time discrimination and behavioral interaction in a free operant situation. *J. comp. physiol. Psychol.*, **1956b**, *49*, 469–476.

Sidman, M. By-products of aversive control. *J. exp. Anal. Behav.*, **1958**, *1*, 265–280.

Sidman, M. *The tactics of scientific research.* New York: Basic Books, **1961**.

Sidman, M., & Boren, J. J. The use of shock-contingent variations in response-shock intervals for the maintenance of avoidance behavior. *J. comp. physiol. Psychol.*, **1957**, *50*, 558–562.

Sidman, M., Herrnstein, R. J., & Conrad, D. G. Maintenance of avoidance behavior by unavoidable shocks. *J. comp. physiol. Psychol.*, **1957**, *50*, 553–557.

Skinner, B. F. *The behavior of organisms: An experimental analysis.* New York: Appleton-Century-Crofts, **1938**.

Skinner, B. F. Superstition in the pigeon. *J. exp. Psychol.*, **1948a**, *38*, 168–172.

Skinner, B. F. *Walden two.* New York: Macmillan, **1948b**.

Skinner, B. F. Are learning theories necessary? *Psychol. Rev.*, **1950**, *57*, 193–216.

Skinner, B. F. *Science and human behavior.* New York: Macmillan, **1953**.

Skinner, B. F. A new method for the experimental analysis of the behavior of psychotic patients. *J. nerv. ment. Dis.*, **1954a**, *120*, 403–406.

Skinner, B. F. The science of learning and the art of teaching. *Harvard educ. Rev.*, **1954b**, *29*, 86–97.

Skinner, B. F. The control of human behavior. *Trans. N. Y. Acad. Sci.*, **1955**, *17*, 547–551.

Skinner, B. F. Freedom and the control of men. *Amer. Scholar*, Winter, **1955–1956**, *25*, special issue, 47–65.

Skinner, B. F. A case history in scientific method. *Amer. Psychologist*, **1956**, *11*, 221–233.

Skinner, B. F. The experimental analysis of behavior. *Amer. Scientist*, **1957a**, *45*, 343–371.

Skinner, B. F. *Verbal behavior.* New York: Appleton-Century-Crofts, **1957b**.

Skinner, B. F. Teaching machines. *Science*, **1958**, *128*, 969–977.

Skinner, B. F. *Cumulative record.* New York: Appleton-Century-Crofts, **1959**.

Skinner, B. F. Pigeons in a pelican. *Amer. Psychologist*, **1960**, *15*, 28–37.

Skinner, B. F. Operandum. *J. exp. Anal. Behav.*, **1962**, *5*, 224.

Skinner, B. F. Stimulus generalization in an operant: A historical note. In D. I. Mostofsky (Ed.), *Stimulus generalization.* Stanford: Stanford U. Press, **1965**.

Skinner, B. F., Solomon, H. C., & Lindsley, O. R. A new method for the experimental analysis of the behavior of psychotic patients. *J. nerv. ment. Dis.*, **1954**, *120*, 403–406.

Smee, A. *Instinct and reason.* London: Reeve, Benham, & Reeve, **1850**.

Sobeloff, S. E. From McNaughten to Durham and beyond. In P. W. Nice (Ed.), *Crime and insanity.* New York: Philosophical Library, **1958**.

Spence, K. W. *Behavior theory and conditioning.* New Haven, Conn.: Yale U. Press, **1956**.

Spence, K. W., & Farber, I. E. Conditioning and extinction as a function of anxiety. *J. exp. Psychol.*, **1953**, *45*, 116–119.

Spock, B. *The common sense book of baby and child care.* New York: Duell, Sloan, & Pierce, **1946**.

Spradlin, J. E. Effects of reinforcement schedules on extinction in severely mentally retarded children. *Amer. J. ment. Defic.*, **1962**, *66*, 634–640.

Standing, E. M. *Maria Montessori, her life and work.* Fresno: American Library Guild, **1959**.

Stein, L., Sidman, M., & Brady, J. V. Some effects of two temporal variables on conditioned suppression. *J. exp. Anal. Behav.*, **1958**, *1*, 153–162.

Strassman, H. D., Thaler, M. B., & Schein, E. H. A prisoner of war syndrome: Apathy as a reaction to severe stress. *Amer. J. Psychiat.*, **1956**, *112*, 998–1003.

Sulzer, E. S. Reinforcement and the therapeutic contract. *J. counsel. Psychol.*, **1962**, *9*, 271–276.

Szasz, T. S. Some observations on the relationship between psychiatry and the law. *Arch. Neurol. Psychiat.*, **1956**, *75*, 1–19.

Szasz, T. S. Psychiatric expert testimony—its covert meaning and social functions. *Psychiat.*, **1957**, *20*, 313–316.

Szasz, T. S. Criminal responsibility and psychiatry. In H. Toch (Ed.), *Legal and criminal psychology.* New York: Holt, **1961a**.

Szasz, T. S. *The myth of mental illness.* New York: Hoeber, **1961b**.

Szasz, T. S. Naming and the myth of mental illness. *Amer. Psychologist*, **1961c**, *16*, 59–65.

T

Taylor, J. A. The relationship of anxiety to the conditioned eyelid response. *J. exp. Psychol.*, **1951**, *41*, 81–92.

Taylor, Katherine W. *Parents cooperative nursery schools.* New York: Teachers College, Columbia U., **1954**.

Toman, J. E. P., & Swineyard, E. A. Effects of alterations in body temperature on properties of convulsive seizures in rats. *Amer. J. Physiol.*, **1948**, *154*, 207–210.

V

Vandenberg, S. G. Great expectations or the future of psychology (as seen in science fiction). *Amer. Psychologist*, **1956**, *11*, 339–342.

Verhave, T. Recent developments in the experimental analysis of behavior. In *Proceedings of the eleventh research conference*. Chicago: Amer. Meat Inst. Found., **1959a.** Pp. 113–136.

Verhave, T. Technique for the differential reinforcement of the rate of avoidance responding. *Science*, **1959b**, *129*, 959–960.

Verhave, T. Is the system approach of engineering psychology applicable to social organizations? *Psychol. Rec.*, **1961**, *11*, 69–86.

Verhave, T. *The experimental analysis of behavior: Selected readings.* New York: Appleton-Century-Crofts, **1965.**

Verplanck, W. S. The control of the content of conversation: Reinforcement of statements of opinion. *J. abnorm. soc. Psychol.*, **1955**, *55*, 668–676.

Viteles, M. S. The new utopia. *Science*, **1955**, *122*, 1167–1171.

W

Walker, H. M., & Lev, J. *Statistical inference.* New York: Holt, **1953.**

Watson, G. Moral issues in psychotherapy. *Amer. Psychologist*, **1958**, *13*, 574–576.

Watson, J. B. *Psychology from the standpoint of a behaviorist.* Philadelphia: Lippincott, **1919.**

Watson, J. B., & Morgan, J. J. B. Emotional reactions and psychological experimentation. *Amer. J. Psychol.*, **1917**, *28*, 163–174.

Wechsler, I. S. *Clinical neurology.* Philadelphia: Saunders, **1952.**

Weihofen, H. *Insanity as a defense in criminal law.* New York: Commonwealth Fund, **1933.**

Weitz, J. Vibratory sensitivity as a function of skin temperature. *J. exp. Psychol.*, **1941**, *28*, 21–36.

Weitz, J. A further study of the relation between skin temperature and cutaneous sensitivity. *J. exp. Psychol.*, **1942**, *30*, 426–431.

Weitzenhoffer, A. M. The production of antisocial acts under hypnosis. *J. abnorm. soc. Psychol.*, **1949**, *44*, 420–422.

Weitzenhoffer, A. M. *Hypnotism: An objective study in suggestibility.* New York: Wiley, **1953.**

Wells, W. R. Experiments in the hypnotic production of crime. *J. Psychol.*, **1941**, *11*, 63–102.

West, L. J. U.S. Air Force prisoners of the Chinese Communists. In Group for the Advancement of Psychiatry, *Symposium No. 3. Factors used to increase the susceptibility of individuals to forceful indoctrination: Observations and experiments.* New York: GAP Publication Office, **1956.**

West, L. J. Hypnosis and the dissociative reactions. *J. clin. exp. Hypnosis*, in press (sic).

Whitehorn, J. C. Goals of psychotherapy. In E. A. Rubenstein, & M. B. Parloff (Eds.), *Research in Psychotherapy.* Washington: Amer. Psychol. Ass., **1959.**

Williams, C. D. The elimination of tantrum behavior by extinction procedures. *J. abnorm. soc. Psychol.*, **1959**, *59*, 269.

Williams, D. R., & Teitelbaum, P. Control of drinking behavior by means of an operant-conditioning technique. *Science*, **1956**, *124*, 1294–1296.

Wiseman, F. Psychiatry and the law: Use and abuse of psychiatry in a murder case. *Amer. J. Psychiat.*, **1961**, *118*, 289–299.

Wolberg, L. R. *Hypnoanalysis.* New York: Grune & Stratton, **1945.**

Wolf, M. M., Risley, T., & Mees, H. Application of operant conditioning procedures to the behavior problems of an autistic child. *Behav. Res. Ther.*, **1964**, *1*, 305–312.

Wolf, S., & Ripley, H. S. Reactions among Allied prisoners subjected to 3 years of imprisonment and torture by Japanese. *Amer. J. Psychiat.*, **1947**, *104*, 180–193.

Wolff, H. G., & Wolf, S. *Pain.* (3d ed.) New York: Charles C. Thomas, **1952.**

Wolowick, A. B. Materials to the study of conditioned reflex activity in children with weak excitatory and inhibitory processes. *Medico-biologichesky Zh.*, **1929**, *1*, 110–119.

Woolf, L. J., Griffiths, R., & Mancrieff, A. Treatment of phenylketonuria with a diet low in phenylalanine. *Brit. med. J.*, 8 Jan. **1955**, *1*, 57–64.

Wykoff, L. B., Jr. The role of observing responses in discrimination learning. *Psychol. Rev.*, **1952**, *59*, 431–442.

Y

Yates, A. J. The application of modern learning theory to the treatment of tics. *J. abnorm. soc. Psychol.*, **1958**, *56*, 175–182.

Young, P. C. Antisocial uses of hypnosis. In L. M. LeCron (Ed.), *Experimental hypnosis.* New York: Macmillan, **1952.** Pp. 376–409.

Z

Zilboorg, G. The reciprocal responsibilities of law and psychiatry. *Shingle*, **1949**, *12*, 79–96.

Zimmerman, Elaine H., & Zimmerman, J. The alteration of behavior in a special classroom situation. *J. exp. Anal. Behav.*, **1962**, *5*, 59–60.